To Oxford friends, old and new

Preface and Acknowledgements

Because I believe that few readers are likely to come to this text without some prior experience of elegy, my introduction, and the commentary as a whole, start from the standpoint of a not-quite-beginner. So, for instance, while Section I of the Introduction lays out some of the basic 'rules' of elegy, it may not be fully understandable to those who have read none of the genre. Its aim is rather to establish common ground for explication of how the standard features of Latin love elegy function in this particular corpus.

Beyond the issue of readership, my main working assumption is that the authors of the corpus are competent, even good, poets. Those who have not read the poems before may find this a surprising place to begin, because we tend to assume that all (published) poetry is written by people who know how to write poetry. Those familiar with the corpus are even more likely to be surprised, since it is often supposed in the scholarship that these 'amateur' poets would surely have been more like Tibullus or Propertius or Ovid if they could have managed it, but that their own limitations prevented them. So, for instance, the fact that Lygdamus' diction is often difficult to parallel might be evidence of his poor Latinity, but I prefer to see in it the mark of a strikingly original poet; similarly, his habit of expanding upon standard tropes at some length is un-Tibullan and un-Propertian, but very Ovidian.

This innocent-until-proven-guilty stance means that I engage with two primary issues in this commentary. The first is to see how these poems do and do not fit into the rest of Latin love elegy as practised by its three primary poets, and to examine those places where it does not reflect standard practice as opportunities to learn what elegy might be and do beyond our expectations of it. I believe this corpus is well positioned to tell us quite a lot about what (some) Roman poets thought elegy actually was. The second, in keeping with my own interests, but also building upon the fact that [Tib.] 3 uniquely presents an elegiac collection written by a number of hands, is to explore the book as a book. This includes, on a surface level, noting how a number of issues and problems recur throughout the collection, especially those that are not otherwise common in elegy, and also treating the somewhat trickier subject of fictive community, that is, the question of what might be gained by imagining that the poems and their authors really do engage with one another.

Part of what is so interesting about this group of poems is that while they are recognizably part of the genre of elegy, they nevertheless stretch its boundaries beyond what readers who have read only the standard authors might expect. The multiplicity of authors in this corpus, too, is a benefit, as it enables the reader to see in a very clear way differences of style that are sometimes obscured by focus on the 'big three' elegists: Propertius, Tibullus, and Ovid (henceforth abbreviated to Prop., Tib., and Ov. respectively); see my brief discussion of style at Section VII of the Introduction. On a more personal note, the more time I spend with this poetry, the better I like it; much of what at first looked to me—and is often considered by others—amateurish and awkward eventually has resolved itself into witty, pointed, and above all, sophisticated poetry written by authors who knew just what they were up to. It is my sincere hope that readers who come to the poetry with an open mind will find their expectations exceeded. My almost-exclusively literary focus necessarily means that I do not have much to say in what follows about textual issues, nor the still contentious questions of priority, dating, and authorship. These are important problems, and I do engage with them where they are directly relevant; readers will always be guided to fuller discussions. But others much more qualified than I have waded into those tricky waters very thoroughly, and yet obtained no conclusive results.

My interests mean that I generally draw comparisons to and cite usages from other erotic elegies, i.e. Prop., Tib., and Ov.'s *Amores*, *Ars Amatoria*, *Remedia Amoris*, and *Heroides*. I also bring in Ov.'s other works (the exile poetry and *Fasti*, and also the non-elegiac *Metamorphoses*) where I think they are illuminating. Plautus, Catullus, Gallus, Vergil, Horace, Statius, and Martial offer much of interest, and I have also looked further afield in some cases, in part to help the reader situate these poets into the context of (other) professional poets. But I have generally not gone beyond the first century CE in citing parallels, except for rare usages. Finally, bearing in mind that the question of dating is a thorny one, I have drawn attention to passages which seem to offer evidence for one period over another. Parallel passages and supporting information about 'normal' Latin usage come from a wider range of authors where closer parallels are not available. At the same time, I have not usually given much space to discussions of primacy in cases of close verbal parallels, preferring instead to quote them and provide bibliography, and to focus on the poets' own contributions.

In keeping with the aims of the commentary as a whole, introductions to individual poems emphasize key issues; lemmata are structured in more or less the same order, beginning with general matters and moving towards particular issues, including citations near the end. Grammatical information is normally last; textual matters vary in location based on their significance for understanding the passage as a whole (and, in cases where variant versions introduce only small differences of meaning, are not discussed at all; again, the reader is usually referred to fuller treatments). The text used is that of Lenz/Galinsky (1971), which is reprinted here, without apparatus and with a few differences as outlined in the Introduction, with kind permission of Koninklijke Brill.[1] In

---

[1] © Koninklijke Brill NV, 1971, Lenz, Friedrich Walther and Galinsky, G. K., *Albii Tibulli Aliorumque Carminum Libri Tres*, 3rd ed.

compiling the commentary I made regular use of the concordances of Tib. (O'Neil 1963), Prop. (Philimore 1961), and Ov. (Deferrari et al. 1939).

The writing of this commentary has been a labour of love, performed on many desks in many locales, and with an even wider variety than usual of assistance. Steve Heyworth read an earlier version of the commentary, and offered countless suggestions for improvement and clarification. More particularly, he asked 'so what?' in ways both small and large; I am grateful for his companionship during two terms at Wadham College in 2014–15, and to the Warden and Fellows of Wadham College for the offer of a Keeley Visiting Fellowship, and for their personal fellowship during my tenure of it. The Institute for Advanced Studies in Princeton provided a congenial home during the spring of 2015; I thank its faculty, staff, and the visiting fellows for their hospitality despite my unofficial status. I thank too Megan Drinkwater, Aline Kalbian, John Marincola, Tim Stover, and Jessica Westerhold, who read earlier drafts of sections of the introduction, and each of whom brought to bear a different and valuable set of skills. Thanks to FSU's Undergraduate Research Opportunity Program, I benefited from the services of three undergraduate assistants, Jenine Massat, Melanie Godsey, and Cassidy Phelps, who expertly gathered data to assist my very preliminary researches.

Further Oxonian thanks are due to the participants in a seminar on [Tib.] 3 at Oxford University in Trinity Term 2015 (co-taught with Steve Heyworth, to whom, along with the Classics Faculty, I am also grateful for allowing me to crash the party). Both formal speakers and lively audience members offered numerous suggestions as well as encouragement of my own ideas. To wit: Tristan Franklinos, principally but not exclusively on 3.1, Jane Burkowski on 3.2, Robert Maltby on 3.4, Melinda Letts on 3.5, Calypso Nash on 3.6, Michael Malone-Lee especially on 3.8 and 9, James Moorwood especially on 3.11, Barney Taylor especially on 3.13, Bruno Currie on 3.16, 3.18, and 3.19, Gregory Hutchinson on 3.19; also Ian Fielding, Peta Fowler, Stephen Harrison, Luke Houghton, Joy Littlewood, Robert Parker, Chris Pelling, and Gail Trimble.

I am grateful for invitations to two conferences, 'Practical Approaches to Tibullus the Idealist' at Manchester and 'Breaking and Entering: Metalepsis in Classical Literature' at Oxford, both in 2015, which allowed me to work out more fully my thoughts on poem 3.4, and provided stimulating discussion and debate. The participants in Craig Williams' Propertius seminar at UIUC in the spring of 2016 were my gracious and helpful hosts, and worked through a number of the Sulpicia-cycle poems with me; thanks to the faculty there, particularly Antony Augoustakis, for the invitation and hospitality. Thanks too to Emory University for the invitation to present some Sulpicia material at its Benario lecture, and to Miami University of Ohio for the same opportunity (both in 2016).

Finally, some more specific obligations: Helen Dixon and Steve Heyworth provided much-needed coaching on textual matters, and Bruno Currie and

Virginia Lewis gave bibliographic assistance on the Greek lyric poets. Eric Walker offered help with Dorothy Wordsworth. Peter Knox, as usual, provided sober and helpful advice, and saved me from a number of errors of fact and mishaps of emphasis. Katherine Geffcken sent me back to the *CIL* just in time (I owe the reference to L. Valerius Cerinthus to her). Special thanks are due also to Megan Drinkwater, writing partner and ideal reader extraordinaire; readers will be especially grateful for her attempts—even where my stubbornness prevailed—to cut out needless verbiage and, contrarily, to fill in the telegraphic pieces. Gareth Williams continues to be a source of wisdom and guidance. Finally, in addition to reading portions of the commentary and all of the introduction, and more importantly, John Marincola regularly reminded me that there are nearly as many ways to conceive of and execute a commentary as there are to skin a cat. (No animals were harmed in the making of this volume.) Thanks are also due to Charlotte Loveridge and her staff at OUP, to Ian Brookes for careful copyediting, Bethan Lee for proofing, and Eduardo García Molina for heroic work on the index locorum.

Contents

Introduction	1
I: Contexts: Elegy and Amatory Poetry	1
II: Contexts: the 'Augustan Age', Patrons, and Poetic Communities	15
III: Theoretical Approaches to Elegy	20
IV: What's in a Name? Name, Pseudonym, and Persona within [Tib.] 3	25
V: Chronology and Authorship: the Composition and Arrangement of [Tib.] 3	35
VI: Women Writing (Latin)	46
VII: Style, Metre, and Syntax	53
VIII: Manuscript Tradition and Text	58
Text	63
Commentary	75
Works Cited	303
Index Locorum	325
Index	377

Introduction

I: CONTEXTS: ELEGY AND AMATORY POETRY

The third book of Tibullus (henceforth [Tib.] 3, but also called *Appendix Tibulliana* and sometimes *Corpus Tibullianum* 3—in this commentary, *CT* refers to all three books) is a kind of poetry formally, that is metrically, known as elegy.[1] While Roman elegy developed along relatively narrow lines, matters are less clear for its Greek predecessor. The word 'elegy' itself purportedly derives from the Greek ἒ ἒ λέγειν, 'to say woe'.[2] So it is connected with lament—and indeed, both Greek and Roman funerary epitaphs are normally written in elegiac couplets (the epigram, normally one or two couplets long, is often considered a separate genre, though it shares a metre with elegy). At the same time, most Greek elegiac poetry (e.g. the work of Callinus, Mimnermus, Tyrtaeus, Solon, and Theognis, its best-known practitioners in the early archaic period), is not lamentation; it covers a variety of topics including proper symposiastic behaviour, the social order and contemporary politics, martial exhortation, political philosophy, historical events, the deeds of the gods, the pleasures of love, and mythological narrative.[3] Indeed, many of these themes also occur intermittently in the Roman elegists, who thus show their engagement with the roots of the metre. Later elegiac fragments do not allow for certainty, but some scholars believe that Hellenistic elegy narrowed its subject-matter, and suggest that Callimachus, Antimachus, and/or Philitas wrote extensively about erotic matters.[4]

From these diverse Greek roots, Latin elegy developed in a particular direction: specifically, it combined the plaintive tone of prior elegy with a predominantly amatory subject matter. Even the 'canonical' elegists, however, wrote other poetry, so that 'Latin love elegy' is best considered a subset of 'Latin elegy' as a whole (Kennedy 1993: 24–6). The poets of this collection locate themselves squarely within the subject-matter of 'mainstream' Latin love elegy, with only one poem, 3.5, containing no amatory material (though here, the 'illness' of Lygdamus may well be metaphorical love-sickness, deriving from his abandonment by Neaera). So our particular set of elegiac poetry can be defined as being poetry about love, and the love is of a very specific kind, that of a man and a

---

[1] On the generic expectations or presumptions of metre, see Hinds 2000 and Morgan 2010.
[2] The etymology is most likely false; see West 1974: 7. But it looks to be the case that Romans believed it; see e.g. Hor. *AP* 75.
[3] See West 1974: 1–21 for discussion.
[4] See especially Farrell 2012 and Hunter 2012 and 2013 on the influences of Greek elegists and the Greek elegiac tradition on Roman elegy.

woman, one per book of poetry (Greek lyric tended to be a bit more promiscuous). Tib. is unique among extant Roman elegists in offering a different named woman in his second book, and in mentioning a male beloved as well. Elegiac love is unhappy, unequal, doomed: hours of despair outweigh moments of joy, and indeed, there are many causes of elegiac misery, from rivals, to trips abroad, forced abstinence in the service of Isis-worship, and the fact that the 'girl' (*puella*) is just plain cruel.

Depending upon how they are counted, we have five, four, or three main practitioners of elegy: Catullus (henceforth Cat.), Gallus, Tib., Prop., and Ov.[5] There is little evidence of Latin elegiac poetry before the Augustan period, and only slightly more after it; it seems to have flourished and died as a major poetic form within a generation.[6] Cat. wrote in a number of metres, but the later four poets wrote exclusively or almost exclusively (barring only Ov.'s *Metamorphoses*) in elegiac couplets. Cat.'s elegiac poetry comprises his poems 65–116 (but generally only 65–8, the 'longer elegiacs', are considered elegy proper; the rest are primarily epigrammatic and have a rather different tone—though we shall see that [Tib.] 3.13–18 share some commonalities with these Catullan poems). Cat. 64, although hexametric, is also important for Lygdamus, the author of [Tib.] 3.1–6 (henceforth L.), who uses its vocabulary and even refers explicitly to it. From Cat.'s broader range of metre and matter, the later elegists (perhaps like the Hellenistic poets before them, or perhaps not) seem to have selected a portion which they considered properly in their purview. We do not know quite how this happened, or why, since we have only ten lines of the shadowy Gallus to cover the half-generation in between Cat. and the latter three poets, who are more or less contemporaries. And there are a number of elegists who exist for us only as names, or are represented by a few lines, most of them mentioned by Ov. in various places.

Gallus is supposed to have written five books of poetry (titled the *Amores*). Reconstructions of the history of elegy often place much of the weight on him, such that anything that is found in the canonical elegists but not in Cat., or is in Cat. in nascent form, tends to be attributed to Gallus. This might or might not be a disservice to later—or earlier—poets (for more on Gallus, see Raymond 2013); we simply do not have enough evidence to judge. Gallus seems to have introduced the conjunction of poet and *amator* as a regular feature of elegiac poetry, and, from what we can tell, to have written about only one woman, whom he

---

[5] There is reason to suspect that the 'canonical' list of four (minus Cat.), first found in Ov., is his own invention; it is taken up by Quintilian and probably does provide an accurate representation of the major elegists. But there will of course have been many others who either dabbled in elegy or were not considered as successful (as Ov.'s catalogues of contemporary poets themselves make clear).

[6] See P. A. Miller 2004, an extended exploration of the question. On post-Ovidian elegy, see Wheeler 2004–5, especially 18–21, and on the post-Ovidian period as an especially fertile one for elegy, Tarrant 1989: 156.

calls a *domina* (mistress, but with head-of-household as well as sexual implications). But the nature and extent of his influence simply cannot be determined from the evidence we have. See Tränkle 1960: 22–30 (which, however, was written before the discovery in 1978 of a further nine lines of Gallus; see Anderson et al. 1979) for a judicious discussion as it pertains to Propertius.

Tib. wrote two books of elegies, the first with ten poems and the second with only six; the standard story, which may well be correct, tells us that death intervened. At some point (see Section VIII below), a number of other poems were inserted into his corpus as a third book, presumably in part because it was so short, but at least one of these poems purports to be written by Tib. (3.19), and others mention his patron Messalla (see Section II below), so their co-location with the genuine poetry of Tib. is not wholly random. Moreover, a number of linguistic and thematic features throughout [Tib.] 3 bear a resemblance to the first two books of Tib.

Prop. wrote four, or five, books of elegiacs in all, of which the first was published separately.[7] And Prop. 4 marks a departure from his earlier elegy, insofar as the poet moves away from strictly erotic themes towards Roman history and mythology, treated in lengthier poems. In terms of subject matter and structure, Prop. 4 may be an important model for the *Appendix Tibulliana*; it is experimental, and written in a variety of voices and modes, some of them female. (See Section IV below, and *ad* intro to 3.8 on the figure of Vertumnus, who also features in Prop. 4.2.) But scholars tend not to find many specific lexical or thematic resonances between [Tib.] 3 and the poetry of Prop., beyond standard elegiac *topoi* and vocabulary. (I am somewhat more generous; see too Navarro Antolín 2005.)

Ov. is the most prolific of the lot—his amatory elegies alone are longer than all the rest of our extant elegiac poetry put together. These are the *Amores* (seemingly first published as five books and later in a slimmer, three-book second edition), the *Ars Amatoria*, a three-book didactic poem purporting to offer instruction to men (in two books) and women (in the third) about how to conduct an elegiac relationship, the *Remedia Amoris*, which claims to offer a way out of this relationship, and the *Heroides*, two series of mythological poetic letters, the first a group of fifteen written from women to the men who have loved and left them, and the second, a group of six, from couples in the earlier phases of a relationship. The *Heroides* too offer a model for [Tib.] 3, insofar as they treat similar kinds of topics from a number of slightly different viewpoints (see Section VI below). Apart from the *Amores*, none of these Ovidian collections is precisely amatory elegy as we might understand it, but the poems show Ov. applying an elegiac mindset to a larger canvas. Then there is another series of Ovidian works written in elegiac couplets, moving further away from classically

---

[7] What we have as a very long Book 2 seems to have once been two books, whose text is corrupt in very many places.

elegiac topics, but often betraying their roots in elegy: the *Fasti*, a poem (incomplete) about the Roman calendar, covering in its current state the first six months; the *Tristia* and *Epistulae ex Ponto*, poetic letters from the poet in exile; the *Ibis*, a work of invective; and a group of other poems which are fragmentary or of dubious authorship. The *Metamorphoses* too, although not written in elegiac couplets, bears a generic affinity to elegy in that many of the characters who people it behave in recognizably elegiac ways. All of the poets of [Tib.] 3 are notably Ovidian in vocabulary and, often, metre (see Section VII below). But Ov.'s elegiacs were extremely influential in the centuries after his death, such that it is not very helpful in terms of dating to say that they are 'Ovidian': all Latin elegiac poems, right up until our own time, are similarly Ovidian (see Wheeler 2004–5). Both Ov.'s amatory and exilic work are important to the poets of the *Appendix Tibulliana*, the latter because they include Ov.'s letters to his wife. (L. positions Neaera, henceforth N., as his wife, perhaps in imitation; see Section IV below.)

The above summarizes poetry written in the elegiac metre, and so provides a general context for locating [Tib.] 3. But metre is not all: there are a number of other kinds of poetry significant for understanding Roman elegy in both general and particular ways. An important precursor is Roman comedy (itself derived from Greek New Comedy), which also treated a portion of the history of a single love affair, and the basic similarity of situation has led many to find in comedy another of the primary roots of Roman elegy.[8] So too, epic is a key genre against which elegy measures itself: although the two metres are in fact very similar, the canonical elegists make much of the 'lopsidedness' of their chosen form (eleven feet over two lines, rather than the even twelve of two lines of hexameter), such that it cannot bear the 'weight' of serious subjects. In this way, elegiac poets present themselves as 'forced' to practise a (slender) Callimachean poetics.[9] The poets of [Tib.] 3 make no mention of the shortcomings of elegy, but I believe that they do in places gesture towards other kinds of poetry (see especially *ad* 3.6). Finally, there are numerous resonances between Greek lyric and epigram and elegy:[10] it is clear that the established elegiac poets knew and used a wide variety of Greek poetry, and I have found reasons to think that the [Tib.] 3 poets did so as well.

***

As we have noted, elegiac poetry could (and in Greek, did) cover nearly any topic, but the [Tib.] 3 poets adhere fairly closely to the subset of it we have

---

[8] See James 1998 and the volume it introduces, with bibliography. See also James 2012.
[9] See Fantham 2001 for some thoughts, and bibliography, on elegiac attempts to escape from the (self-imposed?) straitjacket.
[10] See Day 1938, Cairns 2006b (= 1979: 214–28), and Bessone 2013 on the history of the study of the origins of Roman elegy, a contested subject: essentially the question, alluded to above, is whether we ought to assume that 'subjective' first-person poetry originated in some lost Hellenistic model, or whether Gallus, or even Cat., 'invented' it (Cairns 1979 = 2006b: 216). For recent work on elegy's use of Greek epigram, see the papers in Keith 2011, particularly Maltby 2011.

identified as Latin love elegy. Each of our main practitioners wrote other kinds of poetry: historical, aetiological, religious, to take only a few examples. In this collection, however, we are concerned with poetry 'about the *puella*' (Thorsen 2013: 117). What follows is a series of observations about what this type of elegy tends to focus on, including its most common *topoi*, with marked differences among individual elegists detailed. Quite a number of these 'standard' elegiac characteristics are not, or not wholly, applicable to [Tib.] 3, so we can treat them in brief compass as we begin to put its poems into a generic context.

Elegy, as noted above, focuses on a single relationship between a man who writes poetry (the *poeta*, also known as the *amator*) and (usually) a woman (the *puella*).[11] Tib. uniquely, in 1.4, 1.8, and 1.9, discusses a relationship with another man, and in his second book of poetry, replaces one woman (Delia) with another (Nemesis).[12] [Tib.] 3 follows the usual one-woman, one-man convention, more or less, but because it is written by a number of different hands, it features a number of different couples and so is more heterogeneous than other elegiac collections. In this multiplicity of love-objects, then, it follows Tib.'s *oeuvre* as a whole.

The basic elegiac relationship is by nature illicit (a male rival, the *vir*, is an infrequent but powerful presence in the poetry, and it often raises the issue of deceiving him) and antagonistic: the *amator* would like to have sex with the *puella*, but he does not want to give her what she wants in return (most often, a 'gift'). He regularly complains about the *puella*, and occasionally even claims that he is ready to move on, but seems trapped in an endless cycle of suffering. The parties, or at least the male parties, are deeply implicated; the feelings of the women are generally opaque. Although she is portrayed vividly, the *puella* is rarely given a voice of her own—and of course, even when she is, it is the poet who voices her[13]—so we are left with a lopsided impression of the relationship: she is cruel, making appointments with the lover, but leaving him to sleep outside her door all night; she flaunts other lovers; she is always making up excuses to force him to buy her a present. Cruelty is not a noticeable feature of the depiction of the love-objects of [Tib.] 3, but is implicitly present (perhaps it inheres in the nature of the genre). L. says nothing about how his relationship with N. has ended, which makes it easy for readers to find her at fault (especially as he continues to beg for another chance, and to threaten to kill himself). And the explicit denigration of her as faithless, more usually voiced by the poet himself, is placed by L. in 3.4 in the mouth of the god Apollo, which makes it seem truer (and also less personal, since she is judged by a 'third party'—although here again we

---

[11] But see Gibson 2013 on the ways the elegists themselves undermine the equation 'one man = one woman' throughout their works.

[12] On Roman 'homosexuality' in general, see C. Williams 1999, and on same-sex practices in elegy, Drinkwater 2012.

[13] Much attention has been paid in recent work to this feature of elegy: Lilja 1965; Sharrock 1991; Wyke 2002, and see Section VI also.

simply hear L.'s side of the story). The '*amicus*' of Sulpicia (henceforth S.), to whom are traditionally attributed [Tib.] 3.8–12 (see Section V below), sees only a rosy future for S. and Cerinthus, and so presents very little conflict. S.'s own portrait (given in [Tib.] 3.13–18; see Section V below) is somewhat more varied; of the three major poets of [Tib.] 3 she best depicts the 'ups and downs' of the standard elegiac relationship, dizzyingly happy in one poem and very, very angry in another. The anonymous poems of [Tib.] 3.19 and 20 focus on jealousy and infidelity. Still, despite some noteworthy differences, the relationships depicted in [Tib.] 3 are, like those of elegy, troubled, distressing, and ultimately unsatisfying.

Elegy's originary situation is the struggle between *amator* and *puella* for whether he will have to pay to enjoy her favours.[14] The *amator*'s main strategy is one of persuasion, and this takes many forms. Sometimes he seeks to convince the *puella* that he alone appreciates her, sometimes that his poetry is fair recompense for a night together. The poetry itself therefore can take on incantatory qualities; the elegiac *carmen* is—or would like to become—a close relative to the magical *carmen*.[15] The *puella*, for her part, would prefer some more fungible token of affection. But the standard struggle between the two goals appears in [Tib.] 3 only implicitly; in my introduction to 3.1 I suggest that it is a key if unstated aspect of the dynamic of the L./N. relationship, although 3.2 seems to allude to L.'s wealth (belying the standard elegiac pose of poverty). The structural problem of L.'s relationship is perhaps most like that of Cat.'s with Lesbia, rather than that of the three later elegists: the *puella* is simply not interested, or not interested enough, in the lover, so he tries to gain her attention, or her pity (or even her anger, which would at least show that she feels something for him). N. herself, L.'s beloved, is described even more sketchily than other elegiac women; she is apparently already out of the relationship, and his poetry seeks to win her back. The case of S. is a peculiar one, as she is simultaneously both *poeta/amator* and *puella*, but in this instance at least, her status is unproblematic: she expresses the poet's normal anxiety about a rival for her affections (3.16) and worries that he does not care enough (3.17). The '*amicus*' of S. seems to struggle more with locating her: on the one hand, he presents her as jealous of the time Cerinthus spends away from her (hunting; 3.9), but also portrays her as a passive *puella*. So, for instance, in 3.8 he insists that she deserves all of the luxury goods that the elegiac *amator* is ordinarily concerned to describe as unnecessary, and at 3.10.18 he notes in passing a *credula turba* (who may well be Cerinthus' rivals; see *ad loc.*)

Elegiac poetry is also structured around another implicit struggle: while the *poeta* claims to want only erotic fulfilment, it is clear that more is at stake. If he were ever to 'get the girl' in any kind of final sense, there would inevitably be an end to

---

[14] James 2003, especially 84–98; see Section III for other viewpoints about the status of the elegiac woman.
[15] Well discussed in the literature; see especially Sharrock 1994: 50–86.

elegy. So the desire to write-to-persuade and the desire to need-to-keep-writing are in an anxious equilibrium (Connolly 2000, Gardner 2013). Descriptions of nights of pleasure are vastly outnumbered by angst-ridden soliloquies about whether things are as they seem, and, if so, worries that the situation will not last.

There is also regular, and fruitful, tension in elegy between what the *puella* 'really' is and what the poet would like her to be: the elegiac *amator* wants his *puella* to be faithful, but, if she were, she would not be with him in the first place; we see this as early as Cat. (e.g. 68.136, where he claims to be able to tolerate *rara furta*; see too Rimell 2006). In the poems of [Tib.] 3 this concern appears most clearly in L., who treats the issue primarily in terms of the word *casta*.[16] Elegy is therefore often concerned with the existence of rivals; sometimes they are presented as very real, sometimes only shadows, and it is often not clear whether they exist, or whether the *amator*'s jealousy has invented them.[17] One standard kind of rival, deriving probably from New Comedy, is the soldier: elegists express their surprise that the *puella* could bear to be touched by his bloody hands (e.g. Ov. *Am.* 3.8). But rivals are also sometimes merely rich, posing a threat because of their willingness to give the *puella* the gifts she wants. So too, elegists sometimes hint that in the past they have chosen another woman, or that they might do so in the future, but the context of these statements often makes it unclear whether we should understand them as 'true' or as meant merely to threaten. The poets of [Tib.] 3 recognize amatory competitors in the abstract, but are vague about detail: L. tells us (3.4.58, implied at the start of 3.2) that N. prefers another, but also sometimes believes he can win her back (3.1.19 and 3.4.63, the latter voiced by Apollo). The '*amicus*' is willing to acknowledge potential rivals for S.'s affection (3.10), but not for Cerinthus', a stance in keeping with his 'pro-S.' position throughout. S. herself, however, fears (3.17) or knows (3.16) that she is not the only *puella*, and 3.19 and 3.20 are premised on the existence of other lovers. Here too, elegy's gender roles are somewhat confused: S.'s poetry is angry rather than wounded at the prospect of Cerinthus' infidelity, and she icily points to the status-differences between them (3.16).

While it is not so explicit, or so dramatic, as that found in other elegists, there is certainly a struggle present in depictions of the relationships between L. and N. and between S. and Cerinthus. The L. poems seem to suggest that the relationship is over, rather than in its beginning or middle stage (see especially 3.1.23, *quondam vir*). In this way, the L. cycle is more reminiscent of such non-elegiac poems as Horace's *Odes* 3.9, in which the poet imagines the renewal of an old relationship. And the poems by and about S. both imply a certain degree of elegiac

---

[16] For the paradoxes inherent in framing the elegiac relationship in terms of chastity, see Langlands 2006: 196–204. The quality of *castitas* is linked, of course, to that of *pudicitia*; see Langlands for helpful discussion of the nuances that word can have (far broader than our 'modesty'), 2006: 30 and nn. 127–9 for some differences between the two words.

[17] See Caston 2012 on the mechanics, and especially the gendered implications, of elegiac jealousy.

secrecy and, contrarily, suggest that she is enmeshed in a variety of familial relationships of the kind never seen for the true elegiac *puella*. So the basic elegiac conflict, we might say, is left opaque in [Tib.] 3, sometimes alluded to, but also diffused into other topics.

In addition to the *puella* and the *vir*, another minor, but important, figure of elegy is the *lena*, or procuress. Her existence in elegy probably derives from both New Comedy and from the real lives of sex workers at Rome, and she is an infrequent, but terrifying, visitor in elegy. Her goal is always to appeal to the *puella*'s mercenary instincts, to remind her that her prime earning time is short (see Gardner 2013), and to discourage the presence of poets among the *puella*'s admirers (as often, Ov. provides our fullest example of the type, at *Am.* 1.8, but she is also noteworthy in Prop. 4.5). There is no *lena* in the poems of [Tib.] 3, but some of the ways the '*amicus*' of S. offers her up for display bear similarities to the discourse of the *lena* (see *ad* 3.8 and 3.10; note too Myers 1996 on the ways in which the poet and the *lena* are not wholly distinguishable). The fact that the *puella* is usually alone in the world, sometimes receiving advice from an older woman, provides indirect evidence for one of the most compelling interpretations of elegy, which sees its women as members of a Roman demi-monde, either expensive courtesans or of freed status (that is, explicitly *not* in the category of respectable Roman women as outlined by Augustus' *Lex Iulia de adulteriis coercendis*, which—somewhat arbitrarily—tried to divide women into just two status-based categories, those one could marry, and those who were not respectable; see Kennedy 1993: 92–3 on the mechanics of this 'real' distinction in the elegiac world). The Emperor Augustus' official interest in sexuality brings the issue into sharp focus: he encouraged members of the upper classes to marry and produce legitimate children, and irregular relationships of various kinds came under negative scrutiny. So the question of precisely who these women were is a compelling one. Courtesans could not be married, but might have a temporary or permanent protector, who could be called a *vir* by analogy. And freedwomen, having once been slaves, might be married but could legally have no chastity (see Hor. *Ser.* 1.2.47 on freedwomen as suitable, because safe, love objects).

Another attractive paradigm, deriving ultimately from the identification of Cat.'s Lesbia with one of the Clodiae and with ancient support from Apuleius (*Apol.* 10 equates them, and also tells us that Delia was 'really' a Plania and Cynthia, a Hostia) suggests rather that the elegiac woman was a wealthy and respectable matron engaged in an adulterous affair, referred to by a pseudonym in order to protect her reputation (very few upper-class Romans, particularly women, were unmarried). In this case, the poetry's *vir* would be, precisely, a husband, rather than a primary client or protector. This latter option, although it may fit the Catullan situation, is more difficult to reconcile with the traditional struggle in the later elegists between *amator* and *puella* over money.

The precise legal status of the literary women of elegy is unknowable, because elegy does not provide a historical record of autobiographical events (see Section

III below, and Kennedy 1993: 83–100). The question, however, remains interesting even to those unconcerned with history, because it engages with Augustus' moral reforms: elegy might or might not be illustrating and implicitly advocating a relationship which had recently become illegal, and which was, therefore, very much in the public eye. So the matter ties into larger issues of how we are to understand the relationship between politics and poetry (see Section II below). The lack of clarity about the elegiac woman is itself instructive; it would surely have been possible for the elegists, had they so desired, to leave no doubt about her status, and their decision not to do so may be construed as an act of political disaffection (at the least).

[Tib.] 3 leaves even more questions unanswered about the status of its women than elegy as a whole. Indeed, this collection focuses little attention on the 'blocking-figure' of the *vir*. So too, the poetry of S. is concerned with secrecy, but not deception per se, although, as usual, the '*amicus*' presents a more regularized situation. (3.12 suggests that a *custos* might be on the lookout for S.'s activities, and that her own wishes differ from her mother's.) And some want to read S. as married or engaged to Cerinthus (see Section IV below; this is not wholly prudishness). L., for his part, refers to N. as a *coniunx* (3.1.23, 26–7), which is not standard nomenclature for *puellae* in elegy, and which may therefore be significant (see further discussion *ad loc.*). 3.1 as a whole, in fact, contains most of [Tib.] 3's explicit interest in the issue of marriage. At the start of the poem, L. offers a gift to N. on the occasion of the Matronalia. Some of our evidence suggests that the Matronalia was celebrated only by legally married wives, but the festival seems to have spread throughout the populace fairly quickly, so that the issue remains unclear (see *ad* 3.1.1). Navarro Antolín 1996 suggests that L. and N. are married or, as he prefers, betrothed.[18] Indeed, the fact that L. uses the words *coniunx* and *vir* is part of what has led some, notably Tränkle 1990, to date him quite late, and even to suggest that he does not entirely understand how elegy works. But Ov.'s exile poetry features a number of poems dedicated to his wife, a conceit which may or may not be wholly original to him.[19] By contrast, Knox (forthcoming: 11–13, with bibliography) revives the suggestion

---

[18] 22–3; of his evidence, the most convincing is [Tib.] 3.4.92–4 because it mentions a father, a personage otherwise absent from love elegy. See too Cartault 1909: 70–3, who reconciles the apparent contradictions by suggesting that L. imaginatively portrays the couple as married in accordance with his own wishes, but not with reality.

[19] See e.g. Ov. *Tr.* 1.6, with Kenney 1965, Hinds 1999; on the subject of 'spousal love elegy', see O'Gorman 1997: 115–22; Hinds 1999: 123–4; Petersen 2005; Öhrman 2008, esp. 151–89. Maltby 2009 sees L. as a continuator of Ov. (322, 324). But Ov. *Tr.* 1.6.1–2 suggests a Greek precedent: the late-fifth-century Antimachus of Colophon seems to have written his *Lyde* in honour of his deceased wife (Plut. *Cons. Apollon.* 106b–c; Ath. 13.596a and 598a–b are ambiguous about her status), and the 'Bittis' of Philitas of Cos has sometimes been understood to have been a wife. See too Sklenar 2005 on Ausonius' late-antique refiguring of elegy as poetry about a wife, which may allude to a longer tradition, or may simply refer to Ov. (and L.). There is also Ov. *Am.* 3.13, about attending a festival with his wife (*coniunx*), which most studies of the *Amores* have difficulty incorporating into an understanding of that collection.

that both are freed slaves, and that L. is appropriating the language of the upper classes (see Section IV below for further explication of this scholarly crux).

It is important to remember, however, that the portraits offered of both lover and beloved are literary constructs, and do not have the status of historical truth. So we should not expect to resolve all contradictions to create a tidy 'biography': such questions as whether L. and N. were 'really' married and whether she 'really' cheated on him simply cannot be answered by re-examination of the 'facts' in the poetry, or even by further evidence. The elegists have created their own semi-fictional world, in which erotic relationships bring the feel of danger, but few real consequences (at least for the man). There may, of course, be autobiographical elements in elegy, as there can be in all poetry, but the elegiac system is a closed and narrow one: a series of poems written about a happy relationship would not, whatever its metre, really count as Latin love elegy.

***

Beyond its basic situation, elegy uses a number of structuring metaphors, and operates under a series of unwritten rules.[20] Our main interest here will be to outline, in brief compass, the most frequently occurring of these, and also to detail how the poets of [Tib.] 3 do and do not utilize these *topoi*. One of the habits of elegy is its regular recourse to mythological events as an authenticating gesture; the situation in which the lover finds himself is compared to some mythic paradigm known from literature or perhaps art. Some of these allusions are easy to decode, but others are recondite and presume a significant degree of familiarity with both Greek and Latin literature on the part of author and reader. Interest in the mythological is less pronounced in Tib. than in Prop. and Ov., and less still in the [Tib.] 3 poets as a whole—though recent scholarship has argued for a number of previously unnoticed allusions to mythic narratives within the poems. But L. makes mention of mythology much more often than Tib., and sometimes includes the kinds of catalogues found in Prop. and Ov., as well as metonymies (e.g. Bacchus = wine, see *ad* 3.6.1). The '*amicus*' and S., by contrast, do not mention the gods in their mythological roles, but do envision a strangely close relationship with them, wherein certain gods are invited to intervene in S.'s life or relationship, or affirmed as having done so.[21] We see this somewhat informal treatment of the gods already at Cat. 70 and 72, where the poet reports Lesbia's statement that she would not prefer Jupiter to him, and it reaches full flowering in Ov. While the book as a whole is not much concerned with mythology, and still less with presenting gods and heroes as exemplary, the first part of 3.8 turns on the conceit that S. is fit for divine attention, and goes on

---

[20] See especially Kennedy 1993: 46–63 on the inevitable cross-contamination of metaphor and 'reality'.

[21] See Fulkerson, forthcoming, for further discussion of the role of the gods in [Tib.] 3.

to explore the implications of this, attributing her gifts to Amor himself. And the gods are more present in [Tib.] 3 than they are elsewhere in elegy; in addition to 3.8, Apollo is a significant actor in 3.4 and 3.10, Juno in 3.12 (on which see *ad loc.*), and Venus in 3.13. The minor god Vertumnus also deserves our attention. He appears in elegy elsewhere only in Prop. 4.2, and is invoked in 3.8, as a divine parallel to S.'s ability to look attractive however she dresses herself (see further *ad loc.*).

So too, elegy is often understood as an especially intertextual genre, in which authors regularly refer to their predecessors; Ov. adds the practice of providing 'catalogues' of poets whose work he admires, in part to situate himself as one of them. While elegy is indeed allusive, it is also true that its subject matter is a limited one: successful nights together, nights spent out of doors waiting, worries about a rival, threatened separation, complaints, violent arguments, and the like, provide its main material. And the repetitiveness of the subject matter means that we cannot always tell the difference between inert *topos* and carefully chosen reference (see Hinds 1998). Still, [Tib.] 3 contains numerous intertexts with other elegiac poems, and 3.6 not only alludes to Cat. 64, but even cites its source. The '*amicus*' seems to quote from S. (assuming he postdates her; it is also possible that he simply reports a genuine saying of the 'real' woman), and treats some of the same topics as she does (her illness, her birthday). It has been argued, persuasively to my mind, that S.'s own poetry alludes to the tale of Dido in Vergil's *Aeneid* (Keith 1997); it also contains Catullan and Sapphic echoes. So sophisticated use of referentiality is a noteworthy feature of the poets of [Tib.] 3 as it is of elegy as a whole, though it is far less concentrated in this group of poets.

Servitium amoris, the notion that love is a kind of slavery, is also an important structural metaphor, less for Ov. than for Prop. and Tib. (see Fulkerson 2013). This fantasy that the *puella* is a class above her admirers (which is almost surely a fantasy, given what we know about the legal and social status of most elegists) enables the poet to adopt a variety of different subject positions, first abasing himself and then asserting his genuine authority.[22] The elegists often suggest that the metaphor be taken literally, but that pose is then undermined in a variety of ways. The notion of *servitium amoris* is assumed in the L. poems, but not explicitly invoked until [Tib.] 3.11, and there in a novel way. L.'s poetry itself suggests his abject status on the surface, but a closer look reveals more complicated aspects, and S. presents herself as furious (not resigned) at the prospect of Cerinthus' infidelity. Above and beyond *servitium amoris* or, probably better, as an intrinsic part of it, the elegiac lover is automatically feminized by virtue of the fact that he is at a woman's mercy (and see Section VI below on some of the potential reasons this theme is so significant to elegists). L. and the anonymous

---

[22] This is sometimes as simple as the use of the word *domina*, not yet a dead metaphor in Latin; for early uses, see Cat. 68.68, Gallus 2.6–7, and possibly Lucil. 730 M, with discussion at Lieberg 1962: 179–84.

author(s) of 3.19 and 3.20 are indeed submissive, and in the brief compass of their works, we do not find this trope reversed. The S. poems perform a double-reversal, undoing canonical elegy's enshrinement of the *puella* as *domina* and the male *amator* as her slave.

Elegy also likes to suggest that love is a kind of warfare, *militia amoris*: the *puella* is sometimes a commanding general, but she is also often the booty to be forcibly appropriated. And the hardships the lover endures in her service are reminiscent of the life of a soldier (Baker 1968, Gale 1997). Of the elegists, Ov. uses this metaphor most often (see especially *Am.* 1.9, and Cahoon 1988, with earlier bibliography), but it is almost entirely absent from [Tib.] 3, which may tell us something about the status of its authors, namely that they may not have been subject to, and so familiar with, military service (in the way that Ov. and the other canonical poets, all of the equestrian class, were). On the other hand, the standard metaphors are so fully worked out in extant elegy that it would not be difficult for a poet with no military experience to take them over wholesale; it is probably safer to say merely that the poets of [Tib.] 3 have little interest in the *topos*.

Love in elegy is also conceived of as a kind of hunt, with the *puella* serving as the quarry (see the brief treatment at Murgatroyd 1984). This metaphor is most pronounced in Ov. *Ars*, but it features throughout the elegiac corpus, and makes a brief appearance in [Tib.] 3.9 (probably; the poem refers to Cerinthus' choice to go hunting rather than spend time with S., but it is likely that we should see this as also metapoetic). One of the things this metaphor accomplishes is to emphasize the fundamentally hostile nature of the elegiac relationship: the lover pursues the *puella*, whether she likes it or not. This is, of course, only one facet of the elegiac relationship; in a reversal of the image of the lover as manly agent, elegiac love is also sometimes treated as an incurable disease which afflicts him (see Holzenthal 1967 for extended treatment of the *topos* in elegy). The patient tries everything to be rid of his illness, but, because he does not really want to be free, he remains untreatable. Sickness crops up regularly in the elegists, and is usually understood to be metaphorical, i.e. about love, or poetry, or both (in addition to the fact that it may sometimes be literal, especially when the *puella* suffers it). Both L. and S. describe illnesses in their poetry in ways that lend themselves to metapoetic interpretation.

Beyond these metaphors, there are also a few further regular features of elegy. The first of these, its implicit hostility, has already been alluded to. The power relations in elegy are regularly turned around: when the *amator* is not bemoaning his servitude, he is throwing his authority around, sometimes even threatening violence. More often the violence lies just under the surface.[23] But it is usually discernible, even in the moments when the *amator* presents himself as most vulnerable. And this can be seen also in the poets of [Tib.] 3, especially L.

---

[23] Fredrick 1997; Greene 1998; James 2003; Caston 2012: 93–112.

So for example, in 3.1 L. appears to give N. free choice about whether she wants to continue their relationship, but his threats of suicide in 3.2 and 3.3 can be seen as coercive; beyond this, his reportage in 3.4 of the dream-vision of Apollo, who issues veiled threats against N. should she not be content with L., is surely told with deliberate intent. (Note too the use of Apollo as an 'authenticating' device in that poem; even within the world of the poetry, there may be levels of plausibility or reality.) It is at the very least convenient that Apollo's own wishes cohere so closely to the poet's own. We may attribute the oddity of Apollo's speech to his own amatory incompetence (see *ad loc.* and Fulkerson, forthcoming), but it may also reflect L.'s attempt, conscious or not, to mould N. to his will. Along with sometimes-disturbing suggestions of violence against women, elegy tends to offer an easy, unexamined misogyny. Some of this, as we have noted, is inherent in the nature of the elegiac relationship, which presumes a conflict between what he wants and what she wants. We see this in our poems especially at the end of 3.4, mentioned above, where Apollo voices standard complaints about women's infidelity. The '*amicus*' of S. is often condescending, but not directly misogynistic (see Batstone, forthcoming).

The physical backdrop of elegy is urban life, specifically life at Rome.[24] Generally speaking, the elegists are poets of the city, and the thought of being away from Rome—and especially of the *puella* being away from Rome without them—distresses them. This is especially clear in Ov., particularly in the three books of the *Ars*, which present seduction in a distinctively Roman setting. Outside of this didactic poem, however, we get a gamut of attitudes towards place: Prop. 4 is at one end of this extreme, locating itself very specifically at distinctively Roman locales and engaging with them, and Tib. is at the other, since he regularly engages in fantasies of rural life, in which his *puella* is safe, under his protection, from the temptations of the city. S., however, is an urban creature, complaining of being taken to the countryside, and rejoicing when the trip is cancelled; L. presents himself as ill while his friends are enjoying themselves at a country retreat (regularly a locus of immorality in elegy; see *ad* 3.5.3). So the poems that make up [Tib.] 3 replicate the variations in elegy as a whole in treating Rome as central, but also engaging with various parts of the peripheral world outside of Rome. In addition to physical location, other features of elegy work to impede access to the *puella*: she has a guardian (*custos*), who prevents her from receiving visitors, or a *vir*, which creates a need for secrecy.

Finally, as we have already seen, elegy regularly engages in metapoetic discourse about itself: the difficulties of writing poetry are assimilated to the difficulties of the amorous relationship, and the *puella*, as quasi-Muse, or sometimes as literal Muse, comes to stand for poetry about her.[25] For Prop., the equation is

---

[24] See especially Welch 2012.
[25] See Wyke 1987, 1989a, 1989b, 1994 (now in Wyke 2002); Sharrock 1991; Keith 1994 extends the discussion to poems not usually thought of as programmatic.

aided by the fact that the first word of his first book is *Cynthia*, since ancient poetry books were often called by their first word. So his 'Cynthia' is the story of his Cynthia, somehow the possessor of an awesome and terrifying power over his art. But even where this equation is not explicitly stated, it is regularly assumed. So, for instance, when Ov. discusses his impotence (*Am.* 3.7), we might also understand him to refer to writer's block; a successful night of love-making can also represent a successful night of composition. The *puella*'s individual body parts are often treated metaphorically: her elaborate or simple hairstyles stand for two different modes of poetic discourse; her feet are metrical, and usually of different 'lengths'.[26] So too, when Prop. bemoans Cynthia's inclination to doll herself up in needless luxuries (e.g. 1.2), we might think of him as also explicating his own struggles to produce an unadorned style. The poets of [Tib.] 3 are usually not understood to be capable of such sophistication, but they too employ these common tropes (see especially *ad* 3.8).

Although elegy is poetry about love, it is only very rarely poetry about sex: the language of elegy is not explicit, and most of the 'sex-scenes' are allusively treated. In perhaps the most famous example, Ov. *Am.* 1.5, the poet teases by singling out attractive aspects of Corinna's anatomy, mentions that she was naked, and concludes *quis cetera nescit*, 'who doesn't know the rest?'. The poets of [Tib.] 3 are similarly indirect, a tendency which is most interesting in the case of S., who displays a canny awareness of the politics of hiding and uncovering (Keith 2008): she claims to be unashamed to declare her love from the rooftops, but is nonetheless remarkably elegiac in her vagueness about details. Death, too, is a regular refrain in the major love elegists, mostly in the form of threatened suicide, or in exhortations to the *puella* to seize the day before she is too old (and unattractive). And it is an especially significant theme for L., appearing in those poems even where N. does not.

We can summarize our findings so far by observing that [Tib.] 3 contains most of the standard elegiac building-blocks, but that it also differs, neglecting some and adding others. There is one further example of an important difference, and one further key similarity; the first is a focus on occasional poetry, and the second, genre-bending. Even casual readers of [Tib.] 3 notice its temporal specificity. Whereas elegy often exists in a temporal vacuum, a number of the elegies of the third book focus on a particular day, notably the Kalends of March and the birthday of S.[27] Specific dates, and especially personal ones such as a birthday, give [Tib.] 3 a rather more personal feel, and may contribute to the sense many have that the poetry was composed by a group of friends or a poetic coterie (see Section V below). Prop. (3.10) and Tib. (2.2; see Section IV below),

---

[26] On hair, see Wyke 1989a, Kennedy 1993: 71–7, Boyd 1997: 117–21, Burkowski 2012.
[27] See Allen on the temporal markers used of Prop.'s relationship with Cynthia, and their apparent precision—which is nonetheless irreconcilable (1962: 112–17 = 1950: 148–52); as he notes, there is 'no progression in time' in the story (117). On time in Tib., see Musurillo 1967, and on the gendered nature of time in elegy, Gardner 2013.

among others, also contain references to birthdays, but the prevalence of the motif in the much smaller corpus of [Tib.] 3 suggests a rather different attitude, which focuses on communal life (it remains to be seen whether that community exists in the 'real world', or merely in the poetry). In this way it is similar to the kinds of occasional poetry always written at Rome but perhaps best known to us from Statius' *Silvae*.

The poems of [Tib.] 3 also raise a number of questions about what the genre of elegy really is: like other elegiac poems, they seem to struggle with its narrow constraints. But [Tib.] 3's genre trouble is gendered in form, nowhere more than in the poetry about and by S.: the tension these poems create between her active role as poet/*amator* and her passive role as *puella* is similar to that in certain other elegiac poems, and marks a sharp departure in the particular stance it takes on these topics.[28] The poetry of [Tib.] 3, then, is both recognizably elegiac, taking pains to situate itself in relation to earlier poetry, and subtly different, muting certain canonical themes and developing others which had been underexplored.

II: CONTEXTS: THE 'AUGUSTAN AGE', PATRONS, AND POETIC COMMUNITIES

We move on to a discussion of poetry in the context of Augustan Rome, especially in terms of the development of patronage, of censorship, and of poetic community, by way of offering some historical context into which to locate the poems of [Tib.] 3 (see Section III below for further discussion of historicism). We leave aside for the moment the question of the dating of [Tib.] 3 (Section V below); whenever it was written, it situates itself in the late Augustan period, which is the time when the majority of extant elegy was written. So too, although the elegiac *amator* regularly locates himself outside of normal morality, and the expectations of masculinity, he does so in a context in which other non-elegiac poets are doing the same thing, declaring themselves exempt from or incapable of the social and political roles expected of adult men.

First, Augustan Rome: the historical record is nearly unanimous in suggesting a kind of moral revival under the leadership of Augustus. It is by no means clear what contemporaries made of this, nor is it clear—as used to be thought—that the *princeps* put into place a fully-thought-out programme of reform; more recent scholarship emphasizes its tentative nature. Scholars also have trouble deciding how to interpret what looks like a moralistic streak in the emperor, particularly in terms of his focus on the behaviour of upper-class women. Most

---

[28] See, however, Perkins 2011 for the argument that the opposition between *poeta* and *puella* is always already undermined (her article focuses specifically on Ov. *Am*, but it has larger implications).

relevant for our purposes are the Augustan laws on marriage, *Lex Julia de maritandis ordinibus* and *Lex Julia de adulteriis coercendis* of 18 BCE (later modified, and seemingly mitigated, by the *Lex Poppia Poppaea* of 9 CE), which created legislation on, and so made public, the issue of adultery. In the past, this had been a household problem, handled within the family, but the new laws imposed strict penalties and continued the Augustan practice of acting as if the Roman populace were members of his extended family.[29]

What is most interesting about these laws, at least if the attention of later legal experts is any indication, is that they seem to have attempted to divide women into just two mutually exclusive categories: those of the upper-classes, whom one could marry, and those who were not respectable. The reality was surely a bit more complicated, and elegy, or so it seems, capitalizes upon this confusion. The elegiac relationship certainly looks as if it describes and even advocates adultery, which had not been nearly so much of an issue for previous generations (this is not to say that adultery increased or decreased in the Augustan period, merely that it was being given a lot of imperial attention).[30] It is often observed that elegy's morality is ambiguous: the *vir* could be a husband, but need not be; we might simply be talking about freedwomen, whose personal lives were subject to no official concern. But this is precisely the point: it ought to have been possible for the elegists to allow no ambiguity (e.g. P. A. Miller 2004: 173). So there is at least an implicit tension between (what the elegists present as) Augustanism and their own lifestyle choices. This is also present in the elegiac rejection of the military life (which, however, resurfaces in the figuration of love as war; see Section I above).

***

In addition to the changes brought by Augustus, there are a number of further factors that affect an understanding of the composition of poetry around the turn of the millennium. The Roman world as a whole operated under a system of patronage, which has some rather different implications from its modern relatives. I focus here only on literary patronage; the larger phenomenon is extremely complex and is still not fully understood.[31] It is also unclear to what degree literary patronage is a variant of patronage in general, and to what degree it is a separate entity which adopts some of the vocabulary of patronage. It may well be the

---

[29] This vast series of topics can be discussed here only in the barest outlines; for further insights from a variety of angles, see Zanker 1988, Galinsky 1996: 128–40, O'Gorman 1997, Severy 2003, Milnor 2005.

[30] A useful parallel can be found in Laclos' *Les Liaisons Dangereuses*, an epistolary novel which treats a wide variety of immoral behaviours. The author's moralizing foreword and the tragic end of the two protagonists do little to undermine the joy the narrative seems to take in its own depiction of unconventional behaviour.

[31] On the subject of Augustan literary patronage, see Gold 1987: 111–72, White 1993.

case that the system was flexible enough to operate in a variety of different but immediately recognizable ways: some poets may have needed only encouragement and the presence of an audience, while others required more concrete assistance; so too, patrons may have treated poets more or less like their (other) clients, depending upon status and other factors. But whatever we are to make of Prop.'s claims that he was under pressure to write an epic (and scholars have made many different things of these claims, which appear also in some form in other Augustan poets), it is plain that there is also a story being told about the importance of poetry. And this story is not simply poetic fantasy: doers of great deeds were eager to have them commemorated in a wide variety of media.

So too, there remain many questions about how to understand the elegists vis-à-vis not only Augustanism, but also imperialism; would anything have changed in terms of poetic freedom during the move from Republic to Empire? Our poets mostly offer noisy laments that they are not skilled enough to write important public poetry (often assimilated by them to epic), which is usually taken by modern scholars to indicate a lack of interest in, or perhaps more accurately, a deliberate distancing from, the very notion of panegyric. For instance, some scholars look to elegy as a part of the story of freedom of speech under emperors, and the tale usually told is one of increasing repression.[32] We move from (the Republican, and so—purportedly—'free') Cat., who wrote a nasty poem about Caesar, was told he had offended the great man, apologized, and was invited to dinner (Suet. *Iul*.73), to a less rosy world for poets under Augustus, and thence to what is (again in oversimplified fashion) the wholly circumscribed speech that seems to many to be a feature of Neronian Rome and beyond. Questions of who is allowed to write, and how and why, are always crucial for authors, but concern about them seems to have reached a fever pitch in the Augustan age, as certain acts of what look like censorship suggest.[33] But things need not have been quite as black and white as later authors, writing in a different context, present them. It is also perhaps relevant that while the poets associated with Maecenas engage more directly with political issues (debates about how much and with what intent remain heated), the poets we can connect to Messalla (Tib., Ov., and perhaps the poets of [Tib.] 3) are noticeably apolitical (Hanslik 1952: 36). So it is likely that there is—as is so often the case in the Roman world—a more complicated system of affinities than may first appear.

---

[32] Again, a vexed question: see the sophisticated discussions in Griffin 1984, Nugent 1990, and Feeney 1991, each with further bibliography.

[33] As a counterweight to the evidence often adduced by scholars about Labienus' mimes, burned 6 CE (Sen. *Cont.* 10.*praef*.4–5, Suet. *Calig.* 16.1) and the exile of Cassius Severus in 8 CE (Tac. *Ann.* 1.72.3, 4.21.2, Suet. *Calig.* 16.1) there is Sen. *Ira* 3.23.4–8, on Augustus' patience with the slanders of Timagenes. Scholars debate about whether the emperor's withdrawal of his friendship from the poet Gallus in the early 20s BCE (seemingly based on his political and not his literary failings) is preposterously harsh or exceedingly gentle.

Maecenas is the great literary patron of the Augustan age, and 'supported' (whatever that may mean) Vergil, Horace, and Prop.[34] Tib. dedicates a number of poems to Messalla, who features also in some poems of [Tib.] 3 (see Section IV below). Ov. shows little interest in any patron in his earlier poetry, but in exile claims to have had very close ties with Messalla and his two sons. Scholars sometimes speak of a 'circle of Messalla' like that of Maecenas, but there is no way of knowing whether this actually existed or how formal it was: here again, there are likely to have been variations upon a theme, running the gamut from regular, formal gatherings (or even workshops) of poets to occasional opportunities to meet like-minded people at literary dinners. Later generations of poets focus on the Augustan age as a good time for poets, mostly because of the elite habit of patronizing them; this is sometimes explicit, as with Martial and Juvenal, and sometimes implicit, as with the *Appendix Vergiliana*, which imaginatively situates itself in that period and invokes the patronage of great men. So too, literary gatherings may have had at least implicit political import (as did much else at Rome), at least if later imperial writers' anachronistic re-creations are any basis for judgement: Maecenas may have been the imaginary patron of loyalists of later generations, Messalla that of would-be Republicans.[35]

The question of patronage is relevant to [Tib.] 3 in a couple of ways. First, as has already been noted, some of the S. poems mention Messalla. And second, it has seemed plausible to some that [Tib.] 3 is exactly what it purports to be, a collection of poems written by a group of poets in a context which we might loosely call patronage, perhaps at a 'poetry evening' or perhaps as part of a more formal 'working group'.[36] But this latter may well be an anachronistic theory; there is little evidence to support it. Still, it is worth exploring what can be known about the poetic communities in the Augustan age and later periods. The ancient understanding of the process of writing bears some relationship to our own, but is also subtly different. For one thing, there was normally a presumption that literature, especially poetry, was written with an audience in mind, and designed for public performance. This is especially true for Homeric poetry, archaic Greek lyric, and Athenian drama. But even in later periods, when poetry is more obviously textualized, it is often apparent that a particular, oral performance context is assumed. Beyond this, while it is abundantly clear that Latin poets were keenly engaged with their predecessors and contemporaries, the erudition and allusiveness in a typical poem may reflect large-scale

---

[34] He was also an author in his own right; see André 1983. See Bellandi 1995 on Maecenas' reputation as a patron in the Empire.
[35] I owe this point to Ian Fielding.
[36] Lachmann 1876 seems to have been the first to propose a circle of poets around Messalla (150–1; see Navarro Antolín 1996: 26 on the early and sustained favour it found); see White 1993: 36–8 on the problematic aspects of conceptualizing a patronage 'circle' (primarily, that Romans liked to have influence in as many arenas as possible). See further Section IV below on the 'circle' of Messalla.

Contexts: the 'Augustan Age', Patrons, and Poetic Communities   19

memorization more than, or instead of, the modern image of a desk full of books and papers.

In general, then, late Republican and early Augustan Latin poetry exists on the border between something you read alone in your room (e.g. Ov. *Ars* 1.1–2, *Tr.* 2.259–60), something pre-written for public performance (e.g. Ov. *Ars* 3.345, *Tr.* 2.519–20 and 5.7.25 on the recitation and dancing, *composita cantetur . . . voce* and *saltare*, of portions of his own poetry), and something composed in a group setting (e.g. Cat. 50). Roman poets themselves offer little detail about how they wrote, and there are any number of modern models which may or may not be relevant. For instance, poets might have done a lot of composing in their heads before writing anything down, or they might have had slaves handy to jot down good lines or fragments of lines, or they might have gathered with friends to try bits out, or they might have 'sat down to work' at a particular period of the day, or all of these (or none).

We do know something, however, both about poetic recitations, and about what look like opportunities for poets to share their work with one another. Much of that information is from a slightly later period; from the Augustan era we have Prop. 2.34.65, claiming (before its release to the general public) that the *Aeneid* is something 'greater than the *Iliad*' and also tales from the *Life of Vergil* (not contemporary, but possibly reflecting the Augustan world) about Vergil's reliance on public *recitationes* to help him finish particular lines of poetry.[37] The picture is unclear, but it is at least plausible to assume that contemporary poets might have shared completed work, perhaps even work in progress. The obscure *collegium poetarum*[38] (like other *collegia*) seems to have been something like a union, something like a private club, and may well have provided opportunities for poets to exchange ideas.[39] Finally, in the fictional realm, Ov., I have argued elsewhere, presents for us an analogy for how poetic composition works in his single *Heroides*, where lovelorn women write letters to the men they love; the

---

[37] See Plin. *Ep.* 7.17, which suggests that *recitationes* of a variety of texts proliferated in the High Empire; this might have led to anachronistic attribution of the practice to the Augustan age.

[38] The *collegium* was first housed in a temple of Minerva on the Aventine, seemingly founded in 207, but perhaps this date merely marks a recognition of its importance, which derived from the popularity of Livius Andronicus (Festus 446.32–448.1–4 L; Livy 27.37.7). It seems then to have moved to the temple of Hercules Musarum. Val. Max. 3.7.11 seems to imply that it originated as a theatrical association, perhaps initially including actors (the *schola poetarum* at Mart. 3.20.8 and 4.61.2 is perhaps also relevant); for further discussion see Sihler 1905 (who suggests that the building may have housed busts and even manuscripts), Horsfall 1976 (who posits the association as much less prestigious), and Gruen 1990: 87–91 (who sees it as part of Rome's 'receptiveness to foreign institutions').

[39] See too mentions of a poets' festival at Ov. *Tr.* 5.3, and *sacra* at *EP* 2.10.17, 3.4.67–76, 4.8.81, and Mart. 10.58.13. Gurd 2012, working on a different series of texts, emphasizes the fact that revision often happens in a communal setting (*passim*; cf. esp. 4). This may well mean that a group which is tightly knit prevents us from being able to assign passages or even whole poems to individual hands (see e.g. Sisman 2006, on the regular difficulty in differentiating between Coleridge and Wordsworth).

letters are notoriously similar to one another, which might well be designed to reflect the notion that they were composed communally (Fulkerson 2005).

A final facet of the elegists' self-fashioning that has already been explored is also interesting in the light of patronage: the pose of *servitium amoris* (see Section I above), in which the elegist humbles himself in relation to his powerful mistress, also shares elements of the language and stance of literary patronage (Gold 1993). So too, both Cat. and L. seem to envision their *puellae* as not only *doctae* but as women whose literary opinions matter. L.'s first poem, for instance, is dedicated to N. in a way that conflates the *patronus* with the *puella*.[40]

III: THEORETICAL APPROACHES TO ELEGY

A variety of different theoretical approaches have been central to scholarship on amatory elegy. I summarize here the three that have most frequently and influentially been seen as appropriate to [Tib.] 3 or, usually, to some portion of it. The first, the romantic, or biographical mode of criticism, treats elegy as the sincere, at least semi-autobiographical, record of real events.[41] It recognizes that life is transmuted into art, but believes poetry can, if approached properly, provide insight about the real world. It might, for instance, attempt to count up the number of love affairs Tib. actually had by examining how many different women and men appear in his poetry, and then, perhaps, determining the length of each and arranging them in chronological order; it might even measure this pattern against the love affairs of other poets, arrived at in a similar manner, or gathered from different sources, and use this to come to certain judgements about Tib., e.g. that he was unusually uxorious, or perhaps especially chaste. While this approach has been loudly and repeatedly discredited (especially in the oversimplistic form in which I present it here),[42] it regularly creeps in through the back door, especially when the poetry in question is believed to have been written by less talented poets. (The presumption seems to be that amateurs are not clever enough to make things up.) So too, scholars in fields other than Latin poetry (e.g. historians) and those who read only individual poems often assume that they can take those poems as evidence of something existing in the real world; one example is discussions of the existence or non-existence of a 'marriage law' of the Augustan period, the evidence for which is derived from Prop. 2.7.

---

[40] But note White on the ways the patron is sometimes conceived of as a Muse (1993: 20 and n. 39). For female patrons of literature, see White 1993: 90 and Hemelrijk 1999: 100–3.

[41] I have chosen to treat the 'biographical' approach at greater length than others because it seems such a 'natural' way to read poetry that it requires exposition; other models of interpretation (though some of them are immensely complex) are more readily identifiable as theoretical.

[42] Griffin 1985 has fallen out fashion, but is still well worth reading; I find his explication of Prop. as a kind of 'Antony-figure' both interesting and useful.

This approach, which we might also term 'historicist', believes that fitting the poetry into a context, ideally a historical one, is not only a valid technique, but can generate genuine knowledge. The heyday of elegy's production occurred towards the middle and end of the Augustan period, a time of great interest to many students of the ancient world, and the Emperor Augustus seems to have been interested—as were the elegists, if from a rather different angle—in issues of sexuality and the changing roles of women. It is therefore tempting to look to elegy for information about that world (see Section II above for some of the most prevailing currents in this debate).

The point about artistry being incompatible with amateurism is worth emphasizing in the context of [Tib.] 3: 'good' poets, most literary critics agree, have precise and carefully honed techniques through which they convey a *persona*, one who sometimes gives the appearance of sincere emotion. Indeed, the better the poet, and the more developed the conventions of the genre, the more convincing this appearance will be. But that does not mean that those who come newly to the writing of poetry are unable to create such *personae*, nor that we should assume that all they write is unvarnished autobiography. Latin elegiac poetry is not the result of neurosis, slips of the tongue (or reed), or unguarded moments: it is a highly stylized art form, in which apparent sincerity is part of the mannered effect. But less famous, or perhaps just less experienced, poets are not always given the benefit of the doubt; there is scholarship which claims that, for instance, some of the syntactical oddities in the poetry of L. derive from the fact that he was not a native speaker of Latin. This is, of course, possible, but it is never a solution proposed for Prop., whose text is far more difficult to comprehend.[43]

To be fair, art does tend to capture some of its creators' own experiences (budding writers even today are regularly given the advice to 'write what you know'), and there is no agreed-upon way of separating fact from fiction. For instance, Ov.'s exile poetry is full of first-person autobiographical statements, such as when he tells us that he was married three times, the first two unhappily.[44] Should we believe that this is the literal truth? Can we imagine a reason for him to lie? How might we reconcile this information, whether true or not, with the fact that he has what seems to be an illicit affair with 'Corinna'? While many different genres of poetry are narrative, and so subject to interpretation of a biographical kind, elegy seems especially prone to be understood as telling a 'real' story. This is in part because it is normally written in the first person, but

---

[43] See Tarrant 2016: 105–23 on the history of the text of Prop., whose editorial tradition has been especially controversial; 111–13 contain a list of (seemingly genuine) features of Propertian style which might usefully be compared to certain lines of L.

[44] *EP* 4.10.69–74. This is an especially interesting example, as it was long assumed that such a bald statement must reflect literal truth. But see Hinds 2005 and Fairweather 1987 on some very convenient coincidences in Ovid's autobiography, which suggest motives for fabricating, or perhaps only massaging, the facts.

also because elegiac *personae* often share 'intimate' details and behave with a kind of consistency from poem to poem. So too, the repetition of many 'basic' elegiac situations (see Section I above), lends its own air of genuineness. In the case of elegiac poets, we tend to have little external biographical information about them. Literary critics abhor a vacuum as much as the next person, and the temptation to draw inferences from poetry is difficult to resist. Nor is it always clear that it should be resisted. For instance, Ov. *Am.* 3.9 is a poem about the death of the elegist Tib. Hardly anyone would suggest that it is mere fiction, that Ov. was simply engaging in a rhetorical exercise. And so, based on the other evidence we have for dating Tib.'s death to 19 BCE, it is normally assumed—and probably, with good reason—that *Amores* 3 was published after that date.

Those who reject biographical criticism, on the other hand, might suggest that we can expect to learn nothing—or at least, very little—about an authentic individual through his or her poetry, and this premise in fact gets us to the very heart of some of the problems of interpretation of [Tib.] 3. For instance, to take the most ideologically charged example, and one to which we shall return often, can we understand the poetry of S., voiced in the feminine, as reflecting the biological sex of its author, or not? If so, what can she—the only female pre-Christian Latin poet whose words we have—tell us about women's lives? For many, these are compelling questions, and ideologically worth any amount of effort. Doubters note that it is precisely in contemporary elegiac poetry that we find instances of male poets adopting or 'ventriloquizing' the female voice: Ovid's *Her.* are the most obvious, but there is also Prop 4.3 and, if we extend our parameters more broadly, 1.3, 4.7, 4.8, and 4.11 (see Section VI below). Furthermore, [Tib.] 3 itself engages in the practice of ventriloquism, with a series of poems not only *about* S., but (perhaps) some written in her own voice (3.9 and 3.11) (see Section V below). But engaging in strictly biographical criticism of the S. poems then runs the risk of isolating her work from the category of 'real' poetry; it is all to the good that critics no longer speak about S.'s 'earnest sincerity' or compare her (putatively unselfconscious) 'little elegies' to private letters (e.g. Smith 1913: 83, Luck 1969: 107). Considering her as a separate category from (male) poets seems to me to involve more losses than gains, so—as with the other poets of [Tib.] 3—I mostly seek to incorporate S. into the mainstream.

***

A second and also important way of looking at elegy is more or less the opposite of the previous, and we might call it symbolic or formalist. This stance considers elegy to offer a discourse about discourse; the elegist adopts a series of pre-scripted poses, working them out as so many exercises. There are a variety of scholarly understandings of how and why this methodology is appropriate and how it functions. For some, such as Veyne, elegy is a code, an internally coherent system which is not really transferrable to any other mode of explication;

Kennedy's reading of the use of metaphor in elegiac erotic discourse is similar.[45] Many explicitly theoretical interpretations of elegy fall into this category. So, for instance, the psychoanalytic readings of P. A. Miller and Janan posit elegy as a response to the conditions of contemporary life, but also as expressing a more universal phenomenon in a particular way; for both, elegy marks the rupture between what is real and what people believe/say is real.[46] Another fruitful formalistic approach has been narratology, since elegy seems to be telling a single story (or at least, the consistency of names suggests so). But elegy's narrative is fragmented, in a number of ways: it is not only that we do not get a coherent story from beginning to end, but that it is partial: we hear only the poet/lover's version of events, and a number of elegiac poets hint at the biased nature of the versions they give us.[47]

To some extent, the biographical and the formal approaches must be opposed, as they are mutually incompatible. Those who are able to tolerate the ambiguity, however, can benefit from a mixture of the two: it is rare to find a critic who believes s/he can reconstruct an authorial biography from poetry, but it is also rare to find a critic whose interests are solely in the relationships of poems to themselves, and not to any external reality. Some of the most sophisticated work in Latin elegy picks its way carefully between the two camps—indeed, most of the scholarship that has already been cited has been forced to fit one mould or the other. Even those critics who are not at all interested in biographies of individual authors would often agree that elegiac poetry can tell us important things about the real world. The Augustan marriage legislation has already been mentioned, but there are many other examples: the prevalence of slaves as doorkeepers, messengers, and hairdressers in elegy is likely to reflect their genuine roles in Roman life of the period, and there is much incidental information to be gained about Roman daily life and *mores* from the poetry. Many, whether they acknowledge it or not, strive for a middle path between these two opposites, one which struggles not to make too many biographical statements, but seeks to mine elegiac poetry for bits of useful information. And this makes its own kind of sense (even though it is not always logically defensible).

***

Our third key theoretical approach, feminist and gender theory, can, and in practice does, ally itself with either of the other two approaches, although it

---

[45] Veyne 1988; Kennedy 1993.

[46] P. A. Miller 2004 makes the case that elegy is a poetic response to the unmanning of the elite Roman male in the Augustan period (e.g. 45); Janan 2001 explores the effects of the Lacanian 'divided subject' in the multiple narrative voices of Prop. 4. Janan 2012 offers a very useful introduction to psychoanalytic approaches; her own stance is Lacanian.

[47] Lively 2012: 411–22 treats the S. poems, her limit case for 'fragmentary narrative'; note Caston 2012 on the ways the poets simultaneously express their own jealousy and undermine our ability to find them plausible.

tends to start from a different place. It is eminently reasonable (if you are not wholly a formalist) to believe that the study of elegy can help us to understand *something* about the women of Augustan Rome, and about gender relations in that period: surely they must reflect reality in some fashion or other. But, however unobjectionable in principle, this stance is not especially useful unless we know just how to disentangle the 'real' from the fictive. So, for instance, is the *puella* such a dominating force in elegy because she was in Roman life? If so, does her dominance derive from force of personality, from the simple quasi-economic fact that she has what the lover wants, or from her status? (She might be either higher on the social scale than the *amator*, as the poetry of Cat. seems to suggest, or so low that her movements are unconstrained.) Is her dominance a refraction of some other element of reality, such as a perception among men that women were (newly?) exercising more freedom? Is it simply a joke, deriving humour from its patent absurdity? These are questions well worth answering, but it is by no means obvious how we might go about doing so.

Gendered approaches to elegy, then, encompass a range of critical stances. One pole, connected to our first interpretative frame, reflects a concern with the material realities of actual Roman women (and men), looking at how the women of elegy behave and are treated. James 2003, for instance, suggests that the elegiac mistress is best understood as a courtesan, a cross between the (fictional) world of Roman comedy and the realities of Roman women of the non-elite. Her reading has been extremely influential, and probably provides the single most persuasive interpretation for what the elegiac mistress 'really' is.[48] Another branch of feminist thought suggests that all we ever get are refractions, and that we cannot hope to discover anything genuine about women from male-authored texts; elegiac women are inevitably either symbol or caricature. Even when the elegiac woman speaks, her words are compromised by the fact that they are channelled through (and written by) her male author. For such scholars, the *puella* is only ever textual. This theory of the *scripta puella* or 'written woman' (Wyke 1987, 1994) has also been influential, as has the notion that female characters are 'womanufactured' (Sharrock 1991) to fit the artistic needs of their creators.[49] And some scholars see the disjunction between male and female as emblematic of other concerns, reflecting larger binary oppositions and power differentials, such as those between master and slave, wealthy and poor, emperor and subject, active and passive, and the like, or of the poet's struggle with his (recalcitrant, feminized) poetry.

Although each of the three approaches I have outlined above is backed by a substantial theoretical armature, all are also what we might call transparent: readers without much technical background might well adopt one or more of them

---

[48] See too Adams 1983: 344–8 on the use of *puella* to denote prostitutes.
[49] This discussion is, of course, not unique to Latin poetry; see Gubar 1982 on the trope of woman as art-object and literature as a (man's) way of possessing her.

without intending to ally themselves with an interpretative community. One might, indeed, think one is 'only' reading poetry with the 'normal' assumptions one brings to bear. In this short discussion of theoretical approaches I have therefore not attempted to cover all of the bases, merely those that are most likely to influence 'first' readers of the poems.

IV: WHAT'S IN A NAME? NAME, PSEUDONYM, AND PERSONA WITHIN [TIB.] 3

The poems of [Tib.] 3 are unique in elegy in that they are, at least apparently, by a number of different hands. They are usually known as *Corpus Tibullianum* 3 or *Appendix Tibulliana*, both ways of suggesting a connection to Tib. that may or may not go beyond the fact that these poems eventually formed part of the same manuscript tradition (see Section VIII below). I outline here the traditional divisions within the corpus, before moving on to more highly contested matters. Poems 1–6 are attributed to L. (whose *puella*, or erstwhile *puella*, is N.); 7, not treated in this volume, is a lengthy hexameter panegyric to Messalla which has recently been interpreted as parodic (Peirano 2012: 132–48; see too Section V below); 8–12 is a cycle of poems about a woman named S. and normally ascribed to an anonymous *amicus*, with the even-numbered poems written in the third person, and the odd-numbered poems written in the first person; 13–18 claim to be by S. herself, and focus on her love for a man named Cerinthus. It has become traditional to divide the S. poetry into these two groups, primarily because the poems in the latter group are significantly shorter than those in the former, and because they are rather different in style, but there have been suggestions that one or more of the '*amicus*' poems ought to be attributed to S. (see Section V below). 19–20 round out the collection with two anonymous poems, the first claiming Tibullan authorship. In the fifteenth century, Italian scholars divided the non-Tibullan poems of Book 3 into two books, with the *Panegyric to Messalla* (3.7) and the poems after it separated from the others (see Section VIII on the manuscript tradition); this edition uses the standard, single-book numbering system. These poems are followed in different manuscripts by a funerary epigram for Tib. and Vergil written by Domitius Marsus, a very short prose life of Tib., and/or two of the Priapea (none of which are treated in this volume).[50]

---

[50] The Priapea were seemingly attached to the *Fragmentum Cuiacianum* (see Section VIII below), but are probably not related to [Tib.] 3. The *vita* and epigram (the latter attributed by the *Fragmentum Cuiacianum* to Domitius Marsus; see Fisher 1983: 1931–3 for discussion of both) appear at the end of most manuscripts.

Thus the corpus as it is usually divided. To distinguish between the 'anonymous' poems and poems written by L., S., or her 'friend', however, is somewhat arbitrary, given that we do not know anything about any of these authors other than what we can glean from the poetry itself (see Section V on authorship). Aside from what can be gained implicitly from stylistic considerations and from the regular poetic practice of weaving images and even phrases of previous poets into one's own work, it is not absolutely certain that any of these poets had an influence on those who came later—but of course the question of priority is a difficult one in this corpus; it may well be that the common scholarly assumption that 'bad' poets borrow from 'good' ones—and never the reverse—has blinded us to these poets' importance (see Section V below for extended discussion of the most notorious of these examples). Outside of the corpus, only S., perhaps, is mentioned by a later author: Mart. 10.35 and 38, who also alludes in these poems to a later female poet of the same name (possibly the S. of Sid. *Carm.* 9.261-2, who writes *suo Caleno*); this passage, like nearly everything else about S., has come under scholarly suspicion. And, of course, the *amicus* poetry seems to be predicated upon S.'s own (although in our corpus it precedes it); indeed, 3.13—apparently authored by S.—offers her story to anyone (*si quis*) who would like to tell it.

Authorship in and of the corpus, then, is a tricky matter. It is possible—but unlikely—that each of our poems was written by a different individual assuming one of three or four distinct personae, so that we could have twenty different authors writing the twenty poems, or ten authors writing two poems each. Such a theory is rendered less plausible by the fact that the *personae* are not so distinct or so immediately identifiable that the reason for such a practice is obvious. L., for example, writes like Tib. in places, but also like Ov., and sometimes even like Prop.; if 'Lygdamean' poetry were designed to be a unique subspecies of elegy, we would expect his poetry to be more stylistically distinct. Given the anomalous nature of a woman writing elegy (see Section VI below), the poetry of 'S.', on the other hand, may well fall into the category of being immediately recognizable as a discrete type. So too, the book itself provides us with an example of the practice of writing poetry under an alias, if indeed 3.9 and 3.11 are correctly attributed to the *amicus* rather than to S. herself. And if 3.19 is not genuinely Tibullan (see *ad loc.*), we have another example of the assumption of another's name (see below on the name L. elsewhere in elegy). It is also possible—but for most contemporary scholars, implausible—that the entirety of the corpus was written by a single author. The problem of who wrote what is likely to be insoluble: there is not enough of the poetry to perform reliable statistical analyses, and the stylistic features we can see (such as that S.'s own poetry is extremely compacted) are likely to have been equally obvious to an author trying to write or duplicate 'Sulpician poetry'. So too, we have no clues about how many authors we ought to be searching for, if the obvious cyclical divisions are incorrect.

I therefore adopt here, more for ease of reference than from any strong ideological commitment, the standard authorial/cyclical division, encouraging the reader to bear in mind throughout that we know next to nothing about the actual individual(s) who wrote and/or compiled the collection. I attempt to make the best case I can (see Section V below, but also throughout the commentary), for upholding that traditional division, including treatment of some scenarios by which the poems might have come to be collected as a unit, and attached to the poetry of Tib. On the other hand, I also take note, where I believe it is plausible, of scholarship that proposes different arrangements; these focus especially on reattribution of the '*amicus*' poems (Parker 1994 proposes 3.9 and 11 as genuinely Sulpician, Hallett 2002a: 47 (and elsewhere) that 3.8–12 are all Sulpician).

***

I offer here a brief discussion of the names of each of the major characters in [Tib.] 3, before moving on to discuss ancient theories of persona and anonymous authorship in more detail. None of the names of the characters in the corpus, with the exception of S. and Messalla, is a Roman name (the rest are Greek), but all appear elsewhere in Latin literature. It is usual in elegiac love poetry for the poet to use his own name, but to provide a pseudonym for his *puella*. As has often been noted, those pseudonyms tend to have some larger significance; Prop.'s Cynthia and Tib.'s Delia are feminine versions of cult titles of Apollo (the god of poetry); Cat.'s Lesbia is a way of referring to the Greek poet Sappho; Ov.'s Corinna is the name of a Boeotian poet; Tib.'s Nemesis is a goddess in her own right. And they are also metrically equivalent to the women's 'real' names (see Apul. *Apol.* 10 for the ancient evidence, which does not include Corinna). Tib.'s Marathus, by contrast (= 'fennel', Latin *marathrum*), sounds vaguely pastoral and is attested as the name of a freedman (according to Suet. *Div. Aug.* 79.2 and 94.3, Julius Marathus wrote something like a biography of Augustus); his might well be a real name.

Lygdamus' name, Greek in origin, may be a pseudonym. There is, however, no immediately obvious reason why L. should not have written under his own name, as it is not the practice of other elegists to disguise their identities. If it is his given name rather than a pseudonym, this may suggest a servile origin for the family, but not necessarily for L. himself.[51] Prop.'s Cynthia has a slave named L. (3.6 and 4.7). Indeed, the Greek λύγδος (white marble; adj. λύγδινος, white[52]) has connotations of beauty, which might be appropriate for a Greek slave (often

---

[51] See Della Corte 1972: 694; Knox, forthcoming: 8. Della Corte 1983 draws attention to *CIL* XIV.2298, a poetic epitaph for a freedman of Cotta which bears similarities to a number of Tibullan poems; it is possible that L. is that freedman.
[52] This connection was seemingly first made by Dissen 1835: xxxii.

regarded as a luxury object). Legal status is of course no impediment to literacy in the Roman world; Greeks in particular tended to be teachers, and a slave (or freedman) L. might well have been a member of the household of Messalla, or the Sulpicii, or some family with whom they were in regular contact. His poetry, more like that of standard elegy than the other poems of this corpus in its regular use of mythological exempla (see Section I above), certainly suggests access to the literary world of Greece and Rome. And whatever his origins, L. certainly conceives of himself as a Roman (see 3.1.4, where he refers to *nostris avis*); the phrase is telling even if it reflects only naturalized citizenship.[53]

On the other hand, there are those who see in the name of L. a bilingual pun; translated into Latin, the name would probably be Albus or Albius, which is the *nomen* of Tib. So there is a chance that L. has offered us in his name a clue to his identity (though the style of L. is rather different from that of Tib.). Further speculations abound: Ehwald 1889: 6 etymologizes the name with reference to λύγδην, sobbing. Bickel 1960, followed by Navarro Antolín 1996, suggests that the name is an erudite joke, appropriating the name of a Propertian slave in order to situate L. as the quintessentially elegiac slave of love (see Section I above for the *topos*); Navarro Antolín 1996 opines further that the 'whiteness' of his name is meant to play on the traditional pallor of the lover (21). Evidence about L.'s status from within the corpus is sparse: some understand his apparent claims to wealth at 3.3.4 as the typical freedman's flaunting of newly acquired status and resources (see *ad loc.*).

Neaera, the *puella* of L.'s poetry, may be a pseudonym as well, but hers is also a regular name for courtesans (Hor. *Od.* 3.14.21, for instance, suggests a symposiastic context; Hor. *Epod.* 15.11 and V. *E.* 3.3 one of erotic pursuit; in Greek, see H. *Od.* 12.132–3, where she is a nymph); N. differs from other *puellae*, as L. does from other poets, in having a recognizably Greek name. Phryne in Tib. 2.6.45 may be a relevant *comparandum*; both were the names of famous Greek courtesans, and so may have been adopted by their Roman counterparts, or, if not names chosen by the women themselves, they may have been selected by poets as especially appropriate to the women of elegy.[54] So too, some evidence suggests that 'professional women' had two names: Gallus' mistress, the mime

---

[53] See Postgate for the suggestion that certain difficulties in the language of L. derive from his poor mastery of Latin (1929: xliii). But this probably originates in the belief, common in previous generations, that L.'s poetry is second-rate; see Section III above on the benefit of the doubt normally given to the poetry of Prop., unreadable in parts.

[54] A courtesan N. is known from [Dem.] 59, where she is accused of adulterating the Athenian citizen pool, but there were also eponymous comedies by Timocles (fr. 25–6; Athen. 13.567e, 591d), Philemon (fr. 49; Athen. 13.590a), and Licinius Imbrex (Ribbeck 3.1–2; Gellius 13.23.16). The Athenian courtesan Phryne was the mistress of the orator Hyperides and the sculptor Pheidias; see McClure 2003: 126–36 for the two most common anecdotes about her. Keith 2016 discusses the early Imperial Latin epigraphic evidence for women who have the names of famous predecessors (especially literary ones); these may but need not have been prostitutes. Finally, Postgate 1914 argues that N.'s name may be slang for the female genitalia.

actress Volumnia Cytheris, worked under the name Lycoris (metrically equivalent to Cytheris); the existence of such professional names renders problematic the notion of a pseudonym, as in certain cases it may be better known than a woman's given name (see too McClure 2003: 68–74).

We know even less about N. than we do about other fictional elegiac mistresses: she does not speak, and her physical attributes are not described, nor are L.'s interactions with her detailed in any way; in fact, she is never actually present in the poetry. Some of this vagueness surely derives from the fact that the amatory relationship between the couple has ended—at least temporarily. And here too we see a significant difference in the poetry of L.: elegists often think about whether they ought to continue suffering as they do, but we never see them in a position of wholly frustrated longing (it is always temporary). If Tib.'s Delia is no more by Book 2, she is replaced by Nemesis, and never mentioned again. Prop.'s Cynthia is somewhat trickier: apparently banished from Book 4, she erupts back into it again, returning even from the dead. So N. is not your standard *puella*. But some of what looks like a noteworthy divergence in L.'s poetry from how elegy usually works may derive from the accidents of preservation: it may be that we have only a segment of L.'s tale, and that earlier or later poems would have filled in some of the detail. Still, as it stands, it is noticeable that L.'s poetry presents no moment of joy, or even of togetherness, with N.

The name of **Sulpicia** is perhaps the most striking aspect of [Tib.] 3: In 3.16.4, she names herself *Servi filia Sulpicia*, 'S., the daughter of Servius'. This nomenclature connects her to the Roman citizen body, and so marks her off as distinctly un-elegiac. The Servii Sulpicii are well known in many periods of Roman history, including the late Augustan age.[55] As is usual for questions about S., there is no way of knowing whether the biography that has been constructed for her is an accurate one. But the details offered in the poetry do seem to suggest an Augustan context (for some, in fact, the very number of 'clues' pointing towards Messalla is suspicious—but Roman women always identified themselves through family relations: they took their names from their fathers and, where necessary, a distinguishing adjective from their husbands).[56]

If S. is in fact what her name suggests—a highborn Roman woman—then what we think we know about the 'rules' of elegy will need reconsidering (see

---

[55] Perhaps the most famous of the Servii Sulpicii is the late Republican jurist, cos. 51 (*RE* 95), who died in 43 (see Cic. *Phil.* 9.12). We should probably imagine S. as a grandchild of the jurist, but she may be a daughter; the Servius mentioned at Hor. *Ser.* 1.10.85–6 is the son of a jurist, so perhaps S.'s father or brother (Syme 1981; 1986: 205). Cic. *Mur.* 54 mentions an *adulescens*, who might be the father/brother of S., and also the same as the S. Sulpicius mentioned by Ov. and Pliny as the author of erotic poems (*Tr.* 2.441; cf. Plin. *Ep.* 3.5.3). The jurist married a Valeria. If S. fits into this chronological schema, her father's (grandfather's?) death will have meant that S. (*RE* 114) became the ward of his brother-in-law, her uncle Messalla (first connected by Haupt 1871: 32–4).

[56] Whether S. is a real author or an invented one, her family provides her with literary connections; in addition to the previous footnote, see too Wiseman 1993 on her maternal Valerian connections to Cat. On the guardianship of women, Hallett 1984: 59–60 and n. 34 is a useful resource.

30 *Introduction*

Section I above). But if S.'s name is not meant to convey free birth and very high status, it is even more puzzling: why, of all of the women of elegy, do we have such a distinguished pedigree for the one who seems to present herself most explicitly as freely choosing an extra-marital affair? Some solve the problem by assuming, with no explicit justification in the poetry itself, that S. writes as a young woman about to be married (e.g. Treggiari 1991: 122, 302–3 on the S. poems as 'preliminaries to a marriage'); this speculation is often combined with the identification of Cerinthus with Cornutus (see below). It has also been suggested that we are meant to see the name as an elaborate hoax, that the contradictions between frank expression and high birth are meant to be savoured; if this is correct, the 'S. poems' could be a (tame) Latin version of the notorious sex manuals 'authored' by famous Greek courtesans, titillating in this case precisely because of the incongruity of person and utterance (see Section VI below for other female Latin authors, and for the issue of their explicitness).

Cerinthus, the beloved of S., is again a Greek name (appearing in, among other places, Theognis 1.891.4); the name, as with that of L., may be pseudonymous, servile, or both. (It is attested as a slave name in e.g. Hor. *Ser.* 1.2.81 with Porphyry *ad loc.*; see Cartault 1909: 81–2 and Knox, forthcoming: 28.)[57] Scholars have wanted to see in his name (κήρινθος = 'bee-bread', Davies 1973) an allusion to Apolline poetics of the sort very common for female beloveds in elegy (see above). Roessel ingeniously argues that the pseudonym reflects a different sort of poetic conceit, whereby Cerinthus' waxy name—Romans used wooden tablets covered with a thin layer of wax as an equivalent to our notebooks—puts him at the service of the poet, who inscribes her will upon him (1990: 243, 245). But the word may also be related to the Greek ἕλκος, a festering sore (*L&S II*)![58] If Cerinthus is a pseudonym, this is the most obvious, but by no means the only, example of S.'s plays with Roman gender roles: by giving him anonymity, she seems to suggest that *his* reputation might suffer; in the process, she feminizes him, as well as lowering his status.[59] That is, by being the recipient of love poetry, Cerinthus is implicitly part of the *puer delicatus* tradition of Greek and Latin lyric, i.e. he is being treated as a young and attractive—but also potentially low-status and effeminized—object of erotic attention. Indeed, the Horatian poem in which 'Cerinthus' is mentioned (*Ser.* 1.2.80–2) also focuses on status-difference in love, and seems to put that Cerinthus in the same class as Horace himself (i.e. the 'son of a freedman'). But Porphyry, the Horatian scholiast, suggests that Cerinthus there is the pseudonym of a prostitute, and because of this Boucher

---

[57] See e.g. *CIL* VI.3996, iv.4371 for the name as servile. *Cerinthae ignobile gramen* (V. *G.* 4.63) may also be relevant to the question. And note Fatucci for epigraphic evidence from Arezzo (1976: 157–8).

[58] I owe the point to James Morwood. Note too Bradley's observation that Kerinthos on Euboea is mentioned in the Homeric catalogue of ships (1995: 159).

[59] Hinds intriguingly notes that Cerinthus' name 'sounds like a masculine fusion of Corinna and Cynthia' (1987a: 38).

wonders if his name might be a Roman equivalent of 'Don Juan', such that hearing it tells us all we need to know about the situation (1976: 508, 518). This might, or might not, combine with scholarly suspicions about the identity of S. to render both pseudonymous. On the other hand, *CIL* VI.6.4.3.39011 is a funerary inscription for one L. Valerius Cerinthus and his wife; we have no way of knowing anything about these individuals, but he provides evidence that there was at one point a connection between the Valerii and a Cerinthus. (Messalla is a member of the *gens Valeria* and so too, perhaps, is S.)

In the tradition of elegiac *puellae*, Cerinthus is shadowy and passive (Pearcy 2006: 31–2); we know of him only that he seems to like hunting, that he may prefer a rival to S., and that he is loath to voice his feelings (see *ad* 3.9, 3.11, 3.16). The first is the most significant: it is difficult to reconcile hunting, an upper-class pursuit, with slave origins. Some suggest that Cerinthus' family is not humble, but simply not as noble as the Servii Sulpicii (e.g. Bréguet 1946: 34–5), which means that S. can semi-jokingly taunt him with low status. Finally, Cerinthus has been identified with the Cornutus mentioned by Tibullus in 2.2–3 as about to be married and celebrating a birthday (seemingly first by Gruppe 1838: 27; see further discussion in Hubbard 2004, focusing on similarities between Tib. 2.2 and 2.3 and the S. cycle).[60]

If Cerinthus is Cornutus, this would provide a satisfying coda to the cycle, with everybody living happily ever after (Lowe 1988: 196 n. 21). And the reconstruction is not sheer romantic fantasy: the two names are metrically equivalent (as *puella*-pseudonyms are), share consonants, and, most convincingly, the juxtaposition produces a bilingual pun ($κέρας$ = cornus).[61] And Tib. 2.2 and 2.3 do indeed share some similarities to the poetry of S. (see *ad loc.*). If Cerinthus is a 'Cornutus', he is probably M. Caecilius Cornutus (*PIR*², C34/*CIL* vi.32338), who was in the Arval college with Messalla, or his son (*PIR*² C35/*CIL* vi.2023a and Syme 1980: 2; Scheid 1975: 34–40 furnishes a speculative biography). Given the non-consular status of the Cornuti, we might attribute their election to Messalla's patronage. This theory could also explain S.'s snide comments in 3.18 about Cerinthus' low status—though, on the other hand, her status is so much higher than his that a marriage does not seem likely. This reconstruction, though plausible, cannot be proven or disproven with the information available; some readers will prefer to see the poems as part of a larger narrative, others not. There is one final appealing aspect about positing S. and Cerinthus as betrothed: we have some evidence that engaged Roman couples would have been able to spend unchaperoned time together; there is also the suggestion that physical contact

---

[60] Hubbard argues that 3.13–18 offer a reflection on Tib. 2.2 'through the novel approach of a miniature elegiac cycle in the voice of the bride herself. Just as 2.2.11–20 gives voice to Cornutus' wishes and inner feelings, as Tibullus imagined them, the S. poems do so for the other partner to the marriage' (2004: 185).

[61] Roessel 1990: 244 objects to the connection on the grounds of etymology and prosopography.

and even pre-marital intercourse would not have been unexpected.[62] S., in this scenario, becomes significantly less subversive, but also more comprehensible.

Finally, **Messalla**, the man behind it all (maybe). Messalla (*CIL* vi.32338; *RE* 261; see Syme 1986: 200–16) is well known to us as a patron of poets, a poet in his own right,[63] and as one of the last of the Republican old guard (he was, for instance, a cousin of the tyrannicide D. Brutus). Hammer 1925 provides as full a biography of him as the evidence will allow.[64] He seems to fade from public life in 26 or 25 BCE,[65] and reappears in 2, when he is the author of the proposal that Augustus be known as *pater patriae*. The jurist Servius Sulpicius Rufus married a Valeria, who is probably Messalla's sister, and the jurist's death provides an explanation for how Messalla came to be the guardian of S. (again, this is true whether we understand S. to be real or fictional; she is in the latter case a plausible fiction). As we noted above, the very nature of patronage began to change in the early Augustan period. For many, the Messallan version of it seems 'essentially Republican in nature' (Davies 1973: 25), i.e. it could certainly focus on the accomplishments of the patron in a way characteristic of later panegyric, but was also about private and family events (depending upon the identity of Cornutus, Tib. 2.2 and 2.3 may also fall into this category). Ov., another poet who claims Messalla as a patron, does so only in his exile poetry, written during a time in his life when traditional structures of patronage might have seemed useful;[66] his earlier work does not mention Messalla or members of his family by name, so it is not clear whether the relationship is retrospectively enhanced to serve his later needs.

Scholarship has struggled in vain to create a 'circle of Messalla' similar to that posited for Maecenas (which included Vergil, Horace, and Prop.; see Section II above).[67] The name of Messalla is associated with Tib.'s poetry (1.7 is a poem in praise of Messalla's triumph in September of 27 BCE), and Ov. claims in exilic letters to Messalla's children Messalinus and Cotta to have been supported by their father (*EP* 1.5, 1.7, 1.9, 2.2, 2.3, 2.8, 3.2, 3.5). But one very important difference between the two putative 'circles' is that Maecenas had, however officially or unofficially, encouragement from Augustus to support

---

[62] See Treggiari for the (limited) evidence, and for the conclusion that 'the phobia of pre-marital sex with a *sponsus* does not seem to occur until the empire becomes Christian' (1991: 159–60).

[63] Plin. *Ep.* 5.3.5; the poems were apparently bucolic ([V.] *Catal.* 9.13–20, Baligan 1967b) and perhaps elegiac ([V.] *Catal.* 9.23–4, but see Peirano 2012: 128); he also wrote memoirs, and there are some extant fragments of his oratory (Malcovati 1953 *ORF* 4 # 176). He was known as a stylist (Sen. *Cont.* 2.4.8, Quint. *Inst.* 10.1.113); Quintilian says that he translated famous Greek oratorical speeches into Latin (*Inst.* 10.5.2).

[64] See Hanslik 1955, who interprets somewhat differently, Valvo 1983 for the *status quaestionis* at that point, and Porte 1992 for further thoughts.

[65] He was named *praefectus urbi* in 26, but resigned within a few days (Tac. *Ann.* 6.11).

[66] E.g. Ov. *Tr.* 4.1, 4.4.27–30, *EP* 1.2.75–8, 1.7, 2.2.

[67] See Hanslik 1952 and Davies 1973 for discussion of common 'Messallan' themes, and Duret 1983: 1452–72 on the connections between poets and Messalla, including treatment of Macer (1467–72).

poetry; Messalla was, by contrast, a private citizen (see Section II above on patronage). Still, it is eminently likely that Messalla, interested in the literary arts, spent time with poets, and it is certainly possible that there was some slightly more formal arrangement, whereby he arranged for recitals and the like.[68]

***

We return, briefly, to the question of ancient poetic *personae*, because it has been suggested by a number of scholars that 'S.' may be meant not to denote some individual woman, but is rather a poetic stance available to any poet (most recently and fully argued in Hubbard 2004). Contemporary literary critics tend to assume that poetry is not autobiographical in any uncomplicated sense, even when the author of the poem and a character in it have the same name. For scholars of ancient poetry, too, this is a standard assumption, backed up by assertions in ancient poets themselves (see, e.g. Cat. 16, with nuanced discussion of the *topos* in Mayer 2003: 66–71). At the same time, it also seems to be the case that certain kinds of poetic voice became more easily liable to assimilation by others. This debate is at its most robust within the field of archaic Greek lyric poetry, where there are examples of texts circulating under the name of an author which are either seemingly or certainly not by that author (e.g. the *Anacreonta*, on which see Rosenmeyer 1992,[69] and also the Theognis poems, on which see West 1974: 40–61[70]). But there are also poems which contain a first-person voice but which may not express the sentiments of their authors (e.g. Hesiod and Pindar, to take the most regularly discussed[71]), or which contain 'speaking names' that might or might not reflect a genuine biography (e.g. Archilochus' poetry about Lycambes (= Wolf-Walker) and his

---

[68] The pseudo-Virgilian *Catalepton* 9, a poem written in praise of Messalla, is believed by most to be later than the Augustan period; it too may attest to the vitality of, or at least fantasies about, a 'Messallan' kind of patronage in the Empire (see Section II above).

[69] The *Anacreonta*, unlike some other poems in this category, announce themselves to be homage; the first poem of the collection details Anacreon's initiation of 'me' into the writing of poetry. So this corpus is explicitly about homage and emulation; but see too Rosenmeyer 1992: 21, 50, 70–1 on the ways in which it engages in a narrowing and 'stereotyping' of the complex Anacreontic persona into a more easily manageable unit.

[70] West 1974 is an author-centred study, attempting to separate out the authentic from the inauthentic, and to explain how the two were conflated.

[71] The Hesiodic voice is made more complicated by the fact that, like Homer's, it is likely to be a generations-long accretion of multiple voices; see Lamberton 1988: 23, 61–3 and *passim*; Nagy 1990 e.g. 48, 71, 80. In addition to the broader questions raised by Pindar's epinicians (which voice the 'I' of the chorus which sings them, but also, sometimes, the 'I' of the victor, and perhaps even the city), see Hubbard 2002 on fr. 123 S-M, which he argues is a commissioned poem; what looks to be first-person praise is in fact third-person. See too Scodel 1996: 61 on the 'pseudo-intimacy' deliberately created by poets who compose for larger audiences.

daughter Neoboule (= New Plan)).[72] The phenomenon may also occur outside of poetry; it is worth noting in this context that the genre of the Greek novel includes works by two authors named Xenophon, of whom the better known is Xenophon of Ephesus. Scholars have suggested that the two later Xenophons use the name as a kind of pseudonymic shorthand, borrowing for themselves some of the authority of what is often considered the Ur-novel, the *Cyropaedeia* (written by Xenophon of Athens).[73]

The above examples are Greek, but everything we know about Roman education, which is based on the practice of studying and then imitating exemplars, renders it plausible that the assumption of alternate voices would have been a recognizably Roman phenomenon as well. Indeed, both Ov. *Her.* and Prop. 4.3 are first-person fictions, wherein the poet voices a female subject (see Section VI below).[74] So it is not beyond the realm of possibility that the use of the name S. was a way of denoting a specific kind of poetry rather than a claim to actually being S., and that it was so understood by its original readers; this, in fact, might help explain the existence of another literary S., mentioned by Martial (10.35 and 10.38) as an author of erotic epigrams about her husband (Merriam 1991) and perhaps also the author of the *fragmenta Bobiensa* (see Butrica 2006 for the case that the two women are one). In the absence of further evidence the question cannot be resolved. But for these appropriative models to apply to S., there would need to be some reason for this kind of poetry to circulate under her name. This could be either (now-lost) writings by or about an actual woman named S., or some other tradition, now lost to us, in which Sulpiciae as a whole were seen as particularly prone to illicit love affairs. There is no evidence for either. Perhaps the most interesting part of this problem is the distance it points up between a modern concern with giving credit where credit is due and what looks to be an ancient insouciance about this issue.[75]

Peirano has recently offered a useful take on 'forgeries', including the corpora of texts falsely attributed to better-known authors, and she suggests that we need not assume that an author is attempting to adulterate a pure corpus by inserting inferior imitations under someone else's name; rather, particularly given that

---

[72] This is a matter much debated among specialists; for the standard discussions of what we are to make of the *persona loquens*, see Nagy 1976, Carey 1986; Irwin 1998 provides a history of the question up to that point, and Hawkins 2008 offers a novel interpretation of the relationship between Archilochus and Lycambes. See too Mayer 2003 on the varieties of ancient understandings of literary personae in poetry and prose, with very full bibliography. As he notes, the difficulties in distinguishing between persona and author become more pronounced when poetry is separated from performance, either by time or by context.

[73] See too Peirano 2012: 5–7 on the various kinds of 'pseudepigraphia' that attach themselves to a particular author's name, including the Hippocratic and Orphic texts.

[74] This happens even within the *corpus*: the 'friend' of S. does precisely the same thing (Lowe 1988: 197).

[75] Again, Peirano 2012 is very helpful on the issues; Tarrant 1989 and Janan 2007 make the case that non-contemporary authors who engage with a text by altering it often see themselves as taking part in a conversation rather than engaging in an appropriative gesture.

ancient educational paradigms focused on copying from a model (see too Grafton 1990: 11), the poems may be meant to be understood as tributes, included in a tradition but never intended to be taken as authentic exemplars of it (25–6, and *passim*; see too Tarrant 1987 and 1989 on interpolations within a text). This practice also occurs in Latin prose; to leave aside the notorious difficulties of the *Historia Augusta*, there is the pseudo-Sallustian invective *In Ciceronem*, which presumably was written not to deceive, but to explicate further the differing political positions of the two men. And, as Peirano also points out in her Chapter 3 (which treats [Tib.] 3.7), Messalla, as a well-known patron of literature, is an obvious locus for the work of minor or anonymous authors, either because they are contemporaries who have actually sought him as a patron, or in imitation of the Augustan poets who did so.[76]

V: CHRONOLOGY AND AUTHORSHIP: THE COMPOSITION AND ARRANGEMENT OF [TIB.] 3

Because elegiac poems do not regularly refer to the world outside, it is often difficult to date elegiac collections, either absolutely or relatively. The standard order of the elegists is presented above, in Section I, but it is clear that Tib. and Prop. were, at least in part, working in response to one another; Ov. is usually understood as a later author, but some of his work is contemporary with Tib. and Prop. About the following early elegiac dates, there is sufficient consensus: Gallus wrote at least one poem that can be dated to the return of Caesar from Rome in 45 BCE. Tib. died after 19 BCE (see Section IV above on the Domitius Marsus epigram on the deaths of Vergil and Tib., and Ov. *Am.* 3.9), and it is reasonable to assume that his own poetic output was limited by his early death (he was born between 55 and 48 BCE). Prop. was probably born between 49 and 47 BCE, and his fourth book can be dated to some time after 16 BCE. Ov. was born in 43; his literary chronology is especially tricky as he revised many works, so we cannot always be sure of publication dates. It is unclear, for instance, whether we should understand Ov.'s *Heroides* as influenced by Prop. 4.3 or vice versa. Prop.'s and Tib.'s first books of poetry each seem to come from the early 20s (there is debate about which came first); and Prop. 2 is usually dated to about 26–24.[77]

Dating elegiac poetry is always a tricky business. Given that the poets of [Tib.] 3 are not mentioned outside of their own poetry, and that they do not regularly refer to external events (one exception, maybe, being 3.4, on which see the introduction to that poem), the dating of [Tib.] 3 is a problem of an entirely different order of magnitude. Whereas we know from a variety of external

---

[76] Speyer 1971, which concerns itself with deliberate forgeries, is still instructive.
[77] Heyworth 2012 is especially good on the formation of elegiac books.

sources that Tib., Prop., and Ov. wrote in the late Augustan period, we cannot say even this much about the poets of this collection. To be sure, they situate themselves in the late Augustan period, referring to a Messalla, who must be the Messalla who is Tib.'s patron (M. Valerius Messalla Corvinus; see Section IV above). So too, the poems presume a fundamentally elegiac world view, even where they differ from the norm (see Section I above). And the implicit patronage model within which the corpus as a whole situates itself would fit with an Augustan dating. But it is impossible to determine whether this is the period in which the poems were actually written, or whether they were instead 'set' in a near or distant past.

This degree of suspicion about dating may seem excessive: why not simply take them at their word? But the [Tib.] 3 poems regularly play with questions of authorship and identity, so some caution is warranted. More importantly, many have found in certain parts of [Tib.] 3 stylistic features which seem to indicate a significantly later period (i.e. the Flavian period, around 100 years later; see Section VII below on style). In my own opinion, the stylistic anomalies are not sufficient to date the poetry to this period, not least because of the vast quantities of Latin poetry that are lost to us, some of which may have helped to fill out the picture of what otherwise look like anomalous uses of a word several generations before anyone else uses it. Much of this lost poetry, too, will have been written by less famous poets, and it might give us a rather different picture of how even such things as metre (often seen as a not-fully-conscious element of style, so a good way to catch the anachronism of forgers) were treated by the majority of the poets who wrote Latin verse.

But the evidence is also not sufficient to date the poetry firmly to the Augustan period. We might see [Tib.] 3 as the efforts of a small coterie of poets surrounding Messalla, and it is certainly possible that the miscellaneous poems were always attached to those of Tib. in some informal way; we might imagine, for instance, a series of 'poetry readings', with someone serving as secretary, or we might think of all of the poems as part of the papers of the Messallan household. Our earliest evidence for Tib. mentions only two books (see Section VIII below), but it may mean to refer only to the genuinely Tibullan books.

While it would be nice to have a secure series of dates, relative chronology is probably more important (the two are woven together in what follows); given scholarly interest in elegy's allusive nature, we would like to know which poems serve as source-texts for other poems. To take the primary example (see below), much scholarly ink has been spilt over the question of whether L. took certain of his lines from Ov., or vice versa. It is tempting to assume that the more famous poet must have influenced the less famous, but there is much we do not know about how poetic texts circulated in the ancient world: if two poets are contemporaries, there is always the possibility of less formal circulation of texts preceding publication, and of course, of a more collaborative kind of influence. Ov.'s habit of revising his own works (Martelli 2013) makes this a knottier problem still. And, again, we have lost so much poetry that we can never rule out the possibility that two poets have each found a line somewhere else.

We discuss the arrangement of the poems as a whole before briefly treating the *Panegyric* and then moving to more complex questions of authorship within [Tib.] 3. The poems group themselves by putative author (with the possible exception of 3.9 and 3.11, voiced by S., but which occur in between three poems about her in the third person). Each 'cycle' too, whoever arranged the poems, does have some discernible structure. But at the same time, as is often the case in elegy, the 'story' being told is a non-linear one. A similar case applies to the poetry of Cat., whose poems tell the story of his relationship with Lesbia in fragments rather than in their 'proper' order. It is generally believed that Cat. did not order his poems (rather, they seem to have been grouped by metre, by some later person); this perhaps accidental feature of the Catullan corpus, however, proves influential on later writers, starting with the elegists (see Smith 1913: 44–5, Hooper 1975 on Tib.). Beyond unity of persons, which is maintained within cycles in [Tib.] 3, there are further signs of an organizing hand: all three of the 'first' poems, 3.1, 3.8, and 3.13, contain introductory features (and the first two of these connect to one another; see notes *ad loc.*); 3.1 also speaks of the collection as a unit (however many poems that unit encompasses), and, like many poems that start a book, draws attention to its status as art and artefact in a way we could call programmatic.[78] 3.6, on the other hand, seems to some to end abruptly, with no real closural motives; I suggest *ad loc.* that it does show signs of a transition from one sort of poetry to another, which provide a form of closure. In terms of patterning, poems 8–12 contain 12, 12, 13, 10, and 10 couplets, which may reflect either deliberate composition for a book or deliberate arrangement of already-composed poems.

***

All that we really can know about the composition of [Tib.] 3 is that some individual or individuals understood the poetry of L., the *Panegyric*, the poetry by and about S., and a few other poems, to belong together, so it is worth exploring why. The *Panegyric to Messalla* ([Tib.] 3.7), a 211-line hexameter poem in praise of the literary, oratorical, and military accomplishments of Messalla, has received surprisingly little scholarly consideration. This lack of attention, I think, stems from two main sources: the first is that the poem's historical information is neither unambiguous enough nor detailed enough to be of interest to historians (see n. 81 below for bibliography, and Hammer 1925), and the second is that it has

---

[78] Indeed, while 3.1 may have been designed only to preface the L. poems, its clearly introductory features may have caused its placement (and so, Lygdamus' poems as a whole) at the head of the collection. Dettmer sees 'common themes' and 'common organizational principles' across cycles, as one would expect from a book of poetry (1983: 1971–2), and also argues that the S. cycles 'served as a model' for L. in the writing of his own poetry (1983: 1975).

been thought to share with the other poems of [Tib.] 3 the dubious distinction of being second-rate, and so has received little attention from a literary-critical point of view. So too, the study of ancient panegyric has only recently begun to return to the mainstream; distaste for 'toadying' combines with the poem's anonymity and incongruity within its collection to repel scholarship. 3.7 shares recognizable similarities with later panegyric, a fact which may be due to the repetitive nature of the genre or to its own (actual or 'backdated') influence upon later authors. As with the other poems of the book, the dating of 3.7 is far from clear; there are no obvious anachronisms which prevent it from deriving from Messalla's own lifetime.[79] It is currently not believed to have been written by Tib., although it was probably intended, in some fashion, to be understood as his production.[80] In its own right it is an interesting (and possibly the first extant) exemplar of its genre, a genre which became increasingly important in the Empire.[81]

This commentary, because of its focus on elegy and elegists, continues the scholarly neglect of the *Panegyric*;[82] rather than offering interpretation, I note only that like most of the other poems in the book, 3.7 situates itself in relationship to Messalla. As with the other poems, either this is biographically true, or it is not. But in either case, 3.7's association with Messalla makes it a more natural 'fit' within the book than strict attention to metre or subject-matter might suggest. The question of why the *Panegyric* bisects the elegiac poems also has no obvious answer; possibilities might range from the (real or assumed) dates of composition of the poems, to more abstract principles of arrangement, such as a desire for *variatio*, or decreasing size of the cycles (1–6 = 280 lines; 7 = 211, 8–12 = 114, 13–18 = 40, 19 = 24, 20 = 4), or even that L. was the compiler of the book and gave himself star billing (Cartault 1909: 88–9). Note too that 3.1 is a

---

[79] Not only its actual date of composition, but its purported date remain unclear; scholars suggest dates from 31–26, depending primarily upon whether they see the poem as written before or after Messalla's triumph in 27 (which it does not mention, but may allude to). It also shares language with Vergil's *Georgics*, published in 29 (Duret 1983: 1456, Schoonhoven 1983: 1695–6).

[80] That is, it does not claim him as author, but its presence in [Tib.] 3 gives it status as a (real or fictional) pre-history of the relationship between Messalla and Tib. Salvatore 1948 argues for stylistic similarities with the poetry of Tib., and so, Tibullan authorship. Momigliano believed it to be contemporary with Messalla's lifetime (1950: 39–41), as did Syme (1986: 200, 203) and Schrijvers 2006. See Van Berchem 1945: 33 for the case that the poem was written in praise of his son, Messalinus (cos. 3 BCE), disputed by Schoonhoven 1983 (and most others); Verdière 1954 dates it to the reign of Domitian (64). The most recent thorough study of the poem is Tränkle 1990, who offers commentary and discussion; he dates the poem to the second century CE (which coheres with his views on the dating of the book as a whole).

[81] On the 'pseudepigraphic encomium' see Peirano 2012: 117–72; she argues for the existence of this as a distinct subgenre, written to entertain (119–20). The family continued to be important in the Empire, such that a post-Augustan author might well have seen praise of this Messalla as a deft way to praise some current holder of the name (I owe this point to Ian Fielding); note too [V.] *Catal.* 9 (above, n. 69), which Schoonhoven suggests may be a 'reply' to 3.7 (1983: 1702–6).

[82] That said, I believe the poem is far more interesting than it is usually given credit for; Peirano 2012's suggestion that it is meant as parody may well redeem the text for a new generation of readers.

recognizably 'first' poem in the way no other is (see *ad loc.*; 3.13 is a partial exception); this fact may do much to explain the order as transmitted. As with many of the book's most puzzling questions, a solution may never be found.

Despite the multiplicity of options, the obvious answer to the question of selection principle is probably the right one: whoever arranged the book either gathered disparate poems related to Messalla from a variety of locales, or chose from some larger grouping of poetry already associated with him.

***

The remainder of this section treats the poems in their generally recognized cycles (1–6, 8–12, 13–18), so it is important to note again that this division, while conventional, exists only in the minds of readers: everything that is written about who collected and ordered the poems, and why, is speculation—of varying degrees of plausibility. Heyne 1798 (201–3) was the first to suggest that the book was written by more than one hand, and he was soon followed by Gruppe 1838 (49–50).[83] The poems as a whole do share a number of themes and interests, and principles of arrangement can be discerned (see below), but these may reflect the interests of the compiler more than any of the poems' authors.

Lygdamus ([Tib.] 3.1–6)

Discussions of the chronology of [Tib.] 3.1–6 begin with 3.5.18, in which L. gives the date of his birth; the line is identical with Ov. *Tr.* 4.10.6 (*cum cecidit fato consul uterque pari*, 'when both consuls fell by an equal fate'). The year referred to is 43 BCE in the case of Ov., and is perhaps the same for L.: other dates of historical possibility (i.e. in which both consuls died in office) are 83 BCE, 66 BCE, and 69 CE (Hagen 1954; Knoche 1956, Skutch 1959, Axelson 1960b; see too detailed discussion in Navarro Antolín 1996: 3–20). The history of elegy would need to be entirely rewritten if either of the first two dates were intended: it is unlikely in the extreme that L. invented the conventions of elegy without any notice being taken of it in our sources (some of whom, like Ov., revel in producing lists of important predecessors). The 43 BCE date finds support from those who believe L. to be a pseudonym of the youthful Ov. (or his older brother; Ov. tells us in *Tr.* 4.10.11–14 that he and his brother shared a birthday, and L.'s Latin (*natalem...nostrum videre*) might either refer to a birth date of 43 or the celebration of a first birthday in that year; see Doncieux 1888, Bréguet 1946: 239, and Baligan 1967a: 85; recently revived by Knox, forthcoming: 6). It is also thought by some that both L. and Ov. were coincidentally born in the same year, and that one poet found the line in the other and applied it to himself (or

---

[83] Hence Hubbard's contention about S., that Gruppe 'made her up' (2004: 177).

that both found it in a predecessor[84]). Recent commentators plump for the 69 CE date, and point to distinctively 'Flavian' words and phrases in L. (see Section VII below; Navarro Antolín 1996 covers the question most fully). But it is not always the case that ancient poets tell us the literal, biographical truth about themselves: one poet could have borrowed the line from the other regardless of year of birth. Critics tend to privilege Ov., by far the more influential poet, but it is also sometimes the case that famous authors are influenced by less-famous ones.[85] And who borrowed from whom is not merely a problem of originality; the question takes us directly back to L.'s date of birth: in our cycle, he claims to be 'young' (see *ad* 3.4.73, Lee 1958/9: 20); a precise contemporary of Ov. could know his *Amores*, but the *Tristia*, from which this quotation comes, date to a much later period, and were written at a time when neither Ov. nor L. (if born in the same year) could be described as young.

The issue is made somewhat more complicated by the fact that *Tr.* 4.10 is itself a tricky poem: while claiming to be autobiographical, it also offers Ov. up as simultaneously paradigmatic and influenced by a number of other people.[86] In this context, the line before Ov.'s 'birth announcement' ought perhaps to have raised more eyebrows than it has: *editus hic ego sum, nec non, ut tempora noris* means 'I was put forth here [in Sulmo], and, so that you don't not know the date …'; *nec non* is a strongly positive statement, but it can also be taken literally, emphasizing the not un-knowingness which Ov. here offers to the reader, a claim which differs subtly but importantly from one of facticity. So too, the use of *editus*, with its implications of publication rather than biological processes might hint at a prior literary source, or at least suggest that Ov. is not simply being straightforward.

In the case of one poet quoting another, it is notoriously difficult to determine priority. Who, for example, would not think Cat. 66.39 a cheeky borrowing from the obviously more appropriate V. *A*.6.460, but for the fact that chronology prevents us? Axelson developed a methodology which was designed to make the process more objective (*Prioritätsbestimmung*; 1960a, with application to this question in 1960b),[87] but many now believe that he merely provided a pseudo-scientific veneer for aesthetic judgements. Appropriateness within its context— Axelson's main criterion—proves little help, at least in this case: the L. poem treats the poet's illness and (expected) death, and, while there is no particular reason for him to refer to Ov.'s autobiography, the miasma of death and suffering that hangs over Ov.'s exilic corpus might make it an attractive field for mining.

---

[84] Most recently in Heyworth 2012: 224.

[85] A sampling of scholarly opinions: for Lygdamean priority, Calonghi 1901, Cartault 1906: 166 and 1909: 89, Postgate 1915, Büchner 1965, Parca 1986: 462–3, Somerville, forthcoming; for Ovidian, Ciaffi 1944: 167, Lee 1958/59, Axelson 1960b, Bickel 1960: 311–12, Hooper 1975: ii.

[86] See Fairweather 1987 on Ov.'s self-fashioning vis-à-vis Augustus; Hinds 2005 vis-à-vis Cat.

[87] Lee 1958–9, more or less contemporarily, developed similar arguments, which he applied to Ov. and L.

But the opposite is also true; we can easily imagine the exilic Ov. re-using any and all previous poetry that suggested bodily sufferings.

Especially in the case of a poet such as Ov., seeing where a phrase is 'more appropriate' is an unsteady guide; Ovidian poetics include a regular rupture of decorum. Beyond this, Ov. is a poet of repetition above all.[88] The most relevant aspect of Ovidian repetition for our purposes is his claim to have 'trimmed' the *Amores* from its first, five-book edition to the three books we have (*Am. praef.*, with much discussion in the scholarly literature). This statement has given rise to the suggestion that the line in question appeared in a now-lost poem of the *Amores*, was 'picked up' by L., and then repurposed by Ov. later (Kraus 1957: 197–200; Axelson 1960b: 284, Oliver 1969: 143). One of the things critics seem to like most about this theory is that it allows them to have it all: Ov. is saved the stigma of stealing from an inferior, but L. can still be an Augustan poet.

I have treated these two lines at greatest length because they are the most prominent example of Ovidian and Lygdamean intertextuality; there are a number of others, all discussed *ad loc.* in the commentary. Here I need only say that none of the parallel passages seems to me to resolve finally the question of who predated whom. Hooper 1975: 6–11, followed by Tränkle 1990 and Navarro Antolín 1996, examines the question thoroughly; all follow the lead of Lee 1958–9 and Axelson 1960a and 1960b in singling out 'Silver Latin' phrases in L. (see too Maltby 2009: 327 for the other poets). Navarro Antolín 1996 also argues for the later date for L., finding a number of borrowings in him from Seneca's tragedies, Martial, and Statius (but he also notes that the poems have a 'pre-Ovidian' scansion pattern, 1996: 159–60; see Maltby 2009: 324–6 for echoes of Martial and Section VII below on metrics). Here again, readers must judge for themselves. Some of Navarro Antolín's points about the dating of particular words are more probative than others, but, as I noted above, in the context of all of the poetry we do *not* have, they cannot be decisive.

Beyond the year of L's birth, there is the more complex question of his identity: is he truly unknown to us, or might the name be a pseudonym of some better-known individual? Navarro Antolín 1996: 5–16 offers a brief history of the problem and full citations.[89] An abbreviated list of possible contenders includes: Messalla himself, or one or the other of his sons (Bickel 1960), Ov. (Gruppe 1838, Radford 1920, 1923, 1926, and 1927, Salanitro 1938: 53–4, Bréguet 1946, La Penna 1953, Morgante 1970), Ov's older brother (Doncieux 1888), Tib. (Scaliger 1577, Pepe 1948, Salvatore 1948, Riposati 1967), Ov. or Tib. (Alfonsi 1946: 72–7), Servius Sulpicius (a cousin(/fiancé?) or a brother of S. the poet: Wagenvoort 1917, Witczak 1993; see n. 55 above on family connections), Cassius

---

[88] Fulkerson and Stover 2016; Martelli 2013 and Thorsen 2014 are two recent and in some ways complementary takes on the problems of Ovidian chronology.

[89] To his bibliography, add Bickel 1960 and Butrica 1993. Voss seems to have been the first to suggest that L. was *not* Tib. (1811).

Parma (Oebecke 1832), Valgius Rufus (Doncieux 1888), Julius Calidus (Della Corte 1965), Maecenas or perhaps Augustus (Maleuvre 2001), and nearly every other Augustan poet whose name we know. It is also possible that the name is not a pseudonym at all, but the actual name of an educated freedman (perhaps Tibullus' or Messalla's), or even of Cynthia's slave (see Section IV above).

Sulpicia, by and about ([Tib.] 3.8–18)

Dating can be difficult enough when a poet has a substantial *oeuvre* and speaks of contemporary events. The poetry by and about S. is a small corpus, and one which engages even less with the world of Rome than does the poetry of L. It is unclear by how many hands these poems are authored; scholarship has traditionally divided them into two groups, 3.8–12 (the 'garland' of Sulpicia, written by some third party) and 3.13–18, written by S. herself.[90] But some would see all of the poetry as written by one person, either S. (Hallett *passim*) or the anonymous author (Holzberg 1998: 184); see too Parker 1994 for the attribution of 3.9 and 3.11 to S. for a number of reasons (based on the principle of variation; but also because 3.8, 3.10, and 3.12 share a number of similarities, as do 3.9 and 3.11).[91]

As with L., a wide variety of authors have been proposed for some or all of the poems: for 3.8–12, Tib. (Scaliger 1577, Gruppe 1838, Némethy 1905: 333–5, Cartault 1906 etc., Smith 1913: 79, Zimmermann 1928, Rostagni 1935: 39–40, Ciaffi 1944: 166–71, Ponchont 1968: 168 and n. 1); Ov. (Radford 1920 and 1923, Bréguet 1946: 224, 280, 333); S.'s brother Sulpicius (Butrica 1993); S. (Broukhusius 1708, Hallett 2002a, Parker 1994 and 2006); Cornutus (Hubbard 2004: 188); Cerinthus and S., alternating (Dronke 2003); some Neronian or Flavian author (Tränkle 1990: 258–9, Maltby 2009). For 3.8, 3.10, and 3.12, Tib. (Doncieux 1888: 78–9, Salanitro 1938: 31–4); for 3.9 and 3.11, S. (Doncieux 1891; 78–81, Martinon 1895: xlv–xlvii, Salanitro 1938: 33–4, Parker 1994, Stevenson 2005: 42–4); for 3.13–18, Tib. (Scaliger 1577, Rostagni 1935: 39–40, Ciaffi 1944: 166–71, Hubbard 2004: 181). If S. is not what she appears to be, then we have few clues to her/his real identity (see too Section VI below on women authors in antiquity).

The author of poems 3.8–12 (to keep the traditional division) does not offer us a name; his admiration of S.'s beauty and unreflective encouragement of her love affair suggests that we should understand him as male, and probably not— given what we think we know about the importance of the purity of bloodlines

---

[90] Gruppe 1838 attributed 3.13 also to the '*amicus*', seemingly because of its explicitness (Skoie 2009: 71); Petersen 1849 moved 3.13 to the S. cycle, and Rossbach 1855 (vi, 55) was the first to propose the divisions currently in use.

[91] Parker draws attention to syntactical similarities between 3.9, 3.11, and 3.13–18, which are not shared with 3.8, 3.10, and 3.12 (e.g. *mea lux*, 1994: 48), and expands Lowe's stylistic arguments about 3.13–18 to cover 3.9 and 3.11.

in Roman elite families—as a man with familial ties to her (e.g. *not* her brother); it is, of course, possible that he is a relative untrammelled by traditional Roman morality who supports his sister in her unconventional behaviour. But S.'s invitation to 'anyone' to speak her story need not have been taken up by someone known to her; if her poetry had any circulation, it is possible that the *amicus* poems are the work of a later hand writing in homage. And it seems to some, including me, that the *amicus*, while in support of the affair, is not wholly on S.'s side: he either does not understand much of what is subversive about the S. poems, or actively works to undermine just those qualities (Batstone, forthcoming).[92] At any rate, it is clear that the two sets of poetry, if two sets they are, are connected; the 'garland' poetry is written in response to S.'s own poetry, both in the sense that it picks up on specific themes of that poetry, and more explicitly, in that it responds to Sulpicia's own call to 'anyone' who wants to tell her story to do so (Hinds 1987a). Tränkle 1990: 258 points to a number of Ovidian intertexts in this cycle, including from the (probably late) double *Heroides*, which has implications for dating (in whichever direction). With some hesitation, I treat the two cycles as separate; see Hallett 2002a and Parker for the argument that what looks like stylistic variation can be paralleled within the corpus of Cat., and that S. adopted different styles in different poems (Hallett 2002a: 48; Parker 2006: 26 n. 31, prefigured in Postgate 1929: xli).

Scholarship on the poems by and about S. was long hampered by excessive focus on her sex, and by more or less patronizing remarks about women writing poetry. In many ways the modern scholarly tradition on S. begins with Fredricks 1976 and Santirocco 1979 (who each made the case for the cycle(s) as a unit); this was followed by Lowe 1988 (who offered the first substantive literary assessment of S.'s work, which led him to find it artful rather than artless)— the two latter authors pointed to the relevance of epigram to an understanding of the poems (Santirocco 1979: 238; Lowe 1988: 205). Other notable works include Skoie 2000 (on the history of scholarship on S., and especially (292) on the ways in which S.'s poetry was treated as 'raw material' for the other poet), Milnor 2002 (who focuses on the specifically gendered elements of S.'s *poesis*), and Keith 2006 (a useful summary of the *status quaestionis*).[93]

3.19 and 3.20

These two poems are anonymous elegies, the first placed in the mouth of Tib. (and so, of course, potentially written by him, though contemporary opinion

---

[92] Note too Hallett 2009a, 2009b, and 2011, each of which argue that S.'s poetry was found subversive and objectionable by contemporary and later authors.

[93] See too the 'Petale epigram', which may also be a composition of S.'s (Carcopino 1929: 84–6; Stevenson 2005: 42–4; Hallett 2009c: 187–90). Breguet disagrees (1946: 36–8).

tends not to think so[94]), the second, an anonymous meditation on the quintessential elegiac situation, infidelity. Aside from the mention of Tib., neither gives any indication of authorship; presumably as a result, neither has received much scholarly attention. 3.19 is in many ways more like 'classic' love elegy than the other poems of the book, which fits in with its attempt to be (seen as) Tib. (all the more so if it is not; see again Peirano 2012). Hor. *Od.* 1.33, a poem written to an 'Albius' about his relationship with a 'Glycera', has also been drawn into this discussion. If that Albius is our Albius (contemporary scholarship inclines towards thinking it is), then Glycera might either represent the woman who becomes Delia (or Nemesis), or might treat a different relationship entirely. So some suggest that 3.19 and 3.20 are Tib.'s early efforts, poetry written to Glycera.[95] This is an economical solution, but one susceptible neither of proof nor disproof.

Further Thoughts on the Composition of the Book

One indirect method of dating poetry is, of course, by reference to later authors who seem influenced by it. In the case of allusions, as we have already noted, this is a tricky business, but sometimes poets do us the favour of mentioning important predecessors or of otherwise making clear their later date. This is, unfortunately, not a method that yields results for [Tib.] 3. Navarro Antolín sees the earliest echoes of L. in the poetry of Ausonius and Avienus (both 4th century CE; 1996: 29), but the latest date proposed for L. is in the second century CE, so this does not tell us anything we did not already know. Later mentions of the 'other' poet S. may be relevant; indeed, Hermann suggested that the second S. might have invented the first one (1951: 3–16). On the other hand, the limited influence of [Tib.] 3 is not surprising, given that Tib. himself all but disappeared for much of a millennium (Fisher 1983: 1951–3, and see Section VIII below).

Given the state of our knowledge, it would be rash to attempt to draw any firm conclusions about how this miscellany of poems came together. Two primary, mutually exclusive, hypotheses have found favour over the years.[96] The first is that the poems reflect a genuine poetic community, and were all written by known or unknown members of the 'circle of Messalla' (see Section II above). And there are some internal connections between poems to support this notion of communal composition (see the commentary *passim* and Dettmer 1983).

---

[94] For dissenting opinions, see Cartault 1909: 24 (tentative), Rostagni 1935: 38, and Salanitro 1938: 40 (who further argues that it is about S.). Luck 1969: 114 suggests that both poems are by Tib., and Hermann 1957 argues that both were once a single, Tibullan poem.

[95] See e.g. Gruppe 1838: 217–32; further citations at Fisher 1983: 1930.

[96] Maltby 2009 seems to try to split the difference: while he dates Lygdamus and the author of 3.8–12 to the post-Augustan period (e.g. 324, 333), he also suggests that 3.13–18 are from the late Augustan period (336), and then speculates about household archives (338).

Evidence for this within the corpus includes the inclusion of the *Panegyric to Messalla* and 3.14.5, which claims Messalla as S.'s 'relation'. This theory has in its turn spurred further speculations about the connections of the various persons mentioned in the poetry (e.g. Wagenvoort's, that L. is Cerinthus and S. is N., 1917: 115–18; see above for other suggestions). In the opinion of some, the appeal of the book lies precisely in the intimacy (or pseudo-intimacy; Morrison 2007: 41) that a community of poets creates for external readers.

The existence of a family archive,[97] or simply a box full of papyri that lay unnoticed for some time, is an efficient explanation for this theory, and one that helps to explain certain features of the corpus (especially the 'response' 3.8–12 seem to offer, Dronke 2003: 83), but there is, as usual, no evidence for it. So too, if the varying dates which some have proposed for the different parts of the corpus are valid, it is an impossible hypothesis.

The alternative explanation, that T.'s meagre output was 'filled out' with poetry seen as being 'like' his in some way, is more appealing to a different kind of scholar; see Findley for the suggestion that Book 3, with its focus on elegiac loss, was written to 'fit' into the corpus, rather than incorporated because it already fitted (2002: 151–3). As we have already noted, this theory does not require us to assume malicious intent: our evidence for post-Tiberian elegy is very slim, and it might well have seemed a good idea to some later admirer of the poetry to collect miscellaneous elegies together and attach them to a well-known author (see Section VIII below on the manuscript tradition, which, as usual, does not offer much help). As Lyne notes, the *Appendix Vergiliana* serves as a plausible model for how such a collection of poetry into a book could have worked (2007: 342).

Beyond the unanswerable question of how the poems came to be together, there is the perhaps more compelling one of what we might gain by reading them together. Throughout the commentary, I make the best case I can for reading them as a single book of poetry. Readers are warned, however, that this is more for the sake of the thought-experiment than because I am privy to information unknown to others. What, then, happens when we read this book as a book? First, such a practice reflects the text we have: some individual or individuals believed, for whatever reason, that these poems would gain from co-location. More interestingly, this possibly random assemblage of poems engages with literary critical issues directly related to its own reception. That is, the poems explicitly open up the question of literary ventriloquism: we have, side-by-side, a first-person and a third-person rendition of the same love

---

[97] The notion was seemingly first suggested by Lachmann 1876: ii.150, then Smith 1913: 87, and is thereafter standard (but often implicit); see too Norden 1952: 71 on the book as a 'Hauspoetenbuch Messallas' and White for the importance of the household and family connections to patronage relationships (1993: 4–5, 42–3)—this is of course true for all Roman relationships. For a recent restatement of the case, see Veremans 1998.

affair.[98] The book, taken as a book, suggests that it is concerned with telling details of a relationship in a variety of different ways, from different viewpoints, in a way that is both like and unlike more mainstream elegy.

VI: WOMEN WRITING (LATIN)

For many readers, the most engrossing question of this corpus will be whether S. was in fact a woman. Let me state at the outset that there is no way of resolving the point: most of the scholarly approaches that have been treated as probative reveal more about the scholar than about the text. I consequently prefer to focus on what is at stake in posing the question, and on the various methods that have been suggested to determine an answer. First: the question matters because the poetry of S. might (or might not) offer us the vast majority of the extant non-Christian Latin by a woman, and also some of the earliest female-authored poetry in the Western tradition. This is, of course, not by itself a reason to believe that S. was a woman, but the ideological issues that inhere in the problem do mean that it is wise to proceed with care. On one side are those who accuse doubters of misogyny; on the other, those who use the material realities of women's lives in Rome to convict 'believers' of naivety.

There is substantial information available to us about education in the Roman world, which provides a starting point for the possibility of a woman writing Latin. We have nothing near precise figures for literacy in antiquity;[99] whatever numbers one settles upon, nearly all of those who attained literacy will have been in the upper classes, and an even larger percentage will have been men. At the same time, Hemelrijk persuasively suggests that the issue of women's education was variable by family,[100] and it is perfectly plausible that the Servii Sulpicii, cultured as they were (see Section IV above), educated their daughters as well as their sons. As is well known, Roman elite education focused primarily on public speaking, and women were never expected to master this set of skills. But the rudiments of education, which involved the memorization and replication of 'classics' of prose and poetry, are likely to have been accessible to many more women than the record will ever show, and these practices inherently foster both engagement with literature and the creation of it. Women's education,

---

[98] As Luck notes, this is characteristic of Alexandrian poetry (1969: 110). See Maltby 2011: 89 on possible Gallan precedents, and see below for further discussion.

[99] Harris discusses the evidence for girls' education in the late Republic and early Empire (1989: 239–40), and offers a figure for women's literacy 'below, perhaps far below, 10%' (1989: 259). See Haines-Eitzen 2012: 23–8 on women as authors, library owners, and readers in Christian late antiquity.

[100] For the point that family is a determinative factor in the ancient world for women in particular, see Hallett 1984: 35–61. On the education of women in later antiquity, see Haines-Eitzen 2012: 19–20.

though, may well have been controversial; see e.g. Sall. *Cat.* 25.2-5 on Sempronia, who would probably have been perceived as much less dangerous had she been less cultured: her problem is a moral one, but Sallust suggests that it is indistinguishable from her education. In such a climate, even families that believed in the importance of female literacy may well not have flaunted it. But our examples certainly suggest that a S. of the Augustan period, with the family connections outlined above, is more likely to have attained literacy than many other women in many other periods of history. There is ample evidence that elite Roman women operated in arenas distinct from but overlapping those of their male relatives, including in certain aspects of (what we think of as) the public sphere. So there are no formal barriers to the reality of S., and in fact, it is perhaps more surprising that we know so little about female Roman authors than that we know anything about them.[101]

There are, however, many other facets to the question, of which the most controversial, and also the most interesting, has been whether S. writes in a recognizably female or feminine way. Depending upon how the issue is phrased, it is not as trivial as critics of it sometimes suggest: even without positing a fundamental difference in men's and women's essential natures (or brains, or souls), the radical difference between women's and men's experiences in antiquity might well have resulted in different approaches to life and literature, and so, perhaps, writing that is different in ways we can recognize.[102] But this is slippery ground, not least because any features of language we, at our distance from Latin, can identify as 'feminine' will have been so blindingly obvious as to have been readily, perhaps even unconsciously, available to any native speaker of the language, male or female, who wanted to adopt them.[103] Beyond gendered linguistic markers, studied most fully in the case of Roman comedy,[104] there is a

---

[101] Stevenson 2005, a magisterial study of women writing in Latin, notes that they are often ignored because 'these writers do not fit with either the image of Latin, or the image of women' (2005: 2); see too Farrell 2001 on the incongruity. Lyne 2007: 343-4 offers a short summary of women poets in Rome.

[102] See Russ 1983 and Spender 1989 for some of the reactionary ways in which this supposition, and others, have been used to elide the very existence of women's writing; as Russ notes, active suppression is hardly ever necessary (1983: 18).

[103] For a robust attempt to reconcile the apparently dichotomous critical positions of 'constructionism' (which focuses on the complex realities of lived experience) and 'essentialism' (which posits some unique feature that determines identity), see Fuss 1989, with bibliography about women's reading and writing on 23.

[104] Female characters in Roman comedy swear by a different set of gods from male, and use a greater number of modifiers (Adams 1984); this probably reflects, however stylized, genuine differences between male and female speech. On the related issue of theatrical femininity, see Dutsch 2008, who notes that 'female' characters (played by male actors) 'must have at least attempted to reproduce the discursive practices defining—and defined by—the daily performances of gender by Roman women' (2008: 47). These practices, however, need not be linked to gender: see Hemelrijk 1999: 200 on the use of diminutives as characteristic of those who are trying to persuade others to do things for them (which category often, but not exclusively, includes women).

robust tradition of Greek and then Roman theatre, some of which engages directly with what it means to represent 'woman' mimetically.[105] The important differences between the performance contexts of dramatic poetry and elegy should also not be overlooked: the former has a much wider range of signals available to convey gender to its audience than the latter.

Let us, though, explore the theory of 'ladies' Latin'[106] a little further. It was given support within the context of [Tib.] 3 by the fact that nearly everybody finds 3.13–18 exceedingly difficult poems to construe. The extremely compact nature of S.'s Latin (on which Lowe 1988 is still fundamental) might hint at some larger difference between her and other authors; sex is one obvious place to look for the source of that difference.[107] And so, it was thought that her poems might be some of our only extant remains[108] of an idiolect particular to women, different from Cicero and so hard for us to read. In support of this theory, two points are adduced: that some Latin sources mention women as preservers of archaisms of language (e.g. Cic. *De Or.* 3.45 and perhaps Plin. *Ep.* 1.16.6), and that we have some examples of 'women's speech' (written by men) that contain syntactical peculiarities (see e.g. n. 104 above). But neither of these examples really helps to explain S.'s poetry, which is colloquial more than it is arcane, and the notion of her writing as uniquely feminine is now rather discredited, not least because it seems sexist to many critics to assume that educated women were not competent to write in their own language.[109] But the real problem with the idea that women write a distinct kind Latin from men is that, as noted above, it merely pushes the question

---

[105] I am thinking especially of Aristophanes' *Thesmophoriazousae* and also Euripides' *Bacchae*, which replicate on stage the normal off-stage practices of male actors learning to dress, walk, and speak as women. The latter in particular also calls into question how 'real' any such performance, on stage or off, could ever be. For seminal discussion of some of the most important issues related to the performance of gender in a contemporary setting, see Butler 1990.

[106] The phrase was first promulgated by Gruppe 1838: *weibliches Latein*.

[107] See, however, Miralles Maldonado 1990 on the parallels in male poets to aspects of S.'s writing (among other features, he singles out the double dative, the double negative, the use of *quamvis* and the indicative).

[108] See Hemelrijk 1999: 146–209 on what we have of women's writing from antiquity.

[109] The patronizing tone of much of this scholarship has not worn well; in addition to Gruppe, note Smith 1913: 80–1 on S.'s 'straightforward simplicity', status as 'a genuine woman', 'characteristically feminine' elegies, and 'distinctively feminine' writing style as causing readerly difficulties. The trend continues well into the twentieth century; see Luck 1969: 107 (unrevised in the second edition): 'Written spontaneously by a woman with no literary pretensions, they are a unique document in the history of Latin literature. Sulpicia's poetry does not convey a romantic distillation of life, but life itself speaks forth from these lines, directly, often carelessly, but always believably'. See too Skoie 2002 on 500 years' worth of commentators' treatment of the poetry of S. Batstone, forthcoming: 1, an insightful examination of the question, notes that the more interesting a poet S. has been to scholars, the more ready has been the assumption that she must be a man. So too, a number of ancillary assumptions (her poetry was never intended for publication, it is 'really' love-letters), reflect a specific but often unarticulated set of beliefs about women's 'proper' roles.

Women Writing (Latin)

back a step: articulating a series of practices by which it is possible to 'write like a woman' does not necessitate that only women could write in this way.[110] Still, the fact remains that the S. poems do read rather differently from, say, Prop. 4.3 or Ov.'s *Heroides*, male-authored elegies which assume a female voice (see below).

Perhaps a more promising angle is to examine the gendered aspects of S.'s poetry from a different angle, that of subject matter and authorial positioning; such an approach, as in Milnor 2002 (who compares the poems to Emily Dickinson's *oeuvre*) also has the advantage of making the poetry of S. less anomalous by putting it into a context. In that light, we might be willing to term the disjunction in her poems between showing and hiding, between shouting to the rooftops and keeping silence, a peculiarly 'feminine' strategy.[111] But here as well, the evidence can be interpreted in multiple ways; the sample which the S. poetry offers is statistically so small as to be useless, and feminine 'secretiveness' might well be a male construct. There is little firm ground: we cannot, for instance, tell whether a particular metrical pattern is characteristic of S. or not—not least because we do not know the parameters of the sample. The two most immediately noticeable features of poems 13–18, their syntactical convulsions and their brief length, suggest that they are intended to be discrete from poems 8–12, and perhaps that they were written by a single author, but that argument runs the risk of circularity, since whoever arranged the poems might well have taken length and style into account.

So too, there is the fact that the majority of the ancient Greek poetry authored by women takes as its subject women's friendships and household matters.[112] Alongside this tradition, however, is another, which attributes to women the habit of writing frankly about sex, and this is another noteworthy feature of poems 13–18. Into this category fall, perhaps, the poetry of

---

[110] Farrell 2001: 52–83 treats some of the theoretical problems involved in women writing in Latin, which tend to be 'authenticated'—at least in the versions that come to us—by male narrative frames. See too Stevenson 2005, on the various women writing Latin from antiquity to the eighteenth century, and 19–22 on the ways Latin itself is authorized as a male language (even, perhaps, for native speakers). Flemming 2007 points to similar difficulties with female medical writers, many of whose names prompt questions about authenticity (see especially 269 on the cosmetic remedies of 'Cleopatra').

[111] Gilbert and Gubar's classic study of women writers (1979) may well be anachronistic, as has been suggested, but some of the points they make are at least worth taking into account in a study of S.'s style; most notably, they show the struggle of nineteenth-century women writers against language itself.

[112] Barnard 1978: 205 draws a distinction between classical Greek female poets and their Hellenistic counterparts, suggesting that it is only the latter who concentrate on a 'feminine' subject matter; see too Snyder 1989. Note too the (in)famous argument of Butler 1922, that the *Odyssey*, given its preponderance of domestic scenes and sensible women, was written by a woman (Homer's daughter). West 1977, which suggests that Erinna's *Distaff* was written by a man, seemingly on the grounds that it is a good poem, shows the subjectivity involved in such arguments (see too West 1996, which extends the argument to most other Greek female poets).

Sappho,[113] the sex manuals of 'Philaenis',[114] and the sexual double entendres of courtesans recorded in Athenaeus Book 13. So too, there are the obscene witticisms of Augustus' daughter Julia (Macr. *Sat.* 2.5, admirably discussed by Richlin 1992); indeed, they seem to provide ancillary evidence that Roman women were not quite so limited in their speech and behaviour as is often thought (see n. 63 above on the possibility of pre-marital sex). Even the phrase *docta puella*, generally seen as complimentary when used of elegiac women (see Section II above), may have an edge: the adjective can of course refer to a learned individual, but is also used to signify one who 'has been taught' or 'is experienced'.[115] And (Roman) anxieties about women's reputations take on a new intensity when issues of publication come to the fore (as Habinek 1998 notes, *publicus* is by no means an unproblematic compliment, applied to women or to men).[116]

***

Many readers would prefer to think of S. as a woman, not least because her writings would then be by far the most substantial contribution to Latin literature written by a woman for many centuries. Certainty, once more, is impossible. The best reason for doubt is precisely the context of this corpus, and especially the existence of the 'garland' poetry, which implicitly denies that authorship need have anything to do with poetic *persona*. For one poet to assume the identity of a young woman in love necessarily means that others could, perhaps did, do the same (especially if we accept the corpus's implicit suggestion that its poetry was composed, in some way, by a community). Beyond this, however, there is the distressing fact that this kind of gender-bending is not anomalous in Latin poetry. Other elegists—nearly all of them, in fact—had experimented in various ways with female voices. Cat., first of all, regularly placed himself in the position of a woman, sometimes by implication and metaphor, but sometimes more directly. Drinkwater's 2012 exploration of Tib.'s Marathus poems (1.4, 1.8, and 1.9) as the working out of a series of subject positions from different perspectives provides a different kind of model, one which takes as a starting

---

[113] Note that there is an apparent confusion between Sappho the poet and at least one prostitute Sappho (Ath. 13.596e, Ael. *VH* 12.19), which might have begun with the comic poets (e.g. Diphilus in Ath. 13.599d; cf. the philosopher Chamaeleon in Ath. See McClure 2003: 63–4 on the proliferation of women's names, especially those of *hetairai*, 67 and 85 on the Sapphos, and 83–6 on *hetairai* who were also poets.

[114] See Parker 1992 for explication of these handbooks, which are, as he notes, invariably attributed to women, and most often to Philaenis, whose name becomes a mask for other authors (see Tsantsanoglou 1973: 192–3 for the name applied to prostitutes). Hubbard 2004 applies this model to S.

[115] See Parker 1992: 106 and Habinek 1998 on the ambiguities of women's knowledge and Stevenson 2005: 24 on the phrase *docta puella* as coopted early on in the tradition.

[116] Note e.g. Sen. *Ep.* 88.37 on whether Sappho was *publica* (i.e. a common prostitute; her poetry is conflated with her body as available to all).

point the fundamental repetitiveness of the elegiac scenario. One of the characteristic (but by no means necessary) features of that scenario is that men write poetry about women; given the genre's tendencies towards experimentation, it would not be surprising to find the situation reversed: 'women' writing about their elegiac experience of 'men'.[117]

And in fact, exploration of the female voice is precisely what we find in male-authored poems: there are a number of Latin elegies which do not simply experiment with feminized males, but which, though written by men, take on the female voice (see Jacobson 1974: 343–8 for brief discussion and earlier context).[118] Our most extensive example of such 'transvestite ventriloquism' is Ov.'s *Heroides*, which depict a series of mythical women (e.g. Medea, Dido, Penelope), re-imagined as very like Roman matrons and writing love letters to husbands and lovers, urging them to take some specific action (mostly, to return to the women they have left).[119] *Her.* 15, a letter from the Greek poet Sappho to her erstwhile lover Phaon, is a curious blend of mythic and historical (it has been suggested that its basic subject matter comes from a now-lost poem Sappho wrote about Aphrodite, disguised as an old woman, and ferried without cost by the aged boatman Phaon, to whom in return she granted sexual attractiveness). Sappho herself was probably a real woman, but there is scholarship which argues that her name offered a subject position to male Greek poets when they wanted to explore alternative identities. Here again, we seem to see a conflation of male and female in ways some will find maddening, a poetic move that is simultaneously essentializing in its suggestion that there is a 'feminine' way to write, and 'constructionist' in its assumption that a man can adopt this voice.

In a more homely vein, Prop. 4.3 is the letter of one 'Arethusa' to 'Lycotas', away at war: scholars are puzzled by the Greek names—since the setting is profoundly Roman—but even more so by the form. Prop.'s fourth book also contains poems which are voiced in their entirety by a woman: 4.7 by Cynthia (on which see Rosati 1993) and 4.11 by Cornelia, both dead (not to mention Cynthia's shrewish lament in Prop. 1.3). The mythic women of the *Heroides* and the mythologized women Cynthia and Cornelia might be said to have a clearly literary

---

[117] This is, of course, an argument from silence, and need not imply biological women writing about biological men, merely the assumption of a female subject-position from which to compose elegy.

[118] There are also Greek precedents, most notably Theocritus 2. The fragmentary prose *Carmen Grenfellianum*, dating probably to the second century BCE, is in some ways the most interesting of the potential models (first published in Grenfell 1896); it is the anonymous lament of an abandoned woman, which contains a number of literary *topoi* but/and it might also be autobiographical (see Gigante 1947, Cozzolino 1992, and Esposito 2005 for further discussion).

[119] The phrase 'transvestite ventriloquism' comes from Harvey, who is interested in 'the way male authors create a feminine voice that seems to be—but is not—linked to a whole set of feminine characteristics' (1992: 4). She also notes that such practices tend to silence the voices of actual women (Harvey 1992: 5, 32, and *passim*).

status, but the letter of Arethusa seems to be an attempt at creating a purely fictional character, in a way which might parallel S.

But contemporary practices of writing poetry, if they provide precedents for male ventriloquism of the female voice, also provide reasons to believe that S.'s poetry might have been written by a biological woman. The authors discussed above, while they do adopt a variety of different subject-positions, tend to do so explicitly, in ways that are not likely to mislead unwary audiences; much of the point of these experiments is precisely that the reader is aware of the fictiveness of the identity (the *Heroides* in particular gain much from what we 'already know' about the characters before reading their letters).[120] The poetry of S., by contrast, is easily, and most naturally, read as written by a woman.

Recent scholarship sees stylistic and syntactical similarities between the poetry of S. and the *Heroides* (Piastri 1998, focusing on rhetorical *topoi*, Fabre-Serris 2009 on language). As with so many aspects of this difficult question, this argument cuts both ways: from one angle, it makes sense that male poets wishing to portray a woman's voice in their poetry would be tempted to make use of the writing of a woman if they had access to it; from the other angle, these similarities might attest only to stereotypes about what makes poetry 'feminine', freely accessible to all (male) poets and therefore indicating nothing about biological sex. (See Section III above for the ways these stances affect the interpretation of elegy as a whole.)

Models from later history, while potentially anachronistic, may help us to envision a plausible situation in which S. could have been part of a literary community, and so might have found her way to the writing of poetry. For instance, the late-eighteenth-century Romantic poets William Wordsworth and Samuel Coleridge wrote collectively (*Lyrical Ballads*, though it was first published anonymously, in the second edition bore the name of Wordsworth—although it contains five poems by Coleridge), and both of them seem to have made free use of the diaries of William's sister, Dorothy Wordsworth. Her journals, only recently published under her own name, contain what looks to be the first drafts for a number of themes and even phrases which appear in both men's published work.[121] They seem to have viewed her as a kind of muse, or a storehouse of raw material. She, for her part, gathered and documented sense-impressions for the two men.[122] Christina Rosetti provides another possible family-based model. Sister of the painter Dante Gabriel Rosetti, she was at least an informal part of the (mid-nineteenth-century) pre-Raphaelite circle, which

---

[120] Note too in this light Parker, who argues for the attribution of 3.9 and 3.11 to S.; he notes that it is entirely unparalleled in Greco-Roman poetry to adopt the identity of neither a generic nor a literary, but a specific, known, woman (1994: 44).

[121] See Levin 1987 on the poems, either unpublished or published under William's name, that can be identified as Dorothy's; her journals were first published only in the twentieth century.

[122] See Wordsworth 1987 suggesting that William Wordsworth's best poetry was 'almost like a collaboration between them' (7, introduction R. Trickett); Sisman 2006: 164 and 199 for the two poets' use of her journals.

included writers as well as painters, and many of her family members.[123] We know less about particular influences on her, but it is clear that both women were provided, through their families, with the three things usually identified as central to women's participation in artistic movements: the physical materials with which to work (e.g. paper), mentors from whom to learn, and a community to provide support (Nochlin 1988).

It is, of course, speculative to posit a similar family-based community for the Augustan age, but we have seen that there is some evidence for poetic communities during that time (Section II above). Evidence of women's participation in such communities is, as we would expect, extremely limited, but there is some: Pliny mentions the presence of female relatives in in-home recitations (*Ep.* 4.19.4.; see Hemelrijk 1999: 44–5 for discussion, and 147–53 for three other literary women). Ov. writes *Tr.* 3.7 to a young woman poet, Perilla, thought by many to be his stepdaughter (he refers to himself as her *pater*, 3.7.12, 18); the poem claims that he taught her to write poetry, and corrected her compositions.[124] Even the *puellae* of elegiac poetry are sometimes referred to as authors of poetry (e.g. Prop. 1.2.27–8, 2.3.21–2; see too Perkins 2011). Obviously, then, the models of the eighteenth and nineteenth centuries are not wholly anachronistic, though they will need to be applied with care.

In conclusion, there is nothing in what we know about the Augustan world to prevent the existence of a female poet, and the story [Tib.] 3 allows us to create about S. provides a plausible community for her to have written poetry in. So too, it seems at least possible that S. could have been both a member of the Roman elite and written fairly frank poetry about her amatory interests (note again Julia's jokes). Beyond this, we are in murky waters. The context for S.'s poetry, in combination with its sharp distinctiveness from anything else in Latin poetry, provides evidence for two mutually exclusive hypotheses, and there is no secure method for choosing between them. My own opinion is as likely to be wrong as anyone else's, but it seems to me that much is gained, and little lost, in treating the poetry of S. as an authentically recovered female voice from antiquity.

VII: STYLE, METRE, AND SYNTAX

The commentary as a whole, I hope, will suffice to make the case that the elegies of [Tib.] 3 share a wide variety of stylistic similarities with canonical elegy. In addition to the choice of metre and subject matter, their vocabulary is very

---

[123] See Pollock and Cherry 1988 on the erasure of female agency among the pre-Raphaelites.
[124] See Hemelrijk 1999: 44–5 on literary recitations in private homes and 47–53 on women as readers, especially of poetry. She discusses Perilla at 149–51. Ingleheart 2012, on the other hand, points to the ways in which Perilla is similar to other (wholly literary) elegiac women, such that we may not want to read her as a real person (228); note too Perilla = *per illam*, which may mark her out as a mouthpiece for the concerns of Ov. and other authors about the dangers of readerly reception (239).

similar to that of Prop., Tib., and Ov., and this introduction has already outlined a number of the ways in which the poems cohere to the standard elegiac tropes and understandings of the world. One difference, which might be crucial for interpreting the poems as a whole, is the way in which the poems alter, or perhaps play with, the classic elegiac situation, in which a man pursues a woman for an illicit relationship. L.'s poetry raises the spectre of a marital relationship, while the poetry by and about S. features, at least some of the time, a woman pursuing a man (and some see this relationship as culminating in a marriage as well).

Beyond this general material are some more technical matters, such as metrical patterns and the ways the poets structure their lines and choose words, and it is on these details that this section focuses. Even for those only interested in literary questions, such details are significant insofar as they may provide information about issues of dating and/or authorship. On the other hand, the small size of [Tib.] 3 means that statistical data are not of much use; once the poems are broken into their traditional divisions, this is even more the case. In this summary of the work that has been done on metre and syntax, I make no claim to originality; my goal here is rather to synthesize the fruits of previous studies in the briefest possible compass, and to summarize the meagre consensus that can be gained from them.[125]

The most comprehensive study of metrical structures in the Tibullan poets is Cartault 1911; he shows that the basic metrical and prosodic features of Book 3 taken as a whole cohere with Tib. 1 and 2 (he believes that 3.8–12 were written by Tib.). For instance, synezesis and syncope are both rare in these three books in comparison with Prop. and Ov. (Bréguet 1946: 124 on similarities of sense-units). At the same time, the poems are not wholly Tibullan: the [Tib.] 3 poets tend to avoid a third-foot caesura more often than is the case in Tib. 1 and 2 (Platnauer 1951: 7 n. 1); unlike Tib., they never have bucolic diaeresis (Platnauer 1951: 11); and pentametric endings of more than three syllables are rare (Platnauer 1951: 17).

Once we move to syntactic and stylistic elements, we note that the poems of [Tib.] 3 obey the standard elegiac habit of containing sense-units more or less within couplets; this feature is most prevalent in L., barring certain passages, and least prevalent in S., whose syntax is in general more convoluted (Santirocco 1979; Lowe 1988). Each of the poets has a particular set of 'favourite' words (e.g. S.'s plays on *cura*, etc.); what is more interesting is that a few of them appear across cycles (see Bréguet 1946: 135–51 and 163–241 for the diction and vocabulary of 3.8–12). Diction can provide some information about the dating of the cycles; see Navarro Antolín 1996 (for L.) and Maltby 2009: 327 on 'late' words and phrases (and see Section V above). The book does indeed contain any number of somewhat strange usages (all discussed *ad locc.*), but poetry tends to experiment with language, so it is difficult to know what to make of

---

[125] See especially Maltby 2009, an extremely useful summary.

anomalies. More worryingly, the amount of Latin poetry lost to us is so great that we can never be certain that chains of influence are as they seem; presumably it is often the case that they are much more complex than we imagine, and include authors we know nothing of. So the argument that a certain word or phrase does not appear until a particular period can only ever be an argument from silence; for some scholars there are enough such words and phrases in [Tib.] 3 to raise serious doubts about an early (Augustan) date, but for others, there are not.

***

While I have implicitly argued that the best way to understand the poems of [Tib.] 3 is to put them into the context of 'Latin love elegy', numerous differences exist both among cycles within the collection and between these poems and the rest of elegy. The same is true for metre and stylistics. I summarize some of the more technical points here, dividing by cycle for the reader's convenience.

1–6: While L.'s metrical practices are, generally speaking, very flexible (Cartault 1911: 31) and similar to those of Tib. (Postgate 1929: li), his use of a spondee in the first foot of the hexameter is significantly higher, percentage-wise than is found in Tib. 1 and 2 or in the S. poems, and is also much higher than anywhere in Ov. (Cartault 1911: 11, 83; Platnauer 1951: 38; Findley 2002: 149). He shortens open vowels in the pentameter roughly twice as much as the other authors of the *CT* (also twice as much as Prop., and eight times more often than Ov.; Platnauer 1951: 64). L. very rarely uses a second-foot diaeresis, while in Tib. 1 and 2 and the S. poems it is somewhat common (Platnauer 1951: 18). In L., a weak 'Graecising' caesura in the third foot occurs only twice, whereas it is regular in Tib. 1 and 2 and the other poems of [Tib.] 3 (Platnauer 1951: 9, Maltby 2009: 328). L. never violates Hermann's bridge (Hooper 1975: 61), has a higher percentage of dactylic hexameter openings than the rest of Tib. (44%; Platnauer 1951: 38), and an extremely low percentage of hepthemimeral caesurae (Cartault 1911: 160). L.'s pentameter endings tend towards the disyllabic (this is a feature towards which Ov.'s poetry evolves), and 20% of his pentameters have an internal rhyme (Luck 1969: 29 and Hooper 1975: 61 for discussion). He favours elision of the first syllable of the first foot, but avoids elision of the first short syllable of the first foot; this is noteworthy as it differs sharply from the practice of Tib. (Cartault 1911: 196–7). His percentages of short open vowels at the end of the pentameter are roughly double those of other elegists (except Ov., in whom they are even rarer; Platnauer 1951: 64). In terms of noun/adjective placement, Cartault notes a tendency to end the hexameter with an adjective followed by its noun (1911: 222), as well as the placement of noun/adjective combinations on either side of the caesura (1911: 261). Finally, L., unlike Tib., favours distichs with a single main clause rather than more complex constructions (Cartault 1911: 269–70). Maltby summarizes the metrical practices of L. as fairly repetitive

(2009: 328); Büchner characterizes them as 'typisch vorovidisch' (1965: 102; cf. Maltby 2009: 328). It is worth noting that L. does not allow for the shortening of a final *o*. (Such shortening is characteristic of Flavian poets, so provides evidence against a later date.) There is little that can be concluded from such a small sample, but scholars generally agree that, on metrical and other formal grounds at least, the attribution of the L. poems to Ov. or to Tib. is not probable (see Section V above for dissenting opinions; Cartault 1911: 312–14 on the non-Tibullanness of the cycle—but he does suggest that L. was a pupil of Tib.). More positive identification, including even the century of composition, can only ever be guesswork.

The poet of **8–12** is usually seen as more similar to Ov. than to any other poet (e.g. Bréguet 1946: 60–2), but Tib. also finds favour (e.g. Cartault 1911: *passim*); see Section V above for other suggestions. Among the most noteworthy of similarities to Tib. are the use of penthemimeral caesurae (Cartault 1911: 159) and the distich as a primary conveyer of the sense-unit (Cartault 1911: 278–9). The poet has a wide metrical flexibility, but mostly keeps within the bounds outlined by the major three elegists (Bréguet 1946: 129). He decreases the number of dactyls in the hexameter in comparison to other elegists (Bréguet 1946: 71), and, broadly speaking, his patterns of elision follow those of Prop. (Bréguet 1946: 114; Cartault 1911: 199 notes that he does not elide long syllables). The poet favours symmetrical structures (Maltby 2009: 332), and phrasings similar to the other elegists, especially Ovid (Maltby 2009: 333). Bréguet 1946 offers a detailed discussion of the style and syntax of this cycle, the most important elements of which are discussed in the lemmata (1946: 241–67). She also summarizes the major points of contact between the cycle and other elegies (1946: 267–76). Here again, there is not sufficient evidence, in my opinion, to attribute these poems to any author whose work we have examples of (including S.); I consider it most likely that they are from the hand of an *ignotus*.

As far as the metre of **13–18** goes, Santirocco notes that its pentameters nearly always follow the Augustan predilection towards disyllabism (235–6); the one exception is S.'s name. S. is fonder of internal (pentametric) rhyme than most other poets, following in this Cat. and Prop. 1 and 2 (Bréguet 1946: 111–12; Currie 1983: 1759 n. 24, who suggests it is a Gallan feature). Elisions are rare (Cartault 1911: 185, Lyne 2007: 347, Maltby: 2009: 336), and never of long syllables (Cartault 1911: 199). She has diaeresis after the second foot 20% of the time, which is a relatively high frequency (Hooper 1975: 124), and ends the pentameter with a short vowel much more often, percentage-wise, than other elegists (Lyne 2007: 347; as he notes, the sample is very small, and includes three instances). As a whole, her metrical choices are diverse, but more similar to early Ov. than to anyone else (Maltby 2009: 336), though Cartault notes that she also follows Tib. in a number of particulars (1911: *passim*). Her favoured metrical structures do not precisely match those of any other elegist (Bréguet 1946:

62). Cartault observes a tendency to divide two adjectives and nouns in a hexametric line evenly across the caesura, a feature which distinguishes her from Tib. (1911: 248; e.g. 3.13.3), and ultimately concludes that they are two authors from the same 'school' (1911: 311). S. does not postpone particles, but does postpone conjunctions (Hooper 1975: 89), sometimes to the point of obscurity. This is, in fact, the most noteworthy feature of her style. While her syntax is complex, her diction, by contrast, is simple and concise (Bréguet 1946: 52), and is often described as colloquial (Santirocco 1979: 236, Currie 1983: 1759 n. 24; Maltby 2009: 335 compares it to the less formal writings of Cicero). Bréguet suggests that the syntax is difficult precisely because it *is* colloquial (1946: 48–9), but Lowe seems to be closer to the mark in identifying it as a 'conscious, almost obsessive articulation of form' (1998: 199). See Lowe 1988: 198 and 202 and Lyne 2007: 364–5 on the main hallmarks of S.'s style: subjunctives, particularly jussives, perfect infinitives, temporal adverbs (*iam, nunc*), *quod*-noun clauses, comparative constructions, complex subordination of clauses and particularly conditionals, verbs of which she is not the subject. In keeping with a tendency to view them as 'amateurish', S.'s poems have traditionally been seen as less allusive than elegy usually is (Davies 1973: 26, Tränkle 1990, Santirocco 1979: 237; see also Section I above), but recent work has claimed for them a number of previously unnoticed connections to other texts (Roessel 1990; Merriam 1990, 2005, 2006; Keith 1997; Hallett 2002a, 2002b, 2006, 2009a, 2009b, 2011; Fabre-Serris 2009, with discussion in individual lemmata). As I do with the other poets of this cycle, I tend towards assuming that S.'s poetry is what it claims to be; the political stakes are higher here, and so opinions held more intensely, but in the end there is no secure way of determining authorship.

Far less attention is paid to **19 and 20** than to the other poems, but there is little in them that is sharply inconsistent with Tibullan practice. The confining of sense-units to distichs is always observed in this group (Cartault 1911: 278–9). See Cartault 1911: 306–7 for a summary of the metrical similarities and differences between Tib. and the two poems; his conclusion is that they are Tibullan, and dated between the first and second books (also argued at Cartault 1909: 30). Hor. *Od*. 1.33 might suggest the existence of Tibullan poems outside of the two securely attested books, so one or both of these poems might well be authentically his. Maltby 2009: 337 suggests that the metre of 3.19 is Ovidian rather than Tibullan (or if Tibullan, it is late, which, as he notes, is difficult to reconcile with the biographical tradition).

***

There are, then, clear metrical differences between the poets, and, to a lesser extent, stylistic ones as well. Metre is a subject on which reasonable people may disagree, but I see nothing to preclude Swoboda's conclusion that all of the elegiac poems of [Tib.] 3 are metrically pre-Ovidian (1969–70). In terms of style, each of the poems is more Ovidian than it is anything else, barring certain passages. But this fact is less significant than it may seem given the enormity of Ov.'s influence (see Section I above). In sum, the evidence does not warrant confident conclusions about any of the poems; while it does not contradict the proposition that the collection could have been written by a coterie of contemporary poets working closely together either with or without Tib. himself (see Section V above), it is also well within the bounds of possibility that it is an accretion of later texts carefully assimilated into the work of Tib. along the model of the *Appendix Vergiliana*.

VIII: MANUSCRIPT TRADITION AND TEXT

The transmission and establishment of the text of the *CT* has been well studied (Cartault 1909: 135–47, Reynolds ed. 1983: 420–5, Fisher 1983: 1953–61, Tränkle 1990: 6–9, and Navarro Antolín 1996: 31–40 on this book, with theories about the mechanics of transmission). Complete manuscripts include the *Ambrosianus* from the late fourteenth century, the *Vaticanus* from the late fourteenth or early fifteenth century, and the fifteenth-century *Guelferbytanus* (whose usefulness is disputed by some); all are independent but probably derive from the same archetype. We also have eleventh-century florilegia such as the *Frisingensis*, *Parisinus*, *Thuaneus*, and *Nostradamensis* (the first tantalizingly deriving from a text of a seemingly higher quality than the ones we have), a now-lost fragment from Book 3, the *Cuiacianum* (see Dixon 2006 on the history), and scattered quotations from grammarians (although they do not cite from [Tib.] 3). As often, the *recentiores* are usually deemed inferior (Fisher 1983: 1959). Modern texts are all, more or less, based on Baehrens' edition of 1878.

The point of relevance for this commentary, and so the one that will receive attention, is how early Book 3 was connected to the first two books; if, for instance, an early source mentioned three books of Tib., that would provide some evidence for contemporaneous composition of its books. Alas, the available information is disobliging: as Navarro Antolín notes, the fourth-century authors Ausonius and Avienus seem to allude to poems in [Tib.] 3, and earlier evidence is ambiguous of interpretation (1996: 29; cf. Maltby 2009: 339). So, for that matter, is later evidence; a late-eighth-century catalogue lists two books of Tibullus (Ullman 1954: 25; Codex Diez. B 66, in Berlin), though this may be a scribal error (Ullman 1954: 26; Fisher 1983: 1953), or an identification only of those authentically by Tib.; a twelfth-century list mentions three Tibullan books. There are also *florilegia* dating as far back as the tenth century, and these include [Tib.] 3 (Ullman 1928, Newton 1962). Rostagni (1935) has suggested that the third book circulated independently for a lengthy period, but Tränkle 1990 suggests earlier incorporation.[126]

In terms of the arrangement of poems, there is one oddity worth mentioning: what we know as poem 3.18 is attached in the manuscripts to 3.6; this may in turn indicate the presence of further dislocations of text, and so might call into question the validity of any arguments about arrangement or even cycles.

As noted (Section V above), the abbreviated lengths of both [Tib.] 3 and of Tib. 1 and 2, along with [Tib.] 3's mentions of Tib. and Messalla, might be reason enough for them to have been combined into a unit. *Spuria* are regularly tacked on to manuscripts whose authors we know (Grafton 1990: 31 on the case of Ov.). There is, of course, also the possibility that Tib. 2 is incomplete, and that some portions of Book 3 once belonged to it (especially 3.19, which claims Tib. as its author).

I print Lenz/Galinsky's 1971 Brill text, except as noted below, without apparatus, and with a few, unnoted, alterations of punctuation and orthography.[127]

There are many manuscript variants, especially in the L. poems; in the commentary I discuss primarily those variants printed in other texts, or where an alternative reading has significant implications for meaning. I follow Lenz/Galinsky except in those places where I cannot construe the Latin; alternative readings are listed below.

Differences from Lenz/Galinsky (all discussed in the commentary):

Text printed in this edition	L/G and other texts
3.1.10 pumex et	LG: *pumicet* (Luck *pumex cui*; Tränkle 1990 and Navarro Antolín 1996 *pumex et*)
13 geminae	LG: *geminas* (Luck, Tränkle 1990 and Navarro Antolín 1996 *geminas*)
3.2.15 recentem	LG: *precatae* (Luck, Tränkle 1990 *recentem*; Navarro Antolín 1996 *precatae*)
3.2.18 legant	LG: *legent* (Luck, Tränkle 1990, Navarro Antolín 1996 *legant*)
3.2.19 spargant	LG: *spargent* (Luck, Tränkle 1990, Navarro Antolín 1996 *spargant*)
3.3.36 canunt	LG: *neunt* (Luck *neunt*; Tränkle 1990 and Navarro Antolín 1996 *canunt*)
3.4.64 prece	LG: *fide* (Luck, Navarro Antolín 1996 *prece*; Tränkle 1990 *fide*)

---

[126] See Cartault 1906 for a history of nineteenth-century scholarship on Tibullus, which includes treatment of [Tib.] 3. Knox, forthcoming, suggests a significantly later collection of the three books (41).

[127] © Koninklijke Brill NV, 1971, Lenz, Friedrich Walther and Galinsky, G. K., *Albii Tibulli Aliorumque Carminum Libri Tres*, 3rd ed.

Elegies of the *Appendix Tibulliana*

Text

3.1:
"Martis Romani festae venere kalendae –
   exoriens nostris hic fuit annus avis –
et vaga nunc certa discurrunt undique pompa
   perque vias urbis munera perque domos:
dicite, Pierides, quonam donetur honore   5
   seu mea, seu fallor, cara Neaera tamen."
"Carmine formosae, pretio capiuntur avarae.
   Gaudeat, ut digna est, versibus illa tuis.
Lutea sed niveum involvat membrana libellum,
   pumex et canas tondeat ante comas,   10
summaque praetexat tenuis fastigia chartae
   indicet ut nomen littera facta tuum,
atque inter geminae pingantur cornua frontes:
   sic etenim comptum mittere oportet opus."
"Per vos, auctores huius mihi carminis, oro   15
   Castaliamque umbram Pieriosque lacus,
ite domum cultumque illi donate libellum,
   sicut erit: nullus defluat inde color.
(Illa mihi referet, si nostri mutua cura est,
   an minor, an toto pectore deciderim.)   20
Sed primum meritam larga donate salute
   atque haec submisso dicite verba sono:
'Haec tibi vir quondam, nunc frater, casta Neaera,
   mittit et accipias munera parva rogat,
teque suis iurat caram magis esse medullis,   25
   sive sibi coniunx sive futura soror,
sed potius coniunx: huius spem nominis illi
   auferet extincto pallida Ditis aqua'."

3.2:
Qui primus caram iuveni carumque puellae
   eripuit iuvenem, ferreus ille fuit.
Durus et ille fuit, qui tantum ferre dolorem,
   vivere et erepta coniuge qui potuit.
Non ego firmus in hoc, non haec patientia nostro   5
   ingenio: frangit fortia corda dolor;

nec mihi vera loqui pudor est vitaeque fateri
   tot mala perpessae, taedia nata meae.
Ergo cum tenuem fuero mutatus in umbram
   candidaque ossa supra nigra favilla teget,   10
ante meum veniat longos incompta capillos
   et fleat ante meum maesta Neaera rogum.
Sed veniat carae matris comitata dolore:
   maereat haec genero, maereat illa viro.
Praefatae ante meos manes animamque recentem   15
   perfusaeque pias ante liquore manus,
pars quae sola mei superabit corporis, ossa
   incinctae nigra candida veste legant,
et primum annoso spargant collecta Lyaeo,
   mox etiam niveo fundere lacte parent,   20
post haec carbaseis umorem tollere velis
   atque in marmorea ponere sicca domo.
Illic quas mittit dives Panchaia merces
   Eoique Arabes, dives et Assyria,
et nostri memores lacrimae fundantur eodem: 25
   sic ego componi versus in ossa velim.
Sed tristem mortis demonstret littera causam
   atque haec in celebri carmina fronte notet:
"Lygdamus hic situs est: dolor huic et cura Neaerae,
   coniugis ereptae, causa perire fuit."   30

3.3:

Quid prodest caelum votis implesse, Neaera,
   blandaque cum multa tura dedisse prece?
Non, ut marmorei prodirem e limine tecti,
   insignis clara conspicuusque domo,
aut ut multa mei renovarent iugera tauri   5
   et magnas messes terra benigna daret,
sed tecum ut longae sociarem gaudia vitae
   inque tuo caderet nostra senecta sinu,
tum cum permenso defunctus tempore lucis
   nudus Lethaea cogerer ire rate.   10
Nam grave quid prodest pondus mihi divitis auri,
   arvaque si findant pinguia mille boues?
Quidve domus prodest Phrygiis innixa columnis,
   Taenare sive tuis, sive Caryste tuis,
et nemora in domibus sacros imitantia lucos   15
   aurataeque trabes marmoreumque solum?
Quidve in Erythraeo legitur quae litore concha

    tinctaque Sidonio murice lana iuvat,
et quae praeterea populus miratur? In illis
    invidia est: falso plurima volgus amat.
Non opibus mentes hominum curaeque levantur,
    nam Fortuna sua tempora lege regit.
Sit mihi paupertas tecum iucunda, Neaera,
    at sine te regum munera nulla volo.
O niveam, quae te poterit mihi reddere, lucem!
    O mihi felicem terque quaterque diem!
At si, pro dulci reditu quaecumque voventur,
    audiat aversa non meus aure deus,
nec me regna iuvant nec Lydius aurifer amnis
    nec quas terrarum sustinet orbis opes.
Haec alii cupiant, liceat mihi paupere cultu
    securo cara coniuge posse frui.
Adsis et timidis faveas, Saturnia, votis,
    et faveas concha, Cypria, vecta tua.
Aut si fata negant reditum tristesque sorores,
    stamina quae ducunt quaeque futura canunt,
me vocet in vastos amnes nigramque paludem
    dives in ignava luridus Orcus aqua.

3.4:

Di meliora ferant, nec sint mihi somnia vera,
    quae tulit hesterna pessima nocte quies.
Ite procul, vani, falsumque avertite visum:
    desinite in nobis quaerere velle fidem.
Divi vera monent, venturae nuntia sortis
    vera monent Tuscis exta probata viris;
somnia fallaci ludunt temeraria nocte
    et pavidas mentes falsa timere iubent.
Et natum in curas hominum genus omina noctis
    farre pio placant et saliente sale.
Et tamen, utcumque est, sive illi vera moneri,
    mendaci somno credere sive volent,
efficiat vanos noctis Lucina timores
    et frustra immeritum pertimuisse velit,
si mea nec turpi mens est obnoxia facto
    nec laesit magnos impia lingua deos.
Iam Nox aetherium nigris emensa quadrigis
    mundum caeruleo laverat amne rotas,
nec me sopierat menti deus utilis aegrae:
    Somnus sollicitas deficit ante domos.

Tandem, cum summo Phoebus prospexit ab ortu,
    pressit languentis lumina sera quies.
Hic iuvenis casta redimitus tempora lauro
    est visus nostra ponere sede pedem.
Non illo quicquam formosius ulla priorum   25
    aetas, humanum nec videt illud opus.
Intonsi crines longa cervice fluebant,
    stillabat Syrio myrtea rore coma.
Candor erat, qualem praefert Latonia Luna,
    et color in niveo corpore purpureus,   30
ut iuveni primum virgo deducta marito
    inficitur teneras ore rubente genas,
et cum contexunt amarantis alba puellae
    lilia et autumno candida mala rubent.
Ima videbatur talis inludere palla,   35
    namque haec in nitido corpore vestis erat.
Artis opus rarae, fulgens testudine et auro
    pendebat laeva garrula parte lyra.
Hanc primum veniens plectro modulatus eburno
    felices cantus ore sonante dedit.   40
Sed postquam fuerant digiti cum voce locuti,
    edidit haec dulci tristia verba modo:
"Salve, cura deum: casto nam rite poetae
    Phoebusque et Bacchus Pieridesque favent;
sed proles Semelae Bacchus doctaeque sorores   45
    dicere non norunt, quid ferat hora sequens:
at mihi fatorum leges aevique futuri
    eventura pater posse videre dedit.
Quare, ego quae dico non fallax, accipe, vates,
    quodque deus vero Cynthius ore feram.   50
Tantum cara tibi, quantum nec filia matri,
    quantum nec cupido bella puella viro,
pro qua sollicitas caelestia numina votis,
    quae tibi securos non sinit ire dies
et, cum te fusco Somnus velavit amictu,   55
    vanum nocturnis fallit imaginibus,
carminibus celebrata tuis formosa Neaera
    alterius mavolt esse puella viri,
diversasque suas agitat mens impia curas,
    nec gaudet casta nupta Neaera domo.   60
A crudele genus nec fidum femina nomen!
    A pereat, didicit fallere siqua virum!
Sed flecti poterit – mens est mutabilis illis –

tu modo cum multa bracchia tende prece.
Saevus Amor docuit validos temptare labores,
  saevus Amor docuit verbera posse pati.
Me quondam Admeti niveas pavisse iuvencas
  non est in vanum fabula ficta iocum.
Tunc ego nec cithara poteram gaudere sonora
  nec similes chordis reddere voce sonos,
sed perlucenti cantum meditabar avena
  ille ego Latonae filius atque Iovis.
Nescis quid sit amor, iuvenis, si ferre recusas
  immitem dominam coniugiumque ferum.
Ergo ne dubita blandas adhibere querelas:
  vincuntur molli pectora dura prece.
Quod si vera canunt sacris oracula templis,
  haec illi nostro nomine dicta refer:
hoc tibi coniugium promittit Delius ipse,
  felix hoc, alium desine velle virum."
Dixit, et ignavus defluxit corpore somnus.
  A ego ne possim tanta videre mala!
Nec tibi crediderim votis contraria vota
  nec tantum crimen pectore inesse tuo;
nam te nec vasti genuerunt aequora ponti
  nec flammam volvens ore Chimaera fero
nec canis anguinea redimitus terga caterva,
  cui tres sunt linguae tergeminumque caput,
Scyllaque virgineam canibus succincta figuram,
  nec te conceptam saeva leaena tulit,
barbara nec Scythiae tellus horrendave Syrtis,
  sed culta et duris non habitanda domus
et longe ante alias omnes mitissima mater
  isque pater, quo non alter amabilior.
Haec deus in melius crudelia somnia vertat
  et iubeat tepidos inrita ferre notos.

3.5:

Vos tenet, Etruscis manat quae fontibus unda,
  unda sub aestivum non adeunda Canem,
nunc autem sacris Baiarum proxima lymphis,
  cum se purpureo vere remittit humus.
At mihi Persephone nigram denuntiat horam:
  immerito iuveni parce nocere, dea.
Non ego temptavi nulli temeranda virorum
  audax laudandae sacra docere deae,

nec mea mortiferis infecit pocula sucis
    dexterа nec cuiquam trita venena dedit, 10
nec nos sacrilegi templis amovimus aegros,
    nec cor sollicitant facta nefanda meum,
nec nos insanae meditantes iurgia mentis
    impia in adversos solvimus ora deos,
et nondum cani nigros laesere capillos, 15
    nec venit tardo curva senecta pede.
Natalem primo nostrum videre parentes,
    cum cecidit fato consul uterque pari.
Quid fraudare iuvat vitem crescentibus uvis
    et modo nata mala vellere poma manu? 20
Parcite, pallentes undas quicumque tenetis
    duraque sortiti tertia regna dei.
Elysios olim liceat cognoscere campos
    Lethaeamque ratem Cimmeriosque lacus,
cum mea rugosa pallebunt ora senecta 25
    et referam pueris tempora prisca senex.
Atque utinam vano nequiquam terrear aestu,
    languent ter quinos sed mea membra dies.
At vobis Tuscae celebrantur numina lymphae
    et facilis lenta pellitur unda manu. 30
Vivite felices, memores et vivite nostri,
    sive erimus seu nos fata fuisse velint.
Interea nigras pecudes promittite Diti
    et nivei lactis pocula mixta mero.

3.6:

Candide Liber, ades – sic sit tibi mystica vitis
    semper, sic hedera tempora vincta feras –
aufer et ipse meum patera medicante dolorem:
    saepe tuo cecidit munere victus amor.
Care puer, madeant generoso pocula baccho, 5
    et nobis prona funde Falerna manu.
Ite procul, durum curae genus, ite labores;
    fulserit hic niveis Delius alitibus.
Vos modo proposito dulces faveatis amici,
    neve neget quisquam me duce se comitem, 10
aut siquis vini certamen mite recusat,
    fallat eum tecto cara puella dolo.
Ille facit dites animos deus, ille ferocem
    contudit et dominae misit in arbitrium,
Armenias tigres et fulvas ille leaenas 15

vicit et indomitis mollia corda dedit.
Haec Amor et maiora valet. Sed poscite Bacchi
   munera: quem vestrum pocula sicca iuvant?
Convenit ex aequo nec torvus Liber in illis,
   qui se quique una vina iocosa colunt.
Convenit iratus nimium nimiumque severos:
   qui timet irati numina magna, bibat.
Quales his poenas qualis quantusque minetur,
   Cadmeae matris praeda cruenta docet.
Sed procul a nobis hic sit timor, illaque, si qua est,
   quid valeat laesi sentiat ira dei.
Quid precor a, demens? Venti temeraria vota,
   aeriae et nubes diripienda ferant.
Quamvis nulla mei superest tibi cura, Neaera,
   sis felix, et sint candida fata tua.
At nos securae reddamus tempora mensae:
   venit post multos una serena dies.
Ei mihi, difficile est imitari gaudia falsa,
   difficile est tristi fingere mente iocum,
nec bene mendaci risus componitur ore,
   nec bene sollicitis ebria verba sonant.
Quid queror infelix? Turpes discedite curae:
   odit Lenaeus tristia verba pater.
Cnosia, Theseae quondam periuria linguae
   flevisti ignoto sola relicta mari:
sic cecinit pro te doctus, Minoi, Catullus
   ingrati referens impia facta viri.
Vos ego nunc moneo: felix, quicumque dolore
   alterius disces posse cavere tuo.
Nec vos aut capiant pendentia bracchia collo
   aut fallat blanda sordida lingua fide.
Etsi perque suos fallax iuravit ocellos
   Iunonemque suam perque suam Venerem,
nulla fides inerit: periuria ridet amantum
   Iuppiter et ventos inrita ferre iubet.
Ergo quid totiens fallacis verba puellae
   conqueror? Ite a me, seria verba, precor.
Quam vellem tecum longas requiescere noctes
   et tecum longos pervigilare dies,
perfida nec merito nobis inimica merenti,
   perfida, sed, quamvis perfida, cara tamen!
Naida Bacchus amat: cessas, o lente minister?
   Temperet annosum Marcia lympha merum.

Non ego, si fugit nostrae convivia mensae
　　ignotum cupiens vana puella torum, 60
sollicitus repetam tota suspiria nocte:
　　tu, puer, i, liquidum fortius adde merum.
Iam dudum Syrio madefactus tempora nardo
　　debueram sertis implicuisse comas.

3.8:
Sulpicia est tibi culta tuis, Mars magne, kalendis:
　　spectatum e caelo, si sapis, ipse veni.
Hoc Venus ignoscet: at tu, violente, caveto
　　ne tibi miranti turpiter arma cadant.
Illius ex oculis, cum volt exurere divos, 5
　　accendit geminas lampadas acer Amor.
Illam, quicquid agit, quoquo vestigia movit,
　　componit furtim subsequiturque Decor.
Seu solvit crines, fusis decet esse capillis,
　　seu compsit, comptis est veneranda comis. 10
Urit, seu Tyria voluit procedere palla:
　　urit, seu nivea candida veste venit.
Talis in aeterno felix Vertumnus Olympo
　　mille habet ornatus, mille decenter habet.
Sola puellarum digna est, cui mollia caris 15
　　vellera det sucis bis madefacta Tyros,
possideatque, metit quicquid bene olentibus arvis
　　cultor odoratae dives Arabs segetis,
et quascumque niger Rubro de litore gemmas
　　proximus Eois colligit Indus aquis. 20
Hanc vos, Pierides, festis cantate kalendis,
　　et testudinea Phoebe superbe lyra.
Hoc sollemne sacrum multos consummet in annos:
　　dignior est vestro nulla puella choro.

3.9:
Parce meo iuveni, seu quis bona pascua campi
　　seu colis umbrosi devia montis aper,
nec tibi sit duros acuisse in proelia dentes,
　　incolumem custos hunc mihi servet Amor.
Sed procul abducit venandi Delia cura: 5
　　o pereant silvae, deficiantque canes!
Quis furor est, quae mens densos indagine colles
　　claudentem teneras laedere velle manus?
Quidve iuvat furtim latebras intrare ferarum

candidaque hamatis crura notare rubis? 10
Sed tamen, ut tecum liceat, Cerinthe, vagari,
   ipsa ego per montes retia torta feram,
ipsa ego velocis quaeram vestigia cervi
   et demam celeri ferrea vincla cani.
Tunc mihi, tunc placeant silvae, si, lux mea, tecum 15
   arguar ante ipsas concubuisse plagas:
tunc veniat licet ad casses, inlaesus abibit,
   ne Veneris cupidae gaudia turbet, aper.
Nunc sine me sit nulla venus, sed lege Dianae,
   caste puer, casta retia tange manu, 20
et, quaecumque meo furtim subrepit amori,
   incidat in saevas diripienda feras.
At tu venandi studium concede parenti
   et celer in nostros ipse recurre sinus.

3.10:

Huc ades et tenerae morbos expelle puellae,
   huc ades, intonsa Phoebe superbe coma.
Crede mihi, propera, nec te iam, Phoebe, pigebit
   formosae medicas adplicuisse manus.
Effice ne macies pallentes occupet artus, 5
   neu notet informis pallida membra color,
et quodcumque mali est et quidquid triste timemus,
   in pelagus rapidis evehat amnis aquis.
Sancte, veni, tecumque feras, quicumque sapores,
   quicumque et cantus corpora fessa levant, 10
neu iuvenem torque, metuit qui fata puellae
   votaque pro domina vix numeranda facit.
Interdum vovet, interdum, quod langueat illa,
   dicit in aeternos aspera verba deos.
Pone metum, Cerinthe: deus non laedit amantes. 15
   Tu modo semper ama: salva puella tibi est.
Nil opus est fletu: lacrimis erit aptius uti, 21
   si quando fuerit tristior illa tibi. 22
At nunc tota tua est, te solum candida secum 17
   cogitat, et frustra credula turba sedet.
Phoebe, fave: laus magna tibi tribuetur in uno
   corpore servato restituisse duos. 20
Iam celeber, iam laetus eris, cum debita reddet 23
   certatim sanctis laetus uterque focis.
Tum te felicem dicet pia turba deorum, 25
   optabunt artes et sibi quisque tuas.

3.11:

Qui mihi te, Cerinthe, dies dedit, hic mihi sanctus
  atque inter festos semper habendus erit.
Te nascente novum Parcae cecinere puellis
  servitium et dederunt regna superba tibi.
Uror ego ante alias: iuvat hoc, Cerinthe, quod uror,
  si tibi de nobis mutuus ignis adest.
Mutuus adsit amor, per te dulcissima furta
  perque tuos oculos per Geniumque rogo.
Magne Geni, cape tura libens votisque faveto,
  si modo, cum de me cogitat, ille calet.
Quodsi forte alios iam nunc suspiret amores,
  tunc precor infidos, sancte, relinque focos.
Nec tu sis iniusta, Venus: vel serviat aeque
  vinctus uterque tibi vel mea vincla leva.
Sed potius valida teneamur uterque catena,
  nulla queat posthac quam soluisse dies.
Optat idem iuvenis quod nos, sed tectius optat:
  nam pudet haec illum dicere verba palam.
At tu, Natalis, quoniam deus omnia sentis,
  adnue: quid refert, clamne palamne roget?

3.12:

Natalis Iuno, sanctos cape turis acervos,
  quos tibi dat tenera docta puella manu.
Tota tibi est hodie, tibi se laetissima compsit,
  staret ut ante tuos conspicienda focos.
Illa quidem ornandi causas tibi, diva, relegat,
  est tamen, occulte cui placuisse velit.
At tu, sancta, fave, neu quis divellat amantes,
  sed iuveni, quaeso, mutua vincla para.
Sic bene compones: ullae non ille puellae
  servire aut cuiquam dignior illa viro.
Nec possit cupidos vigilans deprendere custos,
  fallendique vias mille ministret Amor.
Adnue purpureaque veni perlucida palla:
  ter tibi fit libo, ter, dea casta, mero,
praecipit et natae mater studiosa, quod optat:
  illa aliud tacita, iam sua, mente rogat;
uritur, ut celeres urunt altaria flammae,
  nec, liceat quamvis, sana fuisse velit.
Sis iuveni grata: veniet cum proximus annus,
  hic idem votis iam vetus exstet amor.

3.13:

Tandem venit amor, qualem texisse pudori
   quam nudasse alicui sit mihi fama magis.
Exorata meis illum Cytherea Camenis
   adtulit in nostrum deposuitque sinum.
Exsolvit promissa Venus: mea gaudia narret,   5
   dicetur siquis non habuisse sua.
Non ego signatis quicquam mandare tabellis,
   ne legat id nemo quam meus ante, velim,
sed peccasse iuvat, voltus componere famae
   taedet: cum digno digna fuisse ferar.   10

3.14:

Invisus natalis adest, qui rure molesto
   et sine Cerintho tristis agendus erit.
Dulcius urbe quid est? An villa sit apta puellae
   atque Arretino frigidus amnis agro?
Iam, nimium Messalla mei studiose, quiescas,   5
   heu tempestivae saeve, propinque, viae!
Hic animum sensusque meos abducta relinquo
   arbitrio quamvis non sinis esse meo.

3.15:

Scis iter ex animo sublatum triste puellae?
   Natali Romae iam licet esse suo.
Omnibus ille dies nobis natalis agatur,
   qui nec opinanti nunc tibi forte venit.

3.16:

Gratum est, securus multum quod iam tibi de me
   permittis, subito ne male inepta cadam.
Sit tibi cura togae potior pressumque quasillo
   scortum quam Servi filia Sulpicia:
solliciti sunt pro nobis, quibus illa dolori est   5
   ne cedam ignoto, maxima causa, toro.

3.17:

Estne tibi, Cerinthe, tuae pia cura puellae,
   quod mea nunc vexat corpora fessa calor?
A ego non aliter tristes evincere morbos
   optarim, quam te si quoque velle putem.
At mihi quid prosit morbos evincere, si tu   5
   nostra potes lento pectore ferre mala?

3.18:

Ne tibi sim, mea lux, aeque iam fervida cura
   ac videor paucos ante fuisse dies,
si quicquam tota commisi stulta iuventa
   cuius me fatear paenituisse magis,
hesterna quam te solum quod nocte reliqui,   5
   ardorem cupiens dissimulare meum.

3.19:

Nulla tuum nobis subducet femina lectum:
   hoc primum iuncta est foedere nostra venus.
Tu mihi sola places, nec iam te praeter in urbe
   formosa est oculis ulla puella meis.
Atque utinam posses uni mihi bella videri!   5
   Displiceas aliis: sic ego tutus ero,
nil opus invidia est, procul absit gloria volgi:
   qui sapit, in tacito gaudeat ipse sinu.
Sic ego secretis possum bene vivere silvis,
   qua nulla humano sit via trita pede.   10
Tu mihi curarum requies, tu nocte vel atra
   lumen, et in solis tu mihi turba locis.
Nunc licet e caelo mittatur amica Tibullo,
   mittetur frustra deficietque Venus.
Hoc tibi sancta tuae Iunonis numina iuro,   15
   quae sola ante alios est mihi magna deos.
Quid facio demens? Heu heu mea pignora cedo.
   Iuravi stulte: proderat iste timor.
Nunc tu fortis eris, nunc tu me audacius ures:
   hoc peperit misero garrula lingua malum.   20
Iam faciam quodcumque voles, tuus usque manebo,
   nec fugiam notae servitium dominae,
sed Veneris sanctae considam vinctus ad aras:
   haec notat iniustos supplicibusque favet.

3.20:

Rumor ait crebro nostram peccare puellam:
   nunc ego me surdis auribus esse velim.
Crimina non haec sunt nostro sine facta dolore:
   quid miserum torques, rumor acerbe? Tace.

Commentary

3.1:

This poem introduces the collection *in medias res*, and, unlike some poetry (e.g. the *Aeneid*, Propertius 1), its *incipit* does not provide any clue to the meaning of the collection as a whole. (This might or might not have implications for book arrangement; see Introduction, Section V.) To begin an elegiac collection with the word *Martis* is unexpected, suggesting that what follows will be a rather different kind of poetry (a suggestion not fully laid to rest until the poem's third couplet, and especially its fourth, where, in the manner of Ov. *Am.* 1.1, the poem 'veers off' from martial epic). But the first word of Tib. 1.1, *divitias*, is also a 'false start'. At the same time, this is patently a dedicatory poem, introducing the collection, which might originally have consisted only of the first six poems. Still, whoever collected the book into a unit may have seen this poem as prefatory to the whole, especially given its shared occasion with 3.8 (on which see *ad loc.*).

The situation of the poem is elegiac at its heart (unhappy love), as would probably have been assumed given its metre, but the basic situation appears here with a twist: Lygdamus' (L.'s) complaints are not about his relationship with Neaera (N.) per se, but, as we discover in the final lines, that the relationship has ended. And the reference to N. as *coniunx* is unexpected (see Introduction, Section I and below *ad* 26–7). So while aspects of the tone of this poem are familiar, its context, and L.'s attitude towards N., are unique. (Later poems revert to more traditional elegiac themes.) This poem offers the collection to N., who thus combines the roles of elegiac *puella* and of (male) patron (see Introduction, Section II, and below *passim*). Poem 3.1 then discusses its own elaborate appearance and the method by which it should be delivered, and finishes by reflecting upon the current state of the affair and reporting the poet's wish for a different outcome. This first poem, like the book as a whole, partakes in the traditional elegiac focus on a particular named woman, but also displays the elegists' overwhelming concern with the act of writing and making public one's poetry; some of its metapoetic gestures are standard, others strikingly original.

The content of the poem, a discussion of L.'s poetry book and its suitability for N., but also a plea to her to give in to his wishes, is not unusual; 'first poems' of poetry collections often begin by outlining the concerns of the corpus. But the form is worthy of explanation, as is the role of the Muses in L.'s poetry. (Textual difficulties obscure the issue; essentially, it is not clear whether the Muses speak or not; see *ad* 3.1.8 and 12.) L.'s casual invocation of the Muses and familiar tone with them show his poetic ambitions, and perhaps his confidence. Note too Call. *Aet.* fr. 7 where the Graces(?) are asked to wipe their anointed hands on the poetry; there too we see a combination of high and low styles, and a focus on the physical properties of the book. If the Muses *do* speak to L., the advice they give him is first ambiguous (for it depends upon the kind of *puella* N. is), then quotidian: they instruct him on how to prepare his presentation copy, surely the one aspect of the process that he does *not* require their help with. The suggestion that poetry makes the best gift is likely to be approved of by poets, but perhaps not *puellae* (see Introduction, Section I); see *ad* 3.1.7–8.

Poets do sometimes address their own poetic books, and even personify them (e.g. *AP* 4.1, Cat. 1.1, Hor. *Ep.* 1.20, Ov. *Tr.* 1.1, 3.1; see further discussion in Besslich 1974 and *passim* below), but it is rare for a poet to speak about his book to named others (especially to deities such as the Muses); see Cat. 1.9 *patrona virgo*, for a partial exception. Navarro Antolín 1996: 95 notes that such a conversation is sometimes found in Hellenistic epigram, and cites Mart. 10.20 and 12.11, which he takes to be predecessors of this poem, as the first examples of a discussion with Muses about a presentation copy of a volume of poetry. (The tone there is unceremonious, as suits Martial's poetry; see Tränkle 1990: 64–5 for extended discussion, and White 1974 on presentation copies in Martial and Statius.) Even if Martial does precede L., the informality with which L. here treats the Muses requires some explanation, given the different genres in which the two write. It is usually also assumed that this poem depends upon Ov. *Tr.* 1.1, an 'anti-dedication' of the exiled poet's book sent home; see Parca 1986: 466 and Veremans 1998: 12–13 for readings that take the chronology in the other direction (and Introduction, Section V, on dating).

The poem occurs on a specific date, the Matronalia (the same festival as in [Tib.] 3.8—and Hor. *Od.* 3.8—though none of these need to refer to the same year). Amatory elegy tends to avoid tying itself down to a particular time (an exception being festivals of Isis, which directly affect the possibility of a sexual encounter, as in Prop. 2.33; there are also a few celebrations of specific historical or personal events, as in Tib. 1.7, on the triumph—and birthday—of Messalla, 25 September 27 BCE, or the birthdays of Cynthia at Prop. 3.10 or Cornutus at Tib. 2.2, and the festivals of Ov. *Am.* 3.10 and 3.13). But what is rare in elegy as a whole is common in this collection, which is sprinkled liberally, especially in the latter poems, with references to birthdays and other specific days (see *ad* 3.11, 3.14, and 3.15, and Introduction, Section I). This may reflect the influence of Prop. 4 or Ov. *Fas.*, both collections concerned with Roman religious and civic institutions.

The poem can be divided into two even parts: first, the announcement of the collection, and a query, with reply, about what sort of present would be best for Neaera (1–14); then instructions to the Muses about how best to deliver the *libellus*, and what to say (15–28).

"Martis Romani festae venere Kalendae –
2   exoriens nostris hic fuit annus avis –

Martis: the appearance of Mars in elegy deserves attention, particularly as the first word of a poem, since elegy presents itself as 'make-love-not-war', a genre opposed to epic. But this opposition is regularly undermined, especially in Ovid, who often uses the trope of *militia amoris* (see Introduction, Section I, and e.g. *Am.* 1.1.1 and 3.2.49: *plaude tuo Marti, miles!*). Elegiac mentions of Mars tend to refer to his amatory deeds, especially as the lover of Venus (e.g. Ov. *Am.* 1.8.29–30 and 41–2 where the god's place in the zodiac and the city are both subsumed by Venus' authority), or to his fatherhood of the Roman race, thanks to his rape of Ilia, (as the placement of **Romani** implicitly reminds us; see immediately below for further allusions to mythic rapes). *Martiae Kalendae* does not scan, which allows for, but does not require, the proper name. Indeed, Mars has a special place in this poetic book; see *ad* 3.8.1, with citations of his role in elegy. Note too that this first line is heavily spondaic, which lends it grandeur and gravity.

The **Kalendae**, or first, of March is the day of the Matronalia, a festival celebrated to honour the role of the first Roman wives in reconciling the Romans with (especially) their Sabine neighbours, from whom they had been stolen to be brides (mention of the festival does not assist with dating issues; Tert. *De Idol.* 14.6 tells us that it continued into the second century CE). The rape of the Sabine women is well known in Roman mythology (e.g. Liv. 1.9–11.4, Ov. *Ars* 1.101–32, *Fas.* 3.167–258), but we know less about the festival itself (for a summary, see Gagé 1963: 66–80). It is sometimes conceived of as a 'women's Saturnalia' (Mart. 5.84, Suet. *Vesp.* 19.1, and Macr. *Sat.* 1.12.7; Frazer *ad* Ov. *Fas.* 3.169); married women entertained their slaves, and received presents (Plaut. *Mil.* 691), often of flowers (Ov. *Fas.* 3.253–5, Hor. *Od.* 3.8.1–3), but also other things (Juv. 9.50). CRF 57–8 (= Macr. *Sat.* 6.4.13), from a Pomponian farce, suggests women-only rites. Setting this poem on the day of such a festival connects a standard elegiac concern with the value of poetry as a gift (see Introduction, Section I, and below) to a specifically Roman setting. It is not clear what the significance of the Matronalia was to those celebrating it; we may be meant to reflect upon the apparent disjunction between the rape of the Sabines and the free choice offered to N. at the poem's end. The rape of the Sabine women conflates coercion and choice, since the Sabines (according to the story) come to love their violent husbands; L.'s poem similarly seems to want to force N. into choosing him (see *ad* 3.4). See Dougherty 1998 on the ways rape and imperialism are connected throughout Roman literature, and Rimell on Ovid's tendency to stage rape scenes early in his poems (2006: 13).

The Matronalia is associated with Juno, especially Juno Lucina (= the light-bringer, Varro *DLL* 5.69, Isid. *Or.* 8.11.57; see the Praenestine *Fasti* for the dedication of her temple on the Esquiline as the origin of the festival), goddess of childbirth (Ov. *Fas.* 3.247, Festus *De Verb.* 147M, 305M). It is also, obviously, associated with Roman women in their role as bearers of children to their husbands (the month of Mars, the only 'legitimate' child of Jupiter, is thus an especially appropriate time to honour Juno). (Juno) Lucina plays a role later in the book, at 3.4.13, and Juno is important throughout, especially in her role as a personal tutelary spirit. Yet elegy is usually, sometimes explicitly (e.g. the tongue-in-cheek Ov. *Ars* 1.31–4), denoted as unsuitable for matrons (see too Introduction, Section III, as well as *ad* 3.8 for other places where [Tib.] 3 plays with this convention, and for further details on Juno in elegy). Ov. *Ars* 1.405–9, identifying days on which presents might be expected as good times to avoid the *puella*, is a much more typically elegiac interaction with Roman festivals, which get in the way of private enjoyment. (The Ovidian passage may refer to the Matronalia; see Hollis 1977 *ad loc.*) Why does L. place an elegiac poem in such an apparently uncongenial setting? The end of this poem suggests that L.'s relationship to N. differs from the standard illicit elegiac one (he calls her his *coniunx*), so he may be giving us notice right at the start of a new kind of elegy. On the other hand, the evidence admits of several interpretations (see Introduction, Section I, and *ad* 3.1.23 and 3.1.26), and this may be part of L.'s elegiac play with the status of the *puella*. So too, while Roman wives might receive presents only once a year, every day is a Matronalia for the women of elegy, given (what the genre claims is) their constant expectation of costly gifts (see Introduction, Section I).

Venere: alternative (poetic) form of the third person plural, present indicative active. But this form may, especially in conjunction with Mars (and the metre of elegy), remind readers of Mars' affair with Venus, and so, perhaps, of the opening of Lucr. (see further immediately below).

Exoriens...annus: this phrase is unattested (see *TLL* 2.115.78ff for the regular denotations, especially *alter annus*), but is easily comprehensible by analogy with phrases such as Varro *DLL* 9.24.7: *signum exortum hoc anno*, 'a constellation rising in this year', and the regular (*ex*)*oriens sol*. L. notes that the Kalends of March was once the start of the Roman calendar (Ov. *Fas.* 3.135–48, Plut. *QR* 19, Macr. *Sat.* 1.12.3–6, Isid. *Nat.* 4.2); if its 'new-year' implications remained after the change, it would be an especially appropriate time at which to begin a poetic collection. For Lucretius, spring is the time for all living creatures to focus on procreation (1.10–27; cf. V. *G.* 1.1–5).

Nostris...avis: the phrase identifies L. with a Roman viewpoint (see Introduction, Section IV, for speculation about his origins), which does not mean that he must have been a Roman citizen, merely that he assumes a Roman *persona*. **Nostris**: as often, the 'poetic' plural for a singular; see also 3.1.19, 3.2.5, 3.3.8, 3.4.24, 3.4.78 (of Apollo), 3.5.17, 3.6.59, 3.9.24, 3.13.4, 3.17.6, 3.19.2 (possibly a genuine plural), 3.20.1, 3.20.3.

>   et vaga nunc certa discurrunt undique pompa
> 4   perque vias urbis munera perque domos:

Gifts are here personified as wanderers, a conceit which leads the way for the better-attested notion of poems as errant children or slaves (see *ad* 3.1.7). The contrast between **certa...pompa** and **vaga...discurrunt undique** (Maleuvre 2001: 172), with the one suggesting a stately and traditional procession and the other scattered randomness, is nicely reminiscent of the original confusion at the rape of the Sabine women, and also of the controlled chaos of an entire city sending presents to one another (cf. *munera commeant* at Tert. *De Idol.* 14.6, which might depend on this passage but is likelier to describe the actual state of affairs). Luck prints *crebra* for **certa** (see Navarro Antolín 1996 *ad loc.*). So too the repetition of **perque** is, as Navarro Antolín 1996 notes *ad loc.*, elevated, giving a ceremonial feel to the frenetic passage of messengers (see Tib. 1.4.25–6 for the repetition). The couplet may contain a dim echo of Cat. 65.17, where Cat.'s carefully translated poetic gift is not entrusted to *vagis...ventis*.

Discurrunt is an especially Ovidian word (Radford 1926: 160), appearing with **vaga** also at Mart. 4.78.3, *discurris tota vagus urbe* (Fletcher 1965), of the scurrying about of an old man eager to know the news, and 8.33.15, *nec vaga tam tenui discurrit aranea tela*, of the pattern of a spider-web. The Graecism **pompa** is common in Ov. and occurs twice in Prop.

>   dicite, Pierides, quonam donetur honore
> 6   seu mea, seu fallor, cara Neaera tamen."

Pierides refers to the Muses' birth on a Thessalian mountain (Hes. *Scut.* 206); the epithet appears first in extant Latin at Lucr. 1.926 and 4.1, but is not thereafter especially epic in tone; it is not frequent in erotic elegy (Gibson *ad* Ov. *Ars* 3.548), perhaps because, as virgins, the Muses are unsuitable witnesses to elegy's primary activities (Tib. 2.4.15 and 20 explicitly un-invite them if they do not make themselves useful). Prop., on the other hand, denies their virginity (2.30.33–6)—and, perhaps not coincidentally, they visit him frequently (e.g. 3.3, 3.10). Prop. also makes the claim that not the Muses or Apollo, but Cynthia herself is the font of his poetry (2.1.4, *ingenium nobis ipsa puella facit*; cf. Ov. *Am.* 3.12.16), and this, although not often stated, seems to be the general assumption of elegy (see Introduction, Section I, and Lieberg 1962: 91–2, who discusses the trope's origins in Cat.). But the Muses do feature in elegiac discussions of poetic inspiration and craft, as at Tib. 1.4.61–6 (with Maltby 2002 *ad loc.*). The practice of asking the Muses for inspiration is, of course, as old as Homer; L. here does something different, merely enquiring of them who should receive his book. In this he surely refers to Cat. 1.1 (see immediately below), and perhaps also to Meleager *AP* 4.1.1, which asks the Muses where they will bring their fruits and garland of poetry (Maltby 2009: 321).

The manner of L.'s invocation is elevated (among other invocations of the Muses, see e.g. V. *E.* 8.63 and Ov. *Fas.* 2.269 and 6.799, all with identical line-beginning; the first Ovidian example occurs on the Kalends, while the second mentions them); so too **donetur** (see immediately below). Contrast, for example, the—superficially—lowbrow Cat. 1.1, which asks the poem itself to whom the book should be given, *cui dono lepidum novum libellum*. But, despite formal language, L.'s attitude towards the Muses is informal: by the end, they are treated as his errand-girls. Broadly speaking, the closest Latin analogue to this conversation with the Muses is probably in Ov.'s *Fasti*, which features various speaking gods, including individual Muses (e.g. 4.222, 6.501). Navarro Antolín 1996 *ad loc.* finds the treatment of the Muses in this poem inappropriate, and derivative of the 'parodic' invocation of the Muses at Hor. *Ser.* 1.5.51–4, Juv. 4.34, and especially Mart. 3.20 and 8.3 (see too 10.20 and 12.11); Stat. *Silv.* 4.4 addresses its poem/letter, and mentions what the poet's Muses have been up to, so it may also bear some relationship to this poem. Perhaps L. takes such an elevated view of his own abilities that he believes he does not need to treat the Muses with respect. For the argument that the Muses signify literacy (as opposed to Apolline song), which might help to explain their selection as book-carriers, see Konishi 1993.

Honore, when combined with the Muses as addressees, more or less guarantees that the *munera* offered will be poetic. **Donetur** and **honore** (note the continued formality of style) often function in epic as a hendiadys signifying honour as conferred though a gift (seemingly first at V. *A.* 8.617 *ille deae donis et tanto laetus honore*; *OLD* s.v. 2d); [V.] *Cir.* 269 *sceptri donavit honore* shows that the *donum* need not always be physical (there, kingship; see Lyne 1978 *ad loc.*).

Seu mea, seu fallor raises the question much of the rest of elegy has trouble answering: is the *puella* in fact the *amator*'s, or is he wrong? The diction of the line is studiedly ambiguous, covering both the confident 'if I'm not mistaken', and genuine doubt, all the more given the double meaning of **fallor** in elegy (see Pichon 1991: 141–2): both 'I am mistaken (in believing her faithful)' and 'I am being cheated on' (cf. Ov. *Met.* 1.606–7, where Juno offers the near-synonymous alternatives *aut ego fallor/aut ego laedor*; see Paschalis 1986, and also Prop. 2.32.17, where Cynthia is both mistaken *and* deceiving Prop.). So too, **fallor** may be passive 'I am being cheated on' or may have middle nuance: 'I am deceiving myself'—the verb well describes the complexities of the elegiac life. Yet while its nuances are ambiguous, its appearance provides us with the first clear hint that we are dealing with traditional elegiac material. **Fallor** is a leitmotif for L., appearing also at 4.56 and 62 and 6.12 and 46, at 6.12 also with **cara** (see *ad locc.*). For the first time—but not the last! –in L.'s corpus, the question of the elegist's legal relationship to his *puella* is raised: if they are married, it would be peculiar for him to take such a nonchalant attitude towards her adultery (see Introduction, Section I).

Cara is used in the elegists to refer to both family members and romantic partners, so precisely which L. means remains unclear—and elegiac poetry from the time of Cat. is predicated upon this confusion between family relationship and elective affinity (Introduction, Section I). L. claims that even if N. has betrayed him, or is no longer his, she remains precious. **Mea** is standard elegiac usage, perhaps deriving ultimately from Cat. 5.1 (*vivamus, mea Lesbia*); see Pichon 1991 on its semantic range, and Hinds 1998: 25–34 on the limits of intertextual interpretability in (what might or might not be) formulaic language.

The placement of **Neaera**'s name adumbrates her intermediate degree of importance to L.'s poetry. Unlike Cynthia in Prop. 1, she is not the very first word of the book, but neither is she put off, as Ovid's Corinna is, to the fifth poem. In this she resembles Tib.'s Delia, who appears in 1.1, but not as prominently as she might (first at 1.1.57, several lines after Messalla's name). The first mention of the *puella* is normally in the third person, as is appropriate for one relating the story of a love affair. On the name **Neaera**, see Introduction, Section IV.

"**Carmine formosae, pretio capiuntur avarae.**
8   **Gaudeat, ut digna est, versibus illa tuis.**

There is much difficulty in the attribution of lines 7–14; I have given them to the Muses, and accordingly printed Muret's conjecture **tuis** (see below). On the one hand, L.'s question deserves an answer, and who better to provide it than the Muses? But on the other, their advice is banal (which may be part of the point; see below). Postgate's 1915 emendation *novis* dodges the problem by invoking the poetic trope that a new song is best (common throughout ancient literature from the time of Homer, and seen in elegists at Prop. 1.16.41; for comprehensive discussion of the concept of newness in Greek literature, see D'Angour 2011). McKay 1987: 213 proposes *magis*. For further discussion on textual matters, and the attribution of these lines, see Ehwald 1901, Schuster 1968: 150–1, Ponchont 1968: 129 n. 2, Erath 1971: 18 and 51, Lieberg 1980: 141. Lieberg, following Schuster, argues that 7 and 9–14 were spoken by the Muses, 8 by L., which solves the textual difficulty, but is difficult without any change of subject. See *ad* 3.1.12 *tuum* for further pronominal problems.

Carmine is a word of central importance to the elegists, as it refers to their poetry (and to magic; see Introduction, Section I), and also to funerary epitaphs. It is normally presumed that the *puella* likes poetry written about her, i.e. elegy (e.g. Ov. *Ars* 3.533–4). Prop. 1.9.11–12 expresses a similar sentiment (*plus in amore valet Mimnermi versus Homero:/carmina mansuetus lenia quaerit Amor*; cf. too Prop. 2.34); here, as in our passage, no divine inspiration is attributed (though it sometimes is). Other passages are less sanguine about the efficacy of poetry (e.g. Tib. 2.4.19–20: *ad dominam faciles aditus per carmina quaero:/ite procul, Musae, si nihil ista valent*; Prop. 2.24b.21–2: *me modo laudabas et carmina nostra legebas:/ille tuus pennas tam cito vertit amor?*); note too the *lena*'s consistent undervaluing of poetry in comparison with other gifts, as at Prop. 4.5.53–4 and 57–8.

Formosae: often of the *puella* (*CT* 1.1.55, 2.3.65, 3.10.4); of beloved boys at Tib.1.4.3, 1.9.6; specifically of N. at 3.4.57. The word is less elevated than *pulcher* (see further Axelson 1945: 60–1, Pichon 1991: 152–4, Monteil 1964: 23–60, and Knox 1986: 97–100).

Pretio occurs in elegy mostly in situations where the penniless lover is being contrasted with his rich but repugnant rival (a danger implicit in this poem): see, e.g. Tib. 1.9.33 and 52, 2.4.14, 33, and 39; Prop. 3.11.31, 3.13.14, 4.5.29 (*pretiosus* in this sense at 3.13.1 and 4.5.43); Ov. *Am*.1.8.69 and 3.8.30, and especially 1.10.59–64, on the gaucherie involved in the *puella*'s quest for gifts (termed *pretium* at 17–18, 32, 47, and 63). But the situation may not be so black-and-white: *Am*. 2.1.34 suggests that the *puella* sometimes offers herself as a *pretium* for the lover's poetry (a similar notion at Prop. 2.5.5–6). For discussion of the language of gift-exchange in (Plautine) amatory contexts, see Zagagi 1987, with 131 n. 6 on *pretium*. The Muses are exhorted not to sell themselves at Tib. 1.4.62, *aurea nec superent munera Pieridas*.

Avarae is not combined with **pretio** as often as one might expect, given the elegists' struggles with their *puellae* (Introduction, Section I); Ter. *Heaut*. 48–50 (= *Hec*. 49–51) claims that the poet is not greedy: *numquam avare pretium statui arti meae*. But the sentiment sounds proverbial (cf. Publil. Syr. A21: *Avarum facile capias, ubi non sis item* and Mart. 6.63: *scis te captari, scis hunc qui captat, avarum,/et scis qui captat, quid, Mariane, velit*); see Pichon 1991: 91 on *avarus*. On the dangers posed by greedy and beautiful girls, see too Tib. 2.4.35–6, *heu quicquamque dedit formam caelestis avarae,/quale bonum multis attulit ille malis*, with their punishment at 2.4.43–6.

Capiuntur partakes in the elegiac figuration of love as a hunt and elegiac *puellae* as prey (Introduction, Section I; see too *ad* 3.9, and for the verb with this nuance, Pichon 1991: 98–9), or booty acquired by *militia amoris* (Introduction, Section I); cf. Prop. 1.1.1 *Cynthia prima…me cepit*. And for the ability of poetry to captivate, see e.g. V. *G*. 4.348 *carmine quo captae*, Ov. *Am*. 2.1.21–35. This notion conflicts with the end of the poem, where N. is (apparently) free to choose L., or not (see 3.4, which also constrains her choice).

Gaudeat: standard erotic language (see Pichon 1991: 159, Adams 1982: 197–8, *TLL* 6.2.1712.33–53), but cf. Hor. *Od*. 4.8.11–12 for its application to poetry (and note the infinitive there): *gaudes carminibus; carmina possumus/donare*; Prop. 3.2.1–2 *carminis…gaudeat ut solito tacta puella sono*.

Ut digna est may sound a troubling note, especially if we want to press the subjunctive *gaudeat*: 'Would that she is happy, as she ought to be, with the gift of poetry, instead of wanting something else (which I don't want to/can't give)'. This is just what we would expect the Muses to say, given their interests, and L. to want them to say, given his. But the poem leaves this nuance unstated, merely hinting at a shadow-N. who behaves like a typical *puella*. **Digna** elsewhere at

3.8.15, 3.8.24 and 3.12.10 (in verbal form), and 3.13.10, twice; the last instance especially suggests it to be a key concept for the S. cycle.

Versibus is a regular elegiac word for poetry, sometimes suggesting frivolous or unwelcome scribblings (Cat. 6.17, 16.3 and 6, 22.3, and 50.4, Prop. 4.5.57 and 4.7.77) and sometimes more elevated verse (e.g. Prop. 1.9.11 of Mimnermus, 1.16.41, about Prop.'s own poetry, *novo...versu*). It is not clear where Ov. *Am.* 1.11.21 (of the *puella*'s writing) falls. Nemesis is denoted as the source of T.'s *versus* at 2.5.111. And poetry is also persuasive (Stroh 1971 on 'werbende Dichtung').

Tuis is Muret's conjecture for the manuscripts' *meis*, objected to by those who believe that the poem depicts a conversation between Muses and L. I find this reading appealing, especially given that in 3.4 L. also attributes what are likely to be his own opinions to a divine source (there Apollo); never in his own voice does L. criticize N. So too the conceit gives both his poetry and his pursuit of N. divine support. In this case, the Muses answer L.'s query but, like their Hesiodic forebears (*Th.* 26–8; see West 1966 *ad loc.*), they are less than helpful: their options (beautiful vs. greedy) are not mutually exclusive, especially in elegy (see *ad* 3.4.57, with further thoughts on *formosa Neaera*, there put in the mouth of Apollo, and Maleuvre 2001: 173). The question as to which is a more appropriate description of N. is never answered. The couplet also alludes to the poet's elegiac dilemma: as often when poetry is offered, it is not clear whether it will be welcome to the *puella* (see Introduction, Section I). Alternatively, the implicit assertion that N. is *not* greedy, combined with hints scattered throughout the corpus that she is a *matrona*, may mark the contrast between her and other elegiac mistresses.

  Lutea sed niveum involvat membrana libellum,
10 pumex et canas tondeat ante comas,

Poetry is often given as a gift, and is usually attractively presented: see e.g. Cat. 1 and 22.1–8, Hor. *Ep.* 1.20, Ov. *Tr.* 1.1.1–12 and 3.1.13–16 (the latter with similarities *in oppositione*; see G. Williams 1992: 179–82 on the metapoetic nuances of the conceit), Mart. 3.2, Stat. *Silv.* 4.9.7–9; contrast Mart. 1.66 and 11.1. Given the sheer number of precedents, it is humorous to find the Muses (if these lines are attributed to them) urging L. to package the book nicely; that is the part of the process with which he will have least difficulty. Ov. *Tr.* 3.1 bears so many similarities to this poem that it plays a role in the question of relative dating (see Introduction, Section V; Lee 1958–9: 19–20). Kraus suggests that the *Tristia* poem reprises one that had appeared in the first edition of the *Amores*, and was later excised (1957: 199–200).

  Most of the other examples mentioned above invoke poetry as a gift of *amicitia*, not of romantic love, serving as dedicatory poems to a powerful patron (in Ov.'s case, to anyone willing to take on the role). In L., two standard conceptions of poetry as a means of social exchange and as a courtship gift are thus conflated; on the implicit conjunction of romance and *amicitia* in elegy (especially Ov.), see Gibson 1995. Ov., and perhaps also L., does not have a(nother, male) patron; Tib.'s poems in honour of Messalla (1.7, 2.5) do not mention Delia or Nemesis, and Prop.'s gift of poetry to Cynthia is not a grateful return for patronage (but see Tib. 1.1, which elegantly combines the two, though still to two different individuals, Messalla and Delia). The Matronalia might explain the fancy wrapping and patronal language, but we might also read this as another hint by L. that his situation is not that of the typical elegist. Perhaps we are to envision something more like Cat.'s relationship with Lesbia, wherein the woman seems to have a higher status than the man, and so might be envisioned as a quasi-patron (see Introduction, Section II). Or perhaps L., himself powerful, is not in the position of needing a patron (see *ad* 3.3, on his wealth). For the limited evidence of (non-imperial) female patronage of poets at Rome, see White 1993: 90, Hemelrijk 1999: 128–45, and Gold 1993 on female patrons in Propertius.

On the production and decoration of papyrus book-rolls, see Kenyon 1932: 44–64 (mostly dependent on Plin. *NH* 13.23.74–26.83); G. Williams 1992: 184 and n. 27; Johnson 2004: 86–100; on the process of writing and book production and adornment at Rome, Birt 1882: 44–64 (ancient testimonia at 122–33), Kenney 1982: 15–22, and Avrin 1991: 159–75. For the structure of (mostly poetic) books, see Hutchinson 2008, and on the mechanics of book reading in antiquity, see Van Sickle 1980: 5–6. The care with which this book is produced undermines the distinction made in the previous couplet. This volume will be poetry, for a learned girl, and costly, for a greedy one: perhaps N. is both, or L. is taking no chances.

Lutea is the reddish-orange colour associated with Roman brides (e.g. Cat. 61.10 and 188, Luc. 2.361, Plin. *NH* 21.46.6), and perhaps had celebratory connotations in general. Navarro Antolín 1996 suggests that, since the colour most often mentioned for presentation copies is *purpureus* and not *luteus*, we should see L.'s choice as exemplifying his hopes to marry N. (see too Erath 1971: 24–5 and Tränkle 1990 *ad loc.*, with Isid. *Or.* 6.11.4, a choice between *membrana* that are *candida*, *lutea*, or *purpurea*). At Juv. 7.23, however, a finished composition is described as *croceus*. Gellius describes the colour as reddish (2.26.15.1); see André 1949: 151–3 on its precise shade. And on the connections between the adorned female body and an elaborately wrought elegiac text, see Introduction, Section I.

While **membrana** could be used as a writing surface (Cat. 22.7, Hor. *AP* 389 and *passim* in Mart.), the word is here more likely to refer to a leather cover or wrapper around the papyrus itself, as at Mart. 1.66.11 (Birt 1882: 64).

Libellum is the correct word for L.'s six poems (= 290 lines), although elegists usually refer to even longer poetic books with the diminutive. The word's appearance here raises interesting, if unanswerable, questions about the composition of this book: L.'s output is suitably called a *libellus*, but if his poetry was originally composed, as it claims, as a single book(let), how did the remaining poems become attached to it (see Introduction, Section V)? For *libelli* of amatory poetry, see e.g. Prop. 2.13.25, 2.25.3, 3.2.17, 3.3.19 etc., with Pichon 1991: 188, and for another diminutive in L., *ad* 3.6.47 (see Axelson 1945: 39–43 on diminutives).

The *libellus* is **niveum** because it is written on the most expensive papyrus, as we would expect for a presentation copy (see Kenyon 1932: 63 on the probable colour variations in papyrus, and André 1949: 39–40 for the precise nuances of *niveus*). The elision of *niveum* before *involvat* suggests the wrapping of the present.

On the depilatory properties of **pumex** see e.g. Ov. *Ars* 1.506; for its use on papyrus, Cat. 1.2, 22.8, Prop. 3.1.8, Hor. *Ep.* 1.20.2, Ov. *Tr.* 1.1.11, 3.1.13, Mart. 1.66.10, 1.117.16, 4.10.1–2, 8.72.2, Juv. 8.16, 9.95. In many of these passages, metapoetic nuance is likely to be intended, with the 'polishing' reflecting editorial care, and that is probably present here as well; see Batstone 1998, Newlands 1997: 61, and Hor. *AP* 291. Fitzgerald 1995: 40–1 draws attention to the potential foppishness of such attention. The text **pumex et** is printed by Tränkle 1990 and Navarro Antolín 1996 (but not Lenz/Galinsky, who retain the earlier manuscripts' *pumicet*; see discussion in Tränkle 1990 and Navarro Antolín 1996).

Ante is used here, as often, for the adverbial but unmetrical *antea* (Axelson 1945: 20). The papyrus is to be cleaned and polished before being wrapped.

Canas ... comas because papyrus tends to have small fibres sticking out (= human hair, by a flight of the imagination, as at e.g. Tib. 1.2.92, 1.6.86, Prop. 2.18.18, 4.9.52, Ov. *Ars* 3.75–6). Ovid's exilic poetry, being both undecorated and inferior (G. Williams 1992: 186), is *hirsutus ... comis* (*Tr.* 1.1.12). See too **tondeat**, a prosaic word, used by elegists (e.g. Prop. 3.13.29, 3.19.22), though not in a book-making context. The two together humorously humanize the book.

    summaque praetexat tenuis fastigia chartae
12   indicet ut nomen littera facta tuum,

Further decorations of the *libellus*: L.'s name (see below *ad* **tuum**) will appear on at the top of the papyrus, or perhaps on its outside (the meaning of *summa fastigia* is less clear than it might be). See Ov. *Tr.* 1.1.7 for a *titulus* dyed with vermillion; Mart. 3.2.11 for an *index* imagined as proudly reddening, *rubeat superbus*, from its dye. **Chartae**: in favour of the reading *charta* (preferred by Luck 1969, Tränkle 1990, and Navarro Antolín 1996) is the fact that all other parts of the book are personified and serve as subjects of their sentences; it may well be the correct reading. **Summa ... fastigia** is Vergilian: *A.* 1.342 and 2.758 (*summi fastigia* at 2.302 and 2.458), but the closest metapoetic analogue is at Ov. *Met.* 2.3, of the palace of the Sun (*ebur nitidum fastigia summa tegebat*). **Praetexat** has a variety of metaphorical and literal meanings; the closest analogue to this passage is [V.] *Cir.* 100, an invocation to the Muses: *novum aeterno praetexite honore volumen.*

Tenuis is metapoetic, referring both to the desired (Callimachean) style of poetry (see Introduction, Section I) and to the result of its scraping by the pumice; cf. Prop. 3.1.8 *exactus tenui pumice versus eat.* See too *tenui libro* at Ov. *Met.* 1.549, where the phrase refers to Daphne's burgeoning bark, but also to the book of poetry she is becoming part of. And, as Pichon 1991: 278–9 notes, *tenuis* regularly refers to the accoutrements of a *puella*; e.g. Prop. 1.2.2 of Cynthia's *sinus*.

Littera, postponed, serves as the subject of both verbs. **Littera facta** of the writing of letters at Ov. *Her.* 5.2. (For use of the singular with a plural meaning, see *TLL* 7.2.1528.5–84.) **Tuum** indicates that the Muses are speaking (some manuscripts have *meum*); see *ad* 3.1.8 for attribution of these lines. Navarro Antolín 1996 finds a number of difficulties in the manuscript tradition of this distich; see his discussion for details, and Schuster 1968: 151–2; Tränkle 1990 prints **facta** in cruces, while Lenz/Galinsky opts for *picta*. There are good arguments also for Némethy's 1906 *rubra*.

>   atque inter geminae pingantur cornua frontes:
> 14 sic etenim comptum mittere oportet opus."

The language here can be taken on several levels: it refers to the elaborate decorations on a 'presentation copy', but also to the care with which L. has composed the book, and perhaps even, as is regular in elegy, to the metapoetic connections between poetry and *puella* (see Introduction, Section I). The phrasing at Ov. *Tr.* 1.1.5–14, a poem of mourning, reinforces the first of these metaphorical connections; see especially 11, with the identical noun/adjective combination, *nec fragili geminae poliantur pumice frontes* ('nor let your twin edges be polished with the pumice'). **Geminae**: as nearly all commentators on the passage note, it is impossible to accept the manuscript-transmitted **inter** *geminas* with **frontes**, since the **frontes** or edges of the papyrus must lie between the (two) **cornua**; see Tränkle 1990 for defence of the manuscripts' reading, and Erath 1971: 29, Kenney 1982: 31, and Possanza 1994 for further discussion of this vexed passage. Note too the mimetic word order of the line, which, with its postponement of the object of **inter**, may well have led to corruption to *geminas*.

Pingantur: papyri were sometimes coloured at the edges (Ov. *Tr.* 1.1.9; G. Williams 1992: 184). Metapoetic nuance may be felt here, in that there is a tension between the luxuriousness of the present L. gives to N. and the simplicity which is normally urged upon the *puella* (Prop. 1.2 is the originary place in elegy for criticism of the adornment of a *puella*, focusing particularly on excessive make-up). **Cornua** is the standard term for the bosses which attach to the *umbilici*, the sticks to which the papyrus is attached at each end for rolling and unrolling (see Blümner 1916, Besslich 1973, Ishøy 2006); there are two for ease of handling, so that when a papyrus is read all the way through, it must then be re-rolled back to the beginning (as with now-obsolete cassette tapes; cf. Mart. 11.107.1, *explicitum... usque ad sua cornua librum et quasi perlectum,* located near its book-end). Latin authors occasionally make *cornua*-puns at book ends, as at e.g. Ov. *Met.* 2.874, where Europa holds the *cornus* of Jupiter in bull-form, 8.882 where Achelous ends up with only a single horn (Wheeler 1999: 92–3), and *Met.* 15.620–1 of the horns of Cipus (Barchiesi 1997: 187); L. does so at the start of the collection.

Comptum is properly used of anything beautifully arranged (cf. Quint. *Inst.* 8.3.42 for its use as a technical literary term); in elegy, this is often hair (see *ad* 3.8.10 and 3.12.3, both used of S.). Given the well-known connections between poetry and hair (Wyke 1989b: 118–21, Zetzel 1996: 73–81, Hälikkä 2001, Burkowski 2012), many of the elegiac occurrences, including this one, are likely to have metapoetic significance (see McKeown *ad* Ov. *Am.* 1.1.20 and 1.7, with further citations). So the present matches the recipient: both are *compta*. Here, of course, the papyrus' 'trimmed hair' gives the image visual point. See Erath 1971: 30 on the prosaic nuances of **oportet** and **etenim**, which add to the technical, perhaps didactic, feel of these lines. Like Tib., L. uses only *etenim* and *nam* (never *enim*).

Opus refers to poetry from very early to very late Latin (*OLD* 9c); it is regularly used programmatically in the elegists (e.g. Prop. 4.1.67 and 135, Ov. *Am.* 1.*Epig*.2, 1.1.24, 1.15.2, *Ars* 1.29). The apparent disjunction between an elegiac life of *otium* and the *labor* expended in writing poetry (**comptum**) dates back at least to Cat. (cf. the difference between Cat. 1, which announces the care taken with the book, and Cat. 50, where the ludic and extemporaneous nature of composition is emphasized). At least in this poem, L. falls solidly on the 'effortful' side of the equation.

"Per vos, auctores huius mihi carminis, oro
16   Castaliamque umbram Pieriosque lacus,

Némethy 1907 seems to have been the first to note the verbal parallels between lines 13–16 and [V.] *Cul.* 12–19 (note especially *carminis auctor, cornua fronte, Castaliaeque... unda, Pierii laticis,* in a description of the possible locations of Apollo, and then an invitation to the Muses). The question of priority is an open one, given that neither poem is securely dated; Kennedy 1982: 382–5 suggests that both passages, and [V.] *Aetn.* 4–8, similar to *Culex* but not in these lines, depend upon a lost Gallan fragment; see further Erath 1971: 37–40 and Tränkle 1990 *ad loc.*

Per vos: it is strange to beseech the Muses in their own name. **Auctores**: this epic *topos*, whereby the Muses are credited with authorship, is not a normal feature of elegy, whose poets tend to take full credit (see e.g. Prop. 2.10.12, an attempt at loftier poetry; there the poet instructs the Muses how to do their job). This invocation may reflect a move away from L.'s initial 'individualist' stance, a claim about the quality of the poetry, or both. As Navarro Antolín 1996 notes, *carminis auctor* is in poetry most often applied to Apollo, as at e.g. Tib. 2.4.13, [V.] *Cul.* 12, *Aetn.* 4. But this is not exclusive: among other gods as *auctores carminis*, see *inventrix auctorque ego carminis huius* at Ov. *Fas.* 6.709 (of Minerva's invention of the flute), Germ. *Arat.* 2 (of Jupiter). Maleuvre 2001: 173 sees **huius mihi carminis** as deliberately overblown (= 'this my chaunt'?).

Castaliam umbram and **Pierios lacus** are both inspirational locales. Castalia is a spring near Delphi, associated with Apollo because of the woman who threw herself into it to avoid him, and because laurels grew there (V. *G.* 3.292, Prop. 3.3.13, Hor. *Od.* 3.4.61, Ov. *Am.* 1.15.36, Luc. 5.125; also in Greek literature at e.g. Pi. *P.* 1.39). In elegy, it refers to the *aqua* of the fountain, with reference to Apollo (Ov. *Am.* 1.15.36; McKeown 1989 *ad loc.* has further citations), and at Prop. 3.3.13 *Castalia...arbore* provides shade for Apollo (this is the first extant appearance of the adjective); it is also sometimes used as a location for the Muses, as here (e.g. Posidippus *SH* 705.8 = 118.8 A-B, Mart. 4.14.1 *Castalidum decus sororum*). The collocation of adjective and noun provides a salutary example of L.'s diction: although it is a common enough poetic way of referring to Apollo or to divine inspiration, it is attached to *umbra* in only two places in Latin: here, and at Sen. *Oed.* 712–13 (where it is primarily geographic). [V.] *Cul.* 17 has *Castaliae...unda*, and Stat. *Theb.* 8.175–6, in a conjunction of the two phrases above, *lacus...Castalii* (Luck prints *undam*, found in G²). See *ad* 3.1.5 on the *Pierides*, and note the very similar [V.] *Cul.* 18–19 *Pierii laticis decus*; Hagen, followed by others, sees the line as 'Silver' (1954). See Hinds 1987b: 36–8 for puns on *locus/lucus/lacus*, which may also be evoked here; perhaps there is also a pun on *umbra/unda*. As Navarro Antolín 1996 notes *ad loc.*, the pentameter, with two adjectives attached to *-que*, modifying two nouns, has an Ovidian feel.

> ite domum cultumque illi donate libellum,
> 18   sicut erit: nullus defluat inde color.

While it is regular poetic procedure to invoke the Muses, to ask for their help in recalling detail or composing poetry, and to credit them with authorship, L. does something rather different by asking them to serve as messengers. In a sense, the Muses (i.e. his poetry) naturally communicate with N., but the figure is still striking. We may be amused by the fact that where, for instance, Ovid sends a maid as go-between (very common in poetry, and presumably in real life; cf. *Am.* 1.11, and McKeown 1989 *ad loc.* with many further examples, and Prop. 3.6, where a slave named L. plays that role (see Introduction, Section IV)), L. sends the Muses (see too Hor. *Ep.* 1.13; the relative status of Horace and Vinius in that poem is not clear, but part of the point is surely Horace's anxiety). Perhaps, however, a witty compliment is meant: letters and parcels were regularly entrusted to slaves, but also to mutual acquaintances headed in the direction of the recipient. With this couplet L. may suggest that the Muses are regular visitors to both his own and to N.'s house, so they could simply bring his poetry along when they next pay a social call (see too *ad* 3.1.19). Or, more prosaically, L. simply emphasizes that the poem, and the Muses, will belong to N., and so will 'live' at her home.

Ite domum is troubling, as it ought to mean 'to my home'; Maltby calls it 'clumsy' (2009: 326). It is probably best to take **illi** with both verbs, rather than to assume L. and N. share a dwelling. Maleuvre suggests a reference to V. *E.* 10.77, *ite domum... capellae*, and that the poet deliberately assimilates the Muses to goats (2001: 183). This solves one difficulty by introducing another.

Reference to the **libellum** as **cultum** suggests that L. thinks of himself as no ordinary poet (see Mart. 8.72.1–2, whose book is in too much of a hurry to be *murice cultus asperoque/morsu pumicis aridi politus*). It probably also seeks to appeal to the paradigm of the *puella* as *docta*: this is just the sort of poetry book a woman like N. ought to like (cf. e.g. Tib. 1.9.74, Ov. *Ars* 2.175 and 3.51, where the adjective describes a *puella*). **Cultum** also repeats the earlier theme of physical preparation, suggesting not only 'cultured', but also 'cultivation' in personal grooming (*OLD* 4 and 3; e.g. Prop. 1.2.26, Ov. *Am.* 3.7.1, *Ars* 1.511); cf. *ad comptum* at 3.1.14. Book 3 of Ov.'s *Tr.* is instructed not to be *cultior* than its author (who is in mourning, 3.1.14; cf. the dangers of excessive *cultus* in *puellae* at Prop. 1.2.5), and Martial refers to certain kinds of poetry as *cultus* (1.25.2, 1.66.11, 1.117.16, 11.1.1–2, 11.39.16 of the poet himself; see too Hor. *Ep.* 2.2.123). The word is something of a leitmotif among Augustan poets, referring indiscriminately to (women's) appearance, poetry, and the elegiac lifestyle (representative examples at Prop. 1.2.26, 2.22.22, 4.8.75; Tib. 1.4.4, 1.9.74; Ov. *Am.* 1.8.26, *MFF* 7, *Ars* 3.101, 3.127, 3.433, 3.681, *RA* 343); in Tib. the word is used more often of crops (1.1.2, 1.3.61, 1.10.35); see Pichon 1991: 106. Veremans 1998: 12 notes that this poem follows Cat. 1 in its repetition of **libellum** (here 9 and 17, there 1 and 8).

Donate: see *ad* 3.1.5, and *ad* 3.1.8 *gaudeat*, for a Horatian similarity.

Sicut erit may suggest, by contrast to *cultum*, that the poet is aware of his own flaws. The phrase either enjoins speed upon the Muses, as the poetry risks losing its **color** if too much time passes (a possible argument for reading *novis... versibus* at 3.1.8), or it acknowledges that the Muses might be tempted to make some alterations (but for the better, or for the worse?) to L.'s own text. Navarro Antolín 1996 *ad loc.* construes the phrase as exhorting the Muses to take care of the book and not damage it in transit; this would emphasize their servile status.

Color is both a rhetorical term and, here, a personification of the book as a flower, or a person, whose healthful bloom may soon fade (for the erotic implications of the word in elegy, see Pichon 1991: 106). We could take this as an indication of dwindling confidence, or a suggestion that L. does not think his poetry a 'treasure for all time', but we might also read it as indicating L.'s assurance (on the magical properties of poetic *carmina*, see Sharrock 1994: 50–78). Navarro Antolín 1996 *ad loc.* draws attention to the 'marital' nature of the book's colours (yellow for the marriage veil, white for the paleness of lovers).

Defluat: see *TLL* 5.1.364.12ff. for non-liquid uses of this verb, and below *ad* 3.4.81. On Roman processes of dyeing, see *ad* 3.3.17–18. It is possible that L. means with this phrase to suggest also N.'s own colour: he hopes (note the subjunctive) that she will not grow pale at receiving a message from him.

(Illa mihi referet, si nostri mutua cura est,
20   an minor, an toto pectore deciderim.)

The couplet asks for a response, as do a wide variety of written communications both literary and subliterary; for the former, see Ov. *Am.* 1.11–12 (where the answer is negative), and *Ars* 1.437–86 assuring the lover that his letters will eventually receive a reply. Navarro Antolín 1996 *ad loc.* is troubled by the unsignalled switch to the third person and, more significantly, by the mood of the verb. He prefers Skutsch's emendation *referte* (1969: 156; with *illa* as accusative plural); see too Tränkle's (1979: 24–5) defence of the alternative manuscript reading *referat* because it picks up on the increasing hesitation in L.'s poem—a point which becomes clearer by the end of the sentence. But **referet** can have the same nuance, if we understand the future to be a show of confidence, willing N.'s action into being.

Referet can be used for the response to a letter, but may also include an implied *se* if the first of L.'s options holds true: N. may bring herself back to L. Given the inclusive nature of this collection as a whole, however, we may be tempted to take the verb and its invitation as welcoming women into the writing of poetry, an invitation which will be accepted later in the corpus (see Introduction, Section V), and which conflicts with the elegist's regular attempts to silence his *puella* (see Introduction, Section I).

L. is unsure of N.'s response to his poetry, or indeed, to him. This is a frequent elegiac worry, though not one that is often put so bluntly: perhaps she loves him as much as he does her, perhaps somewhat less, or perhaps not at all. For a defence of *sit* instead of **si**, see Tränkle 1990 and Navarro Antolín 1996 (both of whom print the former, and end the line with **cura**). **Mutua** is a standard word in elegy for the desired relationship (at least some of the time; cf. e.g. Tib. 1.2.63, 1.6.76, [Tib.] 3.11.6 and 3.12.8 with notes *ad loc.*, Ov. *Am.* 2.3.2, 2.10.29, and Pichon 1991: 211; see too the erotic uses at Lucr. 4.1201, 4.1205, 4.1216, 5.854, 5.963); at Mart. 10.13.9 the identical line-ending refers to friendship. **Minor** *cura* the elegist will put up with, usually gladly; the third option is what he fears. For L.'s desired *cura* as the regular word for one's beloved, see Pichon 1991: 120–1. There may be an echo here of the Vergilian *nec minor in terris . . . /Aeneae mihi cura tui* (*A.* 5.803–4).

Decederim: the verb is fairly rare in the sense of an emotion departing, and even more so in this indirect manner (e.g. Ter. *Hec.* 505 *decedet iam ira haec*, Hor. *Od.* 2.9.11 *decedunt amores*, Liv. 23.26.8.4, 28.41.9.3, Sen. *Ira* 8.6.2; cf. *OLD* 8a, where none of the examples has an individual as subject). Navarro Antolín 1996 *ad loc.* is probably correct that the phrase derives ultimately from Hom. *Il.* 23.595–6 (ἤματα πάντα ἐκ θυμοῦ πεσέειν, '(for me) to fall out of your whole heart'); it may be colloquial.

Toto pectore is a Catullan (64.69, 66.24), Vergilian (*A*. 1.717, 7.356, 9.276, 9.326), and Ovidian phrase (*Her*. 12.142, *Ars* 2.536, 3.56, *Met*. 1.495, 9.44, 9.244, 10.443, *Fas*. 2.798, 6.464, 6.509, 6.538, *Tr*. 5.4.24, *EP* 1.8.63, 3.1.39), often (Pichon 1991: 228–9) but not always erotic, and perhaps also colloquial (see too Cic. *Fam*. 10.10.2.5, *Att*. 12.35.1.10). The informal tone, if it is informal, may suggest L.'s desperation, or might mimic N.'s own words.

    Sed primum meritam larga donate salute
22   atque haec submisso dicite verba sono:

For instructions on delivering a poem encapsulated within that poem, see Hor. *Ep*. 1.13, Stat. *Silv*. 4.4.10–11, Mart. 12.11.1. L.'s statement, however, is somewhat muddled: Navarro Antolín 1996 suggests *ad loc.* that the normal order of L.'s commands is altered because he begins with what is, to him, the more important part of the Muses' task, 'buttering up' the recipient, and then returns to chronology. On the grandiosity of the verb *donare*, see *ad* 3.1.5; this may soften the impression earlier given that the Muses are simply messengers, or perhaps, if it implies subservient behaviour on their part, reinforce it. For the worry that a letter-carrier will, by choosing the wrong moment, prejudice a letter's reception, see e.g. Hor. *Ep*. 1.13.1–5, with Mayer 1994 *ad loc.* on the importuning crowd of messengers who appeared at the morning *salutatio*.

Meritam: we may see an implied conditional in this sentence, dependent upon her answer: if she will not return L.'s affections, she did not deserve such a lavish greeting, or present.

Larga salute: ablative, as normally with *donare*. Although there is no difficulty in understanding the phrase, the conjunction of adjective and noun is unattested in Latin (unless we read *larga* at Lucr. 5.1215—then the phrase is identical); it may well be colloquial or, as Navarro Antolín 1996 suggests *ad loc.*, **larga** may suggest financial impropriety (L. is willing to buy N.'s love if needed). In either case, the amplitude of greeting is undermined by the next line: is the poem to present itself as jolly or downcast (**submisso sono**—this collocation also unattested elsewhere)? **Submisso** conveys the suppliant tone the Muses should adopt (parallels at Bömer *ad* Ov. *Met*. 5.235), but may also allude to the elegiac love of secrecy (see Introduction, Section I). **Atque**: on *ac* vs. *atque* see Axelson 1945: 82–4. **Haec...dicite verba** an Ovidian phrase, at *Met*. 14.717 (Radford 1927: 359).

'Haec tibi vir quondam, nunc frater, casta Neaera,
24   mittit et accipias munera parva rogat,

It is difficult to know what to make of these lines, which imply a termination of the erotic relationship, something the elegiac poet is rarely willing to countenance. It is possible that **quondam**, normally taken here to refer to the past, refers to the future (*OLD* 2); L. would then emphasize his wishes rather than remind her of their joint history. The word **vir** is of notoriously unclear meaning in elegy: although it ought to mean husband, it is nowhere clear that the elegiac relationship is one of official *coniugium* (see *ad* 3.1.26, and Introduction, Section I). **Frater** is often used of a spouse, or a cousin, in addition to a brother (perhaps N. is L.'s cousin?). In any case, the couplet comes as a surprise, as it seems to acknowledge the end of a relationship without anger or bitterness (elsewhere, the lover is much more agitated; cf. e.g. Prop. 3.24–25 for a typical elegiac break-up).

For a *puella* to be **casta** is more regularly a source of complaint (e.g. Prop. 1.1.5 with Heyworth 2007 *ad loc.*) or insult (e.g. Ov. *Am.* 1.8.43) than a compliment; see Introduction, Section I. **Casta** might claim only that L. is no longer with N., or it might express his wish or belief that she has not replaced him (see Pichon 1991: 101 for its nuances). See *ad* 3.4.23, 43, and 60, 3.9.20, and 3.12.14. In this explicit dedication of the collection to N., we see again the conflation of two normally separate categories, those of the dedicatee and of the *puella*.

Munera parva is easy to understand as the poet's diffidence about his gift (see e.g. [Tib.] 3.7.7, Ov. *EP* 4.8.35, Mart. 4.88.1, 7.17.9, 7.80.5). But this meaning is hampered by the elegiac use of the phrase: in elegy, a *parvum munus* is usually just that, and serves as an attempt to avoid giving a larger present (Ov. *Ars* 2.256 and 261–2; depending on the cost of the ring, Ov. *Am.* 2.15.27 might or might not be a counterexample—or perhaps it simply hopes to teach the *puella* that she should not think of presents in terms of their monetary value). Pygmalion's *munera* to his *eburnea puella* are quintessentially those the *amator* hopes to offer: shells, pebbles, birds, wildflowers, amber (Ov. *Met.* 10.260–1). Other gifts characterized in poetry as small include: offerings to ancestors (Ov. *Fas.* 2.534), eggs and fruit (Mart. 7.49.1), an otherwise unspecified birthday present (Mart. 9.53.1–2), eggs (Mart. 9.54.11), gifts offered to Priapus ([V.] *Priapea* 3.9), a seashore burial (Hor. *Od.* 1.28.3–4), the favours of a slave (Hor. *Ep.* 1.18.75, on which see Porphyry *ad loc.*, who suggests that all gifts are small to the wise man), and the *palladium* (V. *A.* 7.243–4, minimized).

teque suis iurat caram magis esse medullis,
26   sive sibi coniunx sive futura soror,

Another surprise: the relationship not as finished as it might have seemed from the previous couplet (or at least, so L. hopes). Lydia of Hor. *Od.* 3.9 offers an analogy; she had featured in the first book, and, presumably, been discarded, but that poem attempts to begin anew. L.'s tone here seems respectful in contradistinction to the normal elegiac assumption that the *puella*'s decisions are negotiable (see e.g. Apollo's scornful declaration at 3.4.63).

Iurat may add a tone of formality or legality here, but it is also common in amatory contexts, used to promise undying affection (even if often untruthfully, e.g. Cat. 64.143–6, Tib. 1.4.21–4, 1.9.31, Ov. *Am.* 2.16.43, 3.2.61, 3.3.1, 11, 13, 45, *Ars* 1.635, and Pichon 1991: 178); see *ad* 3.6.47 and 3.19.15–18. **Caram** appears again, reminding the reader, or N., of her value.

Medullis is a technical prosaic term but is in regular poetic use for the burning innards of a lover, as at e.g. Cat. 45.16, V. *G.* 3.271, and *A.* 4.66 and 8.389 (see too Pichon 1991: 198); Prop. 1.9.21 and 2.12.17 and Ov. *Met.* 1.473 specify this as the place where the arrows of Cupid fix themselves (see R. Thomas *ad* V. *G.* 3.271 for an Apollonian antecedent). Hor. *Epod.* 5.37, *Ep.* 1.10.28, and Ov. *Tr.* 1.5.9 where the word means 'guts', give a sense of a wider colloquial usage (presumably the erotic nuances predominate here). See too Maecenas fr. 3.1–2, where *visceribus meis...plus...diligo* is used; Courtney 2003 *ad loc.* believes that passage depends upon Cat. 14.1–2 *plus oculis meis amarem*.

The construction with **magis** and *quam* or, as here, an ablative of comparison, appears with particular frequency in this book (see *ad* 3.13.2). As Tränkle 1990 notes, **sive** appears in the *CT* only in L. and 3.7; Tib. uses *seu*.

Coniunx draws attention because it is one of few places in elegy where the poet claims a specific legal status for the relationship, and L. uses the word with greater frequency than other elegists, who do not use it of *puellae*; Prop. 2.8.29 (of Briseis) is an exception that proves the rule; cf. *ad* 3.2.30. See Introduction, Section IV, for discussion of the question, and Introduction, Section I, for elegy written to a *coniunx*. L. offers N. two choices, each of which presumes their continued closeness. **Soror** is not a usual way to refer to a beloved; its appearance here convinces some that the couple are cousins, others that they are slaves. Cf. too Prop. 2.6.42 *semper amica mihi, semper et uxor eris*, which may well influence this line.

> sed potius coniunx: huius spem nominis illi
> 28   auferet extincto pallida Ditis aqua.'"

L. tries once more to convince N. to 'take him back'. The implicit reference to the underworld confirms that we are really still in the melodramatic world of elegy, even if L. has backed off for the moment, and also establishes an important theme in the corpus, L.'s impending death. Büchner 1965: 28 suggests that the notion goes back to Prop. 2.34.91–2 (*et modo formosa quam multa Lycoride Gallus/mortuus inferna vulnera lavit aqua*) and, ultimately, to Gallus. Maleuvre finds the hexameter (deliberately) absurd, pointing to the repetition of *-ius*, the diaeresis, and the difficulty of pronouncing the second half (2001: 174).

Spes is a tricky concept, in part because we tend to import an anachronistically positive nuance to it; see Tib. 2.6.19–28 and Ov. *Ars* 1.445 on its deceptiveness, and (e.g.) Prop. 3.17.12 and Ov. *Ars* 3.477–8 for the alternation of hope and fear that is the standard condition of the lover. Navarro Antolín 1996 *ad loc.* suggests that this distich plays with the proverb *dum spiro, spero*. For the conjunction **spem nominis**, see Cic. *Phil.* 14.28.7, Liv. 5.45.4.5 (*spem ultimam Romani nominis*), Vell. 2.103.1.1 (with *magnis*), Plin. *Pan.* 26.4.1 (*spem Romani nominis*).

Pallida is often associated with death (e.g. 3.5.21, Tib. 1.10.38 of the dead, V. *A.* 4.644 and 8.709 of Dido and Cleopatra just before they kill themselves, Ov. *RA* 602 of Phyllis, just before she kills herself; see too *pallida mors* at Hor. *Od.* 1.4.13 and *pallentes...lacus* at [V.] *Cir.* 333) and fear (e.g. Penelope at Ov. *Her.* 1.14, Medea at *Her.* 12.97), but also with the lover's pallor (of many examples, cf. Prop. 3.8.28); there is a nice conjunction of the two at Ov. *Met.* 4.135, where the amorous Thisbe is *pallidiora* from fear, but also about to die. The fact that a good number of these examples depict women who commit suicide because of amatory misery increases both the feminization of L. (see Introduction, Section I), and perhaps how seriously we should take his veiled threat of suicide. Because his threat ends the poem, it contains an air of finality that might otherwise be mitigated.

Ditis aqua is poetic, but not common, for the waters of the underworld (presumably here Lethe, which causes forgetfulness, on which cf. [Theoc.] 23.19–26, Cat. 65.5–6, V. *A.* 6.714–15, Hor. *Epod.* 14.1–4, Ov. *Tr.* 1.8.36, 4.1.47, *EP* 2.4.23–4, 4.1.17, Luc. 5.221 and 6.768). Mart. 9.29.2 contains the phrase in the same metrical *sedes*; Prop. 3.22.4 ends with *Ditis equos*; see too V. *A.* 6.127 *ianua Ditis*, 7.568 *spiracula Ditis*, 8.667 *ostia Ditis*, 12.199 *sacraria Ditis*, [V.] *Dir.* 66 *omnia Ditis*, *Cul.* 372 *Ditis opacos*, *Aet.* 643 *sub nomine Ditis*, Ov. *Met.* 4.438 *regia Ditis*, 5.395 *raptaque Diti*, Stat. *Theb.* 4.291 *credita Diti*, 7.697 *venerabile Diti*, 7.782 *atraque Ditis*, VF 6.112 *horrida Ditis*, Sil. 13.415 *placamina Diti*, 13.587 *ostia Ditis*, Mart. 12.32.6 *Ditis emersas*. L. later asks for offerings on his behalf to Dis (3.5.33).

3.2:

L.'s writing focuses little attention on happy times, even by comparison to the rest of elegy, and this poem is no exception. Taken as a whole, it treats the elegiac *topos* that life is not worth living without the beloved (see too [Tib.] 3.19 for a less-dramatic version of the same sentiment), and includes an imaginative reconstruction of L.'s funeral (which incidentally provides one of our most complete sources on Roman burial practices). The tone throughout is sombre, with no suggestions of optimism; as often in elegy, the intent is probably manipulative. This poem also has metapoetic implications, as L. seeks to control what is written about him after death, and to link his name irrevocably with N.'s via an epitaph. Elegy often fantasizes about a love which lasts unto (sometimes even beyond) death; see Prop. 4.7, among other elegiac invocations of the *topos*, and Müller 1952: 38–42 for other passages.

Other elegiac death-fantasies with similar elements occur at Tib. 1.1.59–68, a death-scene which features a weeping *puella*, 1.3.5–8, which features Assyrian perfumes but no mourners, 2.6.29–34, about Nemesis' dead sister, Prop. 1.17.19–24, with Cynthia offering hair and roses, 1.19, which is mainly about heroines of the underworld, 2.13.17–36, with instructions about the handling of the body and ashes, including perfumes (there *Syrio*), but also a focus on the funeral march (see Bürger 1905: 321–2), 2.8.17–28, which includes a death-threat, 2.24.35–8, on the lament of the *puella*, 3.16.23–30, about where Prop. would like his bones buried, and 4.7.21–34, where Cynthia gets her turn to be dead. Navarro Antolín 1996 points to [Theoc.] 23, on a cruel beloved and a lover who hangs himself, as a model for this poem. In some of these poems, the poet is dying of abandonment, but in others he is physically sick (though the metaphors of lovesickness and love-as-sickness mean that these cannot always be distinguished; see Introduction, Section I, and Tib. 1.3, as well as notes *ad* 3.10; Ov. *Am.* 2.13–14 about Corinna's post-abortion illness). Tib. 1.3.55–6 is the first extant funeral epitaph in elegy; Ov. *Am.* 3.9.49–54 on the death of Tib. and *Tr.* 3.3.45–76, about the return of the exile's bones, may also be important for this poem, especially in their memorializing functions. Dufallo connects the focus on commemoration here to Prop. 2.1.71–8 (2007: 149 n. 64). These, the passages usually cited as parallels, share general *topoi* and basic vocabulary (e.g. *ossa*, *rogum*, and the like), but not many specific commonalities; L. has created an original, and elaborate, version of a common subject. For the standard Roman take on (elite) funerals, see Polyb. 6.53–4, Houghton 2011, and further below, and on erotic suicides in Roman literature, Hill 2004 (91–104 on elegy).

Poem 3.1 ends with the threat of L.'s death, so we pick up, more or less, where we left off. Here too L.'s wishes are contradictory: presumably, the desire that N. will attend his funeral as chief mourner is really a wish that she continue to care about him, in which case he will have no reason to die. The tone of the poem, especially at the start, is Tibullan (e.g. Tib. 1.10, about the horrors of war, and, implicitly, of the man who is hard enough to leave his *puella* to go to war), but the language, as throughout L., is also Ovidian (Radford 1926). Poem 3.2 is also in many respects similar to Prop. 2.8, about a break-up (or rather, about the theft of a *puella*, followed by Prop.'s threats to die but to take her with him).

The poem falls into three sections: four couplets about the loss of L's *puella*, with the assertion that he cannot bear it; then a lengthy (nine couplets) fantasy about Neaera's behaviour at his funeral; finally, an epitaph (two couplets).

Qui primus caram iuveni carumque puellae
2   **eripuit iuvenem, ferreus ille fuit.**

Formally, 1–4 are a priamel, setting up a disjunction between the kind of man who could bear L.'s sufferings (see next couplet) and himself (who cannot). While generalizing, they are also misleading, since the distinction between the

ferreus who can steal love objects and the **durus** who can bear this treatment is soon elided. This couplet clearly suggests mutuality of affection, but *rapio* (see below) is regularly used for voluntary departure (cf. Eng. 'he stole my girl', which is rarely literal).

Primus implies that the raptor of the *puella* or *iuvenis* is a man, which would fit in with the Tibullan corpus' greater interest in homosexual love (Tib. 1.4, 1.8, and 1.9 are the only Latin elegiac poems which engage directly with the apparently common practice for upper-class Roman men of having male *deliciae*; see Introduction, Section I). Or, given this book's broader conceptions of gender roles ([Tib.] 3.16 worries about a woman stealing a man away), it might simply be a generalizing masculine. On the notion of the *protos heuretes* in Greek literature, see Kleingunther 1933 and Müller 1952: 21, and for two other dangerous elegiac 'firsts', Tib. 1.4.59 (*venerem docuisti vendere primus*) and 1.10.1 (*horrendos primus qui protulit enses*).

On **caram**, see *ad* 3.1.6; it is L.'s regular descriptor of N. **Puellae**: the normal object of elegiac affections, mentioned here first in L. (see Pichon 1991: 244–5). For further details about the elegiac *puella*, see Introduction, Section I.

Eripuit: N. has been snatched away from the passive L. See *TLL* 5.2.791.67–792.17 for the verb in connection with people; it is used in Plautus and thereafter for erotic loss (e.g. Cat. 82.3). Compare the near-identical Prop. 2.8.1 *eripitur nobis iam pridem cara puella* and Ov. *Am*. 2.19.19 *tu...quae nostros rapuisti nuper ocellos*; for the participle (*e*)*repta* (in the next couplet), cf. *abrepto...amore* at Prop. 1.13.2 and *abrepta...coniuge* at Prop. 2.8.29. We might also compare Cynthia's trips away from Prop. at e.g. 1.11 and 12; see too Prop. 3.20, which comforts an abandoned *puella* by offering to stand in for her lost man, and Prop. 3.21, which announces a journey to Athens (there too it is assumed that absence will probably prove fatal to the relationship). As Navarro Antolín 1996 notes *ad loc.*, the verb is also frequently used of death, and so prefigures (what L. presents as) the next logical step in his sufferings.

Ferreus ille fuit: proverbial, but probably a direct reference to Tib. 1.10.2 and 1.2.65 (identical, on which see Brouwers 1978); cf. too Tib. 1.1.63–4 on Delia's heart, which is not *duro...ferro/vincta* (poetic precursors at Murgatroyd 1980 *ad loc.*) and Tib. 2.3.2 on the hardness of the man who can stay in town when his girl is in the country. The image is also frequent in Ov., on whom see McKeown *ad Am*. 1.11.9. The phrase may condemn the Tibullan sentiment: the Tibullan *amator* has himself been **ferreus** enough to leave the *puella* in search of military gains, at least according to 1.3 and 1.7. There are also verbal parallels between this couplet and Ov. *Am*. 2.19.4, a poem directed to the *vir* to encourage him to keep a more careful watch over the *puella*, lest Ov. lose interest: *ferreus est, siquis, quod sinit alter, amat* (see Pichon 1991: 146 for other amatory elegiac uses of the adjective). There, of course, Ov. seeks to increase the dramatic tension of his relationship by inventing obstacles. This poem, at least on the surface, has none of the playfulness of Ov.'s: L. presents himself as being near death because of the impediments to his relationship. **Fuit**: the perfect tenses here and in the next couplet are likely to be gnomic.

> **Durus et ille fuit, qui tantum ferre dolorem,**
> 4   **vivere et erepta coniuge qui potuit.**

Durus, like *ferreus*, is metaphorical of hard-hearted lovers (e.g., probably, Cat. 60.3 *tam mente dura ... ac taetra*), and regular in Tib. and L. (3.4.76, 92, 5.22, 6.7; see too *ad* 3.9.3). On the adjective in Tib., see Leonotti 1990. For a similar sentiment including *dolor*, see Prop. 1.14.18 *illa etiam duris mentibus esse dolor*.

Tantum ferre dolorem: identical phrase at VF 1.766: *potui quae tantum ferre dolorem*, in the mouth of Alcimede, claiming that she could bear the pain of her son's departure but not this new suffering; Tränkle 1990 *ad loc.* believes this to be a coincidence, but Hinds suggests not (1987b: 327; Maltby 2009: 327). V. *A.* 6.464 *hunc tantum tibi me discessu ferre dolorem* (from Aeneas' underworld speech to Dido) is the probable intertext for L. and also VF; it is also possible that the lines derive from V. *A.* 9.425–6 *nec ... tantum potuit perferre dolorem* (Nisus). **Ferre dolorem** tends to appear at line-end; e.g. Lucr. 3.990 *non tamen aeternum poterit perferre dolorem* (of Tityos). Less close, but perhaps still relevant, are Prop. 2.15.35 *nostros ... transferre dolores*, where Prop. cannot transfer his love elsewhere, Luc. 2.39 *neve hunc differte dolorem*, Ov. *Met.* 14.716 *non tulit impatiens longi tormenta doloris*. On the varieties of erotic *dolor*, see Pichon 1991: 132–3 (nearly always erotic in the elegists); see too Tib. 2.4.7 *o ego ne possim tales sentire dolores*; *dolor* is frequent in Prop. (e.g. with *ereptus* at 2.8.36, *tantus in erepto saevit amore dolor*) and regular in L., especially in this poem (lines 6, 13, 29; cf. 3.6.3 and 43). **Ferre** suggests the well-known etymology with *ferreus* (see Navarro Antolín 1996 *ad loc.* for citations).

Vivere et requires elision of the end of the infinitive, which is relatively rare in Augustan elegists (see Smith *ad* Tib. 1.2.72 for discussion and citations). With **vivere ... potuit**, L. may refer to Cat. 68.84, where Laodamia has not had enough time with Protesilaus *posset ut abrupto vivere coniugio*; see too Tib. 1.1.25 *iam modo iam possim contentus vivere parvo*. It is also possible that L. plays off the famous fragment of Q. Caecilius Metellus Macedonicus, recited by Augustus to encourage marriage: *si sine uxore possemus, Quirites, omnes ea molestia careremus; set quoniam ita natura tradidit, ut nec cum illis satis commode, nec sine illis ullo modo vivi possit, saluti perpetuae potius quam brevi voluptati consulendum est* (Malcovati 1953 *ORF* 6). Or it may be a standard phrase: in Plaut. *Mil.* 1241, *Pseud.* 94, the speaker claims not to be able to live without his/her love object; see too Prop. 2.9.3–4, where Penelope *poterat bis denos salva per annos/vivere*, 2.32.55–6, on how no goddess *potuit ... cum solo vivere sola*, and Ov. *Am.* 3.11.39 *nec sine te nec tecum vivere possum* (Barchiesi 2001: 155–9 suggests that the Ovidian passage is a complex commentary on Metellus, and notes Greek versions of the *topos*); see *ad* 3.19.9 *possum bene vivere*.

Erepta coniuge again (see *ad* 3.1.26) suggests the stability of L.'s relationship with N., though that status is again undermined. It is unclear, and will remain so, how N. has become *erepta*, although, as noted above, we need not imagine her as having been taken against her will. The legal issues involved in wife-snatching give the discussion a serious tone, as usage elsewhere may suggest: *ereptum... coniugium* at Cat. 68.106–7; *abrepta... coniuge* at Prop. 2.8.29; *coniunx erepta* or *praerepta* at V. A. 2.738, 3.330–1, 9.138 of Creusa, Hermione, and Lavinia; Ov. *Met.* 5.10 of Andromeda; Stat. *Silv.* 2.6.4 of a generic wife; VF 3.316 of Cyzicus; see too below, line 30. L. is here extremely (and elegiacally) passive: rather than attempting action, he simply bemoans his loss.

Non ego firmus in hoc, non haec patientia nostro
6   ingenio: frangit fortia corda dolor;

The claim not to be **firmus** must be unmanning, even if we are not to see (as we are probably not) a double entendre. In elegy, the adjective often denotes the obstacles arrayed against the lover (as at Tib. 1.2.6 and Ov. *Am.* 2.12.3 of a door), or his resolve to persevere (e.g. Ov. *Her.* 16.170 and 20.86, *RA* 213, 245, 697); see Pichon 1991: 149. Of special interest for this passage is Ov. *Ars* 2.340, which notes that a new love must be coddled, but with proper care, *tempore firmus erit*; cf. too *Ars* 2.652 about how even a *puella*'s faults can strengthen one's love for her, and Ov. *Am.* 2.19.9–18, which explains that the *puella* ought to pretend that there are rivals even if there are not, in order to add piquancy to the relationship. By contrast to these staunch lovers (see too Prop. 2.15.35, quoted *ad* 3.2.3), L.'s affections seem feeble.

Patientia, although not usually with this vocabulary, is a key quality of the *amator*, whose main duty is to suffer (*pati*) whatever trials are thrown in his way, including the removal of his *puella* (for elegiac *patientia*, see Pichon 1991: 227). This connection between patience and suffering, though implicit in the Latin, is not often drawn in elegy (see too *ad* 3.2.3, on *ferreus* and *ferre*): *patientia* does not occur elsewhere in the *CT* or in Prop. But it is an Ovidian term: see *Met* 5.373, *patientia nostra est*; *Met*. 5.667, *non est patientia libera nobis*; *Am.* 3.11.17, where the lover *patienter* clings to the *puella*'s side, and, more pertinently, *Ars* 2.539, where he is urged *rivalem patienter habe*; on the other hand, at *Am*. 3.11.1 the poet claims to have suffered enough (*vitiis patientia victa est*) and to be ready to be rid of the *puella*; note too *impatiens* at Ov. *Met.* 14.716, quoted *ad* 3.2.3. Ov. *Tr.* 5.12.31–2 *contudit ingenium patientia longa malorum*, although in a somewhat different context, is probably also relevant (Radford 1926: 164). [V.] *Aetn.* 411 *tanta est illi patientia victo* (though not of a person) may also be germane. The construction with the dative is awkward; translate 'there is not this patience in my spirit'. See the apparatus of Navarro Antolín 1996 for alternative manuscript readings, including *patiemur et* for *patientia*, which would ease the sense, and discussion at Dell'Era 1996b: 119–20. The verb

Commentary on 3.2.8 99

patior does not occur in the *CT*, aside from one other use in L., at 3.4.66 (on which see below), but is regular in Prop. for the sufferings associated with the lover (e.g. 2.5.19, 2.24.39, 3.19.11); note too Liv. 5.6.5 *et animis et corporibus suis virilem patientiam inesse* (where the sense is eased by the verb).

Ingenio often means something like 'native talent'; it may refer to L.'s poetic abilities rather than merely his spirit. Cf. e.g. Prop. 1.7.7–8 *nec tantum ingenio quantum servire dolori/cogor*, 2.1.4 *ingenium nobis ipsa puella facit*, 2.30.40 *sine te nostrum non valet ingenium*, and many Ovidian examples.

Frangit fortia corda dolor: a generalization: pain makes even the strongest heart break (apparently L. did not have a strong heart to begin with). **Fortia corda** does not appear elsewhere in erotic elegy, but there are many analogues (e.g. *dura corda* at Ov. *Her.* 4.156). The elegiac lover, however, rarely suggests that he is at the breaking point; more normal is the assertion that he can bear anything at all. Where the similar Prop. 2.8 focuses on the fickleness of love in general, L. keeps all the attention on his own sufferings. Its use at Ov. *Tr.* 3.3.57 (*extenua forti mala corde ferendo*) suggests proverbial status (see too *ad* 3.6.16, *mollia corda*). The phrase does, however, appear in later epic: VF 1.315–6 *fortia languent/corda patrum*, Sil. 10.518–19 *cui fortia… haud parvo caluerunt corda vigore*; all of these passages probably depend upon V. *A.* 5.729–30 *lectos iuvenes, fortissima corda/defer in Italiam*. **Frangit… corda** is unattested elsewhere; *corpora* and *animum frangere* are more common, especially in prose; for a similar context in poetry see e.g. Plaut. *Cist.* 222 *[amor] ita meum frangit amantem animum*, Sen. *Troad.* 745 *animos, magna quos frangunt mala*. All of these words are profoundly elegiac: on *cor* see Pichon 1991: 114, *fortis* Pichon 1991: 154, *frangere* Pichon 1991: 155; for *dolor* see *ad* 3.2.3.

> nec mihi vera loqui pudor est vitaeque fateri
> 8   tot mala perpessae, taedia nata meae.

Vera loqui pudor: speaking and not speaking, what is said and what is confessed, are central themes of this book, whose poets draw attention to the fact that they speak the kinds of things that are usually left unsaid. We seem to have here a clarification of what is often implicit in elegy; the elegist behaves shamefully, but does not regularly acknowledge it. The structure of this line, with a concern for speaking of shameful things, is similar to Ov. *RA* 359 *multa quidem ex illis pudor est mihi dicere*, and *Fas.* 5.532 *pudor est ulteriora loqui* (Radford 1926: 164); each treats a topic unsuitable to elegy (ways to wear yourself out sexually, and the group urination of a number of gods).

The use of **pudor** here is especially interesting in the light of S.'s prominent invocation of it at the start of her corpus (see *ad* 3.13.1–2). **Pudor** is a traditionally feminine characteristic (see Introduction, Section I), although it can, of course, be masculine (see Pichon 1991: 242–4 for citations). But the elegist is notoriously lacking in **pudor**, and therefore willing and able to humiliate himself.

Pudor est for *pudet* regularly in Ov. (e.g. *Ars* 3.203 and quotations immediately above).

Vitae...taedia: normally, the elegist fights more successfully against *taedia*, and it is not usually *taedia vitae* (in poetry, the conjunction only at Ov. *Met.* 10.482, 10.625, *EP* 1.9.31 with Gaertner 2005 *ad loc.*, [Ov.] *Nux* 159, Stat. *Theb.* 7.464 (perhaps; there is a textual issue and *visae* may be correct), VF 6.325, Juv. 11.207, all at line-end; Ov. *Ib.* 584 in the middle of the line). The phrase, if correct, provides an early hint of L.'s impending death (it is often used of suicides). See, for instance, Tib. 1.4.16 (where the male lover is encouraged not to be disheartened if his progress is slow); Prop. 1.2.32 (where the *puella* is encouraged to grow weary of her love of *luxuriae*); Ov. *Am.* 2.19.25 (where the *puella* is urged not to be too compliant, lest Ov. get bored); *Ars* 1.718, 2.346 and 530 (similar to the Tibullan passage; the middle one urges the would-be lover to do whatever it takes, however tedious); *RA* 539, encouraging constant sex in order to bring about *taedium* of the *puella*; *Her.* 3.139, where Briseis worries that she has become tiresome to Achilles. (So too the verb, as at *CT* 2.5.93 and 3.13.10, on which see *ad loc.*, Ov. *Ars* 2.325.) In this couplet L.'s persona seems again to differ somewhat from other elegists. But the elegiac usages outlined above also suggest that *taedium* can be put on as a mask, in order not to seem too eager, or that the eagerness of one party causes *taedium* in the other. So L. may be exaggerating his feelings for effect. On the other hand, *taedium vitae* proper does often prefigure a desire for death (see Ovidian citations above, with Bömer *ad Met.* 10.482, Plin. *NH* 7.186, Sen. *Suas.* 6.17, *Ep.* 24.22). For epitaphic parallels of the weariness of life, see Thompson 1911: 11–18 (grief-based), Lissberger 1934: 96–7, and Lattimore 1942: 211–14.

Tot mala is a shorthand for elegiac suffering; cf. e.g. Prop. 3.15.20 and Ov. *Tr.* 3.11.59, in the same *sedes*, and Tib. 2.6.19, Ov. *Tr.* 3.3.56 (elsewhere in the line). For the erotic nuances of **mala**, see Pichon 1991: 195. The closest analogues to this phrase are at Ov. *Tr.* 1.5.47 *tot mala sum passus*, *Tr.* 5.1.33 *tot mala pertulimus* (both at line-start), and Sen. *Phoen.* 465 *tot labores totque perpessus mala*. The word order is intricate, with **perpessae...meae** depending on **vitae** and in turn having **tot mala** dependent upon them; the clause is in indirect discourse with **fateri**. The phrase is likely to derive from Hom. *Od.* 1.1 via a bilingual pun (μάλα πολλά = very many, but μάλα also = *mala*).

Perpessae: *per*- as an intensifying prefix is relatively common in Tib. (*perago, percello, percido, percoquo, percurro*, etc.), although this verb does not appear elsewhere in the *CT*. When the verb appears in elegy, it tends either to identify some specific suffering as too much to bear (e.g. Ov. *Am.* 1.13.25 *omnia perpeterer*), or to underscore what the lover is willing to put up with (Prop. 2.26.35 and Ov. *Her.* 20.83 *omnia perpetiar*); see too Ov. *Tr.* 5.1.33, cited just above, and Prop. 1.20.15–16, *quae miser ignotis error perpessus in oris/Herculis indomito fleverat Ascanio*. The tone here evokes pathos.

Ergo cum tenuem fuero mutatus in umbram
10   candidaque ossa supra nigra favilla teget,

Fantasies about death could not be more elegiac (although not Ovidian): generally, they come from an illness, or sometimes, simply a reflection about how sorry the *puella* will be about her behaviour once the *amator* is dead. L. does not make clear whether he thinks of ending his own life, or whether he imagines that he will simply waste away (see introductory note to this poem); the abruptness of his transition adds to the sense of inevitability. Prop. 2.8 provides a useful *comparandum*: 17–28 detail the poet's death-scene, in which Cynthia gloats and outrages his corpse, until he decides that he must kill her as well as himself. Typically, Prop. resorts to mythical *exempla* to add vividness; L. instead focuses entirely on his own funeral, and imagines N. there as a mourner. Here, as sometimes, the focus is on the funeral itself; there are similar passages at Tib. 1.3.5–10, 53–6 (echoed at Ov. *Am.* 3.9.49–56, on Tib.'s death), and especially Prop. 2.13.17–36, which follow the same general pattern of a description of mourners and the tasks entrusted to them (see Navarro Antolín 2005: 303–5; Erasmo 2008: 16–19). Each of these, though, focuses on different aspects of the procedure (for instance, Cynthia is to accompany the body, but whereas N. weeps with loose hair, Cynthia is instructed to tear her clothing, call Propertius' name, and kiss his lips). Tib. 1.3.55–6 adds the third element, an epitaph (the first in elegy, on which topic see Ramsby 2007 and Dinter 2011); Prop. too has a version at 2.13.35–6. Shorter treatments of different aspects of the funeral occur also at Prop. 2.1.55–6 (Prop.'s funereal train will set out from Cynthia's), and Prop. 2.24.35–8 (Cynthia's imagined speech).

Despite the repetitive nature of the proceedings, specific verbal resonances between funereal elegiac poems are limited; L. differs in his attention to precise corporeal detail. We have surprisingly few descriptions of how Roman funerals actually worked in practice; see Toynbee 1971: 48–50 and Hope 2009: 65–96, especially 84, for a composite picture. On the spectacular nature of elite funerals, see Bodel 1999, and on death in elegiac poetry, Raucci 2011: 122–44. In the Republican and early Imperial periods, the body was normally burned, the pyre drenched with wine, and the bones and ashes collected and placed in a container to be buried or placed elsewhere (see *RE* 18.2.1599–602 and Erasmo 2008: 57–9 on *ossilegium*).

Ergo cum is amusing, or excessively dramatic, as suggesting little difference between weariness of life and the onset of death (Maleuvre 2001: 174; cf. e.g. Prop. 2.13.17, where, however, there may be a lacuna). Indeed, the transition here is extremely abrupt, suggesting that L. does expect death at any moment. The phrase may depend upon Calvus fr. 27, *cum iam fulva cinis fuero* (Hollis 2007). On the scansion of **ergo** (with long *o*; short in later poets) as evidence for an Augustan date for the poetry of L., see Navarro Antolín 1996 *ad loc.*

Mutatus here, as sometimes, for changing one's bodily state (often with *in*; *TLL* 8.1723.30–43), though not regularly in elegy, where the world is rather stagnant (but see the similar phrasing at Ov. *Tr.* 3.3.83–4 *quamvis in cinerem corpus mutaverit ignis/sentient officium maesta favilla pium*); most often it signifies changes of heart on the part of the beloved, or their lack on the part of the lover (from among many, cf. e.g. Prop. 1.12.11, 1.18.9, 2.4.21, 2.24.39; Pichon 1991: 210–11). See too the numerous occasions in Ov. *Met.*, where it is a standard verb for the alteration from one material state to another. The perfect participle may allude to the Roman notion that the dead continued to be present in their tombs (Carroll 2006: 4). **Mutatus in umbram** is a rare collocation: the closest analogue, Hor. *Od.* 3.6.41–2 *sol ubi montium/mutaret umbras*, is not about the same subject. There may be a play on *mutus*, insofar as the dead are silent (except when they are poets, and their words live on; see *ad* 3.2.29–30).

Umbram is used regularly both for shadows caused by the sun, and for the returning dead or undead; it is naturally insubstantial, although the adjective **tenuem** appears surprisingly rarely with it: V. *G.* 4.472, *A.* 6.292–4 (*tenuis...vitas* equated to *umbras*), V. *A.* 10.636 of an image of Aeneas, Prop. 2.12.20 of his attenuated self—but also, implicitly of his small talent, Ov. *Ars* 3.723 of midday shade, *Met.* 6.62 of slight colour variations, Prop. 3.9.29 of Maecenas' humility, drawing himself into the shadows. Cf. *animae tenues* at Ov. *Fas.* 2.565, *levis umbra* at Ov. *Fas.* 5.434, and *gracilis...umbra* at Ov. *Tr.* 4.10.86, all of ghosts; *levis umbra* also at Tib. 2.5.96 (of tree-shade) and 3.7.68 (of the dead), at Sen. *Oed.* 563 and [Sen.] *Oct.* 522 (of the dead), Ov. *Met.* 5.336 (of shade). **Tenuem** is of course emblematic of the kind of poetry many of the elegists think themselves to be writing (see V. *E.* 6.8 for an earlier evocation, and above *ad* 3.1.11), and so it is possible that L. is also making a poetic claim in this couplet (if so, it is rather oblique).

Candida...nigra: there is a regular conjunction in many Latin authors between white and black, light and dark (see Arias Abellan 1984: 112 and 114, a study of Ov., who suggests that *candidus* is the 'bright' version of white and *niger* is the neutral version of black). See Booth and Maltby 2005 for colour-plays throughout the poems of Tib., which they trace to the names of Albius (Tib.) and (Messalla) Corvinus, i.e. white and raven-black. On *candidus*, see André 1949: 31–8, and on *niger*, 52–8 (and for the two in conjunction, 52–3 and 1941: 140–1, which emphasizes the brilliance of each). Pichon 1991: 98 points out that *candidus* is a standard word for the beauty of the beloved. *Niger* is a colour regularly associated in elegy with mourning and death; in this corpus, see 3.3.37, 3.5.5, 3.5.33, and Kubler *RE* 13.2.1698.49–1699.39. **Candida...ossa**: cf. the Homeric ὀστέα λευκά. But here, the connection may be more pointed: L.'s body will be bleached into black and white, by contrast with the bright colours of the book sent to N. when he was feeling more hopeful (3.1.9).

Supra is rare in poetry (but does occur e.g. in Prop. five times); Tränkle 1990 and Navarro Antolín 1996 print the *super* of some manuscripts, and suggest tmesis with -*tego*. **Favilla**: ashes; for their elegiac uses, see Pichon 1991: 143. The tone is markedly funerary (Fletcher 1965: 49, citing *CLE* 1120.4). See Prop. 1.19.19 *quae tu viva mea possis sentire favilla!*—if she felt this way, he wouldn't mind dying. **Nigra** of *favilla* at Ov. *Met.* 6.325, *Fas.* 2.523, Colum. *DRR* 10.354, with *atra* at Ov. *Met.* 13.604, *Tr.* 5.5.36 and Sil. 14.69 (they are also sometimes white, but this would not provide the colour contrast beloved of L.; see especially *ad* 3.4.30).

>   ante meum veniat longos incompta capillos
> 12   et fleat ante meum maesta Neaera rogum.

The mourning of a woman at the tomb is a standard part of the elegiac death-fantasy *topos*, appearing in the examples cited above. This one, however, is rather more detailed than normal. Presumably, although poets rarely draw attention to this, it is part of the point of the death-wish: finally, when he is dead, she will recognize her affection for him. The fantasy about N.'s appearance continues to clarify our understanding of *eripuit* in line 2, since she seemingly has the ability to return to him at will.

While **incompta** is rare in elegy (twice, in Prop.), women's hair is regularly disarranged, in three main scenarios: when in mourning (e.g. Calypso in Prop. 1.15.11 and Cynthia in Prop. 3.6.9; cf. *effusa* of Delia at Tib. 1.3.8, of Venus at Prop. 2.13.56, of Cassandra at Ov. *Am.* 1.9.38, of Dido at Ov. *Her.* 7.70—though she is both mourning and dead—and *longos turbata capillos* at Tib. 1.3.91, also of Delia, but in a domestic scene), when they practise magic (outside of elegy, Hor. *Epod.* 5.16), and when they are about to engage in coitus (e.g. *effusus* at Ov. *Ars* 3.784). (See further Hälikkä 2001, for a typology of disordered hair in Ov., and Burkowski 2012: 182–236 on elegiac hair in disarray.) Here of course the first is meant, but perhaps with some of the implications of the last; often in elegy (especially in Prop.), scenes of bereavement are given an erotic tinge. The alternation between the *comptum opus* of 3.1.14 and **incompta Neaera** here, and the different tones of the poems, may suggest that we are meant to read 3.2 as the result of 3.1; N. has been given free choice and has not accepted the poet, or his work, so now both of them must suffer. Similar phrasing occurs at Ov. *Met.* 4.261, *nudis incompta capillis* at line-end. The adjective also refers to careless poetic composition (V. *G.* 2.386 and Hor. *AP* 446), and we may be meant to feel that nuance here. On **capillos**, see *ad* 3.1.10 *comas*.

Tränkle 1990 *ac loc.* objects to the repetition of **ante meum**, each with different nuance, and suggests that the first be replaced with *ante urbem*; Navarro Antolín 1996 discusses his suggestion at length, but is not convinced, and suggests that the repetition attempts to convey the emotional tone of the passage.

Veniat…fleat: the subjunctives are tentative, a cross between 'I wish she'd come/weep' (optative) and 'she'd better come/weep' (jussive). **Maesta** appears, as one might expect, in scenes of mourning the loss of a loved one (e.g. Tib.

1.3.6, 2.4.44, 2.6.38, Prop. 4.11.9. Ov. *Fas.* 3.134), or of general sadness (usually, in elegy, following the rejection by or departure of a loved one, cf. e.g. Tib. 1.8.53, Prop. 1.5.15 and 1.15.11; Pichon 1991: 193–4). For the suggestion that the adjective can refer to those dead before their time, see Murgatroyd *ad* Tib. 2.6.38. Its frequent use in the 'longer poems' of Cat. (nine times in 63–8) may give it a particular status as an elegiac word.

Rogum is frequent elsewhere in elegy, usually at line-end in Prop. and Ov., sometimes with the suggestion that the poet will live beyond the grave, e.g. Ov. *Am.* 3.9.6 and 28 (of Tib.), *Tr.* 4.10.86, 5.14.6, *EP* 3.2.32; the closest parallel is probably Tib. 2.4.46 *ardendem flebitur ante rogum*. Axelson notes that Tib. prefers this noun to *bustum* (1945: 125).

    Sed veniat carae matris comitata dolore:
14   maereat haec genero, maereat illa viro.

Carae matris genitive, with **dolore** by way of transference (i.e. let her come accompanied by her mother, also in pain). N.'s mother is mentioned again at 3.4.93. Family members are infrequent in elegy, but Tib. imagines his own mother and sister (not) at his funeral (1.3.5–6). Other than this, Tib. mentions only two female relations: Delia has a mother, for whose sake Tib. claims to love Delia (however implausibly, 1.6.57–64), and Nemesis has a sister, tragically dead (2.6.29–40). See Lee-Stecum 1998: 198 for discussion of the possibility that Delia's mother is a *lena*. S.'s mother is mentioned at 3.12.15. This focus on family members may be seen as a feature of the poets of the *CT*, as they are not much mentioned in Prop. (who mentions his parents as dead at 2.20.15; cf. Cynthia's mother at 2.15.20, Arethusa's sister at 4.3.41) or Ov. (in whose *Am.* the most frequent *mater* is Venus, five times; but cf. the *puella*'s mother at *Am.* 1.8.91 and Tib.'s at *Am.* 3.9.51). The presence of female relations here, along with the use of *genero* and *viro*, legitimizes the relationship between L. and N. by placing it in the wider context of Roman marriage (note too the previous poem's use of *frater* and *soror*, lines 23 and 26). On the Roman mother and her relationship with her children, see Dixon 1988. On mourning, and funerary preparations in general, as typically the duty of (lower-class) women, see Richlin 2001 and Šterbenc Erker 2011. L.'s scenario can be seen as a development on Tib.'s: where Tib. had imagined his sister at his funeral, L. fits N. into the roles of both wife and sister. Typically, L. is more explicit, and at the same time, maintains decorum (especially by contrast with such passages as Tib. 1.1.59–62 and 2.13.27–30, which suggest an erotic tone); this may be in keeping with his treatment of N. as a *coniunx*.

Comitata dolore the phrase is awkward, but not unparalleled: *TLL* 3.1815.11–33 and 41–56, which cite Ov. *Tr.* 3.7.47 *ingenio tamen ipse meo comitor*; **dolor** must be metonymic (see Bennett 1905: 77 on *comitor* with an instrumental ablative). On **dolore** see *ad* 3.2.6. For female family-groups of mourners, with a similar construction, see Stat. *Ach.* 2.23 *lacrimis comitata sororum* (Fletcher 1965: 49).

Commentary on 3.2.16–18

Maereat too is difficult, as the commentators note *ad loc.*; the dative (or ablative) is more regularly a thing than a person (*TLL* 8.39.31–71 and 40.47–9; but cf. [Ov.] *Ep. Drus.* 65 *erepta maerentem stirpe sororis*); construe **genero** and **viro** as datives of advantage (or disadvantage). **Genero...viro**: see Introduction, Section IV, and above *ad* 3.1.26 for discussion of the couple's marital status. For the repetition of elements of half-lines in the pentameter, see Wills 1996: 414–8.

Praefatae ante meos manes animamque recentem
16   perfusaeque pias ante liquore manus,

Praefatae: verbs prefixed with *prae-* are relatively common in Tib. (e.g. *praebeo, praecipio*), though this one does not appear elsewhere in the *CT* or in Prop., and is in Ov. only at *Fas.* 6.304, in a prayer to Vesta (see too Cat. 64.382). **Ante** here, as in 11–12, is locative rather than temporal (or, possibly, with Tränkle 1990, to be taken as *antea*, pleonastically with prae*fatae*). The temporal sequence of events is (barely) discernible: weeping, washing of hands, addressing the dead, *ossilegium*, and interment.

Animamque recentem: an Ovidian phrase: Ov. *Met.* 15.846; cf. Ov. *Met.* 8.488 *animaeque recentes* at line-end; Sen. *HF* 722 and Stat. *Theb.* 1.602 and 9.432. **Recentem** is Bach's emendation; *precat(a)e* of the *recentiores* is preferred by Lenz/Galinsky and Navarro Antolín 1996 (the older manuscripts' *rogat(a)e* cannot be right); see Tränkle 1990 for defence of **recentem**.

Perfusae: usually, in elegy, of perfume (*Orontea...perfundere murra* at Prop. 1.2.3, *unguenta* at 2.4.5, love at Cat. 64.330, blood at 64.399) and fairly common in Ov.; see e.g. *Her* 14.127 *perfusa...ossa* for its use in an imagined funeral scene. The word is not used elsewhere in poetry with **manus**. For **perfusae...liquore** and similar phrases, see [V.] *Cul.* 14 *Xanthi perfusa liquore,* Hor. *Od.* 1.5.2 *perfusus liquidis...odoribus,* Ov. *Met.* 3.164 *virgineos artus liquido perfundere rore* (none funereal).

Pias...manus: the adjective is a regular descriptor of those performing a sacred duty or who are in good stead with the gods (e.g. Cat. 76.2, Prop. 3.3.10), though it is not often applied to hands in elegy (the closest parallel at Ov. *Tr.* 5.5.2, *manus ad pia sacra meae*; cf. McKeown *ad* Ov. *Am.* 1.7.3–4 on the Ovidianness of enallage with *manus*). The adjective is used in burial-scenes or to refer to the dead at Prop. 3.7.9, 3.13.18, 3.18.31; in most of these cases *pius* is proleptic. The adjective/noun collocation is first attested in Latin at Cic. *TD* 2.20, a loose translation of Soph. *Trach.* 1046–1102 (possibly Cic.'s own version), but our passage need not refer to that; cf. e.g. V. *A.* 3.42, 4.517, Sen. *Oed.* 226, VF 2.249.

pars quae sola mei superabit corporis, ossa
18   incinctae nigra candida veste legant,

The phrase **pars...sola mei superabit** may remind readers of Hor. *Od.* 3.30.6–7 (*non omnis moriar multaque pars mei/vitabit Libitinam*), Ov. *Am.* 1.15.4 (*parsque* *mei multa superstes erit*), and *Met.* 15.875–6 (*parte tamen meliore mei super alte perennis/astra ferar*), three confident expressions of poetic immortality, each at the end of a poetic book or group of books. If the echoes are deliberate, L. expresses disagreement, claiming that his poetry will not survive his death, or offering a startling variation (my bones alone *of my body* will survive…). In any case, the phrase is striking, and the intertexts may increase our sense that L.'s goals in this poem are not solely about N. For **pars…mei** in less elevated contexts, see e.g. Cat. 63.69 and Prop. 1.4.11.

Ossa…incinctae: hiatus over a line is rare in the *CT* (though elision is even rarer; the poets tend to avoid the situation altogether). **Incinctae** normally means 'girded' rather than 'ungirded'; see Postgate 1929 *ad loc.* for discussion, who suggests the meaning here is colloquial; cf. *TLL* 7.1.911.48–55. The perfect participle appears 13 times in extant poetry, eight times in Ov., with the positive sense.

Nigra here signifies mourning garb, traditionally black for the Romans; cf. e.g. Ov. *Ib.* 100, Stat. *Silv.* 2.1.19, 5.1.19. The conjunction between *niger* and *candidus* is more pointed than in line 10, as the two are juxtaposed, and across the couplet's caesura (see *ad* 3.2.10 on the two colours, and for the connection of **nigra** with death).

The older manuscripts' *legent* (and *spargent* in 19) are unsustainable, both because *parent* in 20 needs a subjunctive and because the confidence inherent in the future tense is inappropriate here; L. is not certain that N. will attend his imaginary funeral. (Postgate's suggestion that the future is used for 'variety' is unsound.) Most modern editors print **legant** and **spargant**. **Ossa…legant**: see V. *A.* 6.228 *ossaque lecta*, Prop. 2.24.50 *legat ossa*, Tib. 1.3.6 *quae legat in maestos ossa perusta sinus*. See too the possible pun in Mart. 4.33.4 *tempus erat iam te, Sosibane, legi*; it may be the case that L. too is making a pun. For details of the ritual of *ossilegium*, see *RE* 18.2.1599.2–1602.55, with citations, and Vahlen 1908: 491–7 for Greek and Latin literary parallels and further citations.

> et primum annoso spargant collecta Lyaeo,
> 20   mox etiam niveo fundere lacte parent,

Primum, like the *prae-* verbs and the *ante* of lines 15–16, and the *mox* and *post haec* of 20 and 21, suggests the precision of the ritual, whose components must be performed properly and in order. **Annoso** is a poetic word, used elsewhere in the *CT* only by L. himself, at 3.6.58 (again of wine, *merum*), but frequently in Ov., of persons and their age (e.g. *senem* at *Ars* 1.14, *anus* at *Fas.* 2.571), trees (e.g. *pinum* at *Met.* 12.357), time (*mora* at *Fas.* 5.144, *vetustas* at *Tr.* 5.2.11), once of wine (*merum*, *Ars* 2.418), and frequently in later poets; the adjective seemingly occurs first at Laber. *Salin.* 99 *non mammosa, non annosa, non bibosa, non procax*. Elsewhere it is used of wine at Plin. *NH* 23.40, Mart. 6.27.5 (*Falerno*); cf. *TLL* 2.1.114.30–65. For **spargant** see *ad* 3.2.18 *legant*.

Collecta: see Tränkle 1990 *ad loc.* on the repetition of *legant* in the previous line (with Ovidian citations); Navarro Antolín 1996 notes that the prefix retains its force.

Lyaeo: a cult name for Bacchus, deriving from the Greek λύω, to loosen, first attested in Leonidas (*AP* 6.154), first in Latin at Enn. *Tr.* 121 *Lyaeus vitis inventor sacrae*, and first metonymically for wine in Latin at Hor. *Epod.* 9.37–8, then frequently; cf. e.g. Prop. 3.5.21, Ov. *Am.* 2.11.49, *Ars* 3.645 (all at line-end) and thereafter, nearly always at line-end. There may be a bilingual etymological pun here in the antonyms **collecta** and **Lyaeo** (see the synonyms at Hor. *Epod.* 9.38 *Lyaeo solvere*). For the sprinkling of wine on funerary ashes, see V. *A.* 6.227, Prop. 4.7.34. For Bacchus as the patron of poets in the lighter genres, which might lead us to seek metapoetic nuance here, cf. e.g. Hor. *Od.* 1.1.29 (with Nisbet and Hubbard 1970 *ad loc.*), Ov. *Tr.* 1.7.2, 5.3.45–6.

Niveo...lacte at V. *E.* 2.20 (where Serv. draws attention to its Homeric antecedent), Ov. *Fas.* 4.151, [Tib.] 3.5.34 (see *ad loc.*). On *niveus*, see *ad* 3.1.9. The pouring of wine was standard in mourning (e.g. Prop. 4.7.34, but see too Plin. *NH* 14.88 on a Numan law interdicting wine); this, however (and 3.5.34), is our only literary evidence outside Stat. *Theb.* 6.210–12 for milk offerings at the time of burial. For epigraphic attestation, see e.g. *CIL* 11.1420.22 (*lactis mellis olei*), and see *ad* 3.5.33–4. On other kinds of offerings made at tombs (flowers, wine, incense, perfume, lamps), see Lattimore 1942: 126–36. **Parent**: strictly unnecessary, and perhaps for variation (we are probably to assume that N. and her mother actually do drench the bones in milk as well as wine, not that they simply plan to do so).

>   post haec carbaseis umorem tollere velis
> 22   atque in marmorea ponere sicca domo.

Carbaseis: the adjective, descriptive of finely woven linen, is rare, appearing at V. *A.* 11.776 (of clothing), Cic. *Verr.* 2.5.30 and 80 (both with **velis**, and of tents), Stat. *Theb.* 7.658 (of clothing); cf. *carabasinis* of clothing at Apul. *Met.* 8.27. The noun *carbasus/um* generally refers to a sail (e.g. Cat. 64.227, of the sail Theseus is to use as a signal to his father), but at V. *A.* 8.34, Prop. 4.3.64 and 4.11.54 it indicates garments, and at Ov. *Met.* 11.48, with *pullo*, mourning clothes; cf. Luc. 3.239, Val. Max. 1.1.7, Curt. 8.9.21 and 24, Plin. *NH* 19.10, VF 5.423 and 6.225 (all referring to cloth). **Velis** here designates simply a broad sheet, of the sort which could be used for nearly anything; as McKeown notes *ad* Ov. *Am.* 1.14.6, this is a rare meaning for the noun (elsewhere at [V.] *Cir.* 35, on which see Lyne 1978 *ad loc.* and Plin. *NH* 35.150). Navarro Antolín 1996 rejects the word as too prosaic, and prints the older manuscripts' *ventis*, which he understands as parallel to *ventus textilis*.

Umorem tollere: conjoined at Lucr. 5.264–5 *quicquid aquai/tollitur in summaque fit ut nil umor abundet*, 6.506–7 *umor/tollitur in nubis*, 6.623–4 *venti... magnam tollere partem/umoris*, 6.627–8 *tollere nubes/umorem* and also in prose

(Vitr. 5.9.6, 8.2.4). Navarro Antolín 1996 notes *ad loc.* that this is our only attestation of the drying of bones before their storage.

Marmorea...domo: *domus* for a tomb is rare in poetry ([Ov.] *Cons. ad Liv.* 73–4), but frequent in funerary epitaphs; see Ov. *Met.* 14.441–2 for *urna...marmorea* as a burial urn. See Toynbee 1971: 50 on the variety of containers for ashes and Vitr. 2.8.10 on the tomb of Mausolus (brick, but finished with marble). Sen. *Ep.* 60.4 has a play on the uses of marble for living and dead: *sic in domo sunt, quomodo in conditivo. Horum licet in limine ipso nomen marmori inscribas, mortem suam antecesserunt*; cf. Petr. 71.7 for a similar point. For **marmorea** see also *ad* 3.3.3 and 16. Cf. V. *A.* 6.228 *ossaque lecta cado texit Corynaeus aëno* for a different container.

> Illic quas mittit dives Panchaia merces
> 24   Eoique Arabes, dives et Assyria,

Perfumes were used in a variety of phases in the Roman funeral, for anointing the body (Ov. *Fas.* 4.853, *EP* 1.9.51–4, Prop. 2.13.29–30 *Syrio munere*), for putting on the flames of the pyre (Prop. 4.7.32; *nardo* absent from Cynthia's funeral, to her outrage), and for burying with the ashes (Ov. *Fas.* 3.561, *Tr.* 3.3.69). For similar phrases, cf. Prop. 4.7.32, Tib. 1.3.7–8, Stat. *Silv.* 2.1.157–62, 2.6.86–93, 3.3.33–5, 3.3.211–13, 5.1.210–16 *Assyrios...odores*, Tib. 2.2.3–4 *urantur odores/ quos tener e terra divite mittit Arabs* (religious, not funereal), and Prop. 3.16.23 *unguenta* (see further Lilja 1972: 54, 88–90).

Dives...dives: *pinguis* is apparently preferred by Postgate 1915, though he prints the manuscript reading in his text; Tränkle 1990 also thinks it might be correct. For Navarro Antolín 1996 *ad loc.*, the repetition of *dives* is original and 'demonstrates the limitations' of L.

Assyria of perfume: Cat. 68.144 *odore*, Tib. 1.3.7 *odores* (funereal), V. *E.* 4.25 *amomum*, Hor. *Od.* 2.11.16 *Assyriaque nardo*, 3.4.32 *litoris Assyrii*, Sen. *Phaed.* 393 *odore*, Stat. *Theb.* 6.209 perfume, *Silv.* 2.4.34 *amomo* (funereal), 2.6.88 *Assyrio manantes germine sucos* (funereal), 3.3.212 *liquores* (funereal), Mart. 8.77.3 perfume, Sil. 11.402 *amomo*. The near-synonymous *Syria* also of perfume: Cat. 6.8 *olivo*, funereal but not perfume at Prop. 2.13.30 *Syrio munere plenus onyx*, [Tib.] 3.4.28 *rore*, 3.6.63 *nardo*, [V.] *Cir.* 512 *amomo*, Hor. *Od.* 2.7.7–8 *nitentis/malobathro Syrio capillos*, Manil. 5.264 *odores*. For the tetrasyllabic ending, see Rebelo Gonçalves 1988: 319. (The word is flagged by Hagen 1954 and those who come after as being both late and prosaic.)

Panchaia (Greek 'all-good') is a fantasy locale, located by Euhemerus in the Indian Ocean (*FGrHist* 63 F 2 = Diod. Sic. 6.1.4; Mela 3.81 places it in the Arabian Sea, at the Gulf of Aden). It was conceived of as rich beyond imagining. Lucr. 2.417 (the place's first mention in Latin, adjectivally—though it may well have occurred in Ennius' translation of Euhemerus), V. *G.* 2.139, 4.379, and [V.] *Cul.* 87 refer to its frankincense; in Ov. *Met.* 10.309 and 478 it is where Myrrha (the mythical source of myrrh) hails from. In this context, *merces* could reasonably refer either to myrrh or to incense, as both are used in funerals. See *RE* 18.3.493–5.

Eoi...Arabes and **Assyria** are real places (in Arabia and Mesopotamia; see Mela 1.2.12 and 14), known to Romans principally for their exotic spices (Arabia was known for balsam, frankincense, and myrrh; Mesopotamia as a primary stop on the journey), obtained through well-established but still perilous trade routes. See J. I. Miller 1969: 101–5 for the spices of Arabia; 119–52 on ancient trade routes; Bowersock 1983: 21 and 64 on the move from land to sea transport. According to Miller 1969: 99, few spices came directly from Persia. Plin. *NH* 12.41.83 notes that *Arabia felix* ironically gains its wealth from producing spices which are burned at funerals. **Arabes** is nominative plural, strictly of the people, but used here metonymically (as at Cat. 11.5 *Arabasve molles*, Ov. *Fas.* 4.569 *turilegos Arabas*; note too Ov. *Her.* 15.76 *Arabum... dona* of perfume, *palmiferos Arabas* of Myrrha's homeland at *Met.* 10.478). **Eoique Arabes** also at V. *G.* 2.115 *Eoasque domos Arabum pictosque Gelonos*; Stat. *Silv.* 3.3.33–5 *tu largus Eoa/germina, tu messes Cilicumque Arabumque superbas/merge rogis*; *Theb.* 6.59–60 *tertius assurgens Arabum strue tollitur ordo/Eoas complexus opes*. Also in non-funerary contexts: Prop. 2.29.18 *afflabunt tibi non Arabum de gramine odores*, 3.13.8 *cinnamon et multi pistor odoris Arabs*; Luc. 7.442 *Felices Arabes Medique Eoaque tellus*, 8.854 *Arabum portus mercis mutator Eoae*; Mart. 3.65.5–6 *quod myrtus, quod messor Arabs, quod sucina trita,/pallidus Eoo ture quod ignis olet*. This is the only instance of **Assyria** as a noun in Latin poetry (in prose it appears first in Pliny); it is not infrequent as an adjective; cf. e.g. Cat. 66.12, 68.144, Hor. *Od.* 2.11.16, V. *E.* 4.25, Tib. 1.3.7 (quoted above), and Mart. 8.77.3. When these places are mentioned in elegy, they usually either signify the wealth of rivals, obtained through trade, or symbolize the luxurious wants of the *puella*; in both cases, they are normally denigrated. The detail and leisurely pace of the poet may suggest his enjoyment of the scene he has created.

  et nostri memores lacrimae fundantur eodem:
26 sic ego componi versus in ossa velim.

Epitaphs make clear that a primary concern the living attribute to the dead is the desire to be remembered. Here, of course, additional point is gained because L. is not genuinely dying or dead; he would prefer N. to remember him while he is still living. The drama and pathos of the situation may therefore be designed to coerce the *puella* into better behaviour: L. only wants to die if he can be assured that N. will weep over him. But, of course, he only wants to die in the first place because she doesn't care for him while he is living.

Nostri memores lacrimae: unattested, and it is bold to have tears personified as 'mindful'; the slightly similar passage at Cic. *Mil.* 34.9 *Valebat apud vox, iudices, Milonis erga me remque publicam meritorum memoria, valebant preces et lacrimae nostrae* helps somewhat. **Nostri memores**: Tib. 1.3.2 *o utinam* memores... mei and Prop. 1.11.5 nostri... memores... noctes; cf. Hor. Od. 3.11.51 nostri memorem funereal, 3.27.14 memor nostri departure, Ov. Am. 2.11.37 vade memor nostri, Her. 11.127 vive memor nostri, Met. 8.586 memores... nostri cure for forgetfulness, 13.380 and 14.730 este mei memores, Tr. 4.3.10 memor nostri departure, Sen. Med. 142 memorque nostri of forgetfulness, Stat. Silv. 4.5.58–9 memor... nostri valediction in letter, VF 1.46 nostri... memor death, Juv. 3.318 nostri memor departure; cf. ad 3.5.31. **Lacrimae** are regular features of elegy, as befitting its putative origin in funerary epigram (see Introduction, Section I, and Pichon 1991: 181–2); they are also suitable to the lamentable situation of the elegist's love life as a whole. For tears at elegiac funerals and death scenes, real and imagined, see Prop. 1.19.18, 1.19.23, 1.21.6, 2.1.77, 4.7.28, 4.7.69, 4.11.1, 4.11.57, 4.11.60, Tib. 1.1.62, 2.6.32, and below *ad* 3.10.21, Ov. Am. 2.10.37, 3.9.11, 3.9.46, Her. 10.119, 11.125, 13.137, 14.118, 14.127, 15.62.

Eodem: i.e. on the spot where the ashes are, L.'s gravesite. **Sic** signifies the end of L.'s reverie, and so summarizes the conditions under which he seeks burial (and perhaps death). In Tib., the word usually starts off the line (note 2.5.122, where it summarizes the poem), which occurs about half the time in L.'s usage.

Componi is used at Prop. 2.24.35–6 of what Cynthia will do with Prop.'s bones, *tum me compones et dices 'ossa, Properti,/haec tua sunt'*, and of Pyramus and Thisbe at Ov. Met. 4.157. But it is also a regular word for poetic composition (Tib. 1.2.53 of a charm, *carmen*, and 91 of *blanditiae*), and also for creation of all sorts (e.g. Tib. 1.1.40 of clay cups, 1.2.22 of a prearranged code, or 2.1.39 of building houses; see Pichon 1991: 111 for several further uses). Cat. seems to have been the first to use the verb of burial (68.98), but it is common thereafter (e.g. Ov. Fas. 5.426). Perhaps it gains additional point here because of the implications of 'piling up' the verb also sometimes contains (e.g. Tib. 1.1.77). The verb is frequent in elegy, but seems to be a particular favourite of the authors of [Tib.] 3, appearing at 3.6.35 (of being forced to laugh when one is sad), 3.7.17 (*componere versus* of future compositions in honour of Messalla, 35 (*componere laudes*), and 100 (forming battle lines), 3.8.8 (of *Decor*'s ministrations to S., 3.12.9 (Juno urged to forge 'equal' fetters for S. and Cerinthus), and 3.13.9 (*vultus componere famae*). Its versatility in this small compass may argue for a programmatic significance: it stands for poetry, but also for falsehood and deception. There are two ways to translate this line: the more obvious 'I, turned into bones, would like to be put to rest in this way', but also, 'and so I would like verses to be composed over my bones'. This latter strains *sic* and *in ossa*, and is perhaps unnecessary given the next couplet, but the juxtaposition of *componi versus* in the line encourages us to take the suggestion more seriously.

The participle **versus** will also, of course, remind the reader of the noun, potentially referring to L.'s own poetry, and prepares the way for his epitaph: the semi-pun asserts that L., changed through death and then cremation, will still exist in poetic form. The phrase **versus in ossa** is similar in tone to line 9's *mutatus in umbram* (Tränkle 1990, Navarro Antolín 1996 *ad loc.*), and so rounds out the excursus; Navarro Antolín 1996 *ad loc.* suggests that *versus in cinerem* would be more appropriate, and posits that L. has written this *metri causa*.

> **Sed tristem mortis demonstret littera causam**
> 28   **atque haec in celebri carmina fronte notet:**

Here again, the language of epitaphic commemoration is reminiscent of that of book-presentation in the previous poem (see the *titulus* of 3.1.12). **Mortis… causam** is an Ovidian phrase (*Her.* 7.195, 18.200, *Ars* 3.40, *Met.* 7.855, 10.380, *Fas.* 3.549, *EP* 1.2.15, 4.6.11), and frequent on epitaphs. **Tristem** and **mortis** are joined in poetry at V. *A.* 11.839, [V.] *Cul.* 209, [Sen.] *Oct.* 101, 351, Luc. 9.762–3 *tristior…/mors*; for *tristis*, see Pichon 1991: 283–4. **Mortis… causam**: prosaic, but at Ov. *EP* 4.7.12, *Ib.* 123, 318, [Ov.] *Ep. Drus.* 458; cf. VF 1.648, Mart. 6.53.3. **Tristem… causam**: Lucr. 5.346–7 *tristior… causa*, Ov. *Am.* 2.14.31 *tristibus… causis*; cf. Prop. 1.18.10, Ov. *Her.* 3.90, *Tr.* 5.4.7 *tristitiae causam*.

    Demonstret occurs in Plaut. and Ter., Cat. 55.2, Prop. 3.16.15, Stat. *Theb.* 10.603 and 12.220, *Ach.* 1.582, and is otherwise prosaic (*TLL* 5.1.503.55–6), possibly epitaphic language. **Littera**: usually, in erotic elegy, of epistles; cf. *ad* 3.1.12 for the singular use.

    The phrase **celebri… fronte**, in its claim that L.'s grave will be well-known, is perhaps less surprising to readers who have picked up on earlier hints that this poem is as much about poetry as it is about a woman; see Clay 2004 for the Greek practice of according cultic status to poets. The phrase may depend upon Hor. *Od.* 1.7.6, *carmine perpetuo celebrare*. *Celeber* occurs elsewhere in Tib. at 2.1.33 (of Messalla) and 83 (of Bacchus); the commentators note that Tib. 2.1 seems to be the first use of *celeber* to mean *clarus*. See too *ad* 3.10.23; the verb is used more frequently, in similar situations (i.e. panegyric and festal); see *ad* 3.4.57 and 3.5.29. Prop. 3.16.25–6 expresses the opposite worry: he wants to be in a quiet spot, lest his tomb be desecrated: *di faciant, mea ne terra locet ossa frequenti/qua facit assiduo tramite vulgus iter*. And indeed, that poem differs from the norm in not containing a concluding epitaph, which Prop. says he does not want. Navarro Antolín 1996 suggests that L.'s phrase refers to the placement of the epitaph on the 'most visible part' of the tombstone, and cites [V.] *Cul.* 411–12 (on which see Seelentag 2010 *ad loc.*) and Prop. 4.7.83–4 as parallels; see too his mention of *inscriptis… notis* at Tib. 1.3.54.

    Because **carmina** can denote anything in verse, the noun describes the immediately following epitaph (e.g. Ov. *Her.* 2.146), but can also be taken as referring to L.'s poetry as a whole.

>   "**Lygdamus hic situs est: dolor huic et cura Neaerae,**
> 30   **coniugis ereptae, causa perire fuit.**"

L. names himself only here in his corpus. Troublingly for some, the name **Lygdamus** is best attested as the name of slaves (see Introduction, Section IV).

The first line of the couplet mimics the language of epitaphs, especially in its first half; indeed, **hic situs est** is formulaic enough to be commonly abbreviated on tombstones, *HSE* (the phrase occurs elsewhere in literature, as at e.g. Ov. *Met.* 2.327). For the epigraphic habit of noting the cause of death, see Lattimore 1942: 142–57, and line 27 above *mortis…causam*. Poetic epitaphs generally blame someone for death, as their purpose is to affect the living. L. suggests that N. is to blame if he dies. **Coniugis ereptae** refers back to 3.2.4, though without further illuminating it. On **dolor** see *ad* 3.2.6; this repetition, as commentators note, provides ring-composition and a sense of closure. On the use of inscriptions in Roman life, and in Latin poetry, see Ramsby 2007; for funerary epitaphs in elegy, see Schmidt 1985 and Ramsby 2007 *passim*, with a list of passages at 34. As she notes, among their other functions, poetic epitaphs can often be an attempt by the powerless to immortalize themselves (114). Perhaps the closest literary parallel to this passage is Ov. *Her.* 7.195–6: *praebuit Aeneas et causam mortis et ensem./ipsa sua Dido concidit usa manu.*

Coniugis returns to one of L.'s main themes, the claim that his relationship with N. is a legitimate one (see Introduction, Section I). It is, of course, possible to imagine a situation like that of the future emperor Tiberius (Suet. *Tib.* 7.2–3), wherein an otherwise happy marriage was ended for political reasons and despite the wishes of both parties, but this goes against what we generally think about the class of both *puellae* and *amatores*; they are generally not important enough to serve as political pawns. Note too Hinds 1999: 139–41, who observes that part of the punch of Ov. *Tr.* 1.3 lies precisely in the comparison between nobodies such as Ovid and his wife and the imperial family.

Causa perire: see Lattimore 1942: 151–8 for the (common) practice of recording unusual causes of death on Latin funerary epitaphs; *TLL* 3.680.58–681.52. As Navarro Antolín 1996 notes, the infinitive with *causa* is unexpected; cf. *TLL* 3.675.74–81, citing V. *A.* 10.90 *causa fuit consurgere* and others. Postgate 1929 suggests that its appearance here derives from the similar Greek construction. For the erotic implications of *perire*, see Pichon 1991: 230–1.

3.3:

This poem expresses a typically elegiac disdain for wealth, and shares specific elements with such poems as Prop. 3.2.11–26, where, however, the focus is rather different. (Prop. notes that although he is not wealthy, he is dear to the Muses, and opines that a mention in his poetry is a greater and more permanent gift than anything tangible.) So too, Prop. 1.5.24 tells Gallus that his *nobilitas* will do him no good with Cynthia; Prop. 1.8 focuses on the evils of a wealthy lover, who takes Cynthia away; 1.14 notes the uselessness of wealth in love. It is also similar to a number of poems in the first book of Tib., which include death-fantasies (e.g. 1.1.59–68, 1.2.71–80) and disdain of wealth (e.g. 1.1.1–6), and of course to the interest in death in [Tib.] 3.1 and 3.2. For the concept of alternative worlds (often fantasies) applied to the elegists, see Glatt 1991 (135–8 on this poem).

Because the poem does not focus much of its attention on N., some have emphasized its philosophical aspects (Navarro Antolín 1996, who compares it to Sen. *Ep.* 90.41, an invocation of the simple life, Bürger 1903: 325, who calls it a quasi-epistle). Note too Hor. *Od.* 2.18.1–11, where the poet claims that wealth is not necessary for a life of contentment (and see Nisbet and Hubbard 1978 *ad loc.* on the Bacchylidean resonances of that poem). The overall tone of this poem is not positive, and it ends, like 3.2, on a decidedly disquieting note. The poem is sometimes examined for what it can tell us about L.'s financial situation (see *ad* 3.3.3); some want to take his claim literally, others not. Postgate 1929 *ad loc.* finds in L. the ostentation of the freedman (see Introduction, Section IV, on L.'s name as potentially indicative of slave status).

Poem 3.3 can be divided into four parts: it begins with a lengthy priamel (twenty-two lines) about what L. has *not* wished for, interrupted by what he *has*, N., (6–10); four lines of recapitulation follow: nothing is worth it without N.; six lines confirm that wealth is nothing to him; and the poem concludes with six lines of prayer to Venus and Juno, undermined by a wish for death.

> Quid prodest caelum votis implesse, Neaera,
> 2 blandaque cum multa tura dedisse prece?

The syntax of the first several lines is complex (and the sentence as a whole quite long for L.—though some editors add a question mark at the end of line 2): L. *has* prayed, but not for the normal run of things, here listed in priamel form. The introductory couplet is reminiscent of, but probably not actually dependent on, a number of Horatian priamels, e.g. *Od.* 1.31.3–8, 2.18.1–11, 3.16.33–8. Where it differs from both them and Tib. 1.1 is in the plaintive tone, and in the religious practices L. claims to have engaged in (though this is not unparalleled in elegy). L. too speaks of a choice of life, but with regret. The first line sounds as though it might reflect only lovers' vows (see especially note on *implesse*), and the second a sick *puella* (both very elegiac themes), but the next couplet clarifies.

Quid prodest begins the poem with a colloquial tone; often, both in elegy and out of it, the rhetorical question implies a negative answer: *nihil prodest*, it wasn't worth it (see too 3.3.11 and 13; the effect is increased by repetition). The question appears elsewhere in Tib. with this nuance (1.2.78, 1.8.9, also in the perfect tense, and see Tib. 1.8.70 *nec prodest* and 3.17.5 *quid prosit*, and Pichon 1991: 241); often the words are separated. Here the mercantile nuance of the phrase gains extra point, as the next couplet shows: there really was no profit to be had from L.'s expenditure. The phrase is often at the line-start; see too Tib. 1.3.23 *quid tua nunc Isis mihi, Delia, quid mihi prosunt* and Ov. *Am.* 3.9.33–4 *quid nunc Aegyptia prosunt/sistra* for other failed interactions with the divine. Among the other pointless pursuits of elegy expressed in this form are: sleeping alone (Tib. 1.2.77–8, Prop. 2.33.17), utilizing artifice to appear beautiful (Tib.

1.8.9–12), artifice in general (Tib. 1.8.61), telling the truth (Tib. 2.4.51), swearing an oath (Ov. *Her.* 21.133), reciting poetry (Prop. 1.9.9), philosophy (Prop. 2.34.27–8), rape (Ov. *Fas.* 2.431), and late learning (Ov. *EP* 2.6.11)—and this covers only the precise phrase; there are many further parallels in and outside of elegy. Given the nature of the difficulties between L. and N., the first word may be reminiscent of Prop. 1.2.1, *quid iuvat ornato procedere, vita, capillo*, a poem about Cynthia's unfortunate tendency to display herself.

The verb **implesse**, not found elsewhere in Tib., Cat., or Prop., is frequent in Ov., most often of filling various spaces with lament or filling out a span of time. **Caelum votis implesse** has no precise parallel; similar language occurs at V. *A.* 9.24 *oneravitque aethera votis* (on which see Hardie 1994 *ad loc.* for the potentially burdensome nature of the repetition) and 9.480 *caelum... questibus implet* (= VF 6.726); Ov. *Met.* 7.428 *muneribus deos implet*; VF 2.167 *tum voce deos, tum questibus implent*. The perfect tense is metrically convenient (and archaizing, Platnauer 1951: 109–12, Perotti 1989), and may not suggest that L. has in fact filled the sky with vows. On the vows of lovers, notoriously unreliable, see Pichon 1991: 300 and e.g. Ov. *Am.* 2.7.27–8. See *ad* 3.4.53, *sollicitas caelestia numina votis*, and below, *ad* 3.3.33.

Neaera's early mention in this poem sets the stage, foreshadowing L.'s ultimate wish: the poem, like its predecessors, features her, but she remains shadowy, her intentions opaque.

Blanda is a standard elegiac word, as is its noun *blanditia*; both are normally used for the seductive speech and behaviour of lovers to one another (*TLL* 2.2038.1–2039.45, and *ad* 3.4.75 with *querelas*); see Ov. *Am.* 2.1.21 and 3.1.46 and *RA* 379, where elegy is characterized as *blandus* or *blanditiae*. (*Blanda prece* is much more common than this poem's **blanda... tura**, which does occur in a religious context at Prop. 4.6.5 *date et blandi mihi turis honores*; cf. Ov. *Her.* 5.60 *blanda fui*—by means of *votis*.) The adjective is more usually amatory, at e.g. Ov. *Met.* 10.642, where Hippomenes' *blandas preces* to Venus help him win Atalanta; cf. the identical phrase not directed to any god at Ov. *Ars* 1.710. L.'s prayers, like these, are for a very elegiac object. On *blandiri*, see Pichon 1991: 94–5, and on *preces*, Pichon 1991: 238–9. **Tura dedisse**: also at Tib. 1.8.70, in the same *sedes*. **Multa... prece**: prayers are often multiplied; cf. e.g. Ov. *Ars* 1.438 *nec exiguas... preces*, Sen. *Med.* 846 *multa prece*, and below *ad* 3.4.64 (where the text may read *fide*).

> Non, ut marmorei prodirem e limine tecti,
> 4   insignis clara conspicuusque domo,

Here we see the elegist's typical lack of concern for the traditional occupations of upper-class Roman manhood, wealth and power (not restricted to elegy: see the similar sentiment at V. *G.* 2.461–6, which begins *si non ingentem foribus domus alta superbis/mane salutantum totis vomit aedibus undam*).

The roof is **marmorei** by analogy, to signify wealth (i.e. it is very unlikely that a roof would be made of marble). But this common word is not much in use in elegy, which suggests its incongruity with the elegiac world: *marmore* at Prop. 2.1.72, 2.31.9; *marmoreus* only in L. of the poets of [Tib.] 3, at 3.2.22 and this poem, 16, and Prop. 2.31.6. The word, both noun and adjective, is more frequent in Ov., but never of the elegist's own home. Compare Prop. 3.2.11ff. (cited *ad* 3.3.13), where the poet's *domus* is explicitly *not* marbled. It is not clear whether L. shares the equestrian status of other elegists, who tend to represent themselves as impoverished (see Introduction, Section I). **Marmorei...tecti**: usually not in the same case, but cf. e.g. Ov. *EP* 1.8.35 *marmora tecta theatra*. **Limine tecti**: paralleled at Ov. *Met.* 5.43 (with *exierat*), 14.254, *Ib.* 615, *Fas.* 1.137 *limina tecti*, all at line-end; Pichon 1991: 189 for erotic nuances of the *limen*. We might also remember L.'s imagined final resting place, the *marmorea...domo* from 3.2.22.

Prodirem: the prefix perhaps gives a formal feel; cf. Varro *DLL* 7.81 *qui exit in vestibulum, quod est ante domum, prodire et procedere dicitur*.

Insignis and **conspicuus** are qualities avoided by the elegiac *amator*, and rejections of wealth and status are common to many kinds of poetry (e.g. Hor. *Serm.* 2.2.10 *contentus parvo* and *Od.* 3.16.18–19 *iure perhorrui/late conspicuum tollere verticem*). **Insignis** is never used by the elegists of themselves, though sometimes of *puellae* (Tib. 1.3.32, Prop. 3.24.4 and 4.11.46 (of Cornelia)) and sometimes of noteworthy objects (Pichon 1991: 173). **Conspicuus** is rare in elegy, and not used of lovers (see Ov. *EP* 3.1.56, on how his fall from grace has made him **conspicuus**, perhaps a hint of the dangers inherent in being visible, and [Ov.] *Cons. ad Liv.* 336 on Drusus' *conspicuum decus*). **Clara...domo**: paralleled at Ov. *Her.* 17.54; further citations at *TLL* 5.1.1983.3–5.

>   aut ut multa mei renovarent iugera tauri
> 6   et magnas messes terra benigna daret,

The second thing L. has *not* beseeched the gods for is wealth of a different kind, the idyllic, rural plenitude sometimes fantasized about by Tib. (e.g. in 1.1). Generally speaking, the non-urban world is of limited interest to the elegists (Introduction, Section I). As Navarro Antolín 1996 notes, line 5 is a 'golden line' (a verb in the middle of the line, preceded by two adjectives and followed by two nouns; see his bibliography *ad loc.*).

Multa...iugera is a Tibullan phrase (1.1.2, 2.3.42), found also at Ov. *EP* 4.9.86 (none in the same *sedes*); cf. also Hor. *Od.* 2.15.1 *pauca aratro iugera*, V. *G.* 4.127–8 *pauca relicti/iugera ruris*, Ov. *Am.* 3.15.12 *campi iugera pauca*, *Fas.* 3.192 *iugeraque inculti pauca*; also prosaic. **Renovarent**: an Ovidian verb, usually of crops (e.g. *Am.* 1.3.9, *Met.* 1.110, 15.125, *Fas.* 1.159, *Tr.* 4.6.13, 5.12.23; cf. Tib. 2.6.41 and Prop. 3.12.35, neither of crops), fairly common in Statius but otherwise not especially poetic. The verb does not appear elsewhere with this direct object.

The adjective **benigna** is used only once in Tib., also of **terra**, at 1.3.62 (in the same metrical *sedes*; see Maltby 1999: 247). Cf. *benignus ager* at Ov. *Am.* 1.10.56, *Parnesque benignus/vitibus* at Stat. *Theb.* 12.620–1. It is not surprising to see the land conceived of as generous, particularly by one who does not actually labour on it; but the uses at Plin. *NH* 18.1.1, 33.1.2, and 35.158, suggest that this is not only poetic fancy (*TLL* 2.1904.22–46).

> sed tecum ut longae sociarem gaudia vitae
> 8   inque tuo caderet nostra senecta sinu,

Old age is a common theme in Tib., especially in Book 1, both in terms of the inappropriateness of love for the elderly (e.g. 1.1.71–2, 1.2.87–96, 1.8.49–50, 1.9.74, 2.1.74, 2.2.19; see Maltby 2002 *ad* the first passage and Murgatroyd 1980 *ad* the second and third passages), and the concomitant notion that the love object will eventually be old and undesirable, so ought to enjoy life now (1.4.29–38, 1.6.77–86, 1.8.42; precursors of this view at Maltby 2002 *ad* 1.1.71–2). But Tib. also invokes old age as a way of suggesting permanence and stability (cf. the end of 1.6, 1.7.55–6 on Messalla's future generations, the image of the old man with his family around him at 1.10.39–48, 2.4.45–50 on a love lasting beyond death, and 2.5.91–4 on family) and of claiming authority (cf. 1.4.79–80—but this sentiment is undermined in the next couplet). [Tib.] 3.5 has a particular interest in old age (see *ad* 3.5.15–16, 25–6). Prop. discusses old age in similar ways, both disparaging it as in general unsuitable for erotic pursuits (2.18.7 and 17, 3.5.23ff., on which see Fedeli 1985 *ad loc.*, 3.19.15), and also invoking the image of long-lasting love even into old age (1.19.17, 2.25.9). Occasionally, as at 2.2.15, he hopes that age will not diminish Cynthia's looks, or invokes the *senes severiores* of Cat. 5, as at 2.30.13. Ov. focuses on the disgustingness (*turpe*) of elderly lovers (*Am.* 1.9.4, *Ars* 2.670); *Am.* 1.13 features an extended joke on the age, and so undesirability, of Tithonus, which is why Eos hastens out of bed each morning. Ov. also notes the decreased desirability of women as they grow older (*Am.* 1.8.53 and 113, *Ars* 3.59–100); we might think of these as representing the standard elegiac 'take' on age. But Ov. is no romantic, so his works contain few assertions of continued love into old age (*Am.* 1.3.17–18 *tecum, quos dederint annos mihi fila sororum,/vivere contingat teque dolente mori,* is a rare exception; there are denials of this kind of scenario in *Tr.* 3.3.43–4, 4.10.73–4). See too Prop. 4.11.64, *condita sunt vestro lumina nostra sinu,* of death surrounded by loved ones, and Nisbet and Rudd *ad* Hor. *Od.* 3.9.24, for further discussion and Greek parallels.

We finally discover what L. *has* prayed for: to be with N. for a long time. **Sociarem** regularly takes an accusative of the thing that is to be shared (*OLD* 1); with **gaudia** nowhere else. The verb is mostly prosaic, but regular in Manil., Stat. and Sil., and has an erotic sense at Ov. *Am.* 2.8.5, *Her.* 3.109, *Met.* 10.635, and Stat. *Theb.* 1.574, 3.282. **Gaudia**, as often in elegy, is probably here used in both its sexual and its non-sexual senses; see *ad* 3.1.8 *gaudeat*. For the conjunction **gaudia vitae**, see V. *A.* 11.180.

Caderet...sinu: the idiom normally equals our 'fall into one's lap' (*OLD* 2a with citations, closest parallel at Prop. 2.28.42); cf. Ov. *Am.* 2.15.14 *inque sinum mira laxus ab arte cadam*, of a ring (and below *ad* 3.13.4). But this sense is not appropriate here, where it must refer to the physical debilities of old age (*TLL* 3.18.37–46), to general decline, or perhaps to death (*OLD* 9a—but normally for battle-death; *TLL* 3.23.9ff.). Whatever the verb means, it is not wholly clear why N.'s lap is L.'s preferred location. The similar phrase *quem.../occupant in parva pigra senecta casa* at Tib. 1.10.39 may help with the sense. *Occupo* at 3.10.5, of illness, and Prop. 4.11.64 *condita sunt vestro lumina nostra sinu*, a death occurring in the loved one's embrace, may also be of relevance (see too Stat. *Silv*. 3.5, about marital bliss in illness, esp. *oculos iam morte cadentes*, 39). However difficult the precise meaning, the general sense is clear enough: old age leads to literal and metaphorical decline, to increased reliance upon others, and eventually to death. The sexual and nonsexual nuances of *sinus* are perhaps both appropriate here; cf. Ov.'s wish to die 'on the job' at *Am.* 2.10.35–8 (without mention of *sinus*). See Pichon 1991: 96 on *cadere* and 264 on *sinus*. For dying in the presence of loved ones, and the elegiac funeral fantasy, see *ad* 3.2. Tib. is more interested in (quasi-)marital love, e.g. 2.2.19–20 *vincula quae maneant semper dum tarda senectus/inducat rugas inficiatque comas* (the concept may be relevant here), but Prop. too sometimes imagines a love unto death.

In(que)...sinu: paralleled at Ov. *Tr.* 4.8.11–12 *inque sinu dominae carisque sodalibus inque/securus patria consenuisse mea*; also *Met.* 10.558.

Nostra senecta: joined in poetry at V. *A*. 11.165–6, [V.] *Cir.* 287, Luc. 9.234, Sen. *Phaed.* 262, Stat. *Theb.* 4.536, VF 1.718, 4.475, 7.65, Mart. 4.25.7, Sil. 6.481; see too Ov. *Tr.* 3.7.35–6 *inicietque manum formae damnosa senectus,/quae strepitus passu non faciente venit*, and *meae...senectae* at Hor. *Od.* 2.6.6. *Senecta* is the more poetic term, *senectus* prosaic, but there are exceptions; for the noun in the *CT*, see Évrard 1978: 134–5 and below *ad* 3.5.17.

> tum cum permenso defunctus tempore lucis
> 10   nudus Lethaea cogerer ire rate.

The (prosaic) collocation of **tum cum** is not common in elegy (all examples listed below); when it does appear, it normally introduces two clauses, e.g. at Tib. 1.9.79 (*tum flebis, cum*...). But the juxtaposition has poetic precedent (e.g. Enn. *Ann.* 6.203, Lucr. 3.681, V. *A*. 11.379, Ov. *Ars* 1.363, *Met.* 6.149, 8.19, 13.592, *Fas.* 2.34, 2.462, 6.732, 6.751, Luc. 2.136, Pers. 1.9, 4.37, all introducing the line; elsewhere in elegy not at line-start at Prop. 2.26.9, Ov. *Am.* 3.13.29, *Her.* 1.5, 3.23, 5.109, *Ars* 1.359, 3.173, *RA* 71, 125, *Fas.* 5.589, 5.625, *Tr.* 1.3.75, [Ov.] *Nux* 7, *Ep. Drus.* 321). The manuscripts' *tunc* may be preferable; cf. *tunc cum* at Ov. *Am.* 3.5.11, *Fas.* 5.273 (possibly spurious), 6.635, *Tr.* 3.11.27, *EP* 1.5.85, *tunc...cum* at Tib. 1.10.19, Ov. *Am.* 2.15.11, *Fas.* 1.247, *Tr.* 4.10.63 (none at line-start).

Permenso does not appear elsewhere in elegy, but the verb is attested in early and late poetry (see *TLL* 10.1.1537.71–3 on the passive use of the participle, with Colum. *DRR* 3.13.13). The phrase **permenso…tempore** is unattested, and with **lucis** somewhat difficult; see *TLL* 10.1.1538.28–35 for parallels, and, for **tempore lucis**, *Il. Lat.* 736 *tempore lucis*, Manil. 4.203 *tempora lucis* (both same sedes), Ov. *Fas.* 3.404 *quintae tempora lucis aget,* and Cic. *Phaen.* 34.288 *exaequat spatium lucis cum tempore noctis*. Note too such phrases as Cat. 64.31 *optatae finito tempore luces*. To understand *lux* as a life is not odd in Latin as a whole (*OLD* 6a, *TLL* 7.2.1910.6–31), though it is not so used elsewhere in *CT*, where the collocation *mea lux* is more common (see *ad* 3.9.15, 3.18.1; 3.3.25 for *lux niveus*). So too Prop. (citations *ad* 3.9.15). Ovidian usage comes closer: *Met.* 6.272, of dying and so leaving *pariter cum luce dolorem*, 14.725 of dying *geminaque simul mihi luce carendum*; see Bömer 1976 *ad* the former passage for similar phrases and Bömer 1986 and Myers 2009 *ad* the latter for the possible dual resonances of *lux* as beloved and life.

Defunctus in this sense at V. *G.* 4.475, *A.* 6.306 (there modifying *corpora*; for substantive (post-Vergilian) uses see *TLL* 5.1.378.56–379.3); parallels at Ov. *Am.* 1.8.107–8 *saepe mihi dices vivae bene, saepe rogabis,/ut mea defunctae molliter ossa cubent* (a female speaker); 2.9.24 *defunctum placide vivere tempus erat*; *Her.* 14.125–6 *dede neci defunctaque vita/corpora furtivis insuper adde rogis*; Hor. *Ep.* 2.1.21–2 *nisi quae terris semota suisque/temporibus defuncta videt, fastidit et odit*.

Nudus: sometimes specified as a condition of entering the underworld (Prop. 3.5.14, Sil. 5.267–9); see too Ov. *Tr.* 5.14.11–12 on how you can't take it with you. Most regularly, the adjective in elegy refers to actual nakedness (often desirable, cf. e.g. Prop. 2.1.13, 2.15.5, 13–16), but can also stand for simplicity or even the poverty nominally favoured by the poets (e.g. Prop. 1.2.8, Ov. *Am.* 1.10.15).

Lethaea may undermine the intended tone of this passage: if indeed all is forgotten (Greek λήθη) then perhaps this life does not matter as much as it seems to? But many poetic underworld scenes, most notably, Vergil's, feature deceased lovers who do not forget their beloveds. The adjective is apparently used first by Cat. 65.5, and then sporadically in poetry (Tib. 1.3.80 with *aquas* and [Tib.] 3.5.24, again with *ratis*, which may derive ultimately from *AP* 9.279.1). The adjective also has a broader sense, sometimes simply denoting the underworld, as at Hor. *Od.* 4.7.27–8.

Cogerer ire rate: see Navarro Antolín 1996 *ad loc.* for Vulpius on 'r' as the *littera canina*, because it sounds like a growling dog (here with allusion to Cerberus), and for other examples in poetry. On force in an amatory context, see Pichon 1991: 105 s.v. *cogi*.

> Nam grave quid prodest pondus mihi divitis auri,
> 12   arvaque si findant pinguia mille boues?

Another series of questions, shorter and personalized (**mihi**), but also generalizing in a philosophical manner: L. is not interested in wealth, either as money or as land. The lines leave unclear whether these are things L. might (have) pray(ed) for, or those he actually possesses. **Nam** is favoured by the poets of [Tib.] 3, who eschew *enim* (**nam** regular in Tib., and at [Tib.] 3.3.22, 3.4.36, 3.4.43, 3.11.8). Ov. prefers *enim*, but Prop. uses both equally; cf. Axelson 1945: 122–3. On **prodest**, see *ad* 3.3.1.

Pondus: a similar phrase at Tib. 1.9.31–2 (*tum mihi iurabas nullo te divitis auri/pondere…vendere velle fidem*); according to Maltby 2002 *ad loc.* the conjunction **divitis auri** originates with Tib. (see too 1.10.7 *divitis hoc vitium est auri* and 1.1.1 *divitias alius fulvo sibi congerat auro*; in both, money is undesirable and unsuitable for the elegist). Here we have a role reversal; L., who seemingly does have money, (now?) realizes that it doesn't matter. Is he thereby placing himself in the (unenviable, in the genre) role of the *dives amator*? **Grave…pondus**: elsewhere in poetry at Hor. *Epod.* 4.17–18, Ov. *Her.* 21.170 (*gravius…pondus*), *Met.* 7.118, Manil. 1.286, Sen. *Troad.* 491, Stat. *Theb.* 1.212–13, Mart. 5.65.9 (*graviora…pondera*); all may derive from Accius 22.2, *ponderitatem gravitatemque*.

Pinguia is often used of fields and agricultural produce in V. *G.* (see R. Thomas *ad* 1.8), and in elegy (of *solum* at Cat. 68.110 and Tib. 2.3.6, of *humus* at Ov. *Her.* 1.54 and *Ars* 1.360, of Campanian soil at Prop. 3.5.5, *nec mihi mille iugis Campania pinguis aratur*, of *musta* at Tib. 1.1.10, of mares at Ov. *Her.* 9.90, and of oil at *Her.* 19.44). The Propertian use is noteworthy, as it also refers to land ploughed (*aratur* there) by a thousand ploughs (*mille iugis*). **Arva…pinguia** elsewhere at V. *E.* 5.33, Hor. *Od.* 3.4.15–16, VF 7.607–8.

Mille: presumably an exaggeration (*TLL* 8.980.69–74); see too Prop. 3.5.5 (quoted above), Tib. 1.3.50 *leti mille repente viae*, 2.3.44 *portatur validis mille columna iugis*, 2.4.60 *mille alias herbas misceat illa*.

> Quidve domus prodest Phrygiis innixa columnis,
> 14   Taenare sive tuis, sive Caryste tuis,

With these lines, L. sets himself apart, at great length, from people who like such wealth. He prefers instead an impoverished old age with N. Given the normal situation of elegiac *puellae*, who have an expiration date, the sentiment may be more pointed than it seems. The first series of questions were parallel; here they are collapsed into a single line each, and the first is then expanded into two further couplets. In addition to passages not otherwise mentioned below which describe lavish dwellings, see Stat. *Silv.* 1.5.34–50 (baths), 2.2.85–97 (a room). On the Roman obsession with marble, see Plin. *NH* 35.1–3 and 36.4–8; on the types of marble, *NH* 36.44–63 (with marble edifices following and statues preceding). The mixing of different colours and patterns of marble increases the luxuriousness of its use. One of these types, *lygdinos*, of brilliant hue, is etymologically related to L.'s own name, and may explain it, if he is using a pseudonym (see Introduction, Section IV).

Innixa: the only use of this verb in the *CT*.; for similar wording see Ov. *EP* 3.2.49 (the temple of Diana *vastis innixa columnis*, Stat. *Silv.* 4.2.38 *innixa columnis* of table-legs, Stat. *Silv.* 1.2.152 *nixa columnis* of a lavish dwelling, all at line-end; further *TLL* 7.1.1698.77–1699.4). It might be a stretch to see here a reference to Cat. 68.72, Lesbia's arrival *innixa arguta constituit solea* (the word's only use in Cat.).

The similarity of phrasing of Prop. 3.2.11–14 justifies quoting it in full: *quod non Taenariis domus est mihi fulta columnis,/nec camera auratas inter eburna trabes,/nec mea Phaeacas aequant pomaria silvas,/non operosa rigat Marcius antra liquor.* There, a rather different point is made: Prop. notes that although not wealthy, he is beloved of the Muses; Hor. *Od.* 2.18.1–5 makes a similar point with different words (see Fedeli 1985: 98–9 for further parallels). See Navarro Antolín 1996 *ad loc* for imitation of these lines in later Latin.

Phrygiis is often used in the elegists of the Trojan war, specifically of Paris' judgement, the rape of Helen, or Aeneas, but also as a shorthand for luxury (*Phrygias... opes* Ov. *Her.* 13.58). The purple marble here mentioned, from the city of Synnas (Strabo 12.8.14, Plin. *NH* 35.3; of marble, see also Plin. *NH* 36.102), appears in poetry at Hor. *Od.* 3.1.41 (see too Porphyry *ad loc.*), Stat. *Silv.* 1.5.37, 2.2.83, Juv. 14.307, Mart. 6.42.11, 9.75.8.

Taenare: Cape Matapan in Laconia (Plin. *NH* 4.16); on its stone, see Strabo 8.5.7. Plin. *NH* 36.135, 158; mentioned also at Prop. 3.2.11 (quoted above), Stat. *Silv.* 1.2.148, Mart. 1.55.5, 6.42.11, 9.75.6–9. It also housed an entrance to the underworld (V. *G.* 4.467, Hor. *Od.* 1.34.10, Ov. *Met.* 10.13 and *Fas.* 4.612, Luc. 6.648, 9.36, Sen. *HF* 587, 663, 813, *Troad.* 402, *Phaed.* 1201, *HO* 1061, 1771, Stat. *Theb.* 1.96, 2.32, 2.44), which may be relevant, given that L. is never far from thoughts of death. The adjective comes to equal 'Laconian' and is used in Ov.'s elegies almost exclusively to refer to Helen (five of six times). The marble from Taenarum came in several colours; see Navarro Antolín 1996 *ad loc.* on which colour is probably meant here.

Caryste: a town on the southern coast of Euboea, known for riotously coloured marble, and for its temple of Apollo Marmarinus (Strabo 10.1.6, Plin. *NH* 4.64, 36.48 and 49 (a quotation from Nepos); for details of the marble see Frazer *ad* Ov. *Fas.* 4.282). It is mentioned otherwise in poetry at Sen. *Troad.* 836, Stat. *Silv.* 1.2.148–50, 1.5.34, *Theb.* 7.370, Mart. 9.75.7. Tränkle 1990 and Navarro Antolín 1996 propose that the regular Flavian conjunction of Carystian marble with the other two mentioned here makes a post-Augustan date likely for this poem. **Tuis... tuis**: direct address of this kind is rare in L., and perhaps elevated.

>   et nemora in domibus sacros imitantia lucos
> 16 aurataeque trabes marmoreumque solum?

The remains of Nero's *domus aurea* (Suet. *Nero* 31, *in ceteris partibus concha auro lita*), notable for its gold, pearl, and gem overlays and for its inclusion of pastures and forests within the compound, shows the extravagance of a later(?)

period (Ward-Perkins 1956, Ball 2003). That was clearly an extreme, but may give us a sense of the luxury that led up to it; as McKay notes, Nero's palace innovated mainly in being an urban villa (1975: 74). See also the imagined house at Prop. 3.2.11–14 (quoted above *ad* 3.3.13). Indoor groves are a sign of luxury at e.g. Hor. *Od.* 3.10.5–6, *Ep.* 1.10.22.

Imitantia: an Ovidian term (Radford 1926) in an Ovidian *sedes*. On the conjunction of **nemora** and **lucos** as quasi-synonyms, see Prop. 4.9.24 (with Enk 1946 *ad loc.*, who finds it a problem, and Fedeli 1965 *ad loc.*, who does not); in addition to Fedeli's citations see also V. *E.* 6.73, 8.86, *A.* 7.82, 8.597–9, Ov. *Met.* 3.176, 8.741–2, *Fas.* 4.751–3, 6.755, Sen. *Troad.* 174, VF 8.24–5, Sil. 3.666, 3.675–6, 3.688, 4.680. **Sacros...lucos**: a poetic phrase (V. *A.* 5.761, 7.778, 8.597–8, Hor. *Od.* 4.15.25, Sen. *Troad.* 174, Mart. 1.53.9, Sil. 14.648; cf. Prop. 4.9.33 *luci sacro...antro* and Ov. *Met.* 15.793 *sanctis...lucis*). Groves sacred to gods remained uncut, and so were traditionally luxuriant.

Aurataeque trabes: cf. V. *A.* 2.448 (same *sedes*), Luc. 10.113 *crassumque trabes absconderat aurum*, Sen. *Phaed.* 496–7 *nec trabes multo insolens/suffigit auro*, *Thy.* 347 *auro nitidae trabes* and 646, Stat. *Silv.* 1.3.35 *auratasne trabes* (in the same *sedes*). Gold roof-beams (V. *A.* 1.726, [V.] *Cul.* 63–4) and marble floors are both luxurious, although not unattested (Cic. *Par. Sto.* 49 *aurata tecta in villis et sola marmorea*). For elaborate ceiling decorations, see also Hor. *Od.* 2.16.11–12, 2.18.1–2, Sen. *Thy.* 457 (and golden walls at Lucr. 2.23–33).

Marmoreumque solum: parallels at Ov. *Met.* 8.702 *adopertaque marmore tellus* of the temple where Baucis and Philemon used to live, 15.672 *marmoreumque solum* of Asclepius' temple (see too Cic. *Par. Sto.* 49, quoted above). Some at least of the houses in Herculaneum are paved with marble, an innovation which seems to date from the second century BCE; Plin. *NH* 36.48 notes the first marbling of interior walls (in the late Republic), and see Plin. *Ep.* 9.39.4 for marble floor and walls; on non-marble flooring, see Plin. *NH* 36.184–189.

> Quidve in Erythraeo legitur quae litore concha
> 18   tinctaque Sidonio murice lana iuvat,

Erythraeo...litore: the Arabian Sea, and especially the Persian Gulf (for the etymology, see Curt. 8.9.14, Strabo 16.3.5, Plin. *NH* 6.28, Arr. *Ind.* 37.3). On pearls, see Plin. *NH* 9.106–124, according to whom those from this region are especially valuable; see too citations below, and *TLL* 6.2.1755.73–1756.14, *RE* 14.2.1687.36–1689.22. Pearls are a profoundly unelegiac gift; see *ad* 3.8.19. The adjective is one of Navarro Antolín's 'late words' (1996: 19; cf. Hagen 1954, Lee 1958–9, Axelson 1960b: 291–2, and Navarro Antolín 1996 and Tränkle 1990 *ad loc.*); it does not appear in Latin before Plin. *NH* 12.70 (earlier authors use *rubro*, as at e.g. Prop. 1.14.12 *legitur Rubris gemma sub aequoribus*, 3.13.6 *et venit e Rubro concha Erycina salo*, Tib. 2.4.30 *vestis et e rubro lucida concha mari*). Poetic occurrences of the adjective referring to pearls are found at Stat.

Silv. 4.6.18 (same *sedes*), Mart. 5.37.4, 8.28.14, 9.2.9, 9.12.5, 10.17.5 (last four in same *sedes*). The noun is first found in Cic. *Verr.* 2.1.49; cf. Varro fr. 388.1. But Butler and Barber *ad* Prop. 3.13.6 suggest accepting *Erythraea* from the inferior manuscripts in place of the difficult *Erycina* there (further discussion at Fedeli 1985 and Heyworth 2007 *ad loc.*).

Concha: metonymy for 'pearl', regularly in the poets (e.g. Ov. *Ars* 3.124 *lectaque diverso litore concha venit*; *OLD* 2b, *TLL* 4.28.41–7; Tib. 2.4.30), but also of seashells proper (see *ad* 3.3.34) and purple. Plin. *NH* 9.53.104 deems shellfish (i.e. their products, notably pearls and purple dye) the greatest source of moral corruption and luxury at Rome (*populatio morum atque luxuria*).

Sidonio: Tyrian dye is the richest in colour, so the most expensive (see André: 1949: 103 on the hue and 92–3 on regional variations in colour, with Gipper 1964); see *ad* 3.8.16 on *Tyros*. Purple is notably associated with the stripes which were worn on the togas of men of the senatorial and equestrian class to indicate their status; Reinhold argues that in the early Imperial period, the wearing of purple indicated affluence rather than status, and that the colour was not yet wholly regal (1970: 48–9 and n. 3). See Reinhold 1970 for a discussion of the origins of the dye (11–12) and its use in the early empire (48–61). Contemporary poetic mentions of Tyre regularly imply luxury and decadence, e.g. V. *A.* 4.262 with Pease 1935 *ad loc.*, and throughout the elegists. Other uses of *Sidonius* for dyed cloth occur in elegy at Prop. 2.16.55, 4.9.47 (gown) and 2.29.15 (evening cap); Ov. *Her.* 9.101 (gown), *Tr.* 4.2.27 (triumphal toga); see too Ov. *Met.* 10.267 *stratis concha Sidonide tinctis* of a bedspread. The adjective often describes Dido in Vergil's *Aeneid*; some of the ominous nuance of her story is surely felt here. Purple is both unelegiac (in that the poets eschew luxury) and elegiac (in that their *puellae* demand it).

Murice: first in poetry for the dye at V. *A.* 4.262 (*Tyrio...ardebat murice laena*); further citations *TLL* 8.1671.5–42 (not elsewhere with **Sidonio**). Tib. 2.4.27–31 contains the normal elegiac criticism of luxury items, including *quicumque...niveam Tyrio murice tingit ovem*, 27–8. **Tincta...murice lana**: parallels at e.g. Hor. *Od.* 2.16.35–7 *te bis Afro/murice tinctae/vestiunt lanae*, Ov. *Ars* 1.251 *consule de gemmis, de tincta murice lana*, *Ars* 3.170 *te, quae Tyrio murice, lana, rubes* (and see Tib. 2.4.27–31 just quoted); **tinctaque** occurs in Ov. at the start of a line at *Her.* 20.236, *EP* 3.1.26, 3.3.106. On the mollusc, and on the dyeing process, see Plin. *NH* 9.60.125–65.141, and Sebesta 1994, especially 66–7, with *RE* 23.2.2000–20.

>   et quae praeterea populus miratur? In illis
> 20   invidia est: falso plurima volgus amat.

This couplet sums up, in quasi-philosophical fashion: the things the vulgar crowd admires are not genuinely valuable; cf. *populo mirante* at Juv. 2.67 (of clothing) and Sil. 16.502 (of Mercury), *miretur vulgus* at Ov. *Am.* 1.15.35.

In elegy **invidia** and its cognates describe those jealous of the lover and/or his beloved (e.g. Prop. 1.12.9, 2.17.11, 2.22.20, 2.26.15, 2.28.10, 3.1.21 with Fedeli 1985 *ad loc.*) but rarely refer to wealth (only, seemingly, at [Tib.] 3.19.7, there too of the common people); Pichon 1991: 174. Prop. sometimes boasts that his relationship is above **invidia** (Prop. 1.12.9, 2.17.11), once he is its victim (1.16.48). Ov. *Am.* 2.6.25, where jealousy has stolen away Corinna's parrot, may also be relevant; many have seen that poem as a doublet of *Am.* 3.9, on the death of Tib. On elegiac jealousy in general, see Caston 2012: it functions in ways sometimes expected, sometimes surprising. See too *HHA* 105, Hes. *WD* 26, Call. *Aet.* Fr. 1.17, on the metapoetic nuances of the word, which also refers to the emotion poets sometimes display towards other poets.

Falso: adverbial ablative (*OLD* lists separately), though it is not so used in Tib. or Prop.; Ov. prefers the ablative to the accusative *falsum* (e.g. *Fas.* 5.683). For erotic nuances, see Pichon 1991: 142. **Volgus**: again, the word has philosophical and distancing nuances.

> Non opibus mentes hominum curaeque levantur,
> 22   nam Fortuna sua tempora lege regit.

Levantur needs to be taken metaphorically with *mentes*. Poetic parallels: Lucr. 2.365 *animum curaque levare*, Cat. 2.10 *tristis animi levare curas*, Hor. *Ser.* 2.5.99 *te servitio longo curaque levarit*, Manil. 4.12 *solvite, mortale, animos curasque levate*, Sil. 8.118 *aegram mentem et trepidantia corda levaret*, and many others with one or the other noun, or *animum*; cf. Pichon 1991: 187.

Fortuna is regularly personified in Latin poetry (though the ancient habit of using only capital letters means we cannot always be certain); she has a similar role as a spoiler of human plans at e.g. Prop. 1.6.25, Hor. *Od.* 1.35, Ov. *Met.* 3.141, 6.195, *Tr.* 5.8.7 and 15, *EP* 2.3.51, 2.7.15, 20, and 41, and throughout poetry (but sometimes favours individuals, as at Ov. *Met.* 5.140, *Tr.* 1.5.27). The word does not appear elsewhere in the *CT* (except at 3.7.182, also personified). **Fortuna...regit** (sometimes also *fors* or *fata*): in poetry as early as Enn. *Ann.* 6.188 (*vosne velit an me regnare era, quidve ferat Fors*), V. *A.* 12.405 (*nulla*), [Ov.] *Ep. Drus.* 51 (*regnat*), Sen. *Phaed.* 978. There is a jingly feel to the pentameter which is usually avoided; the line must be proverbial. Similar sentiments about spurning unnecessary wealth occur at Publil. Syr. L5 *levis est fortuna: cito reposcit quod dedit*, Hor. *Od.* 2.16.9–12, *Ep.* 1.2.47; see Robinson 1946. **Regit**: see Navarro Antolín 1996 for a discussion of the manuscript reading *gerit*. **Sua...lege**: the laws of fortune are a commonplace (e.g. Cic. *TD* 5.25, quoting Theophrastus, Sen. *Cont.* 1.1.5) but rarely expressed as such: in poetry at Manil. 1.56; cf. *ad* 3.4.47 *fatorum leges*.

Tempora: either of one's lifetime (*OLD* 5c) or of particular conditions at the moment (*OLD* 11a). The first is more likely, given Roman perceptions of the vital role played by fortune in human affairs.

Sit mihi paupertas tecum iucunda, Neaera,
24   at sine te regum munera nulla volo.

Sit is troubling: we want a more definite (i.e. future indicative) affirmation. The subjunctive suggests uncertainty: L. *might* like poverty with N. (potential), or he wishes he could (counterfactual), or he would like the opportunity (optative); this latter formulation, the most natural in the context, suggests that N. is the wild-card, which is borne out by the remainder of the corpus (and the *puella* usually prefers luxury to stable poverty). So too, N. may implicitly be equated to Fortuna, since her plans are unclear. (In this way, she is not unlike Tib.'s Nemesis, even more difficult than Delia.)

Virtuous **paupertas** (which does not signify actual deprivation) is laid claim to by a variety of poets, including the elegists; see in particular Tib. 1.1.19 and 37, where his field and table are *pauper*, 1.1.5, where *paupertas* is invoked as a keyword for the poem and for Tib.'s desired lifestyle as a whole, Tib. 1.5, on how the *pauper* will make an especially good lover (61, 63, and 65), Prop. 2.10.24, where he brings only incense, *pauperibus sacris* (see Enk 1946 and Fedeli 2005 *ad loc.*), Hor. *Od.* 2.12.21–8, and 3.3.31 below (which parallels Tib. 1.10.19). There are also, of course, numerous relevant passages without the word, e.g. Tib. 1.2.65–78, Prop. 1.14.15–24. On the motif of poverty in Tib., see Schuster 1968: 81–4. (The word is absent from Cat., for whom the concept might have been more of a genuine concern.)

Iucunda typically denotes the pleasant aspects of the elegiac life (Pichon 1991: 176–7), e.g. Cynthia's conversation at Prop. 1.2.29, Ov.'s illicit love-making with the slave Cypassis at *Am.* 2.8.3, *otium* at *RA* 138. Elegiac usage may derive from Cat.'s fondness for the word (e.g. 14.2, 50.16, 62.26, 62.47, 66.82, 67.1, 68.16, 109.1). It is, of course, not a normal accompaniment of poverty (no other instances), which is what gives it point here. **At** marks a strong adversative: L. gallantly refuses the presents of kings if he is not to share them with N. He is on surer ground when discussing his own wants, so **volo** is in the indicative. As usual, elegists cannot manage to conceive of a middle ground between vast wealth and poverty. For **sine te** as an element of hymns, see Navarro Antolín 1996 *ad loc.* **Regum munera**: the wealth of kings—and their generosity—is proverbial (Otto 1890: 296–7); the elegists focus mostly on the Homeric Alcinous (*Od.* 7 and 8; see Fedeli *ad* Prop. 1.14.24, quoted *ad* 3.3.29), and spurn his wealth (references *ad* 3.3.29).

O niveam, quae te poterit mihi reddere, lucem!
26   O mihi felicem terque quaterque diem!

Only with this couplet does it become apparent that the poem is not a thought-experiment, and that the two lovers are apart, though the reason remains obscure. Repetition of **O** suggests emotional outburst; see Wills 1996: 357–61.

Reddere: an important verb, as Navarro Antolín 1996 notes *ad loc.*, for the L. cycle as a whole, which aims to give N. poetry so that she will give herself back to him; Pichon 1991: 251. **Niveam...lucem** is an accusative of exclamation (as often with o!); the day (*lux* commonly used for *dies*, *OLD* 5) is snowy according to the trope by which certain days were marked as black or white according to the omens or events associated with them (Pers. 2.1 *diem...meliore lapillo*, Plin. *Ep*. 6.11.3; cf. Eng. 'it was a dark day'). The precise conjunction is unparalleled in poetry, but see Aug. fr. Malcovati 5.2 *conviviae, tetricas hodie secludite curas,/ne maculent niveum †nebula corda diem*. *Candidus* is more common with both *dies* and *lux*: cf. Cat. 68.147–8 *lapide...diem candidiore*, 107.6 *o lucem candidiore nota*, Ov. *Her*. 15.124 *somnia formoso candidiora die*, *Her*. 16.320 *candidior medio nox erit illa die*, *Fas*. 5.548 *candida...dies*, *Tr*. 2.142 *nube solet pulsa candidus ire dies*. For *niveus*, see *ad* 3.1.9. **Poterit**: the future instead of a subjunctive adds both vividness and certainty, in contrast with the confusion of mood in the previous two lines.

O mihi: adds to the pathos of **o** and occurs regularly in poetry; for examples at line-start, see V. *E*. 4.53, *A*. 3.489, 8.560, [V.] *Cir*. 286, Ov. *Am*. 2.5.4, *Met*. 12.586, *Tr*. 1.3.66, 1.5.1, 3.4.1, 4.5.1, 5.14.2, *EP* 4.6.22, 4.13.1, Stat. *Silv*. 1.2.163, *Theb*. 3.295, 5.608, 7.363, 11.394, 12.811, VF. 8.10, Mart. 1.15.1, 1.76.1, 11.26.1.

The accusatives of exclamation continue; the phrase **terque quaterque** is standard poetic diction for 'again and again', especially in a *makarismos*; the closest elegiac parallel is *ter quater...felix* at Prop. 3.12.15 of Postumus' luck in his wife, on which see Fedeli 1985 *ad loc*. (cf. too *terque quaterque* at Prop. 3.7.6, of drowning). The phrase appears in Ov. of the shaking of one's locks of hair (*Am*. 3.1.32, *Met*. 1.179, 2.49), usually in anger or sorrow, or of a frenzied action (*Met*. 9.217, 12.288), sometimes without connectives (*Met*. 4.734, 6.133, 12.133, 14.206, *Fas*. 1.576, 1.657, *EP* 4.9.34). But the most likely intertext is Hor. *Od*. 1.13.17 *felices ter et amplius*, of a (similarly imaginary) secure love; cf. too *o terque quaterque beati*, the first speech of V. *A*. (1.94), which goes back to Hom. *Od*. 5.306–7 and 6.154–9; other pathetic occurrences at V. *A*. 4.589, 12.155, Luc. 5.497, Sen. *Phaed*. 694, Stat. *Theb*. 9.881, Sil. 9.159 (also in battle-scenes). The smaller number is sometimes eliminated: Tib. 1.10.63 *quater ille beatus*, Ov. *Ars* 2.447–8 *o quater et quotiens numero comprendere non est/felicem*. The number three has magical, divine, and folkloric associations (as at Tib. 1.2.54 and 1.3.11, Prop. 3.10.4, 4.6.6 and 30, and 4.8.86). **Felicem...diem** also occurs at Ter. *And*. 956, Manil. 5.568, Sen. *Troad*. 470, *Laus Pis*. 159, [V.] *Cir*. 28 (where Lyne 1978 suggests a Calvan origin), *Aetn*. 637; see Pichon 1991: 144 s.v. *felix*.

> At si, pro dulci reditu quaecumque voventur,
> 28   audiat aversa non meus aure deus,

A note of uncertainty is introduced; L. is not sure if his prayers will be answered. On the lover as the 'one who waits', see Barthes 1978: 37–40; this is for the most part true in elegy (though sometimes the poet thinks about setting off for war).

126   *Commentary on 3.3.30*

Dulci is a common word in elegy (Pichon 1991: 135–6); like *iucundus* above (see *ad* 3.3.23), it describes a wide variety of pleasant things, e.g. *coniuge* at Cat. 66.33, *carmen* at Tib. 1.3.60; cf. *ad* 3.11.7 and 3.14.3. **Reditu** occurs elsewhere in elegy in Tib. at 1.3.13, where the omens suggested that the poet would return to Delia alive, and 3.3.35 below; the word appears in a similar context, of a lover's returns (real and imagined), at Ov. *Am.* 2.11.46, *Her.* 2.26, 13.159, 19.165. It is not clear, either here or at line 35, whether there is physical distance to be covered. **Dulci reditu** occurs elsewhere only at Hor. *Epod.* 16.35.

The syntax here is difficult: **quaecumque** serves as the direct object of **audiat** (in a future less vivid protasis). Ancient prayers are most easily understood by reference to the *do ut des* formula; this means that a god might well be conceived of as being pleased by certain projected offerings and less so by others. **Voventur**: cf. Ov. *Met.* 9.675, *Ib.* 129, both in the first person referring to literal vows.

Aversa...aure introduces a traditional thought, namely that the gods may not be paying attention, or may even be deliberately hostile, but the sentiment is phrased differently from elsewhere in elegy: the gods themselves are sometimes *adversi*, as at 3.5.14, Prop. 1.1.8, Ov. *Her.* 7.4, and *EP* 3.2.18. (The idea is used of *Amor* at Prop. 1.14.15, with the same disjunction between wealth and happiness, the latter of which is only possible with love; cf. too the similar *quid Tyrio recubare toro sine amore secundo* of Tib. 1.2.75.) One can refuse to offer one's ears (*immotas* at Ov. *Met.* 15.465), or offer them readily (Prop. 1.1.31, where the god listens *facili...aure*, Prop. 2.13.15, where Cynthia's *aures* are encouraged to be *bonas*, Prop. 3.6.8 with ears *suspensis* from eagerness, *vacuas* ears at Ov. *Am.* 3.1.62 and *Met.* 4.41 and 12.56, *amicas* at *Met.* 4.77, *adrectis* at *Met.* 15.516 and frequently in V.; further citations at Enk *ad* Prop. 1.1.31). Ears can also be deaf (*surdus*: Jupiter's at Prop. 2.16.48 and Ov. *EP* 2.9.25, Prop.'s at 2.20.13, in general at Ov. *Am.* 3.7.61, and proverbially at Prop. 2.16.35–6, *quod aiunt,/turpis amor surdis auribus esse solet*); see Pichon 1991: 91 s.v. *aures* and *avertare* for related expressions. But the prosaic combination of *adverto* and *aures* occurs in elegy only at Prop. 1.1.37, *tardas adverterit aures*, in a poem which may be relevant to this one (cf. too Sil. 11.189); cf. too e.g. *adversum ad Iovem*, Hor. *Epod.* 10.18.

Non meus, i.e. hostile to me. Cf. Ov. *Her.* 12.84 *meosque deos*, TLL 8.918.8–20 and Shackleton Bailey 1954.

nec me regna iuvant nec Lydius aurifer amnis
30   nec quas terrarum sustinet orbis opes.

This couplet recapitulates: without N., wealth is unimportant. But the repetition here gains point from the fact that we now know that he does not in fact have N.

Nec...regna according to Tränkle 1990 *ad loc.*, refers also to Lydia, i.e. the kingdom of the proverbially wealthy Croesus. For the sentiment, see Prop.

1.8.32 (Cynthia swears that without Prop. she would refuse *dulcia regna*), 1.14.23-4 (Prop. himself says *non ulla verebor/regna vel Alcinoi munere despicere*), Tib. 1.8.34 (advice to a *puella* that *regum magnae despiciantur opes*); cf. too [Tib.] 3.7.198-9, where the sentiment is applied to Messalla, whose appreciation is better than *regna/Lydia*, and Greek parallels at Navarro Antolín 1996 *ad loc*. **Iuvant**'s tense reflects reality, suggesting L.'s possession of money (if not the wealth of kings).

Lydius aurifer amnis: probably the Pactolus river in Sardis, reputedly full of gold (Soph. *Phil.* 393, Call. Fr. 814; Otto 1890: 261) because King Midas washed off his 'golden touch' in it (Ov. *Met.* 11.134-145, Hyg. *Fab.* 191); Herod. 5.101 and Strabo 13.4.5, more prosaically, derive the gold from Mt. Tmolus (see too *RE* 18.2.2439-40, with further citations): the Lydian king Croesus (Prop. 2.26.23) was also notoriously wealthy. The word appears first in Latin in the Augustan poets, and esp. in Prop. (e.g. 1.6.32 *Lydia Pactoli tingit arata liquor*; cf. 1.14.11 of Pactolus by name). **Aurifer** is rare in the elegists, occurring otherwise only at Ov. *Am.* 1.15.34 of the Tagus and *Ib.* 300 of the Pactolus; the Hermus was also golden. **Aurifer amnis** only at Cat. 29.19, of the Tagus.

Opes: important to this elegy (and to the genre); the world of elegy is set in opposition to normal Roman values (or perhaps, to what elegists see as the perversion of Roman values into moneymaking and status-related concerns). This poem, however, is one of the more sustained elegiac discussions of the insignificance of wealth if it comes unaccompanied by love (see Introduction, Section I, for other, briefer treatments).

> Haec alii cupiant, liceat mihi paupere cultu
> 32   securo cara coniuge posse frui.

A summarizing *recusatio* (and indeed, this would have been an apt way to end the poem): others may prefer a lavish lifestyle, but L. wants only N. For the juxtaposition **alii...mihi**, see Bréguet 1962.

Cupiant: with the verb, L. marks off greed as an unelegiac sentiment (though the elegist is simply desirous of other things; Pichon 1991: 119).

For **paupere**, see *ad* 3.3.23. The phrase **paupere cultu** appears also at Tib. 1.10.19 in the same *sedes* (see *ad* 3.1.17 for other elegiac uses of *cultus*). In Tib. it refers to statues of the gods made of wood, and dressed in rags; L. has applied this image to himself, perhaps to invoke the world view of Tib. 1.10, which focuses on the virtues of the humble life and simpler times.

Securo: adverbial; this (*se = sine + cura*) is a state almost impossible in elegy (Ov. *Am.* 1.8.95, *ne securus amet*, warns against it, and *Her.* 19.109 wonders *quis enim securus amavit?*; see Pichon 1991: 260 for further citations, most later in the line, and below *ad* 3.4.54, 3.6.31, and 3.16.1). The fact that L. seems to need a guarantee suggests that his poetic persona has not fully assimilated the rules of love elegy (cf. Juv. 6.62 *quod securus ames*). The insecurity of human life is richly attested in the philosophical tradition (in poetry, cf. e.g. Lucr. 3.939, Hor. *Od.* 1.26.6, Tib. 1.1.48 and 77, Sen. *HF* 175, *Phaed.* 521, *HO* 652).

Liceat... posse frui: Tib. 1.5.17 *fruitur... alter amore*; for more on the sexual connotations of *fruor*, see Pichon 1991: 156. As Radford 1926 notes, the position of *fruor* is Ovidian; cf. e.g. *Her.* 20.72 *liceat dum mihi posse frui*. **Cara coniuge**: of Juno at V. *A.* 4.91, Hephaestus at *A.* 8.377, Procris at Ov. *Met.* 7.692, Dryope's husband at *Met.* 9.382, Ceyx at *Met.* 11.727, and Ov.'s own wife at *Tr.* 3.4.53 and *EP* 1.8.32, and standard in funerary epitaphs (see *ad* 3.2.30). On the marital status of N., see Introduction, Section I, and above *ad* 3.1.25–6; both words appear in that poem of N.

> Adsis et timidis faveas, Saturnia, votis,
> 34   et faveas concha, Cypria, vecta tua.

L. appeals to both Juno, goddess of marriage, and to Venus, goddess of sexual desire, using common epithets. While the collocation is attested (see e.g. their shared goals in *Aeneid* 4), their joint invocation prolongs the confusion about the status of L.'s *puella* and his relationship with her.

These **votis** are not, in fact, especially **timidis**; the phrase is Ovidian (*Met.* 9.546, *EP* 2.8.51, the latter in the same *sedes*), the adjective especially so. On *vota*, see *ad* 3.3.1. **Saturnia**: a Latin epic epithet for Juno (first at Enn. *Ann.* 64), often in this *sedes*; here it is aggrandizing but also worrying, given that the epic Juno is terrifying (V. *A.* 1.23 and *passim*, Ov. *Met.* 1.612 and *passim*, Stat. *Theb.* 10.162 and *passim*, VF 1.112 and *passim*, Sil. 2.527 and *passim*; Postgate 1929 *ad loc.* notes that it is 'usually employed where the context suggests a jealous, passionate, or formidable divinity'); see too Amerasinghe 1953 and McKay 1956.

Cypria: as Tränkle 1990 and Navarro Antolín 1996 note, this is a standard cult epithet of Aphrodite/Venus in Greek, but occurs only here in classical Latin; the adjective is common (e.g. Hor. *Od.* 3.29.60, Ov. *Met.* 10.645) and presumably was used in no-longer-extant poetry. The first syllable of **Cypria** is variously scanned short and long in classical poets; Hor., for example, has it both ways. **Concha... vecta**: a fanciful expansion of Venus' birth in the sea (*OLD* 2c; Call. *Epig.* 5, Plaut. *Rud.* 702–4, Stat. *Silv.* 1.2.118, 3.4.5, Mart. 2.47.2); according to Fulgentius she was blown across the waves on a shell (*Myth.* 2.1.40), which may be the precise part of the myth alluded to here. This conjunction does not occur elsewhere; for **concha**, see *ad* 3.3.17.

> Aut si fata negant reditum tristesque sorores,
> 36   stamina quae ducunt quaeque futura canunt,

Si fata negant an Ovidian coinage, seemingly with an epic feel (*Met.* 10.38 *quodsi fata negant veniam pro coniuge*, 10.634 *nec mihi coniugium fata importuna* *negarent*, 13.132–3 *non aequa mihi vobisque negarunt/fata*, the first two about wives); cf. Sen. *Troad*. 511 *fata si vitam negant*, Luc. 7.676 *fatisque negatum*, Stat. *Ach*. 1.549 *sed si fata negant* (same *sedes*), Sil. 1.107 *si fata negarint*, 4.635 *tumulo post fata negato*, 6.116 and 9.18 *fata negassent*.

For **tristes sorores** (not elsewhere) of the Parcae, see *tristes...Parcae* at Stat. *Theb*. 5.274; cf. *nigras...Sorores* at *Silv*. 3.3.21. The Parcae and **fata** form a kind of hendiadys, insofar as the Parcae seem sometimes above fate, and sometimes to work in conjunction with it (van der Horst 1943); cf. Cat. 64.325–6, Tib. 1.7.1–2 *hunc cecinere diem Parcae fatalia nentes/stamina*; V. E. 4.47 *concordes stabili fatorum numine Parcae* (V. A. 12.147 joins *fortuna* and the Parcae), Ov. *Met*. 8.452–3 *in flammam triplices posuere sorores/staminaque impresso fatalia pollice nentes*, Tr. 5.3.17 *dominae fati quicquid cecinere sorores*, Tr. 5.3.25 *scilicet hanc legem nentes fatalia Parcae*, Stat. *Theb*. 1.706, 8.12, *Ach*. 1.255, *Silv*. 5.2.84–5 (cf. *Theb*. 3.241–2 *Fata mihi nigraeque Sororum/iuravere colus*); further discussion at Navarro Antolín 1996 *ad loc*. The Parcae also refuse a **reditum** at Hor. *Epod*. 13.15–16. The Parcae were apparently originally one, a birth-goddess but, assimilated to the *Moirai* (*RE* 15.2.2450.49–2451.5), became three (Clotho, Lachesis, Atropo; Hes. *Th*. 905–6). They spin the threads of fate and therefore determine both length and quality of human life (*RE* 18.4.1417–9; cf. e.g. Mart. 6.58.7–8), and so have a power in some ways above that of the gods themselves. For **tristes**, see *ad* 3.2.27.

Canunt: the Parcae sing while they spin (as, presumably, many ancient females did), most famously at Cat. 64.306ff., where their song prophesies the fate of Achilles (cf. also the examples listed above, Hor. *CS* 25, [Ov.] *Ep. Drus*. 164 (with *neat*), and below *ad* 3.11.3; *CLE* 1141.16). All manuscripts have *neunt* here, emended by Heinsius to **canunt**; for the correct form of the verb (*nent*), see Tib. 1.7.1 and Ov. *Tr*. 5.3.25 (*nentes*), Mart. 1.88.9 *perneverit*, and for further discussion, Navarro Antolín 1996 *ad loc*.

Stamina...ducunt: of weaving, at e.g. Tib. 1.3.86 *deducat plena stamina longa colu*, Tib. 1.6.78 *ducit...stamina torta*, Ov. *Her*. 19.37 *tortaque versato ducentes stamina fuso*, *Met*. 4.34 *aut ducunt lanas aut stamina pollice versant*, 4.221 *levia versato ducentem stamina fuso*, 6.57 *inter stamina ductum*, Juv. 12.64–6, Mart. 6.58.7–8; cf. Maltby 1999: 244 on the vocabulary of weaving in Tib.

> me vocet in vastos amnes nigramque paludem
> 38   dives in ignava luridus Orcus aqua.

L. summarizes: dying is better than not having N. As with his first poem, this one ends with the threat of suicide; the image seems to come from Euphorion fr. 43 Powell, perhaps mediated for L. through Gallus or Prop. (cf. 2.34.91–2).

Vocet: often used of dying, as at e.g. Ov. *Her*. 7.1 (*fata*).

Amnes: see *ad* 3.3.29. **Vastos** of underworld lakes also occurs at [V.] *Cul*. 374, and *Eleg. in Maec*. 1.6. **Nigramque paludem**: also at Sen. *Thy*. 665–6, Sil. 13.573

descendit nigra lentus per stagna palude. On *niger*, see *ad* 3.2.10, and for its association with death, Navarro Antolín 1996 *ad loc.*

Dives: because all human possessions eventually revert to Hades. Both Tränkle 1990 and Navarro Antolín 1996 draw attention to the rarity of a double adjective without conjunction (though see 3.3.27 for another such juxtaposition), and prefer *ditis*; see also Schuster 1968: 153–4 and Courtney 1987: 31 for discussion of *dives*; the latter proposes *livens ignava*, with parallels). In favour of retaining **dives** is that the line then offers a final perspective on the ultimate uselessness of wealth, which turns to nothing in the end.

Ignava: see *ad* 3.4.81; the word often refers in elegy to the speed with which a lover does or does not move (e.g. Prop. 3.11.3, Ov. *Am.* 1.9.43). **In ignava...aqua**: see Navarro Antolín 1996 *ad loc.* for Greek parallels (and the text *ignavam...aquam*, printed also by Luck).

Luridus Orcus: also at Hor. *Od.* 3.4.74–5; cf. *pallidus Orcus* at e.g. V. *G.* 1.277 (cf. *ad* 3.1.28 on *pallida*). **Luridus** is a standard descriptor of the dead, or things related to death, denoting as it can a (sickly) yellowish-green colour (*TLL* 7.2.1861–3, which, however, considers it a synonym of *niger*); cf. Prop. 4.7.2 (*umbra*), 4.11.8 (*porta*), Ov. *Met.* 1.147 (poison; as the commentators *ad loc.* note, it refers to the colour of poison victims), 4.267 (pre-metamorphosis *pallor*), etc.; cf. Sil. 13.560 *Mors lurida*. **Orcus** is an uncommon poetic word for the underworld, throughout antiquity (cf. e.g. Plaut. *Asin.* 606, Cat. 3.14, *Il. Lat.* 3, Ov. *Met.* 14.116, Prop. 3.19.27; a favourite of Hor.).

3.4:

This poem, the description of a dream(?)-visitation from the god Apollo, details a situation very similar to that of Ov. *EP* 3.3, in which Amor comes to visit the exiled Ov. In the Ovidian poem, Amor is about to speak, but Ov. pre-empts him, accusing him of causing his exile and asking why he has come. Amor assures Ov. that neither of them has done anything wrong, and predicts that Augustus' anger will soften. Most of the scholarship on this poem concentrates on the relative dating of these two poems. Many find L. derivative, though others believe that Ov. copied L., or even that the two share a common model (to my mind the most satisfactory solution; see Bürger 1905 for the suggestion that it is Gallan, and Fulkerson, forthcoming, for further explication). *EP* 3.3, with its references to earlier Ovidian programmatic and theophanic poems (*Am.* 1.1.1–4, *RA* 549–58, *Met.* 1.452–76; further examples discussed below and see Kenney 1965: 44–9), seems quintessentially Ovidian, but Ov. has a particular gift for the seamless assimilation of predecessors (Ganzenmüller 1911, among others). On the other hand, L. also seems to have a penchant for picking out and expanding upon notable scenes (as with the tale of Admetus in this poem, discussed immediately below, and the named citation of Cat. in 3.6.41).

Divine epiphanies are of course common in poetry, dating all the way back to Homer and Hesiod. L. incorporates both the expected grandeur and a few whimsical touches. So too, the basic format of the dream is complex: it is both an anxiety dream and a dream of poetic inspiration (Walde 2001: 248). Divine visitations in Latin poetry fall into two basic categories: one in which gods appear to poets, narrated in the first person, to tell them what genre or style of poetry to write; the other in which they appear to heroes, narrated in the third person, to tell them about some particular of their quest (or, indeed, to announce it). The *locus classicus* for the first is Hes. *Th.* 22–34, where the Muses appear (apparently first incorporated into Latin at Enn. 1.3 Sk., where Homer appears, and later at V. *E.* 6.1–5 and Prop. 4.1.135–46, where Apollo and Horos respectively offer advice about what kind of poetry to write), but Latin poets are generally believed to refer to Call. *Aet.* frr. 1–2 Pf., where Apollo and the 'Hesiodic Muses' appear to tell the poet to avoid the well-trodden path. For another non-elegiac but Augustan quasi-epiphany, see Hor. *Ser.* 1.10.31–5, where Quirinus offers poetic advice (with Gowers 2012 *ad loc.*). This poem offers a sophisticated combination of both kinds of epiphany, insofar as L. is a poet, but also the (romantic) hero of the story; in effect, the poem outlines a(n elegiac) kind of heroic quest (see Grillone 1967 and Bouquet 2001 on dreams in Latin epic).

L. does not make it wholly clear whether he was asleep (22 is most naturally taken to mean he was), but the visitation seems to fall into the category of 'epiphanic dream' discussed by Harris 2009: 23–90, with its characteristics described at 36–7 (see too Philo, *De Somnis I*, on various kinds of prophetic dreams in the Old Testament); Versnel 1987: 49–50 notes that divine epiphanies are liable to occur in or near sleep. The ontological status of the event is left deliberately unclear: it might be a divine dream, a divine visitation, what we would call an 'anxiety dream' (genuinely occurring), or, of course, a poetic device made up by L. for his own purposes. See the introduction of P. C. Miller 1994 for discussion of how we might understand dreams as neither logical nor irrational, but rather as providing genuine access to the divine without having to be literally true, and Cic. *Div.* 1.39–70 and 2.120–50 for two radically different ancient views of prophetic dreams and their truth-value (cf. Harris 2003, especially 34 on the functions of poetic dreams); Cicero also treats portents and haruspicy. Van Lieshout 1980 provides a useful background on the study of Greek dreams; Versnel 1987 details what an ancient epiphany actually entailed, and the permeable boundaries between 'hallucination, vision and dream' (48); Cancik 1999 discusses Roman theories about dreams; and Harrisson 2013 treats the Roman understanding of what dreams as a category can mean/do. See too Hanson on the typical setting for similar dream-visions (1980: 1405–13): they tend to include details about the dreamer, the time, the place, and his/her mental state.

Apollo recognizes L. as a poet, but instead of commanding him to write poetry tells him that N. is cheating on him. But, says Apollo, all is not lost, because women are fickle, and L. can probably win her back if he becomes more like the traditional elegiac hero, i.e. persistent and repetitious; the instruction may be about real life or may be a programmatic statement about a change in L.'s poetry. This latter option is, however, only potential; 3.5 and 3.6 have little to say about N., a fact that might imply L.'s rejection of Apollo's advice, and/or of certain aspects of 'standard' Latin love elegy.

Elegiac examples of similar kinds of epiphany or prophecy are at Prop. 3.3 (in a dream, Apollo warns Prop. away from *carminis heroi* and then he visits with the Muses); Prop. 3.10 (the Muses appear to remind Prop. of Cynthia's birthday); Prop. 4.1.135–46 (discussed above); Prop. 4.6.27–54, when Apollo prophesies the Actian victory; Ov. *Ars* 2.493–510 (Apollo offers the advice, through the *praeceptor* Ovid, that would-be lovers must know themselves); Ov. *RA* 555–75 (in a dream, Cupid reminds Ovid that focusing on problems is a good way to fall out of love); Tib. 1.6.43–56 (a divinely inspired priestess of Bellona predicts dreadful things for any man who makes an attempt on Delia). Dreams about unfaithfulness are rare in elegy: the only examples are Prop. 2.26a, in which a shipwrecked Cynthia confesses her infidelity and the potentially un-Ovidian *Am.* 3.5, which is allegorical (and interpreted by an *imaginis augur*, though its meaning seems relatively clear). See too Penelope's allegorical dream at Hom. *Od.* 19.535–62, which, like Ov.'s, requires interpretation, the allegorical dolphin-dream at Ov. *Her.* 19.193–202, and Della Corte 1973 for further poetic examples. Finally, Prop. 4.7, in which the dead Cynthia makes oracular predictions to Prop. in a dream, is also relevant. Apollo positions himself as a *praeceptor amoris*, like (among other gods) Priapus in Tib. 1.4. The extent and range of these examples serve also to make clear L.'s originality; Walde 2001 and Näf 2004 discuss them, and others, at length.

In some ways, the most interesting thing about this poem is what we are to make of Apollo. He is assuredly on L.'s side, but he may be too much so for some readers: his (*delator*-like?) partisanship may undermine his authority, and his (elegiac?) hostility towards N., and perhaps towards women in general, may raise the question of his reliability. So too, Apollo himself, in Ov. *Met.* 2, had made clear that informers are unwelcome even to those they help. Further, we must consider L.'s own motivation: this poem occurs in a collection that L. sends to N. (3.1); so his retelling of the dream can be seen as coercive, threatening her with divine retribution if she does not fall in with his wishes. In keeping with metapoetic tendencies we have already seen in L. (see especially 3.1), one of the main points of this poem may lie in its treatment of the relationship between L. and Apollo; the god not only deigns to show himself to L., but implicitly enhances his status as a poet, and confirms his view of N.'s behaviour. Perhaps surprisingly, however, L. begins the poem by doubting the vision; the need to believe N. chaste overcomes even his desire to be a favourite of Apollo. Navarro Antolín 1996 suggests that Apollo appears in the poem in three distinct roles: first, as a patron of poets, then as a *magister artis*, and finally, as a prophetic *vates* (258 and 291–3). It is not clear whether the physical description of Apollo here would be immediately recognizable as a specific cult image of the god; those at the Palatine temple of Apollo are probably the most significant of these, and also the best-described in poetry (two statues, both depicting Apollo *citharoedus*, are mentioned in Prop. 2.31.5–6, 15–16). If so, that temple, dedicated in 28 BCE (see *ad* 3.4.25) may help with the dating (nominal or actual) of the cycle. We may also want to compare Tib. 2.5, on the installation of Messalinus as a *quindecimvir sacris faciundis*; that poem situates itself in the temple of Apollo, and, like Prop. 2.31 and this poem, is an atypical poem for its author.

The first portion of the poem is much concerned with truth and falsehood, and reasonably so, as L. has had a dream that he is keen to discredit. On the one hand, he wishes to erase the possibility of N.'s unfaithfulness, but on the other, the dream does hint at his ultimate success (whatever that would mean in an elegiac context). But, perhaps to tease us, we do not get the contents of the dream until late in the poem, 43–80 (and this poem is itself notably longer than any of the previous three, further drawing out the suspense).

Structurally, the poem opens with sixteen lines of introduction, speculating about the nature of dreams, and ends with sixteen lines of summary, disbelieving the content of the dream. Lines 17–80, the narrative of the dream itself, can further be divided into the arrival and description of Apollo (17–42), and his words (43–80).

> **Di meliora ferant, nec sint mihi somnia vera,**
> 2   **quae tulit hesterna pessima nocte quies.**

The poem opens prosaically, and apotropaically. Its abruptness helps to set the scene: like L. himself, who has seemingly just woken up, we are uncertain of what is happening.

Di meliora ferant: a commonplace, sometimes without the verb (V. *G.* 3.513) and sometimes with different verbs (Plaut. *Poen.* 1400 *di meliora faxint*; Ov. *Met.* 7.37 *di meliora velint*). **Somnia vera** invokes the gates of sleep from Hom. *Od.* 19.562–7, where, after reporting a dream to her disguised husband, Penelope informs him that true and false dreams have different origins; as Russo et al. 1990 note *ad loc.*, her discourse presumes that dreams at least potentially contain useful messages (see, however, the false dream sent to Agamemnon in Hom. *Il.* 2.8ff. with Kessels 1978: 35–44; normally in Homer, a god assumes the form of a person known to the dreamer). Vergil's invocation of the two gates at *A.* 6.893–901 (*geminae Somni portae, quarum altera... veris facilis datur exitus umbris*) is perhaps more directly relevant; see Austin *ad loc.* for further citations of the proverbial notion. Romans seem to have believed that true(r) dreams happened at dawn (Ov. *Her.* 19.195–6; see *ad* 3.4.17 for the timing of this dream).

Hesterna...nocte is presumably a common phrase; see too Tib. 2.1.12, where (more naturally, for an elegist), it refers to sex and is separated by *gaudia*

134   *Commentary on 3.4.4*

(cf. *TLL* 6.3.2668.28–38 for other citations, including Prop. 2.29.1, featuring the divine epiphany of many tiny cupids, and below *ad* 3.18.5). See too Cat. 50.1, *hesterno die*, a poem also full of tropes of poetic inspiration, and Ov. *Her.* 19.193 *hesternae . . . imagine noctis*, of a dream. **Hesterna** is the reading of some of the manuscripts; *externa* of others makes little sense, but there is good reason to consider *extrema*, found in one manuscript.

Pessima quies: not attested elsewhere (nor is the comparative or positive degree of the adjective with this noun). For most poets, **quies** is beneficial (as shown by the fact that it often appears with *grata*, *muta*, *placida*, *secura*, etc.); night is for the elegists a time of potentially great joy, but also potentially great sorrows; note *mala somnia* of Tib. 2.6.37. **Quies** appears in the *CT* only in this poem, here and at line 22, where it denotes L. falling asleep; the elevation of L.'s diction is noteworthy.

   Ite procul, vani, falsumque avertite visum:
4 desinite in nobis quaerere velle fidem.

Ite: normally at line-start, and often repeated, sometimes in such 'liturgical' phrases; see V. *E.* 1.74, 7.44, 10.77. **Ite procul**: elevated in tone; appears also at line-start at *CT* 1.1.76, 2.4.15, 2.4.20, 3.6.7, Prop. 4.6.9. **Vani** is vocative (the sense would be helped by a noun, e.g. *visus* at the end of the line; see below). See discussion at Schuster 1968: 155–6 (who prefers *vanis*), Tränkle 1990 (who prints *vanum*), and Navarro Antolín 1996 *ad loc*. The adjective appears thrice more in this poem (13, 56, 68, the first two referring to dreams), as well as in 3.5.27 and 3.6.60, so we are entitled to think of it as a favourite word of L. Here it is apotropaic; L. hopes that the dream is untrue. Cf. Prop. 1.3.28 and 3.6.31 for its use of dreams (in the first, Prop. fears that Cynthia is having a bad dream, and in the second—which features a slave named L.; cf. Introduction, Section IV—he hopes his own dreams are not *vanus*). It occurs of night-time *simulacra*, no longer feared by the lover, at Ov. *Am.* 1.6.9, of *somnia* at *Met.* 11.614 in the cave of Sleep, and of the ways the timid are frightened even by *vana umbra* at *EP* 2.7.14. All of these uses are similar, but none provides a true parallel; the text may well be corrupt (without a noun, **vani** ought to refer to the gods).

Falsum . . . visum: prosaic; cf. e.g. Cic. *Div*. 2.121. See Navarro Antolín 1996 *ad loc.* for an argument for reading *visus* (and taking with *vani*), first proposed by Bolle (see Lee 1974: 57 and Navarro Antolín 1996 *ad loc.* who, with Luck, prints *visus*). The adjective is proleptic with **avertite**: L. asks for the dream to be turned away and so made false. Printing *visus* renders **falsum** substantive; this is not impossible, but not ideal (see further Navarro Antolín 1996 *ad loc.*).

Desinite: regularly with an infinitive; cf. Tib. 1.8.7, Prop. 1.15.25, 2.18.29, 2.34.41–2, 4.11.1, Ov. *Am.* 2.2.10, 3.4.11, 3.11.31, *Her.* 15.202, 17.111, *RA* 531, *EP* 1.6.24, 3.6.43, 4.16.48, [Ov.] *Ep. Drus.* 38 for elegiac imperatives at line-start (rare in poetry after the Augustans). See too *ad* 3.4.80, where it is directed to N.

In nobis: for the manuscripts' *in votis*, see Navarro Antolín 1996 *ad loc.*, who prints *in ventis* and discusses other emendations.

Quaerere...fidem: 'don't expect to find credit in us'; for similar phrases, Ov. *Ars* 1.612 *haec tibi quaeratus qualibet arte fides*, Manil. 2.87 *quaerenda fides*, Luc. 9.140 *fidem quaesisse*, Sen. *Phaed.* 826 *quaerit...fidem*, *Oed.* 837 *quaeram fidem*, Stat. *Theb.* 1.502–3 *quaesitam...fidem*. The injunction to stop seeking *fides* has multiple meanings in an elegiac context (Pichon 1991: 147–8). It is not used by the *CT* poets to signify the desired relationship with a *puella* (partial exceptions at 1.9.32, where Marathus has sworn not to sell his—with a nearly identical pentameter ending, *vendere velle fidem*—and at 3.6.49, where Jupiter permits there to be *nulla fides* in the words of a lover), but this is the standard word for it in elegy outside of the *CT*; see e.g. Cat. 64.144, Prop. 1.4.16, 1.18.18, 2.20.4, 18, and 34, 2.26.27, Ov. *Am.* 1.3.6 (with useful further detail *ad loc.* in McKeown 1989), 13, and 16, 2.9.50 (among many examples, the last one undermining the claim as it makes it). We might, without much of a stretch, imagine these to be the words the *puella* would use in a rather different context.

> Divi vera monent, venturae nuntia sortis
> 6   vera monent Tuscis exta probata viris;

In this and the following couplet, L. explicates his oneiric philosophy via a priamel: haruspicy and omens are valid, dreams are of a less secure status (note too Tib. 1.8.3–4 and 2.1.25–6). Divination held an important place in the Roman world, and there is evidence in antiquity for the belief that prophetic dreams tell the truth (see introduction to this poem). It is, however, nearly impossible to distinguish genuine from misleading divine messages (see introduction to this poem for some of the issues, and also *passim* in the commentary on this poem).

Vera monent: see *ad* 3.4.11 *vera moneri* and e.g. Tib. 2.4.51 *vera quidem moneo*. There is some difficulty with the phrase; not all gods give warnings, and L. here seems to be setting up a false dichotomy between gods and (divine) dreams, which are not exclusive; see Navarro Antolín 1996 *ad loc*. **Venturae nuntia sortis**: it is probably best to take **nuntia** as appositional with **exta** (see Navarro Antolín 1996 *ad loc.* for other possibilities). For parallels to the phrase, cf. *nuntia ventura* V. *A.* 8.550 and Ov. *Met.* 14.726, *venturi nuntia luctus* at Ov. *Met.* 5.549; it occurs more commonly with the verb *nuntio*. Note too *eventura* at Tib. 2.1.25; that couplet is a probable intertext. See Navarro Antolín 1996 on the varying punctuation of the hexameter, and for the case for reading *divae vera monent, venturi nuntia, sortes*.

Tuscis: Etruscans were famous for all sorts of divination, but especially haruspicy (Cic. *Div.* 1.3; *RE* 7.2.2432.34–9 and *passim*), although this component of Etruscan identity is not much mentioned by the elegists (the concerns of Roman state religion are not those of the elegists; see Berthet 1991, 94–5 on this passage). There is no need to believe, with some, that L. displays specialist knowledge and so reveals himself to be Etruscan. **Tuscis** appears most often in the elegists of the Tiber (as at 3.5.39), occasionally of the land itself, wars, or individuals. **Viris** is not strictly necessary (Postgate 1915 *ad loc.*), and does not appear elsewhere with the adjective; the noun may be included here in order to distinguish these (legitimate) interpreters from the suspect old women who people elegy (*anus* at e.g. Prop. 2.4.16, Tib. 1.5.12–14, Ov. *Ars* 2.328–30).

Probata: Navarro Antolín 1996 suggests *ad loc.* that the proper perfect participle is *prosecta* (e.g. Ov. *Met.* 12.152), but *probo*, although unusual, gives the proper sense (see *TLL* 10.2.1461.13–57 for a typology). The participle is seemingly technical, and connected to **exta** at Serv. *ad G.* 2.194: *REDDIMVS EXTA sacerdotum usus est verbo; reddi enim dicebantur exta, cum probata et elixa arae superponebantur.*

    somnia fallaci ludunt temeraria nocte
8   et pavidas mentes falsa timere iubent.

In the end of the priamel, L. asserts that dreams are deceptive. On the falseness of dreams, see *ad* 3.4.1 above. Dreams, though a single thing, are given two 'false' descriptors, **fallaci** and **falsa**, to match the double *vera* in the previous couplet. Are they perhaps doubly false?

Ludunt: the verb is transitive (*OLD* 9b), 'to mislead', as often (e.g. Tib. 1.6.9, *TLL* 7.2.1780.1–37); precise parallels occur at Petr. 128.6 *nocte soporifera veluti cum somni ludunt/errantes oculos* and Petr. fr. 30.1–2, *somnia quae mentes ludunt volitantibus umbris/non delubra deum nec ab aethere numina mittunt.* Cf. too Plaut. *Merc.* 225–6 *miris modis di ludos faciunt hominibus/mirisque exemplis somnia in somnis danunt.* **Temeraria**: rare in other elegists (Prop. 2.8.13, and see *ad* 3.6.27) but frequent in Ov.; not elsewhere joined with **somnia**. The adjective may have special point, categorizing dreams: those which come by chance are deceitful (so too, **fallaci** may or may not be limiting). **Ludunt temeraria** and **pavidas timere** are, like the two *veras* and **fallaci/falsa**, doublets of one another.

With **fallaci...nocte**, elegiac vocabulary is used to slightly different effect: normally, nights are deceptive because the *amator* has been cheated of time with the *puella* (a *coniunx* is tricked at Tib. 1.6.15, Tib. by Venus/Marathus at 1.9.83; the (generic) *puella* is *fallax* at 3.6.47 and 51). The dream-Apollo vouches for his own truthfulness below, at 50—but liars often do; cf. in this context the Hesiodic Muses (*Th.* 22–34, the *locus classicus* for deceptive divinities), who claim that nobody can tell the difference between their lies and their truth. This is perhaps a function of the human condition: communications from the gods, whatever lines 5–6 suggest, are never unambiguous (see too line 77, where Apollo seems less confident about oracles). Similar phrases occur at Cat. 64.56 *fallaci...somno* (of Ariadne's awakening to find herself abandoned), Val. Max. 1.7ext.9 *haud fallaci nocturna imagine*, Sen. *Dial.* 1.6.3 *fallacique somnio*; VF 7.213 *velut lenti fallatur imagine somni*.

Pavidas mentes: parallels at Lucr. 6.51 (in response to lightning, viewed as a divine sign), Petr. 89.1.17, superlative at Sen. *Dial.* 3.20.5, *Phaed.* 1082; *TLL* 10.815.49–63 with further examples. The phrase may be proleptic, or may specify the kinds of minds (those already prone to fear) that believe in false dreams. **Iubent** is used in its weakest sense (*OLD* 7: 'ask, bid, invite'); perhaps 'encourage'.

    Et natum in curas hominum genus omina noctis
10   farre pio placant et saliente sale.

Although the meaning is fairly clear, the text as transmitted in line 9 (*natum maturas*, printed only by Postgate 1915 and Tränkle 1990, in *cruces*) is impossible; see Navarro Antolín 1996 *ad loc.* for extended discussion of variants of the manuscript text. Of the numerous suggestions, *vanum metuens* is also plausible (though repeating *vani* from line 3): we badly want something to elucidate *hominum genus*.

    Hominum genus a standard phrase, first in poetry in Lucretius (and so perhaps retaining a Lucretian flavour, especially in this context, one of religious superstition). **Omina** signify dreams only in Ov. *Her.* 9.39–40, Luc. 7.22; *TLL* 9.2.576.36–48. The phrase is unattested, but cf. Prop. 4.4.23, *omina lunae* at line-end (which has nothing to do with dreams). **Omina...placant** paralleled at Plaut. *Epid.* 396 *omen placet*, Serv. *ad A.* 3.262: *aves sunt, eas dicit placandas propter pessima omina*. As Navarro Antolín 1996 notes *ad loc.*, *piare* is the expected verb in this context; it does not scan, and may also be avoided to prevent **pio** *piare* before **saliente sale**.

    Farre is **pio** as a standard offering to the gods (*TLL* 6.1.278.6–11, 37–73), often in the form of cakes made of barley flour and salt (*mola salsa*); cf. V. *A.* 5.745 *farre pio* in the same *sedes*, Hor. *Od.* 3.23.20 *farre pio et saliente mica*, Ov. *Fas.* 1.128 (*farraque mixta sale*, with Bömer 1958 *ad loc.* for further detail and citations), 1.338 (*far* and *mica salis*), 3.284 (*farraque salsa*), and 4.409 (*farra deae micaeque licet salientis honorem*). **Saliente sale**: alliteration is not favoured by L., but he here alludes to the etymological connection (Isid. *Or.* 16.2.3; Maltby 1991 and Ernout and Meillet 2001 *ad loc.*): as salt is heated, its water is released and turned to steam, which makes it crackle and appear to move (*salire*). The figure is avoided at Hor. *Od.* 3.23.20 (quoted above). **Far** and **sal** might be a hendiadys, referring to the single cake, but this makes **saliente** essentially meaningless.

    Et tamen, utcumque est, sive illi vera moneri,
12   mendaci somno credere sive volent,

Utcumque est is a summing-up phrase (prosaic and rare, as is *utcumque sit*); L. doesn't care if the dream was originally true or false, but wants to render it invalid. The hexameter is vexed: **illi** as a dative (of agent) might refer to *genus* of line 9; if nominative, it could denote *timores* of line 13 or, *hominum* by enallage; the problem is exacerbated by difficulty with the verb (*monenti* in most manuscripts; Navarro Antolín 1996 alone among modern editors prints the transmitted reading), and neither eases the sense of the pentameter. There must be some corruption. **Vera moneri**: the passive form of the verb is difficult; perhaps best as an internal (adverbial) accusative.

Mendaci somno: not a common collocation, elsewhere only at Ov. *Her.* 13.107 (Laodamia has *mendaces somnos*, believing in her sleep that her husband is with her; *Am.* 3.6.17 and *Fas.* 6.253 refer to *mendacia vatum*, which are also at issue here); nothing else in the *CT* is *mendax* excepting *ore* at 3.6.35, where L. seeks to hide his sorrows; cf. *TLL* 8.704.65–9.

Volent: the construction of the two parts of the couplet is not quite parallel: the middle-passive **moneri**, if correct, has a different sense from the active **credere**, which needs a subject (it must mean something like 'feel trust in'). See Tränkle 1990 for defence of *volent* (though he prints Postgate's *solent*, as does Navarro Antolín 1996). For amatory uses of *credere*, see Pichon 1991: 115.

    efficiat vanos noctis Lucina timores
14   et frustra immeritum pertimuisse velit,

Vanos noctis…timores: a standard concept, in both Greek (Soph. *El.* 410, AR 4.685) and Latin (closest parallel is Ov. *Am.* 1.6.9 *at quondam noctem simulacraque vana timebam*; cf. Ov. *Her.* 16.344 *vanos…metus*, *EP* 3.6.43 *mitem animum vano infamare timore*; [Ov.] *Hal.* 50 *vani quatiunt…timores*, Sen. *Thy.* 839 *demet nocti Luna timores*). **Vanos** proleptic, to signify the desired effect; L. hopes his prayers will be effective, so must not discount all communication between human and divine.

Lucina, the goddess of childbirth (Capella 2.149, Porph. 3.22.2–3 *Quam ideo Lucinam appellamus, quod lucem nascentibus tribuat*, *RE* 13.2.1648–51; in elegy at Prop. 4.1.99, Ov. *Her.* 6.122, 11.55, *Ars* 3.785, *Fas.* 2.449–51, 3.255, 6.39), is normally identified with either Juno Lucina (Plaut. *Aul.* 692, probably *Truc.* 476, Cic. *DND* 2.68, Ov. *Fas.* 6.39; distinguished from Juno at Ov. *Met.* 9.294; see *ad* 3.1.1) or Artemis Eilithuia or Lucifera (Hor. *CS* 14–15, V. *E.* 4.10 = *Buc. Eins.* 2.38, Isid. *Or.* 8.11.57, quoting V. *A.* 4.511, and see Servius *ad loc.* and MacFarlane 1980 for explanation) or both (Cat. 34.13), and therefore, sometimes with Junonian spring festivals such as the Matronalia (see *ad* 3.1.1; further details in *RE*). Her presence here makes sufficient sense, as her name is etymologically connected with *lux*, i.e. the light of life (Varro *DLL* 5.69, Cic. *DND* 2.68, Ov. *Fas.* 2.449–52, 3.255, 6.39; alternative etymology from *lucus* at Ov. *Fas.* 2.449–50 and Plin. *NH* 16.235). Further, (Juno) Lucina is a kind of tutelary deity in the corpus. But nowhere else is she connected to dreams. Because of her connection to Juno, L. may see **Lucina** as a defender of marital or quasi-marital fidelity

(Sen. *Med.* 1–2 features Lucina as *genialis tori... custos*). Other goddesses seem more appropriate: Luna (Sen. *Thy.* 839, quoted above), or Hecate in her chthonic and ghost-sending capacity (*RE* 7.2.2772.46–2774.34 with citations). Herrmann emends to *Lucifer*, which solves the problem but does not scan. It may simply be that L. wants the etymological pun (see *ad* 3.4.10) or the connection with the Matronalia.

Immeritum: the elegist generally finds it hard to believe that he deserves punishment: Tib. 1.6.72, *CT* 3.5.6, where L. assures Persephone that he does not deserve to die (perhaps the occurrence there is an affirmation of the claim here, or perhaps he is mistaken in both places), Prop. 2.4.3, 2.25.18. L. would prefer to fear for no reason than to find that his portentous dream is real; cf. *si merui* at Tib. 1.2.85.

Frustra: a final long *a* is not often elided before a long *i*; see Platnauer 1951: 75 for examples. **Pertimuisse**: more often uncompounded in the elegists except Ov. (*Her.* 9.74, 12.141, 16.352, 21.1, *Ars* 1.14, 3.526, *Fas.* 2.340, 6.244, *EP* 3.1.156); the verb is regular in Plautus. On the perfect infinitive with present meaning ('I have become frightened'), see Perotti 1989: 142 n. 2.

    si mea nec turpi mens est obnoxia facto
16   nec laesit magnos impia lingua deos.

L. clarifies: he asks for this favour from the gods only if he is innocent. The prevalence of conditionals in this poem perhaps suggests that L. lacks confidence, and the situation is similar to Tib. 1.2.79–86, where the phrase **impia lingua** also appears (see below); in that poem, Tib. asserts his piety, but elsewhere he confesses to impiety, to rather different effect.

Si, according to Navarro Antolín 1996 *ad loc.*, fits poorly here and shows L.'s dependence on Tib. 1.2. Perhaps instead he simply adopts a cautious scepticism (cf. *OLD* 12); one never knows what the gods will object to; cf. Cat. 76.1–6, which begins *siqua... voluptas/est homini*, a passage with similar content and assumptions. 3.5.7–14 make the case for L.'s innocence at greater length.

Turpi... facto: a dative governed by **obnoxia**, 'inclined towards' or 'subject to' (*OLD* 3a with examples; in poetry often in this *sedes*); perhaps here 'guilty of'. *Turpis* occurs regularly in the elegists of the lover's situation or behaviour (this collocation at Ov. *Her.* 9.20, of Hercules' unmanly behaviour; see too Monteil 1964: 261–307, Pichon 1991: 285–6, and *ad* 3.6.37 and 3.8.4). And for a typically elegiac distinction between means and ends, see Ov. *Ars* 3.218 *multaque, dum fiunt, turpia, facta placent*.

Impia is not often used in elegy (Pichon 1991: 171). Tib. uses the word of sacrilegious speech (1.2.82 **impia lingua** in same *sedes*, 1.3.52 *impia verba* in same *sedes*; cf. *ad* 3.4.59) and those being punished in the underworld (1.3.70). L. claims that he is not *impius* at 3.5.14, and depicts Cat.'s Theseus as performing *impia facta* at 3.6.42 (the only other uses of the word in the *CT*). Propertius calls the *puella* (presumably Cynthia) *impia* when he is berating her for not being able to sleep alone for one night (Prop. 2.9.20) and also when she reneges on a promised night (Prop. 2.17.13). Prop. 2.9 may also be relevant in line 63 below, where the possibility of changing N.'s mind is mentioned.

Laesit: gods frequently perceive themselves as being harmed by human impiety, and *laedere* is the word usually used of profanation (e.g. [Tib.] 3.6.26, Ov. *Tr.* 1.5.84, *EP* 1.4.44 *laesi...dei*, 2.3.68 *laesum...deum*; cf. the similar phrases *manes...meos* at Tib. 1.1.67 and *magnorum numen laesura deorum* at Hor. *Epod.* 15.3; Bömer *ad* Ov. *Met.* 1.387 provides further citations, and see too *TLL* 7.2.868.84–869.32). The verb is a favourite of L.'s, with a variety of meanings; see *ad* 3.5.15, 3.6.26, and the opposite statement, that gods do not harm lovers, at 3.10.15.

Magnos a regular epithet of **deos** (*OLD* 12b), first in extant poetry at Enn. *Ann.* 6.190 (*volentibus cum magnis dis*), and regularly thereafter, perhaps with epic implications (cf. e.g. V. *A.* 3.12).

> Iam Nox aetherium nigris emensa quadrigis
> 18   mundum caeruleo laverat amne rotas,

This section begins the description of the disturbing dream with a lengthy, epic prelude. As McKeown notes *ad* Ov. *Am.* 1.5 (with full citations), the phrase *aestus/nox erat* is frequent in erotic contexts; he terms *Am.* 1.5 'an erotic epiphany'; see Stearns 1927: 21–2 n. 65 and Currie 1993 on *nox erat* (which introduces the dream-sequence at Ov. *EP* 3.3.5). The phrase here may, therefore, have misleading implications. For the ancient notion that dreams later in the night are truer, see Mosch. *Eur.* 2–3 with Campbell 1991 *ad loc.*, Hor. *Ser.* 1.10.33, Ov. *Her.* 19.195–6, Philostr. *VA* 2.37 (near dawn, because the body has purged itself of wine), with discussion at Stearns 1927: 51–69. Navarro Antolín 1996 and Tränkle 1990 *ad loc.* see Ov. *Her.* 19.195–6 (quoted *ad* 3.4.21–2) as the main model for this passage, and note that that poem makes clear what is left obscure in L., namely, that the dream is a trustworthy one because of its timing. But the notion seems to be so generally held as to need no specific antecedent. On the neoterics' interest in 'temporal ecphrasis' (here denoted by **iam**), see Parca 1986: 472, and for other examples, usually at the line-start, cf. e.g. Ov. *Fas.* 2.813, [V.] *Cul.* 42, 107, 202, *Mor.* 1.

Aetherium...mundum: for the (grandiose) collocation, see Enn. *Var.* 103 *quod supra mundum erat, quod aether vocabatur*, [V.] *Cul.* 102. **Nox** is regularly personified in Greek and Latin poetry (e.g. Aesch. *Ch.* 660–1, Eur. *Ion* 1150, Enn. *Andr.* 117, V. *A.* 5.721, Tib. 2.1.87 *iungit equos*, all with chariot); where specified in earlier Latin, the chariot is more often a *biga* (as Postgate 1929 notes *ad loc.*) whereas Sol and Aurora drive *quadrigae* (e.g. Plaut. *Amph.* 422, V. *A.* 6.535).

Emensa: a verb not found elsewhere in *CT* or Prop.; *emensas...noctes* occurs at Ov. *Met.* 15.186 *emensas in lucem tendere noctes*, *emensus* at *Fas.* 1.544 (of

Hercules' journey); cf. VF 3.227 *nocte remensa*, Sil. 3.555 *emensi noctes*. As Navarro Antolín 1996 notes *ad loc.*, the verb covers both distance and time, so is especially appropriate here.

Nigris...quadrigis: the horses of night are black, as we might expect, because her chariot travels in the dark, and is unseen (Aurora's, by contrast, are *roseis* at V. A. 6.535); for the horses, cf. Ov. Am. 1.13.40 *noctis equi*, EP 1.2.54 *pruinosi Noctis...equi*. This collocation does not occur elsewhere; on *niger*, see *ad* 3.2.10.
Laverat...rotas: the closest parallels are at V. G. 3.359 *Oceani rubro lavit aequore currum* (of the sun), Tib. 2.5.60 *Solis anhelantes abluit amnis equos*. The trope combines both the care of animals after a journey and the fact that night's chariot ends up in the Ocean.

Caeruleo...amne: of the sea: cf. Stat. *Silv.* 1.5.51, where it describes a river (and V. A. 8.64 for the *figura etymologica caerulus/caelum*); cf. also Morel *Incert.* 78.1 *vallis per imas amne labens caerulo*. On the colour as, despite etymology, referring to a dark, 'midnight' blue, see *OLD* 9b, André 1949: 162–71. By a typical transference from divine being to quality, wherever **Nox** is, it is nighttime (perhaps we are meant to think of the western sky, where the dawn has not yet permeated).

> nec me sopierat menti deus utilis aegrae:
> 20   Somnus sollicitas deficit ante domos.

Lenz/Galinsky print no connective between the lines; in keeping with most other editions, I add a colon. By contrast with Ov. *EP* 3.3.7–8, L. asserts that he was not sleeping until the dawn broke (though his description appears in the same relative location of the narrative as Ov.'s claim to be asleep in *EP* 3.3). There is an odd disjunction between L's claim not to be able to sleep and the prior assertion that it was a dream, which adds to the mystery of this poem. So too, we might wonder why he was (already) sleepless; Apollo's news seems to be no news at all.

Sopierat: a relatively rare verb, appearing in elegy most often as the perfect participle, as at Tib. 2.6.38, where Nemesis' dead sister appears in a dream. The combination **menti...aegrae** can signify insanity (e.g. Cic. *TD* 3.8.12) but also distress (e.g. Liv. 2.42.10.2). In the poets, it mostly signifies mental anguish of various sorts (e.g. Ov. *Tr.* 3.8.25 and 33 and *passim* in the exile poetry; *contra*, *aeger* at Tib. 1.3.3. of a seemingly physical illness), including lovesickness (e.g. Prop. 2.4.11, Ov. *RA* 109, 313–4; Pichon 1991: 81), which may be L.'s malady (La Penna 1951: 206–7). Cf. too 3.5.11, where some manuscripts have *aegros*. *Aeger* also appears with *animus*, of lovesickness (e.g. Enn. *Tr.* 216 *Medea animo aegro amore saevo saucia*); see further Introduction, Section I.

It is surprising to find a **deus** referred to as **utilis**; the adjective is frequent in Ov. (*Fas.* 3.173 *deus utilis armis* at line-end, of Mars, is the closest parallel, but see too *Tr.* 3.3.9 *cibus utilis aegro*, also at line-end). **Somnus**, a kind of gloss on line 19, is personified throughout Greek and Latin poetry (e.g. Hes. *Th*. 211, 758, where he is the son of Night and brother of Death). Perhaps his most memorable personification in Latin poetry is at Ov. *Met*. 11.592–673 (deriving from Hom. *Il*. 14.233–91), where he appears to Alcyone in a vision (Bömer 1980 *ad loc*.). He can drive the chariot of Night (Stat. *Theb*. 2.59, Claud. *Carm*. 15.213–4), and is sometimes part of her retinue (Tib. 2.1.89–90 *postque venit tacitus furvis circumdatus alis/ Somnus et incerto Somnia nigra pede*). Sleep is generally pleasant (e.g. Hom. *Il*. 2.71 γλυκύς), and seen as incompatible with cares (e.g. V. *A*. 2.268–9, Ov. *Met*. 11.624 *quem cura fugit*); here, however, he is imagined as refusing to visit those burdened by anxiety. See too Harrisson on anxiety dreams (2013: 105–6, 155–6).

The soothing sounds of **somnus sollicitas** (despite the meaning of the adjective) suggest L.'s final descent into sleep (there may be a similar effect at the end of Stat. *Silv*. 5.4). For **sollicitas** of anxious lovers or of love itself, see Ov. *Am*. 1.15.38, *Her*. 1.12, 18.196, *Ars* 3.472, 600, *RA* 557, and below, 3.6.36. Insomnia is a regular accompaniment of anxiety (Currie 1993, with citations), and the elegiac lover often cannot sleep: e.g. Tib. 1.2.75–80, 1.8.64, 2.4.11, Prop. 1.1.33, 2.17.3–4, 2.22.47–8, 4.3.29, Ov. *Am*. 1.2.1–4 and McKeown *ad loc*. with further citations, *Her*. 19.55–6, *Ars* 1.735–6; V. *E*. 10.6 *sollicitos Galli dicamus amores* may suggest a Gallan pedigree for the adjective's use in elegy. Note L.'s claim at 3.6.59–61 that he will no longer lose sleep because of love.

Deficit ante domos: the manuscripts' reading; **ante** is variously emended because it does not elsewhere mean 'in the face of'; **deficit** is also sometimes altered to *desit* or *deserit*.

Tandem, cum summo Phoebus prospexit ab ortu,
22   **pressit languentis lumina sera quies.**

Only with the break of day does L. finally fall asleep, which may be connected to the truth-value of early morning dreams (above, *ad* 3.4.17), but also to the fact that Apollo is regularly assimilated to the sun-god, and so an especially appropriate visitant at this time of the day. Ov. *Her*. 19.195–6 has many similarities with this passage: *Namque sub aurora, iam dormitante lucerna/somnia quo cerni tempore vera solent*.

Cum: cf. Ov. *EP* 3.3.9 *cum subito pinnis agitatus inhorruit aër*. **Prospexit ab ortu**: the verb is common with celestial deities (Ceres at Tib. 2.5.58, *Lucifer* at Luc. 10.434, *Phoebi iuga* at Sil. 15.223). **Summo … ab ortu** is somewhat troubling as the sun ought not yet to have risen; Heyne 1798: 203–4 suggests construing as 'from the upper edge of his disc' (and see Navarro Antolín 1996 *ad loc*); Rabirius (230 Hollis 2007, with discussion and citation of Ov. *Fas*. 3.361) may be of help: *Idaeos summa cum margine colles*. **Ab ortu**: frequent, and nearly always at line-end, even outside of hexameter (Ov. *Her*. 16.143, *Met*. 2.112, 6.49, 15.619, *Tr*. 1.2.27, 5.8.25, *EP* 1.4.29, 3.1.127, Germ. *Arat*. 340, *Il. Lat*. 867; Hor. *Od*. 3.27.12). Navarro Antolín 1996 suggests *summa Oeta* as at Sen. *HF* 133

Titan summa prospicit Oeta; see too *CLE* 1109.7–8 (though the relevance of Oeta is not clear); Ov. *Her.* 19.195 (quoted above) provides a similar construction, and AR 1.1273, of the morning-star, may provide a Greek parallel.

Phoebus appears both as the sun-god and as L.'s visitor; for such mixing of aspects, cf. e.g. Achelous in Ov. *Met.* 15.550–9, who (in human form) warns visitors that he (in river form) may drown them. For Apollo as Helios, see the discussion at Navarro Antolín 1996 *ad loc.*, with the first secure attestation in Eur. *Phaeth.* 224–5 Diggle (1970 *ad loc.*).

Pressit: used of falling or being asleep at e.g. V. *A.* 12.908–9 *ac velut in somnis, oculos ubi languida pressit/nocte quies*, Prop. 1.10.7 *labentis premeret mihi somnus ocellos*, Ov. *Met.* 15.21 *pressum gravitate soporis*, VF 5.334 *premit alta quies*; *OLD* 18. The verb, joined with eyes, occurs more regularly of dying (as at e.g. Ov. *Am.* 3.9.49, Sen. *Ag.* 493, Stat. *Silv.* 5.1.196): *CIL* 11.1122.7–8: *nos aetate pares dulcis dum vita manebat/unus amor iunxit nunc premit una quies*; this may be a hint that death, and its vocabulary, are never far from L.'s mind.

Languentis and *languidus* are not uncommon in elegy, especially of post-coital lassitude (Tib. 1.9.56, Prop. 1.3.38, 1.13.15, Ov. *Am.* 2.2.21, 2.10.35, *Ars* 2.692), and of someone simply sleeping in elegy only at Prop. 1.3.2. See *ad* 3.5.28 for the verb used of illness (perhaps metaphorical; see *ad* 3.4.19 *aegrae*).

Sera quies: elsewhere at V. *A.* 8.30 (*seramque dedit per membra quietem*), where Aeneas falls asleep late in the night, and the river-god Tiberinus appears to him with a true and prophetic dream; also Stat. *Theb.* 3.393 *animosaque pectora laxet sera quies*. On **quies**, see *ad* 3.4.2.

> **Hic iuvenis casta redimitus tempora lauro**
> 24 **est visus nostra ponere sede pedem.**

It is striking that although L. has been waiting for the god Somnus, Apollo arrives, unbidden. Although Apollo is not a sleep-bringing god, he does sing to L. (39; possibly a lullaby). Apollo, as a god of poetry, appears with some regularity in poetry (see introduction to this poem). The closest parallels to this depiction in terms of its details are probably Call. *Hymn Ap.* 32–42, Ov. *Met.* 3.420–3, 482–5, 11.165–8 (only the latter actually of Apollo); see Axelson 1960a: 99–101 and Büchner 1965: 107–11 for treatment of Ovidian parallels to this passage. It is also likely that L. refers to one of the statues in the Palatine temple of Apollo (see introduction to this poem).

Redimitus occurs here and at 3.4.87, below, and in Tib. 1.7.45 (of Osiris). Ov. in his elegies generally puts the word in the next metrical *sedes*, but sometimes in this one. Parallels to **redimitus tempora lauro** occur at V. *A.* 3.81 (identical), *G.* 1.349 *redimitus tempora quercu*, Ov. *Am.* 3.10.3, *Fas.* 1.711 and 5.79 *redimita capillos*, *Her.* 6.115, *Am.* 3.11.29 and *Met.* 6.321 *redimita corona*, *Met.* 14.654 *redimitus tempora mitra*, *Fas.* 3.269 *redimita coronis*, 4.661 *redimitam papavere frontem*, Sen. *Oed.* 430 *redimitus tempora sertis*, VF 1.278 *redimitus tempora vittis*;

cf. Sil. 11.484 *lauro redimita* (of a ship). **Tempora lauro**: identical line-ending at Tib. 2.5.5, V. A. 5.246, 539, [V.] *Cir.* 121 (where Lyne 1978 suspects corruption), Ov. *Am.* 2.12.1 (*laurus*), [Ov.] *Ep. Drus.* 459, VF 4.334. See too the description of Apollo at Ov. *Met.* 11.165–6: *ille caput flavum lauro Parnaside vinctus/verrit humum Tyrio saturata murice palla*.

Casta...lauro: not otherwise attested (but cf. *sacra* at V. A. 3.81, and Caes. Strab. fr. 2 Ribbeck, *cum capita viridi lauro velare imperant/Prophetae sancti, caste qui purant sacra*), but unsurprising given that Daphne changed into a tree in order to avoid the advances of Apollo; see *Met.* 1.452–567 for Ov.'s version of the story, mentioned also at Hyg. *Fab.* 203, Parth. *Erot.* 14 (alternative version at Paus. 10.7.8). The ironies inherent in Apollo's lack of amatory success (esp. in Ov. *Met.*; see J. F. Miller 1998), given that he presents himself as an authority, are latent here but come to the fore at 67ff. **Lauro** will tip off most readers that the visitor in question is Apollo, one of whose Greek epithets is *daphnephoros* (although Ovidians might expect Cupid; cf. Cairns 1979: 126 on Ovid's regular move of substituting Cupid for the more standard Apollo as a god of poetic inspiration in *Am.* 1.1.1, *Ars* 1.7–30 and *EP* 3.3, and Armstrong 2004 on Ov.'s take on Apollo as a whole).

Visus takes advantage of the ambiguity of this verb in the passive voice, as normally in dream-sequences (e.g. Enn. *Ann.* 5, V. A. 2.270–1, 3.150–1, 4.467, 5.722, 8.33, Ov. *Her.* 19.200, *Met.* 7.637, 11.672–3, 15.32, 15.653, Prop. 3.3.1, 4.7.3; some of these are divine epiphanies, some dreams, some visitations from the dead). Here, the god was both *seen to* appear (suggesting that he really did) and *seemed to* appear (though perhaps he did not). **Sede**: for a dwelling-place (*OLD* 4b; in elegy at Cat. 67.4 and Tib. 2.4.53).

Ponere...pedem: a ponderous, but not unusual, way of describing arrival; in elegy at Prop. 2.32.48 *hic posuit nostra nuper in urbe pedem*, of a new face in town, and Tib. 1.2.20 *pedem nullo ponere posse sono*. Note that the god puts himself, by means of the verb placement, right in the midst of **nostra...sede**. **Pedem** is perhaps metapoetic: Apollo brings his metre into L's midst, but will soon sing not in the hexameters of his oracle, but in L's own more modest metre.

>   Non illo quicquam formosius ulla priorum
> 26   aetas, humanum nec videt illud opus.

There is some manuscript difficulty in both lines, but the sense is clear; first L. claims that the apparition is more beautiful than any sight seen in previous generations, and then that it cannot be human. *Heroum nec tulit ulla domus* is Lachmann's emendation for the universal manuscript reading **humanum nec videt illud opus**; the verb seems inoffensive and should probably stand (all the more because it increases the ambiguity of *visus* in line 24: the present tense could mean 'never has seen until now' or 'still has not seen', a distinction that highlights the curious nature of this visit (Yardley 1992 *ad loc.*). Given that

Apollo is immortal, and has been seen before, the sentiment is a peculiar one. The details of the description suggest that we are meant to see a specific allusion to the statue of Apollo on the Palatine, a temple built by Augustus and dedicated in 28 BCE (see J. F. Miller 2009: 185–252 for discussion of other poetic treatments of the temple: Prop. 2.31, Ov. *Tr.* 4.2, Hor. *Od.* 1.31, Prop. 4.6, Tib. 2.5). If so, this may help to date the cycle; see Introduction, Section V. This theory also lends support for taking **opus** as referring to a statue, and tells us something about L.'s poetic ambitions: like other poets, he takes official notice of the new temple. See Tränkle 1990 and Navarro Antolín 1996 for further discussion of the distich (Tränkle 1990 prints in *cruces*; Navarro Antolín 1996 prints Heyne's *humanum nec fuit illud opus*).

Formosius is often used for loveliness, both female and male; of the *puella* at Prop. 2.29.25, 3.23.13, Tib. 1.1.55, at *CT* 3.1.7, of N. herself at 3.4.57 (see both *ad loc.*), and of Jason at Ov. *Her.* 12.35 and *Met.* 7.84; it is also used of gods, e.g. Apollo, at V. *E.* 4.57. Use of the neuter form of the adjective for people, especially love-objects, is very common in Ov. (McKeown *ad Am.* 2.2.14, Knox 1986: 100); the idea is that there is no thing, human or not, more beautiful; see Sappho 16 for the conceit, with neuters. (See too above: if the Apollo described is a statue, he might be more likely to receive a neuter adjective.)

Priorum/aetas: partial parallels in poetry occur at Prop. 1.4.7 *quascumque tulit formosi temporis aetas*, Ov. *Met.* 9.225 *prior edidit aetas*, *Fas.* 1.329 *aetate priorum*. **Humanum…opus**: elsewhere at Accius fr. 159 *non facile sine deum opera humana propria sunt bona* and in prose (where the adjective is more regularly in the genitive, with a noun).

  Intonsi crines longa cervice fluebant,
28 stillabat Syrio myrtea rore coma.

Apollo generally arrives with less fanfare; cf. e.g. Ov. *Am.* 1.8.59–60 *ipse deus vatum palla spectabilis aurea/tractat inauratae consona fila lyrae*, and Prop. 4.6.31–2: *non ille attulerat crines in colla solutos/aut testudineae carmen inerme lyrae* (relevant to this passage as a whole). At the same time, this head-to-toe description is not atypical. Most of the descriptions in Latin poetry of Apollo seem to depend, to a greater or lesser extent, on Call. *Hymn Ap.* 32–42. 'Young' gods, and Apollo in particular, have long, flowing hair (Nisbet and Hubbard *ad* Hor. *Od.* 1.21.2 on the mythology; the description ἀκερσεκόμης (with uncut hair) appears first at Hom. *Il.* 20.39). The cutting of human boys' hair marks their move to adulthood and hence mortality, so *intonsus* is a fitting descriptor of a youthful immortal. Poets seem keenly interested in Apollo's hair (Boyd 1997: 123–4 on Ovid). The poetic *intonsus* (*TLL* 7.2.29.52–4) is used of Apollo four times in Tib. (once of Dionysus), and three times in Ov. (once of Dionysus); cf. Prop. 3.13.52 (Dionysus, with further citations at Fedeli 1985 *ad loc.*). **Intonsi crines** occurs at Tib. 1.4.38 (Apollo and Dionysus) and occasionally in later epic of heroes. **Crines** is the most elevated word for hair; see further Pichon 1991: 116–17, and above *ad* 3.2.11 for *capilli* (and e.g. Hor. *Epod.* 15.9 *intonsos...capillos* of Apollo).

Longa cervice: long necks are attractive, apparently in all species; cf. *longa manet cervix* at Ov. *Met.* 11.794 (additional point gained from Mergus' transformation into a diving bird with a long neck), of a horse at Germ. *Arat.* 213, 510, Cic. *Arat.* 34.385, D. Iun. Silan. fr. 41.6–7 (= Colum. *DRR* 6.1.3). **Cervice** is less frequent than *collum* in the elegists but occurs with e.g. *levis* at Prop. 2.3.13 and 3.17.31, *niveus* at Ov. *Am.* 2.4.41, and *eburneus* at *Her.* 20.57. **Fluebant** is used of hair (*OLD* 13a, *TLL* 6.1.971.13–19) at Prop. 2.3.13 (*comae per levia colla fluentes*); see too its use of roses decorating a neck at Prop. 4.6.72 (*blanditiaeque fluant per mea colla rosae*, in a passage where Apollo has just been invoked).

Syrio...rore: Syria was known as a trade route for a wide variety of luxury goods, including especially perfumes (*OLD ros* 4); the use of the same adjective in the same metrical *sedes* at 3.6.63 with *nardo* suggests that it refers to that ointment here as well (Hor. *Od.* 2.11.16–17 *Assyriaque nardo*; see further *ad* 3.2.23–4, on Assyria, and for the confusion between the two; for the phrase elsewhere, see Dioscor. 1.7.1 and Philum. 1.109.9, 2.139.2). (Both here and at 3.6.63 the manuscripts give *Tyrio*.) Similar situations occur at Tib. 2.2.7 *puro destillent tempora nardo* and Ov. *Met.* 5.488 *rorantes comas*. Apollo's hair drips with olive-oil at Call. *Hymn Ap.* 38.

Myrtea...coma appear in this metrical *sedes* in the elegists at Tib. 1.3.66 (there the construction is different) and Ov. *Ars* 2.734 (*sertaque odoratae myrtea ferte comae*); **myrtea** is found in this *sedes* on its own at Ov. *Am.* 3.1.34 *in dextra myrtea virga fuit?* Myrtle, the plant of Venus (e.g. Plaut. *Vid.* 17e, V. *E.* 7.62), has associations with luxury, and is common in garlands. Navarro Antolín 1996 suggests *ad loc.* that L. is depicting Apollo as a *puer delicatus* (his appearance is certainly designed to be breathtakingly attractive, see lines 29–36). Luck, Tränkle 1990 and Navarro Antolín 1996 (see *ad loc.*) prefer *myrrhea* of the *inferiores*, because **myrtea** is not elsewhere applied to hair itself; Postgate 1929 suggests 'myrtle-crowned' (which he terms an 'uncommon use'); more normal are e.g. Tib. 1.10.28 *myrto vinctus*, V. *G.* 1.28 *cingens materna tempora myrto*. Tränkle 1990 suggests that **myrtea** may refer to hair colour (i.e. 'chestnut'), but notes that Apollo is normally blond. But the shrub is appropriate for Apollo because it is an evergreen; like him, it does not show its age. On **coma** see *ad* 3.1.10. Ov.'s Amor appears *nec bene dispositas comptus, ut ante, comas* (*EP* 3.3.16). **Stillabat** is used of hair dripping with unguent at e.g. Tib. 1.7.51, Ov. *Her.* 21.161.

> Candor erat, qualem praefert Latonia Luna,
> 30   et color in niveo corpore purpureus,

Apollo is here said to look like his (twin) sister Diana, here as the moon, a point emphasized by the epithet **Latonia**, which draws attention to their mother: the sun here reflects the moon! The comparison of an individual to an object (which, in spite of the personification, this is) goes as far back in poetry as Hom. *Od.* 6.149–85: Odysseus likens the young Nausicaa first to Artemis and then to a palm tree (163, perhaps not coincidentally, located in Delos at the altar of Apollo). Chloris is compared to the moon at Hor. *Od.* 2.5.18–20, also in terms of her gleaming quality (*nidens/renidet*); at Sappho 96.7–9, also of the moon, the point of the comparison seems to be rosiness. The deliberate asexuality of the Homeric comparison (Odysseus is naked, but he compares Nausicaa to a virgin goddess and to a plant) complicates Navarro Antolín's 1996 suggestion that Apollo is presented as an erotic object. Note again the contrast with Amor's appearance to Ov.: *horrida pendebant molles super ora capilli,/et visa est oculis horrida pinna meis, EP* 3.3.17–18. On the other hand, Maleuvre suggests that the lushness of description assimilates Apollo to Amor, or even Venus (2001: 183–4).

Candor: often of the beauty/whiteness of human skin or, metonymically, of humans themselves (*TLL* 3.247.33–72); a comparison between the warm light of the sun and the cool light of the moon may be adumbrated here (see e.g. [V.] *Cir.* 37–8, *purpureos inter soles et candida lunae/sidera*). It is also possible that **candor** suggests a roseate hue; see above, for Sappho's invocation of the pinkness of the moon, with V. *G.* 4.131 *rubet aurea Phoebe*, Hor. *Od.* 2.11.10 *Luna rubens nitet*, and Ov. *Am.* 2.1.23 *sanguineae...cornua lunae*; further citations at Fedeli *ad* Prop. 1.10.8 *luna ruberet* and discussion at Camps 1966 and Fedeli *ad* Prop. 3.24.7–8 of *roseus...candor* (where outer appearance belies inner falsity). The word also conveys the impression of honesty (*OLD* 4), which is apt for a wisdom-figure (though perhaps not for the Apollo of this poem).

Praefert (*OLD* 3a, *TLL* 10.2.613.11–38, rarely in the poets) is not used elsewhere in quite this sense ('puts on display'). Navarro Antolín 1996 suggests *ad loc.* that it is appropriate here because the verb often implies an attempt at deception. **Latonia**: an epic word; elsewhere in elegy only in Ov. *Tr.* 5.1.57 of Apollo and Daphne, *Ib.* 477 of Delos. This is the word's usual *sedes* in V., Ov. (with one exception), Stat., VF, and Sil. (always). For the *topos* of beauty as outshining the moon, see Hor. *Od.* 1.12.48 with citations at Nisbet and Hubbard *ad loc.*

Color in niveo corpore purpureus: ancients seem to have been particularly struck by the visual contrast between white and scarlet/purple (see e.g. Blümner 1889: 157–8, André 1949: 8). P. Thomas 1979 argues that the combination presages violent death in both Greek and Roman poetry (see Brenk 1990: 219 on πορφύρω, 'to swell or gush'), while Rhorer sees it as associated with shame at the loss of innocence (1980: 79); Edgeworth draws attention to its connections to gods and love (1979: 284). The conjunction of the two appears first in Hom. *Il.* 4.141–7, with the staining of ivory as a metaphor for blood on Menelaus' wound, thereafter of blushes at e.g. Theocr. 7.117, Enn. *Ann.* 361 Sk. (*et simul erubuit ceu lacte et purpura mixta*), and then, notably, in V. *A.* 12.64–71 (67–9 quoted *ad*

3.4.33; see Dyson 1999 for discussion and bibliography of the erotic and violent implications of Lavinia's mysterious colouring). As Skutsch notes *ad* Enn. *Ann.* 361, the metaphorical substances rarely actually mix. The closest parallel to this passage is Ov.'s Narcissus, *Met.* 3.421–3 *et dignos Baccho, dignos et Apolline crines/impubesque genas et eburnea colla decusque/oris et in niveo mixtum candore ruborem*, with Richardson 1964: 165 on Ov.'s interest in blushes). In Tib. the collocation of scarlet and white occurs (implicitly) at 2.4.27–8 (*o pereat quicumque legit viridesque smaragdos/et niveam Tyrio murice tingit ovem*); see too *ad* 3.8.11–12. Zingerle 1877: 30–1 and McCrea 1894: 181 suggest that this colour juxtaposition is especially Ovidian (see further below), although it is present in earlier literature. It is not clear whether Apollo is blushing; given the numerous parallels, and the fact that he is a sun god at dawn (cf. e.g. Prop. 3.10.2, where the sun reddens; Apollo's colour may be the cause or effect of the sunrise), he ought to be (among many, cf. e.g. Ov. *Am.* 2.5.35–6 *conscia purpureus venit in ora pudor,/quale coloratum Tithoni coniuge caelum*, 3.3.5–6 *candida candorem roseo suffusa robore/ante fuit—niveo lucet in ore rubor*, *Her.* 4.72 *flava verecundus tinxerat ora rubor*, 20.122 *niveo … in ore rubor*, 21.217 *candida nec mixto sublucent ora rubore*; further discussion of the colour combination at Enk 1946 *ad* Prop. 2.3.11–12; see Edgeworth 1979 on blushes in Latin literature).

On the other hand, Apollo might simply have a healthy glow from exercise (Stat. *Ach.* 1.161–2 *niveo natat ignis in ore/purpureus*). Or, if the figure being described is (also) a statue, it/he is likely to be brightly painted. Note too, with Navarro Antolín 1996, that boys described as Apollo is here are nearly always erotic objects, and see Bömer *ad* Ov. *Met.* 10.594–6. Cf. in this context Ov. *Am.* 1.5, which begins as a quasi-divine epiphany but turns erotic (McKeown 1989 *ad loc.*, Hinds 1987c: 7–11); perhaps there is always something arousing about the appearance of a god.

Niveo: of body parts at Tib. 1.4.12 (a boy's chest) and 1.5.66 (Delia's feet); see Maltby *ad* Tib. 1.4.12 for the suggestion that this Catullan adjective is also particularly Alexandrian. Propertius uses *niveus* more usually of people (3 people: 2 animals), and Ovid does the reverse (10 people: 37 animals). On the semantic range of the adjective outside of the elegists, see André 1949: 39–40, and on the preference for *niveus* over other terms in Ovid, Silius, and Statius, André 1949: 388. Apollo is *niveus* also at e.g. [V.] *Catal.* 9.1. See Otto 1890: 244.

Purpureus: never of a person in Tib. or Prop.; Ov. is particularly fond of the adjective and of juxtaposing it with white-coloured words, sometimes of persons, who either redden in shame (normally the *puella*, as at *Am.* 1.4.22, 2.5.34 and cf. 37–8, 3.3.6, but sometimes also Ov. himself, *Am.* 1.3.14, or his wife, *Tr.* 4.3.70), from exertion (Atalanta, at *Met.* 10.596), or because they are naturally of high colour (especially Amor, *Am.* 2.1.38, 2.9.34, *Ars* 1.232). On the range of **purpureus** outside of the elegists, see André 1949: 90–102, and on the preference of epic poets for this word over other colour terms, André 1949: 388; see

Pichon 1991: 247 on its erotic nuances. And for the (rare) polysyllabic pentameter ending, see Platnauer 1951: 42–5. Note the sound patterning of c- and p-, and the alliteration in **Latonia luna**.

>   **ut iuveni primum virgo deducta marito**
> 32 **inficitur teneras ore rubente genas,**

This couplet draws a few of the parallels cited above into sharper light; **inficitur** is normally used for dyeing, which makes the Homeric and Vergilian resonances (the latter quoted *ad* 3.4.33) clearer, and the erotic implications of the Vergilian passage as well. The lines give, perhaps intentionally, the confused impression of a dream, mixing the colours of sunrise (when L. finally falls asleep), the slightly androgynous looks of Apollo, and L.'s ultimate fantasy of marriage with N. (though Roman weddings seem to occur in the evening, not dawn). By contrast with Apollo's general air of untouchability, Ov.'s Amor in *EP* 3.3 has been roughly handled, at least in terms of his feathers: *qualis in aeriae tergo solet esse columbae,/tractatam multae quam tetigere manus*. The contrast, from whichever direction it originates, is surely pointed.

On the precise meanings of **virgo**, see Watson 1983; the word itself is epic. **Deducta** is a semi-technical term, so rare in poetry, for the process by which the bride is accompanied to her new home (which in part constitutes the wedding ceremony). Cf. Ov. *Fas.* 4.153 *cum primum cupido Venus est deducta marito*; Cat. 68.143 *nec tamen illa mihi dextra deducta paterna*. Much is known about marriages in Rome (Treggiari 1991 provides a starting-point): the presumption, at least in upper-class families, is that bride and groom will not know each other particularly well. Brides might have been even more likely to blush then than now, given the obscene verses which accompanied the marital couple to their bed (e.g. Sappho 112; cf. too Ov. *Am.* 2.5.34–42, where Aurora as blushing spouse and a *puella* looked at by *sponso...novo* are *comparandae*; note too Cairns 2005 on the mention of weddings as a cause of blushes). In this context, **deducta** is also metapoetic, symbolizing the 'drawing down' of Apollo from his usual epic themes to less elevated personal elegiac poetry.

Iuveni...marito: poetry often presumes that the groom is young (e.g. Cat. 61.56, Hor. *Od.* 3.11.37, though he is likely in real life to have been significantly older than the bride).

Inficitur: middle with an internal accusative. Navarro Antolín 1996 notes that this is the only instance of the verb in the middle with this meaning, and suggests that L. means to hint at the falsity of the bride; for the active verb cf. e.g. Luc. 5.214–15. **Teneras...genas**: a Tibullan (1.1.68, 1.4.14, 1.10.55) and Ovidian (*Am.* 2.5.46, 2.6.4, *MFF* 100, *Ars* 1.532, 2.452, 3.568) phrase, nearly always in this *sedes* (also in Seneca's tragedies and Statius). Both young men and women blush regularly in antiquity; the blush was seen as a sign of good breeding, and as instantiating the youthful virtue of *pudor*. In addition to the passages cited above, see Cat. 65.24, *huic manat tristi conscius ore rubor*, where a maiden blushes at the discovery of a love-apple; Lavinia's blush at V. *A*. 12.67–9 also has marital connotations. On *genae*, see Pichon 1991: 160; *tener* Pichon 1991: 277–8.

Ore rubente: otherwise only at Mart. 5.2.7; for the verb in this context, V. *A*. 12.68 (quoted *ad* 3.4.33–4); *rubens* Pichon 1991: 255.

> et cum contexunt amarantis alba puellae
> 34   lilia et autumno candida mala rubent.

These two lines make the allusion even more specific: this juxtaposition of colour terms, and of flower-picking, is regular to scenes of erotic violence. So, for instance, Lavinia, the woman over whom Aeneas and Turnus will go to war, blushes *indum sanguineo veluti violaverit ostro/si quis ebur, aut mixta rubent ubi lilia multa/alba rosa, talis virgo dabat ore colores*, V. *A*. 12.67–9; see too Enn. *Ann*. 361 Sk., quoted *ad* 3.4.30, and examples below, including the rape of Persephone.

Et: the difference in meaning between *et* and Puccius' conjecture *aut* would be slight. Most lists of comparative metaphors, however, use *aut* (e.g. Ov. *Am*. 2.5.35–41, quoted below), so it may be preferable; Luck prints *ut* in both 33 and 34. **Contexunt**: the verb alludes to weaving, a regular task of women; for its use of flower-garlands, see Cat. 64.292 and *TLL* 4.692.9–17. More literally, it alludes to the garland worn by Apollo (probably; see *ad* 3.4.28 *myrtea*).

Amarantis (amaranth) which ranges in colour between purple, red, and gold, takes its name from the Greek, *amaraintos + anthos* = unfading bloom (Plin. *NH* 21.47 with Maltby 1991: 27); as Navarro Antolín 1996 *ad loc*. notes, it is an appropriate plant because Apollo does not fade either (see too *ad* 3.4.28 *myrtea*). The flower is rarely mentioned, but occurs at Ov. *Fas*. 4.439, where it is one of those that Persephone's companions pluck; Hagen 1954 sees the word as 'Silver'.

Alba...lilia: regularly joined in the poets (Prop. 2.3.10, V. *G*. 4.130–1 (same *sedes*), *A*. 12.68–9 (quoted above), Petr. 127.9, VF 6.492; see Otto 1890: 193 and Büchner 1965: 108–10). Lilies are in Prop. juxtaposed with poppies (and *candida*, 1.20.37–8) in the narrative of the beautiful boy Hylas' capture by the nymphs (where *poma* are also present; see immediately below). Ov. is particularly fond of invoking the flower in situations with beautiful young (doomed) innocents: Narcissus' complexion is like lilies in glass (*Met*. 4.355), Persephone innocently gathers violets or white lilies just before she is kidnapped (*Met*. 5.392; cf. her choice of lilies at *Fas*. 4.442, but some of her companions prefer, among others, violets, poppies, hyacinth, amaranth, and roses)—again, the colour combination seems normally to presage violence. Hyacinthus droops like violets or poppies or lilies (*Met*. 10.191), and at *Met*. 10.212 he is turned into a flower with the shape of a lily but a brilliant hue, *purpureus*). In a passage that brings together all of this imagery, Ov. describes Corinna blushing (*Am.* 2.5.35–41; see McKeown 1998 *ad loc.*): *quale coloratum Tithoni coniuge caelum/ subrubet, aut sponso visa puella novo;/quale rosae fulgent inter sua lilia mixtae,/ aut ubi cantatis Luna laborat equis,/aut quod, ne longis flavescere possit ab annis,/Maeonis Assyrium femina tinxit ebur,/hic erat aut alicui color ille simillimus horum*. On the colour *albus*, see André 1949: 25–41 and Pichon 1991: 82.

Candida mala: unusual colouring for an apple (more usually e.g. *roscida*, as at Prop. 1.20.36), but see Ov. *Met.* 3.482–4: *pectora traxerunt roseum percussa ruborem,/non aliter quam poma solent, quae candida parte,/parte rubent*, where, however, there is no blushing but rather redness from blows. Ov.'s next simile is grapes partly ripe and partly unripe, and it may be that the apple here is also just starting to ripen. The fruit of Cat. 65.19, which provokes a blush, is also an apple, so that passage is probably relevant (see too Sappho 105, important for the Catullan passage, where a young woman is compared to a ripe apple, high up on a tree, desired but unreachable, and Theocr. 7.117); *poma*/**mala** are love-gifts at Prop. 1.3.24 and 2.34.69. Biblical associations may hamper our comprehension: for Latin love poets the most important apple is that of Callimachus' Acontius and Cydippe—the ardent lover Acontius had inscribed the words 'I swear by Artemis that I will marry Acontius' onto an apple, and rolled it to Cydippe's nurse. She picked it up, and the unwitting girl read its inscription aloud, thus binding herself to Acontius (Call. *Aet.* frr. 67–75, Ov. *Her.* 20 and 21, with a comparison at 21.215–7, and brief mentions at *Ars* 1.457–8, *Tr.* 3.10.73). The golden apples of the Hesperides (Prop. 2.24.26) may also be pertinent; they were used by Hippomenes to woo the swift Atalanta (*Met.* 10.650–77). Finally, Hermaphroditus' blush at Salmacis' boldness is also relevant (*Met.* 4.331 with commentaries, *hic color aprica pendentibus arbore pomis*)—both Hippomenes and Hermaphroditus are attractive young men who are about to be victimized.

We can draw some conclusions from these numerous parallels (more in Bömer *ad* Ov. *Met.* 3.423): Latin poets are exceedingly fond of the juxtaposition of red/purple and white, and use them in scenes of eroticism, desire, and suppressed violence. They recur in descriptions of both masculine and feminine beauty, but the closest parallels to this passage are masculine; in either case, they seem to depict an erotic object newly made self-conscious of her or his appeal. But it is not clear whether such nuances are appropriate to Apollo; presumably it is his desirability and not his vulnerability that is alluded to. **Rubent**: see *ad* 3.4.32.

>   Ima videbatur talis inludere palla,
> 36   namque haec in nitido corpore vestis erat.

Ima...palla refers to the bottom-most edge of Apollo's garment. The *palla* (= Greek *peplos*; *RE* 18.3.152–5) was normally worn as an outermost garment by respectable women (but not prostitutes; Ov. *Am.* 3.13.26), by men not entitled to wear the toga (i.e. non-citizens), and by poets, seers, and other artists; as the latter it is the regular clothing of Apollo the lyre-player (*TLL* 10.1.120.3–31; on Apollo's clothing, see Ov. *Am.* 1.8.59–60 *ipse deus vatum palla spectabilis aurea/ tractat inauratae consona fila lyrae*, *Met.* 11.166 *verrit humum Tyrio saturata murice palla*). Apollo's *palla* is rarely described in poetry, but often depicted visually (*LIMC* 2.1.203–8; cf. Prop. 2.31.16 *in longa...veste* of the Palatine Apollo; McKeown *ad* Ov. *Am.* 1.8.59–60 suggests it too describes the statue). A Greek nuance may be regularly present in invocations of the *palla*, but Apollo is also firmly Roman, with long-standing temples, worship, and a (perhaps) recent boost in status as a result of Augustan patronage. For discussion of the Augustan poets' conceptions of Apollo, see J. F. Miller 2009. *Pallae* were normally floor-length, as here: *veste fluente pedes* Prop. 3.17.32, *fusa sed ad teneros lutea palla pedes* Tib. 1.7.46, Ov. *Met.* 11.166 (quoted above), and *palla imos ferit alba pedes* VF 1.385.

Inludere: on the 'play' of clothing, cf. [V.] *Cir.* 144 with Lyne *ad loc.*, *suspensam gaudens in corpore ludere vestem*; Lyne suggests a Calvan origin. While the uncompounded *ludere* can also have this sense (V. *A.* 11.497, Sil. 16.363, both of horse's manes rippling), *alludere*, first proposed by Cyllenius, would be the more usual verb (*OLD* 1a-b, *TLL* 1.1698.65–1699.1, e.g. Cat. 64.67 and Ov. *Met.* 4.342), and Navarro Antolín 1996 prefers it (see too Allen 1906: 455–6 for discussion). **Inludere** more often refers to mockery (*TLL* 7.1.390.9–13, e.g. V. *G.* 1.181, Ov. *Met.* 3.650 and 9.66, Manil. 4.263); if correct here, the verb must be extended to mean 'play at' or 'tease'. This hints that we are not to take Apollo wholly seriously. Note too that the book as a whole engages in sophisticated play with the ways clothing can both conceal and reveal (see Introduction, Section I, and *ad* 3.8.13 and 3.13.1–2).

The verb **videbatur** reintroduces the note of uncertainty (cf. *ad* 3.4.24)—did the *palla* actually drag against Apollo's ankles? Did he, in fact, appear at all? **Nitido** is, in effect, not much different from *candidus* or *albus*, again emphasizing the whiteness and splendour of the god (used of Apollo at Ov. *Met.* 4.348, of Sol at *Met.* 14.33 and *Tr.* 3.5.55, and of Lucifer at Ov. *Am.* 2.11.55); note too Navarro Antolín 1996 *ad loc.* on the word as 'equivalent to *Phoebus*'. **Nitido corpore**: otherwise unattested, but cf. Enn. *Tr.* 136 *nitidant corpora*; V. *G.* 1.467, Hor. *Od.* 1.4.9, Tib. 1.8.16, Ov. *Met.* 13.838, 15.30, and *Il. Lat.* 158 pair it with *caput*, Ov. *Ars* 3.74 and Sen. *Phaed.* 376 with *ore*, Ov. *Tr.* 4.3.9 with *vultus*; the adjective is also frequent with hair.

> Artis opus rarae, fulgens testudine et auro,
> 38   pendebat laeva garrula parte lyra.

If the bay leaves did not clue us in, the attributes will: the lyre is quintessentially Apollo's (though invented by Hermes, it was given by him to Apollo; see *HHH*

41–54, which contains assembly instructions, and Call. *Hymn Ap.* 253–4); there is an ancient version which has Apollo as the inventor (Diod. Sic. 3.59.5–6, 5.75.3, Plut. *De Mus.* 1135f), but see Hägg 1989 for a different version. This one is lovely; its description as **artis opus rarae** sounds like a tag line, but the phrase is unattested, although it has an Ovidian feel. Note the similar phrasings with *artis opus* at Ov. *Ars* 1.266, 2.14, *Met.* 13.290 (with Bömer 1982 *ad loc.*) *artis opus tantae*; *Fas.* 1.268 *callidus artis opus*, 6.662, *RA* 16 *Ne pereat, nostrae sentiat artis opem*; *opus rarum* at Ov. *Fas.* 3.820 *erudit et rarum pectine denset opus*; *ars rara* at Ov. *Am.* 2.4.17 *places raras dotata per artes*. On the erotic nuances of *ars*, see Sharrock 1994, Pichon 1991: 90, and for *rarus*, Pichon 1991: 250.

The lyre shines, **fulgens**, both because of the gold (presumably plating, suggested by *artis...rarae*), and because tortoise-shell, the material of the soundbox, can be polished to a very high sheen. On the composition of bowl lyres see Maas and McIntosh Snyder 1989: 94–9 and West 1992: 56–9; they are, as the latter notes, the standard domestic instrument, but are also sometimes the instrument of Apollo and the Muses. **Testudine**: the proper basis of a lyre at e.g. *HHH* 33, Hor. *Od.* 1.32.13–14, 3.11.3, Paus. 8.54.7, by metonymy at Ov. *Ars* 3.147 (and see *ad* 3.8.22). Ov. *Met.* 2.737 suggests that tortoise-shell was also used as wall inlays (see Bömer 1969 *ad loc.* for citations). **Auro**: for Apollo's golden lyre, see Hes. *Scut.* 203, Call. *Hymn Ap.* 32–3, Pi. *P.*1.1–2, Prop. 3.3.14, Ov. *Ars* 2.494, and note the epithets χρυσοφόμιγξ at Sim. 511a.5 Page and χρυσολύρας at Aristoph. *Thes.* 315. Apollo's lyre is inlaid with ivory and gemstones at Ov. *Met.* 11.167 (quoted below), and contains both **testudine** and **auro** at Hor. *Od.* 4.3.17–18: *o testudinis aureae/dulcem quae strepitum, Pieri, temperas*.

Pendebat: of musical instruments (*TLL* 10.1.1030.46–64) at Hor. *Od.* 3.19.20 and V. *E.* 7.24 (*fistula*), Tib. 2.5.29–30 (Pan's pipe), Prop. 3.3.28 (the Muses' *tympana*), the latter two in the same *sedes* (and a favourite word of Prop.). **Laeva**: cf. Ov. *Met.* 11.167–8 *instructamque fidem gemmis et dentibus Indis/sustinet a laeva, tenuit manus altera plectrum* (with Bömer 1980 *ad loc.*). Lyres are normally held in the left hand, and on the left side, so that they can be played with the right hand (see West 1992: 64–70 and Maas and McIntosh Snyder 1989: 92–4, with illustrations at 100–112). Shields are also carried on the left side (Ov. *Met.* 4.782, 13.347, and 15.163), as are quivers (*Met.* 8.320). There is, however, the possibility that *laeva*, which also means 'ill-omened', is invoked to hint at the unhappy tidings already alluded to at the start of the poem. (Cupid similarly lays his left hand on Ov.'s bedpost at *EP* 3.3.14.) **Laeva...parte**: Ovidian: *Met.* 4.655, 7.241, 7.357, 8.220–1, 9.82, 14.102, *Tr.* 1.4.19; poetry often omits the noun.

The instrument is described as **garrula**, a poetic word which Maltby *ad* Tib. 2.5.30 suggests Tib. was first to apply to a musical instrument (*garrula silvestri fistula sacra deo*, of Pan's pipes; see *TLL* 6.2.1699.32–9 for further citations); see too Hor. *Od.* 3.11.3–5 where the *testudo* is *nec loquax olim*. In elegy, the adjective is normally used for troublesome or delightful *puellae* (Prop. 2.23.26,

3.23.18), gossipy old women, or the babble of children or servants (cf. Tib. 1.5.26 and Prop. 4.7.42), but also for birds, especially the crow (Apollo's bird) at Ov. *Am.* 3.5.22 and *Met.* 2.547; often, especially in Ov., the excessively chatty are punished (*Am.* 2.2.41–60, *Ars* 2.606 of Tantalus, *Met.* 3.360 of Echo, 5.678 of the Pierides; see Keith 1992: 99–103 and *passim* on informers in *Met.* 2). Generally, the word is not flattering. See too *ad* 3.19.20. **Lyra**: a Greek word, but common in elegy, often in this *sedes*. Apollo's lyre is often mentioned by Latin poets (see *ad* 3.8.22); for some representative passages, see Hor *Od.* 1.21, Prop. 2.31.6 (of the statue of Apollo Palatinus, where the *lyra* is *tacita*; the correction here may be pointed, suggesting L.'s own more intimate relationship with Apollo), Ov. *Am.* 1.8.60 (probably also of the statue; Tib. 2.5 is also set at the temple), *Ars* 2.494, *EP* 4.8.75; see Bömer *ad* Ov. *Met.* 8.15 for further parallels.

      Hanc primum veniens plectro modulatus eburno
40   felices cantus ore sonante dedit.

Veniens: see Tränkle 1990 *ad loc.* on the difficulties of this passage, including the participle and the oddities of the mechanics; Postgate 1929 *ad loc.* notes that the construction is Greek. At this point L.'s and Ov.'s poems diverge: Ov. accuses the god before he can speak, while L. listens to the music of Apollo.

    The *plectrum* can be made from a variety of materials, ivory being among the best because most durable (Maas and McIntosh Snyder 1989: 98; West 1992: 65 and n. 78, who notes that Apollo's is golden at *HHAp.* 185). **Plectro** is a technical term, but used five times by Prop., seven times by Ov. (elegies and *Met.*), and in e.g. Horace, Seneca, Statius, and Silius. **Modulatus** is also technical, but is used in poetry of playing an instrument (in the ablative): e.g. V. *E.* 10.51 *carmina pastoris Siculi modulabor avena*, Tib. 2.1.53 *primum est modulatus avena*, Ov. *RA* 181 *inaequali modulatur harundine carmen*, *Met.* 11.154 *inaequali, cerata modulatur harundine carmen*; of singing at Ov. *Met.* 14.341 *feminea modulatur carmina voce* and 14.428–9 *cum lacrimis ipso modulata dolore/verba*, Hor. *Od.* 1.32.4–5; and of both playing and singing at V. *E.* 5.14.

    Felices cantus: *felicia carmina* is more usual: at Cat. 64.382, of another song that contains as much woe as happiness, and Ov. *Am.* 2.17.27. Elegy is the metre for *tristia verba*, but we might expect Apollo to sing epic song; the placement of **felices** as the first word of the pentameter (the line which defines elegy as elegy) emphasizes his artistic licence, and the change of expected subject matter. But 41 soon clarifies: Apollo can, and does, sing different songs, but he will adapt himself to the constraints of this poem's genre. Further on *felix*, see *ad* 3.3.26. **Cantus...dedit**: e.g. V. *A.* 1.398 *cantus dedere*, 9.618 *dat tibia cantum*; cf. Cat. 64.306 *edere cantus*. **Ore sonante**: a regular phrase: Ov. *Met.* 8.533–4 (Bömer 1977 *ad loc.* offers similar idioms in Ov.): *non mihi si centum deus ora sonantia linguis/ingeniumque capax totumque Helicona dedisset*; Ov. *Fas.* 1.571–2: *quis ubi nil agitur, patrias male fortis ad artes/confugit, et flammas ore sonante vomit*. Note too Prop. 2.31, which features two singing Apollo(-statue)s, and Tib. 2.5, which looks also to be describing a Palatine statue, with J. F. Miller 2009: 201–2 and 235–6.

> Sed postquam fuerant digiti cum voce locuti,
> 42   edidit haec dulci tristia verba modo:

Postquam in prose usually takes the perfect indicative, but here (as often in poetry) a double pluperfect; see Tränkle 1990 and Navarro Antolín 1996 *ad loc.* for citations.

Digiti...locuti: not elsewhere of the making of music with one's hands (though the phrase here is made less difficult by **cum voce**). See Ov. *Ars* 1.137 *nil opus est digitis, per quos arcana loquaris* and *Tr.* 2.453 *digitis saepe est nutuque locutus* (each in an erotic context), both of silent communication (and Ov. is often interested in speech which is aberrant, hampered, or suppressed). West 1992: 67–70 discusses lyre-accompanied singing; see too Landels 1999: 65–6 on the probable range of the instrument. **Cum voce** of a lyre player at Ov. *Met.* 5.112, *citharam cum voce moveres.*

Edidit: of epic (or grandiose) speech (*TLL* 5.2.86.79–87.60): e.g. Ov. *Fas.* 3.856 (of an Apolline prophecy), *Met.* 1.637 (of Io), 8.703 (of Jupiter), 12.577 (Nestor), Tib. 1.4.73 *deus edidit ore* with Murgatroyd 1980 *ad loc*. For the conjunction **edidit...dulci** (with the more regular *ore*, of Nestor), see Bömer *ad* Ov. *Met.* 12.577. **Edidit...verba** in poetry at Tib. 1.9.26 *ederet ut multo libera verba mero* and Ov. *Met.* 5.105–6 *semianimi verba exsecrantia lingua/edidit*; cf. Ov. *Fas.* 1.444 *facili dulces editis ore modos.*

There is a nice juxtaposition between **dulci** and **tristia** (cf. V. *A.* 12.802, Manil. 4.527 (not adjacent), Sil. 6.67; the adjectives do not share a line elsewhere in Latin poetry). Some modern editors accept the older manuscripts' *tristi dulcia*; see Schuster 1968: 156 and Navarro Antolín 1996 *ad loc*. On *dulcis*, see *ad* 3.3.27; it ought not to apply either to the metre/melody of elegy or its subject matter, but presumably—if the word is correct—L. means to suggest a kind of haunting beauty to Apollo's poem. **Tristia verba**: also at [Tib.] 3.6.38, Hor. *AP* 105–6, Ov. *Tr.* 1.3.80 (the same form in the same *sedes*), 2.133; on *tristis*, see *ad* 3.2.27 and 3.3.35. Here Apollo shows his versatility, first in non-elegy (*felices cantus*) and then, in a metre L. can reproduce, **tristia verba**. **Dulci...modo**: Hor. *Od.* 3.9.10, Ov. *Fas.* 1.444 (quoted above), Sen. *Ag.* 584. L.'s phrasing leaves it unclear whether the disjunction is only in content, or whether Apollo has also switched from song to metrical speech; **modo** can be used for both (but is strongly suggestive of verse). On the alternation between fingers and plectrum, see V. *A.* 6.647.

> "Salve, cura deum: casto nam rite poetae
> 44   Phoebusque et Bacchus Pieridesque favent;

Cura deum: also at e.g. V. *A.* 3.476 (Anchises), Ov. *Am.* 3.9.17 (*divum cura*), *Ars* 3.405 (both of poets), *Met.* 4.574 (vengeance), 8.724 (Baucis and Philemon); cf.

Tib. 2.5.113 *divum servat tutela poetas*. The claim is aggrandizing; see Baligan 1948: 28–9, Axelson 1960a: 102–3, Büchner 1965: 506–7 on Ovidian echoes, and Ov. *Ars* 3.539–50 and Hor. *Od.* 1.17.13–14 on the moral purity of poets. **Cura** becomes an elegiac word (see *ad* 3.1.20 and *TLL* 4.1475.42–57).

Casto...poeta: appropriate to poets, but perhaps an odd choice in elegy, given its usual objectives; the phrase emphasizes L.'s faithfulness to the cheating N., and may derive from Cat. 16.5, where Cat. claims that a sacred poet (*pium poetam*) must be chaste, though his verses need not be. (On the chastity of the Muses in Tib., see Lieberg 1980: 144–6; see also Ov. *Ars* 3.539–50 for their moral superiority.) On the other hand, note the erotic subject matter of the Muses' song at Prop. 2.30.27–30, and discussion of their sexual experience at 33–6. There may be an implicit *figura etymologica*, with *casto* alluding to the Muses' Castalia (S. Heyworth, private communication; see *ad* 3.1.16). The elegist rarely claims to be *castus* (note that he does not here either); this is a quality much more desirable in the love object and his or her surroundings; cf. Tib. 1.3.83, 1.6.67 and 75, 3.9.20, Prop. 2.6.28, 2.19.3, 2.32.60, 3.12.15 and 37. In a different but related usage, Prop. had famously been taught *castas odisse puellas* by Cynthia (Prop. 1.1.5, but cf. 1.11.29 *contra*, with discussion of both at Langlands 2006: 197–8), a passage that may relate to [Tib.] 3.1.23, where N. is unfortunately *casta* vis-à-vis L.; see above *ad loc*. Ov. is more suspicious of *castitas*: he characteristically notes *casta est quam nemo rogavit* (*Am.* 1.8.43), suggests that the *vir* might as well believe the *puella* to be *casta* (*Am.* 2.2.14), and then claims that guards will not make a girl so (*Am.* 3.4.3, 36, and 41). A religious sense is also sometimes present, as it probably is here: things related to religious ritual or to certain gods are regularly *castus*: *CT* 2.1.13, 2.5.122, 3.4.23, 3.12.14 (the latter two of Apollo), Prop. 2.29.27, 3.20.7, 4.8.13, Ov. *Am.* 1.7.18, 3.13.3, and *casta laurus* above, line 23. N. will later in this poem be criticized for not being *casta* (60), so the contrast between her and L. is pointed.

Postponement of **nam** occurs first in Cat. (where it may be designed to avoid a fourth-foot spondee; L. has no such interest, as the first dozen lines of 3.1 make clear); on L.'s use of **nam** and *etenim*, see *ad* 3.1.14, and on the conjunction, see Axelson 1945: 122–3, Platnauer 1951: 93–6. **Rite** ('duly') has both religious and non-religious implications; here we are probably seeking a combination of the two, since poets have some connection to the divine. The word usually characterizes the way men behave towards gods, not vice versa.

Phoebus: Apollo names himself first, perhaps in a foreshadowing of the following couplet, which will claim that he is the more useful friend to have. Other juxtapositions of **Phoebus**, **Bacchus**, and the **Pierides**, the three main sources of poetic inspiration, occur at Call. *Iamb.* 1.7–8, [V.] *Catal.* 9.59–60, Prop. 3.2.9 and 15–16, 3.3.13–26, 4.6.75–6, Ov. *Am.* 1.3.11, *Ars* 3.347–8 (with Gibson 2003 *ad loc.*), Stat. *Silv.* 1.5.2, 5.1.25–6. Phoebus and the Muses are obvious friends to poets, Bacchus perhaps less so, at least for the followers of Callimachus; his kind of poetic inspiration tends to be more frenzied and less controlled than the others'.

Bacchus: connected to poetry and poets at e.g. Hor. *Ep.* 1.19.4, *Od.* 1.1.29–30, 2.19.1–2, 3.25, Prop. 4.1.62, Ov. *Am.* 3.1.23, 3.15.17, *Ars* 1.525 of Liber calling *suum vatem* (who assists lovers), *Fas.* 3.714 and 789–90, *Tr.* 5.3. **Pierides favent**: same line-ending at Ov. *Ars* 3.548, also a generalization about poets. On the **Pierides**, see *ad* 3.1.5.

    sed proles Semelae Bacchus doctaeque sorores
46   dicere non norunt, quid ferat hora sequens:

Apollo here sets himself apart from L.'s other well-wishers: he alone can prophesy. The Hesiodic Muses' claim to tell the future is ignored (Hes. *Th.* 66–8), as is the possibility that poets might have access to this knowledge as well.

    Proles Semelae: Ov. *Met.* 3.520 *proles Semeleia, Liber* with Bömer 1969 *ad loc.*; the noun adds epic grandeur. For the preference of some editors (including Luck) for the Greek genitive *Semeles*, see Navarro Antolín 1996 *ad loc.*; the homoioteleuton is unattractive. The Muses are frequently **doctae sorores**: (e.g. Cat. 35.17, 65.2, *Buc. Eins.* 1.35, Manil. 2.49, Ov. *Met.* 5.255, *Fas.* 6.811, *Tr.* 2.13, Stat. *Theb.* 9.317, Mart. 1.70.15, 9.42.3); at Tib. 1.4.61 they love poets because they too are learned; *doctus* describes poets and poetry as early as Lucr. 2.600. The *puella docta*, famous in elegy (and relevant to the learnedness of the Muses; see Introduction, Section II), is not explicitly mentioned in Tib., but appears in [Tib.] 3.12.2, and at Cat. 35.16–17, Prop. 1.7.11, 2.3.20 (of her poetic composition), 2.11.6, 2.13.11, and at Ov. *Am.* 2.4.18. The lyre of Apollo is *docta* at Prop. 2.34.79, as is Cat. at [Tib.] 3.6.41 (see *ad loc.*).

    Dicere non norunt: as often, the infinitive after a verb of knowing means 'know how (to tell)'; similar phrasing at Ov. *Her.* 6.124 *fallere non norunt*.

    Hora sequens for the future in general, but also suggesting the immediacy of these future events (cf. Prop. 1.4.3 *vitae quodcumque sequetur* for a similar phrasing). **Sequens**: as Navarro Antolín 1996 notes *ad loc.*, this is the only adjectival participle at pentameter-end in L. (though they are common in Vergil, Prop., and Ov.; see Platnauer 1951: 45–7).

    at mihi fatorum leges aevique futuri
48   eventura pater posse videre dedit.

Fatorum leges: also at e.g. V. *A.* 12.819 *fati...lege*, [V.] *Cir.* 199 *fatorum lege*, Ov. *Met.* 3.316 and 10.203 *fatali lege*, and elsewhere in epic, suggesting an elevated tone. The relationship between Jupiter and the Fates had been difficult to sketch out from as early as Homer (see *ad* 3.3.36); either the Fates are in charge, and Jupiter has limited ability to change things, or Jupiter is in charge, and the Fates enforce his will. Apollo's gift of prophecy and his healing abilities make him a powerful ally, although when (as in Ov. *Met.*) he attempts to use them for his own benefit, they inevitably fail. Prophecies direct from the mouth of Apollo are rare; much more common is a divine message from the Delphic oracle, which apparently always told the truth (though sometimes in a form unrecognizable, and so useless, to its hearers). On the Delphic oracle, see Fontenrose 1978.

Aevique futuri/eventura: more grandiose than *hora sequens*, showing that Apollo can make long-term predictions as well. Commentators generally dislike the phrase, finding it 'pompous', a 'monstrosity' (Navarro Antolín 1996) and 'inelegant and incorrect' (Postgate 1929). Partial poetic parallels occur at Lucr. 3.486 and Ov. *Her.* 4.131 *aevo…futuro*, V. *A.* 8.627 *venturi…aevi*, Ov. *Met.* 7.96–7 *futuri/eventus*. **Eventura** is often used in passages of prophecy (e.g. Tib. 2.5.11 with *vides*, where Maltby 2002 *ad loc.* notes that Tib. seems to have been the first to use the word in this way, Ov. *EP* 4.3.113; *ventura* used in the same way at Ov. *Met.* 5.146); cf. 3.4.5 above.

Pater: prophecy as a gift from Jupiter/Zeus also occurs at e.g. *HHH* 471–2, Aesch. *Eum.* 19, fr. 86R, Ov. *Met.* 3.336–7; perhaps this fact undermines Apollo's authority, as Navarro Antolín 1996 suggests *ad loc.*, but it might also confirm it by connecting him with a higher power (the same 'chain of command' at e.g. V. *A.* 3.251–2, *quae Phoebo pater omnipotens, mihi Phoebus Apollo/praedixit*). **Posse videre dedit**: cf. Ov. *Met.* 14.843–4 *si modo posse videre/fata semel dederint* (where the seeing is literal). For **videre** of prophecy, see e.g. Liv. 6.12.8, Stat. *Theb.* 1.398–9.

> Quare, ego quae dico non fallax, accipe, vates,
> 50   quodque deus vero Cynthius ore feram.

Prophetic self-authentication is fairly frequent in other kinds of poetry, though perhaps unnecessary coming from Apollo, who is a god, and has already made a fairly impressive first impression (note the judgement of Postgate 1929 that Apollo is too prolix). Beyond this, these two lines are troubled, and consensus impossible. See Navarro Antolín 1996 *ad loc.* for discussion of the most serious problem, the two subordinate clauses dependent upon **accipe**, and their tautology. (The problem is more serious if the clauses are not parallel, as they are not with *quamque*.) Postgate 1912: 42 defends *quamque* and Brouckhous' *ferar*; further alternatives are *quidque* and (the transmitted) *ferat*; further discussion at Fletcher 1931: 50–1 and Tränkle 1990 *ad loc.* (who prints *quidque…feram*). Whatever text is preferred, the point ought to be that Apollo claims two separate kinds of authority, the first as a *vates*, the second as a god.

Quare ego: the elision of a final vowel before a short initial vowel is rare (Platnauer 1951: 74), although before *ego* at the start of a line it is more common. **Quare** is not as prosaic as commentators suggest: seven times in Prop. (six times in this *sedes*); six times in Vergil (always in this *sedes*), thirty-one times in Ov. (never in this *sedes*); not otherwise in *CT*.

Non fallax is a significant phrase, especially with **vates** (on which see Newman 1967: 99 on this poem; it is first used of Apollo at V. *A.* 6.12, *Delius…vates*). The noun is not much used in elegy: in the *CT* **vates** appears

Commentary on 3.4.52

only to describe Apollo or one of his authorized representatives (here, possibly at 3.4.9, and at Tib. 2.5.18, 65, and 114 of the Sibyl). In Prop. the word refers to famous seers or priests of Apollo (2.2.16, 2.3.51, 4.1.51, 4.6.1 and 10, 4.9.57), to Prop. himself and the fame he will gain (2.10.19, 4.1.75 and 117), and also to a 'prediction' that the *puella* will disappoint (2.17.3) and to Prop.'s susceptibility to charlatans (*fallaci... vati* 2.4.15). In the *Amores*, Ov. appropriates the word to refer to himself and other poets, often incongruously: 1.1.6 and 24, 1.8.57 (in the mouth of Dipsas), 2.1.34, 2.4.21, 2.18.18 and 35 (the latter of Macer), 3.1.19 and 67, 3.9.5 and 41 (of Tib.), 17, 26, 29 (of Homer), 3.12.41, 3.15.1; elsewhere in the *Amores* the word appears only at 1.8.59 of Apollo, god of poets, and at 3.6.17, of the false tales of old. **Fallax** occurs (negatively) with Apollo elsewhere at e.g. V. A. 6.343–4 *fallax haud ante repertus*, and see ἀεὶ δ᾽εὔορκος Ἀπόλλων at Call. *Hymn Ap.* 68, from which it may originate.

Accipe: portentous, and standard to introduce oracles, prophecies, and other divine communications (*OLD* 18–19; cf. e.g. Enn. *Ann.* 1.32, Cat. 64.325, Germ. *Arat.* 612, V. *E.* 6.69 (perhaps hinting at a Gallan precedent), *A.* 6.136, Prop. 4.2.2, Ov. *Her.* 16.42, *Am.* 1.1.24, *Met.* 14.318, *Fas.* 1.115, 5.449, Calp. Sic. 2.34, *Il. Lat.* 126.

Vero...ore, a final authenticating gesture, suggests that what follows will be something in the order of a testimonial, but instead, the prophecy abruptly begins; apparently, Apollo expects it to prove his case. Similar phrases are used of Apollo's prophecies (*vero...ore* at Ov. *Met.* 10.209; *non mentito...ore* at *Fas.* 6.426) and of mortal claims to truthfulness (Ov. *EP* 2.7.23; see *ad* 3.6.35 *mendaci...ore* and Ov. *Am.* 3.3.44 about the *puella* speaking *mendaci...ore*). Given that elegy is a genre much concerned with truth and lies, there may be good reason for Apollo to emphasize his veracity (all the more so if we think of him as L.'s creation, designed to frighten N. into submission); the poem offers no confirming evidence of the truth of Apollo's prophecy, and, in fact, L. later claims to hope that the god lies.

Apollo is **Cynthius** from Mt. Cynthus, on Delos, the place of his birth (citations at Maltby 1991: 171). The epithet is used in a variety of Apolline contexts, perhaps most relevantly at V. *E.* 6.3 in a poetic initiation scene, at Prop. 2.34.80 where Apollo plays his lyre, and at Ov. *Ars* 2.239 in the narrative of his affair with Admetus (also Ov. *Fas.* 3.346, 3.353; Greek occurrences are late). The fact that this cult epithet makes him the 'brother' of Prop.'s Cynthia—at least in name—may not be accidental: she too speaks authoritatively but perhaps deceptively. (See too 3.9.5 for mention of Delia, the name of Tib.'s *puella*, and line 79 below for Apollo as *Delius*.)

   Tantum cara tibi, quantum nec filia matri,
52   quantum nec cupido bella puella viro,

The word order of nouns is particularly pleasing, as each girl is placed next to the person who loves her most. **Tantum...quantum**: an obvious model—especially given the prosaic nature of the phrase—is Cat. 37.11, *amata tantum quantum* *amabitur nulla*; as Navarro Antolín 1996 notes *ad* 51–60, this passage has numerous Catullan echoes. The couplet is reminiscent of L.'s concern throughout with familial relationships (see Introduction, Section I, and note Cat. 3.6–7 *suamque norat/ipsam tam bene quam puella matrem*). N. has already been denoted **cara**, at her first mention (see *ad* 3.1.6). Since the word is not generally used for *puellae*, and appears frequently of N., its use here may add a note of intimacy: Apollo, omniscient god as he is, is aware of L.'s pet names for his girlfriend. But the detail might also make us suspicious, either of Apollo—'reading up' before delivering a prophecy—or of L. himself, who forgetfully speaks *in propria persona* when he is supposed to be recounting a dream.

Filia matri might pick up on Hor. *Od.* 1.16.1 *o matre pulchra filia pulchrior* (see Nisbet and Hubbard 1970 *ad loc.* with further citations), especially given the rarity of mothers in elegy (see *ad* 3.2.13). For another amatory family metaphor, cf. Cat. 72.3–4 *dilexi tum te non tantum ut vulgus amicam/sed pater ut gnatos diligit et generos*, and Cat. 3.7, quoted immediately above.

Cupido: a comic, and then Catullan word, frequent in elegy (*TLL* 4.1427.10–30; with *vir* at Ov. *Am.* 2.5.26, *Ars* 3.88, Tib. 1.1.76 (in a different context), and cf. Ov. *Am.* 2.6.56 *cupido...mari*, *Her.* 3.26 *cupidi...amantis*, 5.129 *iuvene...cupido*); see Pichon 1991: 119–20 and below *ad* 3.9.18 and 3.12.11. **Cupido...viro** elsewhere at *Priap.* 16.6. **Bella puella**: the adjective is informal (Axelson 1945: 35) and Catullan (Ross 1969: 110–11); this conjunction is rare (perhaps avoided because of homoioteleuton), occurring only in Cat. 69.8, 78.4, Ov. *Am.* 1.9.6 with McKeown 1989 *ad loc.* (all in same *sedes*), Mart. 1.64.4 *neque bella nec puella es*, 2.87.1 *bellas...puellas* (but often in adjacent lines; see Baligan 1950: 283). **Bella** also occurs at Tib. 1.9.71 and [Tib.] 3.19.5 (see *ad loc.*) in amatory contexts; see Monteil 1964: 221–40 and, for elegiac context, Pichon 1991: 93. **Puella viro**: see too *ad* 3.4.58.

>   pro qua sollicitas caelestia numina votis,
> 54   quae tibi securos non sinit ire dies

Sollicitas is a regular word for constant attention, religious or otherwise (*OLD* 2b), and the verb is favoured by L. (see *ad* 3.4.20, 3.5.12, 3.6.36 and 61; otherwise it occurs in *CT* only at 1.7.30 and 3.16.5, but is frequent in Ov.). With this verb Apollo suggests L.'s obsessive behaviour; see too *ad* 3.3.1, *caelum votis implesse* with **votis** here. We might wonder why, given that other elegists make vows for their *puellae* only in illness, L. engages in such behaviour. **Caelestia numina**: a common way of referring to gods: [V]. *Aetn.* 339, Ov. *Her.* 20.181, *Fas.* 6.251, *EP* 3.6.21 (all same *sedes*). For **numina** elsewhere in [Tib.] 3, see *ad* 3.5.29 and 3.6.22.

Securos...dies are of course a *desideratum* in elegy, but not present in its reality: the phrase is attested elsewhere only at Mart. 5.20.2 *securis liceat frui diebus* and Plin. *Pan.* 68.2 *securus tibi et laetus dies* (on the peculiarities of *securus*, see *ad* 3.3.32). Prop. and Ov. seem by contrast to relish the volatile nature of their relationship, even inventing obstacles. **Non sinit ire**: cf. Prop. 3.25.8 *tu* *bene conveniens non sinis ire iugum*, Ov. *Tr.* 4.3.24, *EP* 1.3.36, *Ibis* 8, 12 (all without *ire*, most in the same *sedes*).

> et, cum te fusco Somnus velavit amictu,
> 56   vanum nocturnis fallit imaginibus,

The dream-vision discusses the act of falling asleep (cf. Patroclus at Hom. *Il.* 23.69, drawing attention to Achilles' sleep, and Cynthia at Prop. 4.7.13, drawing attention to Prop.'s), which may reinforce the urgency of the god's message—N. is faithless *right now*. It is appropriate for **Somnus** to have a **fusco...amictu**, as he generally travels in darkness (*OLD amictus* 5, *TLL* 1.1901.13–50 for the poetic extension of the word; cf. μελάμπεπλος δὲ Νύξ at Eur. *Ion* 1150); the image of him wrapping his victims in a cloak is compelling, and unattested, but perhaps derives from Tib. 2.1.89 (where, however, Sleep has wings, of a different colour: *tacitus furvis circumdatus alis*, probably deriving from Call. *Hymn* 4.234); **fusco** is not otherwise connected to **somnus**, nor is *furvis* (nor does either colour describe an *amictus*). But other cloaks real and metaphorical mimic the rainbow: *purpureus* (V. *A.* 3.405 *purpureo velare comas adopertus amictu*, [V.] *Cul.*172, Stat. *Silv.* 5.3.119, Sil. 7.447; cf. *Tyrius* at Ov. *Ars* 2.297 and Stat. *Silv.* 3.4.55), and *puniceus* (Stat. *Silv.* 2.1.132 *puniceo velabat amictu*), *glaucus* (V. *A.* 8.33 *glauco velabat amictu*, 12.885, Stat. *Silv.* 1.3.71), *roseus* ([V.] *Lyd.* 176), *croceus* (Ov. *Ars* 3.179 *croceo velatur amictu*, *Met.* 10.1 *croceo velatus amictu*), *auratus* (Ov. *Met.* 14.263 *aurato circumvelatur amictu*), *niveus* (Ov. *Fas.* 3.363 *niveo velatus amictu*, Stat. *Silv.* 3.3.3), *sanguineus* (Stat. *Theb.* 3.125), *niger* (Stat. *Theb.* 3.416), *flavus* (Stat. *Silv.* 2.3.16), *albens* (Stat. *Silv.* 5.2.67), *ater* (VF 6.745, Sil. 7.687, 15.284; cf. Sil. 5.36 *atrae noctis*). Night has a cloak more often than Sleep does (e.g. Eur. *Ion* 1150, Sil. 12.613 *terras caeco nox condit amictu* and cf. 15.284). Lucr. 6.1134 *caeli mutemus amictum* (for moving to a new location) and V. *A.* 1.412 (Venus) *multo nebulae circum dea fudit amictu* are rather bold and may have inspired L., as might Ov. *Met.* 1.611, of the couch of Sleep. As Lyne notes *ad* [V.] *Cir.* 250 (*velavit amictu*), the collocation is regular at line-end, and seems to be felt as especially suitable for poetry; among his citations see Cat. 64.266, V. *A.* 3.545, VF 1.659, and those quoted above (all with the verb).

Vanum: possibly adverbial, but Ov. *EP* 2.9.29, *vana...si fallat vota* [*Ceres*], suggests that Apollo may refer proleptically to L.'s prayers, 'making it that you have prayed in vain'. Taking the adjective with **te** is also attractive, 'you, when you are at leisure'. Some connective would help with construal, either between **fallit** and the preceding **velavit** or the following **mavolt**. **Fallit**: Apollo either falsifies L.'s claim not to have slept earlier that night or, more probably, the present tense is generalizing; N. behaves this way on a regular basis, whenever L. is asleep. Sleep here assumes some of the characteristics of the deceitful *puella*.

Nocturnis...imaginibus: Cairns 2006a: 80, 160, 230 sees this line as Gallan and draws a comparison to Prop. 1.5.24 (*nescit Amor priscis cedere imaginibus*) and 1.20.41–2 (*nescius undis/errorem blandis tardat imaginibus*). The phrase occurs elsewhere at Ov. *Am*. 3.5.31 and 33; cf. such phrases as *imago noctis* (e.g. Ov. *Her*. 19.193) and *nocturnis...somnis* (e.g. Hor. *Od*. 4.1.37). Note too the connection to 7–12, which are generalizing.

> carminibus celebrata tuis formosa Neaera
> 58   alterius mavolt esse puella viri,

Apollo lets the cat out of the bag: N. wishes to be, perhaps already is, someone else's girl (it is amusing that the lengthy preamble has led up to this succinct message; line 58 tells the whole story). Of course, this is not privileged knowledge; L. has suspected this from the start. Why does Apollo tell (see *ad* 3.4.38 on the punishment of informers in Ov. *Met*., notably the raven in Apollo's own liaison with Coronis, 2.612–15, 631–2)? He ought to know that his news is unwelcome (indeed, this may account for his lengthy preamble, which now looks like nervousness at having to get to the point). The elegiac lover would usually prefer not to know about the infidelities of his *puella* (see *ad* 3.20). Although there are no common words, most readers see allusion to V. *E*. 10.21–3, where Apollo appears to Gallus (with no preamble at all, *venit Apollo*) and informs him that *tua cura Lycoris/perque nives alium perque horrida castra secuta est*. As always with *E*. 10, this suggests the possibility of a (lengthier) Gallan treatment, which may influence L. here.

Carminibus...celebrata: echoes the statement at 3.1.7–8 (see *ad loc*.). Poetry is the only gift the lover (says he) can give (Introduction, Section I); cf. Prop. 3.2.17 *fortunata meo si qua es celebrata libello*; Ov. *Am*. 1.10.59 *est quoque carminibus meritas celebrare puellas*; Pichon 1991: 103. The noun-verb conjunction is of course not found only in elegy (e.g. V. *A*. 8.303, Hor. *Od*. 1.7.6, Ov. *Met*. 2.252, Sil. 15.276), but in its generic context, **celebrata** is ambiguous: the poet seeks a certain degree of notoriety, and Messalla is positively *celeber* at 2.1.33 (perhaps first in this sense in Tib.; see commentators *ad loc*.), but it is not always desirable for the *puella* to be well-known (cf. Corinna, made famous throughout the town to Ov's detriment, in *Am*. 3.12.7–10). On the other hand, claims of the 'public' nature of the *puella* also serve as poetic self-advertisement: elegiac women become known through the dissemination of men's poetry about them (e.g. Prop. 3.2.17, quoted above, and see Introduction, Section I). On the use of **celebrata** to refer to a book of poetry currently under way, see Prop. 3.2.17.

On **formosa**, see *ad* 3.1.7. Given *celebrata* above, we may be meant to draw a connection between (the much less ambiguous) *famosa* and **formosa** (first apparently in Lucil. 11.419, *et formosus homo fuit et famosus*); for L's suppression, and employment, of alliteration, see *ad* 3.4.10. **Alterius mavolt...viri**: paralleled by Hor. *Od*. 3.24.22 *alterius viri* (in a rather different context); Ov. *RA* 772 *esse quod alterius coeperat illa viri*. The use of the semi-technical **puella** suggests the normal elegiac situation, i.e. that N. prefers another, and **viri** often signifies the rival with some 'official' claim on the **puella**, as opposed to the poet-lover (Introduction, Section I). But note that the language is ambiguous: N. might, despite **puella**, be considering (divorce and re-)marriage. Thus far in the corpus, N. has not been much like other elegiac mistresses; here she proves to share their most salient characteristic, that of faithlessness (and this may encourage us to reread 3.1 in a different light—perhaps L. was simply lying to himself, pretending, like Cat., that his relationship was quasi-marital (see Introduction, Section I)). For **puella viri** at line-end, see *ad* 3.4.52.

>   diversasque suas agitat mens impia curas,
> 60   nec gaudet casta nupta Neaera domo.

Suas, the manuscript reading, is beloved of no editor (Tränkle 1990 terms it a stopgap); **diversas** ought probably to have a dative, rather than another adjective modifying the same noun (Lipsius' emendation *tuis* provides this). The text printed emphasizes N.'s independence from L., drawing attention to her disobedience of the marital formula *ubi tu Gaius, ego Gaia*; unlike a proper *coniunx*, she retains her own concerns.

   Agitat mens: V. *A.* 9.187, Sen. *Med.* 47, Sil. 13.399; for the verb as mental (= *cogito* + *acturum*), see Varro *DLL* 6.42, *TLL* 1.1335.80; elegiac usage at Pichon 1991: 82 and cf. Prop. 1.7.5 *nostros agitamus amores*, primarily of love poetry. **Agitat...curas**: attested in poetry only elsewhere at Sen. *HF* 138; otherwise in Liv. **Mens impia** is harsh language; on **impia**, see *ad* 3.4.16 and 3.6.42. We may find the accusation more, or less, shocking placed in the mouth of a god: L. avoids responsibility for the attribution, but it gains emphasis when spoken by such an authority. **Mens impia** occurs elsewhere in poetry at Cat. 67.25 of an incestuous father-in-law and [Sen.] *Oct.* 225 of Nero, spoken by Octavia. As those citations suggest, *pietas* often entails familial or conjugal obligations (see too, in elegy, Prop. 2.9.19–20, *impia* of Cynthia, with Fedeli 2005 *ad loc.*, Ov. *Tr.* 1.2.37 (*coniunx*), and Pichon 1991: 171); perhaps L. (or Apollo) wishes again to suggest the formal nature of the relationship with N.

   Diversas...curas: i.e., other than those shared with L. (they are **suas**), but often simply of a variety of concerns (Ter. *And.* 260, V. *A.* 12.487). Or possibly this is an extension of the elegiac use of *cura* for love object (see *ad* 3.1.19), and Apollo means to suggest that N. has many other lovers.

   Gaudet and its noun are used in elegy, especially in Ov. *Am.*, for the pleasures of sexual intercourse (*Am.* 1.10.32, 2.3.2, 2.5.29, 2.9.44 and 50, 2.19.58, 3.6.88, 3.7.63; the only exception is at 3.15.7–8, where it refers to Mantua's pride in Vergil, Verona's in Catullus, and Paelignia's in Ovid; see too the memorable Ov. *Her.* 15.109 *mihi nescioquis 'fugiunt tua gaudia' dixit*, where *gaudia* refers by metonymy to Phaon). In Prop., about half of the occurrences of *gaudium* have sadistic or other unpleasant overtones (e.g. 1.3.23, 1.12.16, 2.8.18, 2.24.17, 3.6.23, 3.8.35, 4.8.63). Note too 2.1.8, *gaudet laudatis ire superba* *comis*, and 3.2.2, *gaudeat ut solito tacta puella sono*, both of which combine the notion of poetic fame and of female rejoicing (each in a slightly different manner). For Tib., however, the concept is non-sexual: e.g. Tib. 1.6.81, 2.5.83 (at 2.3.49 he inveighs against *puellae* who *divitibus...gaudere*). L.'s slightly peculiar diction (*esse* should be understood) perhaps seeks to capture both (what ought to be) N.'s pride in being chosen by L. and her unfortunately out-of-control sexuality. Or **nec gaudet** simply means 'she doesn't want to', or perhaps Apollo simply likes the word (cf. line 69, where he uses it again). Note too L.'s claim, via the Muses, that poetry causes *formosae* to rejoice (3.1.8), which is also undermined by Apollo.

Casta: transferred to **domo**, as at Cat. 64.384, V. G. 2.524, Hor. Od. 4.5.21, and Prop. 2.6.28 (each word in the same *sedes*), Luc. 9.201; cf. Cic. Cael. 9 *castissima domo*. On *casta*, see *ad* 3.1.23; the word is one of L.'s regular descriptors of N., and Apollo's denial of it to her may make us revise our opinion of her, of L.'s judgement of her, or of Apollo himself. The mention of **domo** again raises questions about the precise parameters of the relationship (see Introduction, Section I): if N. is in fact a *nupta* in L.'s own *domus*, he should not need a dream to arouse his suspicions about her behaviour.

Nupta raises, not for the first time, the question that troubles many readers of elegy: what, precisely, is the legal status of the elegiac relationship? As has become increasingly clear, this is a question to which the poems (especially these poems) give so many opposing answers that we simply cannot make a final determination (see Introduction, Section I). That said, it is rare to find such technical terms outside of L. (see his use of *coniunx* in 3.1.26–7, and discussion *ad loc.*); other elegists prefer more ambiguous terminology (see Pichon 1991: 216–17 s.v. *nubere*). The more precise term here, of course, need not induce us to believe that L. intends to convey a biographical truth. Rather, he regularly makes use of vocabulary and imagery which invoke the marriage bond; see too 79, *promittit coniugium*. On **nupta** as wife or bride, see Cat. 61.78b, 66.87, Prop. 3.13.23, Ov. Ars 3.613 (where it must refer to legitimate wives), RA 774 (Helen and Menelaus), Fas. 2.794 (Lucretia).

>   A crudele genus nec fidum femina nomen!
> 62   A pereat, didicit fallere siqua virum!

L. has the dream-Apollo engage in a stereotypical anti-woman polemic (Otto 1890: 231). Perhaps the most famous example of this kind of negative generalizing about women can be found in the mouth of another god, when Mercury succinctly warns Aeneas against Dido at V. A. 4.569–70, *varium et mutabile semper/femina* (the commentators note *ad loc.* that this is the first use of *mutabile* in the neuter of people, and *mutabilis* is in the same *sedes* in 63 of this poem), but the concept dates back to Agamemnon's underworld curse of women at Hom. Od. 11.405–56. For similar thoughts in elegy, see Prop. 2.25.22 (*credule, nulla diu femina pondus habet*, with Fedeli 2005 *ad loc.*), 3.13.23 (*hoc genus infidum nuptarum*), and for an earlier Latin version, Plaut. *Mil.* 456.

The first sentence has only limited grammatical structure, which hints at L.'s/Apollo's agitation; **a** introduces two nouns either complementary or appositional to **femina** (with *est* supplied); for the poetic nature of the particle, see *TLL* 1.1441.41–7, 1.1442.23–48 (1.1443.19–24 for repetition); Kershaw 1980 and 1983 on Augustan usage. See too *ad* 3.4.82, 3.6.27, and 3.17.3.

Crudele genus alludes to the notion, found first in Hesiod's myth of Pandora, that women and men are distinct species; the phrase occurs elsewhere only at V. *A.* 6.359, of a barbarous race. The adjective is frequently used of men who abandon women, e.g. Theseus (*crudelis...mentis*) at Cat. 64.136–7 and (*crudelem*) Prop. 1.8.16, Aeneas (*crudelis*) at Ov. *Her.* 7.182, or do not return affection, e.g. V. *E.* 2.6, Ov. *Met.* 3.442 with Bömer 1969 *ad loc.*; on *crudelis*, see Pichon 1991: 117. (The elegists more commonly use *saevus*; see line 66 below).

Fidum...nomen: appositional with **femina** (see V. *A.* 7.717 for another example of **nomen** used appositionally); the noun/adjective combination occurs elsewhere only at Stat. *Theb.* 6.372 (in the plural). As Axelson notes, **femina** is the term preferred to *mulier* from the Augustan period on (1945: 53–7; cf. Adams 1972: 239). On elegiac uses of *fidus*, see Pichon 1991: 148.

Pereat may simply be exaggeration, or it may, especially when combined with Apollo's other comments, imply personal hostility towards N. (the generalizing **siqua** does not necessarily mitigate the claim). Either way, it is peculiar in the mouth of a god, who could simply dispense with optative subjunctives and kill her; once again, L.'s focalization is intrusive. The verb appears frequently in the elegists for curses, e.g. Tib. 1.1.51 (riches), 2.4.27 (those who amass riches), Ov. *Her.* 19.105 *a potius peream* (before you love another), *Ars* 2.272 *a pereant* those who use gifts sneakily, 3.494 *a pereant* those who make it necessary to disguise your handwriting in love letters, *Fas.* 4.240–1 *a pereant* at each line-beginning of Attis, referring to his offending genitalia (see *TLL* 1.1442.66–74 for the regular combination of **a** and **pereat**).

Didicit fallere is a Tibullan notion (*non ego fallere doctus*, 1.9.37; cf. *fingere...didicit, perdidicit* 1.9.65), also found in other elegists. Generally, however, the elegist has taught the *puella* her tricks, which she uses to play him false. As is typical for the elegiac persona, Apollo sets himself up as a *praeceptor amoris*, but also betrays his own fallibility. Ov. *EP* 3.3.53 denies, of his books, *didicisti fallere nuptas*.

Fallere...virum: cf. Ov. *Ars* 1.310 (Pasiphae), 3.484 (*est vobis vestros fallere cura viros*, not of husbands), *Tr.* 2.461–2 Tibullus *docetque/qua nuptae possint fallere ab arte viros*; see *ad* 3.1.6. It is strange to find the elegist referring to himself with the noun **virum** given what that noun usually means (see Introduction, Section I). **Siqua**: a misleading use of the indefinite: Apollo has a specific woman in mind, and has already told us who. His generalization may seek to soften the hostile tone, or to allow for the possibility that his knowledge is incorrect.

Sed flecti poterit – mens est mutabilis illis –
64   tu modo cum multa bracchia tende prece.

Abruptly, Apollo changes tack, assuring L. that it is not too late. This has two effects: (1) Apollo has suddenly become the spokesman for elegiac (i.e. insecure) love, rather than simply allowing L. to make up his own mind. The assertion that women are fickle means that L. can attempt to win back N.'s affections, so in some ways this poem (re-)creates the usual situation of elegy. (2) It allows Apollo to continue railing against women for a different failing. His words here are very close to Mercury's at V. *A.* 4.569–70 (quoted at 3.2.61); note too Ov. *Met.* 2.145–6 *si mutabile pectus/est tibi*, Ov. *Her.* 7.51 (Dido to Aeneas: *tu quoque cum ventis utinam mutabilis esses*), *Fas.* 4.601 (Demeter: *non est mutabile pectus* about the desirability of Hades as a son-in-law), *Tr.* 5.13.19–29 *neque enim mutabile robur…pectoris esse tui*. See *ad* 3.2.9. Prop. 2.9.35–6, *feminea non constat foedus in ira*, may also be relevant—although it is used in that poem to make the opposite point: Prop. criticizes the *puella* for so easily changing her mind, while N.'s potential mutability may work to L.'s advantage.

Flectere: for this metaphorical usage, see *OLD* 9a, *TLL* 6.1.893.25–60. Cat. 64.136–7 *nullane res potuit crudelis flectere mentis/consilium?* is a probable inspiration for this line. **Flectere** can be used in elegy for both the alienation (Prop. 1.19.24) and return (Prop. 1.8.39) of a *puella*'s affections; see Pichon 1991: 150. As at 59, it is N.'s **mens** which is defective; see *ad* 3.3.21.

Tu modo: with the imperative typical of didactic moments (e.g. Prop. 2.20.14, 4.2.20); see *ad* 3.10.16. **Bracchia tende**: ancient suppliants held forth their arms, palms up (rather than together at face or chest height), so this phrase, and gesture, are not as peculiar as they might seem. The imperative mood is especially appropriate from a god (though it may be better to take Apollo's words as merely advice). The phrase is especially frequent in Ov. *Met.*, occurring on average more than three times in every book (if *tendere manus/palmas* are included), but not normally in the imperative, and with a number of meanings (see further Anderson 1993). It is first attested at V. *G.* 2.296, of an oak's branches (note too Cat. 66.10, *levia protendens bracchia*, of Berenice's prayers and vows). See Pichon 1991: 96 on *bracchia*.

Multa…prece (Lenz/Galinsky *fide*) is more suitable to a god than a mortal, but the *puella* is sometimes assimilated to a goddess (Lieberg 1962, focusing on Cat.). It is possible that L. is not to pray to N., but to a god (as at Tib. 1.5.18, where Tib. has prayed for Marathus' safety); see below, line 76. In Prop. *preces* are used almost interchangeably for gods and mortals, and sometimes ambiguously (perhaps similar to our 'I beg of you?'); cf. *ad* 3.3.2. On the regular manuscript confusion between *prece* and *fide*, see Tränkle 1990 and Navarro Antolín 1996 *ad loc.*, and below *ad* 3.6.46.

Saevus Amor docuit validos temptare labores,
66   saevus Amor docuit verbera posse pati.

The suffering of love (with here a glancing suggestion of the trope of *servitium amoris*, further developed as Apollo continues) is quintessentially Propertian (Navarro Antolín 2005: 309–11). But the vocabulary of physical abuse is Tibullan: 1.6.37–8 *non saeva recuso/verbera, detrecto non ego vincla pedum*; 2.3.80 *non ego me vinclis verberibusque nego*; cf. too *saeva... verbera* at Ov. *Am.* 1.7.6. The couplet as a whole evokes a number of genres: first elegy (**Amor**), then didactic (**docuit**), then epic (**temptare labores**). The hexameter is missing in the manuscripts and supplied by the *Fragmentum Cuiacianum* (see Introduction, Section VIII). **Saevus Amor docuit**: while love is often, at least implicitly, savage in elegy (*saevus* is frequent in Propertius), this phrase is Vergilian (*E.* 8.47–8; same metrical *sedes*; see Lee 1958–9: 16–17), with noun-adjective combination deriving from Enn. *Med.* 216 Jocelyn (*saevo amore* of Medea; cf. Sen. *Med.* 850), but with a long Greek tradition as well (see Navarro Antolín 1996 *ad loc.*). Prop. 1.1 contains both the notion of *Amor* as a teacher—or, perhaps better, tamer— (1.1.5 with Fedeli 1980 *ad loc.*, Lee 1958–9: 16, and Parca 1986: 472) and of love's savagery (1.1.27), but they are combined more intimately in this poem. Love (personified, insofar as we can tell) is **saevus**, often programmatically: also at Tib. 1.6.3, Ov. *Am.* 1.1.5, 1.6.34, and 2.10.19, *Ars* 1.18, *RA* 530, VF 7.307, Stat. *Theb.* 1.128 (there *amor regendi*); for **saevus** in elegy, see Pichon 1991: 257–8. On the unpleasantness of (personified) **Amor** in general, see Ov. *Am.* 2.9.1–6, [V.] *Cir.* 135–6 (with Lyne 1978 *ad loc.* for an alternative interpretation). For the repetition of a phrase at line-start, see Wills 1996: 180–2. We may also be meant to think of the Ovidian 'battle' between Amor and Apollo in *Met.* 1, which tells the story of Amor's victory over Apollo in the person of Daphne.

Validos appears in Tibullus only of farm animals, implements, and chains, and is found elsewhere in the *CT* only at 3.11.15, and once in Prop., at 2.34.48, of a snare or noose. **Labores** can stand as a shorthand for *militia amoris* (e.g. Tib. 1.2.33 and 1.4.47 *duros subisse labores* with Maltby 2002 *ad locc.* for further parallels and discussion, Prop. 1.1.9, Ov. *Ars* 2.66; cf. Tib. 2.3.79 for agricultural labours); the notion is also Vergilian (similar constructions at V. *A.* 6.437 *duros perferre labores*, 8.291 *duros mille labores*, [V.] *Cir.* 291 *duros passa labores*, all of which are likely to derive from Lucr. 3.999 *durum sufferre laborem*—and note too *E.* 10.1, which may suggest a Gallan tone). The notion that the lover will spare no effort appears in Latin first for us at Plaut. *Merc.* 858–63, but is presumably a commonplace (see Zagagi 1988: 204 n. 43 for Greek citations). In Ovid's amatory elegies, the word tends to be used for any expense or effort. **Validos labores**: otherwise unattested, but a neat variation; the standard phrase uses *durus*; see Pichon 1991: 180–1 on the amatory nuances of *labor*. **Temptare labores** is rare in prose as well as poetry, but see *temptare laborem* in the same *sedes* at V. A. 5.499. The verb may suggest epic endeavours (see e.g. *quis [=quibus] labor Aonios seno pede ducere cantus*, Stat. *Silv.* 5.3.92), not least among them those of Hercules (note **labores**).

Verbera posse pati: closest parallel at Tib. 1.6.37–8 *non saeva recuso/verbera*; see Pichon 1991: 290, and see above. For **pati** see Pichon 1991: 226–7.

>   Me quondam Admeti niveas pavisse iuvencas
> 68   non est in vanum fabula ficta iocum.

Apollo now launches into a story about his own unhappy love affair, suggesting that the object of the previous couplet is himself as well as (potentially) L. Readers may wonder how appropriate his tale is, not because it is about same-sex love (indeed, Tib. treats a variety of amatory relationships), but because the point of the narrative seems to be that Apollo was unhappy in love too, and that that is simply how love works, which is not much comfort. Hellenistic poets (Call. *Hymn* 2.47–54 with F. Williams 1978 *ad loc.*, Rhianus fr. 10 Pow., *Schol. Eur. Alc.* 1) seem to have been the first to make this a love-story (otherwise a punishment; see Eur. *Alc.* 1–14); Ov. *Her.* 5.151–2, *Ars* 2.239–41, Sen. *Phaed.* 296–8, and Stat. *Silv.* 3.3.58 do not specify, and at Ov. *Met.* 2.679–83 Apollo, distracted by love, does not pay attention to the cattle, which allows Mercury to steal them. The love-story takes over (e.g. Plut. *Num.* 4.8), presumably under the influence of Callimachus.

Beyond this, however, readers of elegy will find this story very familiar, as Tib. tells it in 2.3.11–28 (where it is noteworthy for being his only foray into extended mythic narrative; it is of course possible that this poem precedes that, but traditional dating schemata have L. as derivative). In that poem, Nemesis is in the country, and Tib. fantasizes about being with her, even at the cost of blisters on his soft hands (2.3.10). For, he says, Apollo, although beautiful, did manual labour because of his love of Admetus, despite his sister's embarrassment and mother's grief, and to the neglect of his other duties. There, the emphasis is on the details of rustic life; here, on Apollo's willingness to undergo sufferings. The first-person narration reads as a direct challenge to the Tibullan poem: as Apollo explicitly claims, the *fabula* is not simply designed for empty entertainment, but real-life experience (see Solimano 1970 on the elegiac versions of the tale). Apollo hereby puts himself in the tradition of the elegiac expert in love (see Introduction, Section I); see, most notably, Ov.'s observation at *Ars* 1.23–30 that he will not claim poetic inspiration, but real-life experience (*usus*), and Prop.'s similar claim at 2.1.3–4. But it is comical for a god, especially a god of prophecy, to select scenes from his own biography in order to persuade his listener; further, we may hear in Apollo's claim that his fall from glory is not funny (**non est in vanum ... iocum**) the god's own touchiness about what must surely be a sensitive subject. (Apollo was notoriously unsuccessful in love; this is a leitmotif of his appearances in Ov. *Met.*: Daphne in Book 1, Coronis in

Book 2, Hyacinthus and Cyparissus in Book 10; see J. F. Miller 1998, Fulkerson 2006).

Niveas...iuvencas: joined in Vergil (*E.* 6.46, *G.* 1.15) and Ov. (*Am.* 2.12.25–6 *niveus* of a cow, 3.13.13); there is variation as to which animals Apollo pastures; see F. Williams *ad* Call. *Hymn Ap.* 48, where (following Homer) they are horses. For *niveus*, see *ad* 3.1.9. **Pavisse**: the pasturing of cattle is a detail on which Latin poets focus when they mention this tale: e.g. V. *G.* 3.2, Ov. *Her.* 5.151, *Ars* 2.239 (same *sedes*). L.'s version of the tale begins here, as does Tib.'s (*pavit et Admeti tauros formosus Apollo*, 2.3.11), but L. quickly moves on to his own feelings. Apollo speaks of himself, using a (possibly distancing) infinitive construction, which allows him to allude to previous poetry as he tells his own story, and shows him as a critical interpreter of both Tib. and, potentially, L. himself.

Fabula ficta: on the lies of poets, see Ov. *Met.* 13.732–4 with Bömer 1982 *ad loc.*, Ov. *Fas.* 3.738 *non habet ingratos fabula nostra iocos* (relevant but on a different topic); the notion appears first, of the Muses' poetry, at Hes. *Th.* 27–8 (with vast bibliography). As Tib. notes, this story is now famous, whatever Apollo here claims: *Fabula nunc ille est: sed cui sua cura puella est,/fabula sit mavult quam sine amore deus*, 2.3.31–2; if the Tib. poem post-dates L., the noun would have even more point. On the elegiac nuances of *fabula*, see Pichon 1991: 140.

Iocum: used at Cat. 42.3 when a woman does not take Cat.'s threats seriously, Prop. 2.24.16 of being tricked by a *puella*, Ov. *Fas.* 6.320 *est multi fabula parva ioci*; see Pichon 1991: 175.

> Tunc ego nec cithara poteram gaudere sonora
> 70   nec similes chordis reddere voce sonos,

While he was in love, Apollo gained no joy from his usual musical pursuits; a similar sentiment is expressed of him in the third person at Tib. 2.3.12: *nec cithara intonsae profueruntve comae*. Here, however, matters are more serious: he was not able to play his normal instrument, but rather had to resort to the bucolic reed-pipe (see *ad* 3.4.71). The lines are surely metapoetic, hinting at generic constraints, and refer also to the necessity for L.'s composition of elegiac laments (see Introduction, Section I). Further, Apollo here finds himself in the position of the elegist, who cannot help himself with his own poetry—but also in the position of his mythic self, where, although the god of prophecy, he cannot see that his love for Daphne is doomed (Ov. *Met.* 1.491), or, although a god of healing, he cannot cure either his own lovesickness (*Met.* 1.523–4) or even the wound he has inflicted upon another (*Met.* 2.618). The former *topos* is frequent elsewhere (e.g. at Ov. *Her.* 5.149–50 where the healer Oenone cannot medicate her lovesickness). The epic adjective **sonora** is not much used: it appears first in V. *A.* 1.53, 12.139 (winds and rivers), 12.712 (bronze shield), Stat. *Silv.* 1.5.4 (*ferae...sonorae* of a tortoise-shell lyre). On elegiac uses of *gaudeo* see *ad* 3.4.60; the echo may be deliberate, emphasizing the difference between the joys of the faithless and the sorrows of the faithful.

Similes...sonos: elsewhere at Ov. *Met.* 11.734–5 *maesto similem plenumque querelae/ora dedere sonum*, and occasionally in Imperial prose authors; cf. Ov. *Met.* 1.708 *sonum tenuem similemque querenti*. **Reddere voce**: the accusative is much more common in prose and poetry (esp. *reddere voces* at line-end: e.g. Cat. 64.166, Lucr. 4.577, Cic. *Div.* 1.13.11 = *Arat.* 3.4, Var. Atax fr. 15.5 Courtney (quoted *ad* 3.4.72), V. *A.* 1.409, 6.689, [V.] *Cir.* 255); for the ablative (where, as here, there is another direct object), see Hor. *Od.* 4.11.34–5 *modos, amanda/voce quos reddas*, Ov. *Tr.* 1.8.26 *parili reddere voce vale*.

    sed perlucenti cantum meditabar avena
72   ille ego Latonae filius atque Iovis.

Sed, as often in Latin, here carries an adversative sense: 'No, and in fact'. **Perlucenti**: the word means either 'transparent', as at Ov. *Met.* 4.313 (same *sedes*) and 411, 'shining', as at Cat. 68.57 and below, 3.12.13, or, as here, 'capable of being seen through because not solid' (*OLD* 1b; elsewhere at e.g. Plaut. *Rud.* 102, Sen. *HF* 1001, Juv. 11.13, and Varro *DRR* 3.5.13); here it denotes the loose weave binding the reed-pipe together but allowing for light to pass through (*avena*; *fistula* more common and prosaic; see Coleman *ad* V. *E.* 1.2, the ultimate model for this line, but Lee 1958–9: 21 sees this usage as 'Silver'). Luck and Navarro Antolín 1996 prefer Huschke's *permulcenti* (Dissen 1835: 356); Delz 1991: 62 suggests *praecludenti*. Perhaps, given the pastoral situation, we are to imagine the pipes as bound by vines (according to West 1992: 111–12, cloth or wooden frames were standard, but Landels 1999: 70 mentions twine and straw as well). It is perhaps surprising after his emphasis on musical inability in the previous couplet to find that Apollo continues to make music (if of a different kind). He has switched to bucolic (or rather, a kind of hybrid bucolic-elegy), in the fashion of Gallus in V. *E.* 10 (see below). On the materials and composition of the pan-pipe, see West 1992: 109–12, and on its lowly and rustic status, 110–11; Landels 1999: 70–1 also observes its more restricted musical range than the lyre, and Eur. *Or.* 146 suggests the limited volume of the instrument (which will metapoetically also signify its limited pretensions).

Meditabar avena: an echo of V. *E.* 1.2 and 10.50–1 (in the same *sedes*): in the first (*meditaris avena*), Meliboeus envies Tityrus, who is able to remain in the rustic world and play his pipes; in the second, more directly relevant but with a different verb, Gallus claims that he will play his *Chalcidicus...versus* on Sicilian pipe (*Siculi modulabor avena*). See too *modulatus avena* at Tib. 2.1.53 and *modulemur avena* at Calp. Sic. 1.93 (both same *sedes*), and VF 4.386 *modulatur carmen avena*; the phrase is evidently a marker of bucolic song. **Meditabar** (*TLL* 8.579.75–580.3; also at e.g. V. *E.* 6.8 *agrestem tenui meditabor harundine Musam*; cf. *Phoebo...meditante* at *E.* 6.82, [V.] *Lyd.* 6, Ov. *EP* 3.4.45–6 *meditata* *querellas/ . . . lyra*) is perhaps chosen by L. (or Apollo) as an Alexandrian marker, emphasizing his poetic effort (cf. *ad* 3.15.13); note too Var. Atax fr. 15.4–5 Courtney: *At tunc longe gratissima Phoebi/dextera consimiles meditatur reddere voces*, seemingly about the similarity of the lyre to the music of the spheres.

Ille ego: used in poetry to make an aggrandizing claim (but note Austin 1968: 110 on the 'fall from grace' implicit in other such statements): e.g. Tib. 1.5.9 (the poet saved Delia's life), 1.6.31 (the poet lay outside all night), Prop. 4.9.38 (Hercules boasts about his labours), Ov. *Am*. 2.1.2 (staking a poetic claim), *Her*. 16.246 (Paris reveals himself), *Met*. 4.226–8 (the Sun boasts to Leucothoe), but especially V. *A*. 1.1a-b *ille ego, qui quondam gracili modulatus avena/carmen*; it is not clear how old these latter lines are, but some attribute them to V. himself (the phrase's recurrence at Ov. *Am*. 2.1.2 and *Tr*. 4.10.1 helps with this claim); cf. Stat. *Silv*. 4.3.76–7. Apollo, or L., inverts Vergil's career, moving from the high to the low genres (see Putnam 2010, with ample bibliography).

Latonae filius atque Iovis: gods (and mortals) often cite genealogy to show status: here there is a disjunction between being the son of Jupiter and playing pastoral strains. The line, which Apollo's identity fully occupies, has a Homeric feel. But from a metrical point of view, Apollo's claim becomes comical, for he complains about performing one inferior mode of poetry (pastoral, normally in hexameter) in another (elegiac couplets, more elevated in subject matter but demeaned by metre). And Apollo's regular poetic association with rustics (Daphne, Oenone, Gallus) undermines his claim to be an outsider in this world. **Latonae**: Apollo's mother is also mentioned at Tib. 2.3.27, where she is horrified by his behaviour; cf. line 29. **Latonae filius**: apparently first at Liv. Andron. *Od*. 21.1 *Mercurius cumque eo filius Latonas* (cf. *Latonae puerum* at Hor. *Od*. 4.6.37). **Atque**: on the lack of elision, see Platnauer 1951: 78–82 (elegy usually elides the form; not doing so may be a deliberately 'epic' gesture). Butterfield 2008: 397 n. 33 suggests that this instance is amateurish and *metri causa* (his text mistakenly refers to an occurrence at 3.5.72, rather than in this poem).

> Nescis quid sit amor, iuvenis, si ferre recusas
> 74   immitem dominam coniugiumque ferum.

Apollo continues in his role as elegiac teacher (see Introduction, Section I). Given that elegiac love tends to be painful, Apollo's words make sense in this context, though his own experience with Admetus does not precisely match L.'s with N. (the former is a case of *servitium amoris*, the latter of suspected infidelity). The difficulty is eased by the notion of *labor* (see *ad* 3.4.65), which covers all efforts elegiac lovers make; they often imagine themselves undergoing literal physical toil. Apollo assures L. that love is simply like this; his (possibly deliberate) conflation of elegiac language (**dominam**) with legalistic (**coniugium**) continues the elegiac, and especially Lygdamean, trend of obfuscating the *puella*'s status (see Introduction, Section I).

Nescis quid sit amor: V. *E.* 8.43 *nunc scio, quid sit amor* in the same *sedes* (deriving from Theocr. 3.15) is important for this couplet. **Iuvenis** is one of the few hints anywhere in elegy about the age of the *amator*. (L. suggests his youth at 3.2.1–2 and uses *iuvenis* again at 3.5.6.) Normally, we assume the *amator* to be a bit older than this (and, in the case of Tib. 1.8.31–2, to be himself attracted to *iuvenes*)—but the term is vague, and covers men throughout the whole period in which they might be in military service, i.e. up to the mid-forties. Apollo is himself described as *iuvenis* at line 23, which reinforces the parallelism suggested between man and god.

Ferre recusas: when conjoined in poetry, always in this *sedes*, but not normally in an erotic context; the phrase is literal at Ov. *Met.* 10.171 (Apollo does not refuse to carry nets for Hyacinthus); cf. Sen. *Phaed.* 135. **Recusas**: cf. Tib. 1.6.37–8 *non saeva recuso/verbera*; the verb is not found in Prop. but frequent in Ov.

Immitem dominam: the elegiac mistress is normally cruel, though her behaviour is not usually expressed with this conjunction of words (but see Hor. *Od.* 1.33.2 about *immitis Glycerae*, who is cruel to an Albius, normally assumed to be Tib.; see Introduction, Section V). **Dominam**: Apollo invokes the standard elegiac trope of *servitium amoris* (see Introduction, Section I, and Pichon 1991: 134).

Coniugiumque ferum: cf. Ov. *Met.* 4.515 (a simile, *utque ferae sequitur vestigia coniugis*); each word is Ovidian; see *ad* 3.1.26. **Ferum**: the elegiac relationship is normally an uncivilized one (see *ad* 3.4.65 *saevus Amor*). But at Tib. 1.5.5, the poet names himself *ferum* when he had thought he could live without Delia (see Maltby 2002 *ad loc.* for the potential wordplay there between *ferus* and *ferreus*; there may also be wordplay between *ferus* and *ferre*). The word appears again in 86, in a simile describing how L. is *not*. There is thus inconsistency in the elegiac system: love is cruel, but the lover is not—and this may adumbrate his ultimate inability to succeed. As usual in this poem, Apollo uses harsher language about the elegiac relationship than those involved in it.

>   Ergo ne dubita blandas adhibere querelas:
> 76 vincuntur molli pectora dura prece.

Apollo resumes his precepts, and returns to the concept of praying mentioned at 64: be prepared to suffer, but complain, in case it makes her relent (a similar statement in the first person at Prop. 1.18.25–6: *omnia consuevi timidus perferre superbae/iussa neque arguto facta dolore queri*). So too, Apollo obliquely encourages L. to continue writing love poetry: **querelas** often denote lovelorn laments (women's in Cat. 64.130, 195, 223, and 66.19; see Pichon 1991: 248–9); they come to signify the elegiac poet's *oeuvre*, which is also (a representation of) his sorrow (= *elegiae*; cf. e.g. Tib. 1.2.9, 1.4.71, 1.8.53, and throughout Prop. and Ov.; see too the verb at 3.6.37 and Introduction, Section I). For **blandas ... querelas**, see Tib. 1.2.9 *ianua, iam pateas uni mihi victa querellis*, 1.4.71–2 *blanditiis vult esse locum Venus: illa querellis/supplicibus, miseris fletibus illa favet*; 1.8.53 *maestas... querellas*. Similar phrases at Cat. 64.139 (*blanda promissa*), Ov. *Am.* 2.1.21 (*blanditias elegosque levis*), *Met.* 3.375–6 (*blandis accedere dictis/et mollis adhibere preces*), 14.18–19 (*promissa precesque... blanditiasque meas*), Hor. *Od.* 2.9.17–18 (*mollium... querelarum*), Stat. *Silv.* 2.1.45.

Ne dubita: see McKeown *ad* Ov. *Am.* 1.7.63 on the Ovidianness of this verb and the archaic construction. **Adhibere** is used most often in the poets to mean 'pay attention'; perhaps Apollo, god of healing, uses it in a medical sense (McKeown *ad* Ov. *Am.* 2.13.15); cf. Ov. *Met.* 3.376 *mollis adhibere preces* and immediately below.

Vincuntur: a present general: hearts normally do melt because of prayer (but Apollo makes no claim of efficacy in this particular case). The verb is standard elegiac language, based on the analogy of love as war (Introduction, Section I), and may derive from V. *E.* 10.69, *omnia vincit Amor*, though the meaning is rather different here. Tib., by contrast, thinks gifts are the way to win out (1.5.60), but notes that love conquered Apollo's medical skill when he sought Admetus (2.3.14). Perhaps allusion to that poem gives the reader pause: how has Apollo, there unsuccessful, suddenly become an expert? But there is regularly a disjunction in the elegists between claims to knowledge and inability to apply it for their own benefit. See too *ad* 3.6.16: *vicit et indomitis mollia corda dedit*, and Pichon 1991: 294–5 on *vincere*.

Molli prece: the adjective has an active sense, 'softening' (as at Ov. *Met.* 3.376, cited above). Usually one or another is a verb (e.g. *mollire* at Sen. *Phoen.* 141); cf. Ov. *Am.* 2.2.66 *quid precibus nostris mollius esse potest?*, *Tr.* 5.8.28 *molle cor ad timidas sic habet ille preces*. See *TLL* 8.1376.45–68 for this sense of *mollis*; see also *ad* 3.6.16, and Pichon 1991: 204–6. On *preces*, see *ad* 3.3.2.

Pectora dura: the concept is common in poetry, not always erotic, and expressed in a variety of ways (Ov. *Am.* 1.11.9 *durum in pectore ferrum*, *Her.* 21.229 *durius... ferro... pectus*, *Met.* 14.693, 14.758, *EP* 4.12.31 *duro... pectora ferro*, Luc. 10.72, Sen. *Phoen.* 113, Stat. *Theb.* 1.613, Sil. 11.481–2 *durata... pectora*). The line has enveloping word order, with hearts surrounded by prayer; see *ad* 3.1.20 and 3.4.84 for *pectus*. For the quintessentially elegiac conjunction of *mollis* and *durus*, see Cairns 2006a: 232–4.

> Quod si vera canunt sacris oracula templis,
> 78   haec illi nostro nomine dicta refer:

This use of **si** to express something akin to 'given that' (*OLD* 12) is perhaps undermined by the **quod** and by the fact that Apollo, as mediated through L., seems distressingly *un*certain about his statement (although they are his oracles and he is the god of prophecy). So too, Apollo might have realized that the message would be more plausibly received by N. if it were to come through a regular channel rather than second-hand from the (hardly objective) L. The lack of clarity here may influence our evaluation of the veracity of any part of this dream; **canunt** is the word for both prophecy and poetry, and the 'point' of this poem is presumably a reminder to N. that the god approves of her relationship with L. (and no other). The collocation **vera canunt** is regular in poetry, though it is more often a positive assertion than, as here, an *aporia* (cf. e.g. Tib. 2.5.63, where the sibyl concludes her prophecy with the authenticating *vera cano*, Ov. *Ars* 1.30, where the poet claims that his own experience assures *vera canam*, *Ars* 3.790, where he claims that neither the oracle at Delphi nor that at Ammon will tell *vera…quam mea Musa canet*, Hor. *CS* 25). The sentiment is sometimes phrased *si non vana* (e.g., notably, Prop. 3.6.31, in the mouth of Cynthia and addressed to a slave named L.); see O'Hara 1990: 55–6.

Sacris oracula templis: for a similar construction, see Ov. *EP* 3.1.131 *non semper sacras reddunt oracula sortis*. **Nostro nomine**: three times in elegy in the same *sedes*; three times elsewhere in the line, but not elsewhere meaning 'under my authority'. *Nomen* is an important concept to the elegists (and Cat.), particularly in relation to fame and reputation; note e.g. Ov. *Am.* 1.3.21 where Io, Leda, and Europa *carmine nomen habent*. **Dicta**: cf. Cat. 11.16 *non bona dicta*.

    hoc tibi coniugium promittit Delius ipse,
80   felix hoc, alium desine velle virum."

Apollo's final message, at least, is clear: he promises (i.e. prophesies) this **coniugium**. Or perhaps not—the probably inappropriate legal term again raises questions (whatever L. wishes for), nor do we know whether the union is past, present, or future. So too, while it is always nice to have divine approval, Apollo is not the god of marriage, nor have his own romantic relationships been noticeably stable. **Promittit** can stand for *spondeo* (*OLD* 2b; Ov. *Her.* 21.139), but also occurs elsewhere in the context of Apollo's promises (Hor. *Od.* 1.7.28–9 *certus enim promisit Apollo*). **Delius** is one of L.'s regular terms for Apollo (see *ad* 3.6.8), and occurs throughout Latin poetry, sometimes (as here) as a substantive; whereas Apollo was *Cynthius* (50), he is now **Delius** (again with the play on *puella* naming conventions). **Ipse**: as Navarro Antolín 1996 notes *ad loc.*, the use of *ipse* here is emphatic, and also authenticating: Apollo makes this promise in his own person.

Felix hoc: ablative of cause; the adjective means 'lucky' more than 'happy', and is yet another way of conveying her aberrance to N. Grammatically, the suppressed verb could be indicative ('since she is [objectively] fortunate'), or an imperative ('she had better be happy'), or even a conditional ('if in fact she decides that she is content'); the ambiguity lends Apollo's utterance a properly oracular quality. Navarro Antolín 1996 *ad loc.* makes too much of the potential ambiguity. For Ov., *felicitas* can be associated with marriage (*Met.* 9.333, *EP* 4.11.22). On **felix**, see *ad* 3.3.26.

Desine velle: common enough diction (see 3.4.4), but cf. Cat. 73.1 (in a scene of disappointment), Ov. *Am*. 1.10.64 (frustration). **Velle** is used with a person as direct object at Ov. *Am*. 2.19.1–2 and *Ars* 1.110. Here again the verb is ambiguous: N. is either 'willing to' entertain other possibilities, or she 'wants to'. Perhaps mimicking this confusion is the way the verb looks at first to have **coniugium** as its direct object, but this switches at the end of the line to **virum**: what N. wants remains opaque, even to the god.

   Dixit, et ignavus defluxit corpore somnus.
82   A ego ne possim tanta videre mala!

Apollo delivers his final message and disappears; either he, or L., does not want to dwell on the distressing news (and L. will go on to express his horror and disbelief). On the other hand, Apollo has given very elegiac advice, and promised a *coniugium*, which news L. can pass along to N. **Dixit**: a typical way to end epic speech (twenty times in V. *A*., thirty-three times in Ov. *Met*. at line-start immediately following a speech). So, although this is elegy, L. gives *gravitas* to Apollo's speech. But it is also the standard way of ending a dream vision or interpretation (e.g. Ov. *Am*. 3.5.45, *dixerat interpres*, *EP* 3.3.93 *dixit, et*).

We see L.'s 'reaction shot', expressed with a negative optative subjunctive (as at Tib. 2.4.7, *o ego, ne possim tales sentire dolores*) and preceded by the dramatic **a**: he wishes he could 'unsee' his vision. The sentence, and in particular the verb **videre**, means that he hopes these evils have not happened, but also, along the lines of the Ovidian *vir* of *Am*. 3.4.43–8 and Ov. himself in *Am*. 3.14.1–2, that the lover might prefer not to face the truth (see too *ad* 3.20 below).

Ignavus . . . somnus: it is peculiar to term L.'s sleep **ignavus**, given how hard-won it was; although we might expect sleep to be lazy, the adjective and noun are paired only at Ov. *Met*. 11.593, in the same *sedes*; see *ad* 3.3.38 for other elegiac examples of the adjective. The gradual way we sometimes wake up is well captured by **defluxit**, but the verb is used elsewhere only at Stat. *Ach*. 1.620 *totis ubi somnus inertior alis/defluit in terras mutumque amplectitur orbem*; see *ad* 3.1.18 on *defluat . . . color*. *Somnus abit* is an Ovidian phrase, usually at line-start (*Met*.7.643, 9.472, 15.664, *Fas*. 3.23, 6.389; at line-end at *Tr*. 4.3.22, *EP* 3.3.12; cf. *TLL* 1.70.27–50).

A ego: hiatus is found regularly in elegists after interjections, usually to pathetic effect: e.g. Tib. 2.3.5, 2.4.7, Ov. *Am*. 2.5.7, 2.9.2, 3.1.16, *Ars* 3.347 (all with *o*, at line-start); see Platnauer 1951: 57 and Ross 1969: 49–63. See too *ad* 3.17.3. Suffering **tanta mala** (cf. *tot mala*, 3.2.8)—although it is by no means clear that this referent is always active—becomes for L. very personal, and presumably has the same kind of Odyssean resonances as Tib. 1.3. The phrase occurs, sometimes in the form *tanta malorum*, as early as Plautus (e.g. *Aul*. 732; *Men*. 902, mentioning Odysseus), and is sprinkled throughout prose authors; it is infrequent in earlier Latin poetry outside of Plautus, and is rare in epic, despite its Homeric pedigree (e.g. Cic. *Att.* 8.11.3 *non multo, inquam, secus possum vaticinari; tanta malorum impendet* Ἰλιάς). For Cat., the *tanta mala* which are his brother's death (65.4) prevent him from composing poetry—although he tells us this in a poem. The phrase becomes something of a leitmotif for Ov. in exile to refer to his (Odysseus-like) journeys and sufferings; cf. *Tr.* 1.1.48, 3.13.24, 4.1.88, 4.4.38, and it is picked up on by Seneca in the tragedies, where it is also frequent.

    Nec tibi crediderim votis contraria vota
84   nec tantum crimen pectore inesse tuo;

The suspicion that L.'s ignorance was his bliss is reinforced by this couplet, using the (rare) perfect subjunctive **crediderim** with potential meaning: he would rather not believe what he has heard. The couplet also suggests that L. has not really believed his own words in the previous three poems. On **crediderim**, see Prop. 1.1.23 *tunc ego crediderim* and further citations at *TLL* 4.1147.37–61; see also *ad* 3.4.12.

 The precise syntax here is difficult: **tibi** is a dative of reference or possession, with the infinitive *esse*, and perhaps also *nobis*, omitted (Heyne emends **votis** to *nobis*): 'I couldn't believe that you had vows against my vows'. **Votis contraria vota** restates 59: N. has been plotting (or perhaps simply wishing) against him. Elsewhere in elegy at Prop. 1.5.9 (Cynthia may not be *contraria* to the *votis* of her potential suitor Gallus); in poetry it occurs otherwise only at Luc. 9.115, but see V. *A.* 1.239 *fatis contraria fata*. For **contraria**, see Pichon 1991: 112, and for repetition with **contraria**, Wills 1996: 201–2. On **vota** see *ad* 3.3.1 and Pichon 1991: 300–1. For a use of this phrase in Ausonius, see Green 1977: 444; it may be allusion or, as Postgate 1915 suggests, simply a common phrase.

 A precise translation for **crimen** is always difficult: it refers both to the commission of a crime and to the accusation (i.e. it does not always imply guilt—though here it seems to). It is a standard elegiac linguistic move to appropriate vocabulary from other areas of life into amatory discourse (see Kennedy 1993), so infidelity becomes viewed as a criminal act (see *ad* 3.20.3). Then again, the elegists are also notoriously coy about the legal status of the *puella* (see Introduction, Section I), and L. persists in using conjugal language, which might mean that the metaphor is not dead (as, perhaps, in Tib. 1.6.41, seemingly its first use in elegy, and *passim* in all three elegists; see Pichon 1991: 116). Depending upon dating (and of course upon the relationship of L. and N.), the noun may be meant to refer to Augustan legislation (Introduction, Section II). The first Latin application of **crimen** to love seems to be at Publil. Syr. A29: *amare iuveni fructus est, crimen seni*. **Crimen...inesse** is an Ovidian phrase (*Her.* 17.218, *EP* 3.1.20 and 3.3.70; as Radford notes, the verb is rare in poetry except in Ov. and Lucr. (1927: 359).

 Pectore is a regular location for plans and thoughts (*OLD* 3b). As Postgate 1915 and Navarro Antolín 1996 note *ad loc.*, **inesse** normally takes the preposition *in*; for counterexamples, see *inest foribus* at Tib. 1.6.34 and *corpore inesse* at Lucr. 1.590 and 3.634.

nam te nec vasti genuerunt aequora ponti
86   **nec flammam volvens ore Chimaera fero**

This couplet introduces one of the longer sentences in L., running to line 94, and in it L. indulges in the 'hard-hearted' *topos*, which derives for the elegists at least partly from the abandoned Ariadne of Cat. 64.154–7 (*quaenam te genuit sola sub rupe leaena?/quae mare conceptum spumantibus expuit undis,/quae Syrtis, quae Scylla rapax, quae vasta Charybdis,/talia qui reddis pro dulci praemia vita?*), alluded to also by Ov.'s Ariadne at *Her.* 10.1, 131–2 (beasts, rocks, and sea). Cat. 60, Scylla (e.g. in Ov. *Met.* 8), and Dido's soliloquy at V. A. 4.365–7 (Caucasus mountains and tigers) are also key moments (the latter picked up on by Ov.'s Dido at *Her.* 7.37–9, where rocks, oak, beasts, and the sea appear), and the theme had been common in Greek literature (first at Hom. *Il.* 16.33–5, Patroclus' address to Achilles and also, notably, Eur. *Med.* 1358–60). As will be seen from perusal of these examples, there is a standard set of components (normally focusing on nature, barbarians, and mythological monsters), shuffled about, so that it is difficult to determine what is specific allusion and what are simply standard elements of the genre (see Hinds 1998 for treatment of the problem). The list of monsters, applied to a woman, may derive from Anaxilas fr. 22 K (Chimaera, Charybdis, Scylla, Sphinx, Hydra, lioness, echidna, harpy), and there are other possible precedents.

L.'s specimen is noteworthy for being negative—since (**nam**) N. is *not* all of these things, L. finds it inconceivable that she could be so cruel. L. expands upon his predecessors both in detail and in number of comparanda, so we are perhaps to understand him as carried away; his focus on female monsters may express his negative fantasies about N. (earlier displaced onto Apollo). L. mentions the following as irrelevant to N.'s birth: (1) sea, (2) Chimaera, (3) Cerberus, (4) Scylla, (5) lioness, (6) Scythia, (7) Syrtes. Four of these (5, 1, 7, 4) appear in the Catullan example (which adds Charybdis). Among other examples of the *topos*, one of the earliest extant in Latin, Cat. 60.1–3 features the lioness (5) and Scylla (4) (*num te leaena montibus Libystinis/aut Scylla latrans infima inguinum parte/tam mente dura procreavit ac taetra*; see Weinrich 1959, Quinn 1973, and Lieberg 1966, the latter on Theoc. 23), Ov. *Met.* 8.120–5 (*non genetrix Europa tibi est, sed inhospita Syrtis,/Armeniae tigres austroque agitata Charybdis./Nec Iove tu natus, nec mater imagine tauri/ducta tua est: generis falsa est ea fabula! Verus,/[et ferus et captus nullius amore iuvencae]/qui te progenuit, taurus fuit*) contains the Syrtes (7), tigers, and Charybdis. (This version is especially pleasing because placed in the mouth of Scylla, who is herself often an exemplum in these narratives, and because she adapts her insult specifically to Minos; cf. Bömer 1977 and Kenney 2011 *ad loc.*, and Ov. *Met.* 7.32–3 where Medea uses tiger, rock, and stone to urge herself to assist Jason.)

'Negative' versions of the *topos* appear at e.g. Tib. 1.1.64 (*nec in tenero stat tibi corde silex*), Ov. *Met.* 9.613–15 (*neque enim est de tigride natus/nec rigidas silices solidumve in pectore ferrum/aut adamant gerit, nec lac bibit ille leaenae*), using tiger, rock, iron, adamant, and a lioness (5); the sheer length of the excursus here suggests that L. is or presents himself as having become carried away. Use of such *adynata* is not necessarily tied to love; as its first appearance, Patroclus to Achilles (sea and rocks) shows (Hom. *Il.* 16.33–5). See too V. *E.* 8.43–5, where Amor himself is born of the cliffs, Ov. *Tr.* 1.8.37–44 to an unnamed betrayer (Pontic rock, Scythia (6), Sarmatia, flint, iron, tigress), *Tr.* 3.11.3–4 to an unnamed betrayer (cliffs, beasts, flint). Ov. *Tr.* 4.7.11–20, about a friend who has not written, contains a wide range of mythological exempla: Medusa, Scylla (4), Chimaera (2), Centaurs, Geryon, Cerberus (3), Sphinx, Harpies, giants with snake feet, Gyes, and the Minotaur, all of which Ov. thinks more likely to exist than that his friend has abandoned him.

The *topos* is frequent in Greek literature as well; cf. e.g. Eur. *Med.* 1341–3 (lioness and Scylla), *Bacc.* 987–91 (rocks). But L. inverts the usual form: N. is *not* born from monsters or stone but from perfectly normal parents. For a mild version of the same complaint, intended persuasively, cf. Hor. *Od.* 3.10.11–12. L. may here be influenced by the Lucretian discussion of dreams and simulacra in Book 5; there, Lucr. notes that such things as Centaurs, Scyllas, and Chimaeras do not exist (5.890–924), except in dreams and as ephemeral combinations of visual matter. We may, indeed, wonder to what extent N. is herself an imaginary creation for L., given that she is a mixture of the stereotypical qualities of an elegiac *puella* and of a wife.

It is perhaps relevant to L.'s point that even inanimate natural elements were thought to be susceptible to poetry; in addition to the tale of Orpheus, note Cic. *Arch.* 19 *saxa et solitudines voci respondent* (and see too *ad* 3.4.91 *barbara*).

The sea is particularly apposite as a first example, as Aphrodite was born from the sea, and she is a notoriously unfaithful spouse. **Vasti ... aequora ponti**: the sea is viewed as cruel as far back as Hom. *Il.* 16.34, and is a foundational element in the *topos* (see e.g. Ov. *Met.* 14.711 for this notion in an erotic context); for the Roman mistrust of the sea, see Nisbet and Hubbard *ad* Hor. *Od.* 1.3. **Aequora ponti** (poetic plural) is elevated language, occurring at line-end at e.g. Lucr. 1.8, 2.772, 6.440, V. *G.* 1.469, Ov. *Met.* 2.872 with Bömer 1969 *ad loc.*, and in various other cases and locations (*TLL* 1.1023.84–1024.6); **ponti** first at Enn. *Ann.* 225. *Maria vasta* occurs at Cat. 63.48 but probably the epic tone predominates here. **Vasti ... ponti**: noun/adjective combination at V. *G.* 4.430, Manil. 1.166, Sil. 2.572, 4.80, 10.321. *Aequor* is joined with *vastum* at Prop. 3.9.3, Tib. 1.7.19, V. *A.* 2.780, 3.191, 7.228, Ov. *Fas.* 4.419, *EP* 1.4.35 (the adjective is often used of desolate, featureless expanses, *OLD* 2).

Genuerunt: used of giving birth as early as Enn. *Ann.* 1.107, but it is probably also a specific allusion to Cat. 64.154, quoted above.

Commentary on 3.4.88 179

The **Chimaera** was a mythical monster formed of the combination of a lioness, a goat, and a serpent or dragon (Lucr. 5.905–6, Hyg. *Fab.* 57.3, 151.1, Apollod. 2.3.1), who breathed fire from either the lion's or the goat's mouth (this latter in the middle of her body, Serv. *ad A.* 5.118). She was killed by Bellerophon as a part of his heroic quest, Hom. *Il.* 6.179–82; cf. Hes. *Th.* 319–25; for a naturalizing explanation (a fiery mountain) see Plin. *NH* 2.236.5 and 5.100.2. Her poetic invocations focus on the difficulty of fighting against her (e.g. Hor. *Od.* 1.27.21–4), or simply mention her multiform appearance or fire-breathing (e.g. Ov. *Met.* 9.647–8 *quoque Chimaera iugo mediis in partibus ignem,/pectus et ora leae, caudam serpentis habebat*; *Tr.* 4.7.13–14, *Chimaeram,/a truce quae flammis separet angue leam*. Charybdis and Chimaera are used of a woman at Hor. *Od.* 1.27.18–24. **Flammam volvens**: V. *G.* 1.473, Ov. *Met.* 7.109; metaphorical at Sil. 9.446 (*volvit flammas ad sidera*); cf. *volvit...ignem* at V. *G.* 3.85 (*OLD* 7a and *TLL* 6.1.869.43). It probably derives from Hes. *Th.* 319. **Fero** is repeated from 74, where it describes marriage.

    nec canis anguinea redimitus terga caterva,
88   cui tres sunt linguae tergeminumque caput,

Cerberus, the three-headed canine guardian of the underworld (first mentioned at Hom. *Il.* 8.368), is referred to obliquely, as often, and then expanded into a full couplet. He is sometimes given snakes, sometimes not (elegiac mentions of his snakes at Tib. 1.3.71: *tum niger in porta serpentum Cerberus ore/stridet* and Ov. *Her.* 9.93–4: *inque canes totidem trunco digestus ab uno/Cerberos implicitis angue minante comis*; see Murgatroyd 1980 *ad* the former and Casali 1995 *ad* the latter for further citations). L.'s description is fairly standard, his language unique; for **canis** of Cerberus, see *TLL* 3.257.12–31; see Navarro Antolín 1996 *ad loc.* on the concentration of 'r', the *littera canina*, and of 's', imitative of snakes. Cerberus is a common element in descriptions of the underworld, and also serves to explain the difficulty of a task; sometimes his existence is denied. (The two are combined at Stat. *Silv.* 2.1.184: death is not to be feared because Cerberus does not exist.) Cerberus is unusually friendly at Hor. *Od.* 2.19.29–33, but his visitor there is the god Dionysus: *te vidit insons Cerberus aureo/cornu decorum leniter atterens/caudam et recedentis trilingui/ore pedes tetigitque crura*. For the etymology (= *kreo + boros*, meat-eater), see Serv. *ad A.* 6.395. He does not occur in the 'cruelty' *topos* elsewhere, so L. probably has a particular reason for inclusion: perhaps his thoughts are again reverting to his own impending death.

    Anguinea: rare: the manuscripts transmit *consanguinea* but it is universally emended, normally to **canis** + some word related to *anguinis*. In poetry it is found elsewhere only at *Il. Lat.* 891 (where it is also an emendation; Hagen 1954 sees the word as 'Silver'); cf. Ov. *Tr.* 4.7.12 *anguineis* of Medusa's hair. Cerberus' snakes are often on his back, as here (e.g. *schol. ad* Hes. *Th.* 311), but some traditions have snakes on his head: e.g. Hor. *Od.* 3.11.17–18, V. *A.* 6.419 (*colla*), Tib. 1.3.71–2 *tum niger in porta serpentum Cerberus ore/stridet et aeratas excubat ante fores*. **Caterva** in elegy at Prop. 4.11.98, Tib. 1.2.49 and 69, 1.6.81, Ov. *Am.* 1.9.27, always in this *sedes*; nowhere else joined with **anguinea**. **Tergeminum**: often of Cerberus: Prop. 4.7.52 *tergeminusque canis*, Ov. *Ars* 3.322 *tergeminumque canem*, Stat. *Theb.* 2.31 *tergemino...somno*, 7.783 *tergeminos...hiatus*, *Silv.* 3.3.27 *tergeminus custos*; cf. too Ov. *Tr.* 4.7.16 *tergeminumque virum tergeminumque canem* of Geryon and Cerberus.

    Scyllaque virgineam canibus succincta figuram,
90   nec te conceptam saeva leaena tulit,

L. returns to a single *exemplum* per line (such variation in length is normal, to add variety). **Scylla**: one composite dog follows another. Latin poets often—seemingly deliberately—confuse the two Scyllas, one the Megarian daughter of Nisus who becomes a bird, the other a nymph loved by Glaucus and turned into a monster by the jealous Circe. Megarian Scylla's story occurs at V. *G.* 1.405, Ov. *Met.* 8.1–151, and [V.] *Cir*; the nymph's at e.g. Ov. *Met.* 13.900–14.74. But Ov. also gives the daughter of Nisus a snaky groin at *Am.* 3.12.21 and *Ars* 1.333, as do V. *E.* 6.74 and Prop. 4.4.39, and the monster-dogs are called *Nisaei* at Ov. *Fas.* 4.500 (see Bömer 1958 *ad loc*). The monstrous Scylla is often paired with Charybdis, from Hom. *Od.* 12.85–110 on, as double dangers for sailors on the straits of Messina between Italy and Sicily (paired also at e.g. V. *A.* 3.420–1, Ov. *Am.* 2.11.18, *Met.* 7.62–5 *cinctaque saevis/Scylla rapax canibus Siculo latrare profundo*, and *passim*).

    Succincta (i.e. *sub-cincta*) is exceptionally well-chosen, as it is from her nether parts that the dogs begin (the Homeric monster has many heads (*Od.* 12.90–2), but from the Hellenistic period the dogs are relocated to her groin); the same verb is used of Scylla at Lucr. 5.892, V. *E.* 6.75, and Ov. *Met.* 13.732; see Bömer 1982 *ad loc*. Here it is restored from F by Scaliger; other readings are *submixta*, *commixta*, and *commissa*. The compound verb, used as early as Ennius and Plautus, does not appear elsewhere in *CT*, but **canibus succincta** is in the same *sedes* at [V.] *Cul.* 331 (further citations *TLL* 3.256.55–72); see too [V.] *Cir.* 59 *candida succinctam latrantibus inguina monstris*.

    Those who know the myth as told in Ov. *Met.* 13–14 will be entertained by the use of **virgineam**: it adds pathos, emphasizes that N. could not have derived from this monster, and alludes to the fact that it was in trying to take control over her own sexual status that Scylla became a monster. There is an implicit lesson here for N. **Virgineam...figuram**: see Ov. *Met.* 13.733 *virginis ora gerens* of Scylla, and cf. Ov. *Met.* 3.607 *virginea...forma* of the disguised Dionysus, Stat. *Ach.* 1.743–4 *vestigia magnae/virginis aut dubia facies suspecta figura*; [V.] *Cir.* 71, Ov. *Tr.* 4.7.13, and Stat. *Silv.* 3.2.86 use *virgo* of Scylla.

    Conceptam: as often in Latin, the past participle is used where English prefers two main verbs; the phrasing here is similar to Cat. 64.155 (*mare conceptum*).

Leaena: lionesses feature in the abandoned lover's laments at Cat. 60.1 and 64.154. See too 3.6.15, with note *ad loc.* Byblis' complaint of the hard-heartedness of her brother also includes a lioness (Ov. *Met.* 9.613–15, *neque enim est de tigride natus/nec rigidas silices solidumve in pectore ferrum/aut adamant gerit, nec lac bibit ille leaenae*, with Bömer 1977 *ad loc.* for further citations). **Saeva leaena**: cf. V. *G.* 3.245–6 (*leaena/saevior*), *lea* at Ov. *Met.* 4.102, *Il. Lat.* 396, VF 6.148, and Eur. *Med.* 1342–3 on Medea's savagery, like that of a lioness and worse than Scylla.

> barbara nec Scythiae tellus horrendave Syrtis,
> 92 sed culta et duris non habitanda domus

A final two examples, the last (**Syrtis**) referring back again to Cat. 64.157; the two places appear together also at Luc. 1.367 to signify the ends of the earth. **Barbara... Scythiae tellus** is a traditionally barbarous land, usually mentioned in poetry for its coldness (e.g. V. *G.* 3.349, Ov. *Met.* 1.64 with Bömer 1969 *ad loc.* for further citations, 2.224) and overwhelming mountains (e.g. Prop. 4.3.47; Prometheus was said to have been chained to the Caucasus mountains in Scythia). Ov. *Tr.* 1.8.39–40 and Sen. *HO* 143 seem to be the only two other mentions of Scythia in the cruelty *topos*. (It is, of course, especially appropriate for Ovid, who often conceives of his place of exile as Scythian.) **Barbara** is used of Pontus and its inhabitants at Cic. *Verr.* 2.5.150, Ov. *Tr.* 3.11.7, 5.2.31, *EP* 1.3.38, Sen. *Phaed.* 166, [Sen.] *Oct.* 980 (*TLL* 2.1737.18–46). *Scythia* is notable for being the homeland of Medea (e.g. Ov. *Her.* 12.29, *Met.* 7.53, where it is also *barbara*, VF 1.43), and where Ov. is exiled (e.g. *Tr.* 1.3.61), both by some extension of the actual geographical area. See Pichon 1991: 93 on *barbarus* as 'rustic' and 'cruel'. Cic. *Arch.* 19 claims that *nulla umquam barbaria violavit* the status of poet (*poetae nomen*).

Horrenda Syrtis: two shallow gulfs in North Africa (Sidra and Gabes), sandy and so dangerous for boats, especially in rough weather (Prop. 2.9.33, Ov. *Am.* 2.11.20; full discussion in Pease 1935 *ad* V. *A.* 4.41). The Argo became stranded there (AR 4.1235), and Cato marched there (see, most conveniently, Nisbet and Hubbard *ad* Hor. *Od.* 1.22.5); they serve as a typical place to avoid at e.g. Ov. *RA* 739, *Fas.* 4.499, Hor. *Od.* 2.6.3. They are mentioned in Ariadne's hard-hearted *topos* at Cat. 64.156, Scylla's at Ov. *Met.* 8.120 (Bömer 1977 *ad loc.* for further detail). Cf. V. *A.* 4.41 and Ov. *Met.* 8.120 for *inhospita Syrtis* at line-end. **Horrenda** is mostly an epic word (throughout the tradition), used sometimes by other poets in less elevated circumstances, but of a place-name only at Ov. *Met.* 1.216 (Maenala) and Stat. *Silv.* 1.4.78–9 (Armenia).

It is not very common for a sentence extending over a number of couplets to change course in the middle of one (the switch being heralded by **sed**). We move from epic myth to L's domestic concerns: N. has none of these terrifying origins, but instead comes from a civilized home. As Navarro Antolín 1996 notes, mentions of family in the cruelty *topos* are regular, but a *domus* is not. **Culta**: opposed to *barbara* above (and often in prose; in poetry at V. F. 1.70–1, Ov. EP 2.7.69), the adjective is most frequently applied in Tib. to crops, but also to hair (1.4.4, negatively, 1.8.9), to a *puella* (1.9.74, ironically), and to *amor* (*colendus*, 2.4.52). L. uses the participle elsewhere only of his book, 3.1.17, but it is also applied to S. (3.8.1).

Duris, by contrast, is used frequently by Tib. and even more frequently by Prop., of doors closed, labours, restrictions, and of the *puella*. N.'s heart (cf. *dura pectora* at line 76) contrasts with her context, and the gerundive **non habitanda** may suggest that her kind-hearted family would, or should, deny her a home if her behaviour becomes aberrant. As is typical for L., the grand, 'epic' word is placed into the pentameter. **Habitanda domus**: V. E. 2.29 the first use of *habitare* in elevated poetry; cf. Hor. *Epod.* 16.19 *habitandaque fana*. On *domus*, see *ad* 3.3.4.

et longe ante alias omnes mitissima mater
94   isque pater, quo non alter amabilior.

It is not clear what conclusions we should draw from these lines about N.'s family or upbringing; they may serve merely to point up the contrast between N.'s cruelty and her kind parents. Interestingly, although mothers and other female relatives of *puellae* appear in elegy, fathers (and other male relatives) do not (for exceptions that prove the rule, see *Am.* 1.15.17, where the continued existence of the type of the *durus pater* is listed among the reasons why Menander is read, and at *Am.* 3.8.31, where money (= Jupiter, in a shower of gold) would have overcome even the *durus pater* of Danae). We might take this as significant in explaining either the status of *puellae*, or the fact that the elegists do not feel that they need to explain it: elegiac *puellae*, excepting N. (and S.; see *ad* 3.14.5, and Introduction, Section I), do not have male relatives to take care of them. **Pater**, however, is appropriate to the marital scenario L. evokes. Veremans 1998: 23 notes that—in keeping with elegy's inversion of the relative 'weights' of each line of the couplet—N.'s mother receives the (manly) hexameter, her father the (feminine) pentameter.

Ante: as Tränkle 1990 and Navarro Antolín 1996 note, the use of the preposition for preference is originally colloquial, and becomes common in poetry (*TLL.* 2.135.68–136.8), e.g. V. E. 3.78, A. 3.321, 11.821, 12.391, Cat. 68.159 (*longe ante omnes... carior*), Tib. 2.4.24, Ov. *Am.* 2.6.12, *Ars* 3.534, *Met.* 5.476, 8.23, 10.120 (all with *alios*). See too *ad* 3.19.16.

In keeping with traditional Roman gender roles, we might expect mothers, or women in general, to be **mitissima** (Ov. *Her.* 14.55, *Met.* 10.510); contrast *immitis* at 74. Fathers, as noted above, are not so; see the (perhaps standard) counterexample at e.g. Sen. *Cont.* 7.1.11.1; note too Pichon 1991: 203–4. **Is** is not frequent in the poets, except in Ov.; see Axelson 1945: 70–3; Platnauer 1951: 116–17.

Quo non alter amabilior: the structure of the phrase is Vergilian: cf. V. *A.* 1.544–5 *quo iustior alter/nec*, 6.164 *quo non praestantior alter*, 7.649–50 *quo pulchrior alter/non fuit*, 9.772 *quo non felicior alter*, 12.639 *quo non…mihi carior alter*, Ov. *Met.* 12.405 *qua nulla decentior*, 14.623–4 *qua nulla/…sollertius*. **Amabilior**: informal language (Axelson 1945; 102–3); cf. e.g. Plaut. *Stich.* 736, Lucr. 1.23, Cat. 65.10 of his brother, Hor. *Od.* 2.9.13, *Ep.* 2.2.132, Ov. *Ars* 2.107, 723 (not in Vergil, Tib. or Prop.). See Pichon 1991: 83 for the nuances of *amabilis*; here it presumably means not that he is loveable or delightful, but that he is in favour of *amor*, and so the opposite of what we would expect of a *durus pater*.

Haec deus in melius crudelia somnia vertat
96   **et iubeat tepidos inrita ferre notos.**

L.'s prayer, which might seem as conventional after the description of an unpleasant possibility as our 'bless you' after a sneeze, gains additional point from the fact that he has just been in conversation with a god. **In melius…vertat** sounds like standard language, but there are only one or two parallels: Suet. *Aug.* 23.2 *se res p. in meliorem statum vertisset*, Serv. *ad G.* 1.198 *vis…quae contra naturam vertuntur in melius*, 2.59 *modo 'degenerant' vertuntur in peius; alias in melius*. The phrase is seemingly a cross between *di melius* and *di vertant* (Navarro Antolín 1996 *ad loc.*), both very common; see Mosch. 1.27 for a prayer to the gods to offer a favourable outcome to a disturbing dream (with further citations in Campbell 1991 *ad loc.*).

Crudelia somnia: the adjective appears four times in the *CT*: 1.4.35 (of the gods), 1.8.7 (of the god burning more cruelly), and twice in this poem (see 61, above). Given the other *CT* uses, the reader might well conclude that gods are more likely to bring cruelty than to disperse it (so too Prop.: of his seven uses, six pertain to some aspect of love, and only one is used negatively, in an assertion that the god Neptune is not cruel to those in love, 2.26.45). The closest literal parallel to this passage occurs at Ov. *Her.* 10.111, where *crudeles somni* prevented Ariadne from knowing of Theseus' departure. The juxtaposition is arresting, as sleep is usually presented as a kindly respite from cares (see *ad* 3.4.19).

Tepidos…notos is a quintessentially Ovidian noun/adjective combination: *Am.* 1.4.12 (see McKeown 1989 *ad loc.*), 1.7.56, 2.8.20, *Her.* 11.76 (all in this *sedes*), *EP* 4.10.43, *Ib.* 34 (elsewhere in the line). The adjective gives the sense of a pleasant breeze, but Hor. *Od.* 1.3.14 calls the wind *rabiem*, and Ov. *Am.* 2.6.44, 2.11.52, 2.16.22, *Her.* 2.12, 2.58, 10.32, *Met.* 1.264–5, *Fas.* 2.300, *Tr.* 1.2.15 and 30 make things sound significantly more violent; L. is seeking a very powerful wind to blow his dream far away (note Tibullus' dreams of life with Delia, blown away by Eurus and Notus, 1.5.35). More often, especially in elegy, it is promises, or the faithless words of lovers, rather than dreams, that are carried away by the winds (Otto 1890: 364–5). Given that L.'s dream has ended with reassurances from Apollo, it is peculiar that he wants it undone.

Iubeat: cf. Ov. *Am.* 1.4.11–12 *nec Euris/da me nea nec tepidis verba ferenda Notis*, 2.8.19–20, *Ars* 1.631–4 (Jupiter commands the perjuries of lovers to be carried away by the winds, *et iubet Aeolios irrita ferre notos*; see *ad* 3.6.49). For similar notions without the verb, see Cat. 30.10 *ventos irrita ferre* and 70.3–4 *sed mulier cupido quod dicit amanti/in vento et rapida scribere oportet aqua*.

3.5:

This is the first discussion of illness in [Tib.] 3, where it becomes a leitmotif (see too 3.10 and 3.17, with discussion of the elegiac theme at Müller 1952: 58–80 and especially Holzenthal 1967; this poem at 27–34). The poem, continuing L.'s earlier focus on death, is reminiscent of Tib. 1.3, where Tib. lies ill, his punishment for leaving Delia and going off to war; as with that poem, there may be metapoetic nuance here. There, the poet takes the blame for causing his situation; in this poem L. does not, perhaps because he has not abandoned his *puella* or his craft (or perhaps we are to draw some larger conclusion about him). There is also a difference in that L. seems to be announcing his illness to those who do not know, whereas Tib. is being left behind by his friends (1.3.1 *ibitis...sine me*).

The *puella* is more regularly ill in elegy than the lover, although the ('lovesick') condition of the lover is itself often assimilated to illness, particularly in its symptoms (*pallor, dolor*, and the like; see Introduction, Section I). It is difficult to determine when illness in the elegists is meant to be literal, and when metaphorical; places such as Ov. *Ars* 2.319–36, where the poet leaves the unpleasant aspects of ministering to a sick *puella* to his rival, are difficult to understand metapoetically, but Ov. *Am.* 2.13–14, on Corinna's abortion, may well refer to the creation or destruction of poetry, and poems such as Ov. *Tr.* 3.3 and 5.13, on the poet's illness and decline, could reflect physical ailments, but also embody his soul's suffering at being away from Rome. L.'s symptoms, however, are those of quartan fever (malaria, but not a life-threatening variety; see Celsus 3.15.6, Sallares 2002: 12); see Grmek 1989: 1–16 on the difficulties with modern conceptualizations of ancient symptoms, and 281 on the prevalence of malaria in the Greek world. But the disease ordinarily broke out later in the year than spring, the time in which L. sets the poem (Sallares 2002: 62, 135–6; see *ad* 3.5.2). We may thus be meant to see his illness as genuine, but also—in his mind at least—as simultaneously caused by love. The focus on death in this poem is typical for L.

One surprising element of this poem is that N. is not named in it (Alfonsi 1946: 66). Some have even suggested that the poem is not by L. (Doncieux 1888: 129). Rather, the poem addresses itself to a largely unspecified *vos*, on vacation, at a hot spring (described as the next-best-thing to Baiae, a place where *puellae* often go to cheat; see e.g. Prop. 1.11). But note Zgoll 2002: 109–10, who plausibly suggests that *vos* may refer to N. and L.'s rival(s); given L.'s obsessive concern with N., we should probably understand *vos* to be a group of friends that includes N. The model of Tib. 1.3 might lead us to expect address to a patron (and see *vos... amici*, which is almost certainly not N., at 3.6.9), but none comes. In a related vein, it is not clear whether we should understand this poem as a continuation of the previous one, that is, as L.'s putting into practice Apollo's advice to continue suffering—the tone of this poem is perhaps more resigned than the previous four, and may well continue from its main point, the unfaithfulness of N.—or as his rejection of that advice and development of other areas of poetic interest (see Introduction, Section V, on the order of the poems). The final two poems of L.'s corpus move slightly away from amatory elegy, and so his trajectory parallels in miniature that of both Prop. (whose fourth book claimed to leave personal amatory poetry wholly behind) and Ov. (who claims in the last poem of the *Amores* to be moving on to other things (*Am.* 3.15.1), but differs from that of Tib. (who had always interspersed a broader range of poetry, and whose amatory elegies did not confine themselves to a single *puella*, but included two, and a *puer*).

While the Romans were keen on natural hot springs in all circumstances, they seem also to have believed them curative of illnesses of various kinds (e.g. Liv. 41.16.3, with further citations at Navarro Antolín 1996 *ad* 3.5.3). It is a sad coincidence that L.'s friends are enjoying the benefits of a spa, while he himself is in need of one.

The poem is tripartite in structure, with invocation of friend(s) at start and end (two couplets each) bookmarking L.'s treatment of his illness and pleas to the gods to spare him; the first and third sections are a kind of priamel, distinguishing L.'s situation from that of others. Navarro Antolín 1996 suggests Mart. 4.57.1–3 as the main parallel for this poem (Martial is at Baiae, his addressee at Tibur). But Mart. 6.43 features the poet at his farm writing to a friend at Baiae, which suggests that Romans often took holidays and wrote poetry, and that we need not seek a particular model (see *ad* 3.5.3). See Cartault 1911: 314 (with evidence discussed *passim*) on this poem as stylistically distinct from the five other Lygdamean elegies.

Vos tenet, Etruscis manat quae fontibus unda,
2   **unda sub aestivum non adeunda Canem,**

The poem begins with a geographical excursus and is, in form, a priamel (**vos** swimming in the Tiber, contrasted with *at mihi* in line 6). **Vos tenet**: cf. Tib. 1.3.3 (*me tenet*), Tib. 1.6.35 (*te tenet*), both at line-start, not a usual place for this verb in Latin poetry. The placement of **vos**, as the first word of the poem, suggests that it may well include N., who has been L.'s primary concern up to this point (see introduction to this poem). For **tenet** of geographical location, *OLD* 4a. **Etruscis**: an Italic people, influential upon the early Romans in a number of ways, including providing a number of kings. Although the adjective appears nowhere else with **fontibus** (nor does the equivalent adjective *Tuscus*, on which see *ad* 3.4.6 and 3.5.29), the area does contain a number of hot springs (Strabo 5.2.3 and 5.2.9; for their continued use into the middle ages, see Boisseuil 2002); it is unclear which L. intends (Prop. 1.14 is written to Tullus, at Tibur). The water at sources is, naturally, more healthful than elsewhere (and ancient medical texts connected malaria with stagnant pools; Sallares 2002: 55 with citations). But Tuscany was known, at least in the fifth century CE, as a place where malaria was rampant (Sallares 2002: 64, 70, 192–200), so there may be an unintended irony here. **Fontibus** may have a metapoetic nuance: not only bathers, but poets, are keenly interested in untainted pools (see *ad* 3.5.57–8), and in tracing things to their sources.

Manat…unda: the phrase is Catullan (*manans alluit unda pedem*, 65.6), and also appears at [V.] *Cul.* 148: *his suberat gelidis manans e fontibus unda*. As Navarro Antolín 1996 notes *ad loc.*, this couplet has a pleasing aural effect, with *a*-vowels and repetition of *-unda* reproducing the lapping of the waves (see too Bömer *ad* Ov. *Met.* 11.496 for similar effects elsewhere); the figure occurs early in Latin, but has Greek roots. **Unda/unda…non adeunda**: L. engages in a kind of etymological pun (for this kind of epanalepsis, see Wills 1996: 159–67). As Radford 1926 notes, this participle is very Ovidian, often in this *sedes*; see too Tib. 1.6.22 *non adeunda* in this *sedes*. **Sub** here with an accusative of time (Postgate 1915).

Canem refers to Sirius, the dog-star, also at Tib. at 1.1.27, 1.4.6 and 42; the first two in conjunction with **aestivum** (the second time directly modifying *canis*; Maltby *ad* 1.4.6 notes that this replicates a Greek phrase κύων ὀπωρινός), and the third with the similar *arenti* (at Tib. 1.7.21 it is called Sirius and *arentes…findit…agros*); see too the similar *Canis aestifer* at V. *G.* 2.353, *aestivo…sidere* at [Ov.] *Hal.* 117, *aestiferi canis* at Sen. *Oed.* 39. Sirius' rising in mid-July was a dangerous time in the Mediterranean, as it often coincided with extremely hot and dry weather (Hom. *Il.* 22.26–31 is the *locus classicus*; see too poetic mentions by name at e.g. Tib. 1.7.21, V. *G.* 4.425, *A.* 3.141 and 10.273, and an explanation of how the heat in humans mirrors that of the earth at Theophr. *CP* 1.13.5–6); more importantly, it is the time when the annual malaria epidemic broke out in Rome (Sallares 2002: 62), and the time when most wealthy Romans left town for the countryside. **Aestivum**, therefore, probably refers both to weather and to malarial fever (as at line 27 below). On the various mythological origins of Sirius, see Frazer *ad* Ov. *Fas.* 4.939. Where moderns might think the hottest part of the summer to be ideal for playing in or near the water, ancients do not; this is when they stay inside or, at the very least, in the shade. See Pichon 1991: 81 on the erotic heat connoted by *aestus*.

> nunc autem sacris Baiarum proxima lymphis,
> 4   cum se purpureo vere remittit humus.

As Tränkle 1990 and Navarro Antolín 1996 note *ad loc.*, **autem** appears only here in the *CT*. **Sacris…lymphis**: the waters at Baiae are also called sacred at Mart.

4.57.7 (*sacri fontes*; cf. 4.57.8 *Nympharum partier Nereidumque domus*) (to Hercules; Postgate 1915). **Proxima**: Schoppes' emendation for the manuscripts' *maxima*, accepted by most editors; see Tränkle 1990 and Navarro Antolín 1996 *ad loc.* for further discussion. For **lymphis**, see *ad* 3.5.29 and 3.6.58.

Baiarum: a pleasure resort near Cumae, valued for its volcanic hot springs (according to Strabo 5.2.9 they were the most famous of all, and Mart. 6.42.7 mentions *principesque Baiae*), and infamous as a place of vice (see D'Arms 1970: 42–3 and 119–20 with nn., Schmatz 1905 and Borriello and d'Ambrosio 1979 for topography); among many citations, see e.g. Cic. *Cael.* 27 and 35, Prop. 1.11, and Ov. *Ars* 1.255–6, with commentators.

Spring is often **purpureo** because of its brightly coloured flowers: for the conjunction **purpureo vere** see V. *E.* 9.40, Colum. *DRR* 10.256 (dating ultimately to Pi. *P.* 4.64 φοινικανθέμενου ἦρος); *purpureos...colores* at Tib. 1.4.29, *purpureis...floribus* at Ov. *Fas.* 5.363. The adjective refers to a wide variety of other things, including the complexion typical of youth (see *ad* 3.4.30, and *passim* in Vergil), and the light of sunrise or sunset, and in e.g. Cicero it has a decidedly luxurious and louche tone, which may be relevant here given the contemporary resonances of spas, and may also be conveyed by the use of **remittit** (for the noun and verb, see Ov. *Fas.* 4.126 *vere remissus ager*). **Remittit humus** also at Colum. *DRR* 12.15.1; on the 'loosening' of spring, cf. Hor. *Od.* 1.4.1–10, V. *G.* 1.43–4, with commentators: here we are probably meant to understand the weather as increasing the romance of the scene.

    At mihi Persephone nigram denuntiat horam:
6   immerito iuveni parce nocere, dea.

This couplet marks the abrupt change to the subject that occupies the majority of the poem, seen in the contrast between *vos*, the first word of the poem, and **at mihi** here. **Persephone**, as queen of the underworld, is found in Latin poetry as a death-bringing figure elsewhere at Hor. *Ser.* 2.5.109–10 (*trahit*), V. *A.* 4.698–9 with Pease 1935 *ad loc.* (*nondum...crinem/abstulit*), Prop. 2.28.47–8 (paired with her husband and asked for *clementia*), Ov. *Her.* 21.46 (*nostras pulsat...fores*, where she comes prematurely), Gratt. *Cyn.* 373–4 (*letum...extulit*), Stat. *Silv.* 2.1.147 (*crinem tenet infera Iuno*), and *Theb.* 8.10 (*furvo...poste notarat*). As Navarro Antolín 1996 notes *ad loc.*, Persephone fulfils a dual purpose: she tells of L.'s death but also, as often (implicitly here), serves as a harbinger of spring. This is the Greek form of her name; Latin *Proserpina* is also used by the poets; see Rebelo Gonçalves 1988: 312.

The phrase **nigram horam** (note contrast with *purpureo*) is not otherwise attested; *niger* in the *CT* is often associated with death and with evil omens (e.g. the *nigra manus* of death, Tib. 1.3.4, the black funeral garments of 3.2.18). The adjective appears three times in this poem, more often than in any other poem of the *CT* (and see *ad* 3.2.10). **Horam** refers to death at Tib. 1.1.59 (*suprema* *hora*); there are a number of similar phrases in poetry: *extrema... hora* at V. *E.* 8.20, *dubiae... horae* at Prop. 2.13.45, *fatalis... hora* at Luc. 9.87, *gravis... hora* at Stat. *Silv.* 2.1.54. The phrase is also related to *atra dies* at V. *A.* 6.429 and *niger... dies* at Prop. 2.24.34.

The difference between *nuntio* and **denuntiat** is that the latter is more official, a kind of 'announcing from on high' (though Persephone comes from the underworld). The verb is very common in prose, and not otherwise used in *CT*; but Arethusa at Prop. 4.3.61 claims that when an owl hoots, *illa dies hornis caedem denuntiat agnis* (and cf. [Ov.] *Hal.* 60).

L. is not willing to submit to his fate: he protests that he is young and has done no wrong. **Immerito**, which appears also at Tib. 1.6.72 and 3.4.14, sets the tone for the next several couplets. On **iuveni**, see *ad* 3.4.73 (not otherwise with *immeritus*).

Parce is an especially elegiac verb, as the elegist often seeks help (see too *ad* 3.5.21 and 3.9.1). For **parce nocere**, cf. Prop. 2.5.18, and on **nocere**, Pichon 1991: 214. **Dea**: Persephone is not often addressed in poetry (but see Prop. 2.28.47–8, where her *clementia* is beseeched).

>   Non ego temptavi nulli temeranda virorum
> 8   audax laudandae sacra docere deae,

The next few couplets may be an extended allusion to such Tibullan passages as 2.4.21–6, where the poet decides to turn to a life of sacrilegious crime in order to offer gifts to the *puella*; note too Koenen 1968 on their similarities to the sacral language of Egypt (and see Introduction, Section I, on religion in elegy). L., at least by his own portrayal, is wealthy (see *ad* 3.3), but still cannot get what he wants. Tib. questions his own innocence at 1.2.81–4 and protests it at 1.3.51–2; cf. Stat. *Silv.* 5.5.3–7, Petr. 133.3 (quoted *ad* 3.5.11). L., for his part, denies all wrongdoing; Ov. *Am.* 2.2.63–5, *EP* 2.2.9–16, and 2.9.67–72 detail a similar range of crimes not committed (poison, drawn swords, mythological acts of hubris, poison, forgery); see too Ov. *EP* 1.1.51–8 on confession and divine forgiveness.

L. has not tried to teach (nor, presumably, to learn) about the rites of the Bona Dea (here alluded to by use of **laudandae**—but see below for another suggestion). Her rites, imported into Rome during the second Punic war, were forbidden to men (e.g. Prop. 4.9.25–6); but see Staples 1998: 14–15 with nn. for the epigraphic evidence, which suggests male worship. L. uses this example, by metonymy, as a way of showing that he has not betrayed the secrets of the gods. The Bona Dea is mentioned in elegy as offering a handy excuse to *puellae* wanting to sneak out (e.g. Tib. 1.6.22). We know more about this cult than we otherwise would because of Clodius' supposed transvestitism at the celebration of the rites of the Bona Dea in 62 BCE. For full discussion of the goddess, her worshippers, and the cult, see Brouwer 1989, *RE* 3.1.686.64–694.8; sensible treatment also at Wiseman 1974: 130–37.

Commentary on 3.5.10–12

Non ego: see *ad* 3.2.5. **Temeranda**: frequent in Ov.; see McKeown *ad* Ov. *Am.* 1.8.19 and Ov. *EP* 2.2.13 *temeraria dextera* (Diomedes'). **Audax**: almost wholly negative in the elegists, denoting those bold beyond reasonableness. **Docere**: Tränkle 1990 *ad loc.* obelizes and wants something such as *vulgare* (which does not scan) as at e.g. Hor. *Od.* 3.2.26–7 and Ov. *Ars* 2.601; other emendations are *noscere* (Heyne), *movere* (Voss), and *subire* (Heinsius).

Laudandae...deae: Postgate 1915 suggests that this does not refer to the Bona Dea (Tib. 1.6.22 *Bonae...Deae*), but rather to Persephone (with her Greek epithet ἐπαινή translated *laudanda*). The rites would then, presumably, be those of the Eleusinian mysteries. This is appealing, but on the other hand, poison (see next couplet) is traditionally conceived of as a 'woman's crime', so there may be point to reference to the Bona Dea (see too above). For elegiac *laus*, see Pichon 1991: 185.

> nec mea mortiferis infecit pocula sucis
> 10   dextera nec cuiquam trita venena dedit,

L. seems to be reacting to the impious lover of Tib. 1.2 and 1.3. Beyond religious crimes (mentioned first, perhaps, in order to reassure the gods about what most concerns them), L. has also been guilty of no profane ones.

Nec: for this repetition (over the next four lines), see Wills 1996: 414. **Mortiferis...sucis**: the combination is unattested, and the adjective is rare in elegy (Prop. 3.13.17, Ov. *RA* 26, *EP* 3.1.26). Sen. *Med.* 717–18 features the two words in close conjunction, in a passage where the Nurse describes the horrors of Medea's magic. **Sucis** of poisons is Ovidian (most often those of Medea and Circe). **Infecit**: a regular verb for poisoning (*OLD* 4a; *TLL* 7.1.1413.42–1414.9); cf. e.g. Ov. *Her.* 9.142 and *Met.* 2.784. The verb is combined with **pocula** at V. *G.* 2.128, with *venenis* at V. *A.* 7.341. **Pocula** is a favourite word of L., used here and in line 34, and below at 3.6.5 and 18; cf. Tib. 1.5.49–50 *ore cruento/tristia cum multo pocula felle bibat*.

Dextera: Navarro Antolín 1996 suggests *ad loc.* that for the right hand to administer poison is especially cruel, since it is the hand of *fides*.

Trita venena: see Bömer *ad* Ov. *Met.* 14.44 for the frequent use of this verb in magical contexts, and, in elegy, Prop. 2.17.14 *trita venena* in the same *sedes* (and Fedeli 2005 *ad loc.* for further citations of the perfect participle). Older manuscripts transmit *certa*, which is somewhat odd with poisons (**trita** in the *Fragmentum Cuiacianum*; Luck prints *taetra*); see Navarro Antolín 1996 *ad loc.* for discussion.

> nec nos sacrilegi templis amovimus aegros,
> 12   nec cor sollicitant facta nefanda meum,

This couplet is vexed, with a variety of manuscript readings. L. may refer to removing sick people from temples (as printed), or bronze (*aera*), or sacred fire

190   *Commentary on 3.5.14*

(*ignes*), or may speak of burning temples (*admovimus ignes*). See Tränkle 1990 and Navarro Antolín 1996 for discussion, and for defence of the last option, from the humanist manuscripts, as being the most extreme, and so the most likely example for L. to choose. The line seems to echo Tib. 1.3.51–2: *timidum non me periuria terrent,/non dicta in sanctos impia verba deos*. The closest parallel to the second line, however, is at Petr. 133.3, *non templis impius hostis/admovi dextram*, which Parca 1986: 467 sees as an adaptation of this couplet. See Schuster 1968: 157–60 for further discussion of the printed text; given the context of this poem, concern with the ailing might be most relevant (see esp. Val. Max. 2.5.6 on temples of Fever). But any of the other readings might also be correct.

Sollicitant: cf. Ov. *Tr.* 4.8.6, Sen. *Phaed.* 438, Luc. 6.806, Mart. 7.54.2 *animum sollicitentque meum*, and see *ad* 3.4.20. **Facta nefanda**: at Ov. *Her.* 14.16 and *Fas.* 2.850, both in the same *sedes*; the two are not elsewhere joined. For **cor** see *ad* 3.2.6.

    nec nos insanae meditantes iurgia mentis
14   impia in adversos solvimus ora deos,

L. moves towards verbal crimes against the gods. **Insanae ... mentis** is a constitutive feature of the elegiac lover (V. *E.* 10.22, using the verb to describe Gallus, is the *locus classicus*; *insana mente* at Tib. 2.6.18), especially if he is Propertian (1.5.1, 1.9.16, 2.14.18, 2.22.16, 4.1.34; 1.4.17, 1.6.16, 2.20.3, 3.8.2, 3.17.3 of the *puella*); in Ov.'s amatory elegies the adjective is present but less prominent (*Am.* 1.12.21, *Ars* 1.372; *Am.* 3.6.58 of the *puella*). With the negative, perhaps L. makes the claim to a significant difference from other elegists. So too, he may be disavowing the impious behaviour of elegiac lovers such as that mentioned at Tib. 1.2.81–2; see Pichon 1991: 172–3. Luck and Navarro Antolín 1996 print *insana ... mente*; see the latter *ad loc*. **Meditantes** is not used in the *CT* except by L. (also at 3.4.71). For sacrilegious speech in elegy, see Tib. 1.3.52 *non dicta in sanctos impia verba deos*, 2.6.17–18 *tu me mihi dira precari/cogis et insane mente nefanda loqui*, Prop. 1.1.8 (quoted below), 2.28.9–12.

Iurgia only here in the *CT*, but in Prop. (1.3.18 *expertae metuens iurgia saevitiae*, where it takes a similar genitive of characteristic, 2.6.32, 3.6.18, 3.8.19) and Ov. (*Am.* 2.2.35, 2.9.45; *Ars* 1.591, 3.374, *RA* 35), normally of lover's quarrels and, as Pichon 1991: 178 notes, to describe the complaints of the offended lover. For religious uses, see *TLL* 7.2.666.44–667.2.

Impia ... ora: probably modelled on *impia lingua* at Tib. 1.2.80 (and see *ad* 3.4.16) and *impia verba* 1.3.52 (quoted above). **Solvimus ora**: a common phrase for breaking silence. The verb from Ov. onward is reserved for speaking: e.g. Ov. *Met.* 1.181, 7.190–1, 9.427–8, *Tr.* 3.11.20, Sen. *HF* 664, *HO* 724, Luc. 5.140, Stat. *Ach.* 1.524–5, Sil. 15.455, 17.339–40.

Adversos deos: see Prop. 1.1.8, where his love for Cynthia has caused him *adversos ... habere deos*, Ov. *Her.* 7.4 *adverso movimus ista deo*, *EP* 3.2.18 *adversos extimuere deos*, Liv. 9.1.11; for this meaning of the adjective, see *OLD* 9c, *TLL*

1.870.12–23, and cf. *offensos…deos* at Ov. *Her.* 21.48, *offenso…deo* at *Fas.* 1.482, *offensi…dei* at *Tr.* 1.10.42, *offendatur…deus* at *Tr.* 1.5.38.

> et nondum cani nigros laesere capillos,
> 16 nec venit tardo curva senecta pede.

Picking up from *immerito iuveni* of 6, L. moves from the crimes he has not committed to discuss his youth. This couplet offers the only physical detail L. provides about himself (description, even of the *puella*, is rare in elegy). We might want to connect the poet's youth to the untimely death of Tib. (attested not merely in his biographical tradition, but in Ov. *Am.* 3.9), especially as we are nearing the end of L.'s cycle, and this poem contains a number of closural elements. Some have seen 3.5 as particularly disjointed by contrast with the previous four, which might argue for actual illness or, more plausibly, for the careful planning out of how one might reflect illness in a poem. (3.6, in which the poet is 'drunk', is even more scattered.) Perhaps instead the structure has simply been missed: L. returns to his point of departure. See Lee for extended discussion of Ovidian parallels in this and the next two couplets (1958–9: 17–18); in each case he finds L.'s usage inferior and therefore derivative.

Cani: white hair is a typical symbol of old age; usually, in elegy, it is the marker of the elderly (and risible) lover; cf. e.g. Tib. 1.1.72, 1.2.94, and Prop. 3.5.24 with Fedeli 1985 *ad loc.* for Greek models, and Burkowski 2012: 127–81. The image here is vivid, differing from but similar to those at Tib. 1.6.77 and 1.10.40 (see *ad* 3.3.8 for more on old age in [Tib.] 3, and a brief but telling description at Ov. *Met.* 3.275–8). **Cani nigros…capillos**: *cani capilli* at Ov. *Ars* 2.117, and cf. *Tr.* 4.8.2 *inficit et nigras alba senecta comas* and 4.10.93–4 *iam mihi canities pulsis melioribus annis/venerate, antiquas miscueratque comas*. As often, L. juxtaposes colour-words.

Laesere is a vivid verb (*OLD* 1a and *TLL* 7.2.867.56–868.2); see *ad* 3.4.16, 3.6.22, 3.9.8, and 3.10.15, and McKeown *ad* Ov. *Am.* 1.7.40. L. prefers to highlight the psychological impact of aging over the more literal rendering at Tib. 1.8.42 *heu cum vetus infecit cana senecta caput* and Prop. 3.5.24 *sparserit et nigras alba senecta comas*.

The second line of the couplet mirrors Ov. *Ars* 2.670, a passage which asserts that love is not appropriate to the elderly: *iam veniet tacito curva senecta pede*; see Lee 1958–9: 17 for discussion which assumes Ovidian primacy, Doncieux 1888: 130 for the opposite claim. **Tardo…pede**: elsewhere at Tib. 1.8.48 (*non tardo labitur illa pede*), Ov. *Am.* 2.19.12 (*cunctantem tardo iussit abire pede*), and *Tr.* 1.3.56 (*indulgens animo pes mihi tardus erat*). *Tacito* is used more commonly by Tib. and Ov.: Tib. 1.9.4 *sera tamen tacitis Poena venit pedibus*, 1.10.34 *imminet et tacito clam venit illa pede*, Ov. *Tr.* 4.6.17 *tacito pede*, *Tr.* 4.10.27 *tacito passu*.

Curva senecta: other than the parallel from *Ars* 2.670 cited above, see Stat. *Theb.* 4.419 *incurva senecta*. But the basic notion occurs elsewhere in elegy: Prop. 2.18.20 *anus... curva*, Tib. 2.2.19–20 *vincula quae maneant semper dum tarda senectus/inducat rugas inficiatque comas*; cf. Ov. *Tr.* 3.7.35 *damnosa senectus*.

>   Natalem primo nostrum videre parentes,
> 18   cum cecidit fato consul uterque pari.

Line 18 problematically = Ov. *Tr.* 4.10.6. See Introduction, Section V, for extended discussion, and Lee 1958–9: 17–18, 20–21. **Natalem primo** is most naturally taken as the day of birth, but it could, by a stretch of the Latin, mean first birthday (Traina 1966 for earlier history of the problem, Navarro Antolín 1996: 10, Knox, forthcoming). On **primo** as a temporal adverb for the more regular *primum*, see Bömer *ad* Ov. *Met.* 15.106, Ov. *EP* 3.6.45. L. presumably chooses it to distinguish from **nostrum** and to avoid homoioteleuton. **Cecidit fato**: both in regular usage for death, but together in poetry only at Ov. *Tr.* 1.2.53 *fato... cadentem*, 4.10.6, Sen. *Oed.* 780 *aliquisne cecidit regio fato comes?*, 787 *quo cadat fato*. **Uterque pari**: at line-end also at Ov. *Fas.* 5.704.

>   Quid fraudare iuvat vitem crescentibus uvis
> 20   et modo nata mala vellere poma manu?

This couplet is logical only if it is kept on its most literal plane: one avoids picking unripe fruit in order to be able to enjoy it later, when ripe (see McKeown *ad* Ov. *Am.* 1.10.55–6 for the conjunction of grapes and apples). But death seems especially interested in taking the young and/or beautiful away from the world (cf. e.g. Kaibel 1878: 575).

   Fraudare (*TLL* 6.1.1264.1–26 for the construction, and Bömer *ad* Ov. *Met.* 7.250) expresses L.'s frustration at dying with 'unfinished business'; the verb does not otherwise occur in *CT* or Prop., but is common in Ov., especially in the near-identical *Am.* 2.14.23–4: *quid plenam fraudas vitem crescentibus uvis,/pomaque crudeli vellis acerba manu* of a fetus (where it is, as commentators note, more appropriate than applied, as it is here, to a grown man; see McKeown 1998 *ad loc.* and Lee 1958–9: 17). But we need not accuse L. of incompetence; the image fits his mood, in which he sees himself as just having begun life (see too Cic. *Sen.* 71, on age as 'ripening' a person, and on *poma... cruda... vix evelluntur*, and e.g. *AP* 12.205 and Hor *Od.* 2.5.10 for the young as unripe grapes). As with much of this section of the poem, the lines are relevant to the Ov./L. chronology debate; see Ramorino 1899: 277 for the suggestion that they were in the first edition of the *Amores* (further discussion in Enk 1950 and Lee 1958–9; Büchner 1965: 93–4 suggests L.'s priority). For the contrary sentiment, see Tib. 1.1.7–8 *ipse seram teneras maturo tempore vites/rusticus et facili grandia poma manu*. For elegiac *fraudes*, see Pichon 1991: 155. **Fraudare... vitem** elsewhere only at Ov. *Am.* 2.14.13; perhaps a pun on *vitis/vita* is intended.

Iuvat is L.'s main change from the Ovidian line (assuming Ov. predates): it suggests that L., in his illness, has come to see the world as conspiring against him, taking pleasure in his suffering. **Crescentibus uvis**: the phrase does not occur elsewhere (besides Ov. *Am.* 2.14.24, where it also ends the line). *Crescentibus annis* is Ovidian (*Ars* 1.61, *Met.* 10.24); the same phrase at Mart. 1.88.1 suggests its use on epitaphs. **Mala... manu**: for *malus* as synonym of *crudelis* (*OLD* 3b), see V. *E.* 3.11, and note Ov. *Am.* 2.14.24, quoted above; L. ascribes malevolent intent to the hand that plucks his life away. Does he choose the adjective because of the homograph noun *malum*?

    Parcite, pallentes undas quicumque tenetis
22   duraque sortiti tertia regna dei.

The change from singular **parce dea** (6) to plural (**parcite**) signifies the broadening of L.'s pleas to any underworld god (**quicumque**) willing to hear them; for the verb's use in Tib., see Hellegouarc'h 1989.

Pallentes: in Tib. always participial in form; never in Prop., and split almost evenly in Ov. Although the underworld contains both paleness and liquid, **pallentes...undas** occur elsewhere only at Sil. 9.250. See *ad* 3.1.28 for the underworld rivers.

Dura...tertia regna: elsewhere only at V. *A.* 6.566 *durissima regna*; **tertia** because Hades obtained the third (least favourable) lot when he, Zeus, and Poseidon divided the world amongst themselves (Hom. *Il.* 15.187–93; Sen. *HF* 609 and 833 *tertiae sortis*). **Tertia regna**: an Ovidian phrase: in the same *sedes* at Ov. *Am.* 3.8.50 and *Fas.* 4.584; cf. *triplicis... fortuna novissima regni* at *Met.* 5.368; Sil. 8.116, 13.437. See *ad* 3.2.3 for *durus*. Translate 'and you who live in the difficult third kingdom of the god who won it by lot'. **Sortiti**: suggests a more particular referent than **quicumque**, i.e. Hades (and perhaps also Persephone); see Navarro Antolín 1996 *ad loc.* for the plausible suggestion that we should understand *estis*. See Bömer *ad* Ov. *Met.* 2.241 for the epic tone of the participle.

    Elysios olim liceat cognoscere campos
24   Lethaeamque ratem Cimmeriosque lacus,

In the other elegists except Ov., **olim** always refers to the (far-distant) past; Ov., in keeping with usage elsewhere, uses the word for the distant past (*Ars* 3.405), the recent past (*Her.* 8.41), and the future (*Am.* 3.11.7). The use of the adverb at V. *A.* 1.20 for the future glory of Troy may suggest that this meaning has an epic flavour; L.'s subjunctive incorporates both the wish/expectation that he will reach the Elysian fields, traditional post-mortem locale for the blessed, *and* that this should not happen for a long time.

Elysios...campos: the *locus classicus* is Hom. *Od.* 4.561–9; see Heubeck et al. 1988 *ad loc.*; mentioned in Latin poetry first at V. *G.* 1.38 and then Tib. 1.3.58

194   *Commentary on 3.5.26*

(*ipsa Venus campos ducet in Elysios*; Tib. fantasizes that Venus herself will take him there because he has always honoured her). As Navarro Antolín 1996 notes *ad loc.*, the concept of a special Elysium for poets in love is likely to derive from the Tibullan passage (Henderson 1969; V. *A.* 6.441–9, the *lugentes campi*, where those who die from love go, may also be relevant). Ov. uses the adjective *Elysius* four times, only at *Ib.* 173 with *campi*. Ov. *Am.* 3.9.60, on the death of Tib., which claims *in Elysia valle Tibullus erit*, and Domitius Marsus' epitaph for Vergil and Tib., with the same *iunctura*, suggest that the phrase was seen as Tibullan.

Lethaeam ratem: cf. *ad* 3.3.10 for the same noun/adjective combination, unique to L. The two phrases of this line are grammatically parallel, and also have parallel meanings; the line's construction is Ovidian. **Cimmeriosque lacus**: the adjective is used of the Sea of Azov, the Black Sea, and of the underworld, because the Cimmerians (like the dead) never saw the sun; *RE* 11.2.397–434. The adjective occurs elsewhere at e.g. Hom. *Od.* 11.14–19, [V.] *Cul.* 232 *Cimmerios lucos* (and see Hinds 1987b: 36–8 for puns on *locus/lucus/lacus*), Ov. *Met.* 11.592–3 with Bömer 1980 *ad loc.*, Ov. *EP* 4.10.1–2, [Tib.] 3.7.64; Otto 1890: 83. **Lethaeam** and **Cimmeriosque** are flagged by Hagen 1954 as late words; both, however, occur in earlier poetry: the former with e.g. *gurgite* at Cat. 65.5, *liquor* at Prop. 4.7.10, *stagna* at Prop. 4.7.91, *aquas* at Tib. 1.3.80 and *passim*; the latter occurs as early as Naevius (fr. 18.1).

           cum mea rugosa pallebunt ora senecta
    26   et referam pueris tempora prisca senex.

Olim of line 23 is now given a specific meaning: L. should die long in the future, when (**cum**) he is wrinkled with age, telling stories to the young. This focus on the positive aspects of growing old is characteristic of Tib. among the elegists (e.g. 2.2.19–20 *vincula quae maneant semper dum tarda senectus/inducat rugas inficiatque comas*), as is the presence of young children (e.g. 1.7.55–6 *at tibi succrescat proles quae facta parentis/augeat et circa stet veneranda senem*, 1.10.43–4 *sic ego sim, liceatque caput candescere canis/temporis et prisci facta referre senem*, 2.5.93–4 *nec taedebit avum parvo advigilare nepoti/balbaque cum puero dicere verba senem*). The middle passage from Tib. is a close match, and L.'s may well depend upon it. In Prop. and Ov., the *rugae* of age more often signify powerlessness and potential lovelessness (Prop. 2.18.6, 3.25.11–14, 4.5.59, 4.5.67; Ov. *Am.* 1.8.112, 2.14.7, *Ars* 1.240, 2.118, 3.73, 3.785). The only other conjunction of **pallebunt** and **senecta** occurs at Sen. *Ben.* 7.27.3 *senes pallidos*.

Rugosa…ora senecta: cf. *sulcavit…cutem rugis* at Ov. *Met.* 3.276, *rugis peraravit anilibus ora* at *Met.* 14.96, *ruga senilis* at *Fas.* 5.58, *Tr.* 3.7.34, and *EP* 1.4.2.

Are the **pueris** his children/grandchildren? If so, L. is asking more than it first seems: not only not to die now, but to have a long-term relationship which flourishes into future generations. For the image of old men instructing children, or simply enjoying their company, see the Tibullan examples above. **Tempora prisca**: for the conjunction, see Tib. 1.10.44 (quoted above); that line as a whole is nearly identical to this one; the phrase occurs elsewhere in poetry at Ov. *Fas.* 1.197 and Sil. 4.55.

> Atque utinam vano nequiquam terrear aestu,
> 28   languent ter quinos sed mea membra dies.

L. returns to the present moment, wishing his fever to be the symptom of no greater illness. **Atque utinam** is in the elegists nearly always at line-start (see too *ad* 3.19.5); thereafter not so frequent. **Vano** was something of a leitmotif of 3.4; perhaps this too is a (feverish) dream. For the pleonastic use of **vano** and **nequiquam**, see Cat. 64.111, *nequiquam vanis*. **Vano... aestu**: this striking phrase is not found elsewhere; it suggests L.'s frustration with the illness, which neither goes away nor kills him.

Terrear: for medical use, see *OLD* 2b; the subjunctive may indicate a counterfactual or a genuine wish. Luck and Navarro Antolín 1996 print the alternative manuscript reading *torrear* (see the latter *ad loc.*). **Ter quinos... dies**: not simply, *pace* Navarro Antolín 1996, poetic language, but a precise description of quartan fever, which has affected L. three times, in five-day periods. He is, therefore, worn out; for other descriptions of the symptoms, see Hipp. *Prog.* 20, Galen *De Praecog.* 2–3 (at 3.1 Galen notes that the third attack of the fever makes most doctors give up hope of the patient). The fever is, however, not usually fatal; L.'s anxiety may reflect a degree of hypochondria, or his sense that life is not worth living without N. On **languent** see *ad* 3.4.22; for the verb's use of illness, *ad* 3.10.13 and Ov. *Am.* 2.2.21 (*TLL* 7.2.921.77–922.12). **Sed**: see Tränkle 1990 *ad loc.* on the placement of the connective; it is emphatic, confirming that the fever is not *vano*. Might we see in L.'s assertion that *his* symptoms signify a genuine illness a comment on Tib.'s illness in 1.3?

> At vobis Tuscae celebrantur numina lymphae
> 30   et facilis lenta pellitur unda manu.

L. ends emphatically (**at vobis** marks a dramatic change in subject) with a return to his addressees, lazing about in the water. Is this in spite of his illness, or out of ignorance? If ignorance, is the point of this poem (whatever it says) to summon aid (perhaps especially N.)?

On **Tuscae**, see *ad* 3.4.6; not otherwise used with **lymphae**. **Numina lymphae** is also unattested; Heinsius' conjecture *flumina* is attractive. On **celebrantur**, see *ad* 3.4.57; the verb in this sense is sometimes religious (= *venerare*, *OLD* 1a; see Tränkle 1990 *ad loc.*) and sometimes not (= *frequentare*, *OLD* 4; see Navarro Antolín 1996 *ad loc.*, and Bömer *ad* Ov. *Met.* 1.172), and **numina** leaves that ambiguity present (for Baiae as *cana...nympha*, see Mart. 6.43.1–2); see too Ov. *Fas.* 4.865 *numina, volgares, Veneris celebrate, puellae*. For Greek and Roman polytheists, all bodies of water and most trees have a divine spirit in charge of or associated with them, so (if the word is correct), however fanciful L. is being, he is not incorrect.

Facilis...unda: *OLD* 5b, *TLL* 6.57.44–69; cf. Prop. 1.11.11–12 *aut teneat clausam tenui Teuthrantis in unda/alternat facilis cedere lympha manu*; this phrase occurs at Luc. 1.222 and Stat. *Silv.* 3.2.84. Note too *facili...liquore* at Prop. 1.20.47 and Plaut. *Rud.* 170 (*facile enabit*). The phrase is reminiscent of the more elegiac *placida...aqua* (Tib. 1.2.80, 1.4.12, quoted below, 1.7.14, Ov. *Her.* 19.82, *Ars* 3.386, *Tr.* 3.4.16, *EP* 2.2.30, 3.6.44. In elegy, nothing is especially *facilis* (Pichon 1991: 141); the adjective may suggest that L.'s friends, whoever they may be, do not really belong in his world.

Lenta...manu: there is surely a pointed disjunction between L.'s condition, languid through illness, and the voluntarily minimal movements of his friends. This phrase is prosaic: Petr. 18.5, 26.5, 138.2, Sen. *Cont.* 3.pr.10.4, [Sen.] *Oct.* 820 (of soldiers). **Lentus** (unlike *facilis*) is a main characteristic of the elegiac beloved; see Pichon 1991: 186. See too *lenta...bracchia* of swimming at Ov. *Her.* 19.48, *Met.* 4.353–5 with Bömer 1976 *ad loc.*, and Rut. Nam. 1.248.

Pellitur: cf. the (erotic) image of a boy swimming at Tib. 1.4.12 (*hic placidam niveo pectore pellit aquam*); see too Ov. *Ib.* 589 *per alternos pulsabitur unda lacertos*.

> Vivite felices, memores et vivite nostri,
> 32   sive erimus seu nos fata fuisse velint.

L. suggests that remembering him is not incompatible with happiness for his friends (**felices** presumes their continued good fortune), a contrast with his earlier notion that his untimely death would be a tragedy for all. Perhaps he is putting his best face on things, or perhaps the end of the poem brings him acceptance and peace; Navarro Antolín 1996 *ad loc.* sees the lines as a quasi-propempticon (see e.g. Prop. 1.6.31–6, where he does not know where Tullus will go, only that he will stay). This would have been a fitting place to end the poem.

Vivite felices: especially appropriate in funerary contexts: V. *A.* 3.493 (also at line-start); cf. Hor. *Od.* 3.27.13–14 *sis licet felix, ubicumque mavis,/et memor nostri, Galatea, vivas* (farewell without death). Further on *felix*, see *ad* 3.3.26. **Vivite**: the contrast between the poet's own death and his friends' continued life gains particular point from its difference from such passages as the *vivam* at Ov. *Am.* 1.15.42 and *Met.* 15.879; there, the poet is confident of immortality through writing, but here L. hopes only that his friends live beyond him.

Memores...nostri: see *ad* 3.2.25; the repetition may reinforce the impression that L. addresses himself to N. **Erimus...fuisse**: a particularly poignant use of the perfect infinitive to indicate death; cf. *Eleg. in Maec.* 2.14.

Fata…velint: cf. Prop. 1.6.30 and 1.14.14 (in both of which passages the infinitive comes in between); elsewhere at Ov. *EP* 4.6.3 *voluit miserabile fatum*, Luc. 2.544, also Ov. *Met.* 10.634 *fata…negant*; cf. *Fortuna* with the verb at e.g. Plaut. *Pers.* 515, Prop. 1.6.25, Mart. 4.18.5, and Juv. 7.198. *Fata sinunt* is a much more regular phrase; L.'s change perhaps reflects the sense of being actively persecuted despite his innocence.

> Interea nigras pecudes promittite Diti
> 34   et nivei lactis pocula mixta mero.

Nigras pecudes: black offerings are made to chthonic gods (Hom. *Od.* 10.524–9; cf. too e.g. Lucr. 3.52–3, V. *G.* 4.546, *A.* 5.97, 5.736, 6.153, 6.249, Tib. 1.2.62 with Smith 1913 and Murgatroyd 1980 *ad loc.*, Ov. *Met.* 7.244–50). The offerings to the gods of the dead hint at the closure that L. does not directly mention.

Diti: see *ad* 3.1.28; L. returns to themes of 5 and 21–4. **Nivei lactis**: see *ad* 3.2.20. On black and white and the contrast between them, see *ad* 3.2.10 (there *niger* and *candidus*); André 1949 does not discuss this juxtaposition. For milk as an underworld offering see *ad* 3.2.20.

Pocula mixta: same *sedes* at Ov. *Tr.* 5.3.50, Mart. 8.39.4, also at Sil. 14.661. **Mixta mero**: something of a paradox, as *merum* is unmixed wine (cf. Mart. 3.57.2); joined also at Tib. 2.1.46, *mixtaque securo est sobria lympha mero*. **Mero**, the final word of the poem, perhaps connects it to 3.6 (as do the sustained references to liquids in this poem, both water and wine).

3.6:

This poem begins as a cletic hymn (Men. Rh. 334.25–336.4, Cairns 1972: 137, 192–6) invoking the god Bacchus, but soon moves to N., and thence to love in general (for other elegiac hymns, see e.g. Tib. 1.2, 1.7, Prop. 3.17, 4.6, 4.9, Ov. *Tr.* 5.3, with Littlewood 1975 and J. F. Miller 1991 on Prop. 3.17, the closest parallel to this poem, both discussing precursors, and Navarro Antolín 2005: 311–14 on the Propertian intertexts). Hor. *Od.* 2.19 and 3.25, two other hymns to Bacchus, help to show the uniqueness of this poem, as they focus throughout on the god—and indeed, the poem as a whole bears noticeable linguistic and stylistic resemblances to Horatian symposiastic poetry. It is a fitting conclusion to the cycle, confirming earlier hints in L. that his relationship with N. is doomed. (Prop. 3.17 is also often read as the 'beginning of the end'.) The poem suggests a divine contest between Amor and Liber, both to be understood metonymically (and perhaps also more literally), in which wine can serve as a *remedium amoris* (a common theme in elegy as a whole, especially Ov.). See, for instance, the interplay between Bacchus and Amor played out in Prop. 1.3, where the drunk poet (*ebria cum multo traherem vestigia Baccho*, 1.3.9) returns to his jealous *puella*: *et quamvis duplici correptum ardore iuberent/hac Amor hac Liber, durus uterque deus…* (1.3.13–14). We might also compare Ov. *Am.*

3.1, in which Ov. envisions his decision about whether to continue writing elegy or to turn to tragedy as a battle between the two, personified as women vying for his affections. And all of these scenes, are, of course, replays of the famous 'choice of Heracles' between Vice and Virtue (see Philostratus, p. 496; Xen. *Mem.* 2.1.21).

This poem exemplifies two contradictory beliefs about wine and love, both frequently found in elegy (and epigram before elegy): that wine helps to dull the pain of unhappy love (e.g. *AP* 12.49–50, Tib. 1.2.1, 1.5.37–8, Prop. 3.17.3–4), and that it makes one vulnerable to love (e.g. *AP* 5.93, Ov. *Her.* 16.231–2, *RA* 809–10; see too Müller 1952: 33–8); Prop. 3.17.5 contains both sentiments (*per te iunguntur, per te solvuntur amantes*). Unusually for elegy as a whole (but less so for Tib.), the poem has a dramatic development: L. envisions a scene which involves other people, and seems finally to come to a decision about his love, and his poetry. L.'s invocation of Liber is somewhat informal, but this is in keeping with the way he, and the poets of [Tib.] 3 as a whole, address the divine (see Fulkerson, forthcoming); a notable parallel is Tib. 1.7, particularly in the way that poem glides from Messalla to Osiris to Bacchus to the metonymy of wine (see Murgatroyd 1980 *ad* 49–50), to Messalla's Genius.

Links with Tib. 1.2 are probably important: there, too, drunkenness is imitated to poetic effect, and the poet seeks to warn others. But Tib.'s woes are less severe: Delia is locked away, but not uninterested (and he spends most of the poem fantasizing about her escape). Throughout the poem, L. plays with the notion of a sober poet imitating a drunken symposiast (see e.g. *ad* 3.6.5 and 3.6.33–6): the deterioration of the poem from its complex and elevated hymnic structure shows the effects of the wine.

Although we know nothing about the intended arrangement of the poems, the disjunction between 3.5 and 3.6 is just as marked as that between 3.4 and 3.5. The previous poem ended with L. fearing death, which he envisioned as impending. Here, he is at a party (though still suffering, apparently not physically), encouraging others to drink. So too, although the train of thought of the poem is confusing at moments (mimicking, presumably, the increasing drunkenness and confusion of L.), there is a clear denouement. L. expands upon the elegiac topic of wine's relationship to love in a fashion more typical of Greek and Roman lyric poetry (which often presumes a sympotic setting). L., like other elegists (e.g. Ov. *Am.* 3.1, Prop. 4.1), signals his move away from elegy to a more elevated genre, in this case, lyric. Unlike them, however, he does not continue writing a different sort of poetry (at least, not that we know of). The closing lines (especially) are rife with symposiastic vocabulary and themes (see Giangrande 1967 for a survey).

The poem is difficult to divide into large sections, as its structure is deliberately unfocused. Broadly, the first six lines invoke Bacchus; the next six include the poet's friends, if they are willing to drink as well; the following six praise either Bacchus or Amor (or both; see *ad loc.*); the following six describe the power of Bacchus; the next eight threaten N. and then wish away the threat; the following six note the difficulty of feigning joy; the next four mention Ariadne; the next eight complain about faithless girls; the next six regret the loss of a faithless girl; and the final eight return to the joys of wine.

> Candide Liber, ades – sic sit tibi mystica vitis
> 2   semper, sic hedera tempora vincta feras –

Other poetic invocations of Bacchus (in addition to the hymns listed above) occur at Tib. 2.1.3–4, Ov. *Met.* 4.9–30. For parallels to **candide Liber**, see *candide Bacche* at Ov. *Fas.* 3.772, *candida formosi… ora Lyaei* at Sen. *Oed.* 508, and see *ad* 3.4.34 on the nuances of the adjective and god; he is termed *pulcherrime* at Ov. *Tr.* 5.3.43. See too *candide Bassareu* at Hor. *Od.* 1.18.11 (and the explanation at the end of that poem, that wine's liquid surface sparkles). The epithet **Liber** is also significant: L. seeks liberation from his unhappy romance, and from the elegiac prison. **Ades**: standard language for invoking a god; cf. e.g. Tib. 1.7.49, 2.1.35, etc. **Sic sit**: both normal for Ov. (four times) and for the language of prayers and vows.

The **vitis** of Dionysius is **mystica** because related to divinity (though the two are not elsewhere joined until Christian literature, which may mean that there is corruption of the text here; the adjective is *candida* in some manuscripts, the noun *victis*; see Navarro Antolín 1996 *ad loc.* for further details). The adjective is relatively rare (first attested in Latin at Accius 688R, associated with the *vannus Bacchi* at V. *G.* 1.166), in elegy only at Ov. *Ars* 2.640 (where the *praeceptor* claims not to divulge anything about his *furta*) and *Her.* 2.42 (of the *sacra* associated with marriage rites). The difficulty seen by some with the adjective (that it ought, strictly speaking, to refer to mystery rites, none of which involves a vine, so far as we know) is slight; it can refer to divine things in general (*TLL* 8.1759.7–24). Navarro Antolín 1996 prints, and makes a good case for, *rustica*. *Vannus* is also possible in place of **vitis**.

Semper refers both to the immortal nature of the gods or, with the comma placed before the word instead of after, to the evergreen nature of ivy. **Hedera** is regularly associated with Dionysus, perhaps because it grows in a luxuriant and uncontrolled manner (see Ov. *Fas.* 3.769–72 for the explanation that the god loves it because his cradle was hidden from Juno by ivy). Bacchus favours poets (see 3.4.44), and ivy therefore becomes associated with them as well (e.g. Prop. 4.1.62, Hor. *Od.* 1.1.29, *Ep.* 1.3.25, Ov. *Tr.* 1.7.2, 5.3.15).

Tempora vincta: conjunction unattested elsewhere; *vinctus* with *tempora* as a retained accusative occurs at V. *A.* 12.120 *verbena tempora vincti*, Ov. *Her.* 6.44 *tempora vinctus*, [Ov.] *Ep. Drus.* 334 *tempora vinctus*. There are also manuscript difficulties in the pentameter; most editors prefer the text as printed here; see Castelli 1973 and Tränkle 1990 and Navarro Antolín 1996 *ad loc.* for further discussion.

> aufer et ipse meum patera medicante dolorem:
> 4   saepe tuo cecidit munere victus amor.

These lines are also vexed: Wacker's emendation *affer… merum, pater, et medicare…* is an elegant and quite possibly correct solution, which Luck prints; Tränkle 1990 prints the text as above except for *medicare* and Navarro Antolín 1996 prints the above text. **Aufer:** the imperative (where we might expect an optative subjunctive) is common in poetic addresses to the divine. **Ipse,** i.e. in person; the injunction to a god to oversee something personally is also standard.

Patera medicante is found in the *recentiores*, preferred by a number of recent editors; the older manuscripts' *medicando* is unmetrical and difficult to construe, probably arising from dittography. Birt's *patera medicare* is also attractive (see too Dell'Era 1996b, who supports *metum pariter medicare*). Further discussion at Schuster 1968: 160–2 and Navarro Antolín 1996 *ad loc*. On **dolorem,** a standard descriptor of elegiac pain, see *ad* 3.2.3.

Munere is a regular manner of denoting boons from the gods, including Bacchus (e.g. V. *G.* 3.526–7 *Massica Bacchi/munera*, Ov. *Ars* 1.565 *munera Bacchi*); also in Greek δῶρα Διωνύσου (Hes. *WD* 614; see Navarro Antolín 1996 *ad* 3.6.17–18).

L. makes the well-known claim that drinking to oblivion can (temporarily) banish love (see introduction to this poem). While the original text would not have distinguished between **Amor** and **amor,** capitalization would suggest, along with **victus,** that the metaphor has changed from medicine to warfare, and Amor is envisioned as suffering defeat (note too the martial language of **cecidit**); see Hollis *ad* Ov. *Ars* 1.231–2. For the alternative opinion, see V. *E.* 10.69 *omnia vincit amor*, Ov. *RA* 260 *nec fugiet vivo sulpure victus amor*, and for the two notions conjoined, Prop. 1.1.

> Care puer, madeant generoso pocula baccho,
> 6   et nobis prona funde Falerna manu.

Care puer: of a beloved slave at Mart. 1.88.7; here, of a slave (Skutsch 1966: 144–5): *puer* is a standard term for slave boys, by analogy to Greek symposia, at e.g. Hor. *Od.* 1.38.1, 3.14.17, 3.19.10); see too 3.6.62. The combination occurs first of Pallas at V. *A.* 8.581; cf. VF 4.53, Stat. *Silv.* 3.4.60, 5.5.79, Sil. 4.475, 6.537, of Achilles at Stat. *Ach.* 1.252 and 1.273. The tone of **care** is either beseeching (L. wants more wine) or, potentially, erotic. Among Greek precedents, Alcaeus 366 LP is likely to be important, as is Theocr. 29.1 (both of which suggest that wine brings with it truth; see too *ad* 3.6.33–6, on the complicated game L. is playing here with imitation and representation). Perhaps confusingly, the most frequent *puer* in amatory elegy is Amor himself, so it may be the case that L. is undermining his own wishes. **Puer:** of Bacchus also at Ov. *Met.* 4.18. **Puer** is regular in this *sedes* throughout poetry, often after a vocative epithet (see too

3.9.20). For the conjunction of a (slave-)boy and Falernian wine, see Cat. 27.1–2, Hor. *Od.* 2.11.18–20, Mart. 9.93.1, 14.170.2.

Madeant: often in poetry for wine and those drinking it (especially in Horace; cf. Tib. 2.1.29–30, 2.2.8, 2.5.87 (adj.)). Generally, it is drinkers, and not their cups, who are soaked (*TLL* 8.34.18–44). **Madeant pocula** is a strikingly original phrase; cf. Prop. 2.33.39 *largius effuso madeat tibi mensa Falerno* and, possibly, Xen. 1.4 κρατὴρ δ'ἕστηκεν μεστὸς εὐφροσύνης.

Generoso... baccho: cf. Ov. *Met.* 4.765 *generosi munere Bacchi*; the noun is here metonymic, but the adjective (common for wine, *TLL* 6.2.1801.82–1802.8, but also meaning 'well-born') also refers to the god, and perhaps to the long tradition of poetic verse about him (i.e. **generoso** is also metapoetic). **Pocula baccho**: see V. *A.* 3.354, [V.] *Cir.* 229, and Ov. *Fas.* 3.301 for *pocula Bacchi* at line-end; VF 1.260 for *pocula baccho*, Stat. *Theb.* 5.257 *pocula Bacchum*.

Et: Navarro Antolín 1996 *ad loc.* prefers Müller's *en*, noting that the parallelism which normally links clauses is missing. That may well be the correct reading; as he notes, it is regular with imperatives. **Nobis** is either dative of advantage with the verb or possessive with **Falerna** (or both, making nice use of the ambiguity of Latin).

Prona... manu: unusual, signifying with the hand turned upside down, or leaning forward (to ensure that all the wine pours out, *OLD* 2b); *plena manu* is preferred by some, but Hor. *Od.* 3.29.2 provides a kind of parallel (*non ante verso lene merum cado*), though a much less bibulous one, as does Prop. 2.33.39 (quoted above). **Falerna**: one of the best Italian wines, coming from Campania, mentioned quite a lot in Horace (Nisbet and Hubbard *ad* Hor. *Od.* 1.20.9); see Plin. *NH* 14.62 on its quality, and Navarro Antolín 1996 *ad loc.* with many further citations.

>   Ite procul, durum curae genus, ite labores;
> 8   fulserit hic niveis Delius alitibus.

L. here refers to the well-known *topos* of wine as a banisher of cares; see introduction to this poem. **Ite procul**: see *ad* 3.4.3 and, for the 'pastoral' repetition, Wills 1996: 99–100. The bucolic diaeresis of the line adds to its eclogic feel.

Durum... genus: also at V. *G.* 1.63, of the human race, with Thomas 1988.1 *ad loc.*, *A.* 9.603, Ov. *Met.* 1.414 with Bömer 1969 *ad loc.*, and note too the similar phrase *gens dura*; see *ad* 3.2.3, 3.4.76, 3.4.92, 3.5.22, 3.9.3 on *durus*. The collocation **curae genus** is unattested except at Quint. *Inst.* 11.3.22 (where it refers to exercise); **Curae** seem to be an especially Gallan notion; the word appears in V. *E.* 1.57, identified as the *schema Cornelianum* (an enclosing apposition; see Skutsch 1956: 198–9 and Solodow 1986), as does the repetition of **ite**. On **labores**, see *ad* 3.4.65. And the conjunction of care and labour also seems Gallan (see V. *E.* 10.1, 22, 28, and *passim*).

Fulserit: as the commentators note, the manuscripts' *pulserit* must be wrong (unless some other part of the couplet is corrupt and Apollo is asked to propel away cares and labours); see Tränkle 1990 *ad loc.* **Niveis...alitibus**: Apollo is sometimes accompanied by white swans (Sappho 208 LP, Call. *Hymn* 4.249, Himerius 48.10–11), though it is not clear why they would appear here. Taking Apollo as the sun-god (Tränkle 1990 *ad loc.*; cf. *Cynthius* at Ov. *Fas.* 3.346 and 353), drawn across the sky by swans, is one possibility (cf. e.g. *LIMC* Apollon/ Aplu 76), as is understanding the phrase to refer to his (winged) horses, though this is unattested; see Navarro Antolín 1996 *ad loc.* for extensive discussion. **Delius**: cf. [Tib.] 3.4.79 for this epithet. Beyond the difficulty of understanding this line, it is odd to invite Apollo into a poem thus far dominated by Bacchus (who will continue to be important); Baehrens conjectures *Euhius*. Venus would also be an obvious referent (cf. e.g. Sappho 1), or perhaps Amor.

    Vos modo proposito dulces faveatis amici,
10   **neve neget quisquam me duce se comitem,**

Here we see the possibility that L. is moving from one genre to another; this poem, in addition to its symposiastic context, displays a lyric sensibility about friendship; for the elegist, friends are almost inevitably either hindrances to love (e.g. Prop. 1.1.25–6, 1.4) or rivals (e.g. Prop. 1.5). So too, travel is unimaginable when there is love (e.g. Prop. 1.6). Ov. *RA* 151 reintroduces friends and 213–48 suggests travel to the man who wants to fall out of love; Cat. 11 and Prop. 3.21 combine the two. **Modo**: L. here situates himself as *magister bibendi*, master of the revels (Greek, but well-attested in Roman culture; e.g. Hor. *Od.* 1.4.18, 2.7.25–6, Ov. *Ars* 1.581–2). On the scansion of **modo** (short), see Navarro Antolín 1996 *ad loc.*; examples at e.g. [Tib.] 3.4.64, Prop. 1.7.4, Ov. *Her.* 2.101.

    Proposito...faveatis: the phrasing occurs also at Ov. *Fas.* 1.468 (*propositoque fave*); apart from in Ov., **proposito** is not frequent in poetry, and seems to be a legal (or perhaps religious) formula; cf. Sen. *Dial.* 2.9.4, Plin. *Pan.* 95.3. **Dulces amici**: seemingly formulaic (frequent in Cic. *De Am.*, and at e.g. Cat. 30.2, Hor. *Ser.* 1.3.139–40, *Ep.* 1.7.12, Ov. *EP* 1.8.31, Pers. 5.23; *TLL* 5.1.2194.37–2195.21). L. uses the adjective persuasively, perhaps like *care* in line 5. See Pichon 1991: 85 on *amicus*, and notes *ad* 3.3.27, 3.4.42, 3.11.7, and 3.14.2 on *dulcis*.

    Me duce: personal pronoun with ablative is standard in elevated, especially epic or epic-like, contexts (e.g. V. *E.* 4.13, *A.* 10.92, Ov. *Am.* 2.12.13, *Met.* 8.208, 14.112). **Se comitem**: the military metaphor in **duce** is continued; for the construction, see e.g. Hor. *Od.* 1.35.22 *nec comitem abnegat*, Ov. *Ars* 1.127 *comitemque negabat*.

    aut siquis vini certamen mite recusat,
12   **fallat eum tecto cara puella dolo.**

L. is casual about an event that, when it might have applied to him in 3.4, caused such misery. Perhaps this loftier view emphasizes his new generic affiliation as symposiast (cf. e.g. the joking curse at the end of Hor. *Epod.* 3).

Certamen mite: not elsewhere, and deliberately paradoxical: compared to the *certamina* of love, this one is gentle. **Vini certamen** is also unattested, but note *certamine bibendi* at Plin. *NH* 36.156, and *bibendoque superavit* at Cic. *Flacc.* 92; L. means the competitive drinking games that accompany symposia. But the phrase also hints at the struggle between wine and love going on in L. himself. On **mite**, see *ad* 3.4.93, and on **recusat**, *ad* 3.4.73.

Fallat... tecto... dolo: for the phrasing, see Ter. *And.* 493 *fallere incipias dolis*, V. *A.* 1.684 *falle dolo*, Sil. 3.233–4 *docilis fallendi et nectere tectos... numquam tarda dolos* (also in prose); on *fallere* in elegy see *ad* 3.1.6, and for the quintessentially elegiac notion of *furtivus amor*, Pichon 1991: s.v. *dolor* 133, *furta* 158. For similar elegiac wording cf. e.g. Ov. *Am.* 1.2.6 *tecta... arte*, Prop. 3.23.18 *blandis... dolis*, 4.7.16 *nocturnis... dolis*, Tib. 1.9.24 *occultos... dolos* (Maltby 2009: 327).

Eum in elegy only at Prop. 2.29.8, 3.20.1, Ov. *Fas.* 4.551, 6.584, 6.755 (latter two times in same *sedes*), never in Tib. (see on *is ad* 3.4.94). **Cara puella**, the normal denotation of L's beloved N., is a detail which shows that this context is rather different from L's usual style.

> **Ille facit dites animos deus, ille ferocem**
> 14 **contudit et dominae misit in arbitrium,**

Ille: as Navarro Antolín 1996 notes *ad loc.*, repetition of pronouns is regular in hymns and prayers (and derives from Greek poetry); cf. V. *E.* 1.6–10, Tib. 1.2.17–22 with Murgatroyd 1980 *ad loc.*, Prop. 1.14.17–21 with Fedeli 1980 *ad loc.*, Ov. *Am.* 1.6.7–8 with McKeown 1989 *ad loc*. **Ille... deus**: despite the apparent specificity of this phrase, it is not at all clear to which god L. refers; it seems to be the case that Dionysus and Amor alternate, with no indication of the changes (so Tränkle 1990 and Navarro Antolín 1996). The power of wine is discussed at Hor. *Od.* 1.18.5, 3.21.14–20, Ov. *Ars* 1.237–44, and the power of love is a regular *topos* in elegy. The first **ille** seems to refer to Bacchus (the notion that love enriches the spirit is not a Roman one), but it might also be Amor. The second is similarly unclear: Bacchus is traditionally a tamer of animals, but Amor tames even the gods (and the mention of **dominae** must refer to him). This is, presumably, the point: in the very act of distinguishing between the spheres of the two gods, L. finds himself unable. Bacchus is valued by L. for his role in (diminishing) love, but wine can also enhance *amor*. The symposiastic feel of the poem as a whole is enhanced by these deictic particles ('this god'... 'this (other) god'), which could, in the context of performance, refer to statues or other representations of two gods likely to be present in some form at a drinking party.

Dites animos: unattested, and peculiar (though see a similar sentiment at Hor. *Od.* 3.21.18, *virisque et addis cornua pauperi*). The closest parallel, though not especially helpful, is probably Ov. *Ars* 1.237 *vina parant animos. Mites* appears in no manuscripts, but is favoured by some as a more elegiac notion, and as providing better contrast with **ferocem**. This reading is likely to be preferable; the whole couplet would then refer to Amor, who does 'soften' those previously unaccustomed to love.

Ferocem/contudit: it is perhaps too much to see in these lines an allusion to V. *A.* 6.853 *debellare superbos* (but note the similarities to V. *A.* 1.263–4 *populosque feroces/contundet*); cf. Prop. 1.1.10 *saevitiam…contudit* and Ov. *Ars* 1.12 *animos placida contudit arte feros* (Chiron of Achilles, but Ov. of Amor by implication). Tib. prefers *ferreus* to denote one uninterested in love (see *ad* 3.2.2), but for this sense, see Pichon 1991: 145. On *contundere*, see Pichon 1991: 112.

Dominae…in arbitrium: *arbitrium* with a genitive is mostly prosaic (e.g. Cato *Agr.* 144.1 *arbitratu domini*; note, however, Ov. *Ars* 1.504 *arbitrio dominae* and *ad imperium dominae* Tib. 2.3.79). Here again, L. suggests *servitium amoris* (see Introduction, Section I), as a punishment for misbehaviour, not as the normal state of affairs. On **dominae**, see *ad* 3.4.65 and 74.

> Armenias tigres et fulvas ille leaenas
> 16   vicit et indomitis mollia corda dedit.

Armenias tigres: also at V. *E.* 5.29, Prop. 1.9.19, Ov. *Am.* 2.14.35, *Met.* 8.121, 15.86 (both in same *sedes*), Sen. *HO* 241–2; the region had many of them (Varro *DLL* 5.100 says the word *tigris* is Armenian), and they were associated with Dionysus, at least in Latin literature (e.g. Hor. *Od.* 3.3.13–14, Ov. *Am.* 1.2.47–8, *Ars* 1.550, 559; see Bömer *ad* Ov. *Met.* 3.668 on the animals of Dionysus).

Fulvas…leaenas: also at V. *G.* 4.408; cf. the descriptor of lions at Lucr. 5.901 (*corpora fulva leonum*), V. *A.* 2.722, 4.159, 8.552–3 (*fulva leonis/pellis*), Hor. *Od.* 4.4.14 (*fulvae matris*), Germ. *Arat.* 149, Ov. *Her.* 10.85, *Met.* 1.304, 10.551, 10.698–9 (*fulvae/…iubae*), *Fas.* 2.339, Sen. *Oed.* 920 (*fulvam…iubam*), *HO* 1933 (*fulva…iuba*), Stat. *Theb.* 1.397, Sil. 2.193–4, 7.288, 16.237 (*fulva…colla*). The choice of lionesses here rather than lions is likely to be significant, in keeping with the reasons for L.'s complaint: lionesses do tend to be fiercer than lions, but L. is also suffering from what he sees as the behaviour of a woman. Lions are also associated with Dionysus, but the taming of lions is especially characteristic of Cybele (Cat. 63, V. *A.* 3.113, Ov. *Met.* 10.704, Gratt. *Cyn.* 19); see too the Punic lions tamed at [V.] *Cir.* 135 with Lyne 1978 *ad loc.*, the Numidian lions at Ov. *Ars* 2.183, and other lions subdued at Ov. *Met.* 7.373, 14.538, *Tr.* 4.6.5. Dionysus is more likely to be meant here, but there is visual evidence for Amor seated on lions (*LIMC* s.v. Eros 257–76, Eros/Amor Cupido 335). On *fulvus*, see André 1949: 132–6.

Tigres…leaenas: the two wild animals occur together at V. *E.* 5.27–9, *G.* 2.151–2, Hor. *Od.* 1.23.9–10, Ov. *Met.* 1.304–5, 15.86, Luc. 6.487, Sen. *Phaed.* 344–8, [Sen.] *Oct.* 86, Stat. *Silv.* 2.1.8, *Theb.* 6.787–8, 9.16. Both are tamed at Hor. *AP* 393 *dictus ob hoc lenire tigres rabidosque leones*, Ov. *Ars* 2.183 *obsequium*

tigresque domat Numidasque leones, *Buc. Eins.* 2.37 *mordent frena tigres, subeunt iuga saeva leones*.
    Mollia corda: the phrase in the singular is Ovidian: *Her.* 15.79, *Tr.* 4.10.65–6, 5.8.28, *EP* 1.3.32 (*TLL* 4.941.47–50); cf. Juv. 15.131 *mollissima corda... dare*.

        Haec Amor et maiora valet. Sed poscite Bacchi
18   munera: quem vestrum pocula sicca iuvant?

L. clarifies: Amor is responsible for many great things. But the ambiguity remains, as L. has throughout conflated love and wine. **Et** perhaps signifies that Amor can achieve even greater things (e.g. taming the gods). **Maiora valet**: the internal accusative is regular with the verb, but this phrase is unattested and probably colloquial, though a recognizable variant of *haec valet*. On the **Bacchi/ munera**, see *ad* 3.6.4.
    Vestrum: here a partitive genitive, 'which of you'. **Pocula sicca**: cf. Petr. 92.5 (*siccatoque avide poculo*), where the participle suggests the emptying of cups; but cf. *siccus* for sober at e.g. Hor. *Od.* 4.5.39 and *Ep.* 1.19.9. While the meaning is opposed to *madeant... pocula* at 4, the sense here is pleasingly ambiguous; L. is noting that not-drinking pleases nobody, and that, once having begun to drink, stopping pleases nobody.

        Convenit ex aequo nec torvus Liber in illis,
20   qui se quique una vina iocosa colunt.

The standard procedure for the gods is to honour (or at least, not to punish) those who honour them. Euripides' *Hippolytus* provides one of the more spectacular examples of the consequences of not showing honour to a god, but there are many others. **Convenit**: 'arrives', but perhaps also with the sense of *OLD* 4b, 'be on good terms with', reinforcing **ex aequo** (on the Ovidianness of which, see McKeown *ad* Ov. *Am.* 1.10.33); the closest parallel is at Luc. 8.232 *ex aequo me Parthus adit*.
    Torvus: more usually of animals (e.g. Prop. 2.3.6, of a boar) than of gods. But there are human and divine applications, usually of 'scary' gods (e.g. V. *A.* 7.415 of Allecto's *facies*, but note too Ov. *Am.* 3.1.12, of the brow of Tragedy, and *Ars* 2.453, of the angry eyes of the *puella*). Of gods proper, the adjective is used of Mars at e.g. Hor. *Od.* 1.28.17, Pluto at Juv. 13.50, Juno at Stat. *Silv.* 4.6.54, her gaze at Ov. *Met.* 4.464, Diana at *Met.* 6.415. L.'s portrait of Bacchus is meant to unnerve, even as it reassures with the **nec**. On **Liber**, see *ad* 3.6.1.
    Quique: emphasizes the democratic nature of the god, and the ease of worshipping him. **Una**: 'along with him'; one could pay honour to Dionysus with hymns or cult offerings, but he is very closely associated with wine. **Vina iocosa**: not elsewhere; the adjective occurs in amatory elegy at Tib. 2.1.85, Ov. *RA* 387, and note *iocoso... Lyaeo* at Hor. *Od.* 3.21.15–16 and *iocosi munera Liberi* at

4.15.26. For the poetic plural, see Navarro Antolín 1996 *ad loc.*; on *iocum*, see too *ad* 3.4.68 and 3.6.34. Luck prints Bolle's *verba*. **Colunt**: as often, of divine worship (*OLD* 6a); but also in a more prosaic sense, of paying careful attention to (*TLL* 3.1670.52–80).

> Convenit iratus nimium nimiumque severos:
> 22   qui timet irati numina magna, bibat.

With most editors, I adopt Lachmann's **convenit** for the manuscripts' hopeless *non venit*; the parallelism with the previous couplet is pointed. **Nimium nimiumque**: only elsewhere at Ov. *Her.* 1.41 and Mart. 8.3.17 *nimium nimiumque severi* (Radford 1927: 361, Maltby 2009: 325).

By contrast to his geniality with the drunk, Bacchus is angry at the austere. Presumably we are meant to think of the Catullan *senes severiores* of 5.2. **Severos** (Livineius' *severis* may be preferable; see Tränkle 1990 and Navarro Antolín 1996 *ad loc.*, who print it) does not appear elsewhere in the *CT*; its other uses in amatory elegy, especially in Ov. (e.g. *Am.* 2.1.3, 3.4.43, 3.8.31) suggest that the word has the particularly elegiac meaning of 'hostility to love'. So wine and easy love are again equated, if only implicitly—and this is itself a lyric position. Note too the similar statement at Hor. *Od.* 1.18.3 *siccis omnia nam dura deus proposuit*.

Qui timet: the problem has an easy solution: drink! Gods are regularly envisioned as angry, both in and out of elegy. And Bacchus can certainly punish; as we shall see. But L. perhaps also alludes to the fact that those who did not drink wine were often seen as suspicious, in part because of the connections between symposia, friendship, and politics. (Note too Euripides' *Hippolytus*, where the eponymous hero is doomed because he prefers not to engage in the pleasures of Aphrodite.) Cf. e.g. Cat. 27.5–6 *lymphae/vini pernicies*, and the tales of Bacchus' revenge in Ov. *Met.* 3–4.

Irati: for the substantive, see Tib. 2.1.74 with Murgatroyd 1994 and *TLL* 7.2.374.57–67. **Numina magna**: elsewhere in poetry at V. *A.* 2.623 (unfinished) and *passim*, Ov. *Am.* 2.8.18 in same *sedes* (with *per*).

> Quales his poenas qualis quantusque minetur,
> 24   Cadmeae matris praeda cruenta docet.

L. provides an example which is likely to have already occurred to the reader thinking about the savagery of Dionysus. The distich, with its repeated alliteration of q- and c-sounds, is emphatic, perhaps to mimic the god's anger. **Poenas**: elegiac punishments are not normally so serious; see Pichon 1991: 235. **Qualis** comes from the *Fragmentum Cuiacianum* (see Introduction, Section VIII); other manuscripts have *deus hic quantasque* (printed by Luck). **Quantusque** to signify the changes in Bacchus: in his anger, the jovial god has become a different entity (as occurs also in Eur. *Bacc.*). This phrase is epic rather than elegiac: V. *A.* 3.641, Ov. *Met.* 3.284; cf. VF 4.603–4.

Cadmeae matris: Agave, the mother of Pentheus, who, under Bacchus' spell, killed her son with her bare hands (being under the impression that he was a lion). The phrase occurs elsewhere at Sen. *Oed.* 436 and 1006; according to Axelson 1960a: 106 the formulation is a blending of Ov. *Fas.* 3.721 *Thebanae mala praeda matris* of Pentheus and *Fas.* 5.178 *Libycae praeda cruenta ferae* of Hyas (Lee 1958–9, following Hagen 1954, sees it as 'Silver'). Büchner 1965: 506 posits Gallus as a common source for both authors.

Praeda cruenta: Ovidian (*Fas.* 5.178, quoted above) and otherwise prosaic (Liv. 8.38.15, Plin. *Pan.* 36.1). **Docet**: see too the exemplary nature of Pentheus' story at Ov. *Met.* 4.429–30 *quidque furor valeat, Penthea caede satisque/ac super ostendit.*

>   Sed procul a nobis hic sit timor, illaque, si qua est,
> 26   quid valeat laesi sentiat ira dei.

As often, the mention of a divine act of vengeance, or of its possibility, prompts an apotropaic wishing it away, often with the quasi-formulaic *procul sit* (or *ite procul*, as at 3.4.3 and 3.6.7 and 52). L. specifies that such punishments properly fall upon those who reject Bacchus. Other poetic examples of **procul … sit** occur at e.g. Cat. 63.92, [Tib.] 3.19.7 (see *ad loc.*), Ov. *Ars* 2.107 *sit procul omne nefas*, *Fas.* 4.116 *a nobis sit furor iste procul*, Lucr. 4.255 *procul absit*, 6.767, Luc. 10.525 *procul absit*.

Si qua est: parenthetical, and meaning presumably 'if there is any [Agave] around here', but better taken as referring to any blasphemer (or indeed, to any *female* blasphemer, automatically letting L. off the hook). Indeed, there is one woman who has sinned against both L. and the gods: N. has not as yet been introduced into the dialogue, but her presence in the poem has been foreshadowed by the mention of love, and she is surely implicated by **illa**, and by L.'s immediate repentance in the lines that follow. See Courtney 1987 for an alternative suggestion (*illaque questa*), Watt 1991 for *illaque si quae est* and Navarro Antolín 1996 *ad loc.* for discussion of other emendations.

Laesi: on this verb for gods, see *ad* 3.4.16, 3.5.15, and 3.10.15. The phrase **ira dei** (and synonyms) is frequent in Ov.: *Met.* 4.8 *laesi … numinis iram*, 10.399 *ira deum*, *Tr.* 1.5.84, 1.10.42, 5.12.14, *EP* 1.4.44, 2.8.76 *ira dei* (same *sedes*), *Tr.* 3.6.23 *numinis … laesi … ira.*

>   Quid precor a, demens? Venti temeraria vota,
> 28   aeriae et nubes diripienda ferant.

L. immediately thinks better of his selfish prayer; he does not feel any ill-will towards N. (and perhaps it is safer not to have any angry gods around at all). **Quid precor**: at line-start also at Ov. *Her.* 2.103 *quid precor infelix* and VF 7.437 *quid, precor, in nostras venisti, Thessale, terras?*

A demens: also at V. E. 2. 60, [V.] Cir. 185, Prop. 2.30.1, Ov. Her. 21.72. Tr. 5.10.51, EP 4.3.29, Sen. Med. 930; cf. V. E. 2.69 *quae te dementia cepit* and *quid facio demens* at 3.19.17, and note *ad loc*. On **a** see Kershaw 1980 and 1983. **Demens**: in Tib. and Ov. Am. usually applied to the elegiac lover, but not so in Prop; see too Pichon 1991: 126. **Precor**: not elsewhere combined with **demens**.

The conjunction between **venti** and **vota** is common in the poets (who like the alliteration, here emphasized by word arrangement): e.g. Luc. 5.491, Manil. 1.77, Ov. Her. 19.95, Fas. 3.593–4, Tr. 1.2.17. And erotic poets are accustomed to their vows remaining unfulfilled: Cat. 30.10 (*ventos irrita ferre ac nebulas aerias sinis*); 64.142 *quae cuncta aerii discerpunt irrita venti*, Tib. 1.5.35–6 *quae nunc Eurusque Notusque/iactat odoratos vota per Armenios*, Ov. Am. 2.6.44 *vota…rapta Noto*). On **vota**, see *ad* 3.3.1; not otherwise with **temeraria** (on which see *ad* 3.4.7).

Aeriae…nubes: V. A. 7.704–5, Sil. 17.341; TLL 1.1063.6–15; *aerii…venti* at Cat. 64.142. Similar thoughts, with **diripienda**, at Prop. 4.7.21–2 *fallacia verba/ non audituri diripuere Noti*, Tib. 1.6.54 *ut hic ventis diripiturque cinis*, Stat. Theb. 5.366–7 *obnixi lacerant cava nubile venti/diripiuntque fretum*.

> Quamvis nulla mei superest tibi cura, Neaera,
> 30   sis felix, et sint candida fata tua.

The obscurity of the previous lines resolves: N. has been the unspoken *illa*, the cause of L.'s hearty encouragement to drink. Perhaps this is not a surprise: the indefinite future now seems negative to L., although he had given hints as early as the opening lines of the first poem of this cycle; cf. too 3.1.19–20.

Quamvis with the indicative shows L.'s belief in his own statement; the syntax is rare in prose but frequent in poetry (e.g. Cat. 12.5). **Cura, Neaera**: for the beloved as **cura**, see V. E. 10.22 (plausibly dated to Gallus; see Ross 1975: 68–9), and above *ad* 3.1.19. Navarro Antolín 1996 *ad loc*. suspects that L. did not understand the allusion because there is no apposition here, but Parca 1986: 468 thinks he did. **Superest…cura**: Stat. Ach. 1.218 *altera consilio superest tristemque fatigat cura deam*, VF 5.52 *si tenui superant in imagine curae*.

Felix: see *ad* 3.3.26, 3.4.40 and 80, 3.5.31, 3.6.43, 3.8.13, 3.10.25; for **sis felix**, cf. Cat. 68.155 *sitis felices*, Hor. Od. 3.27.13 *sis licet felix*, Prop. 1.13.35 *sit felix*. The phrase is a correction of *illa…sentiat* of lines 25–6.

Candida fata: elsewhere at Ov. Tr. 3.4.34 *dignus es et fato candidiore frui*; cf. Tr. 5.7.4 *candida fortunae pars*, EP 2.4.30 *non ita pars fati candida nulla mei est*. On **candida**, cf. 3.4.34 and *ad* 3.3.25 *niveam lucem*. L. may refer to a wedding in N.'s future (see *ad* 3.4.31).

> At nos securae reddamus tempora mensae:
> 32   venit post multos una serena dies.

At, as often, is resumptive, denoting a change in topic: L. returns, mentally, to the party. **Reddamus tempora**: one regularly gives time (*tempus dare*: Plaut.

Bacch. 676, Ter. *And.* 556; Ov. *Met.* 7.662–3 *lucis pars ultima mensae/est data*); the noun occurs less frequently with compounds such as *reddere*. **Securae… mensae**: *mensae* are not elsewhere **securae**; the collocation involves a synecdoche in which *mensa* stands for the symposium as a whole. L. may also use the word proleptically: 'Let us pay attention to the pleasures of the table, which will, I hope, make *me* carefree'. For the adjective, see *ad* 3.3.32, 3.4.54, and 3.16.1.

L. invokes the proverbial calm after the storm (Otto 1890: 113, Theocr. 4.41–1); cf. Ov. *Tr.* 2.142 *candidus…dies*, Sen. *Ep.* 107.8. As it stands, line 32 must assume some adjective meaning the opposite of **serena**; otherwise, L. is saying that there have been many nice days in a row (*multus* cannot really mean 'many *other* kinds'). So too, many object to the feminine gender (*dies* elsewhere is masculine in the plural); **multos** is an emendation for the manuscripts' *multas*, but still not fully satisfying (Tränkle 1990 prints the feminine). Housman 1890: 19 conjectured *pluvias*, which gives the required meaning, and Luck prints Santenis' *nimbos*.

> **Ei mihi, difficile est imitari gaudia falsa,**
> 34   **difficile est tristi fingere mente iocum,**

Another abrupt, 'Tibullan' change of mood: the tables are not carefree after all, and L. remains troubled. **Ei mihi**: regularly in poetry (e.g. Prop. five times, Tib. twice, Ov. forty-six times); see McKeown *ad* Ov. *Am.* 1.6.52 for its tone.

Difficile est is a standard beginning for a catalogue (here very abbreviated); cf. V. *G.* 2.257, Hor. *AP* 128, Manil. 3.548, and especially Ov. *Met.* 2.447 *quam difficile est crimen non prodere vultu*! On amatory difficulties, see Pichon 1991: 130, and for **difficile est** introducing the problems of moving beyond love, Cat. 76.13–14.

Imitari is a regular verb for the dissimulation of feelings (*OLD* 3 a and b), but not often in elegy (a different meaning at 3.3.15). See McKeown *ad* Ov. *Am.* 2.4.15; the closest analogue to this passage occurs at Ov. *RA* 497 (*positosque imitare furores*) and cf. Tac. *Ann.* 1.24, *maestitiam imitarentur*, for feigning an expression, Sen. *Oed.* 419, *creveras falsos imitatus artus*, for a broader dissimulation. We are probably to understand a metapoetic nuance, with L. drawing attention to the sophistication of mimicry: while difficult to pretend not to be sad when you are, it is even more difficult to feign drunkenness and sadness when you are neither.

Gaudia: although a regular elegiac word for sex, it has a different meaning here (3.9.18, 3.13.5); see *ad* 3.3.7 for other meanings. For **gaudia falsa**, see Plaut. *Poen.* 1258, Ter. *And.* 180, *Hec.* 842, V. *A.* 6.513–14, Prop. 1.8.29, Ov. *Her.* 13.108, and on the metre, Holmes 1995. **Tristi…mente**: elsewhere at Ov. *Her.* 12.148; for the adjective see *ad* 3.3.35, 3.4.42, 3.6.38, 3.10.7, 3.10.22, 3.14.2, 3.15.1, 3.17.3.

Fingere iocum is apparently parallel to our 'make a joke'. But the verb is especially apt, as L. is feigning his feelings as well (and L.-the-poet presents us with false persona of L.-the-drinker). **Iocum** too is a word appropriate to the bedroom (e.g. Cat. 8.6, Ov. *Her.* 15.48).

>   nec bene mendaci risus componitur ore,
> 36 nec bene sollicitis ebria verba sonant.

Nec bene is presumably used to avoid the repetition of *difficile est* and infinitive. **Mendaci...ore**: elsewhere at Ov. *Am.* 3.3.44 and *Met.* 9.322 (the latter in same *sedes*); *TLL* 8.703.34–42.

The metaphor implied by **risus componitur** is an interesting one—the laugh (or smile; *surrisus* does not exist in classical Latin) is constructed or arranged on a face, which is then deceitful because of the intrusion of external matter. See further on **componitur**—a key word for this corpus—*ad* 3.2.26, 3.8.8, 3.12.9, 3.13.9, and on **risus**, Pichon 1991: 253.

L. undermines his earlier claim by suggesting that drunkenness is for those already without cares (rather than helping to dispel them), and inappropriate for **sollicitis** (we might call this a 'religious' way of looking at things, insofar as L. suggests that one needs to have the proper mindset to worship the god). Perhaps L.'s excessive drinking has made him maudlin (note Navarro Antolín 1996 *ad loc.* on the repetitiveness of language as showing drunkenness). **Ebria verba**: cf. Ov. *Fas.* 6.408, same *sedes*; *TLL* 5.2.14.51–60; Pichon 1991: 136 *ebrius*.

>   Quid queror infelix? Turpes discedite curae:
> 38 odit Lenaeus tristia verba pater.

This couplet helps to clarify the previous one; L. is trying to pull himself together, but his *secura mensa* turns out to be no such thing. **Queror** is an elegiac keyword; the etymology of *elegia* is often invoked to help explain why (see Introduction, Section I). See especially the recurrence of the noun *querella* as a leitmotif in Cat. 64 (130, 195, and 223) and throughout the elegists. In his last elegiac poem, L. asks why he is writing elegy: if there is no amatory suffering, there is no elegy.

Infelix: this *sedes* favoured by Ov. (e.g. *Am.* 3.2.71 *quid facis, infelix*, *Her.* 2.103 *quid precor infelix*, 11.51 *quid faciam infelix*, 14.93 *quid furis, infelix*), and the word is often in the vocative in elegy. The word also has pre-elegiac associations, most notably Calvus fr. 9 Courtney, *a virgo infelix* (picked up at V. *E.* 6.47 of Pasiphae, which might be its first significant amatory usage), and becomes the *mot juste* for Dido.

Turpes...curae: not elsewhere joined; L.'s love-woes are not shameful in themselves, but inappropriate to the celebratory context of the symposium. On **turpes**, see *ad* 3.4.15. **Discedite** in this sense at Hor. *Serm.* 1.1.18, Ov. *Met.* 10.336; *TLL* 5.1.1283.78–1284.10.

Odit: Bacchus hates (= shuns) sad words because they are not sufficiently festive at a symposium; elegy is not a Bacchic genre. We are probably meant to think of Cat. 85 (*odi et amo*), particularly given the occurrence of *amat* at line 57.

Lenaeus is another cult-name for Bacchus, as at V. *G.* 2.529, 3.510, *A.* 4.207, Hor. *Od.* 3.25.19, Ov. *Met.* 4.14 with Bömer 1976 *ad loc.*, *Ib.* 329, Stat. *Silv.* 4.6.80. From the Greek Λήναιος, the name of an Attic month and festival, which included comic performances, and deriving ultimately from λήνος, a tub or wine-vat (Maltby 1991: 333). This epithet refers us directly back to the god's most salient attribute. **Lenaeus pater**: also at V. *G.* 2.4 and 7, Ov. *Met.* 11.132, Colum. *DRR* 10.430; for Bacchus as **pater**, see *TLL* 10.1.685.68–686.6 (first for us at Enn. *Ath.* 120).

Tristia: again, an elegiac keyword, even before Ov.'s *Tristia* (note e.g. Cat. 65.24, 66.30, 68.56). We usually render with 'sad', but the word can also mean harsh, etc. **Tristia verba**: also at Hor. *AP* 105, Ov. *Tr.* 1.3.80, 2.133. L. may here signal a move away from elegy, the metre of *tristitia* par excellence. But L. may also be mistaken about the preferences of his chosen saviour, since Ariadne's **tristia verba** are what first drew Bacchus' attention to her. The sentiment is peculiar in the context, as it hints at an Ariadne punished by Bacchus, rather than saved by him (see Maleuvre 2001: 185–6 and immediately below).

> Cnosia, Theseae quondam periuria linguae
> 40 flevisti ignoto sola relicta mari:

The connection between this couplet and the previous is not clear; presumably the reader is meant to be reminded of the relationship between Ariadne and Bacchus, and so, perhaps, to see future happiness in store for L. as well. The obvious poetic referent is Ariadne's lament in Cat. 64, and in fact, L. will go on to 'cite' it in a way unparalleled in extant elegy. L.'s apostrophe strikes many as inept, given that Theseus abandoned Ariadne, not the other way around. Two factors help to explain L.'s mention of her here: the first is that he continues, and makes more explicit, the regular Catullan practice whereby the poet feminizes himself vis-à-vis his 'active' and so masculinized lover; L. is counting on Bacchus to rescue him from his plight, to save him from abandonment as he did Ariadne. This enables L. to envision a brighter future for himself (as Ariadne) and punishment for N. (as Theseus). The other is that there are several variants on the Catullan story: one in which Ariadne has abandoned the god for Theseus (Hom. *Od.* 11.321; see Webster 1966 for discussion), and another in which he betrays her (Ov. *Fas.* 3.465–516). L. may thus suggest the elegiac nature even of Bacchus' relationship. (Prop. 3.17 also mentions the story, leaving unclear which variant he intends.)

Cnosia: Ariadne and Theseus feature regularly in elegy, often with apostrophe, under the influence of Cat. 64 (see e.g. Prop. 1.3.1–2); the topic seems also to have been popular in wall-painting. See too Prop. 1.15.9–22 (no direct address), Ov. *Ars* 3.35–6 *quantum in te, Theseu, volucres Ariadna marinas/pavit, in ignoto sola relicta loco* (where Lee 1958–9: 18 sees Lygdamean copying). **Cnosia**: 'Cretan girl' (from Cnossos), a regular way of referring to Ariadne (Ov. *Her.* 15.25, *Ars* 1.556, 3.158, Manil. 1.323, 5.263a, Sen. *HF* 18, Stat. *Silv.* 1.2.133, 5.1.232, *Theb.* 12.676). For confusion between *Cn* and *Gn*, see Housman 1928 (his arguments not accepted by all).

Theseae: *Thesea* in the same *sedes* at Prop. 1.3.1, so this line incorporates an allusion to the passage (immediately overshadowed by the citation in the next line, but still important).

Quondam might, in the Contean manner, indicate allusion (Conte 1986: 57–69): once, i.e. in Cat. 64.

Periuria is bound to remind the reader of Cat. 64 (135, 148 in same *sedes*, 346), although the word becomes common in elegy (e.g. Tib. 1.3.51, 1.4.21, 1.9.3, and below, 3.6.49) and epic, usually in this *sedes*. The treachery of Theseus is legendary (Otto 1890: 347: Ov. *Am.* 1.7.15 *talis periuri promissaque velaque Thesei*, *Her.* 4.59 *perfidus Aegides*, 10.75–6 *Vivimus, et non sum, Theseu, tua—si modo vivit/ femina periuri fraude sepulta viri*, *Ars* 3.457 *Parcite, Cecropides, iuranti credere Theseo*, *Fas.* 3.461 *periuro... coniuge*, 3.473 *periure et perfide Theseu*, Stat. *Silv.* 3.3.179–80). Note his also-proverbial faithfulness to Perithoos. **Periuria linguae**: see Ov. *Her.* 7.67 and *Met.* 14.99 (same *sedes*); Pichon 1991: 231.

Flevisti: frequent action of an abandoned lover, e.g. Ov. *Am.* 1.7.16 and *Her.* 10.43 (both of Ariadne); Calypso weeps over the lost Odysseus with the same verb at Prop. 1.15.10. For the verb as transitive, see *TLL* 6.1.901.18–61.

Ignoto... mari: the island of Naxos, where Theseus and Ariadne had only recently landed, was (like Crete) in the Aegean, but in a part unfamiliar to her. There may also be a hidden pun in that the phrase looks like *ignoto marito*, a standard elegiac situation, or perhaps she is weeping to/for Bacchus, as yet unknown to her ('to an unknown man'; **mari** as dative of *mas*). We might also want to link **ignoto** to *quondam* in the previous line: once this had been an untold story; now it is all too familiar (and also personally felt by L.).

Relicta is another frequent descriptor of Ariadne, the ur-heroine of abandonment since Cat. 64 (see e.g. Cat. 64.180, 200, 299, Ov. *Her.* 2.76, 10.80, 10.129, *Ars* 3.36, 3.158). For the participle applied to other elegiac heroines, see Prop. 1.6.8, 2.24.46, Ov. *Am.* 2.18.22, *Her.* 1.8, 3.66, 5.29, 7.84, *Ars* 3.460, *RA* 583, 785, *Met.* 8.108, 11.423, usually in this *sedes*.

> sic cecinit pro te doctus, Minoi, Catullus
> 42   ingrati referens impia facta viri.

What might have seemed like an allusive game (however obvious) is here ended, as L. cites his source. It is not common for the elegists to cite poetic predecessors in quite this way; usually when they do, it is as part of a list of (general) important influences. Ov. does so most frequently, normally in a catalogue and normally for a specific purpose, such as locating himself in a genealogy (see Introduction, Section I).

Sic refers back to 39–40, but perhaps also has a wider application: 'Catullus also sang, just like I am doing here'. **Cecinit**: one of the regular verbs for the recitation or composition of poetry (often epic).

Pro te: like most elegists, L. takes the side of Ariadne, praising Cat. for publicizing Theseus' dirty deeds (see Parca 1986: 468 for the suggestion that it means 'speaking in your name'). Here again, we note L.'s implicit feminization, and perhaps identification with Ariadne (note the apostrophe, and see *ad* 3.6.39–40): having been abandoned, he also hopes for rescue from Bacchus (in liquid, if not divine form).

Doctus: a regular descriptor of poets (e.g. Hor. *Od.* 1.1.29, Tib. 1.4.61 with Murgatroyd 1980 *ad loc.*; *TLL* 5.1.1758.17–45), and *puellae* (or Muses; see *ad* 3.4.45 and 3.12.2), and of **Catullus** at Ov. *Am.* 3.9.62 (*docte Catulle*) and Mart. 7.99.7, 8.73.8, 14.100.1, 14.152.1. At first, this looks like a clumsy gesture (rather than alluding, L. points his reader to the source). But it may be more: by naming Cat., and only Cat., L. suggests that he is post-Catullan (rather than post-Ovidian, post-Tibullan, etc.). This might be the mark of a later author trying to insert himself into a tradition, or might suggest that L. is genuinely writing in the same period as Tib. and Ov. (Ov. also tends not to name contemporaries.) Horace seems to play on the phrase (of an unknown bore): *simius iste/nil praeter Calvum et doctus cantare Catullum*, *Ser.* 1.10.18–19. Or perhaps both allude to a lost source. See further, Introduction, Section V, on the dating of this cycle.

Minoi: relatively rare of Ariadne: Cat. 64.60, Prop. 2.14.7, 2.24.43, Ov. *Her.* 16.349, 17.193, *Ars* 1.509, *Met.* 8.174, VF 7.279. L. offers a taste of his *doctrina* (a rare form, and a Greek one), in homage to Cat.

Ingrati: a Catullan adjective (64.103, 68.142, 73.3, 76.6 and 9, and thereafter common in the elegists); Pichon 1991: 169–70. **Ingrati…viri**: of Theseus at Ov. *Fas.* 3.462; also at Prop. 1.6.10, Ov. *Her.* 12.124, *Fas.* 1.622. **Referens**: standard to describe what is told in poetry (*OLD* 18), and perhaps evoking Ariadne's repetitive laments (Conte 1986: 57–69).

Impia facta: Catullan, also at Lucr. 1.83, V. A. 4.596, Ov. *Her.* 10.99–100, *Fas.* 2.38; not simply e.g. *mala*, because Ariadne had saved his life, so deserved better treatment. The adjective is common in L. (see *ad* 3.4.16, 3.4.59, 3.4.96, and 3.5.14).

> Vos ego nunc moneo: felix, quicumque dolore
> 44   alterius disces posse cavere tuo.

Elegy has a long didactic tradition; see Introduction, Section I. The phrasing is proverbial; it is indeed a good idea to learn from the mistakes of others (cf. e.g.

Ov. *Ars* 3.455 *discite ab alterius vestras timuisse querellis*), but L. does not specify whether he means for his audience to learn from Ariadne's mistakes, or his own (perhaps, indeed, he continues to conflate them, suggesting that there is a single lesson to be learned). L.'s words are amusing, as he seems to fail to learn from his own *exempla*, precisely as he urges others to do so.

Nunc: resumptive; L. returns to his present companions. There may also be a play with *quondam* (39) and *cecinit* (41): L. distils the advice of previous poets, updating it for a new generation. **Moneo**: a didactic verb, appearing in the first person in the context of advice about love at Tib. 1.8.69, 2.4.51, Prop. 1.1.35–6 (*hoc, moneo, vitate malum: sua quemque moretur/cura*), an especially important parallel, 1.20.1 (plural), Ov. *Ars* 1.387 and 1.459. **Felix**: cf. *ad* 3.6.37 *infelix*. The adjective regularly introduces a general statement, as here with *quicumque*; direct reference to V. *G.* 2.490 may be intended (*felix qui potuit rerum cognoscere causas*) with the windowpane reference to Lucr.; if so, drunk-L. shows his poor assimilation of didactic poetry.

Dolore: used for both physical and mental pain; in the elegists, it is not always clear which, since it describes lovesickness; see *ad* 3.2.3, 6, 13, and 29, 3.6.3, 3.16.5, and 3.20.3. It occurs frequently in Ov., usually in this *sedes*. **Disces**: presumably, from L.'s poetry. L. may intend to draw a contrast between *doctus Catullus* (whose most learned poem provides L.'s source-text) and himself: Cat. had only written about suffering, while L. has lived it. (This is, of course, to miss Cat.'s own point, taking overly seriously the contrast between 'Alexandrian' and 'personal' poems in the corpus.)

Cavere: the manuscripts transmit *carere*; the *Fragmentum Cuiacianum* (see Introduction, Section VIII) had *cavere tuos*; see Navarro Antolín 1996 *ad loc.* for further discussion: 'whoever you are who will be able to learn from the pain of another to avoid your own (pain)'.

>   Nec vos aut capiant pendentia bracchia collo
> 46   aut fallat blanda sordida lingua fide.

The poet shifts abruptly to a favourite theme, the perfidy of women. After displaying sympathy for Ariadne, L. has now returned to the contemplation of his own situation: women are as deceitful as men are.

Capiant...fallat: negative jussive subjunctives: 'don't let...'. **Capiant** (see *ad* 3.1.7), **fallat** (see *ad* 3.1.6, 3.4.7, 3.4.49, 3.4.56, 3.4.62, 3.6.12, 3.6.47, 3.6.51, and 3.12.12), and **blanda** (see *ad* 3.3.2 and 3.4.75) are all elegiac keywords. **Blanda...fide**: *prece* is often confused with *fide* in manuscripts; here A and the majority of others have *fide*. See *ad* 3.4.64, and Navarro Antolín 1996 *ad loc.* The word need only mean 'protestations of faithfulness', not actual trustworthiness.

Pendentia bracchia belong in an elegiac situation (though the precise phrase is found only at Ov. *Tr.* 3.5.15 *bracchia...pendentia collo*), but it is not clear how they relate to L.'s own circumstances: N.'s crime seems to be neglect, not deception (see 3.4.64 *tende bracchia* for the envisioned scenario). **Bracchia collo** in this *sedes* is Ovidian: *Her.* 16.167, *Met.* 1.762, 3.389, 9.459, 9.605; see too *Met.* 3.428–9 *captantia collum/bracchia*; for similar phrases, Prop. 3.12.22 with Fedeli 1985 *ad loc.*, Ov. *Her.* 2.93, *Met.* 6.479, 11.386, *Fas.* 2.760, and Pichon 1991: 105 s.v. *collum*.

Sordida lingua has manuscript authority but is not attested elsewhere (and so there are a number of conjectures for the adjective, e.g. Bergk *perfida*, Heinsius *subdola*, the latter being preferred by Luck and Tränkle 1990; see Tränkle 1990 *ad loc.*). The meaning comes closest to *OLD* 7; see Ov. *Am.* 1.10.48 with McKeown 1989 *ad loc.*

    Etsi perque suos fallax iuravit ocellos
48   Iunonemque suam perque suam Venerem,

Here again L. seems to miss the point, or perhaps to undermine it: Ariadne had declaimed against the untrustworthiness of men; L. appropriates her (feminine) voice to say the same about women; the gender reversal is typically Catullan.

Etsi 'even if' (see Axelson 1945: 88 and 123); at line-start in Ov. *Am.* 3.14.50, *Ars* 3.753, *Met.* 2.322, 3.238; only here in the *CT* and twice in Prop.

Fallax iuravit: the swearing of false oaths is connected in elegy to Theseus (Ov. *Ars* 3.456–8, *Fas.* 3.487). **Ocellos**: one often swears by one's own eyes; cf. e.g. Ov. *Am.* 2.16.42–6, 3.3.9–14, Tib. 3.11.8, and Prop. 1.15.33 with Fedeli 1980 *ad loc.*; the long Latin tradition seems to begin at Plaut. *Men.* 1060. The diminutive (here **ocellos**) is relatively rare in elegy (cf. *libellum* at 3.1.9 and 17) and may be a pointed echo of Prop. 1.1.1.

Iunonem…suam…suam Venerem: Juno, as the female equivalent of a man's Genius (see *ad* 3.11.8), mentioned also at Petr. 25.4, Sen. *Ep.* 110.1, Plin. *NH* 2.16, Juv. 2.98, in inscriptions, and perhaps alluded to at Plaut. *Cas.* 408; see too *ad* 3.12.1 and 3.19.15, and *RE* 10.1.1115.11–42. See Dumézil 1966: 292–3 for discussion of the possibility of an individual Juno for women existing much earlier than the Augustan age, and Nitzsche 1975: 9 for its connections to fertility and childbearing. Swearing by one's 'Venus' is unattested, although the use of the goddess's name metonymically is regular (Pichon 1991: 289–90); cf. Ov. *Her.* 2.39–41 for both goddesses in an oath. **Suam** may stack the cards in the *puella*'s favour (*OLD* 13c) or simply acknowledge that she is naturally associated with love (*OLD* 11).

    nulla fides inerit: periuria ridet amantum
50   Iuppiter et ventos inrita ferre iubet.

The faithlessness of lovers' oaths (Skiadas 1975, with precedents in Greek and Latin) and the corruption of Jupiter himself (see immediately below) are frequent topics of love poetry, and these lines are accordingly very allusive (the two tropes implicitly combined at Cat. 70). **Nulla fides**: at Cat. 87.3 and Ov. *Ars* 3.377 in a similar context; Hor. *Ep.* 1.17.57 and Manil. 4.577 (with **inerit**, same *sedes*) provide the closest parallels. **Fides** might refer to the (lack of) divine reinforcement of the oath, or—since the word refers both to trustworthiness and an oath—might simply be a tautology (i.e. she will swear, but you won't believe her). Either way, the phrase comments on the inherent disequilibrium of the elegiac situation.

The repetition of **periuria** here is puzzling, as earlier L.'s sympathy had been wholly with Ariadne; here, he almost blames the naive victim of lover's lies. But she did not know any better; we, on the other hand, have examples (like Ariadne herself) to warn us. **Periuria ridet amantum**: also at Ov. *Ars* 1.633, in the same *sedes* (also Jupiter). But note the ominous tone of Prop. 2.16.47–8: *non semper pladicus periuros ridet amantes/Iuppiter*. **Periuria...inrita** are carried off by the winds also at Tib. 1.4.21–2 (*venti*) and Ov. *Ars* 1.633–4 (*Aeolios...notos*); Lee sees Lygdamean imitation of the latter (1958–9: 18–19).

Ridet.../Iuppiter: a poetic commonplace; sometimes it is Jupiter himself (Tib. 1.4.21–6 (where he is surprisingly joined by Diana and Minerva), Ov. *Ars* 1.631–4, and a rare intervention at Prop. 2.16.47–56), sometimes Venus (Ov. *Am.* 1.8.85–6), sometimes an unspecified group of gods (Tib. 1.9.1–6, Ov. *Am.* 3.3.11) who permit the lover to swear falsely without punishment (for the Greek tradition, see e.g. Pl. *Phlb.* 65c, *AP* 5.6.3–4). Jupiter probably stands by metonymy for the divine order as a whole (given that these oaths are sworn by Juno and Venus), but he is also an especially likely supporter of infidelity. Note too the Catullan precedent of Jupiter's intrusion as a force acting against poet/lovers (70 and 72).

   Ergo quid totiens fallacis verba puellae
52   conqueror? Ite a me, seria verba, precor.

L. attempts to face reality—even the gods are against him—and to return to a festive spirit. **Quid...conqueror**: L. complains because he is an elegiac poet, because the situation of elegy is one of complaint; see *ad* 3.6.37 on *queror*, and Introduction, Section I. The compounded form appears elsewhere in elegy at Tib. 1.10.54; there it is a woman who laments the violence of love; cf. Cat. 64.164 (Ariadne's lament), Ov. *Ars* 1.739 (in love right and wrong are confounded), *Met.* 9.147 (Deianeira's lament). **Totiens**: the repetitive nature of elegy is obvious (Introduction, Section I), and often acknowledged by the elegists themselves (e.g. Prop. 2.1.1); see Heyworth 2013, with discussion of the elegiac vocabulary of repetition, and Conte 1986.

The **fallacis...puellae** is a regular feature of the genre; without her and the related *dura puella* (or strict guardianship) it could not exist. She is only so named, however, at Tib. 1.6.15 and above, line 12. See too *ad* 3.4.7 and 49 and

3.6.47. Navarro Antolín 1996 prints his conjecture *iura* for **verba**, finding the repetition otiose (and suggests a copyist's error).

Ite...precor: on the surface, L. is simply attempting to change the subject away from his unhappy love affair (see discussion of *procul* at Tränkle 1990 *ad loc.*, printed by Luck and Navarro Antolín 1996). But—in keeping with the symposiastic theme of this poem—**seria verba** are both 'words of business' (*OLD* 1) and 'sober words' (*OLD* 2); Hor. *AP* 106 finds them characteristic of *severi*; the conjunction is found nowhere else in poetry, but at Hor. *Ser.* 2.2.125 *contractae seria frontis* are smoothed out by wine, and at Ov. *Fas.* 5.341 *nulla coronata peraguntur seria fronte*. **Seria** are, presumably, also words that could be taken seriously, including the oaths of a *puella* which, as we saw above with *fides*, might be genuinely intended even if they are not taken to be so.

  Quam vellem tecum longas requiescere noctes
54 et tecum longos pervigilare dies,

Quam vellem is a subjunctive of exclamation, similar to our 'how I wish!' (and with a similar estimation of its implausibility); L. hereby returns again to his fantasy world, and, perhaps, to *seria verba*. Repetition of **tecum** is emphatic; cf. e.g. Prop. 2.21.19 *nos...nos...tecum*, Tib. 1.1.57–60 *tecum...te...te*, Ov. *Am.* 3.2.3 *tecum...tecum*. For a similar sentiment see Ov. *Am.* 1.3.17–18 *tecum, quos dederint annos mihi fila sororum,/vivere contingat teque dolente mori*, where life and death take the place of night and day.

Longas noctes: the phrase is Propertian (1.12.13, 2.15.24; cf. 1.3.37 *longa...tempora noctis*) and Ovidian (*Am.* 2.19.22, *Her.* 16.317, 17.181; cf. *Am.* 1.2.3 *noctem quam longa*); it may be Catullan in origin (*nox est perpetua una dormienda*, 5.6; *noctibus in longis avidum saturasset amorem*, 68.83), but also occurs at Lucr. 5.699, Hor. *Od.* 1.25.7 (where it is likely to be playing with the elegiac feel of the passage), 4.9.27, and often in later poets. **Longos dies**: not ordinarily conceived of as erotic, which makes the Propertian point that the relationship is a serious one: cf. Ov. *EP* 2.4.25–6 *longa dies citius brumali sidere, noxque/tardior hiberna solstitialis erit*. For an elegiac day and night together, see Prop. 3.10, and for night-time events occurring in the day, Ov. *Am.* 1.5.

Requiescere: often in the elegists, sometimes in an amatory context, and usually in this *sedes*: e.g. Prop. 1.8.33, 2.17.15, but also of lying awake alone, e.g. Cat. 68.5, Prop. 1.16.15; see Pichon 1991 s.v. *quiescere*. This occurrence may well allude to V. *E.* 1.79, *requiescere noctem*, an offer of hospitality.

Pervigilare: only here in the *CT* (uncompounded form at 1.2.78 and 3.12.11). Again, the word can signify in elegy both staying awake for sex (Cat. 88.2) and staying awake from amatory torment (Cat. 68.8, Prop. 1.16.40, Ov. *Am.* 1.9.7). It is perhaps odd to **pervigilare dies**; presumably L. means something along the lines of Cat. 32 and Ov. *Am.* 1.5 (neither of which use the verb); on *vigilare*, see Pichon 1991: 294.

perfida nec merito nobis inimica merenti,
56   perfida, sed, quamvis perfida, cara tamen!

The couplet may be corrupt (Postgate prints with *cruces*). Among its difficulties are the move from plural **nobis** to singular **merenti**, and (less dire) the repetitiveness of **merito...merenti**. But the wordplay in the pentameter, if correct, is nice (and often pointed out by commentators as one of L.'s few really good lines). See Navarro Antolín 1996 for discussion of possibilities, the best of which is *nec amica* for **inimica** (which he prints, along with Luck); repetitiveness is clearly important to this part of the poem. This angry tone is often found in the elegists before and during a break-up (which is, of course, rarely definitive).

   Perfida: see *ad* 3.6.39 (*periura*); Pichon 1991: 231. **Nec merito**: what precisely the elegiac lover does deserve is up for grabs; Prop. 1.9.7, 1.17.1 claim that he suffers appropriately, 2.29.13 that he does not deserve the girl; cf. Tib. 1.6.82 (the *puella* deservedly punished) and the application of the adjective to N. at 3.1.21; note too *immeritus* at 3.4.14 and 3.5.6.

   Inimica: rarely of the *puella* (Prop. 2.9.44); it is usually displaced onto other objects or people (e.g. Prop. 1.8.12, 1.11.29, 2.6.38, 2.13.16); see Pichon 1991: 160, and Introduction, Section I, on the necessary antagonism between the elegiac couple. **Cara** is one of L.'s standard descriptors for N.; cf. 3.1.6 (also with **tamen**), 3.1.25, 3.2.1 (twice), 3.2.13, 3.3.32, 3.4.51, 3.6.5, 3.6.12 (also of others, 3.8.15, 3.12.19). Note too the way this couplet provides an implicit (negative) answer to the question posed at the end of 3.1 (Büchner 1965: 67); see Wills 1996: 69–71 for corrective repetition (here over a significantly longer stretch of text).

Naida Bacchus amat: cessas, o lente minister?
58   Temperet annosum Marcia lympha merum.

L. returns to gaiety, reassuring himself that he is no longer upset. **Naida**: L. refers to the regular Greco-Roman practice of mixing water (here personified as water-nymphs; more usually in Latin poetry *nymphae*, as at [V.] *Dir.* 67, Prop. 3.16.4 with Fedeli 1985 *ad loc.*, Mart. 6.43.2 and 6.47.1) with wine (= Bacchus); see e.g. *AP* 9.258, 9.331, and 11.49.3 for the conceit; in 9.331 the baby god is first saved from the thunderbolt that destroys his mother and then washed in river-water. But, given that the god has featured earlier in the poem, and his bride Ariadne has also been mentioned, and given that naiads are often members of the Dionysiac retinue (Pratin. 708.4, Hor. *Od.* 3.25.14), and suffer the sexual attentions of satyrs, the phrase is striking (all the more so because the conceit, and vocabulary, are unelegiac). Navarro Antolín 1996 suggests *ad loc.* that the addition of water means that L. wishes to turn away from Bacchus (and so towards Amor), but the poet may also hint at an attempt to abandon the elegiac world—and indeed, the remainder of the poem posits him as a lyric poet in the mould of Horace and the Greeks, enjoying a series of love affairs but taking none seriously. On the Callimachean preference for water-drinking poets (and their subject matter) over those who drink wine, and its echoes in Latin poetry, see Heyworth 1994: 63–7, with citations and bibliography; Knox 1985 dates the *topos* later.

Bacchus amat: the phrase usually refers to the personified god, who loves Ariadne (Ov. *Her.* 15.25) and garlands of flowers (Ov. *Fas.* 5.345), but also to grapes/wine, as at V. *G.* 2.113 (*Bacchus amat colles*) and Mart. 4.82.6 (*sua cum medius proelia Bacchus amat*). For **amat** of things, see *TLL* 1.1955.58–1956.19 and *OLD* 11, and for a different personification, Ov. *RA* 143 *Venus otia amat*.

Cessas suits a sympotic setting, as at Mart. 9.93.1 *addere quid cessas, puer, immortale Falernum?* The verb may also be a comment on the poem's length, or the poet's failure to move on (see too *iam dudum*, line 63). **Lente**: an elegiac word; see *ad* 3.5.30 and 3.17.6, but also a pastoral one (e.g. V. *E.* 1.5). Here, of course, the word is simply literal (contrast Hor. *Od.* 2.11.18 *ocius*), but this perhaps emphasizes L.'s new poetics (see *piger* in the same context at Mart. 11.36.5). **Minister**: often used of wine-pourers (e.g. Cat. 27.1, Mart. 1.11.3, 10.98.1, 11.11.3); the direct address to a slave is perhaps best known in Latin poetry from Hor. *Od.* 1.38 (see too Abel 1930: 94).

Marcia lympha: the Marcian aqueduct, built 144–40 BCE by Q. Marcius Rex, originated in the Paelignian mountains to the east of Rome, and was restored several times. The aqueduct served NW Rome (Plin. *NH* 36.121). It was considered the purest (and coldest) water available at Rome (Plin. *NH* 31.41); see further Ashby 1973: 88–158, Evans 1994: 83–93, de Kleijn 2001: 14–18, with ancient sources. It is mentioned by poets more frequently than any other source of water (e.g. Prop. 3.2.14, 3.22.24, Mart. 9.18.6, Stat. *Silv.* 1.3.65, 1.5.26–7), though this phrase occurs only here. It is (barely) possible that the reference is meant as homage of some kind to Messalla, who was made *curator aquarum* in 11 BCE (Front. *Aq.* 99), and so may perhaps have repaired it.

Temperet is not the regular word for mixing wine, in or out of elegy (but see *OLD* 6); its use here may suggest a metapoetic nuance, whereby L. seeks to combine (Callimachean) fonts of inspiration with (Horatian) symposiastic lyric. **Annosum**: i.e. aged, so of high quality. The word appears elsewhere in the *CT* only at 3.2.19 (also of wine; see *ad loc.* for other elegiac uses), so we might conclude that it is a favourite word of L.

    Non ego, si fugit nostrae convivia mensae
60   ignotum cupiens vana puella torum,

What L. will not do is postponed to the next couplet, perhaps for suspense (and to emphasize that, given his vacillation in the poem, we—or he—may really not know what he will actually do); he is unable to escape from thoughts of N. **Non ego**: this placement emphasizes the negative; others (elegiac lovers?) may put up with flighty *puellae*, but L. for his part will not (Adams 1999: 100–4 for postponed *ego*).

Fugit is relatively rare for the action of a *puella*, despite her regular disappearance from the scene: e.g. Cat. 37.11, Ov. *Am.* 2.11.7, Tib. 1.8.62 and 1.9.74 (where she flees a *senex amator*); the verb also appears of Theseus' departure at Cat. 64.183, of Prop.'s at 1.17.1, and of Protesilaus' at Ov. *Her.* 13.4 *me cum fugeres*. See too *ad* 3.19.22. Navarro Antolín 1996 *ad loc.* prefers *fugiat*, found in some late manuscripts, as emphasizing the hypothetical nature of L.'s statement; the indicative seems more appropriate. The verb is also less active in meaning (*OLD* 11a 'avoid'), and so the implication might be that she has never even tried the pleasures of L.'s table, rather than that she has left from them.

Convivia mensae continues the sympotic atmosphere (Mart. 8.39.1, same *sedes*), but is also an elegiac phrase: Prop. 2.16.5 and 3.25.1, Ov. *Ars* 1.229, *Ib.* 431 (all same *sedes*); see too *TLL* 8.739.63–740.10 for **mensae** as festal tables, and on **convivia**, Pichon 1991: 113.

Ignotum...torum: 3.16.6 is the only other instance of this phrase. As Navarro Antolín 1996 notes *ad loc.*, the adjective means either 'new' or 'inferior'; perhaps, in fact, L. means both.

Cupiens: the participle is used elsewhere in the *CT* only at 3.18.6, in the same metrical *sedes*; there S. has left because she wants to hide her true feelings for Cerinthus. If the two passages are related, we are offered the possibility that L. is mistaken about the cause of N.'s absence (but the participle is common in e.g. Ov., so the connection may be illusory). **Vana**: frequent in L. (see *ad* 3.4.3, 3.4.13, 3.4.56, 3.4.68, 3.5.27), though not of the **puella**, or applying to her (but cf. Ov. *Am.* 3.11.21 *vanae...linguae*); for the meaning ('fatuous', 'lacking judgement'), see *OLD* 6a and Pichon 1991: 287.

> sollicitus repetam tota suspiria nocte:
> 62   tu, puer, i, liquidum fortius adde merum.

L. is done mourning for N., a point emphasized by the fact that this is the second-to-last couplet of his last poem.

Sollicitus: cf. *ad* 3.4.20, 3.6.36, and 3.16.5; the earlier passage in this poem marked L. off as still affected, but here he is not. The adjective is a regular descriptor of the lover (Prop. 3.7.1, 3.17.42, Ov. *Am.* 1.15.38, *Her.* 3.137, *Ars* 3.472, 3.600) and of elegiac love (Prop. 1.16.40, Ov. *Her.* 1.12, 18.196, *RA* 557).

Repetam...suspiria = *suspirare*: Ov. *Met.* 2.125 (with Bömer 1969 *ad loc.*) and 13.739 are the only other examples (both *repetens suspiria*); cf. Prop. 1.3.27 (*ducere suspiria*), Ov. *Am.* 2.19.55 *traham suspiria*. On sighs as a sign of love, see Pichon 1991: 172. Here L. finds repetition (**re-**) as he tries something new. **Tu puer**: see *ad* 3.6.57. **I**: as Navarro Antolín 1996 notes *ad loc.*, the manuscripts' *et* is meaningless; see his discussion *ad loc.*; he opts for the text as printed, as does Tränkle 1990, but Luck prints *i puer et*, following Huschke (which = Prop.

3.23.23). **I** intensifies the infinitive: 'go ahead and' (cf. e.g. Ov. *Am.* 3.3.1, *esse deos, i, crede*).

Liquidum: usually in the elegists of water; with **merum** at Ov. *Tr.* 2.490 and Mart. 12.60.8; cf. Ov. *Met.* 13.639 *liquido... Baccho*; the point here seems to be that it would flow (more?) freely if only the pourer would permit it to. On **merum**, see *ad* 3.5.34, 3.6.58, 3.12.14. **Adde merum** at Tib. 1.2.1 is surely relevant, coming at the start of that and the end of this poem; cf. the same phrase at Ov. *Am.* 1.4.52, where the *puella* is advised to get her *vir* drunk. The verb is commonly used for wine-pouring (Mart. 9.93.1, 10.98.1, 14.170.2). **Fortius**: suggests a kind of metapoetic competition with the previously cited passages: if poets are going to get drunk/write sympotic poetry, L. will do it better.

Iam dudum Syrio madefactus tempora nardo
64   debueram sertis implicuisse comas.

For (funereal) perfumes, see *ad* 3.2.23, and on symposiastic garlands, see e.g. Hor. *Od.* 1.36.15–16 (combined at Hor. *Od.* 2.7.7–8, 21–5, 2.11.14–17, 3.9.3–4); see too Lilja 1972: 58–96 on the symposiastic and celebratory uses of perfumes. **Iam dudum**: a prosaic construction, not found elsewhere in *CT* or in Prop., but at Cat. 64.374 and Ov. *Fas.* 3.507, 4.207. The point, especially given that this is the end of L.'s corpus, may be that a finish (at least to this kind of poetry) is long overdue. **Syrio... nardo**: Syria was the standard source for nard; see *ad* 3.4.28, *Syrio... rore*.

Madefactus is an especially appropriate verb in this context, used here literally, for the liquid nard (cf. Tib. 2.6.32 *madefacta... serta,* there of tears), but often refers metaphorically to heavy drinking (cf. English 'soused', 'pickled', and e.g. Ov. *Ars* 3.765). For the participle, see *ad* 3.8.16. **Tempora nardo**: cf. *distillent tempora nardo* at line-end at Tib. 2.2.7; for Greek precedents, see e.g. Alcman 362, Anacr. 363.

Sertis implicuisse: twining a garland, in the hair, or arms, around a neck (Pichon 1991: 171). Elegiac **sertis** are often symposiastic, e.g. Tib. 1.3.66, 1.7.52, 2.2.6, Ov. *Ars* 2.734 and, for Greek precedents, e.g. Alcman 362, Anacr. 352, 396, 397, 410. **Implicuisse**: Ov. *Fas.* 5.220 *sertaque caelestes implicitura comas.* On hair, see *ad* 3.1.10 and 3.8.9–10. **Comas** perhaps echoes the last word of Hor. *Od.* 3 (3.30.16), which is in turn an echo of χαίταν at Pi. *Ol.* 14.24 (Nisbet and Rudd *ad* Hor. *Od.* 3.30.16, drawn to my attention by S. Heyworth).

3.8:

The next five poems are usually thought to form a cycle that focuses on S. and her relationship with Cerinthus (see Introduction, Section IV); the point-of-view alternates, beginning here with a description of S. in the third person, which in the next poem changes to first person. The poem shares a number of verbal similarities with Tib. 2.2, the poem about Cornutus' birthday, which has led many to conclude that both poems refer to the same couple (see Introduction, Section IV, on the potential connections between Cornutus and Cerinthus). There may be Homeric resonances (see *ad* 3.8.1); Hallett also suggests that the presence of Venus, Amor, and a Tyrian *palla* are meant to be reminiscent of Vergil's Dido, but leading in this case to a rather different outcome (2002a: 52).

This poem, which introduces S. to the corpus, is puzzling in a number of ways. In elegiac fashion, her name begins the cycle (see Introduction, Section I), but the name itself is very unelegiac, insofar as it is a Roman gentile name (see Introduction, Section IV), rather than a metrically equivalent Greek pseudonym. Even from its first word, then, the cycle presents a tension: S. is seemingly both an elegiac *puella* and a respectable woman, two categories which have not yet met in elegy (see Introduction, Section I). So too, beginning with a woman's name, while it is a Propertian gesture, is here given a lyric twist, as the '*amicus*' does not—or at least, not explicitly—have an amatory interest in her; she is a *puella* but not his *puella*, a point which might suggest that she is everyone's *puella* (see Introduction, Section IV on the ambiguities of S.'s presentation in this cycle, and *ad* 3.13 below for another example of S.'s availability to appropriation). S.—despite the status conveyed by her name—appears as a *puella*, decorated for the admiration of others; the visual nature of the description almost forces readers to look at her. See, e.g. Prop. 1.2 on the ambiguities this situation creates for the poet, who has a stake in the pleasing appearance of the *puella*, but is neither willing to pay for her accoutrements nor to allow others to do so; still less is he willing to allow her to be admired by others (see Introduction, Section I).

And since *puella* is also poetry (Introduction, Section I), the elegist's jealous feelings are undermined by his own attempts to publicize his *puella*: if he keeps her to himself, she will never increase his reputation. So this poet, like other elegists, *wants* S. to attract attention among a community of men (and gods!) because of her tasteful ornamentation (*cultus*), especially insofar as he can claim responsibility for it. Our poet is less conflicted, however, since (at least on the surface) he has no erotic interest in S. But the fact that S. is presented, even in this cycle, as also having her own poetic voice, complicates the issue, raising provocative questions about the poet's relationship to his (and her) poetic material.

This poem, with its broadly hymnic structure, goes further than many elegies in the religious liberties it takes (Hinds 1987a: 31 terms it 'slightly outrageous'), for it recommends S. to the attention of the god Mars (cf. Cat. 70 and 72); this is a trope which derives ultimately from mythical stories of the gods' earthly visitations, which normally involve the rape of mortal women. Gaertner 2000a suggests that the poem has close relations with Ov. *Fas.* 3 precisely in the context of Mars making an appearance to mortals; while [Tib.] 3.4, 3.10, and 3.12 also hint at personal relationships between divine and mortal, this poem goes the furthest. There are also some similarities with the *Homeric Hymn to Aphrodite*.

But erotic violence is, if present at all in this poem, only implicit. S. is identified as fit for divine attention, and the poem explores the implications of this stance, as well as its cause (Amor himself, with various assistants). The pose of 'intimate distance' is in keeping with the attitude of the author of this poem of admiring S. from afar and observing the progress of her affair, rather than presenting himself as an *amator* (Hinds 1987a: 31); note too Introduction, Section VI, on 'third-person elegy'.

At the same time, our author is not quite disinterested: his suggestions in this poem about the luxury which S. deserves suggest the faint whiff of the *lena* (see Introduction, Section I, and Myers 1996), as does his willingness to enumerate, and so display, S.'s charms for the god Mars. (Note the ways this cycle as a whole picks up on the invitation of 3.13, to 'anyone', to tell S.'s story: with these poems, S. becomes public property.) Here again, the question of S.'s status arises: as a woman, she is by definition the regular object of a desiring gaze, but it is not clear whether she is being presented as potentially marriageable, or instead available for less regular liaisons. As Hinds 1987a notes, S. is first presented to us as 'disguised'. But is she a matron disguised as a *puella*, a courtesan disguised as a matron, or a male poet disguised as both (Introduction, Section VI)? So too, we never learn whether the author has any particular interest in S. himself, or whether he is simply an amused bystander. The fact that none of this poetry is addressed to her is surely noteworthy; the author prefers to speak to other men and male gods about S. (Hinds 1987a: 39; see too Keith 2008: 115–38 on the homosociality inherent in elegiac poetry). It is probably not plausible, as some have done, to imagine that the author is S.'s brother; everything we know of Roman social relations among the upper classes argues against a brother who is complicit in an unmarried sister's love affair (however metaphorically we manage to take S.'s own language). Dronke intriguingly suggests that this (and the other two third-person poems of the cycle, 3.10 and 3.12) are written by Cerinthus himself (2003: 92).

The introduction of Vertumnus in line 13 of this poem further complicates matters, as he is a god of changeability of various kinds (especially, in Augustan poets, gender transformation, see Introduction, Section VI); perhaps we should understand him as the patron god of S.'s gender-troubled poetic discourse, wherein women write poetry and men are pursued. Perhaps, however, Vertumnus is meant to resolve the paradox noted in the previous paragraph about S.'s disguises: S., like the god, can be whatever she (or the author) likes. On the ways all of the S. poetry plays with elegy's expectations about gender, see Introduction, Section VI. Ruiz Sánchez suggests that the similarities with Prop. 2.1 (see *ad* 3.8.5–12) point to a larger programmatic significance (1996: 381–3).

Finally, the poem's occasion is the same as that of 3.1, the Kalends of March (although not necessarily in the same year); see the introduction to 3.1 for further details. It is not at all clear whether the Matronalia was celebrated in all periods exclusively by matrons (see Tränkle 1990: 257; Hinds 1987a); if it was, the festival is a puzzling way to introduce S., who is presented throughout as a *puella* (but see Watson 1983 on the precise meanings of *puella* outside of elegy, which do not preclude marriage or even giving birth).

The poem can be divided into three sections: the first two couplets introduce S. and the occasion; the majority of the poem (eight couplets) describes her appearance and clothing; the final two couplets praise her to Apollo and the Muses.

>   **Sulpicia est tibi culta tuis, Mars magne, kalendis:**
> 2 **spectatum e caelo, si sapis, ipse veni.**

Beginning with a woman's name, **Sulpicia**, locates us squarely in the world of elegy (Hinds 1987a: 30; Navarro Antolín 2005: 316–17 for the case that it is specifically Propertian elegy): in this poem, S. is silent, requiring a poet to transmute her into art (Batstone, forthcoming). Yet *puellae* are normally given (Greek) pseudonyms; starting the cycle with a Roman gentile name offers its own kind of inversion, suggesting a disruption of elegiac norms and perhaps making the metapoetic case that Romans can compete with Greeks even in Roman poetry. Given that this cycle, if it were ever to have stood on its own, could be known by its first word, **Sulpicia**, it is not inapposite to see an act of appropriation here (however neutrally intended): S. will (3.13.6) invite aspiring authors to tell her story, but, presumably, not in order to be silenced herself (see too below, *ad* **culta**).

The poem is addressed to **tibi** (Mars), and therefore might be understood to dedicate the poem, or cycle, to him. If so, this is a much less formal dedication than is customary for humans, let alone gods. If not, it is strange to address him so prominently. As is discussed below (see too *ad* 3.1.1), Mars might seem a peculiar choice as dedicatee for erotic poetry, but his two most notable conquests, Venus and Rhea Silvia (one the goddess of desire, the other the progenitor of the Roman race), are thereby each suggested as comparanda for S.

On **culta**, see notes *ad* 3.1.17 and 3.4.92. The quality is associated with taking care with one's appearance, but also with the *docta puella*, the object of elegiac poetry. A metapoetic claim is implicit: the poetry about S. is also carefully wrought, such that praise of her is also praise of the corpus (see Introduction, Section I). Batstone (forthcoming) may be right to see here a further claim made by the author of these poems about the lack of *cultus* of the later S. cycle (i.e. poems 13–18). Finally, on a literal level, religious festivals were naturally a time for dressing up and parties. Hinds notes that **est...culta** may instead mean 'Sulpicia has been worshipped by you' (1987a: 34), a notion which finds support in the lines that follow.

Mars Magne is unattested as a cult title (*RE* 14.2.1927–8); the adjective may be meant to assimilate him to various Roman generals who were also thus called. When Mars is mentioned in elegy (only in Ov.), he is generally metonymic: *Her.* 3.45, 16.372, *RA* 153, *Fas.* 5.59, *EP* 1.8.15, *Ib.* 215 (exceptions immediately below, and see further citations and discussion *ad* 3.1.1). The beginning of Ov. *Fasti* 3 invokes Mars as the patron of its month, and makes the case that, just as Minerva both wages war and engages in *ingenuis artibus*, so too can Mars appreciate poetry in addition to fighting; Rhea Silvia is later mentioned in that book as something Mars found to occupy his time with other than warfare (*Fas.* 3.171). Generally speaking, Mars plays little role in love, or poetry about love, with the exception of his long-standing affair with Venus (first in Hom. *Od.* 8; see too the rape of Rhea Silvia, mentioned throughout Latin poetry and told at Ov. *Fas.* 3.11–42, and the failed encounter with Minerva at *Fas.* 3.675-96—both narrated in 'his' month). The Mars/Venus story was very popular in art, and is alluded to also at Ov. *Her.* 15.92, *Tr.* 2.295, 2.377. At Ov. *Am.* 1.1.12, Mars is mentioned as *in*appropriate to poetry (*Aoniam Marte movente lyram*). The hexameter, particularly with its **magne**, invokes an epic Mars, but the pentameter puts him squarely in the world of elegy.

The trope of *militia amoris* is implicit in the invocation of Mars; elegiac love is a kind of war, in which the *puella* (and Amor) become metaphorically both enemy and commanding officer (see Introduction, Section I). So while Mars is at first look a surprising addition to this poem, he does fit in with its generic assumptions in a broader sense. Extending the metaphor, we might think of Amor's attentions to S. later in this poem as a kind of Homeric 'arming-scene', preparing her for her confrontation with admiring men and gods (cf. Hera's similar Homeric pre-seduction scene, *Il.* 14.159–223); S. is also thereby assimilated to the tradition by which the *puella* is treated as divine or quasi-divine (Introduction, Section I).

The **Kalends** of March are also mentioned at 3.1.1 as an occasion for poetry; this poem is perhaps meant to be or to introduce a similar kind of gift, although it does not contain the same intensity of programmatic language. So too, 3.1 was primarily interested in the festival, whereas this poem focuses on the god himself, as a potential admirer of S.

Spectatum, a supine of purpose (as at Ov. *Ars* 1.99, *spectatum veniunt*; Hallett 2006: 42 suggests that the Ovidian phrase derives from this), encourages the god of war to leave his usual occupations. The word suggests the theatre (note the context of the Ovidian passage); metapoetic implications also inhere, implicitly, since Mars is typically more interested in love than in poetry (though he is not as notorious as some gods for his sexual liaisons). Indeed, his selectiveness may have particular point here, as the poem suggests that S./this group of poems will be worth his effort; Mars is plainly envisioned as an audience rather than a practitioner of poetry. Thus far, the status of S. as passive object remains unchallenged: whether as poetry or *puella*, she exists to arouse the interest of others.

Si sapis is informal in an address to a god: it usually, at least in elegy, accompanies a warning from an equal or superior. The verb appears elsewhere in *CT* only at 3.19.8, in a similar construction (see *ad loc.*). The closest comparanda (Prop. 2.16.7, advising Cynthia to fleece her praetor for all she can; 2.17.10, claiming that you should wish to be a lover least of all, *si sapias*, and Ov. *Met.* 14.675, Vertumnus in disguise recommending himself to Pomona, *si sapies*) suggest that the phrase may be a regular feature of colloquial speech about love affairs (cf. too the phrase at Ov. *Am.* 2.2.9 and 3.4.43, both pandering).

Ipse veni: cf. Tib. 2.5.6 *ad tua sacra veni*; Ov. *Her.* 1.2, 8.24 both *ipse veni*, at line-end, encouraging a too-slow lover. Again, the language is probably colloquial. See Hinds 2006 for a potential etymology with Venus here, as goddess of *venia* (and below *ad* 3.8.10 *veneranda* and 3.8.12 *venit*). Note too the verbal parallels with Ov. *Fas.* 5.549–51: *fallor, an arma sonant? non fallimur, arma sonabant:/Mars venit et veniens bellica signa dedit./Ultor ad ipse suos caelo descendit honores*; that passage continues with his inspection (*perspicit* 561, *videt* 563 and 565, *spectat* 567) of various grand, public objects.

> Hoc Venus ignoscet: at tu, violente, caveto
> 4   ne tibi miranti turpiter arma cadant.

The poet claims that **Venus** will not mind Mars' attention to S.; the two gods had been romantically entangled as far back as Hom. *Od.* 8 (with offspring attested at Hes. *Th.* 933–7). But Venus is traditionally jealous: note the sufferings of Psyche (as told in Apuleius' *Golden Ass*), who is simply beautiful, and not even direct competition. In fact, the lovelier S. is, the worse it is likely to be for her. But the author probably does not mean us to make such a leap; S. herself in her 'own' cycle, 3.13.3–5, presents Venus as keenly interested in her poetry, and life.

Ignoscet is the usual verb for pardoning or forgiving, elsewhere in the *CT* at 1.2.12 and 1.6.29. Prop. 2.28.3 (*hoc tibi vel poterit coniunx ignoscere Iuno*), wherein the poet insists that Juno would forgive Jupiter for sparing the sick *puella*'s life, may also be relevant here (and that poem's focus on illness fits in well with the concerns of this corpus, if not of this particular poem). Hinds notes that Venus has two things to forgive: not only has the author intruded into her relationship with Mars, but she is the goddess who ought to be summoned for amatory assistance (1987a: 32)—and in fact, she is, later in the book (see *ad* 3.13.3–4). Note too the lengthening of the last syllable of **ignoscet**; this does occur, especially when a pause is emphasized (see Smith *ad* Tib. 1.10.13; Platnauer 1951: 59–60), but the line may contain a corruption. As Bréguet 1946: 259 notes, **at tu** is a verbal tic of this poet at sense-breaks (3.9.23, 3.11.19, 3.12.7, each at line-start; cf. 3.10.16 *tu* at line-start).

Violence is a regular, if normally unexpressed, feature of the elegiac world (see Introduction, Section I), and also a characteristic of Mars (although, as

Smith 1913 notes *ad loc.*, **violente** is used as his epithet only elsewhere at Sen. *Troad.* 185; see too Val. Max. 7.2.2.5 *error violentiae Martis* and Bréguet 1946: 211 for the argument that it is a Greek usage). Note too the word-placement: the epic **violente** appears in hexameter (see below on the placement of *arma cadant* in the pentameter).

Caveto: the future imperative is formal, the sentiment less so, suggesting as it does that Mars might make a fool of himself through inappropriate behaviour. Combined with the vocative **violente**, it reinforces the notion that Mars is out of place. *At tu... caveto* at Tib. 1.2.89, which warns a bystander that he will some day suffer the wrath of Venus, is a likely intertext (with disturbing implications for both Mars and S.).

Miranti retains its core meaning of wondering at or being amazed by (*OLD* 3 and 4); Mars has not seen anything like S. before! For S. to be proffered to the male gaze (even that of a god) gainsays her apparent status; see Introduction, Section IV.

Turpiter goes with *cadant*, but word-order might tempt us to take it with *miranti* (which would increase the impression of Mars' awkwardness). For **turpiter** elsewhere in the book, see *ad* 3.4.15 and 3.6.37. Compare Ov. *Ars* 3.79–80, urging the passing of time as a reason to take a lover: *carpite florem,/ qui, nisi carptus erit, turpiter ipse cadet.*

Arma cadant inevitably reminds one of Mars' normal role, perhaps too of the first line of the *Aeneid*, *arma... ca-*, and of Ov.'s quick shunting aside of *arma* for *amor* in *Am.* 1.1.1–2, especially the way in which *arma* are neutralized in the 'elegiac' pentameter. (See Pichon 1991: 90 on the elegiac, and erotic, nuances of *arma*, most of which play on its epic connotations.) Finally, note the frustration of the elegiac expectation that '*arma*' (= penis) will rise, not fall, in the presence of an attractive *puella*. The couplet as a whole echoes Lucr. 1.33–8, in which Mars puts his armour aside to sit in Venus' lap. So too, this elegy is in tune with the multiple Ovidian efforts to fashion Mars as an elegiac lover (see *ad* 3.8.1, with citations). If we read these lines in the light of Ov. *Am.* 1.1.1, where, at Cupid's insistence, Ovid will abandon *violenta... bella* for love poetry, we might see them as providing an implicit *recusatio*: Mars is welcomed into this poetry, but only a peculiarly elegiac version of Mars, who drops his weapons at the first sight of a pretty girl. Smith 1913 and Tränkle 1990 *ad loc.* note some intertexts, all of lovers who cause destruction and pain: Prop. 4.4.21 (Tarpeia drops her water jug at the sight of Tatius), Ov. *Her.* 16.253 (Paris drops his drinking-cup at the sight of Helen's breast), *Met.* 14.349 (Circe drops her herbs at the sight of Picus); the Helen intertext refers also back to the tale of Menelaus dropping his armour at the sight of Helen's breast (see Michalopoulos *ad* Ov. *Her.* 16.249–54, with Greek citations). See too *Anacreonta* 4, about a beautiful woman overcoming the sword and fire (especially given the following lines); this may be a commonplace. See above *ad* **violente** on the arrangement of this couplet.

Illius ex oculis, cum volt exurere divos,
6   accendit geminas lampadas acer Amor.

Amor takes responsibility for S.'s beauty, and thereby provides another hint that she is meant to be passive (cf. Prop. 2.29.17–18, where Amor creates perfumes, and the sequence at Prop. 2.3.23–32). The subject(s) of the next few couplets is not immediately clear: it is possible to take S. as the subject of *volt*, but Amor is more natural, especially given that *illius* must refer to her. On the other hand, Amor works most naturally through others, using one person to enflame another; even the gods are susceptible (see, among many examples, Ov. *Met.* 1.452ff., where Amor takes Apollo down a peg by hitting him with an arrow that makes him love the reluctant Daphne). By way of comparison, Pi. fr. 123 S-M, lines 13–15 suggest that Peitho and Charis 'dwell' (ἔναιεν) in the son of Hagisilas; that poem is usually understood to be erotic, but might also be encomiastic (Hubbard 2002).

The notion of love as a flame (and eyes as torches) is common in love poetry (see **exurere** at *TLL* 5.2.2126.7–14; see Hubbard 2002: 269–72 with nn. for scientific and philosophical theories about the eyes as exuding fire), though, as Tränkle 1990 notes *ad loc.*, it is not used in quite this way elsewhere in ancient poetry; for some partial parallels, see Pichon 1991: 77 s.v. *accendere* and 301 s.v. *urere*, and V. *A.* 4 *passim*. Prop. 2.3.14 shares the conjunction of *oculi* and *geminae…faces*. Torches are also symbolic of marriage, so we may be meant to discern conjugal imagery as well. The situation here is slightly different from the norm, however, in that Amor is actively involved, as with Daphne in Ov. *Met.* 1; he uses S. as a weapon against other gods. Stranger still, her eyes are presented as the source of his flames, rather than the other way around (see *AP* 9.15 for a more typical use of the conceit, and Porc. Licin. fr. 7 Courtney for a further variation); S. thus becomes the originary source of enflaming visual stimulus: let Mars beware indeed! See too Ov. *Met.* 1.498–9 *videt igne micantes/ sideribus similes oculos*, Ov. *Her.* 20.57–8 *hoc oculique tui, quibus ignea cedunt/ sidera, qui flammae causa fuere meae*. The line shares diction with Ceres' use of trees as torches at Ov. *Fas.* 4.493 *illic accendit geminas pro lampade pinus*.

Lampadas, a Greek word, appears in elegy only in Ovid, normally of genuine lamps or torches (once of the moon); it is used at Ov. *RA* 552 and Varro *Men.* fr. 204.2 of Amor's torches; see *TLL* 7.2.909.52–64 for nuptial torches, 909.83–910.12 for the torches of love, and Pichon 1991: 183 for erotic uses.

Acer is used for things bitter, keen, fierce, sharp, or difficult (often of beasts); see Pichon 1991: 78 for its erotic nuances. It describes *Amor/amor* at Tib. 2.6.15, Prop. 1.9.26, 2.3.46, Ov. *Her.* 4.70.

Illam, quicquid agit, quoquo vestigia movit,
8   componit furtim subsequiturque Decor.

The notion that the beloved is attractive is common in elegy; the closest in tone to this sentiment, and surely a key referent, is Prop. 2.1.15–16: *seu quidquid fecit sive est quodcumque locuta,/maxima de nihilo nascitur historia* (Navarro Antolín 2005: 317–18 notes *AP* 5.260, also focusing on hair). Here the subject of *agit* and *movit* changes, to S.; this awkward disjunction is made less so by the early introduction of *illam*. (It is probably stretching the Latin too far to retain *Amor* as the subject; S. then becomes little more than an automaton.) But **Decor** quickly takes over from S. as subject. As Tränkle 1990 notes *ad loc.*, the pentameter has an Ovidian feel; see e.g. Ov. *Am.* 3.13.30 *ipsa sacerdotes subsequiturque suas* for a partial parallel.

Vestigia is used regularly for footsteps and the tracks of animals ([Tib.] 3.9.13), and by a logical extension, for feet themselves (e.g. Cat. 64.162, [Tib.] 3.7.12–13); also in elegy of the remnants of the battle of love (Cat. 66.13, Tib. 1.9.57, Prop. 1.5.25, 2.29.35 and 45, Ov. *Her.* 10.53, *Am.* 1.8.97). Looking forward in the corpus, we may want to understand S.'s *vestigia* here as her writing, the literary traces she leaves of her love for Cerinthus. The phrase **vestigia movit** is, however, prosaic and associated with military activities (e.g. Liv. 10.36.3.5, 21.44.7.1, Curt. 10.2.13.5).

Componit applies both to the arrangement of one's person (Ov. *Am.* 2.17.10 of the face, Prop. 1.15.5, Ov. *Her.* 12.156, *Ars* 2.303, and *RA* 679 of hair) and to creative activity (e.g. Tib. 1.2.55 of a *cantus* given by a witch, 1.2.93 of a *senex amator* crafting love-speeches, Prop. 1.7.19, 1.9.13, Ov. *Am.* 2.1.1, 3.15.3, *Tr.* 2.361–2, 5.1.8 of love poetry; also in prose at e.g. Quint. *Inst.* 1.11.19); presumably both nuances are to be felt here (see *ad* 3.2.26 for more on the verb).

Furtim paints a portrait of S. as unaware of her charms; in this she differs radically from the normal elegiac *puella*, who is deliberately artificial. (Ov. *Ars* 3 contains typically misogynistic elegiac thoughts on women's adornment, especially those aspects of it which might cost the lover money.) Or, possibly, the adverb is to be focalized through the viewer/poet, who cannot work out how S. (and **Decor**) manage their magic. The word **furtim** is quintessentially elegiac (Pichon 1991: 158), but normally refers to illicit love-making, especially in the *CT* (e.g. Tib. 1.2.10 and 19, 1.5.65, 1.6.5, 1.8.35, to take only the adverb, in only one book of elegy; see nn. *ad* 3.9.21 and 3.11.7, and the probable antecedent in Cat. 68.136).

Personifications of abstract nouns are frequent in both Latin and Greek, but **Decor** is not normally one of them (appearing, or rather, not appearing, at Stat. *Theb.* 2.286: neither she nor Amor have fashioned a baneful necklace). **Decor** has taken over from Amor in the fashioning of S., serving as subject of *componit* and *subsequitur*; elegiac *puellae* tend to be somewhat more self-directed than this (e.g. Prop. 1.2.5), and it remains unclear what we are to make of S. The repeated changes of subject present S. as a doll, decorated by various gods for the amusement or befuddlement of others. If we are meant to think of Pandora's creation and adornment by the gods (Hes. *Th.* 570–93 and *WD* 59–82), the picturesque image becomes a disturbing one: S. is then a dangerous, liminal figure, bringing evil to man. This is perhaps an excessive conclusion to draw, but one which fits in with the latent misogyny of elegy (Introduction, Section I) and with the uncanny depiction of S. in this poem.

                  Seu solvit crines, fusis decet esse capillis,
10   seu compsit, comptis est veneranda comis.

S. is the most probable subject of this sentence (especially given **veneranda**), but it might still be *Decor* in the hexameter. For different women's hairstyles, and their ability to charm, see *AP* 5.260, Ov. *Am.* 1.5.10, *Ars* 3.135–58 with Gibson 2003 *ad loc.*; Tib. 1.8.15–16 *illa placet, quamvis inculto venerit ore/nec nitidum tarda compserit arte caput*. The construction with *seu...seu* and description of the various 'looks' of the *puella* recalls Prop. 2.1.5–16, quoted in part below.

Women's hair is often loose when they are (1) in mourning (Tib. 1.1.67–8, Prop. 3.13.18); (2) performing magic (Ov. *Met.* 7.183); or (3) in intimate or domestic settings (Ov. *Ars* 3.236, *Met.* 9.90, *fusis utrimque capillis* at line-end); see the comprehensive study of elegiac hair at Burkowski 2012 (loose hair at 182–236). The couplet, as Smith 1913 notes *ad loc.*, is Ovidian in its anaphora and chiasmus; among his parallels see especially *Am.* 2.5.43 and *Ars* 2.297–8 (cited below). Apollo's comments at Ov. *Met.* 1.497–8 suggest that arranged hair was considered more attractive (*spectat inornatos collo pendere capillos/et 'quid, si comantur?' ait*). See too Ov.'s advice on hairstyles at *Ars* 3.133–68 (which suggests that different styles are attractive on different women, but makes clear that all women need to put forth effort; even the 'careless' look is deliberately wrought). See *ad* 3.8.8, on *componit* and the arrangement of hair, along with Introduction, Section I, and Zetzel 1996 and Gibson *ad Ars* 3.133, 135 and *passim* for parallels between style, linguistic decorum, and coiffure.

If *Decor* is involved, it is natural that S. **decet**; this is almost but not quite a *figura etymologica*; see Pichon 1991: 123–4 s.v. *decere*. For hair as the *decus* of Bacchus and Apollo, see Tib. 1.4.38.

Veneranda may suggest quasi-divinity (for the treatment of the *puella* as a goddess, seemingly originating in Cat., see Lieberg 1962 and Introduction, Section I). Given the couplet's metapoetic implications, it may put S. into the position of Muse, inspiration for our author's poetry, and/or draw attention to the probable status differences between the Servii Sulpicii and the (usually equestrian) elegiac poet (see Introduction, Section IV). Note too the etymological connections with Venus (Hinds 1987a: 33), with the concomitant suggestion that S. may replace Venus in another sphere, and see *venit* in line 12, also sometimes linked with Venus.

Sive is repeated in a similar dressing scene at Ov. *Ars* 2.297–8: *sive erit in Tyriis, Tyrios laudabis amictus:/sive erit in Cois, Coa decere puta* and Prop. 2.1.5–8 *sive illam Cois fulgentem incedere cerno,/totum de Coa veste volumen erit;/seu vidi ad frontem sparsos errare capillos,/gaudet laudatis ire superba comis*. Both share individual points, but also the conceit that the *puella*'s appearance, whatever the details, demands a tribute of poetry; see too Prop. 2.3.43–4 on the charms of his mistress, as a painter might display them: *sive illam*

Hesperis, sive illam ostendet Eois,/uret et Eoos, uret et Hesperios. Our author combines specificity with the Propertian use of two exclusive opposites.

    Urit, seu Tyria voluit procedere palla:
12   **urit, seu nivea candida veste venit.**

Urit is standard elegiac language for the effects of love (see Pichon 1991: 301, and above *ad* 3.8.5 *exurere*); S. is presented as a force of nature, indiscriminately burning all in her path. Hallett 2002a, implausibly to my mind, sees a connection between the couplet and Cat. 68.71; the language is rather formulaic.

    Palla: for Ov.'s thoughts on women's attire, see *Ars* 3.169–92 (mostly focusing on colour) with Gibson 2003 *ad loc*. The *palla* was worn by Roman women in public (and also by certain gods and bards; see *ad* 3.4.35 on Apollo's *palla*). See *ad* 3.3.18 on Tyrian purple, with Ov. *Ars* 2.297–8 (quoted *ad* 3.8.9–10) on its suitability for *puellae* (and the importance of praising them when they wear it). See too *ad* 3.4.34 on the favoured status of the juxtaposition between purple and white in Latin, *ad* 3.6.1 (especially) on *candidus* of a person, *ad* 3.1.9 for *niveus*, and *ad* 3.2.10 for *candidus*. Tib. 2.5.38 has *niveae candidus* juxtaposed in the same *sedes*. Hallett suggests a connection to **candida** at Cat. 68.70, seeing the presentation of S. as similar to that of Cat.'s quasi-divine Lesbia (2002b: 146).

    Talis in aeterno felix Vertumnus Olympo
14   **mille habet ornatus, mille decenter habet.**

The appearance of **Vertumnus** is at first sight confusing, but, I believe, central to an understanding of the Sulpician cycles. He is a male god, but one who regularly appears in the garb of a female (for details, see *RE*). So, like S., he tends to subvert traditional gender roles, and his external appearance can mislead about his inner self (e.g. in Ov. *Met*. 14.623–772). He also potentially reflects the status of the '*amicus*' of S. of 3.9 and 11, cloaking himself in a female identity (and of S. 'herself' in 13–18, assuming the—automatically male—identity of a poet). Note especially in this context Prop. 4.2.21–4: *opportuna mea est cunctis natura figuris:/in quacumque voles verte, decorus ero./indue me Cois: fiam non dura puella;/meque virum sumpta quis neget esse toga?* (with Navarro Antolín 2005: 318–19). Vertumnus was considered by the Romans to be an Etruscan god (Varro *DLL* 5.46, Prop. 4.2.4, Plin. *NH* 34.34), transferred by *evocatio* from Volsinii just before its sack, and with a temple on the Aventine founded on 13 August 264 BCE. He also had a statue on the *Vicus Tuscus*, and shopkeepers made offerings to him (Prop. 4.2.13). Many literary discussions of him play on his etymological connection to *vertere*, which may or may not reflect his actual duties and functions. **Aeterno** does not appear elsewhere with this noun, and Vertumnus is nowhere else claimed to live **Olympo**; this may be simply the poet's way of combining Roman with Greek (see too *ad* 3.8.1 *Sulpicia*), or perhaps **in** suggests not domicile but visitation, and we are to imagine a scenario in which Vertumnus (like S.) shows up and excites various gods by his different guises. The appearance of Vertumnus might, of course, merely suggest variability, without any special meaning for the cycle (cf. e.g. Hor. *Ser.* 7.13–14).

Felix: see notes *ad* 3.3.26, 3.4.40, 3.4.80, 3.5.31, 3.6.30, 3.6.43, 3.10.25. Here the word probably contains its original implications of fertility (and perhaps hints at successful seduction) as well as blessedness (*OLD* 1); cf. *felicior* applied to Vertumnus at Ov. *Met.* 14.642.

Ornatus, like *compono* above, plays on a double meaning; Vertumnus does alter his clothing, and the poetry of and about S. alters traditional gender roles and even speaking voice. A number of elegiac poems discuss the *cultus* of the *puella*, which is a flashpoint of tension for the elegiac poet, as well as part of what makes her desirable (see introduction to this poem). By invoking the easy abundance of Vertumnus, the poet seems to suggest that S., unlike the usual *puella*, can afford to buy her own finery in large quantities (see James 2003 on the ways it is very much to the poet's advantage to make this claim, whether it is true or not).

Mille: cf. *ad* 3.3.12. The word is also reduplicated at Ov. *RA* 526, *Met.* 8.628–9, perhaps with a Catullan feel. **Decenter**, related to *decor*, is repetitive after the proper noun and verb (see *ad* 3.8.9), emphasizing the etymological wordplay; its presence here may also be explained by its use at Prop. 4.2.25–6, of Vertumnus' garland, *nec flos ullus hiat pratis, quin ille decenter/impositus fronti langueat ante meae* (cf. Cartault 1909). For a similar Ovidian repetition with **decenter**, see *Am.* 2.5.44: *maesta erat in vultu—maesta decenter erat*.

>   Sola puellarum digna est, cui mollia caris
> 16   vellera det sucis bis madefacta Tyros,

These lines reiterate the suggestion that S. might be (mis?)taken for an elegiac *puella*, and the poem as a whole offers a *puella*'s eye view of the elegiac situation, from an apparently disinterested admirer. S., if she is to be understood as a *puella*, is fortunate to have at least one person who believes she ought to be showered in luxury (perhaps because it is not his responsibility to provide it). Stat. *Silv.* 1.2.122–9, placed in the mouth of Venus, claims that the earth has not provided jewels sufficient for Violentilla.

Digna est: frequent in comedy, perhaps colloquial. The phrase **sola…digna** is found in a variety of poetic contexts, notably at V. *E.* 8.10 (songs alone worthy of Sophocles) and *A.* 7.389 (Bacchus alone as deserving to marry Lavinia; this provides a potential intertext with this poem, in its focus on the divine attention certain women deserve). In Prop. the word **sola** is often used of those who can bear comparison to the gods, and that nuance is surely present here as well.

Dignus, while not common in Tib. (only at 2.6.43) occurs often in [Tib.] 3 (see *ad* 3.1.8). Hallett connects its use here to Cat. 68.131 (2002b: 146).

Cui introduces a relative clause of characteristic (or, possibly, a jussive); the comparative of *dignus* is more common with the subjunctive (*OLD* 2b). **Tyros** serves as the subject of the clause, offering its cloth for double-dyeing; the phrase may introduce a certain distance between admirer and recipient of the gift, and so emphasize through replication the author's disinterested stance.

Caris…sucis is not attested elsewhere. *Sucus* (literally juice) occurs regularly for dye and herbal remedies, and in [Tib.] 3.5.9 for poison. *Tyrio…suco* occurs at Ov. *Met.* 6.222–3, for the dye on equestrian accoutrements. **Carus** here has both its 'elegiac' sense ('pleasing' or 'precious') and its more standard meaning of 'expensive' (*OLD* 2 and 1 respectively). There is similar phrasing at Stat. *Silv.* 3.2.139–40: *quo pretiosa Tyros rubeat, quo purpura suco/Sidoniis iterata cadis*, but the two passages are probably independent.

Vellera…madefacta is not an unreasonable way to describe the dyeing process, although the phrase is unattested. *Madefacio* (see *ad* 3.6.63) is slightly less common in the elegists than *madeo*, and much more common than *madesco*, but the three mean essentially the same thing and are used most frequently of drunkenness or freely flowing tears (see *ad* 3.6.5). For similar phrases, see Tib. 2.1.62 *molle…vellus ovis*, Ov. *Fas.* 2.107 *induerat Tyrio bis tinctam murice pallam*, Sil. 11.40–1 *madefacta veneno/Assyrio maribus vestis*.

Bis: the double-dyeing process would render the garment richer in colour, and so, even more valuable (see Plin. *NH* 9.135–41 on the differing qualities of different shells and dye methods, and above *ad* 3.3.18 for purple dyes in general). The cloth so dyed is known as δίβαφος; see Plin. *NH* 9.137 for a brief history.

>   possideatque, metit quicquid bene olentibus arvis
> 18   cultor odoratae dives Arabs segetis,

Possideat suggests a resolution of the elegiac contradiction between soi-disant poverty and the desire to ornament one's beloved (but note the vagueness inherent in the subjunctive, leaving unclear the mechanism by which S. might come to have these things); generally the elegists assure us that *puellae* are most appealing when dressed least expensively. The difference, as noted above, may derive from the fact that the author of this poem is not S.'s *amator*, so will not have to provide the gifts he thinks she ought to have. (Indeed, we might think of him as a *lena*-figure, trying to make a good bargain for her; see the introduction to this poem.) As is usual with elegiac gifts, the proposed presents are all luxury items, designed to make the *puella* more decorative without actually giving her financial independence.

The repetitiveness of **olentibus** and **odoratae** may be meant to suggest the overpowering nature of the perfumes; see *ad* 3.2.23–4. Both noun *odor* and verb *odoro* occur in elegy of perfumes and the lands which produce them; see

234   *Commentary on 3.8.20*

e.g. Cat. 68.144 (*Assyrio...odore*); Tib. 1.5.36 (*odoratos...Armenios*), Prop. 2.29.17 (*Arabum...odores*) and 3.13.8 (*pistor odoris Arabs*).

Metit (from *meto* not *metor*) occurs only here in *CT*; in elegy at Prop. 4.10.30, Ov. *Am*. 3.10.40, *Her*. 6.84, *Ars* 2.322, *Fas*. 2.519 and 2.706. **Dives**: see *ad* 3.2.23–4, 3.3.11, 3.3.38, 3.15.3; the word is used with *terra* at Tib. 2.2.4; see *ad* 3.8.19 and Hubbard 2004: 185 for other similarities to that poem.

Arabs: masculine nominative singular, of a person also at Prop. 3.13.8 and Tib. 2.2.3–4 in similar contexts: *cinnamon et multi pistor odoris Arabs; urantur pia tura focis, urantur odores/quos tener e terra divite mittit Arabs* (and see *ad* 3.2.24 for the land, with further detail). The word is almost wholly poetic, mostly in the context of sacrificial or funereal incense (e.g. Sen. *HO* 793 for the former, Stat. *Silv*. 5.3.43 for the latter (also using *odoratas*)), but for its use of perfume that is worn, see Prop. 2.29.17: *afflabunt tibi non Arabum de gramine odores* (see *ad* 3.8.6 for context). Also similar is Sen. *HF* 909–10: *quidquid Indorum seges/ Arabesque odoris quidquid arboribus legunt* (of a sacrifice to the gods).

     et quascumque niger Rubro de litore gemmas
20   **proximus Eois colligit Indus aquis.**

Tibullan themes recur here, especially the notion of gathering wealth from everywhere (though for Tib., this has little point; cf. e.g. 1.1.1–6, wherein the poet allots the accumulation of resources to others, for whom it might make better sense than it does for him). Tib. 2.2.15–16 is a probable intertext: *nec tibi, gemmarum quidquid felicibus Indis/nascitur, Eoi qua maris unda rubet* ('nor would you [Cornutus] prefer for yourself all the pearls which are born in fortunate India, where the waters of the red sea blush'); some of those who see more intimate connections between Cornutus and S. (Introduction, Section IV) view these lines as a description of his wedding presents to her. The **gemmas** of the sea are pearls (on which, see *ad* 3.3.17). Again, jewellery is not usually recommended to the *puella*, presumably because the *amator* might then have to purchase it.

Rubro...litore refers here, as often, not to the Red Sea but to the Indian Ocean, particularly the Persian Gulf and Arabian Sea (as at V. *A*. 8.686; see Casson 1989: 16 on Indian pearls in general, commentary *ad* 35.11.26–7 on the location of the so-called 'Pearl Bank', and *ad* 59.19.22–3 on pearls at the southeastern tip of India). Note the juxtaposition of **niger** and **Rubro**, a common device among poets (and see *ad* 3.2.10, and *passim*, on black and white, *ad* 3.2.10 on *niger*, and André 1949: 75–8 on *ruber*). The two words are sometimes placed near one another in prose; in poetry elsewhere only at Mart. 7.30.4 (*a rubris et niger Indus aquis*), possibly an intertext with this line. Maltby suggests that the line is likely to be earlier than 3.3.17 (2009: 333). Hallett, on the other hand, sees Ov. *Ars* 3.129–30 (*nec caris aures onerate lapillis,/quos legit in viridi decolor Indus aqua*) as alluding to this couplet (2006: 42); cf. too *Tr*. 5.3.24, with similar line-ending.

Proximus Eois...aquis: the Indian Ocean was traditionally considered the border between West and East, and is regularly connected with its native Indians: in addition to Tib. 2.2.15–16, cited above, see Prop. 4.3.10 *tunsus et Eoa decolor Indus aqua*; Ov. *Ars* 1.53 has *nigris...Indis*.

> Hanc vos, Pierides, festis cantate kalendis,
> 22   et testudinea Phoebe superbe lyra.

We move from the material gifts of which S. is worthy (whether she receives them or not) to her worthiness for song. In a manner reminiscent of epic, the Muses are urged to do precisely what the poet, in invoking them, does himself (i.e. sing of S. on the Kalends). At the same time, as many have noted, S. is herself put into the position of a god receiving hymn (Bréguet 1946: 283–4; Lieberg 1980: 146). On the **Pierides**, see *ad* 3.1.5.

Festis...kalendis: see introduction *ad* 3.1 for more on the Kalends of March, and for the phrase *festae...kalendae* in the same metrical *sedes*. It remains unclear whether the author considers S. worthy of song in her quasi-divine capacity, adumbrated earlier, or simply because of the Matronalia (which, again, may or may not be a festival for *puellae*; see *ad* 3.1.1).

Cantate: as Hinds notes, the move from S. as worshipper to divinity, while a common *topos* for *puellae*, 'is very elegantly done' here (1987a: 33). **Phoebe**: at the end of the poem, Apollo is invoked, suggesting a kind of ring-composition with the invocation of Mars at its start (but an odd one, since S. was there presented as a potential erotic object of the war-god; perhaps the mention of Apollo will inspire Mars to hurry up). **Testudinea...lyra**: on the tortoise-shell lyre of Apollo, see *ad* 3.4.37–8 and, for a Propertian intertext, *ad* 3.4.27–8; the phrase occurs in the identical *sedes* at Prop. 4.6.32.

Superbus signifies Apollo's pride in his instrument; the modern negative implications of pride are probably inappropriate here (the word is also used of Apollo at 3.10.2 and Ov. *Met.* 1.454, just before he takes a fall; his sister is *superba* at *Met.* 2.442), although we may wonder how this haughty god will react to being brought in so casually at the end, to finish the job of the '*amicus*' in singing of S. In elegy, the adjective is reserved mostly for difficult love objects (Tib. 1.8.77, 1.9.80, 3.11.4, Prop. 1.18.25, 2.1.8, 2.8.16, 2.21.7, 3.8.36, 3.24.2, 3.25.15, 4.8.82), which further complicates the situation: presumably we are not to see it as introducing a disjunction between the unfussy Mars and the more discerning Apollo as regards S.'s charms.

> Hoc sollemne sacrum multos consummet in annos:
> 24   dignior est vestro nulla puella choro.

The poem concludes with a strange image: although many festivals feature humans singing hymns in honour of gods (in the Greek world, see, notably,

Alcman frr. 1 and 3), the reverse is here imagined. We do not know enough about the Matronalia to determine whether choruses were a regular feature of it; I suspect not. For thorough discussion of what we know about Greek female choruses, see Calame 1997; we know little about any Latin counterpart. So too, the notion of singing *about* S., while flattering in that it suggests her similarities to a goddess, might also be seen as silencing her own poetic voice (depending, of course, upon whether we are to imagine her as composing the choral song). The author of this poem thus locates himself in an intermediate place: he is clearly influenced by the poetry of S.—or at the very least, he seems to know of it—but he does not manage to conceive of her as writing her own poetry. The confusing polyphony of voices (the Muses and Apollo, plus the author—and perhaps also S.) is emblematic of the concerns of this cycle of poetry as a whole, which is willing to act as an advocate for S. but not to allow her full subjectivity; this may support the theories of those who view S. as (in 'real life') marrying Cornutus (Introduction, Section IV). It is perhaps significant too that ancient choruses normally do not sing their own words; like this cycle, they separate authorship from voice.

Consummet: see Tränkle 1990 for discussion of the corrupt manuscript reading *haec sumet*, and other conjectures. **Dignior**: once again, the poet asserts S.'s worthiness, perhaps because her role in this cycle is so extraordinary. **Choro**: though common in Ov., usually in this *sedes*; see too V. *A.* 6.657. In his exile poetry, Ov. (e.g. *Tr.* 5.3.10, *EP* 1.5.58 seems to suggest a community of poets, which may be relevant here.

3.9:

The cycle continues in the first person: 'S.' (though for some, S. herself; see below) addresses first a boar, in mock-epic apostrophe, then her beloved Cerinthus. The poem invokes the elegiac love-as-hunting *topos* (Introduction, Section I; see too Bréguet 1946: 294–304 and Davis 1983) with the gender switch made famous by Phaedra (Euripides', Ov.'s, and perhaps Seneca's; critics have seen verbal echoes of Ov. *Her.* 4.41–4 and Sen. *Phaed.* 110–11 in this poem; see below). Given the relative dearth of hunting poems in Latin literature, Bréguet suggests a Greek, perhaps an Alexandrian, model for this poem and for Ov. *Her.* 4 (1946: 295, 303). The first two lines also share some notable linguistic similarities with Prop. 4.9, on the founding of the Ara Maxima, (see below for details). Fabre-Serris suggests a sustained series of intertexts between this poem and several others (Prop. 2.19, on hunting, and especially Ov. *Her.* 4 and 15, each purporting to be written by a woman pursuing a man), behind all of which she sees the influence of Gallus, in part via V. *E.* 10 and Prop. 1.1 (2009: 158). Note too her suggestion that the interruption of hunting for love-making is a Gallan trope (2009: 159). As Hinds 1987a: 34 notes, the poem, like many of its relatives, both opposes loving to hunting and conflates the opposition.

Beyond this, however, the poem offers a first voicing of S., who was in the previous poem simply a passive object of admiration. Here, in her own person,

S. expresses a typically elegiac jealousy and shamelessness (the latter all the more surprising when put in a woman's voice). As in 3.8, the gods are readily imagined as taking an active interest in S.'s life: indeed, Diana is cast almost in the mould of a rival. Some of the mythological intertexts are puzzling, and it is not always clear that the speaker of the poem is fully in control of their deployment. (The author, presumably, is, and so we are presented with a situation like that in Ov.'s *Her.*, where the female speaker voices utterances of whose ironic nuances she is unaware, while author and audience know more.) Specifically, the allusions to Venus' love for Adonis and Phaedra's for Hippolytus are appropriate to this situation insofar as they engage with desiring female subjectivity (see Bernays 2004: 211 on the former). But in both cases the woman is much older and in a position of power relative to her love object; perhaps more worryingly, he is more or less unwilling. The Venus-allusions also set up a contrast, deriving ultimately from the story of Hippolytus, between (S.'s anxieties about) a young man's choice between what Artemis and Aphrodite symbolize (Fredricks 1976: 777; see e.g. Hor. *Od.* 1.1.25–6 for the trope in Latin poetry). Hinds 1987a: 35 also draws attention to the Homeric love affair of Ares and Aphrodite, revealed to all in *Od.* 8. Finally, Hallett 2009b sees disparaging allusions to S. in Ov.'s treatment of Thisbe's active pursuit of Pyramus in *Met.* 4.

This poem, and 3.11, are usually attributed to the *amicus*, writing in S.'s voice in the first person (i.e., they are presumed to be written by the same author as 3.8, 3.10, and 3.12). Parker 1994, however, has suggested that we might instead attribute them to S. herself; Hallett, in a series of articles (2002a, 2002b, 2006; 2009b, 2011), argues that 3.8–3.12 are all written by S.; 2006: 40 points to connections between this poem and V. *A.* 4. In a somewhat different vein, as Hinds 1987a: 34 notes, the transition between the end of 3.8, which suggests women's voices, leads nicely into this poem, written in S.'s voice. Dronke sees this poem as a direct response, written by S., to the previous: Cerinthus (see introduction to 3.8) compares S. to Venus, and notes that Mars would have a hard time choosing; S. responds by playing Venus, and casting Cerinthus in the role of Adonis (2003: 92). Maltby notes that most of the evidence for the Neronian or Flavian dating of this cycle comes from this poem (2009: 333–4); the parallels are, however, mostly of rare words, and so may not carry much weight.

The poem falls into three sections: the first, ten lines, sets up the situation and the complaint; the second, eight lines, indulges in a fantasy of love-making in the wilderness; the final six lines return to the author's main point, that Cerinthus is better off not hunting at all.

> Parce meo iuveni, seu quis bona pascua campi
> 2   seu colis umbrosi devia montis aper,

Parce meo: cf. *parce meo, iuvenis, temerarius esse periclo* at Ov. *Met.* 10.545, Venus to Adonis (a key intertext for this passage, although with a different construction). While Venus' love too is doomed, she has at least had the sense to appeal to someone who might comprehend her pleas. **Parce** appears often in elegy, usually in this *sedes*; Fabre-Serris 2009: 162 suggests that the verb (which appears also at Ov. *Her.* 4.162 and 167) has a particularly Gallan flavour in this context.

Iuveni too is potentially alarming: while it can be used to describe an elegiac lover (e.g. Prop. 1.9.6, Tib. 1.2.17), it also sometimes refers to the transitional period when young men begin losing their attractiveness to men, and become attractive to women (Tib. 1.4.33, 1.9.55; Tib. 1.8 outlines the difficulties that can ensue). So one of the difficulties the speaker faces (even if only imaginatively) may be that Cerinthus is too young to be interested in her.

Quis: here addressed to the boar: 'whether you inhabit...' with **colis** supplied from the next line. **Bona pascua**: not attested elsewhere; the noun is prosaic. **Pascua campi**: also unattested; presumably a variant of the epic *aequora campi* (first at Enn. *Ann.* 124 Sk. and frequent thereafter, usually in this *sedes*).

Colis: *TLL* 3.1672.46–52 of the habitations of animals. **Umbrosi devia montis** invoke a pastoral landscape, but perhaps also a sacred space (for the former, see, e.g. Prop. 4.9.24–7, containing *umbroso*, *nemus*, and *devia*). **Umbrosi... montis**: also at *Il. Lat.* 654. **Devia montis**: not elsewhere; **devia** features in descriptions of hunting scenes (e.g. Ov. *Met.* 3.146, which, since it describes Actaeon, may also hint at a threat to Cerinthus; Maltby 2009 notes the adjective at Luc. 4.161 and Stat. *Theb.* 5.248). Note too Prop. 2.19.2, *devia rura coles*, of Cynthia hiding herself in the countryside (same *sedes*).

Aper and the act of hunting introduce an ominous note into the world of elegy. Generally, elegiac hunting is metaphorical, referring to the pursuit of women (Introduction, Section I, and e.g. Ov. *Ars* 1.46); the actual hunt is, however, dangerous (see e.g. the Calydonian boar hunt at Ov. *Met.* 8.270–424). Elegy sometimes addresses non-humans, most usually a door; this is the only extant elegiac address to a boar. As Hinds 1987a: 34 notes, this poem begins by looking like a hymn; only the last word of the couplet changes our understanding. The boar is an extremely dangerous animal (Smith 1913 *ad loc.*; see too Xen. *Kyn.* 10 and Sen. *Ira* 1.1.6); the death of Adonis hovers around these lines (mentioned in elegy at Prop. 2.13.53–4, but also known from Bion's lament, and from Ov. *Met.* 10.519–739; see Bréguet 1946: 300–3 on Bion and this poem). The Vergilian Gallus plans to hunt boars (*E.* 10.56), which may be relevant to their presence here (see *ad* 3.9.7–8); but cf. boar-hunting as an innocuous hobby at Hor. *Epod.* 2.29–38.

> nec tibi sit duros acuisse in proelia dentes,
> 4   incolumem custos hunc mihi servet Amor.

The sentence is a funny combination of plea and command. **Tibi sit**: perhaps more regular to have a noun in the nominative, such as *impetus* or *desiderium*, but the construction is acceptable as is (a partial parallel at Prop. 1.20.13–14).

Lines 4–5 introduce Diana and Amor, while 18–21 return to them; the two quasi-prayers mark the start and end of the poem.

Duros…dentes: elsewhere in poetry at Lucr. 5.1064, V. *G*. 1.261–2 (of a plough), 2.378–9. **Acuisse**: sometimes used in love poetry for the arrows of Cupid, as at Prop. 2.9.38, Ov. *Ars* 3.516, *Met*. 1.470, 5.381. **Acuisse…dentes**: also at Hor. *Od*. 3.20.10 (lioness), Sen. *Ira* 1.6 (boars), Sen. *Phaed*. 346–7 (boar); cf. Hom. *Il*. 11.416 of a boar. So too, **proelia** in Tib. and Prop. (but not Ov.) can refer to love battles (Tib. 1.3.64, Prop. 2.1.45, 3.5.2; see Pichon 1991: 241); the literalization here is jarring. See *ad* 3.2.3, 3.4.76, 3.4.92, 3.5.22, 3.6.7 for the elegiac nuances of **duros**.

Incolumem custos: perhaps a *figura etymologica*? **Custos** is removed from its normal elegiac usage (wherein it signifies the doorkeeper who blocks access to the *puella*, so an object of importuning and derision; e.g. *ad* 3.12.11, Pichon 1991: 121). When **Amor** is conceived of as a **custos**, his role does not benefit the lover (at Prop. 2.30.7–9 he sits upon the lover; at Tib. 1.6.51 he guards the *puella* for the lover, but not well; **custos** is also sometimes used of deities, as Apollo at Prop. 2.34.61). And the word order, wherein **custos** is surrounded, undermines any suggestion of his ability to protect.

Mihi servet Amor: same line-ending at Tib. 1.6.76: there, the *puella* is envisioned as feeling a *mutuus…amor* which will keep her faithful, whereas here the *puer* needs assistance.

    Sed procul abducit venandi Delia cura:
6   o pereant silvae, deficiantque canes!

Postgate 1915 posits a lacuna before these lines; the connective is obscure. (Smith 1913 sees no trouble.) The couplet introduces a disquieting note: the speaker is not simply concerned for the safety of her *iuvenis*, she is primarily upset that he chooses to hunt instead of being with her. The tone of the second line may be 'childish' as some suggest—and so charming—or it may rather disturb by its vitriol.

For **procul**, see *ad* 3.4.3, 3.6.7, 3.6.25, 3.14.6, 3.19.7; **procul** at V. *E*. 10.46 in the same *sedes* may add to the evidence for a Gallan source for this passage (see next couplet). **Procul abducit** is a (rare) prosaic construction. The mention of **Delia** is striking; it refers, as often, to Diana, but the author must know that *Delia* has another significance in elegiac poetry (namely, that of Tib.'s mistress in Book 1; see *ad* 3.4.50 and 79); other elegists tend to avoid the adjective in the feminine (of the goddess only at Ov. *Her*. 4.40, 20.97, *Fas*. 5.537; at Ov. *Am*. 3.9.31 and 55 of Tibullus' *puella*). Heinsius conjectured *in devia*, which Luck prints.

The verb **abducit**, common in comedy and elegy (Prop. 2.20.1, Tib. 2.3.61, Ov. *Am*. 1.9.33, *Her*. 8.86, 16.343, *Ars* 2.403, *RA* 777, *Tr*. 3.10.65, mostly about Briseis; see *ad* 3.14.7 and *ad* 3.2.2 *eripuit*) suggests an amatory rivalry between

Diana and S. (perhaps figured as Venus, with a pun on **venandi**). The conjunction **venandi Delia** is thus potentially jarring. On the other hand, Diana does enjoy the company of young men (cf. e.g. Hippolytus), and this cycle envisions the gods as especially likely to interact with human beings. This divine hands-on approach might, or might not, explain S.'s jealousy; compare the story of Cephalus and Procris, best known to us from Ov. *Met.* 7.672–865, with Davis 1983 on variant versions of the myth. On **venandi**, see Pichon 1991: 288. **Venandi...cura**: also at Manil. 5.204 (same *sedes*); **cura** is the instrumental ablative.

O pereant: see *ad* 3.4.62 (especially on the emotional tone of the particle). **Pereant silvae**: not surprisingly, no other passage in Latin wishes that the forests would disappear.

Deficiantque canes is also unattested. The expression is odd; while **deficiant** might simply mean 'disappear', it can also be equivalent to *perire* (*OLD* 6, *TLL* 5.1.329.32–330.46, with Sil. 14.495 and Plin. *NH* 10.37, and Maltby 2009: 333–4).

> Quis furor est, quae mens densos indagine colles
> 8   claudentem teneras laedere velle manus?

This distich, somewhat irregularly for this cycle, does not contain two discrete sense units; instead, in the manner of a net-hunter, the reader must close in on meaning from the edges.

Quis furor est: Tib. 1.10.33, Ov. *Am.* 3.14.7, *Ars* 3.172 (same *sedes*). It is noteworthy that the phrase often occurs when a poet recalls him- or herself from potentially impious or dangerous speech; this poetic persona, by contrast, finds nothing troubling in the previous lines. **Furor** is normal in elegy (and epic), though it usually signifies love-madness (e.g. Prop. 1.1.7, 1.4.11; Pichon 1991: 157–8); note too its presence in the Gallan scene at V. *E.* 10.60. **Quae mens**: same *sedes* at V. *A.* 2.519, where the addressee is (also?) doomed; on **mens**, see *ad* 3.3.21, 3.4.8, 3.4.15, 3.4.19, 3.4.59, 3.4.63, 3.5.13, 3.6.34, 3.12.16.

Densos...colles: not elsewhere in poetry; Tränkle 1990 *ad loc.* notes Sen. *Phaed.* 506 and *Thy.* 413 as parallels for the adjective with this meaning ('thickly wooded'). See Tib. 1.4.49 *claudere valles* (with Hubbard 2004: 192). **Indagine**: technical language, in poetry mostly confined to epic; cf. V. *A.* 4.121 *indagine cingunt* (same *sedes*), which scene may have resonances with this one given that erotics are combined with hunting there as well. The other poetic occurrences of the word are: Ov. *Met.* 7.766 *latos indagine cinximus agros*, Luc. 6.42 *indagine claudit* (same *sedes*), Stat. *Theb.* 2.553–4 *clausas indagine profert/...feras*, 12.451, *Silv.* 2.5.8 *indagine clausus* (same *sedes*), *Ach.* 1.459–60 *feras indigo latentes/ claudit*, Sil. 10.80, 13.141, 14.368 *claudens...indagine* (same *sedes*).

Teneras...manus: first attested at Cat. 61.211, of a child, and Lucr. 6.795, of a woman working; thereafter at Prop. 3.3.34 (Muses), 3.7.48, *et duro teneras laedere fune manus* (Paetus), Tib. 2.3.10 (Tib. himself), [Tib.] 3.12.2 (S.), Ov.

Am. 1.13.18 (boys working), *Her.* 15.216 (Cupid), *Fas.* 4.120 (Venus), 4.774 (girls making clothing), *EP* 4.12.24 (Ov. himself). On *tener* see *ad* 3.4.32, 3.10.1, 3.12.2, and note the *teneras...plantas* of V. *E.* 10.49 (with note immediately below). *Insuetas...manus* at Tib. 1.4.48 in a similar context. **Laedere...manus**: Prop. 3.7.48; the use of the verb at V. *E.* 10.48 (and in Apollo's speech to Daphne, Ov. *Met.* 1.508) may suggest that it had a Gallan flavour. On **laedere**, see Pichon 1991: 182–3, and *ad* 3.9.17 *inlaesus*.

Quidve iuvat furtim latebras intrare ferarum
10   candidaque hamatis crura notare rubis?

Quid...iuvat: a standard poetic question (see *ad* 3.3.18, 3.5.19); Fabre-Serris 2009: 158 sees a connection between the question here and that at Ov. *Her.* 4.87–8 (and also draws into the equation Prop. 2.19.17–18 *ipse ego venabor: iam nunc me sacra Dianae/suscipere et Veneris ponere vota iuvat*); in her view the similarities point to a Gallan source.

Furtim normally refers to a more elegiac activity, such as illicit love-making, both of the love the elegist and his mistress enjoy without the knowledge of others (a good thing: e.g., Cat. 68.136, 145, Tib. 1.2.10, 1.5.7, 65 and 75, [Tib.] 3.11.7 and see *ad loc.*, Prop. 2.9.42, 4.7.15, Ov. *Am.* 1.4.64) and of the love she enjoys apart from him (a terrible thing: e.g., Tib. 1.6.5, Prop. 2.32.17); note the hunting implications of Tib. 1.6.5–6 *nam mihi tenduntur casses; iam Delia furtim/nescioquem tacita callida nocte fovet*. See too *ad* 3.8.8, 3.9.21, 3.11.7.

Latebras...ferarum is poetic, but not elegiac; cf. e.g. Lucr. 6.766, Luc. 2.153; but note *latebris captivarumque ferarum* at Ov. *Met.* 1.475 of Daphne's familiar haunts, and especially in Jupiter's speech to Io at *Met.* 1.593: *quodsi sola times latebras intrare ferarum* (key for Hinds 1987a: 36). This latter intertext (Jupiter is just about to rape Io) perhaps suggests that this poem brings danger to Cerinthus. Adonis' boar found *latebris* at Ov. *Met.* 10.710; for erotic nuances see Pichon 1991: 184. For likely places to find boars, see Xen. *Kyn.* 10.6. **Intrare** has, at least potentially, erotic undertones at Ov. *Her.* 8.96, *Ars* 1.720, 2.358, *RA* 503, *Met* 3.177, 7.814, 14.656.

Crura: objects of elegiac desire in Ov. (*Am.* 1.4.43, 3.2.27, 29, 31, *Ars* 1.156, 3.775, *RA* 317). **Crura candida**: unattested, but see Ov. *Met.* 12.403 *color est...cruribus albus* (cf. *ad* 3.2.10, 3.2.18, 3.4.34, 3.6.1, 3.8.12, 3.10.17 on **candida**). Apollo's speech to Daphne, in which he worries *ne...indignave laedi/ crura notent sentes*, is similar (Ov. *Met.* 1.508–9; cf. Nonn. 16.91–3). There, of course, Daphne is fleeing to protect her virginity, while S.'s love-object gains his wounds in the service of a hobby. Given ancient associations of men with outdoor pursuits (e.g. Hor. *Od.* 1.8.3–4), praise of Cerinthus' limbs as *candidus* may be effeminizing (see too Telephus at Hor. *Od.* 1.13.2–3, who has *cerea... bracchia*, and Introduction, Section IV, on Cerinthus' name).

Hamatis... rubis not elsewhere in poetry; the participle is usually metaphorical in elegy of weapons by which the lover is caught (Cupid's arrows in Prop. 2.12.9, hooks for fish (= women) in Ov. *Ars* 1.47; see Pichon 1991: 163 on these nuances). **Rubis** is not common in elegy; Prop. 4.4.28 describes a similar situation, wherein Tarpeia is scratched on her water-carrying journeys (multiplied beyond necessity by her desire to see Tatius, so the model may be more appropriate than it seems).

Notare occurs with a similar meaning at Prop. 1.6.16, 3.8.6, Ov. *Am.* 1.7.50, 2.6.4, and 3.6.48, mostly of injuries sustained in elegiac *rixae* (*OLD* 4); cf. *crura notent* at Ov. *Met.* 1.509, quoted above. There may also be metapoetic nuance: rather than scratching himself, C. could join S. in scratching out poetry.

> Sed tamen, ut tecum liceat, Cerinthe, vagari,
> 12   ipsa ego per montes retia torta feram,

The couplet contains a lovely inversion of the themes of love/hunting/*militia*, here perhaps even more incongruous than usual in the mouth of S. Similar passages are found at e.g. Tib. 1.4.49–50 *nec velit insidiis altas si claudere valles,/dum placeas, umeri retia ferre negent*, Ov. *Her.* 4.41–2 (written by Phaedra 'herself') *in nemus ire libet pressisque in retia cervis/hortari celeris per iuga summa canes*, *Her.* 5.19–20 *retia saepe comes maculis distincta tetendi;/saepe citos egi per iuga longa canes*, *Met.* 8.331–3 *quo postquam venere viri, pars retia tendunt/vincula pars adimunt canibus, pars pressa sequuntur/signa pedum* (of a boar-hunt), 10.535 *per iuga, per silvas dumosaque saxa vagatur*. Note too Sen. *Phaed.* 110–11 *iuvat excitatas consequi cursu feras/et rigida molli gaesa iaculari manu*, and Phaedra's wishes in a number of sources to be free to roam in the woods (e.g. Eur. *Hipp.* 208–11, Sen. *Phaed.* 394–7). The Milanion exemplum (Prop. 1.1) shares no common words, but is thought by many (e.g. Ross 1975: 61–5 and *passim*) to contain allusions to Gallus, which may also be relevant here; for the *topos* with genders reversed, see e.g. Pi. *P.* 9.5 and Nonn. 16.82–5.

Cerinthe: S.'s *iuvenis* is here first given a name; see Introduction, Section IV. **Vagari**: often of aimless wandering (e.g. Tib. 1.2.25, Prop. 2.29.1, Ov. *Met.* 3.370), perhaps implying S.'s opinion of the pointlessness of the activity, but also used for hunting at Ov. *Met.* 3.146, and of erotic flightiness at Prop. 1.5.7.

Ipsa ego: Fabre-Serris 2009 sees this as Gallan (by way of Prop. 2.19.17, quoted *ad* 3.9.9). **Retia**: usually metaphorical in the elegists (Pichon 1991: 253), but literal at Tib. 1.4.50, and Ov. *Her.* 4.41 and 5.19, all quoted above; cf. 3.9.20. **Torta** normally (in indicative form) of a lover's torments: e.g. Tib. 1.4.81, 1.5.5, 1.8.49, 2.6.17, Prop. 3.6.39, 3.17.11; see *ad* 3.10.11 and 3.20.4. **Retia torta**: elsewhere at Calp. Sic. 7.53–4. On hunting-nets, see Xen. *Kyn.* 2.4–9, Gratt. *Cyn.* 25–33. For **feram** in this context, see Tib. 1.4.50, quoted above.

> ipsa ego velocis quaeram vestigia cervi
> 14   et demam celeri ferrea vincla cani.

It is amusing to note the vocabulary of love as a hunt being used literally here. **Velocis...cervi**: also at V. *A.* 5.253, Ov. *Met.* 1.306 *crura...velocia cervo*; cf. *veloces...dammas* at Sen. *Phaed.* 62. **Vestigia cervi**: cf. Cat. 64.341 *celeris vestigia cervae*, Ov. *Tr.* 5.9.27 *vestigia cervae*, Stat. *Silv.* 2.3.22 (all same *sedes*). The change from boars to deer suggests both allusion to the tale of Venus and Adonis at Ov. *Met.* 10 and S.'s own desire to deflect Cerinthus' hunting towards a less dangerous subject. **Vestigia** may, as often, denote the poetic re-use of familiar material; this scenario is well-trodden ground.

Celeri...cani (a collective singular): phrase in plural at Ov. *Her.* 4.42 (quoted *ad* 3.9.11) and *Fas.* 2.232. **Ferrea vincla**: not attested elsewhere. On *ferreus*, which implies an anti-elegiac stance towards the world, see *ad* 3.2.2.

> Tunc mihi, tunc placeant silvae, si, lux mea, tecum
> 16   arguar ante ipsas concubuisse plagas:

S. is even willing to spend the night out of doors! For the rarity of repetition of **tunc**, see Wills 1996: 109. **Placeant silvae**: a quotation from V. *E.* 2.62 (elsewhere only at Cic. *De Or.* 3.18).

Lux mea is standard elegiac language, probably deriving from its uses in Cat. 68.132 and 160 (see Pichon 1991: 193). That said, the noun is rare in the *CT* and usually signifies actual light (e.g. 2.1.5, 3.3.9, 3.3.25); S. herself uses *mea lux* at 3.18.1 in the same way as here. *Mea lux* occurs at Prop. 2.14.29, 2.28.59, 2.29.1 and Ov. *Am.* 1.4.25, 1.8.23, 2.17.23 (reversed at *Ars* 3.524), each time interjected into the middle of a direct address.

Arguar: found in the elegists (especially Ov.), otherwise prosaic; passive uses at Ov. *Her.* 20.79, 20.224. It is also puzzling: does she mean that she will be proved to have been there (*OLD* 1), or that she can claim to have been there (*OLD* 2)? The verb suggests an interest in public disclosure mirroring that found elsewhere in S.'s poetry (see especially *ad* 3.13.1–2 and 10); see Pichon 1991: 89. Hinds 1987a: 35 suggests that the verb may be meant to remind us of Ares and Aphrodite in Hom. *Od.* 8: 'Sulpicia is still Venus; but as her fantasy moves towards the moment of fulfilment, Adonis is discarded and, with the nets poised to close the trap, Cerinthus is recast in the role of Mars'.

Concubuisse always has an erotic meaning in elegy: Tib. 1.8.35, Prop. 2.15.16, Ov. *Am.* 2.17.18, *Her.* 16.204, *Ars* 2.632, 3.522, *Fas.* 2.592, 4.32, 4.172, 5.86, 6.574, *EP* 4.10.14. **Plagas**, like *retia*, are usually metaphorical snares (e.g. Ov. *Ars* 1.270); see Pichon 1991: 234. Batstone (forthcoming) suggests that this poem reacts to S.'s own poetry, first 3.14 (which wonders why one would ever leave the city), then 3.13 (reacting to S.'s interest in exposure by dressing her in 3.8, and now, by undressing her).

> tunc veniat licet ad casses, inlaesus abibit,
> 18   ne Veneris cupidae gaudia turbet, aper.

S. makes clear her real motivation: as we might have suspected, she's not really interested in hunting. Insofar as the boar has moved from aggressor to (safe) prey, he and S. have switched roles. It is left unclear, perhaps deliberately, whether the boar would in fact interrupt them, or whether Cerinthus would show more interest in the boar than in S.; the (possibly playful) rivalry between *puella* and beast continues below.

Ad casses: again, usually amatory in elegy, pertaining to hunt metaphors (e.g. Tib. 1.6.5, Ov. *Ars* 1.392; see Pichon 1991: 100). **Inlaesus**: it is comic to envision the boar as unharmed (given that the couple are not likely to bother him if they are making love, and he was always more danger to them than they were to him); the contrast between *incolumem* at line 4, applied to Cerinthus, his wish *teneras...laedere manus* (his own) at line 8, and the now-safe boar is amusing, since S. has, unwittingly, placed them both in grave danger.

Veneris cupidae gaudia: cf. [V.] *Lyd.* 59 *dulcia...veneris...gaudia*; **veneris... gaudia** is an Ovidian phrase (*Am.* 2.3.2, *Ars* 2.459, 3.797–8, 3.805, *Met.* 12.198, and thereafter found in Petronius and Martial); cf. Prop. 2.19.17–18 *Veneri ponere vota iuvat*; on **gaudia** see *ad* 3.1.8 and 3.13.5. Fabre-Serris sees this as one of the key words that connects Ov. *Her.* 15 to the S. cycles (2009: 163). **Veneris cupidae**: unattested elsewhere (but for similar play with *cupido*, see e.g. Colum. *DRR* 7.6.3 *immatura veneris cupidine*, Ov. *Met.* 14.634 *Veneris...cupido*, Curt. 6.5.32 *ad venerem...cupido*, Plin. *NH* 28.119.6 *cupiditates veneris*); on *cupidae*, see Pichon 1991: 117.

Turbet: cf. the similar use at Prop. 1.3.17, of waking a sleeping Cynthia.

> Nunc sine me sit nulla venus, sed lege Dianae,
> 20   caste puer, casta retia tange manu,

Nunc: adversative; similar to the Greek νῦν δέ ('but as it is' *OLD* 11a). **Nulla... venus**: cf. Valerius Aedituus 2.5–6 Courtney *at contra hunc ignem Veneris nisi si Venus ipsa/nulla est quae possit vis alia opprimere*, V. G. 4.516 *nulla Venus, non ulli animum flexere hymenaei*, Ov. *Her.* 4.87–8 *quid iuvat incinctae studia exercere Dianae/et Veneri numeros eripuisse suos?*, Prop. 1.14.16 *nulla mihi tristi praemia sint Venere*; cf. Hor. *AP* 320, where the noun has the Catullan meaning of 'charm'. The sentiment may be a response to 3.13.5–6, in which S. had imagined her desire as available to all, at least in poetry (Batstone, forthcoming). **Lege Dianae**: the phrase is otherwise unattested, but this is not surprising; see too Ov. *RA* 199–200, quoted *ad* 3.9.23. Construe with **caste**, 'chaste according to the law of Diana' (and note too the ring composition of *Delia* in the third couplet and **Dianae** in the third couplet from the end). The 'laws' of Diana require chastity, from both male (e.g. Hippolytus) and female (e.g. Callisto) followers.

Caste puer: the use at Hor. *CS* 6 suggests a religious import, but Hor. *Ep.* 2.1.132 seems less specific. The similar-sounding Mart. 8.46.2 *Ceste puer, puro castior Hippolyto* hints that the Phaedra story continues to lurk underneath S.'s words; on *castus*, see *ad* 3.1.23, 3.4.23, 3.4.43, 3.4.60, 3.12.14. The adjective undermines the speaker's wishes. **Casta...manu**: in poetry at Varro *Men.* fr. 27.1, Ov. *Her.* 20.10, *Fas.* 4.260, 4.324, 6.290, Sen. *Phoen.* 222 (note too the ominous Sen. *Phaed.* 261 *castitas vindicem armemus manum*), and occasionally in prose. There is a typical metonymy of **manu** for *mente vel sim*.

> et, quaecumque meo furtim subrepit amori,
> 22 incidat in saevas diripienda feras.

This couplet is surprising, putting a curse on a rival we didn't even know existed; one wonders just how vague *quaecumque* is meant to be. **Furtim**: note the parallel between Cerinthus' underhand behaviour at line 9 and that of this unnamed 'she', which may suggest broader connections between the two (i.e. perhaps they have been sneaking around together). Cf. Tib. 1.6.5–6, *nam mihi tenduntur casses; iam Delia furtim/nescio quem tacita callida nocte fovet*, where Tib. has been (metaphorically) dragged to the country, and finds a rival. See too Prop. 4.3.69–70, in which Arethusa asserts that she only wants Lycotas to return home safely if he has been faithful to her.

Subrepit: as often, the prefix *sub-* carries a notion of sneakiness (cf. in elegy Cat. 77.3 *sicine subrepsti mi*, Tib. 1.1.71); note too the verb's similarity to *surripio*, used of theft, as at Ov. *Am.* 1.1.4, where Cupid removes a foot from Ovid's poetry, and Cat. 99.1 and 16, of stealing a kiss (and see Dell'Era 1996a: 99). Luck prints *Fragmentum Cuiacianum*'s reading *subrepet*.

Diripienda: there is a nice disjunction between the sly *-rep-* of S.'s rival and the *-rip-* she will suffer; in elegy, the verb is usually less violent (Tib. 1.2.84, 1.6.54, 1.10.60; see *ad* 3.6.28). The poet may be thinking of Actaeon (Ruiz Sánchez 1996: 388). On the grammar of the gerundive, see Tränkle 1990 *ad loc*. **Saevas...feras**: apparently first at Tib. 1.10.6 (same *sedes*); cf. Ov. *Her.* 4.38 *est mihi per saevas impetus ire feras*, where the import is rather different, 7.38 (different case, same *sedes*), *Met.* 4.404 *servarum simulacra ululare ferarum*, 7.387 *saevarum more ferarum*. The parallelism between Cerinthus' desire *latebras intrare ferarum* at line 9 and the punishment of the unknown woman is well-crafted.

> At tu venandi studium concede parenti
> 24 et celer in nostros ipse recurre sinus.

The final couplet is even more disturbing, as S. turns sweetly back to Cerinthus. Note again the 'unelegiac' hexameter contrasted with the 'elegiac' pentameter. **Venandi studium**: parallel to *venandi...cura* of line 5; cf. too Ov. *RA* 199–200 *vel tu venandi studium cole: saepe recessit/turpiter a Phoebi victa sorore Venus* with Hinds 1987a: 37.

Concede: the verb is also used at Ov. *Her.* 4.35–6 *si mihi concedat Iuno fratemque virumque,/Hippolytum videor praeposita Iovi*, a reversal of the Catullan *topos* whereby Lesbia claims to prefer Cat. to Jupiter himself. For *concedere* as something the lover wants the beloved to do, see Pichon 1991: 108. **Parenti**: notable because elegy tends not to mention family members (Introduction, Section I); the unelegiac word suits the unelegiac figure. Dell'Era 1996a: 99 discusses the alternative *parumper*.

Celer...recurre: the desired behaviour is precisely parallel to that of a hunter or, more ominously, to prey; the alliteration suggests the speed with which *Ce*rinthus ought to move. The verb is found uncompounded at Prop. 3.20.10 (*in nostros curre, puella, toros*) of a first encounter; the prefix here shows the relationship to be already extant.

In nostros...sinus: see *ad* 3.3.8 on **sinus** and especially *ad* 3.13.4, where the Muse has put Cerinthus there (both with *noster*); cf. 3.19.8, this phrase is also found at Prop. 1.17.12, Ov. *Am.* 2.12.2, 3.2.76, *Her.* 19.62. Fabre-Serris 2009: 165 claims that Ov. *Her.* 15.95, *huc ades inque sinus, formose, relabere nostros*, bears 'striking similarities' to this line; it might merely be an elegiac phrase.

3.10:

Illness is a main theme of this collection (see introduction to 3.5). This poem seems to correspond in some way to 3.17, also about S.'s sickness. Here Apollo is solicited to come and heal S. (and indeed, he may respond; see *ad* 3.10.15). The summoning of Apollo makes sense on a number of levels: he is the god of healing, of course (with a temple in Rome from 431 BCE), but he has also appeared as a god with a special interest in poets, in 3.4. Gaertner 2000b sees the poem as dependent upon Tib. 2.3, esp. lines 9–14. Elegiac girlfriends are ill with some frequency: Tib. 1.5.9–20, [Tib.] 3.17, Prop. 2.9.25–8, 2.28, Ov. *Ars* 2.315–36 (Ov. *Am.* 2.13–14 is a special case, as Corinna is ill from an abortion), and so are poets, though they are usually explicitly lovesick: Cat. 76.25, Tib. 2.5.109–10, Prop. 2.1.58, 2.4.9–16, perhaps Cat. 50.11–16). Here, of course, as throughout her poetry, S. has an ambiguous place, somewhere between *puella* and poet. On the genre of sickness poems, see Yardley 1973 and 1990, the former of which locates it within Hellenistic friendship treatises; see too Holzenthal 1967: 76–85 on this poem. Elegiac poetry regularly plays with the similarities and differences between love and illness; see Introduction, Section I.

The poem continues the cycle's alternation between poem-about-S. and poem-in-her-voice. It is possible, if somewhat strained, to read the poem as a first-person prayer using third-person descriptors (although this is not done in commentaries or in scholarship on the poem; cf. Tib. 1.8). Fredricks 1976: 763 suggests that it is experimental, most especially in its 'objective', third-person treatment of elegiac situations, without an autobiographical commitment on the part of its author, and believes that this calls for a rethinking of the cycle as a whole. She also suggests that this poem marks a more optimistic turn to the collection (780–1). Hallett 2002a: 53 sees in the poem allusions to Dido, particularly in the different effects of *vota* (3.10.12; see *ad loc.*), and in 2002b: 144 suggests a pun on the Valerii Sulpicii in 3.10 and 3.17 (see too *ad* 3.17); Hallett 2009a suggests connections between this poem and Ovid's rendition of Thisbe in *Met.* 4. Dronke 2003 (see introduction to poem 3.8) suggests that the poem is written by Cerinthus, in response to S.'s illness.

The speaking voice of the poem seems to envision a broadly elegiac scenario, but hastens to reassure Cerinthus that S. loves him alone. If this voice is to be trusted, it marks a sharp disjunction from normal elegiac practice, where nothing is secure. So too, the poem continues the objectification of S. found in 3.8; once more she is passively awaiting the action of one or more men.

The poem can be divided into three parts: the first, fourteen lines long, is a prayer to Apollo to heal the sick *puella*, along with a list of the steps he might take; the second, six lines long, reassures Cerinthus that she will both recover and that she loves him; the third, six lines long, again asks Apollo for help and promises the couple's gratitude for it.

> Huc ades et tenerae morbos expelle puellae,
> 2   huc ades, intonsa Phoebe superbe coma.

Compare Prop. 2.28.1, *Iuppiter, affectae tandem miserere puellae* (Navarro Antolín 2005: 320–1).

Huc ades: a regular formula of appeal to a god (Tib. 1.7.49, of Osiris (?); Ov. *Am.* 1.6.54, Boreas; Ov. *Am.* 2.12.16, Triumph; 3.2.46, Venus; *Tr.* 5.3.43, Liber; Caesius Bassus fr. 2.1, Bacchus) or human (V. *E.* 2.45, Alexis; 7.9, Meliboeus; 9.39 and 9.43, Galatea; Tib. 2.1.35, Messalla; Ov. *Her.* 15.95, Phaon), almost always at line-start. It is not elsewhere repeated in consecutive lines (but see V. *E.* 9.39 and 43).

Expelle: the verb is used of Apollo at Tib. 2.3.14a, but of his pastoral duties, *stabulis expellere vaccas* (and so, perhaps, adds an odd resonance here), and at Cat. 44.7 of a cough; cf. the uncompounded forms at Ov. *RA* 115 *pellere morbos* and *Fas.* 3.827 *Phoebea morbos qui pellitis arte*, and a different prefix at V. *A.* 9.328 *depellere pestem*. The verb, with various prefixes, is technical (*TLL* 5.2.1635.34–47), as in Cato, Celsus, Pliny, and Caes. *BG* 6.17 (*Apollinem morbos depellere*).

On **tenerae**, see *ad* 3.4.32 and 3.9.9; also used with **puellae** at 3.12.2. **Intonsa...coma**: used of Apollo's hair at Tib. 2.3.12; see too *ad* 3.4.27. For **superbe** of Apollo, see *ad* 3.8.22 (there of his lyre); note too Prop. 2.1.8, of the *puella* who glories in her hair.

> Crede mihi, propera, nec te iam, Phoebe, pigebit
> 4   formosae medicas adplicuisse manus.

Crede mihi: slightly informal in an address to a god, but otherwise regular in elegy, especially in Ov., usually at the start of the line; the informality of tone may suggest the urgency of the case. **Propera** also suggests that time is of the essence. Combined with **nec...pigebit**, it reintroduces the suggestion of 3.8 that S. is a desirable object that any god would be pleased to get his (healing) hands on. **Phoebe**: Apollo, as god of medicine, is naturally appropriate, but as a god of beauty and youth he might also be expected to care about the loss of S.'s beauty.

For **formosae**, see *ad* 3.1.7; Prop. 2.28.1–2 provides context (*Iuppiter,.../tam formosa tuum mortua crimen erit*). **Medicas...manus**: a Vergilian phrase (V. *G.* 3.455, *A.* 12.402); cf. *TLL* 8.547.27–548.56, probably connected to the temple of Apollo Medicus (Liv. 40.51.7). But note too Tib. 2.3.13–14, of Apollo's inability to heal his lovesickness, *nec potuit curas sanare salubribus herbis:/quidquid erat medicae vicerat artis amor*. **Adplicuisse manus**: not otherwise found together, but see Quint. *Decl. Mai.* 1.11, and similar Greek phrases at Pi. *P.* 4.272, Solon 13.62.

    Effice ne macies pallentes occupet artus,
6   neu notet informis pallida membra color,

Macies can be used both for illness and for lovesickness (the former at Ov. *Met.* 3.397, at 7.290 and 14.578 combined with *pallor*; the latter at Prop. 4.3.27, Ov. *Ars* 1.733, *Met.* 9.536, 11.793); see Pichon 1991: 193 on amatory wasting away. Note too Ov. *Ars* 2.660: *sit gracilis, macie quae male viva sua est*, and 3.267 with Gibson 2003: 197–204, where being *nimium gracilis* is one of many flaws that affect women's bodies (see esp. *ad loc.* for other evidence that thinness was unattractive). **Macies...occupet**: elsewhere only at Hor. *Od.* 3.27.53–4, *antequam turpis macies decentis/occupet malas*; in elegy *occupare* is used of sleep and age stealing over a person (Tib. 1.2.2 and 1.10.40); so too Tib. 1.10.50 of rust gradually wearing down metal and Prop. 2.6.36 of weeds encroaching. There may also be metapoetic nuance; see Call. *Aet.* fr. 1 on the desirability of slim poetry, which becomes a leitmotif for late Republican and early Augustan poets (see too Cameron 1991 (revised 1995: 488–93) for jokes about thinness, some of which have poetic import, and Cameron 1995: 307–31 on the *Aetia* prologue in this context).

The *pallor* of illness is quite different from the normal *candor* of a beautiful person, the former better described by the colour *albus*; **pallentes...artus** is unparalleled, but cf. Ov. *EP* 1.10.27–8: *parvus in exiles sucus mihi pervenit artus/ membraque sunt cera pallidiora nova*. Note too Juv. 15.101, of siege victims: *pallorem ac maciem et tenuis...artus*. *Luto* describes one sick with love at Tib. 1.8.52.

Informis: contrasted with *formosae* of the previous couplet; the word occurs in elegy only at Prop. 1.5.16 and 2.8.33, in the same *sedes*, referring to Gallus after he has felt the wrath of Cynthia, and to the body of Patroclus (see too Holzenthal 1967: 121–8 for the potential role of Gallus in illness poetry). For extended discussion of the word, see Monteil 1964: 66–8. **Informis...color**: not otherwise together, but on **color**, see *ad* 3.1.18 and 3.4.32.

Pallida membra: Ovidian (*Her.* 21.15, *Met.* 4.135, *EP* 1.10.28). Some editors cannot tolerate the repetition in the manuscript reading; Luck prints the attractive *languida*, Tränkle 1990 *tabida*. See Vahlen 1907: 360, Tränkle 1990 *ad loc.*, and Dell'Era 1996b: 121–2. For **membra**, see *ad* 3.5.28.

> et quodcumque mali est et quidquid triste timemus,
> 8   in pelagus rapidis evehat amnis aquis.

Quidquid triste timemus is an indirect way of speaking around what is feared; **quodcumque mali est** (or rather, *quid mali*) is much more familiar (both phrases are prosaic). On **mali**, see *ad* 3.2.8, 3.4.82, 3.17.6, 3.19.20; on **triste**, *ad* 3.2.27, 3.3.35, 3.4.42, 3.6.34, 3.6.38, 3.10.22, 3.14.2, 3.17.3.

Pelagus is a grandiose, epic and didactic word (*TLL* 10.1.990.3), from the Greek πέλαγος; in elegy it occurs only in Ov., but frequently there. **Rapidis**: frequently used of flowing water (e.g. with *mari* at Tib. 1.2.42, *fluminis* at Tib. 1.2.46, *undis* at Ov. *Am.* 3.6.51). **Rapidis ... aquis**: also at Cat. 70.4, Ov. *Am.* 1.15.10, 2.4.8, 3.6.80, *Ib.* 514, Mart. 10.103.2, Sil. 4.596. **Amnis aquis**: a Tibullan and Ovidian line-ending: Tib. 1.4.66 (*aquam*), 1.9.50 (*aqua*), Ov. *Am.* 1.8.50, *Ars* 3.344 (*aquas*), 3.386 (*aqua*), *Fas.* 1.292 (*aqua*), 3.652 (*aquas*), *Ib.* 78 (*aquae*). There may be a Callimachean resonance in the disprivileging of rapid, well-publicized waters (among the bibliography, see esp. Knox 1985, Poliakoff 1980 for the argument that it derives from Pindar).

Evehat: in elegy at Prop. 3.7.63 (see Heyworth 2007 *ad loc.* for discussion of the proper prefix); other verbs are more common with water (e.g. *deferre* at Ov. *Fas.* 6.228).

> Sancte, veni, tecumque feras, quicumque sapores,
> 10   quicumque et cantus corpora fessa levant,

Apollo is requested to do much more actual nursing than we might expect (compare, e.g. Venus in V. *A.* 12.411–22, in which—with much better motivation to intervene personally—she stealthily adds a medicating herb).

Sancte veni: used of Bacchus at Tib. 2.1.81 in the same *sedes*; **sancte** is used of the birthday Genius and Juno at 3.11.12 and 3.12.7 (feminine; see *ad loc.*); of Theseus at Cat. 64.95; of Augustus at Ov. *Fas.* 2.63 and 2.127; of Terminus at *Fas.* 2.658; of a friend at *Tr.* 3.14.1. The word is something of a favourite of the poets of [Tib.] 3; in addition to the instances just listed, see 3.10.24, 3.11.1, 3.12.1, 3.19.15, 3.19.23.

Sapores: normally of flavours (cf. e.g. Tib. 1.7.35), but also of pleasing smells; in poetry, usually in this *sedes* (e.g. V. *G.* 4.62). **Cantus** can refer to incantations as well as love poetry; see Pichon 1991: 98 s.v. *canere* and, for affirmations of their efficacy, Hom. *Od.* 19.457–8, Cato *Agr.* 160.

Corpora: see *ad* 3.2.17, 3.4.30, 3.4.36, 3.4.81, 3.10.20, 3.17.2; **fessa** is in elegy non-erotic (as opposed to *lassus*): e.g. Tib. 1.2.2, 1.3.88, Prop. 1.3.42, 3.12.8, 3.24.17, Ov. *Am.* 2.9.19, *Her.* 18.162, 19.56, 21.14. **Corpora fessa**: see 3.17.2 (same *sedes*); also in poetry at Cat. 64.189, Lucr. 4.848, V. *A.* 4.522–3, Gratt. *Cyn.* 473, Ov. *Met.* 11.624–5, Luc. 4.623. Note too Hor. *CS* 63–4 [*Phoebus*] *qui salutari levat arte fessos/corporis artus*, of illness. See Axelson 1945: 29 on the poetic tone of the adjective.

>   neu iuvenem torque, metuit qui fata puellae
> 12 votaque pro domina vix numeranda facit.

Here we discover, perhaps to our surprise, that the *amor* of previous poems is mutual; up to now, we had not known whether Cerinthus' desire to hunt was inspired by, or masked, a lack of interest in S.

On the elegiac **iuvenem**, see *ad* 3.2.1. **Torque** often describes what elegiac lovers do to one another (e.g. Tib. 1.8.49 *neu Marathum torque*); see *ad* 3.9.12 for a different use, and Pichon 1991: 281. **Metuit** is also quintessentially elegiac; see Pichon 1991: 200–1. For **fata** as equivalent to death, see *OLD* 6, *TLL* 6.1.359.22–360.77.

For **vota**, see *ad* 3.3.1, 3.3.33, 3.4.4, 3.4.53, 3.4.83, 3.6.27, 3.11.9, 3.12.20. **Vota** are regularly made during the *puella*'s illnesses: e.g. Tib. 1.5.10 and 15–16, Prop. 2.9.25, 2.28.59–62, Ov. *Am.* 2.13.24, *Ars* 2.327. **Vota…facit**: cf. e.g. Cic. *Att.* 8.16.1 *illo aegroto vota faciebant* for the practice. See *ad* 3.4.74 on **domina**.

Numeranda: on the countlessness of the lover's feelings, see Cat. 5 and 7 (with *numerus* at 7.3), Ov. *Her.* 18.107 (*gaudia noctis* are *non…numerari*). **Vix numeranda**: not elsewhere; **vix** with the gerundive in elegy appears at Prop. 4.8.72, Ov. *Her.* 7.143, 16.178, 18.8, *Fas.* 1.556, *Tr.* 3.3.22, 3.4.42, *EP* 1.4.28, 1.8.12.

>   Interdum vovet, interdum, quod langueat illa,
> 14 dicit in aeternos aspera verba deos.

The repetition of **interdum** does not occur elsewhere in elegy. **Langueat** is often used in an erotic sense, of satiety (e.g. Tib. 1.9.56; Pichon 1991: 183–4), and, in Ov., of illness real and metaphorical (cf. Tib. 2.6.49, where the *puella* feigns illness). See too Ov. *Am.* 3.7.27, *Ars* 2.336 and *RA* 511, where the verb is used of a waning of erotic interest or arousal. And see *ad* 3.4.22, 3.5.28. For causal **quod** with the subjunctive, see e.g. Tib. 2.3.9 (noted by Smith 1913 *ad loc.*).

Aeternos deos: also at Tib. 2.3.30, Ov. *RA* 688, *Fas.* 3.804, 4.954, 6.322 (same *sedes*). **Aspera verba**: mostly prosaic; in same *sedes* at Ov. *EP* 2.7.56 and elsewhere at *EP* 2.6.8, Sil. 10.272. For **aspera**, see Pichon 1991: 91. Note too the similarities to Tib. 1.3.52 *non dicta in sanctos impia verba deos* (with Maltby 2009); there the sick poet claimed that he had not spoken sacrilegiously; here the poet says that the *amator* has. He seems, however, unconcerned with the blasphemy.

Pone metum, Cerinthe: deus non laedit amantes.
16   **Tu modo semper ama: salva puella tibi est.**

Generally speaking, narrative tension is created by the fact that the elegiac lover never knows what will happen. But this cycle is more optimistic than elegy as a whole. It is, further, not clear whether we are to understand the next six lines as spoken by the poet, or by the god (presumably the former); see Fredricks 1976: 771–3.

    Pone metum: an Ovidian phrase, usually in this *sedes*; note especially at *Her.* 20.1, also of illness. Dronke 2003, who sees the lines as self-address, adduces *miser Catulle* (Cat. 8.1) as a parallel.

    Deus non laedit: probably the singular for plural, as usual, but Apollo may be meant, since he has already been invoked. Might we also be meant to hear a hint of the Hippocratic 'first, do no harm'? See *ad* 3.4.16 on *laedo* of harming the gods (rarer with this reversal, but cf. Ov. *Met.* 14.40). **Non laedit amantes**: for parallels, see Prop. 3.16.11 *nec tamen est quisquam, sacros qui laedat amantes*; *contra*, Ov. *Ars* 2.515 *plus est, quod laedat amantes*. It is fairly rare in elegy, and in the *CT*, to have a sense-break at the end of the hexameter.

    Semper ama: the first half of the pentameter has a gnomic feel; similar passages occur at e.g. Ov. *Am.* 1.3.2 *aut amet aut faciat, cur ego semper amem*, 2.4.10 (*centum sunt causae, cur ego semper amem*), *Her.* 15.80 (*et semper causa est, cur ego semper amem*), 17.254 (*bella gerant fortes, tu, Pari, semper ama*); note too Prop. 2.13.52 *fas est praeteritos semper amare viros*, 2.22.18 *mi fortuna aliquid semper amare dedit*. It is part of the elegiac condition to always love (even if, as the passages show, it is not always a single love-object).

    Salva puella: in same *sedes* at Prop. 2.28.44, of recovery from illness, and Prop. 2.9.3, of preserved chastity; perhaps both senses are meant here (note too Tib. 1.5.19, and *salvo grata puella viro* at Prop. 4.3.72).

21   **Nil opus est fletu: lacrimis erit aptius uti,**
22   **si quando fuerit tristior illa tibi.**

The couplet is almost universally transposed here, where it makes significantly more sense; for brief discussion, see e.g. Cairns 1972: 155 and Yardley 1977: 396–7.

    Fletu: lacrimis: as per generic expectations (see Introduction, Section I), the lover is often in tears (see especially Prop. 3.8.24, *sive tuas lacrimas sive videre meas*, which demands that one party or the other cry). Sometimes these tears are designed to manipulate the *puella* (Ov. *Ars* 2.325–6 *et videat flentem, nec taedeat oscula ferre,/et sicco lacrimas conbibat ore tuas*); **uti** suggests a certain premeditation on the part of Cerinthus. **Lacrimis**: see *ad* 3.2.25. For *aptus*, see Pichon 1991: 88.

Si quando is not common in elegy, but does occur (Prop. 1.17.27, Ov. *Am.* 1.13.6 in this *sedes*). **Tristior** has its standard elegiac meaning here, i.e. if she is unfavourable to you (e.g. Tib. 1.6.2, 2.3.33); it marks a noteworthy change from line 7, where real life has intruded (but also suggests that this relationship does bear affinities to the elegiac norm). On the other hand, the comparative may suggest a limit to elegiac misery ('somewhat upset'). Further on *tristis*, see *ad* 3.2.27, 3.3.35, 3.4.42, 3.6.34, 3.6.38, 3.14.2, 3.15.1, 3.17.3.

    At nunc tota tua est, te solum candida secum
18   cogitat, et frustra credula turba sedet.

At nunc often has a resumptive sense: i.e., 'but as it is' (cf. *ad* 3.9.19). But the temporal nuance is also important: (only?) 'right now', in keeping with the ominous tone of the previous couplet. **Tota tua est** is unusual in elegy, which is predicated upon uncertainty and suspicion; note too 3.12.4 *tota tibi est* (and the opposite situation, *ad* 3.1.20, where L. has fallen away from N. *toto pectore*); cf. Prop. 4.8.48 *totus eram* with Heyworth 2007 *ad loc*. It is not clear whether the author is optimistic, or simply ill-informed. Note the alliteration of *t-*, *s-*, and *c-* sounds, which gives the lines an incantatory quality.

Te solum: again, an uncommon phrase (and presumably, sentiment) in elegy: elsewhere only at 3.18.5, where it means 'by yourself'. **Candida**: see *ad* 3.2.10; here probably not physical, but something like 'innocent', as at Ov. *Am.* 2.18.29 of Penelope. **Secum/cogitat**: as Smith 1913 notes *ad loc.*, this construction is extremely rare, for metrical reasons, in dactylic metres; the verb is also relatively rare.

This **credula turba** is puzzling, and raises again questions about S. Were she a normal elegiac *puella*, it could be her host of admirers (see e.g. Prop. 2.6.3, where the noun is used of the devotees of prostitutes), but that seems inappropriate for one of her status; **turba** does not easily lend itself to senatorial suitors. The noun is frequent in Tib., and normally describes the lower classes, unsavoury groups, or children; partial exceptions occur at 1.4.9 (*puerorum... turbae*, always loveable), 1.4.80 (those who surround the *magister amoris*), 2.1.16 (of a religious procession); see too 3.10.25 and 3.19.12. On the other hand, Prop. 3.14.29 claims that no Roman girl can leave the house without a *circumdata turba* protecting her, and Ov. regularly uses the noun for a small group (e.g. *Am.* 1.1.6). The fact that S.'s is **credula** suggests that it is composed of would-be lovers fondly imagining that she might be thinking of them, rather than of bodyguards or matrons. **Credula**: often in elegy of those being deliberately deceived (e.g. Prop. 1.3.28, 2.21.6, 2.25.22); note Ov.'s observation *credula res amor est*, *Her.* 6.21 and *Met.* 7.826; see Pichon 1991: 115. **Credula turba** also occurs together at Ov. *Fas.* 2.716, of Romans misunderstanding an oracle, 4.312 of our habit of believing the worst (dangerous to the Vestal Claudia Quinta), and *RA* 686 on our tendency to flatter ourselves (all same *sedes*).

Sedet: we may be meant to think of the participle at Cat. 51.3 and its Sapphic model; there a rival is certainly meant. In amatory elegy, the verb can refer to the elegiac practice of waiting for the *puella* to open her door (Tib. 1.1.56). *Adsideo* is the more regular verb for sitting by a patient's bed (e.g. Ov. *Her.* 20.134, 137, 21.191; *TLL* 2.877.35–878.51).

> Phoebe, fave: laus magna tibi tribuetur in uno
> 20   corpore servato restituisse duos.

Fave: a verb regularly applied to the gods: Tib. 2.5.1, on Messalinus' installation as a priest of Apollo, has the identical first two words. L.'s use is somewhat different, in that he prefers the subjunctive (3.3.33 and 3.3.34 for gods, 3.6.9 for mortals; 3.4.44 in the indicative). Imperatives also at [Tib.] 3.11.9 and 3.12.7; cf. also *ad* 3.19.24. Imperatives occur in the same *sedes* also at Prop. 4.1.67 (*Roma*), Ov. *Fas.* 3.714 (*Bacche*), 4.1 (*Alma*), 6.249 (*Vesta*) and not in the same *sedes* at Ov. *Fas.* 1.468, *Am.* 2.13.21, *Ars* 1.146. The author leaves unclear whether the favour of Phoebus will be shown by his mere appearance, his healing talents, his allowing the happy couple to stay together, or all three (the remainder of the couplet suggests healing).

Laus: praise—presumably in poetic form—is suitable for both gods (Apollo at Tib. 2.5.4) and mortals (Tib. 1.9.47), though it is less frequently offered as a bribe for specific services rendered. **Laus magna**: mostly prosaic; in poetry at V. A. 5.751, Hor. *Serm.* 2.3.99, Ov. *Am.* 2.9.16, *EP* 4.13.48, VF 1.104–5, 5.83, Sil. 17.188. **Laus...tribuetur**: in poetry only at Prop. 3.24.3 *noster amor talis tribuit tibi, Cynthia, laudes*, Manil. 4.141–2 *praemia laudis/...tribuet*.

In uno...duos: the image of two saved in one occurs also at Prop. 2.28.41–2, and becomes beloved of Ovid; see Ov. *Her.* 20.233, *Met.* 3.473, 11.388 (explicit at *Am.* 2.13.15, with a twist at *Her.* 11.60). On the history of the *topos*, see Bréguet 1962.

Corpore servato: not otherwise joined, though various similar phrases exist with noun and verb. **Restituisse**: Ennian (*Ann.* 12.63, of Fabius); thereafter common in poetry, but especially Ov. (*Am.* 1.12.4, *Her.* 4.8, *Ars* 2.492, *Fas.* 1.626, 2.86, 2.242, 3.16, 3.68, 6.288, *Tr.* 3.3.22, *EP* 3.6.36, 4.13.38 in this *sedes*; often elsewhere).

> Iam celeber, iam laetus eris, cum debita reddet
> 24   certatim sanctis laetus uterque focis.

Iam seems to suggest that Apollo requires the praises of S. and Cerinthus in order to be **celeber** and **laetus**. **Celeber**: of Messalla at Tib. 2.1.33, and Cupid at 2.1.83; otherwise in erotic elegy primarily of places, poems, and festivals (with an exception at Ov. *Her.* 5.3, where Oenone uses it of herself); see *ad* 3.5.29. It is also used of other gods throughout poetry, e.g. Diana at Hor. *Od.* 2.12.20, Isis at Ov. *Met.* 1.747 (*celeberrima*). **Laetus**: for the satisfaction of the gods, see e.g. Ov. *Tr.* 2.72 (Jupiter, because he is praised in gigantomachies); for elegiac nuances, Pichon 1991: 183. There is something vaguely troubling about the application of **laetus** to both mortal and god; Martini's conjecture *gratus* may be preferable in line 24 (see Cartault 1909: 251 for defence of the text as printed).

Debita reddet: prosaic (e.g. Cic. *Verr.* 2.2.51); similar phrases in poetry usually contain a noun (or two), e.g. Prop. 2.28.60 (*munera...debita redde choros*; cf. Cartault 1909), V. *A.* 2.538 *praemia*, Ov. *Fas.* 4.898 *vina*, *Tr.* 2.160 *amor*; cf. Ov. *Fas.* 5.596 *voti debita solvit*. **Certatim**: a somewhat rare adverb in poetry; Cat. 64.392 (the Delphians welcoming Liber) offers the most relevant parallel: *cum Delphi tota certatim ex urbe ruentes*.

Sanctis focis: a combination found also at Tib. 1.2.84 and 1.8.70, Ov. *Fas.* 3.734, 4.296, and *EP* 2.1.32 in same *sedes*, and see *ad* 3.10.9, where the adjective is used of Apollo. **Focis** reminds us of the (apparently) private nature of this poetry (see too 3.11.12 and 3.12.4).

> **Tum te felicem dicet pia turba deorum,**
> 26   **optabunt artes et sibi quisque tuas.**

Picking up on *laetus* in the previous couplet, the poem ends with the suggestion that Apollo is competing with the other gods for mortal favour. Indeed, **felicem**, which means 'blessed by the gods', is strange applied to a god (citations at *OLD* 2 and *TLL* 6.1.439.16–48 all mean 'propitious' rather than 'fortunate'); see *ad* 3.3.26 and *passim*.

Pia turba: Prop. 3.13.18, Ov. *Fas.* 2.507, *Tr.* 5.3.47, [Ov.] *Ep. Drus.* 296, Luc. 8.79, VF 1.750, Sil. 10.592, all in same *sedes*, and generally of those worshipping gods rather than gods themselves. **Turba deorum**: elsewhere in poetry at Ov. *Fas.* 2.667–8, *Tr.* 4.1.54, [V.] *Aetn.* 62, Sen. *Thy.* 843, Stat. *Silv.* 3.1.108–9, Juv. 13.46 (cf. *divum/turba* at e.g. VF 6.626–7).

Optabunt artes: a seemingly unattested phrase, but see e.g. Ov. *Am.* 1.1.7–12 for the (ridiculous) prospect of gods switching roles, and note too Mars' encroachment upon Minerva's duties at Ov. *Fas.* 3.171–6.

3.11:

This is another poem about a particular day, which happens quite often in [Tib.] 3 and sometimes in Tib. (1.7, 2.5); see Introduction, Section I. Like 3.9, it is focalized through S., and its occasion is Cerinthus' birthday. See Cairns 1972 index s.v. *genethliakon* on birthday poems, which we first find in Latin and Greek in the Augustan period (others include Hor. *Od.* 4.11, V. *E.* 4 (at least in part a birth poem), Prop. 3.10 with Cairns 1971 and 1972, Tib. 2.2, Stat. *Silv.* 2.7; for the first Greek examples, see Crinagoras *AP* 6.227, 6.261, 6.345, all accompanying presents). Quite a number of these occasions are, however, also public holidays, or at least are publicly celebrated; *tectius* and *clam* of 17 and 20 situate this poem in a rather different context. Cesareo 1929 and Argetsinger 1992: 180–5 discuss Roman birthday poems, and Bowerman 1917 surveys Latin poetry in which birthdays are mentioned; see too Müller 1952: 68 on birthdays as an elegiac theme. On the contemporary resonances of birthdays and other anniversaries in the Augustan period (shortly after the Julian reorganizing of the calendar in 45 BCE), see Hinds 2005: 221–2; Feeney 2007: 148–51, 156–60. Martial suggests that birthdays were celebrated on their respective Kalends (8.64, 9.52, 10.24, 12.60), at least in the Flavian period. So the birthday poems in this cycle may be more closely connected to the two Kalends of March poems (3.1 and 3.8) than at first appears.

If Cerinthus were a *puella*, his birthday would be an occasion to avoid him, because he would want gifts (Ov. *Ars* 1.405); S. is a typical *amator* in considering poetry to be an appropriate present. Like much of this cycle, the poem thus poses the question of which of the pair of lovers is the appropriate subject and which the object of love poetry: S., who has primarily been the object of various kinds of gazes (admiring, concerned), suddenly becomes an agent, as well as the speaker: she is the active party in this poem in a way that she was not in 3.9. Indeed, S. displays a remarkable degree of forwardness and confidence about the reciprocity of her love; unlike in most elegy, she proclaims herself secure in the knowledge that her love is mutual. (The hopeful aspects of her diction can be paralleled from other elegies, the assertive ones less easily.) Dronke 2003, following Parker 1994, suggests that this poem should be counted among the works of S. (rather than her *amicus*); see Introduction, Section V.

The poem falls into two halves: the first five couplets celebrate the birthday of Cerinthus, while the second five question, then affirm, his feelings for the *puella*.

>   Qui mihi te, Cerinthe, dies dedit, hic mihi sanctus
> 2   atque inter festos semper habendus erit.

Cerinthe: Cerinthus, the addressee, despite this direct address, is curiously passive. **Dies dedit:** Fredricks 1976: 778–9 notes that the poem is not, at its start, obviously a genethliacon; at first we are more likely to think it commemorates the day the two lovers met. **Hic:** as Smith 1913 notes *ad loc.*, the deictic indicates that the poem was written (or presented) on the day itself. **Sanctus:** used of birthdays at Hor. *Od.* 4.11.15–17 *dies... sanctior*; **dies... sanctus:** elsewhere at Afr. 141R (*sanctum diem Dianae*). The adjective is common in [Tib.] 3; see *ad* 3.10.9.

Festos is used of a variety of celebratory occasions, some general and some specific, e.g. Tib. 2.1.29, 2.1.81, 2.5.36, 2.5.87, 2.5.99; cf. *ad* 3.1.1 and, for amatory nuances, Pichon 1991: 258. **Habendus erit:** an Ovidian line-ending (*RA* 376, 564, 630; the gerundive often in this *sedes*).

> Te nascente novum Parcae cecinere puellis
> 4 servitium et dederunt regna superba tibi.

Te nascente: unparalleled, but the conceit suggests such mythic parallels as Adonis or Phaon, who even as babies attracted the attention of Venus; perhaps this poem continues the role-playing of 3.9.

Novum…servitium: elsewhere at VF 2.180–1 (but see *servitus…nova* at Hor. *Od.* 2.8.18); this couplet marks the introduction of the quintessentially elegiac notion of *servitium amoris* into the book (see Introduction, Section I). Beyond that, though, it objectifies Cerinthus in a way that is traditionally feminine, despite its overt suggestion of him as a master: as an object of the gaze of *puellae*, Cerinthus has a power of his own, but it is essentially passive (Hinds 1987a: 38). Girls are here envisioned as trapped or captured into love rather than, as is normal in most genres of ancient poetry, as trapping others. Batstone (forthcoming) suggests this line may be a response to 3.16.4, which denotes S. as *Servi filia* (see *ad loc.*).

Parcae cecinere: the Parcae often sing as they weave the fates; here their singing and their weaving are combined into a single action; cf. Cat. 64.303–22 and 383 *carmina divino cecinerunt pectore Parcae*, Tib. 1.7.1–2 *hunc cecinere diem Parcae fatalia nentes/stamina, non ulli dissolvenda deo*; Ov. *Tr.* 5.3.25–6 *scilicet hanc legem nentes fatalia Parcae/stamina bis genito bis cecinere tibi*. On **Parcae** as present at birth (note their etymological connection with *partus*; Varro *apud* Gell. 3.16.10), see V. *E.* 4.46–7 '*talia saecla*' *suis dixerunt* '*currite*' *fusis/concordes stabili fatorum numine Parcae*, Ov. *Met.* 8.451–6, *Tr.* 5.3.14 *nascenti…mihi Parca fuit*. They are also wedding-divinities, which may be implicit in the context here; in addition to Cat. 64, see Aristoph. *Av.* 1731–4. **Puellis**: in elegy, the possibility of (multiple) rivals is never far; note the line-ends *puellis* and *tibi*, which establish the basic situation: one man, many eager *puellae*.

Dederunt: parallel to *dedit* on line 1; see Platnauer 1951: 53 for the shortening of 'e' in perfect plurals. **Regna superba**: also at Tib. 1.9.80 and Prop. 4.1.88 in the same *sedes*; *superbia* has before now in [Tib.] 3 been characteristic only of Apollo (3.8.22, 3.10.2). But *puellae* are often arrogant: Tib. 1.8.77, Prop. 1.18.25, 2.1.8, 3.8.36, 3.24.2, 4.8.82, Ov. *Am.* 1.6.58, *Her.* 5.92, 21.33, *Ars* 3.302, 3.509, and especially Tib. 1.9.80 *et geret in regno regna superba tuo* (a *puer*). For the idea of beauty giving **regna** to the *puella*, see Prop. 3.10.18, Ov. *Am.* 2.17.11 *si facies animum dat et omina regni*; also Ov. *Am.* 1.1.13 and 2.9.53 (to Cupid).

> Uror ego ante alias: iuvat hoc, Cerinthe, quod uror,
> 6 si tibi de nobis mutuus ignis adest.

The lines seem to suggest a decrease in confidence. **Uror**: S., who used to burn others (see *ad* 3.8.11–12, where the verb is also repeated), now herself burns, but the flame is mutual (or, more precisely, she is pleased *if* it is); Dronke sees the allusion as more specific, and suggests that in this poem S. responds directly to

Cerinthus' words, reframing herself as also a victim of love (2003: 95). While the flames of love are a common trope, they do not appear in L.'s poetry; cf. *ad* 3.17.17, 3.19.19, and e.g. Tib. 2.4.6 *uror, io, remove, saeva puella, faces*. See Adams 1999: 125 on the placement of **ego** as 'contrastive emphasis'. On **ante** as a comparative see *ad* 3.4.93. Fabre-Serris 2009: 155 and 163 sees here influence from Sappho 2.44 and on Ov. *Her.* 4.19–20 and *Her.* 15.9–10 (both with *uror*). Such phrases as Ov. *Her.* 19.5 *urimur igne pari* may suggest that it is simply a *topos,* but Sen. *Phaed.* 415 *mutuos ignes ferat* adds weight to the Phaedra implications here.

Iuvat more regularly introduces an infinitive or even a condition, but a causal *quod* clause is not unparalleled. This line is unusual in the number of elisions, which the poets of [Tib.] 3 tend to avoid.

De nobis: the phrase is slightly obscure; presumably it is an ablative of cause, and Cerinthus is to be understood as catching fire from S. (see above on *uror*, with Dronke's interpretation). The notion is common enough, but not elsewhere phrased so vividly. **Mutuus ignis**: a common wish, even if not elsewhere in these words (excepting Sen. *Phaed.* 415, quoted above); see Pichon 1991: 165–6 s.v. *ignes*. Hallett 2002b: 147 sees a specific allusion to Cat. 45. Note too the imagery of *mutua vincla* at 3.12.8.

> Mutuus adsit amor, per te dulcissima furta
> 8   perque tuos oculos per Geniumque rogo.

The couplet uses the Ovidian trick of repeating words in successive lines. **Adsit**: the subjunctive perhaps suggests a lack of confidence, which is either overcome or covered over by the end of the poem.

Per te: not, as it first seems, the object of the preposition; rather, **te** is the object of **rogo**, and the object of **per** is postponed. **Dulcissima furta**: part of the standard elegiac vocabulary (Prop. 2.30.28, V. *G.* 4.346, Ov. *Met.* 9.558); see *ad* 3.3.27, 3.4.42, 3.6.9, 3.14.3 on *dulcis*, and *ad* 3.8.8, 3.9.9, 3.9.21 on *furta*). Swearing by one's own infidelity also occurs at e.g. Tib. 1.5.7 *per te furtivi foedera lecti*. Hallett 2002a: 53 may be correct to see V. *A.* 4.172 *furtivum ... amorem* as a model. **Tuos oculos**: on swearing by a loved one's (or one's own) eyes, see *ad* 3.6.47; Ov. *Am.* 3.11.48 has **perque tuos oculos** in the same *sedes*.

Genium: the role of the *Genius* in Roman religion is not entirely clear; see *ad* 3.6.48. Rose 1923 and Nitzsche 1975:7–8 see its origins in fertility and family preservation; see Cesareo 1929: 43–63 for discussion of poetry about and for the Genius. Other citations at Plaut. *Capt.* 977 *per tuom te genium*, Ter. *And.* 289 *per ... genium tuom*, Hor. *Od.* 3.17.14–16, *Ep.* 1.7.94 *te per Genium*, Prop. 4.8.69, Petr. 37.3, 53.4, 57.11, 62.14, 74.14, 75.2, Sen. *Ep.* 12.2; he is explicitly a birthday god at Tib. 1.7.49 and 2.2.5, Pers. 2.3. Smith 1913 suggests *ad loc.* that, especially given its predominance in Petronius, the birth-god is appropriate to those of freed status rather than the freeborn; there is no way of knowing, but if correct, this would tell us something important about Cerinthus.

>   Magne Geni, cape tura libens votisque faveto,
> 10   si modo, cum de me cogitat, ille calet.

The speaker adopts a more formal tone, as befits a direct prayer. While swearing by someone else's Genius does occur, prayers to him are otherwise unattested (as we would expect, given the extremely personal nature of the god). **Magne Geni**: unattested in the singular; see Smith 1913 and Tränkle 1990 *ad loc.* for discussion of the manuscript reading *mane* (an older form of the adjective) and other conjectures. But **magne** is frequent for direct address to the gods (most often Jupiter); cf. *ad* 3.8.1 for its use of Mars.

  Libens: the participial form is relatively rare, occurring in elegy only at Prop. 1.2.28 and 2.24.27. On **votis**, see *ad* 3.3.1.

  De me cogitat: elsewhere in elegy with this construction only at Ov. *Ars* 2.686 (*de lana cogitat*); not uncommon in poetry (*OLD* 2), though mostly prosaic (*TLL* 3.1462.4–33). **Calet**: while the metaphor of love as a flame is an old one (see *ad* 3.8.6 and 3.11.5–6, and Pichon 1991: 97), this verb appears only infrequently in elegy: Tib. 1.10.53, Ov. *Her.* 18.90, 18.177, *Am.* 3.6.83, *Ars* 1.526, 3.571; cf. Petr. 79.8, Sen. *HO* 377.

>   Quodsi forte alios iam nunc suspiret amores,
> 12   tunc precor infidos, sancte, relinque focos.

The couplet hints at jealousy, as in 3.9. (This emotion has so far only been attributed to S. by her poet, with what grounds remains unclear.) **Suspiret**: used in amatory contexts at e.g. Cat. 64.98 (*in flavo…hospite*), Prop. 2.24.5 (*nobis*), Ov. *Ars* 3.675, *Fas.* 1.417 (*in illa*), and see *OLD* 1c; it is not often used with the accusative, but see e.g. Tib. 1.6.35 (*te tenet, absentes alios suspirat amores*) and [V.] *Lyd.* 3 (*nostrum suspirat amorem*); see too *ad* 3.6.61 *suspiria*. There is manuscript division between **suspiret** and *suspirat*; the subjunctive is probably better than the indicative as suggesting S's unwillingness to believe.

  Infidos: of the **focos** because they have refused to fall in with her plans. Smith 1913 suggests *ad loc.* that the Genius also looked after the bed, so that the poet, or S., can conceive of infidelity as sacrilege (see further *ad* 3.12.4). For *infidus*, see Pichon 1991: 169.

  Sancte: regularly of gods or their locales (with *focis* at Tib. 1.2.84 and 1.8.70, possibly influencing this passage), and in the vocative of Cupid at 2.1.81; see *ad* 3.10.9, 3.11.1, 3.12.1, 3.12.7, 3.19.23. **Relinque**: it is not at all clear what it would mean for a birth-spirit to leave; matters may be as benign as at Tib. 2.3.64: *tu quoque devotos, Bacche, relinque lacus*, which would result in spoilt wine, but there may be a hint that the desertion of his Genius would mean the loss of his life (not exactly parallel is the story of Meleager, told at Ov. *Met.* 8.451–525). Whatever the poet means, the sentiment is ill-omened (see too the verb at e.g. V. *E.* 5.35); cf. the curse of forests placed in S.'s mouth at 3.9.6, and of the rival at 3.9.22.

Nec tu sis iniusta, Venus: vel serviat aeque
14   **vinctus uterque tibi vel mea vincla leva.**

This couplet can be seen as a radical reinterpretation of the usual understanding of *servitium amoris*, in which the trope represents not hierarchy but intimacy (see Fulkerson 2013, which also argues that this state is in fact what the elegists ultimately desire). S., at least as she is described here, is not interested in elegiac suffering. Alternatively, the multiplicity of possibilities might express S.'s uncertainty (see *ad* 3.1.19–20).

Iniusta: see Tib. 1.5.58 *saevit et iniusta lege relicta Venus*, Pichon 1991: 170 (179 s.v. *iustus*), and below *ad* 3.19.24; injustice is the standard complaint of the elegiac lover (e.g. Prop. 1.7.12, 2.5.14). See too Tib. 1.2.99–100 *at mihi parce, Venus: semper tibi dedita servit mens mea*, 2.3.29–30 *felices olim, Veneri cum fertur aperte servire aeternos non puduisse deos*, 2.4.4 *et numquam misero vincla remittit Amor*, and, from another genre, Hor. *Od.* 1.33.10–12 *sic visum Veneri, cui placet imparis/formas atque animos sub iuga aenea/saevo mittere cum ioco*. **Venus**: once again, the Olympian gods are envisioned as having a direct personal interest in the poets of the collection.

Serviat: this slight variation on the *topos* of *servitium amoris* may owe its existence to Cat. 45.14, where both lovers are envisioned as slaves (*huic uni domino usque serviamus*). **Tibi**: for service to Venus, see Tib. 1.2.99 (and below *ad* 3.12.10). **Aeque**: not a word much used in elegy, where the relationship is typically one of (alternating) dominance and submission; cf. *ad* 3.18.1. Cat. 45.20 (*mutuis animis amant amantur*) may be a model, and, from the Greek tradition, see Theocr. 12.15, ἴσῳ ζυγῷ, *AP* 5.68, 5.88, and 5.286. Pichon 1991: 81 notes that *aequus* normally refers to one who is willing to fall in love. Fabre-Serris 2009: 157 sees a parallel between the repetition of **uterque** here and in line 15 and the *pariter... uterque* of Ov. *Her.* 4.28.

Vincla: of lover's chains at Prop. 2.29.6, 3.11.4, 3.15.10, and 3.20.23 (La Penna 1951: 187–90); the newer term *vincula* is also common in Prop.; see *ad* 3.9.14. (For Propertius, the difference is more than one of metrical convenience: the older term is mostly used of erotic bonds, the newer non-erotic. Ov., on the other hand, uses them interchangeably; cf. *RA* 213 and 294.) Hubbard 2004 draws attention to the similarity between this image and Tib. 2.2.18–19 (a poem written for Cornutus; see Introduction, Section IV). For the ancient etymology connecting Venus to *vincio*, see Hinds 2006. We may even be meant to see allusion to the tale of Venus' adultery with Mars in Hom. *Od.* 8.256–366; there the couple are trapped by the cuckolded Hephaestus and held in chains as a spectacle for other gods. If so, it is either very clever or very foolish of the poet to remind Venus of the incident. **Leva**: often in elegy of gods who do (or do not) alleviate one's miseries, but these are not usually amatory; cf. Ov. *Fas.* 1.367, *Tr.* 4.1.19 and 49, *EP* 1.1.57 and above, 3.3.21. The phrase **vincla leva** is essentially prosaic; cf. e.g. Cic. *TD* 1.118, Liv. 9.9.7.

Sed potius valida teneamur uterque catena,
16   **nulla queat posthac quam soluisse dies.**

While the poem puts into S.'s mouth a preference for servitude that is somewhat different from that typically seen in elegy, the fact that she feels comfortable dictating its terms is quintessentially elegiac.

Valida: in Tib., the word is used mostly of labouring animals, but Tib. 2.6.25 uses *valida...compede* of the chaining of a (literal) slave. See *ad* 3.4.65. **Catena**: cf. Tib. 2.4.3, where the poet is held (*teneor*) in chains, and Pichon 1991: 102 on the amatory nuances of the noun. **Valida...catena** not elsewhere joined. For the sentiment, see Prop. 2.15.25–6 *atque utinam haerentis sic nos vincire catena/ velles, ut numquam solveret ulla dies*, Hor. *Od.* 1.13.17–18 *felices ter et amplius/ quos irrupta tenet copula*, Ov. *Met.* 4.678–9, where Perseus differentiates between the chains of prisoners and those of lovers (*non istis digna catenis,/sed quibus inter se cupidi iunguntur amantes*), Stat. *Silv.* 5.1.43–4 *vos collato pectore mixtos/ iunxit inabrupta concordia longa catena*.

Posthac is rare in elegy, appearing only three times, in Cat. 65.9, 65.11, and 99.16. **Soluisse dies**: see quotation of Prop. 2.15.26 above.

Optat idem iuvenis quod nos, sed tectius optat:
18   **nam pudet haec illum dicere verba palam.**

The poet seems to regain confidence as the poem draws to a close. But we are faced with the question of why this **iuvenis** is so quiet about his feelings: either he is in fact not as interested as S., or (traditionally feminine) bashfulness (cf. **pudet**, with Hinds 1987a: 40) is being attributed to him (cf. e.g. Ov. *Ars* 1.276, where women love secretly: *tectius illa cupit*; the passage continues by noting that if men were not active, women would assume this role, with Hinds 1987a: 41). It is not clear why Cerinthus would feel the need to conceal his love, although there has been much speculation, mostly focusing on potential status differences between him and S. (see Introduction, Section IV). Speaking and silence are central issues in [Tib.] 13–18, in an explicitly gendered way; cf. especially 3.18, where she is ashamed to speak, and 3.13, where she is not (with introductory notes to those poems). Hinds 1987a: 40–1, 43 notes the speechlessness and passivity of Cerinthus throughout this cycle, but especially here.

Optat idem: same line-start at Ov. *Tr.* 5.11.27, but in a rather different context. **Tectius**: the sentiment is broadly similar to Cat. 61.169–71.

Dicere verba: elsewhere in poetry only at Tib. 2.5.94 and Mart. 8.7.2, both in same *sedes*. **Palam**: also at Tib. 2.1.84–5, where there is a disjunction between open and covert speech: *palam pecori, clam sibi quisque vocet/aut etiam sibi quisque palam*. Cf. Cat. 61.196 (in a marital context).

>   At tu, Natalis, quoniam deus omnia sentis,
> 20   adnue: quid refert, clamne palamne roget?

The couplet is either an appeal to the god to grant Cerinthus' wish, which he hasn't expressed, or, perhaps, a confession that S. has not expressed hers out loud either. We do not know whether Romans conceived of a 'birthday wish' as having extra force.

At tu, Natalis: Tib. 1.7.63 *at tu, Natalis multos celebrande per annos*, 2.2.1 *venit Natalis ad aras*, 2.2.21 *eveniat Natalis*. **Natalis** personified also at Ov. *Tr.* 3.13.2, 5.5.13.

Deus omnia sentis: while many gods are omniscient (cf. e.g. Ov. *EP* 1.2.71 *quamvis deus omnia novit*, *EP* 4.9.127–8; outside of elegy at e.g. Hes. *WD* 267, Archil. 177.2–3W, Plaut. *Capt.* 313), it is not clear that such a minor being as a personal guardian spirit would be; the poet perhaps seeks to flatter him.

Adnue: S.'s beloved is often identified with the Cornutus of Tib. 2.2 (see Introduction, Section IV); *adnuat* appears in that poem, at line-start in 9 and then *annuit* in 10, where his Genius must assent to all of his requests (Hubbard 2004: 184); cf. *CT* 2.5.121 and 3.12.13, where the verb is in the imperative, the first addressed to Apollo and the second to Juno. In general, the elegists tend to make the verb the first word in its line, and it refers to gods more often than not. (The verb appears more often in Ov. *Fas.* than in the rest of elegy combined.)

Clamne palamne: attested nowhere else. The sentiment is surprising, as it ought to make a difference (both to S. and to the gods) whether Cerinthus expresses his wishes in words or they must intuit them. Dronke, however, points out that S. does not claim that Cerinthus has *never* voiced his sentiments, only that he has not done so in this poem (2003: 95).

3.12:

Once again, S. becomes an object of poetry's attention rather than its subject; here it is her birthday and (as in 3.8), the poet speculates about her inner life. It is best understood as paired with 3.11, as the two poems express many of the same sentiments, with the same wording. Dronke suggests that this poem is a 'flashback', written by an outside observer, to a period in which the lovers had not yet become a couple (2003: 95). If so, the poem's end brings us back to the present (conceived of as the future), namely, the following year's birthday. There is also the possibility that S. herself is meant to be the speaker.

The presentation of S. vacillates between goddess and *puella* (see Lieberg 1962 and Introduction, Section I). Her physical attributes are only hinted at, but the elegiac world of deceit is explicitly invoked. Or the poem may provide a transition to a new kind of *docta puella*; as the next poem demonstrates, S. is so *docta* that she becomes an author (see Introduction, Section VI). Juno continues to be important in this book (cf. e.g. *ad* 3.1.2). Poem 3.12 can be divided into three roughly equal sections: the poet first sets up a contrast between S.'s stated purpose (dressing for her birthday to honour Juno) and her real one (impressing her lover, 1–6), with a prayer to Juno to understand and support the relationship (7–14); then follows a description of the offerings, a reiteration of the disjunction between voiced and silent wishes found in 3.11, and a further prayer (15–20).

> Natalis Iuno, sanctos cape turis acervos,
> 2   quos tibi dat tenera docta puella manu.

Natalis Juno: parallel to the Genius for men (*ad* 3.11.8–9); see *ad* 3.6.48 (where she seems to be a tutelary spirit, but is not connected with birthdays per se). Juno's presence here may be meant to invoke the Matronalia, featuring in 3.1 and 3.8 (on which see *ad locc.*). She is not a goddess who appears frequently in amatory elegy; outside of this book, she appears primarily in reference to Io (Prop. 2.33.9, 3.22.35–6, Ov. *Am.* 2.2.45, 2.19.29; to the peacock at *Am.* 2.6.55), to Ixion's attempted rape (Tib. 1.3.73–4), to religious rites (Prop. 4.8.16, Ov. *Am.* 3.10.46, 3.13), to Hercules (Prop. 4.9.43 and 71–2), and as Lucina (Prop. 4.1.99–102; cf. *ad* 3.1).

Sanctos is something of a leitmotif in [Tib.] 3: cf. *ad* 3.4.4, 3.10.9, 3.10.24, 3.11.1, 3.11.12 (it also appears below at 3.12.7, 3.19.15, and 3.19.23). **Acervos** are important to Tib. (1.1.9, 1.1.77 of grain, 2.5.89 for a religious festival) as evidence of a life frugally and piously lived; *sanctos...acervos* is not otherwise attested. **Turis acervos** at line-end at Ov. *Met.* 5.131, Stat. *Silv.* 2.1.21, *Theb.* 11.222, Mart. 7.54.5; see too Tib. 1.8.70 *sanctis tura dedisse focis*; Ov. *Met.* 3.733 *turaque dant sanctasque colunt Ismenidas aras*, *EP* 2.1.32 *tura prius sanctis imposuisse focis*, 3.1.161–2 *prius imposito sanctis altaribus igni/tura fer*.

Tenera...manu: see 3.9.8 for the conjunction applied to Cerinthus. **Docta**: see 3.4.45; **docta puella**: see Introduction, Section VI.

> Tota tibi est hodie, tibi se laetissima compsit,
> 4   staret ut ante tuos conspicienda focos.

Tota with dative, presumably meaning 'all yours' (*in* + ablative is more usual, *OLD* 4b); cf. 3.10.17 for the more common *tua*. The sense is strained enough that the emendation *lota* may be preferable (so Luck, and see Schuster 1968: 165 and Tränkle 1990 *ad loc.*, who also prints *lota*); 'bathed' is in an ancient context not as silly as it first seems, and fits well with **compsit**. For washing before worshipping the gods, see e.g. Prop. 3.10.13; Liv. 5.22.4.

Tibi: must refer to Juno, but the next couplet suggests that S. has another in mind as she beautifies herself. Indeed, if we take **compsit** metapoetically, as playing on the regular association between hair and poetry (see *ad* 3.1.14, of L.'s poetry, and 3.8.10, of S.), the pronoun may refer to her audience: S., now polished in the manner of a Callimachean poem, is a sight to behold; on this verb, see Pichon 1991: 107. On **laetissima**, see *ad* 3.10.23 and 24.

Conspicienda (in context here, 'waiting to be seen'): not for the first time, nor the last, the S. poetry offers a sophisticated meditation on visibility and discretion (without a limiting pronoun, S. is presented not only to Juno, or Cerinthus, but to the reader as well). Tib. 1.2.70 uses the gerundive of the soldier who is rival for Delia's affections, 2.3.52 of Nemesis' desire to flaunt her expensive clothing. Juno is the final god to whom S. will be offered for inspection in this cycle; if it is correct to see S. as soon to be married (Introduction, Section IV), she is also the most appropriate. **Focos**: see *ad* 3.10.24 and 3.11.12. The juxtaposition between a *puella*-like interest in public attention and the domestic sphere implied by **focos** is typical for S.'s own self-presentation in the following cycle. If the hearth is in a sacred space, as the language here might suggest (*OLD* 3), it is worth noting that temples were among the few neutral spaces where men and women could meet in public (see, for instance, the tale of Acontius and Cydippe told in e.g. Ov. *Her.* 20–1).

> Illa quidem ornandi causas tibi, diva, relegat,
> 6   est tamen, occulte cui placuisse velit.

S. claims that she has taken such care in honour of Juno, but in fact, it is for Cerinthus. Her secrecy is notable, since readers have already heard all about him, not least in the previous poem (where he was silent). So too, given the intrusion from an omniscient narrator, this begins to look like an elegiac relationship, where secrecy is both required and pleasing.

Ornandi: Tib. objects to excessive cultivation in Pholoe (1.8.11), as does Prop. in Cynthia (1.2.1, 2.18.36); the gerund hints at the elegiac woman's status as a luxury object, and also, since that desire is here dissembled, at the elegiac worry that the *puella* may seek attention from multiple men (note Claudia Quinta's excessive ornamentation as provoking inquiry into her chastity, Ov. *Fas.* 4.309). The verb is also metapoetic, for the elegiac poet wants his *puella*/ poetry to be known; see Introduction, Section I. For this sense, see Ov. *Tr.* 1.1.9. **Ornandi causas** also has a technical, rhetorical meaning, found often in Cicero.

Diva: commonly used of goddesses (e.g. Prop. 2.14.27, of Venus), but with a specifically elegiac tone (Cat. 68.70), whereby the *puella* is assimilated to a goddess; see *ad* 3.4.5, 3.8.5. **Relegat** (here meaning 'attribute responsibility to', *OLD* 3b) is prosaic and sometimes technical (e.g. Ov. *Tr.* 1.7.8). Its use with the simple dative is unusual; Tränkle 1990 adduces as a parallel Liv. 28.42.15 (though there is a textual problem). In poetry, the verb is mostly in this *sedes* except in Ov. **Occulte** is not as common as one might expect in elegy, given its covert nature; see Pichon 1991: 218 for the adjective. There may be a wordplay on S.'s *cultus* (see *ad* 3.8.1). The lines provide a noteworthy difference between S.'s own poetry, which speaks what is usually unsaid, and the image of a dutiful, silent daughter (at least on the surface).

Placuisse velit: similar to Tib. 1.9.71 *non tibi sed iuveni cuidam vult bella videri*. Things become even more personalized, and more divine, at Prop. 4.8.16: *causa fuit Iuno, sed mage causa Venus*.

> At tu, sancta, fave, neu quis divellat amantes,
> 8   sed iuveni, quaeso, mutua vincla para.

For **sancta,** see *ad* 3.10.9. The requesting of support from Juno, goddess of marriage, for what looks like an extra-marital affair, is odd (see Introduction, Section IV, for discussion of this cycle as pre-marital). Perhaps Romans understood the birth-Juno as wholly distinct from her Olympian eponym, or perhaps we are meant to conclude that S.'s relationship is licit (despite the elegiac vocabulary used of it here). So too, the relationship of S. to this poet is puzzling: she might be the speaker, but if she is not, the speaker would need to be close enough to S. to divine her inner thoughts and wishes (e.g. a brother or cousin); in this case publishing them would be anathema to him.

Fave: see *ad* 3.3.33–4, 3.10.19, 3.11.9 (the first addressed to Juno as Saturnia, and also requesting her support for an elegiac relationship). **Divellat**: not an especially elegiac word, occurring only at Ov. *Tr.* 3.9.27 (twice, of Medea's slaughter and dismemberment of her brother); see Pichon 1991: 132. But it is used of love by Hor. *Od.* 1.13.18–20 (*nec malis/divulsus querimoniis/... amor*), and 1.36.18–19 (*nec Damalis novo/divelletur adultero*), 2.17.14–15.

Iuvenis: see *ad* 3.2.1–2 and *passim*. **Mutua vincla**: continuing the themes of 3.11.13–15, and confirming that S.'s feelings are less opaque than Cerinthus'.

> Sic bene compones: ullae non ille puellae
> 10   servire aut cuiquam dignior illa viro.

This sentiment—that a couple is perfect for one another—does not much occur in elegy, in part because elegy seems to be about couples who are not well-suited, and in part because it is usually written in the first person, and focuses more attention on negative parts of the relationship. Ov. *Ars* 2.385 notes that cheating loosens *bene compositos...amores*; cf. *Fas.* 3.484 *tam bene compositum sollicitare torum* and [Ov.] *Ep. Drus.* 301 *par bene compositum*, of a married couple.

Compones: of personal cultivation (see *ad* 3.8.8), poetry (see *ad* 3.2.26), and here, arrangement in general; the goddess is urged to keep up the good work. **Ullae**: as Smith 1913 notes *ad loc.*, this is the only place in Latin where this feminine dative occurs; it is probably a medieval corruption.

For the notion of *servitium amoris* inherent in **servire**, see *ad* 3.9.4, and for the possible wordplay on the Sulpicii Servii, see *ad* 3.16.4. **Dignior**: a word of some importance in this book of poetry, possibly deriving from Cat. (e.g. 68.131; Hallett 2002a: 49), possibly from Gallus (fr. 2.6–7, *c[ar]mina...*/*domina... digna mea*), possibly neither; see *ad* 3.1.8, 3.8.15, 3.8.24, 3.13.10. *Dignus* with the infinitive also occurs at Tib. 2.6.43 (*digna est foedare*) and is frequent in Ov. The juxtaposition between *dignus*, which implies high status, and *servitium*, which implies low, is probably deliberate (and recurs in a different form at 3.16.4).

    Nec possit cupidos vigilans deprendere custos,
12   fallendique vias mille ministret Amor.

Cupidos: see *ad* 3.4.52. **Vigilans**: elsewhere in *CT* at Tib. 1.2.77–8 (*quid... prodest cum fletu nox vigilanda venit*); closer parallels at Prop. 4.5.47 (*ianitor ad dantis vigilet*) and Ov. *Am.* 1.9.27–8 (*custodum transire manus vigilumque catervas/militis et miseri semper amantis opus*). **Vigilans...custos**: see, in a different context, Cat. 62.33 *vigilat custodia*. **Custos**: a guardian who watches *puellae*, thereby serving as a blocking character to the elegiac relationship; see Tib. 1.2.5 and 15 (*tu quoque ne timide custodes, Delia, falle*), 1.6.10, 1.8.55, 2.1.75, 2.4.32–3, Prop. 1.11.15, 2.6.37–9, 2.23.9, Ov. *Am.* 2.2, 3.1.49, 3.4, *Ars* 3.611–66.

    Deprendere: not elsewhere in *CT*, although of course the notion is common. The verb is often used in Ov. of catching lovers in the act (e.g. *Met.* 3.6, *Am.* 1.9.39, *Ars* 2.557); cf. Pichon 1991: 127.

    Eluding guardians and **fallendi...vias mille** are Tibullan themes (e.g. 1.2.15 quoted above, 1.8.56 *ipse dedit cupidis fallere posse deus*, 2.1.75–6 *hoc duce custodes furtim transgressa iacentes/ad iuvenem tenebris sola puella venit*), and part of elegy as a whole; cf. Ov. *Tr.* 2.447–50. These lines make clear that illicit relations of some kind are envisioned and sanctioned by the poet; cf. *inque modos venerem mille figuret amor* at Ov. *Am.* 3.14.24. **Fallendique**: *-que* here carries an adversative tone (i.e., let not... but instead...). On *fallere* see *ad* 3.1.6. **Vias mille**: at V. *A.* 12.753, of Turnus' flight.

    Ministret: also with **Amor** as subject at Tib. 1.10.57–8 (*at lascivus Amor rixae mala verba ministrat,/inter et iratum lentus utrumque sedet*), where, however, he prolongs fights (but is also implicated in the making-up process), and with Natalis as subject at 2.2.21 (where he looks after the offspring of Cornutus and his wife; on Cornutus' potential relationship to these poems, see Introduction, Section IV). While the verb is not, strictly speaking, educative, the concept is (*OLD* 3; *TLL* 8.1020.54–1021.9).

    Adnue purpureaque veni perlucida palla:
14   ter tibi fit libo, ter, dea casta, mero,

Adnue: what gods do to show their assent; see *ad* 3.11.20.
    Purpurea: see *ad* 3.4.30. **Purpurea...palla**: not otherwise in poetry, also at e.g. Cic. *Verr.* 2.5.31, 2.5.86, 2.5.137 (all of Verres' effeminate dress), Fronto *ad*

Ant. de Eloq. 2.14.2, and *punicea...palla* of Achilles at Stat. *Ach.* 2.5. On gods (esp. Apollo) wearing the **palla**, see *ad* 3.4.35 (it is not common for Olympian goddesses: Venus at VF 2.106 and Diana at Ov. *Met.* 3.167; minor goddesses include Thetis (VF 1.132), Circe (Ov. *Met.* 14.262), Nox (Stat. *Theb.* 2.527), Tisiphone (Ov. *Met.* 4.483, Stat. *Theb.* 1.110 and 11.495), Discordia (V. *A.* 8.702), Tragoedia (Ov. *Am.* 3.1.12). At Silius 7.77, however, the Romans offer to Juno a *palla*, so the rarity of goddesses in *pallae* may be coincidence. The repetition of *p, r,* and *l,* and of **ter**, provides an incantatory quality to the lines.

Perlucida: for the verb, see *ad* 3.4.71. The adjective, not common, is often associated with divine things (e.g. Jupiter as a bull at Ov. *Met.* 2.856, Diana's grove at *Met.* 3.161). On the use of *per-* as an intensifier, see Axelson 1945: 128. There may be a hint in -*lucid-* of Juno as the principle of *aer*, aether (=Ἥρα; see e.g. Cic. *DND* 2.66.1, quoting Euripides, and Feeney 1991: 150 and 329 with further citations).

Ter, thrice, is a number of ritual significance; cf. e.g. V. *G.* 4.384. **Libo**: almost exclusively of sacrificial offerings in elegy (exceptions at Ov. *Fas.* 3.670, *Am.* 1.8.94, and *Ars* 1.429, though the latter two, birthday cakes, may also be offerings; see Ov. *Tr.* 3.13.17 and 4.10.12). Cf. Tib. 2.2.8 (with *mero*, both in same *sedes*), of Cornutus' birthday (see Introduction, Section IV, and Hubbard 2004: 184, who sees 3.11 and 12 as 'in some sense renewing the birthday wish of 2.2').

On **casta**, see *ad* 3.1.23, 3.4.23, 3.4.60, 3.9.20. **Dea casta**: also of Juno at Ov. *Am.* 3.13.3 (*casta...Iunoni festa*), Stat. *Theb.* 10.58; while Juno is notoriously chaste, it is perhaps especially surprising to have her invoked in this context, which seems to be one of illicit love. On the other hand, she is a regular in this collection, and the mythographers do detail her pre-marital affair with her brother Jupiter (though elegists never mention it). The adjective is also used of e.g. Lucina at V. *E.* 4.10, and Minerva at Ov. *Am.* 1.7.19 and [V.] *Cir.* 23. **Mero**: see *ad* 3.5.34, 3.6.58, 3.6.62.

praecipit et natae mater studiosa, quod optat:
16   illa aliud tacita, iam sua, mente rogat;

It now becomes even clearer that Juno, goddess of marriage, is being asked to help a girl deceive her family. **Praecipit**: here in the sense of 'advise or order' (as at Ov. *Her.* 17.175) and not, as often with this verb, pre-emptively. Et is regularly postponed to the second word of the line (e.g. Tib. 1.1.77).

Mater introduces a hymeneal theme (see e.g. Cat. 62.60–5, where the disjunction between the wishes of the bride and her parents also occurs). Here, however, we have heard nothing of S.'s family (see Introduction, Section IV, on Messalla as her guardian—which does not, of course, preclude a living mother). **Studiosa**: also *ad* 3.14.5 *nimium Messalla mei studiose*, where S. finds Messalla overbearing. There may, but need not, be a scholarly tone to the adjective (see e.g. Cat. 116.1 and Ov. *Her.* 15.1, where it is used of poetic composition); it can also suggest that doctitude runs in S.'s family. Hallett 2002b: 147–8 suggests, in fact, that here and throughout, the poetry alludes to Cat. 45 and 116, and to the family of the Valerii. **Mater studiosa**: not otherwise together; the phrase suggests a mother's ambitions for her daughter (which, in the Roman world, are sure to be marital).

Optat refers either to what S. wants or, more likely, her mother's wishes. *Quid optet*, an indirect command, is a better reading; *optat* at 3.11.17 aids in the corruption (see Tränkle 1990 *ad loc.* for discussion of the text, which both Luck and he print). **Optat**/*roget* at line-end in 3.11.17 and 20 add further to the parallelism between the two poems. **Tacita…mente**: the phrase also occurs at Cat. 62.37, in a marital context. In Ov., however, the phrase is associated entirely with illicit relationships: Ov. *Am.* 1.4.23 of a lover's complaint (silent because her *vir* is present), 3.7.63 of erotic fantasies, *Ars* 1.602 of curses of a rival, *Fas.* 3.634 of Lavinia's (unfounded) jealousy. As will be seen, silence is a key theme in the poems about and by S. **Mente rogat**: in the same *sedes* at Tib. 1.9.84, where Venus is asked to preserve *grata…mente* towards the poet.

> uritur, ut celeres urunt altaria flammae,
> 18   nec, liceat quamvis, sana fuisse velit.

Uritur: for the flames of love, see *ad* 3.11.5. But this simile is somewhat unusual; the religious tone both reminds us of Juno and alludes to the description of S. at 3.8 and elsewhere as a quasi-divinity. The transference of the simile is an easy one—flames do not actually burn an altar, which is fireproof—but perhaps also hints at the all-consuming nature of the passion. **Celeres…flammae**: a Lucretian phrase: 2.192, 5.301, 6.224; also at Ov. *Tr.* 1.2.45 *quam celeri micuerunt nubilia flamma*, of lightning.

Sana: only here in the *CT*; compare the (now archaic) 'heart-whole'. Metaphors of love as an illness or form of madness are exceedingly common, in elegy and outside of it: with *sanus*, see Cat. 83.4, Prop. 1.1.26, 2.12.12, 3.24.18, Ov. *Met.* 7.18, 8.35, 9.542, 9.600, *Fas.* 4.7, *RA* 493, 504, 546, 621, 794; cf. too [Tib.] 3.17, where S. does not want to be well (there, *evincere morbos*) except under certain circumstances.

> Sis iuveni grata: veniet cum proximus annus,
> 20   hic idem votis iam vetus exstet amor.

Nearly every word in this vexed hexameter has come under suspicion; see Schuster 1968: 167–9 and Tränkle 1990 *ad loc.* for discussion. Probably the most plausible suggestion is Gruppe's *Iuno grata* (which is, however, unmetrical); **sis** comes from F; Ambr. and V have *si iuveni*. Perhaps emending to *sit*, or even *sim*, is the best solution (S.J. Heyworth, *per litteras*). Or perhaps the birthday is encouraged to return on the following year. Tib. 1.9.83–4

HANC TIBI FALLACI RESOLUTUS AMORE TIBULLUS/DEDICAT ET GRATA SIS DEA MENTE ROGAT provides an example of the kind of vow one might deliver when extricated from an elegiac affair (though this is surely not the sense here); if we (implausibly) take **iuveni** as feminine, referring to S., Ov. *Ars* 1.63 provides a parallel. Cf. Tib. 1.9.84 *grata sis dea menta rogat*.

Proximus annus: see Gardner 2013 on the passage of time in elegy. On **grata**, see Pichon 1991: 160–1. **Idem**: elegiac love seems to thrive on the principle of constant change; it is not clear whether the poet knows this: perhaps he wishes the couple a different kind of relationship. On **votis**, see *ad* 3.3.1.

Iam vetus: after the passage of a year; cf. Prop. 1.1.7 *toto...anno*. **Vetus... amor**: a phrase well-attested in poetry: Cat. 96.3 and Tib. 2.4.47, both of a bond ended only by death; Ov. *Her.* 16.257, *Met.* 5.576, and Stat. *Silv.* 1.2.90 of mythic love stories; Ov. *RA* 108 of the difficulty of rooting out an old love; cf. Manil. 1.358, where Perseus is mindful of his old love for Andromeda. Despite elegy's normal assumption that the elderly are repugnant, it does also sometimes envision long-term affairs (e.g. Prop. 2.25.9–10). **Exstet amor**: the verb an emendation of Baehrens (cf. Tib. 2.4.38, where Cartault emends to this text). The manuscripts have *esset*; *adsit* of the *recentiores* is also worth consideration.

3.13:

S. speaks in her own voice, as she did in 3.9 and 3.11. But scholars generally separate out 3.13–3.18 (see Introduction, Section V, for other divisions) as the work of S. herself; these poems are as a group shorter (scholars often term them 'epigrammatic' or 'epistolary') and are generally difficult to construe (see Lowe 1988 for discussion of their syntactic peculiarities). Milnor 2002 has compared them, usefully, to the poetry of Emily Dickinson, which is also somewhat tortured in expression, and concerned with issues of visibility and hiding (especially present in the current poem). Dronke compares this poem to the letters of Eloise and Abelard (2003: 86). Those who see 3.8–3.18 as all written by S. point to the Catullan precedent of differing lengths and tones, and alternations of person between poems (e.g. Hallett 2002a: 47–8, 2002b: 141).

It is unlikely that authorship of poetry about S. will ever be satisfactorily resolved. But this poem differs from the previous five in a number of ways. First, S. here takes a more active role: it is her poetry that has brought her what she wants. By contrast, Cerinthus, somewhat shy in 3.8–3.12, is now literally turned into a passive and nameless object and bodily transported into S.'s lap (Hinds 1987a: 43). Second, S. manifests a distinct lack of concern for what people will say; indeed, where earlier poems (at least those in the third person) had been careful to preserve her modesty, this one throws caution to the winds. Third, these poems are noticeably shorter than the previous grouping. (We might again adduce the model of Cat., in whose corpus poems are divided by length; on the other hand, it is not clear who arranged the poems of Cat. or when, so it is hard to know if he would have served as a model for later authors.) Fourth, their syntax is noticeably more difficult. But the division may nonetheless be arbitrary; a number of these points may depend not on different authorship, but on the fact that Amor has now arrived, so the game has changed.

Although S. has often been thought to compose 'artlessly', recent scholarship has argued against this: Tränkle 1990 sees allusions to Sappho in this poem; Keith 1997 to Vergil's Dido; Merriam 2005 to the Iliadic Helen and Paris. Working from the other direction, Hallett 2006 sees allusions to this poem in Ov. *Ars*, Hallett 2009a to Ov. *Am.* 3.14, Hallett 2011 to Liv. 39, and Fabre-Serris 2009 sees the poem as influential upon Ov. *Her.* 4 and 15 (two poems in which a woman declares her love for a man, and which show concern for *fama* and *pudor*; 2009: 151). Beyond this, it has a broadly Catullan tone. Dronke suggests that the poem is a meditation on the different nuances of *fama* (reputation, literary fame, gossip) in the light of S.'s complex identity (2003: 85), i.e. a very typical subject for a poet, but with a few interesting twists. The poem is also programmatic for the cycle, introducing most of its major themes: a re-reversal of the elegiac reversal of gender expectations; feelings which are alternately hidden and displayed; and S.'s own ambiguous role as *poeta/amator/puella*. Lyne, in fact, suggests that it is 'an opening and *publishing* poem' (2007: 343 and 348; his italics; cf. Hinds 1987a: 43 on this poem as 'a statement of intent to publish'). This seems plausible: the placement of this summing-up poem first suggests a deliberate arrangement.

The poem announces that S. is ready to proclaim her love, finally arrived (*venit*), to the world. It does so in language that seems to many readers disturbingly indiscreet if authored by a Roman woman (see Introduction, Section VI). Indeed, what to make of the disjunction between what is expected of a woman of S.'s status (see Introduction, Section IV) and S.'s own words has long bedevilled interpreters; a plausible solution, along the lines of Dronke 2003, would be to treat S.'s discussion of love as (also) about love poetry, and the poem as (re)presenting her new-found poetic voice. Lowe too notes that the poem 'is about discourse, a series of loosely interlocked paradoxes and conceits on the theme of being talked about in its multiple guises and implications. On the one hand, Sulpicia wants to shout her love from the rooftops; on the other, she is bound to avoid public talk of her affair to avoid damage to her moral reputation' (1988: 204). In this vein, Milnor suggests that this poem 'transforms' the (male) conventions of authorship by replicating the use of the female body as an 'authenticating' gesture (2002: 261, 267–8), a trope familiar but made strange by the fact that S. is at least potentially both exploiting poet and exploited female body; see too DeBrohun for discussion of the undoing of an apparently closed binary system as it occurs in Prop. 4 (2003: 24–8 for definition and application). Interestingly, it is only with *digna*, in the final line of the poem, that it becomes clear to a first reader that the speaking voice of this poem is female.

Generations of editors have assumed that this, seemingly the first poem, comes chronologically last in the 'story', because of its erotic implications; see

Skoie 2013 for extended discussion. As often in elegy, the arrangement of the poems prompts readers to pose biographically-based questions that cannot be answered; see Introduction, Section I. Although we know nothing about who ordered the cycle (Introduction, Section V), this poem fits well as an introduction: S.'s poetry, which follows, has (already) been proven, and got her what she wants (compare Sappho fr. 1, which details a long chain of successful love affairs/poems, with reminiscences *ad locc.*). Poets are not shy about proclaiming their own abilities (see e.g. Hor. *Od.* 3.30.1–9, Ov. *Am.* 1.15, *Met.* 15.871–9), but it is surprising to find such a claim at the *start* of a poetic collection rather than at its end, before the reader can have amassed sufficient evidence to agree. Finally, the poem is noteworthy in containing the invitation to 'anyone' to speak of S.'s love, and so calling into being the previous '*amicus*' poems (see Introduction, Section V). In apparent disregard of her reputation, S. professes herself eager to be spoken about (see further *ad* 3.13.5), and indeed, anticipates *fama* by speaking about herself (Lowe 1988: 203–4). Ov. *Am.* 1.5, which undresses Corinna for the audience's delectation, is a partial parallel, and Prop. 1.13, in which Prop. witnesses the affair of Gallus, may also be relevant. But we might instead see allusion to Cat. 5.2–3, with its faulting of those who would pry into the relationship. The distinction between 'speaking' and 'writing' may be important, but is not fully articulated: ancient poetry is often described as sung rather than written, and the verb *narro* (line 5) is not unusual in these contexts. Is S. encouraging her audience to gossip, or to compose poetry, or both?

The poem can be divided into two parts: first, an announcement of S.'s love, and poetry, assisted by Venus (1–6); then a brief meditation on written and spoken tales of love (7–10). For other 'victory' poems, cf. Prop. 2.14, Ov. *Am.* 2.12 (both, however, framed as military triumphs, though the former includes a dedication to Venus).

    Tandem venit amor, qualem texisse pudori
2   quam nudasse alicui sit mihi fama magis.

The convoluted nature of the sentence, not atypical for this group of poems, has led some to opine on the intrinsic differences between men's and women's writing (see Introduction, Section VI): either because of incompetence or womanly duplicity, S. simply cannot say what she means. It is more likely to derive, as Milnor 2002 and Batstone (forthcoming) note, from S.'s keen awareness that, given her station in life, to voice her own desire is literally to attempt to say the unsayable (and this is true whether S. is biologically female or a man assuming a feminine role). The sentiment is nearly impossible to convey in idiomatic English: 'Love has come at last, of the sort that the rumour that I have hidden it,/Would be more of a source of shame to me than to have exposed it to anyone'. See Lowe, who observes that we see the poem 'slithering off after three forthright words of uncharacteristic lucidity into a syntactic morass'; as he discusses at length, S.'s language is exquisitely balanced between expression and obscurity (1988: 203).

Tandem: given the convention of naming groups of poems after their first word, this opening is strange, and may indicate that this is *not* the first poem of a formal cycle. So too, the adverb works well to connect the wished-for *vetus amor* from the final line of the previous poem; finally the impatient poet has obtained what she wants, whether that be poetry or love or both (see too *ad* 3.14.1, and next couplet). For similarly impatient bursts of joy beginning a poem, see e.g. Prop. 2.8b and 2.14 (though it is notoriously unclear in that book as a whole where poems start and end). We may be tempted to connect the word to Gallus fr. 2.6 (... *tandem fecerunt carmina Musae*, 'at last the Muses have made poetry [worthy of my mistress]'), because of this poem's later mention of poetry's worth, and of the Muses; V. *E.* 10.69 strengthens the Gallan case (Fabre-Serris 2009: 149). Lyne sees Prop. 1.1 and Ov. *Am.* 1.2, both introductory poems, as parallel (2007: 350). See too Allen 1962: 112–17 (= 1950: 148–52) on the regular confusion of chronologies in elegy. Alfonsi compares S.'s impatience with bourgeois morality with that of Sappho in L-P 16 (1946: 95).

Venit: see Hinds 2005 and 2006 for wordplay with the name of Venus here (which appears in line 5); Cic. *DND* 2.69 for the etymology. See too Fabre-Serris 2009: 150–1 for discussion of an allusion to Sappho 2.46, which begins with ἦλθες, 'you came'. **Tandem ... venit** also at Tib. 2.5.46 of a divine epiphany (as perhaps here; see immediately below).

Amor: as often, it is unclear whether this is the god or the feeling/sexual act; Lyne sees a pun on this ambiguity, cashed in by the confusion of pronoun in line 3, and reminiscent of both the aftermath of a cletic hymn and, with **nudasse** in the next line, naked cupids (2007: 351, citing Nonn. 7.275, 48.107; *AP* 207.1, Prop. 1.2.8, Ov. *Am.* 1.10.15). Readers will probably eventually take it as a common noun, but the proliferation of hands-on gods in [Tib.] 3 (Venus and the Muses in this poem alone) might continue to give pause. As noted in the introduction to this poem, we might (also) take this couplet metapoetically: S., waiting for her Muse, has at last been inspired, and so casts off her feminine reluctance to write because the quality of her poetry is simply too good to keep under wraps. The Muse is traditionally, of course, a Muse and not Amor, but perhaps this is another of S.'s sex-changes; note too the closeness between Amor and S. in 3.8, and Ov.'s frequent claim to an especially intimate relationship with the god (Armstrong 2004). Fabre-Serris draws attention to Ov. *Her.* 4.19, *venit amor*, which she sees as post-dating this poem (2009: 153–4). The first three words of this poem, **tandem venit amor**, work against one another grammatically; *tandem* suggests that it has been a long time coming; *venit amor* is inceptive.

Qualem: relative clause of characteristic which, combined with the double dative (but see below, on **pudori**) and two perfect infinitives, makes for extremely complex syntax. The precise nuance of the adjective is difficult; S. probably means only that her lover is well-suited to her, but the word might also imply that he is relatively equal to her in status (a contention undermined elsewhere in the cycle; see Introduction, Section IV).

Texisse: used regularly of metaphorical covering, i.e. hiding (e.g. Tib. 1.9.28, 3.11.17). S. draws a distinction between hiding and making bare (**nudasse**), yet manages to accomplish both of these mutually exclusive acts, not least by means of syntax. By the end of this poem, she will have both laid herself bare and disclosed no details about her relationship (except, seemingly, its consummation). The perfect tense suggests precedence in time not to *venit* but to **fama** (but see Lowe 1988: 204, who suggests that the tenses show the distance between past action and current effects). For the suggestion of a connection between **pudori** and **fama** in this poem, and Ov. *Her.* 4.9 and 18, see Fabre-Serris 2009: 152–4. **Pudori**: the text as printed gives a double dative construction ('a source of shame to me'); this structure is also found at 3.16.5. *Pudore* in V (also seemingly corrected in Ambr.) is probably to be preferred (Lyne 2007: 351 for discussion): it would provide an ablative of cause (further on chastity, see Introduction, Section I, and Kaster 2005: 28–65). Metapoetically, the Roman virtue of *pudor* (being too bashful to make one's work public) gets in the way of acquiring authorial *fama* (on which see further below). Hallett 2009a: 5 sees Ov. *Am.* 3.14.17–18 and 21–2 as dependent upon these lines.

Quam: as a comparative relatively uncommon in Tib. (e.g. 1.1.52, 2.3.32) but frequent in S: see 3.13.8, 3.16.3–4, 3.17.4 and 3.18.5. **Nudasse**: the verb means to strip something of its covering; it is surely not accidental that it has corporeal implications as well; S. is 'exposing herself' to the reader (see Flaschenreim 1999: 38 on the preponderance of semi-clothed women in elegy, and *passim* on the ways this poem simultaneously exposes as it hides). In addition to its regular meaning, the verb appears in elegy of revealed body parts at Cat. 66.81, Tib. 1.3.92, Prop. 2.15.5, 3.11.15, 3.14.13, 4.8.47. Ov. *Am.* 2.5.5 is probably the closest metapoetic parallel: *non male deletae nudant tua facta tabellae*, 'it is not a poorly erased note that lays bare your deeds'—and the parallel may be closer than is at first apparent, given the connection made later in this poem between exposure and writing. Hallett sees an allusion to this verb in Liv. 39.15.4, also in the context of public revelation of illicit sexuality (2011: 86). However literally the verb is meant, it is bold, particularly, as Milnor 2002: 260 notes, in the context of the expected *pudor* of the respectable Roman woman. Note too, with Snyder 1989: 130–1, that despite the rhetoric of 'telling all', S. does not provide Cerinthus' name until the following poem.

Alicui offers another surprise: S. will have exposed herself not merely to her lover, but to some anonymous other person in order to gain *fama*: the suggestion in the previous S. poems about her availability to various gods is shockingly, if vaguely, literalized on the human plane. Here again, we may see a metapoetic nuance: once having written and made writing public, the writer/ the writer's work is exposed to anyone who comes along (as Hor. *Ep.* 1.20 and

Ov. *Tr.* 1.1 make abundantly clear). This is an especially vulnerable position for a female writer (see Introduction, Section VI, on the nuances of *docta puella* and *publica*).

Fama magis: the notion of comparative degrees of fame does not appear often in poetry, but a similar phrase at Ov. *EP* 4.16.3, *famaque post cineres maior venit*, suggests metapoetic implications (cf. too Prop. 3.1.23–4). The basic—and unresolvable—tension between **fama**'s positive and negative implications gives the poem much of its obscurity. For a woman, *fama* and the exposure it brings are generally bad (Batstone, forthcoming), but for a poet such publicity is necessary (note that Tib. does not use the word). My translation 'rumour' above attempts to finesse this, but one might rather read S. as (ironically) suggesting that 'the bad press about me would be greater if I hid this than if I exposed it'; this construal would require reading *pudore*. For the negative implications of **fama**, see e.g. Ov. *Am.* 1.8.15, 2.2.50 (of a woman); for positive, e.g. Prop. 3.1.9, Ov. *Am.* 1.10.62, 1.15.7, 3.9.5 (of a poet), 1.14.50 (of a woman). **Fama** appears throughout amatory elegy; on its particularly elegiac nuances, see Pichon 1991: 142. Keith claims that whereas Dido becomes the object of **fama**, S. manages to remain its subject (1997: 302); Hallett 2009a sees Ov. *Am.* 3.14.6 and 36 as referencing this poem. The couplet as a whole might also be translated to bring out its latent metapoetic hints: loosely, 'finally (the ability to write) love poetry has come, of the kind which will make my fame so great that it would be a greater shame to keep it to myself than to show it to the world'. **Magis** with the double dative (if **pudori** remains) is a primarily prosaic construction (Bréguet 1946: 48–9 with citations).

Exorata meis illum Cytherea Camenis
4 adtulit in nostrum deposuitque sinum.

In these lines, Merriam sees an extended reference to Hom. *Il.* 3.373–82, 3.410–12, and 5.311–14 (in which Venus removes her son Aeneas and also Paris from danger, and in which Paris and Helen are thrown together; note Helen's reluctance by comparison with S.'s own at 3.18, on which see *ad loc.*). She also connects the passage to Cat. 65.19–24 and Callimachus' tablets at fr. 1.21–2 (2005: 161–3). For Merriam, the story of Paris and Helen provides material for S. to construct an imaginative fantasy of her own (2005: 167). Reference to Sappho is also likely (Merriam 2005: 163; see *ad* 3.13.5–6). The lines might also suggest the previous cycle and hint at its effectiveness (esp. e.g. 3.11.13–16).

Lyne notes an 'abAB pattern of adjectives and noun' in 3 (2007: 352); **illum** and **nostrum** are also each the centre word of their line. There may be play here with the notion of a poetic 'sphragis', here anonymized.

Exorata: elsewhere in elegy, mostly Ovidian, of prayers to the gods (e.g. Ov. *EP* 4.8.22) or human begging (e.g. Ov. *Am.* 3.11.43, where the *puella*'s face pleads for forgiveness), but not otherwise used of poetry; see Pichon 1991: 139 on the elegiac nature of pleading. The **ex-** prefix implies successful entreaty, and the bald statement that poetry has been efficacious in securing love is rare in the elegists, who tend to be more hesitant in such claims, or to deny them altogether: see e.g. Ov. *Am.* 1.8.57–62 (a *puella* taught that presents are better than poems), 1.13 and 3.6 (the poet is wholly unsuccessful in persuading Aurora to rise later or a river to abate its flow so that he may cross), and 3.8.1–8 (the soldier preferred to the poet); by contrast, see e.g. Prop. 1.8.28 and 41–2 (Prop., through his prayers, which are later glossed as Muses, has convinced Cynthia to remain in Rome). Prop. 3.2 and 3.3 are about the efficacy of poetry more generally. Lowe astutely observes that poetry brings S. both her love object and an avenue of escape from the strictures of *fama* (1988: 204).

Illum: Smith notes *ad loc.* that the pronoun is vague, as we do not yet know to whom it refers (Amor?), and speculates that this is because for S. 'there can be but one "him"'; there are, however, any number of Catullan and elegiac parallels. Lyne, by contrast, suggests that both this pronoun and *meus* in 8 may be 'a designed inducement to the reader to proceed further' (2007: 350). S.'s main focus is perhaps not Cerinthus, but her own poetry, focalized through *amor/ Amor* (see *ad* 3.13.1); we may also think of Amor, disguised as Iulus, in Dido's lap in *A.* 4.83–5; see Keith 1997 for Sulpician allusions to the Dido narrative, 302 on *sinus*. Note too Prop. 1.1.1–4, where Cynthia, subject of the first couplet, is changed without notice to Amor in the second.

Cytherea: see Pichon 1991: 121 for other elegiac citations (in Ov., often in this *sedes*). Venus' epithet is an old one, from the Aegean island sacred to her (Hes. *Th.* 198). It appears in Greek as early as Homer (*Od.* 8.288), in Sappho (fr. 86 and 140a; Merriam suggests that the word may have been especially Sapphic, 2005: 168 n. 8), and regularly in Latin, especially Vergil and Ov.; for the epithet in connection with an amatory promise, see Ov. *Her.* 16.20 (Paris to Helen) *pollicita est thalamo te Cytherea meo*. Merriam suggests that the double naming of Venus, Greek and Latin, signals S.'s 'multilayered literary allusion' to both Sappho and Hom. *Il.* 3 (2006: 12–13). Hallett sees Ov. as picking up on the epithet at *Ars* 3.43–4, where Cytherea orders Ov. to teach women how to love (2006: 42). Fabre-Serris finds a Gallan allusion, seeing a playful reference both to the Muses' intervention in his life and, with the name **Cytherea**, to his mistress Lycoris (the mime actress Volumnia Cytheris, 2009: 150).

While the poet of the previous cycle was at pains to draw the attention of Mars and Apollo to S., once she takes matters into her own hands, S. attributes her success to Venus, who is indeed the most appropriate god for this office; cf. e.g. her offer to Sappho in fr. 1. Venus is also suitable given her own active pursuit of young men (Anchises and especially Adonis), and, as a woman, may provide S. with a more congenial model for assuming a subject position in love. Merriam suggests that Roman poets saw Venus as especially beneficent to women (2005: 164–5).

Meis...Camenis: the Camenae were originally Roman water-nymphs, who lived in a sacred grove outside the Porta Capena (*RE* 3.1427–8), but were early on identified with the (Greek) Muses as inspirers of poetry (see the first line of Liv. Andron. *Od.*, Enn. *Ann.* fr. 487, and Naevius' epitaph). They appear regularly in later poetry, in hexameter (e.g. V. *E.* 3.59) and elegy, and especially in Hor. *Od.* For *Camenae* referring to a personal poetic gift, see Hor. *Od.* 4.9.8 and Ov. *EP* 4.13.33; Varro *DLL* 6.75 and 7.26-7 provide a (surely false) etymology from *cano*, which Ov. *Met.* 14.434 reproduces: *nomine de nymphae veteres dixere Camenae. Meae Camenae* also occurs at [Tib.] 3.9.24, Calp. Sic. 3.42, Mart. 7.68.1 (*nostrae* at e.g. [Tib.] 3.7.191, Stat. *Silv.* 4.7.21); see too Lieberg 1980: 150-2 on this passage. Alliteration with Cytherea may account for their mention here, but their appearance at Prop. 3.10.1, a poem about Cynthia's birthday (a common theme in [Tib.]), may also be relevant. While the poem seems to be introductory of this cycle, some see this phrase as referring to the book's earlier poetry, especially to 3.9 and 3.11 (e.g. Holzberg 1998: 186). Flaschenreim notes that the two proper nouns work to position S. within both Greek and Roman poetic traditions (1999: 40).

The mostly prosaic **attulit** and **deposuit** attribute a remarkable lack of subjectivity to S.'s love object; the act of dropping a beloved in someone's lap seems to be unique (and ought furthermore to take the ablative). *Deponere sinu* is found elsewhere only of children: without preposition at Ov. *Fas.* 2.404, where the Tiber releases Romulus and Remus from his embrace; *in sinu... deposuit* at Sen. *Cont.* 2.4.3.5 for the entrusting of a baby; and *sinu... conde depositum meum* at Sen. *Troad.* 521 when Andromache asks Hector, in Hades, to guard their child. The somewhat similar phrasing at Prop. 1.6.23-4 (*et tibi non umquam nostros puer iste labores/afferat et lacrimis omnia nota meis*), is notably different in tone, but may be relevant. Pichon notes that *deponere* on its own is generally used for putting love aside (1991: 127). Cat. 68.132 has similar phrasing, but there the mistress moves of her own volition: *lux mea se nostrum contulit in gremium*.

Nostrum: for the plural, see *ad* 3.1.19. **Sinum**: the word may be meant sexually, or at least erotically (see Tib. 1.1.46 *et dominam tenero continuisse sinu*; common in Ov.) but the *sinus* is also the place where one would hold a child. Cat. 37.11, Prop. 1.8.37-8, and Ov. *Her.* 16.158, all of leaving from the *sinus* of a man, lack the potentially obscene tone of *sinus* applied to a woman (note too Cat. 65.19-24, with amatory nuance, adduced by Merriam 2005: 161). It may also be metapoetic; see Roessel 1990: 245-8 on the fact that one normally carries a book-roll *in sinu*. For other meanings of the word, see *ad* 3.9.24. The accusative *sinum* (instead of an ablative) is perhaps by assimilation to *adtulit* (Lieberg suggests that it is used for vividness, 1980: 152).

    Exsolvit promissa Venus: mea gaudia narret,
6   dicetur siquis non habuisse sua.

Not surprisingly, this couplet has provided fuel to those who see S.'s poetry as authored by a male or group of males, who hereby authenticate their work, giving permission to themselves to 'speak' of S.'s love (see Introduction, Section V, on communally authored poetry). The tone is perhaps rather that of Cat. 5.2–3, where the *senes severiores* are not sympathetic. It could also, of course, explain 3.8–12 as the response to (a genuine) S.'s encouragement (see Introduction, Section V).

The phrase (**ex/per)solvit promissum** is prosaic, appearing elsewhere in poetry only at Ov. *Met.* 14.810–11, *Fas.* 3.391–2. The mention of a promise from Venus makes the link to Sappho 1 stronger (see *ad* 3.13.3 *Camenae*); in that poem, Sappho and Aphrodite seem to have a relationship of some longevity and intimacy, wherefore Aphrodite regularly comes to Sappho's amatory aid and causes a string of women to reciprocate her affections.

Mea gaudia narret: a striking statement, because elegy is nearly always 'first-person' poetry, but also because it calls the rest of the poems into being, particularly 3.8, 3.10, and 3.12 (Hinds 1987a: 42). Here again questions of cycle-division and attribution come into play. Ancient poetry is often figured as spoken, and just as our 'say' is used of writing, so *narro* is used of poetry at e.g. Prop. 1.18.29 (but not elsewhere in the *CT*). On the other hand, it also means 'gossip' at Prop. 2.18.37, Tib. 1.5.42 (Lyne 2007: 353). It is unclear exactly how the first part of the line connects to the second: Venus has done her job and S. has had joy, but why does this mean someone else should tell the story? Lowe terms it 'apodotic to an open future condition, leaving it still uncertain whether she intends to commit her sins to *fama*' (1988: 204). Perhaps S. suggests that having attained her erotic object, she has no further interest in poetry (misleadingly, given what follows); if so, her utilitarian emphasis on the efficacy of her poetry is unparalleled (see *ad* 3.13.4). In either case, the subjunctive, urging that her story be told, contradicts our expectations about S.'s concern for her reputation, but confirms the first couplet. In the elegists, **gaudia** are normally sexual, or metonymic for the loved one; see *ad* 3.9.18. Fabre-Serris 2009 suggests that these lines influence Ov. *Her.* 15.109–10. Given the difficulty most (modern) readers have in explicating S.'s meaning, the words may also carry a challenge: 'let anyone narrate my story [if he can understand it]'.

Dicetur is strained, but fits in with S.'s concern throughout this poem with reputation, her own and others'. It is sometimes suggested that this is an 'extra' verb *metri causa*, but the contrast with *ego* in line 7, and S.'s consistent concern with who talks about whom, suggest otherwise (so too, the trisyllabic molossus hardly deflects attention from itself). The construction may be distancing (S., occupied with her own affair, doesn't know or care about anyone else) or welcoming (S. encourages anyone, ever, **si quis**—note the future tense—who wants to write love poetry, to do so). Either would be surprising: elegiac poetry tends to predicate itself upon *puella*-as-muse (see Introduction, Section I), but also on 'autobiographical' experience, such that it ought not to be available to any chance passer-by to write S.'s story in the third person (but note Prop. 1.10, a poem written about Prop.'s observation of Gallus' affair). And yet, here it is. So perhaps S. means to displace the love-object as muse (and to replace her/him with Amor or Venus). More boldly, Flaschenreim suggests that S. means by **quis** to indicate that 'both sexes may find their experience represented' in her poetry (1999: 41; cf. Pearcy 2006: 33 on this as S.'s attempt to tell the story of those who have no voice). In any case, this is a surprisingly generous model of poetic composition, wherein a body of material is made available to a community constructed simply by its willingness to use it (and one that may mimic, or call into being, that of the composition of [Tib.] 3). We might contrast the elegiac poet's more typical jealousy about his *puella*/subject matter (Batstone, forthcoming). On the other hand, elegiac poetry also positions itself as didactic and even remedial (e.g. Prop. 1.7.13–14, 3.3.19–20, and especially Ov. *Am.* 2.1.5–8); Paris conceals his own desire for Helen under the names of others (Ov. *Her.* 16.243–6). Lyne suggests Cat. 5.2 as a comparandum: nosy people with nothing better to do are welcome to gossip about S. (2007: 353).

> **Non ego signatis quicquam mandare tabellis,**
> 8   **ne legat id nemo quam meus ante, velim,**

The distich is difficult (and plays an important role in discussions of 'female Latin'; see Introduction, Section VI) because it is unclear where the emphasis lies: one possibility is that S. expresses a traditionally feminine worry about committing herself to writing (Lowe 1988: 205, seemingly). See Farrell 1998 on the dangers women can cause themselves through writing, and such passages as Ov. *Am.* 1.11.23–4, which limits the amount women should write; Prop. 3.23, a poem about a lost notebook, points up one danger of elegiac writing, and Ov. *Am.* 1.12, which suggests that a visit in person would have been more persuasive, another. We might translate this 'I would not want to put anything in writing, lest anybody read it before my lover'. The other possibility, which is more in keeping with what the remainder of the poem suggests, is that S. claims that her personal communication is not personal at all, i.e. 'I would not want to *seal* my tablets to prevent anybody from reading it before my lover' (so Lyne 2007: 349). The ambiguity is probably unresolvable; perhaps the larger point is that S. has written so as to present herself as dutiful or not, depending on what her reader expects. Interestingly, here again Cerinthus' role is downplayed; he is not even to be the privileged recipient of intimate communication, but is rather simply part of S.'s reading public (Hubbard 2004: 180). Lowe terms the couplet 'mischievous', especially in the coy subjunctive *velim* (1988: 204). Dronke notes the triple negatives, which emphasize S.'s rejection of public opinion (2003: 85).

Mandare: in elegy, usually in the participle, of orders or advice given (e.g. Tib. 1.3.15); a similar phrase in the same metrical *sedes* occurs at Prop. 3.23.11 (*mandata tabellis*, which Lyne 2007: 350 suggests alludes to this passage; cf. *OLD* 2). **Tabellis** resemble notebooks; they are flat, thin sheets of wood covered over with wax and scratched into with a stylus to write short notes and poetry (and they were often perforated and gathered together to make booklets). In elegy they are the standard means of written communication between *amator* and *puella* (e.g. Ov. *Am.* 1.11.7 and 15, 1.12.1 and 7)—though they do not usually designate polished poetry. The diminutive is a neoteric device, often at line-end. *Tabellae (ob/con)signatae* and/or *mandatae* occur frequently in Plautus, usually as a key element of a plot for obtaining money (writing in Plautus is regularly deceptive). For Holzberg, the word explains the 'format' of poems 14–18, which are letters (1998: 186; their epistolary quality is also noted by Smith 1913 *ad loc.* in a dismissive vein). Lyne, on the other hand, putting emphasis on **signatis** (cf. Prop. 3.23.4), notes that 'open' poetry means published poetry (2007: 348). (See Introduction, Section VI, for the dangers inherent in women coming to writing.)

Ne...nemo: Smith 1913 *ad loc.* and Dell'Era 1996b: 125 note some parallels for the emphatic (and colloquial) double negative (including *nemo non* at Prop. 2.19.32); Bréguet 1946: 49 suggests that it may be based on Greek usage. For (rare) lengthening of the *o*, see Platnauer 1951: 50 (the Prop. line also lengthens). *Me* appears instead of **ne** in Ambr. and V; the reading *me legat ut* (Barney and Postgate), where *ut* is a conjecture, removes the ambiguity entirely. The metapoetic gain, whereby S. becomes a *lecta puella* (cf. Ov. *Am.* 2.1.5) may be worth the loss in wordplay.

Meus: for parallels, cf. e.g. Ov. *Her.* 5.4, *Ars* 1.322, *Fas.* 2.752 (all of love-objects); cf. also *ad* 3.1.6. **Quam ante**: *ante* is postponed at Lucr. 3.973, 4.884, Mart. 9.35.6, and otherwise prosaic; on *ante* for *antea* see *ad* 3.1.10. The word order is neat, emphasizing the priority of **nemo** over **meus**.

    sed peccasse iuvat, voltus componere famae
10   taedet: cum digno digna fuisse ferar.

The poem ends, as it began, with a juxtaposition between the desire for secrecy and the need to tell all. **Sed** continues on from *velim* of 7; S. did not want that; she does want this. We might recall Sappho 16, which foregrounds female erotic choice even when it conflicts with the constraints of society.

Peccasse iuvat is significant as evidence for S.'s admission of potentially 'inappropriate' behaviour. In the elegists, *peccare* generally describes an adulterous (or quasi-adulterous) affair, or the cheating activities of one or another party; cf. e.g. Tib. 1.6.16 for the former and 1.6.71 for the latter, and Ov. *Am.* 2.7.19–20 for *peccasse...iuvet* of potential cheating (Hallett 2009a: 5 sees Ov. *Am.* 3.14.1 as dependent upon these lines). Hor. *Od.* 1.27.17 seems to use *peccare* less explicitly, of falling in love (without any physical component), but *Serm.* 1.2.63 undermines this interpretation. Language suggesting wrongdoing of this kind has not yet made an appearance in [Tib.] 3, which seems to treat of (more) licit affairs, but it recurs at 3.20.1; the verb suggests that S. understands the subversive and disruptive potential of her poetry/behaviour. So too, **iuvat**

rejects an entire code of conduct: S. will act in defiance of society's norms, and she will enjoy it. While the sentiment is Catullan (5.2), the effect is rather different when it is voiced by a woman, who would suffer more serious repercussions than a man. Note too the appearance of indicatives, rare in S., to make clear her choice (Lowe 1988: 205 terms the lines 'a burst of almost capricious impersonalized subjectivity'). Fabre-Serris sees a close connection between the verb and Ov. *Her.* 15.133–4 (2009: 165), one of the more explicitly sexual lines in Latin poetry.

For **componere** as assuming a false expression, see *ad* 3.6.35; on its metapoetic nuances, see *ad* 3.2.26, and on the notion of hiding in this cycle, see also 3.18. **Componere voltus** appears in poetry at Ov. *Met.* 13.767 (*feros…componere vultus*) of the care Polyphemus, newly in love, takes with his appearance (there with at least implicit deception), *Fas.* 5.30 (*voltus composuisse suos*) where the gods arrange their faces to resemble that of Maiestas (in emulation more than dissimulation), Manil. 3.214 *vultus…componere certos* (of depicting the precise features of the stars), and Manil. 5.451 of the influence of Cepheus rising on a person's physiognomy. It is otherwise prosaic, and occurs primarily in contexts of deliberate deception (e.g. Sen. *Dial.* 12.17.1, Plin. *Ep.* 2.20.3, Suet. *Cal.* 50.1, Tac. *Ann.* 1.7.3; it is more positively viewed—but still deceptive—at Sen. *Ep.* 66.5, Plin. *Ep.* 3.16.5, 7.1.6, Quint. *Inst.* 9.1.21). On *vultus*, see Pichon 1991: 303.

Famae: for the more usual *ad famam*. Working out the precise emphasis of **taedet** is again difficult: it could mean 'how annoying that I have to—and will continue to have to—pretend', or could announce a change in behaviour ('I'm tired of pretending, and so I'm finished'). The final words of the poem confirm that it is the latter; for more on **taedet**, see *ad* 3.2.8.

Digno digna: Currie notes that alliteration is not common in S., and suggests that this effect is 'especially found in antique or homely contexts' (1983: 1759 n. 24; his citations are Plautine). For the repetition of adjectives, see Wills 1996: 225–41; it occurs in Tib. with nouns at 1.8.26, 1.9.80, 2.1.37, 2.5.117, and is frequent in Ov. For the 'epitaphic' qualities of the final statement, see Flaschenreim 1999: 44–5, with Prop. 4.11.36 *uni nupta fuisse legar* (and see too Plin. *NH* 35.115, of the painter Marcus Plautius, *dignis digno loco picturis*). Hubbard suggests that the phrase may be marital (2004: 185, with citations). Häußler 1968: 85 and 252 lists the phrase as colloquial (see Bücheler 1891: 243). Keith 1997: 302 connects this line to V. *A.* 4.191–2 (*venisse Aenean Troiano sanguine cretum,/cui se pulchra viro dignetur iungere Dido*), Hallett 2002a to Cat. 68.131–2 (*aut nihil aut paulo cui tum concedere digna/lux mea se nostrum contulit in gremium*). Fabre-Serris 2009: 155 suggests the importance of the Gallus fragment, which includes *digna* (quoted in part *ad* 3.13.1), and sees this line as influential upon Ov. *Her.* 15.39–40; Batstone (forthcoming) draws attention to its monumental qualities. If it is correct to see a hint of class-consciousness in the *qualem* of line 1, this phrase redefines it.

Fuisse: see Varro *DLL* 6.80 for the euphemism *cum muliere fuisse* of sexual intercourse. It is difficult, but just barely possible, to imagine that S. does not mean the verb in a sexual sense. Lowe notes S.'s control over *fama* in her final words: she herself provides 'the hitherto coyly hinted-at tidbit of gossip on her own terms in her own poem' (1988: 204)—though without any kind of detail. As Maltby notes, the phrase is a colloquialism, appearing frequently in Plautus and at Cic. *Fat.* 30, Ov. *Am.* 2.8.27, *Ars* 3.664 (2009: 335).

Ferar is closural, and normally taken as a subjunctive; Milnor 2002: 276 suggests attention to the full ambiguity of the form, which might also be future (as *moriar*, *vitabit*, *crescam*, and *dicar* are at Hor. *Od.* 3.30.6–10, and *vivam* at Ov. *Am.* 1.15.42 and *Met.* 15.879; cf. Lyne 2007: 350 with further citations); note too *ferar* at Hor. *Od.* 2.20.1. Like these other statements, S. leaves it unclear whether she *will be* spoken about, she *might be*, or she *wishes to be*. In the light of the progressive reinterpretations of *fama* occurring throughout the poem, we might see this as a final definition: scurrilous gossip has turned into poetic reputation. And this is itself a radical envisioning of the function of elegiac poetry: if the *puella* is as available as S. proclaims herself to be, there is no need for poetry to woo her.

3.14:

3.14, another genethliacon (see 3.11), is paired with 3.15, which apparently resolves the problem presented in this poem. See Santirocco 1979: 232 on the verbal echoes, and on the contrasts between the two in addressee and tone. He also points out the stylistic differences between the two: the first poem includes 'the pathetic fallacy, the stock contrast of city and country, the facile generalizing about the timeliness of travel, and the rather overdone ending'. The juxtaposition of birthday and unhappiness is also striking (Lyne 2007: 354). Note, however, that the text as transmitted leaves unclear whose birthday it is; the phrasing of 1–2 certainly suggests S.'s, but 3.15.1 claims it as Cerinthus' (it ought to be the same in both cases, or much of the point of the poems is lost). The poem has a very clear opening; less marked is its end.

This poem, presumably, is one reason critics assume that S. is a rather young woman; its petulant tone suggests that of a spoilt child. But—aside from the fact that this is a modern stereotype (note too the necessity for all Roman women to be under some man's guardianship, which tends inevitably to suggest infantilization)—that may not be all that is going on in this poem: the *puella* often departs from Rome only in order to be with a rival, leaving the lover to fret. In this respect, the two poems provide a parallel to Prop. 1.8, often split into two poems, where a trip is proposed and cancelled; Prop. 2.19 is another '*puella* departure' poem. But this and 3.9 are the only elegiac poems which purport to offer a '*puella*'s-eye' view of the elegiac situation of separation (for partial parallels see Prop. 4.3 and the *Heroides* of Ov.). Here, however, S. makes clear that it will not be her choice, that the *rapta puella* really was taken against her will, raising again questions about how similar she really is to other elegiac women (Batstone, forthcoming). Note too Barthes' suggestion that, because movement is a quintessentially masculine activity, the one who is left behind is always feminized (1978: 13–14; cf. Lipking 1998: xix: 'When a man is abandoned, in fact, he feels like a woman').

The question remains open whether we are to imagine Messalla as cognizant of S.'s relationship with Cerinthus or not: is this an attempt to separate the lovers, or an innocent avuncular treat? As Batstone notes, our ignorance probably parallels S.'s own; Messalla is not likely to have explained his motivation.

> Invisus natalis adest, qui rure molesto
> 2   et sine Cerintho tristis agendus erit.

Invisus natalis, not surprisingly, is unattested elsewhere in Latin literature. For an unhappy **natalis** elsewhere, see Ov. *Ib.* 217 *lux quoque natalis, ne quid nisi triste videres*, and see the conjunction of the noun and **tristis** at 3.15.1–3, Ov. *Tr.* 3.13.1–10, 19–20; for **tristis** see *ad* 3.2.27, 3.3.35, 3.4.42, 3.6.34, 3.6.38, 3.10.7, 3.17.3.

Rure molesto: unattested, although this is a judgement with which the elegists, excepting Tib., would agree (see Introduction, Section I). **Molesto**: probably colloquial (*TLL* 8.1352.73–1353.64); often used in e.g. Plautus of annoying persons and circumstances. At Cat. 51.13, *otium* is so described, and it appears throughout Prop. and especially Ov. for those who interfere in erotic matters (e.g. Prop. 1.5.1, Ov. *Am.* 2.3.15).

Sine Cerintho: obviously the aspect of the countryside which colours all else, making it hateful; cf. *sine* at 3.9.19. As with his first mention at 3.9.11, he is fleeing or absent (Pearcy 2006: 34). **Agendus**: the gerundive here is perhaps legalistic, prompting Hallett 2011: 84 to note that S. may be playing upon the fact that her father is a jurist (cf. *OLD* 41, 42, 44). On the other hand, Cic. *Fin.* 2.101.7 *dent quod satis sit ad diem agendum natalem suum quotannis mense Gamelione* cf. *OLD* 30 and Juv. 4.66–7 *genialis agatur/iste dies*) suggests that this is normal usage for a particular special day.

> Dulcius urbe quid est? An villa sit apta puellae
> 4   atque Arretino frigidus amnis agro?

These lines, typically for S., are full of questions. We might read them as a rejection of Tib. 1.1, a poem which, at least in fantasy, privileges country life—or, more broadly, as a rejection of Tibullan elegy. But see e.g. Tib. 2.3.64–7, which claims that wine is not worth removing girls from the city for.

Dulcius: again, somewhat colloquial; see 3.3.27, 3.4.42, 3.6.9, 3.11.7. For the sweetness of a city in different contexts, see Cic. *De Leg.* 3.19.2 (*nihil erit iis urbe,* *nihil domo sua dulcius*), and Liv. 4.12.7 (*dulcedine contionum et urbis*). For the conjunction of *tristis* and *dulcis*, Lyne 2007: 355 notes Gallus fr. 2, which may or may not come from the same poem; the papyrus marks a separation between the two words); note too 3.4.42.

Villa: the only other mention of a *villa* in the *CT* is at Tib. 2.3.1: *rura meam, Cornute, tenent villaeque puellam*, of which this is likely to be an echo (on the special status of Tib. 2.3 in regard to the S. poetry, see Introduction, Section IV). The word is not in Prop. or in Ov.'s amatory works; it conjures suggestions of rusticity, but presumably a **villa** of Messalla would be exceedingly comfortable. **An…apta**: brings out the question of how generically appropriate the country is to elegiac poetry; see *ad* 3.10.21. **Sit** may be preferred to *est* as expressing the extreme unlikelihood of the statement, or simply its hypothetical nature. **Puellae**: see *ad* 3.2.1: S. here locates herself with the quintessential elegiac term. Lyne 2007: 355 wonders if the *puellis* of H might be more appropriate, as 'fitting Sulpicia's (humorously) indirect argumentation', and cites Tib. 2.3.66 for the plural as a notional singular.

Arretino…agro: also at Sall. *Cat.* 36.1 (though there is probably no connection). For discussion of Arretium, and the inscriptional evidence that the Sulpicii had property there, see Fatucchi 1976; this may explain the specificity of the location, which is usually eschewed in elegy.

Frigidus amnis: the river is the Arno, eight kilometres north of Arezzo (mentioned as a source of grapes, wheat, and a healing herb at Plin. *NH* 14.36, 18.87, 26.87). Commentators often wonder why S. singles out the river (e.g. Lyne 2007: 355); some prefer Scaliger's *annus* (see Lyne for discussion and parallels). But rivers have a distinguished pedigree in elegy: see *ad* 3.6 (hints of metapoetic imagery in this poem at Pearcy 2006: 34). Messalla presumably imagines that **frigidus** will be pleasing to S., but she is associated with heat (flames at 3.8.5–6, fever at 3.17.2). The possibility of either cooling down or being 'healed' of her lovesickness by running water (cf. 3.10.8) may be part of S.'s objection. Compare Cat. 44, in which the poet goes to the country to recover from a cold.

> Iam, nimium Messalla mei studiose, quiescas,
> 6   heu tempestivae saeve, propinque, viae!

Messalla: this line marks the first intrusion of Messalla into this cycle. (He had already appeared as the dedicatee of [Tib.] 3.7.) He is normally presumed to be the same Messalla as Tib.'s patron, and here S.'s guardian; see Introduction, Section IV. Maternal uncles are ideally imagined as special sources of protection and affection (Hallett 1984: 151–5 and *passim*), a fact that may be in play here. But see also Santirocco 1979: 232 on the 'interfering uncle' of Hor. *Od.* 3.12.3, which is surely another potential model.

Studiose: has metapoetic implications, as at Cat. 116.1 and Ov. *Fas.* 2.15 (see too *ad* 3.12.15, with Hallett 2002b); it occurs with notions of patronage, in the vocative and in the same *sedes*, *Tr.* 3.14.7 and *EP* 2.5.63, and with a notion of keenness for Ov.'s poetry, *Tr.* 5.1.1. **Mei studiose** may recognize S. as a subject, and author, of poetry, i.e. 'a careful reader of my poetry' in addition to 'paying attention to me'. Finally, **nimium ... studiose** suggests the disjunction between Messalla's intent—giving S. a pleasant surprise for her birthday—and its effect, which is to make her miserable: Messalla is both paying her too much attention, and not enough. If we take **mei** as referring to poetry as well as person, we might conclude that Messalla has not understood S.'s poetry (or alternatively, has understood it too well!): she expects him to know that she would not relish a trip to the countryside.

Quiescas: here intransitive, metaphorical, and perhaps comically colloquial ('give it a rest'); usually in elegy of those dead or resting. The closest elegiac parallel occurs at Ov. *Her.* 12.196, of Jason's soothing of the dragon (there transitive); for the intransitive use see *OLD* 6b, with examples from comedy, and Hor. *Ser.* 2.1.5 (where it is an instruction to stop writing poetry).

Tempestivae ... viae: the sentiment sounds gnomic, but is attested only at Apul. *Met.* 8.21. The adjective is mainly prosaic (perhaps with a rustic flavour, given its association with temporal cycles in the agricultural writers); in elegy it is compounded to its opposite, *intempestivus*, except at Ov. *Tr.* 4.10.81. The two main manuscripts, followed by nearly all modern editors, read *neu* for **heu**, which gives the required negative (but inappropriately adds a connective); see Cartault 1909: 256, Schuster 1968: 169–70, Vretska 1957: 84–6, Tränkle 1990 *ad loc.* (who prints *neu tempestive sepe propinque vie* in cruces), and Lyne 2007: 356 for discussion. We could supply 'and also recognize that...', but the line remains vexed.

Saeve: strong language from a ward; it might be better replaced with the manuscripts' *saepe* (as Luck has it). **Propinque**: of relatives at Cat. 41.5 (where they are in some supervisory role over the *puella*), Hor. *Ser.* 2.3.218 (also in the context of tutelage), Prop. 1.22.7, 2.6.7, 4.1.79, Ov. *Fas.* 2.618-19 (and see *TLL* 10.2.2022.51–66); at first look it appears too formal and vague, especially in a direct address, but perhaps equivalent to our 'cousin' of any number of familial relations. Cf. the first Propertian example, *mei ... membra propinqui*. Note too the tantalizing fragment of Caesar Strabo (almost surely a coincidence): *deinde propinquos nostros Messalas domo deflagrata penore volebamus privare*, from a speech against P. Sulpicius Rufus (Malcovati 1953 *ORF* 73.14.1).

Hic animum sensusque meos abducta relinquo
8   arbitrio quamvis non sinis esse meo.

Animum sensusque: a fairly common phrase (e.g. V. *A.* 4.22, Ov. *Met.* 14.178); see Pichon 1991: 86 s.v. *animam*.

For **abducta**, see 3.9.5; the perfect participle is a nice way to suggest S.'s subjectivity, but also the uncertainty the (male) elegiac lover normally has about why the *puella* is leaving him—is she really unwilling, or is that simply what she tells him (see *ad* 3.2.2 and 3.9.5)? Tib. 2.3.61, with *abducis,* is less certain. So too, the participle may suggest S.'s powerlessness (as at Prop. 2.20.1). See Milnor 2002: 264 on the fact that S.'s abduction here (compare the theft of N. at 3.2.30) removes her from an affair rather than forcing her into one.

Arbitrio...meo: S. succinctly objects to her formal status as *femina in tutela* (Introduction, Section IV; note too *arbitrium* of Hermione's legal status at Ov. *Her.* 8.32); she is also, of course, complaining about Messalla's overzealous performance of his duties. See 3.6.14 (also Prop. 4.1.143, Ov. *Ars* 1.504, Hor. *Od.* 3.6.40), where it is imagined that one could be under the *arbitrium* of a woman (legally, of course, this is not possible). In Ov., the word can stand for poetic judgement (*EP* 3.9.48 *arbitrio variat multa poeta suo*); cf. *Tr.* 4.4.22 of a letter Ov. wrote, *non fuit artibrii...tui*. Note too Ov. *RA* 380, where personified Elegy is encouraged *arbitrio ludat amica suo*. See too Publil. Syr. A5, who notes *amor animi arbitrio sumitur, non ponitur*: S. is also expressing her choice (see Pichon 1991: 88 for *arbitrium*). The case is difficult (more regularly genitive); cf. Tränkle 1990 *ad loc.* for parallels in the jurists. Perhaps this is another instance of 'legal' language.

Sinis: see Statius' emendation *sinit* (which would require *quam vis*). See too *ad* 3.15.2. For **quamvis** with indicative, see *OLD* 4; the sense here is that S. is not allowed to have an opinion (**arbitrio**), but she does anyhow. Luck prints *arbitrii quin tu me sinis esse mei*, derived from later Italian manuscripts and Heinsius; Tränkle 1990 has the text as above except for *quoniam* in place of **quamvis**.

3.15:

The poem expresses S.'s joy at the change of plans; now she will spend the birthday with Cerinthus. As Santirocco 1979 notes, although this poem is clearly paired with the previous one, it differs in tone and style (though both poems have a clear beginning and a less clear end). Poems expressing unalloyed happiness are rare in elegy, and, like most of them, this one is preceded and followed by poems with darker tone. So too, unlike similar poems in Prop. (e.g. *vicimus* 1.8.28), S. does not take credit for affecting the world with her poetry; the not-trip has occurred, like the proposed trip, unbeknownst to her (Batstone, forthcoming).

> Scis iter ex animo sublatum triste puellae?
> 2   Natali Romae iam licet esse suo.

The question mark is, of course, modern punctuation: this might be a simple statement of fact. The brevity of the poem, however, and the *forte* of line 4, suggest rather that S. is eager to convey her news. **Scis** is an informal beginning to a poem, reflecting the suddenness of the change of plans, and S.'s excitement. **Iter...sublatum**: otherwise only at Cic. *Att.* 16.4.4. **Iter...triste** elsewhere at Ov. *Tr.* 3.9.32, Sen. *HF* 1136, *Oed.* 657, and Mart. *Spect.* 12.6; the phrase responds to *natalis...tristis* of 3.14.1.

Ex animo: construe with **sublatum**; the journey is no longer a matter of concern; cf. Eng. 'cares lifted away'. **Ex animo** normally means 'sincerely' (e.g. Cat. 109.4), but it is here more literal (e.g. Plaut. *Cas.* 23, *Truc.* 454, Lucr. 4.908, Hor. *Ep.* 1.5.18 (and for a pun on these two meanings, see Cic. *De Or.* 2.260; that pun may also be here).

Romae: locative. The city, a constant focus of the elegiac world (Introduction, Section I), is rarely mentioned by name.

Suo: the manuscript reading *tuo* is hard to reconcile with the previous poem, where it is S.'s birthday. (Huschke's *meo* also possible, as is *tuae*, read by Luck in some Renaissance manuscripts.) See discussion at Schuster 1968: 171–2 and Tränkle 1990 *ad loc.*

    Omnibus ille dies nobis natalis agatur,
4   qui nec opinanti nunc tibi forte venit.

Omnibus ... nobis: peculiar (but the only manuscript reading), as S. has so far been interested only in two persons, herself and Cerinthus. The phrasing suggests rather a larger community (perhaps the *solliciti* of 3.16.5). Dell'Era 1995 suggests *optimus* (paralleled at Cat. 14.15 of the Saturnalia). **Dies ... natalis agatur** cf. 3.14.2; Lyne suggests *genialis* for **natalis** along the lines of Juv. 4.66 (2007: 358).

Nec opinanti: mostly prosaic. See Tränkle 1990 *ad loc.* for a defence of the conjecture *necopinata*, which Luck and he print. **Nec opinanti ... forte**: It is odd to suggest that a birthday (**dies ... qui**) comes unexpectedly and by chance, since they occur with some regularity (particularly after the Julian calendar reforms; cf. Hinds 2005 on Ov.'s birthday in *Tr.* 4.10). Presumably the repetition is meant to emphasize the poet's delight at her changed circumstances, and her anticipation of Cerinthus' delight upon hearing that they will be together. **Tibi** is also peculiar, given the **nobis** of the previous line. Luck prints *sorte*.

3.16:

Perhaps the most difficult of the poems to construe (scholars have offered at least three distinct interpretations), 3.16 uses sarcasm to make S.'s point: she is *delighted* that Cerinthus seems to feel so secure in her affections that he can pursue another woman. No other elegy uses language in quite this way, a fact that leads some critics to speculate about the indirectness of women's speech in Latin (or about the heightened emotion that is being conveyed). But the basic situation—a suspected rival—is extremely common in the elegiac world. Batstone (forthcoming) suggests that the poem means to convey some of S.'s own difficulties in coping with the fact, or supposition, of Cerinthus' infidelity. Whose fault is this, exactly? Was she a fool to believe what she used to believe? Could there be a reasonable explanation? Beyond this, he suggests that it expresses precisely the situation of a female poet, who is not able to demand a response from others. Those looking for a coherent narrative often place this poem chronologically just before [Tib.] 3.13, such that the couple has fought and (then) made up; Hubbard connects this poem to the epithalamic Cat. 61, wherein the groom is reminded that he must discontinue relationships with slaves (2004: 187). This poem is also part of the long tradition of women's lament, which begins in the *Iliad*, finds full flowering in Greek poetry, especially tragedy, and takes an erotic turn (in elegy at e.g. Prop. 1.3, Ov.'s *Heroides*, and many others); see Holst-Warhaft 1992 on the tradition of women's funerary laments.

The poem also contains S.'s full name (and assertion of her status), and perhaps provides further information about the *credula turba* of 3.10.18. This might, indeed, be key to interpretation: perhaps S. has expressed her willingness to flout convention by engaging in an illicit physical relationship, only to discover that Cerinthus has found a lower-class woman to oblige instead. (See Ov. *Am.* 1.8.43, *casta est, quam nemo rogavit*, and *passim* in the *Ars* for the opinion that women are much easier to seduce than they seem.)

Santirocco 1979: 233 points out both the wordplay (*cadam* in 2, *cedam* in 6; *securus* in 1, *cura* in 3, *solliciti* in 5; cf. Lowe 1988: 201 on *securus...de me* and *solliciti...pro nobis*) and the way S. conveys the vast chasm between her own aristocratic status and 'the concrete representations of her rival's lowly status: *togae, pressum quasillo, scortum*, and *ignoto toro*'. (See too Flaschenreim 1999: 47 on the ways the two women are not so very different.) The quasi-legalistic language may derive from the juristic interests of Ser. Sulpicius Rufus (see Introduction, Section IV). Keith 1997 suspects a connection to the anger of the Vergilian Dido (*A.* 4.305–30, 365–87). Perhaps most interestingly for the collection as a whole, Hinds 1987a: 46 finds in the poem hints at cross-dressing in the word *toga*, and notes that at some periods the Kalends of March (important to this cycle, and to the book as a whole; see *ad* 3.1.1 and 3.8.1) provided an occasion for men to dress as women. But the evidence is mostly Christian (Schneider 1920); Macr. *Sat.* 6.4.13, from a Republican Atellan farce (which context may be relevant here) is of unclear import. See further discussion at *RE* 14.2.2308–9 and Hinds 1987a: 46. If, however, the practice can be dated to the time of this poetry, we may have a hint about the nature of its authorship.

Gratum est, securus multum quod iam tibi de me
2 **permittis, subito ne male inepta cadam.**

Gratum est: a colloquial phrase, attested in prose at e.g. Cic. *Att.* 14.20.2, 15.7.1, *Fam.* 13.16.4, in poetry at e.g. Plaut. *Capt.* 454. Generally, however, it is used of actual pleasure, rather than sarcastically.

Securus: key to this poem, but of unclear import: construed with **de me**, it means 'confident I won't cheat too'; alone, 'confident you won't be caught'. In Tib., the word is unironic and pertains to freedom from care or toil (*OLD* 4b;

perhaps 'unconcern'). In L., however, the adjective relates to fidelity to one's lover (see *ad* 3.3.32, 3.4.54). Ov. is, as usual, more specific: *Her.* 19.109 wonders *quis enim securus amavit?*; *Am.* 1.8.95 and *Ars* 2.443 and 3.609 provide the detail that a rival prevents complacency in love. As usual, S. seems to know the standard elegiac conventions, but to eschew them. Note too the etymological connection with *cura* (and perhaps a wordplay with Cerinthus). The legal sense of the word ('immune', *OLD* 5b) may also be relevant here, given S.'s probable connection to a juristic family (Introduction, Section IV). **Quod**: usually taken as the conjunction, explicating what is **gratum** (as is the case in the majority of the Ciceronian examples), but it might also be the relative pronoun, 'what you allow yourself'. **Multum quod iam tibi de me**: the initial sense, 'very secure for your part about me', must be revised in the second line, when the verb gives sense. **Multum** might also be construed with **securus**: 'exceedingly confident'.

Permittis: often with a reflexive and an accusative, 'allow yourself' (*OLD* 6a; *TLL* 10.1.1557.19–41: Ov. *Her.* 8.39 *quem sibi permisit...amorem*; closer parallels in prose at e.g. Sen. *Ep.* 51.3 *sibi plurimum luxuria permittit*, *QN* 1.pr.1 *multum permisit sibi*, with **de** at Cic. *Att.* 12.27.2. Piastri 1999: 327 suggests reading *mihi* of the older manuscripts for **tibi**, which she construes as adding to the sarcasm ('thanks for allowing me this much for myself'). **De me** might also be construed with **securus**, 'secure about me'. Ending a line with two monosyllables is unusual in elegy; see also 3.17.5.

Subito: of the suddenness of S.'s fall and perhaps also of her discovery. **Ne**: possibly with **securus** but better with **permittis** as a kind of final clause, explaining why it is **gratum** (Lyne 2007: 360). **Male**: somewhat colloquial and intensifying; cf. Cat. 10.33, Hor. *Serm.* 1.3.45, 1.4.66 (both modifying adjectives), with Tränkle 1990 for discussion. **Inepta** can cover both S.'s mistakes in her personal life and (a lack of) poetic craftsmanship. For erotic stupidity, Cat. 8.1, Tib.1.4.24, Ov. *Ars* 1.306, *RA* 472; for bad hair days (perhaps with metapoetic implications), Prop. 2.18.28, Ov. *Am.* 1.14.36; see Pichon 1991: 167–8 for further nuances.

Cadam: usually taken as a purpose clause, dependent upon *securus* or *permittis* (Lyne 2007 prefers the latter); it could also be an indirect command 'that I shouldn't fall'. Smith 1913 adduces Caes. *BG* 5.31.5 for the sarcasm. Commentators generally understand the verb to mean our 'become a fallen woman' (*OLD* 11a and 24; Plaut. *Pers.* 656 and various wordplays in Sen. *Cont.* 1.3, but otherwise unattested in Classical Latin), and therefore assume that S. has preserved her virginity up to this point. But note the legal sense (*OLD* 11b, 'to fail in legal proceedings'). Or S. might simply mean 'be diminished' (*TLL* 3.25.34–26.42; Lowe 1988: 201). The confusion is probably not simply our own; as often, S.'s vocabulary allows a variety of meanings to be understood. Batstone (forthcoming) notes, 'If Sulpicia has no place to stand in this effort to preempt Cerinthus, she has many places to fall'. See too the introduction to this poem for wordplays on **cadam** and *cedam* of line 6. Ellerman 1982 defends *credam*.

Commentary on 3.16.4

        Sit tibi cura togae potior pressumque quasillo
4   **scortum quam Servi filia Sulpicia:**

Sit is heavily ironic, either jussive or an (insincere) optative subjunctive (Luck prints P's *si*). **Cura**: see Introduction, Section VII, for the importance of the word to this poem.

    Togae: the garb of citizen men and prostitutes (e.g. Hor. *Serm.* 1.2.63, Cic. *Phil.* 2.44); commentators often assume S. refers to the latter (i.e., that the phrase is a hendiadys), but this may be because they see Cerinthus as not a citizen; S. may rather warn him to pay attention both to his status and his whore (a zeugma; Hinds 1987a: 45 notes that she is also drawing attention to her own transgression of gender norms within this cycle); Batstone (forthcoming) sees a more intimate connection between the two meanings: citizen status means precisely the ability to enjoy oneself with a prostitute, *securus*. It may or not be relevant that Hor. *Serm.* 1.2.80–2 makes mention of both a Cerinthus and a toga (Hallett 2006: 40–1 argues for allusion). If both meanings of **togae** are intended, S. also reverses the elegiac lack of concern with one's citizen duties, positioning herself as a disapproving representative of the Roman elite. **Potior pressum**: the plosives hint at S's rage (as do the repeated *c* and *s* sounds throughout).

    Pressum…scortum: there is an anacoluthon in the couplet, in that this ought to be the same case as **togae**; see Tränkle 1990 *ad loc.* for parallels. **Scortum** is not an elevated word (in poetry mostly in satire and comedy; cf. Cat. 6.5 and 10.3 and Pichon 1991: 260). It strikes an especially harsh tone when juxtaposed with S's formal name (here appearing for the first time in the poetry). Hallett suggests that Liv. 39.9.5, which refers to Hispala Faecinia as a *scortum*, is an allusion to this passage (2011: 86).

    Quasillo: in elegy elsewhere only at Prop. 4.7.41, where Cynthia's replacement punishes certain slaves with heavier wool-baskets. The word is rare in Latin, appearing elsewhere at Cato *Agr.* 133.3, Cic. *Phil.* 3.10, Petr. 132.3, Plin. *NH* 17.98 (see Tränkle 1990 *ad loc.* for debate about its gender). The Pliny passage suggests that these are among the lowest-status slaves; for the connections between spinning and prostitution (in that both were professions available to poor women), see *AP* 6.283–5. Although this is clearly not the sense here, wool-working in elegy is also sometimes linked to matronal virtue (e.g. Prop. 1.3.41, Tib. 1.3.85–7). On the diminutive at line-end, see *ad* 3.13.7.

    Servi filia Sulpicia: the 'seal' on S's poetry; its importance explains the odd caesura. But **Servi filia** undermines S's attempt to assert her aristocratic status; the phrase is normally used to describe slaves (Hinds 1987a: 45) and, as Batstone (forthcoming) notes, is also used for prostitutes: even where she appears to offer unambiguous declaration, S. remains difficult to pin down. So too, as Hinds notes, this moment of potential authorial triumph contrasts sharply with the tone of the remainder of the poem (1987a: 44); see too Batstone (forthcoming)

Commentary on 3.17

on the way S. (like all Roman women) cannot identify herself except in terms of her relationships to men.

> **solliciti sunt pro nobis, quibus illa dolori est**
> 6   **ne cedam ignoto, maxima causa, toro.**

For the hyperbaton of the couplet, cf. Ov. *Tr.* 3.5.23–4 *si tamen interea, quid in his ego perditus oris—/quod te credibile est quaerere—quaeris, agam*, *Ib.* 3–4 *nullaque, quae possit, scriptis tot milibus, extat/littera Nasonis sanguinolenta legi* (Housman 1972: I.140–1, with further examples).

Solliciti: see *ad* 3.4.20, 3.6.36, 3.6.61 for elegiac meanings (and note Publil. Syr. A34 *amor otiosae causae est sollicitudinis*). Keith 1997 connects this couplet to V. *A.* 4.35–8, where Dido mentions other potential suitors. It is unclear if this is S.'s referent; commentators generally assume that she means members of her aristocratic family. But, if family, they ought rather to be concerned with S.'s illicit affair, rather than its potential endangerment (see Hinds 1987a on the 'interested parties' the lines adumbrate as poetic audience). For the plural **nobis**, see *ad* 3.13.4.

Dolori: dative of cause; for the noun, see *ad* 3.2.3, 3.2.6, 3.2.13, 3.2.29, 3.6.3, 3.6.43, 3.20.3 (all of emotional pain). See Schuster 1968: 172–3 on the choice between *dolori est* and *doloris* (the latter of which Luck prints).

Ne cedam ignoto maxima causa toro: for the word order, seemingly Gallan, see commentators *ad* V. *E.* 1.58 (with Skutsch 1956: 198–9); this construction also occurs at 3.17.1. **Ne cedam**: implied fear clause (so positive, 'lest I give way'), dependent upon *dolori* (Lyne) or *solliciti sunt*. S. may mean 'be replaced by' a rival or 'give (myself) to' a relationship (see below); the verb is used of marriage at e.g. V. *A.* 3.297 and 12.17. Note again the potential wordplay with Cerinthus. **Maxima causa**: Prop. 1.16.35 *maxima causa doloris*, Ov. *RA* 322 *odio... maxima causa*, 768 *aemulus est nostri maxima causa mali*, *Tr.* 5.12.46 *maxima causa fugae*.

Ignoto... toro: paralleled only at 3.6.60, on which see *ad loc*. But there is no need to conclude, with Wagenvoort 1917: 115–18, that this means L. and S. are a couple. **Ignoto** most explicitly refers to the (unnamed) rival, but the word may have particular point, if it is correct that Cerinthus' status is significantly lower than S.'s. **Toro** could refer either to Cerinthus' bed or, metonymically, to S.'s rival (this will depend on the meaning of the verb *cedam*; see above). Or perhaps both: **ignoto, maxima causa, toro** could reflect the opinions of the **solliciti**, eager to see her preserve her reputation, but S., may misconstrue them to signify that she should act against the rival so as to preserve her relationship. Finally, there may be a metapoetic tinge to **ignoto**: S. could here express worries about her own poetic reputation.

3.17:

3.17 provides a neat reversal of the standard sick-girlfriend poem (see 3.10 for the genre; the two poems may refer to the same incident): here, the *puella* writes of her own illness and so expands upon the trope of love-as-disease (Introduction, Section I; Holzenthal 1967: 72–6 on this poem). S. would, it turns out, only like to recover if she knows that Cerinthus loves her. Keith 1997 suggests that this poem may depend in part upon V. *A*. 4.1–5, and Tschiedel 1992: 96 sees a close relationship to Tib. 1.3.

The poem uses technical medical language (as Maltby 2009 notes, we have only late parallels), and a number of Catullan phrases. Hallett 2002b: 144 sees a pun on the name of the Valerii ('healthy ones') in this and 3.10. Santirocco 1979: 233 connects this poem to the previous one, insofar as both present a 'relation under strain'. Finally, Lowe 1988: 200 notes 'the careful patterning of pronouns, the chiastic echo of *euincere morbos*, the artful variations of enjambment' as evidence of the poet's sophistication.

> Estne tibi, Cerinthe, tuae pia cura puellae,
> 2   quod mea nunc vexat corpora fessa calor?

Estne: regular in comedy, so perhaps colloquial (elsewhere in poetry at line-start at e.g. Cat. 66.15, Sen. *HF* 621, 697, *Troad*. 979, Stat. *Theb*. 10.238). Importantly, S. does not know what C. feels for her: the uncertainty is typically elegiac although the use of questions is not (Batstone, forthcoming). **Cerinthe**: see *ad* 3.9.11.

Pia cura: cf. Ov. *Am*. 2.16.47 *si qua mei tamen est in te pia cura relicti*, *Her*. 8.15 *cura mei si te pia tangit*; note too V. *A*. 2.536 *si qua est caelo pietas quae talia curet* and Auson. *Parent*. 19.13 in a funerary context. **Cura** has its usual elegiac meaning; see 3.1.19, 3.2.29, 3.3.21, 3.4.9, 3.4.43, 3.4.59, 3.6.7, 3.6.29, 3.6.37, 3.9.5, 3.16.3, 3.18.1, 3.19.11. **Pia** adds a different tone; see 3.2.16, 3.4.20, 3.5.7, 3.10.25: so far in this corpus, it has referred only to religious things. Many see a Catullan emphasis to the mention of *pietas* (Santirocco 1979: 233, Hallett 2002b: 147), or even a Vergilian note (Santirocco 1979: 233). But it also occurs at e.g. Ov. *Ars* 2.321 of fidelity (Lyne 2007: 362–3, who also discusses the manuscript reading *placitura* here; **pia cura** is a Renaissance emendation).

Vexat: of a variety of troubles in elegy: mythical, metaphorical, and physical. The participle describes a sick Cynthia at Prop. 2.28.15, is used of increasing a lover's interest at Ov. *Am*. 2.19.15, and, perhaps most interestingly, describes tackling a hackneyed poetic theme at Ov. *Tr*. 2.318; perhaps there is also metapoetic nuance here. **Vexat corpora**: rare, and prosaic (citations at Lyne 2007: 363); Celsus 7.26.5 (*si valens corpus est neque magnopere vexatum*) suggests that it is technical.

Corpora fessa: at 3.10.10, also of S's illness. The adjective is perhaps especially appropriate in this location, which may take us towards the end of the last elegies we have for a generation (note too the metapoetic implications of **corpus**). Note too *defessa* at Tib. 1.5.9, also of illness.

Calor is the standard medical term for fever (*OLD* 4, *TLL* 3.181.15–39; e.g. Juv. 12.98); but is also used in elegy to describe passion (*OLD* 6, *TLL* 3.182.25–36;

e.g. Prop. 1.12.17, 3.8.9; Ov. *Ars* 1.237). Given the identity tricks some see as inherent to the composition of this corpus, there may also be a pun on *cal(l) idus* here.

> A ego non aliter tristes evincere morbos
> 4   optarim, quam te si quoque velle putem.

A ego: a neoteric construction, denoting a situation of great emotion; see *ad* 3.4.82. **Non aliter...quam**: note the same construction in 3.16.3–4; it is not common elsewhere in elegy outside of Ov.; see *ad* 3.13.2.

Tristes...morbos: also at Tib. 1.5.9, V. *G.* 4.252, Ov. *Met.* 7.601; the noun is used of illness in elegy at 3.10.1 (see *ad loc.*), Ov. *Ars* 2.323; of lovesickness at Cat. 76.25, Tib. 2.5.110, Prop. 2.1.58, Ov. *RA* 81, 115. It is not possible fully to distinguish the two usages; the *RA* itself is an extended play on the double meaning of the concept. **Evincere morbos**: otherwise medical: Celsus 3.22.8, Colum. *DRR* 6.5.2, Veg. *Mulom.* 4.3.6. Similar phrasing occurs at Ov. *Met.* 1.685: *molles evincere somnos*, also at line-end, of Argus' struggles to stay awake.

Optarim: elsewhere at Tib. 1.6.74, Ov. *Her.* 17.109, Hor. *Ser.* 1.1.79. See Tränkle 1990 *ad loc.* for the hyperbaton of **quoque** in poetry.

> At mihi quid prosit morbos evincere, si tu
> 6   nostra potes lento pectore ferre mala?

This final couplet does not add much; perhaps it is a marginal rewriting of the previous couplet that has crept into the manuscripts. See Tränkle 1990 *ad loc.* and Lyne 2007: 364 for alternative manuscript readings. **Si tu**: two monosyllabic words rare at the end of a hexameter; see Tränkle 1990 *ad loc.*, who discusses similar endings in the first three books of Prop. and in Gallus (see too Norden 1957: 448–9).

Lento pectore: elsewhere at Ov. *Her.* 15.169–70 (*versus amor fugit lentissima mersi/pectora*). **Lento** means both pliable and slow; in the latter sense (*OLD* 8; *TLL* 7.2.1163.14–53) it is a standard elegiac word for the lover who is less ardent: e.g. Tib. 2.6.36, Prop. 1.6.12, 1.15.4, 2.14.14, 2.15.8, 3.8.20, 3.23.12, Ov. *Ars* 1.732 (with the opposite meaning at Prop. 2.14.22, where the *puella* does not respond to others). On **mala**, see *ad* 3.2.8, 3.4.82, 3.10.7, 3.19.20.

3.18:

This poem has a complex structure (a single sentence, with multiple subordination; see Lowe 1988: 198 on the way S. uses 'complications of syntax to which elegy is not normally hospitable to nest, embed, and interlock rhetorical ideas and build complex emotional puzzles out of restricted epigrammatic technique'). The temporal structure of the poem is also complex: Lowe 1988: 199 outlines 'four moments of experience': *iam, hesterna nocte, paucos ante...dies,* and *tota iuventa* (with correspondingly intricate syntactic structure). Lyne 2007: 365, on the other hand, suggests that the difficulties reflect colloquialism. As usual for S., the poem highlights a disjunction between seeming and being, and its conclusion leaves the reader uncertain about the status of the relationship (did she ruin things?). Many have wanted to see this poem as chronologically preceding 3.13 (see Milnor 2002), and some have even rearranged the poems to fit this theory, but this imposes a closure that is not present in the text we have (see Skoie 2002). In fact, the poem, potentially the last of the S. cycle, is not especially closural (Lyne 2007: 343). Its placement in the manuscripts is various; it is usually joined to 3.17 and sometimes also placed after 3.6.

The elegiac lover regularly expresses desire, but usually with more directness; we might also be reminded of Cat. (Tränkle 1990, Gaertner 1999, Lyne 2007). Santirocco notes that this poem violates the typical elegiac tendency to use a couplet as a sense-unit, attributing it to the poet's desire to seem 'breathless' (1979: 234). (This should not, of course, be mistaken for artlessness.) Hallett 2009a sees the poem as having prompted Ov. *Am.* 3.14, a poem that criticizes female sexual liberation and has 'Sulpician' language and themes.

> Ne tibi sim, mea lux, aeque iam fervida cura
> 2   ac videor paucos ante fuisse dies,

The lines are difficult to translate: 'Lest I be as fevered a concern as I seemed to be to you a few days earlier, my darling…' **Ne tibi sim**: see Lowe 1988: 198 on the characteristic Sulpician use of subjunctives, especially in this poem. Tränkle 1990 *ad loc.* and Lyne 2007: 365 note a number of parallels for the *ne…si* phrase (*ne* OLD 4), and the latter observes that this construction is 'a real colloquialism' not otherwise found in poetry. Here, it introduces a negative purpose clause serving as the apodosis. **Mea lux**: see *ad* 3.9.15; Lyne 2007: 366 notes that only elsewhere at Ov. *Ars* 3.523–4 is it addressed to a man. Hallett 2002a sees a specific allusion to Cat. 68.160 here in the use of the vocative. Note too the play with **dies** in the next line.

Aeque…ac: in poetry, mostly found in comedy, but also at Cat. 22.16, Hor. *Ser.* 2.3.47, *Ep.* 1.1.92–3. For the differences in tone between *ac* and *atque*, see Axelson 1945: 82–4; see too *ad* 3.11.13 for a similar use of **aeque**. **Fervida**: at Ov. *Am.* 1.2.46 of the arrows of Cupid, and Prop. 3.17.13 of wine, but less common for passion than one might expect in the elegists (see Pichon 1991: 147). **Fervida cura**: unattested, but see Hor. *Od.* 1.30.5, where Amor is termed a *fervidus puer*. The adjective suggests that this might be seen as a companion to the previous 'illness' poem; it is also tempting to connect this passage with the *cura* wordplay in 3.16. For **cura** in the elegiac sense, see *ad* 3.17.1, and Ov. *Am.* 2.16.47.

Videor: here the poet again raises questions of appearance and reality (see *ad* 3.13). **Paucos…dies**: common, and prosaic; also found in comedy and at e.g. Cat. 13.2, [V.] *De Rosc. Nasc.* 47, Juv. 10.343–4, 13.160, Mart. 1.15.4. For **ante**, see *ad* 3.1.10 and 3.2.11–15. **Fuisse**: on the infinitives in this poem (three, each in the same place in its couplet), see Lowe 1988: 199 and Lyne 2007: 365 (especially on elegiac perfect infinitives).

    si quicquam tota commisi stulta iuventa
4   cuius me fatear paenituisse magis,

Si quicquam: in elegy at line-start at Cat. 96.1, 102.1, 107.1, elsewhere at Prop. 2.21.9, Ov. *Tr.* 3.4.3, *EP* 1.6.19. Merkelbach 1984: 95 suggests replacing **si** with *nil* (which Luck accepts). **Tota...iuventa**: also at VF 3.682.

Commisi: the word can have sexual implications (*TLL* 3.1902.60–70), which may be present here (note also Sall. *Cat.* 24.3 *Sempronia, quae multa saepe virilis audaciae facinora commiserat*). With the perfect, S. seems to suggest that the period of her youth is past in a way similar to L. in 3.5. **Stulta** refers regularly in elegy to those uninterested in love, as at Tib. 1.2.68, 1.4.34, or incompetent at it, as at Tib. 1.9.45, 1.9.65, [Tib.] 3.19.18; we may be meant to connect it with *inepta* of 3.16.2. Here, as with *digna* towards the end of 3.13, is this poem's solitary grammatical indication that its speaker is female. The focus on the stupidity of youth is reminiscent of Cicero's tactics in the *Pro Caelio* (e.g. 10, 25–30). **Iuventa**: uncommon; see *OLD* 1 for its diachronic meaning '[whole] youth'. But, as Lyne notes, one can refer to one's youth even while still in it (2007: 348).

Cuius introduces a relative clause of characteristic. **Fatear paenituisse**: probably not, as Lyne 2007: 365 suggests, merely for the sake of metre: the S. cycle is keenly interested in issues of telling and not-telling. **Paenituisse**: relatively uncommon in love elegy outside of Ov. *Her.* (where it appears eight times; otherwise Tib. 1.4.47, Prop. 4.2.3, Ov. *Am.* 3.7.46, *Ars* 2.592). **Magis**: a 'Sulpician' word; see *ad* 3.13.4.

    hesterna quam te solum quod nocte reliqui,
6   ardorem cupiens dissimulare meum.

The pentameter is an especially pleasing end to the S. cycle. As usual, the poet challenges expectations: we might expect her to regret foolish deeds (especially given *commisi* of line 3), but instead, she regrets *not* having done them. **Hesterna...nocte**: see *ad* 3.4.2; here surely referring to Cat. 50.1, another poem called into being by an emotional encounter. **Te solum...reliqui**: Lyne 2007: 367 suggests comparison with Cat. 64.200, *quali solam Theseus me mente reliquit* and Prop. 2.24.46 *sola relicta*; see too *ad* 3.6.40. While the elegiac *puella* does leave her *amator*, it is rare for her to do so under her own volition (see *ad* 3.2.2 *eripuit*). So too, departure is rare for the *amator*, who wants union any time, all the time: should we understand this as a temporary manifestation of S.'s *pudor* (3.13.1)?

Ardorem: on the 'fires of love', see *ad* 3.8.6 and 3.11.5–6, (and note the disjunction between **nocte** and **ardorem**, parallel to the conjunction of *lux* and *dies* in lines 1–2). At the end of her cycle, S. attempts **dissimulare**, as opposed to 3.13, where she wanted to make all public (or did she?). Are we to read the poems chronologically, and, if so, is this new stance accounted for by the deepening of her feelings, or something else? **Dissimulare** is more commonly used in elegy of the tricks lovers use to hide their relationships, as at e.g. Ov. *Am.* 2.2.18, 2.7.8, 3.11.24; cf. Pichon 1991: 131 and Ov. *Ars* 1.276 on women as better able to hide their desire (*vir male dissimulat: tectius illa cupit*). S., with this poem, uncovers her attempt to cover things over, continuing the elegiac cycle of deferral. **Cupiens dissimulare**: prosaic and rare (Cic. *Verr.* 1.21, *Flacc.* 21.14). **Ardorem...dissimulare** not otherwise attested. Note too Lowe 1988: 199 and Lyne 2007: 367 on the ways successive pentameters in this poem grow shorter (line 2 has six words, line 4 has five, this line has four).

3.19:

This poem (or fragment), which claims to be by, or is at least put in the mouth of, Tib. (line 13), is generally assumed to be spurious (of recent participants in the debate, see Knoche 1956 against Tibullan authorship; Eisenhut 1977 for, with Smith 1913 and Lenz 1932 for some of the earlier history). If genuine, it may be either early work or, possibly, once have formed part of the (extremely short) Tibullan Book 2. Among the evidence against authenticity, Knoche 1956: 174 and Tränkle 1990 note that it is shorter than most genuine Tibullan poems (excepting 2.2), Maltby 2009: 337 draws attention to some metrical differences, and Knoche 1956: 175 finds its clarity of expression un-Tibullan. These points are not probative one way or another. Those who want to see the poem as belonging to early Tib. adduce Hor. *Od.* 1.33 and its suggestion of a 'pre-Delia' relationship with Glycera, though that poem's *Albi* may or may not be Tib., and it is not clear how Glycera is to be fitted into the narrative; see Nisbet and Hubbard *ad loc*. Ov. *Am.* 3.9.32 *altera cura recens, altera primus amor* tends in the other direction, confirming the impression of Tib.'s own poetry that Delia and Nemesis are it; see Introduction, Section V (though Glycera could of course be one or another of these women).

As with most of the poems in this book, there are echoes of other poems which could be read in two different chronological directions. The poem does not seem a deliberate forgery, or a cento (*pace* Gaertner 2002): Tibullan echoes are equalled by those of other poets, and there are not quite enough of them to suggest consistent and conscious emulation. Rather, the poem utilizes, as does much of erotic elegy, a series of familiar *topoi*.

The poem itself deals with a typical elegiac situation, though the elegiac *amator* is here even more abject than usual: he flaunts his powerlessness in a way that is artful (for, of course, he could simply have destroyed the poem if it were really 'giving away' his secret): note e.g. Ov. *RA* 11 *nec te, blande puer, nec nostras prodimus artes*. He also succumbs to erotic servitude (which, incidentally, has the effect of guaranteeing, at least on his part, the continuance of the relationship; Fulkerson 2013). The poem falls into two sections: the author first assures the *puella* of his love, swearing by Juno to be faithful (eight couplets); he then bewails the fact that his careless speech has given the *puella* an unfair advantage (four couplets).

> Nulla tuum nobis subducet femina lectum:
> 2   hoc primum iuncta est foedere nostra venus.

Tuum: the addressee is unclear; Tib. has two *puellae*, Delia and Nemesis, but there is also Glycera of Hor. *Od.* 1.33 (see introduction to this poem); cf. e.g. Knoche 1956: 173 and below, *ad* 3.19.22, where her 'known'-ness is (for us, ironically) emphasized.

Subducet: future; there will be no rival. See e.g. the more regular construction *nec mihi rivalis certos subducet amores* (Prop. 1.8.45, which Lee 1963: 7 sees as the original). The verb with this direct object is unattested in Latin (and more naturally suggests the theft of furniture); for a Greek parallel, see Soph. *El.* 114. The line may reference Hom. *Od.* 23.177–204, the immovable bed of Odysseus, which could not be 'stolen away'; if so, the sentiment gains extra point and sophistication. For erotic thievery, see Pichon 1991: 270. **Femina** is not as common as *puella* in the elegiac poets, but not unattested (and may support the Odysseus–Penelope connection): see *ad* 3.4.61.

Lectum: the only occurrence of this word in [Tib.] 3, although it is frequent in other elegists, both literally (e.g. Tib. 1.1.43) and metaphorically of a romantic relationship (e.g. Tib. 1.5.7), often in this *sedes*; see Pichon 1991: 185–6. It appears with a similar sense at Prop. 4.11.85 *seu tamen adversum mutarit ianua lectum*.

Primum: Postgate 1880: 282 notes that the word is Propertian, and here 'very doubtful Latinity' for *primo*. **Iuncta...venus**: Tib. 1.9.76 *venerem iungere*, Ov. *Ars* 2.679 *venerem iungunt*, *RA* 407 *venerem...iunge*; cf. Cat. 78.3 *iungit amores*, Tib. 1.1.69 *iungamus amores*, Ov. *Tr.* 2.536 *quam legitimo foedere iunctus amor*. **Venus** is repeated in the final couplet, which may be a closural device (i.e. it may indicate that we have a complete poem rather than, as some think, a fragment).

Foedere: standard for lovers' pledges (Pichon 1991: 152); cf. e.g. Prop. 3.20.21 *foedere lectus*, Tib. 1.5.7–8 *per te furtivi foedera lecti,/per venerem quaeso compositumque caput*, 1.9.1–2 *quid...foedera,...clam violanda, dabas?* Prop. 3.20, which seems to allude to such a contract, should probably not be taken literally (though see Racette-Campbell 2013 on its similarities to extant Greco-Roman marriage contracts).

> Tu mihi sola places, nec iam te praeter in urbe
> 4   formosa est oculis ulla puella meis.

Tu mihi sola places: an elegiac tag-line. It is, of course, possible to take the sentiment as sincere, but Ov. *Ars* 1.42, *elige cui dicas 'tu mihi sola places'*, suggests the fungibility of the elegiac woman. Even Prop. 2.7.19 conveys a certain sense of doom: *tu mihi sola places: placeam tibi, Cynthia, solus* (with line 6 below). Cf. too Prop. 1.7.11 *placuisse puellae*, Ov. *Am.* 3.4.32 *sola placet*. **Sola** here, however, has additional point: the poet will go on to exclude all but the *puella* from his world.

Iam: the temporal reference is jarring; does the poet mean to suggest that he used to find other girls beautiful? (If so, this would be very elegiac: however much the elegist swears fidelity, the relationship always has a short shelf-life.) **Praeter** is un-Tibullan, but appears in Ov. **Urbe** is significant as locating this poem within a larger (usually inexplicit) urban world. It may also play on the pun *orbs in urbe*; see e.g. Ov. *Ars* 1.174 *ingens orbis in urbe fuit*, and *Ars* 1.55–60 on the abundance of *puellae* at Rome; for the delights of the city, see *ad* 3.14.3.

Formosa...oculis...meis: Postgate 1903 sees an imitation of Prop. 4.4.32 *et formosa oculis arma Sabina meis*; Tränkle 1990 *ad loc.* suggests Ov. *Met.* 9.476 *ille quidem est oculis quamvis formosus iniquis*. On **formosa**, see *ad* 3.1.7; it is a favoured word of L. **Ulla puella**: same *sedes* at Tib. 1.1.52.

> Atque utinam posses uni mihi bella videri!
> 6   Displiceas aliis: sic ego tutus ero,

See Prop. 2.7.19, quoted *ad* 3.19.3, about the rarity of elegiac fidelity. **Atque utinam**: frequent in Prop., occasionally in Ov.; in the *CT* only here and 3.5.27, in the same *sedes* (where it is also unclear whether the subjunctive introduces a real or an impossible wish). Smith 1913 *ad loc.* notes that **uni mihi** always replaces *soli mihi* in Tib., but not elsewhere in the *CT*. **Bella videri**: cf. Cat. 8.16 *cui videberis bella?*; Tib. 1.9.71 *non tibi sed iuveni cuidam vult bella videri*; on the prosaic **bella**, see *ad* 3.4.52; cf. Call. *Epig.* 29.3–4 Pf. for a parallel.

Displiceas: used of a lack of erotic interest at Tib. 1.8.75, Prop. 4.5.49, Ov. *Her.* 13.46, *Met.* 8.493, 9.527, *Tr.* 1.1.50, 2.140; see Pichon 1991: 131. Is **tutus** too much to ask for in elegiac love? Prop., who uses the word with some regularity, does so ambiguously; sometimes it is to be wished for (e.g. 2.4.19), sometimes attained (e.g. 2.13.14), and sometimes impossible for Prop. himself (e.g. 1.1.32). See too Ov.'s famous statement that he sings of *venerem tutam* at *Ars* 1.33, and Prop. 2.13.14 *domina iudice tutus ero*. Ov. *Ars* 1.752 suggests that if you don't trust anyone with your girl, *tutus eris*, 2.58 that by following his instructions, *tutus eris* (both same *sedes*). **Ero**: future indicative perhaps to emphasize the keenness of the poet's wish.

> nil opus invidia est, procul absit gloria volgi:
> 8   qui sapit, in tacito gaudeat ipse sinu.

The rejection of boasting is not especially elegiac; normally the *amator* cannot wait to tell the world of a successful night (cf. e.g. Prop. 1.8.42 *Cynthia rara mea est*). (We might see this poet-lover as smarter than the usual run, but the remainder of this poem undermines that characterization.) On **invidia**, see *ad* 3.3.20; here, as there, the intent is to avoid the evil eye.

Procul (with *absum*): a Tibullan formulation (1.6.39, 1.9.51, 2.1.11). **Gloria vulgi**: the common people, unlike our author, gossip about their affairs; indeed, they do so in this very corpus (as also does he). Cf. Tib. 1.5.2 *at mihi nunc longe gloria fortis abest* (the poet has falsely boasted that he can separate from Delia); Pichon 1991: 160.

On **sapit**, see *ad* 3.8.2; the present general is didactic, applicable to anyone in a similar situation. **In tacito...sinu**: Ov. suggests keeping your mouth shut during the good times at *Am.* 3.12.7 and *Ars* 1.741–2; Prop. during the bad at 3.21.32. Further on **sinu** see *ad* 3.3.8, 3.9.24, 3.13.4. On **gaudeat**, see *ad* 3.1.8, 3.4.60, 3.4.69. The phrase is proverbial: cf. e.g. Prop. 2.25.29–30 *quamvis te diligat illa/in tacito cohibe gaudia clausa sinu*, Cic. *TD* 3.51 *in sinu gaudeant, gloriose loqui desinant*, Sen. *Ep*.105.3 *invidiam effigies...si scieris in sinu gaudere*; Hom. *Od.* 22.411 (Otto 1890: 324).

> Sic ego secretis possum bene vivere silvis,
> 10   qua nulla humano sit via trita pede.

The couplet proposes a quasi-Tibullan retreat from the city, which throws into contrast the urban setting of the poem (cf. e.g. Tib. 1.3). But even Tib. imagines a kind of civilization, on a rural farm, while this poet seems to want to steal the *puella* away from all possible temptation, perhaps in the manner of Acontius, hiding out in the woods and carving the name of Cydippe (Call. *Aet.* fr. 72, 73, seemingly also important for Gallus; see V. *E.* 10.50–4 and Prop. 1.1.9–12, with commentators). The *puella*, for her part, almost never shares the *amator*'s joy at being away from Rome (see too *ad* [Tib.] 3.14–15).

Sic ego: an Ovidian locution, also in Tib. and Prop. **Secretis...silvis**: Ov. *RA* 591 has *secretae...silvae* in the same *sedes* (where, however, they are detrimental to a lover); cf. Ov. *Met.* 7.75 *secretaque silva*, Mart. 12.18.23 (where the sense seems to be erotic). Note too Hor. *Ep.* 1.4.4 *tacitum silvas inter reptare salubres*, in a poem addressed to an Albius often believed to be Tib. At a metapoetic level, the solitude sometimes craved by the elegist is in contradiction to the audience he needs for publication; cf. e.g. Prop. 1.18, with similar sentiments.

Possum: placed in the indicative, presumably, to assert certainty. **Bene vivere**: frequent in prose, especially philosophical, and also in poetry; cf. e.g. Cat. 61.226 *bene vivite*, Tib. 1.3.35 *quam bene Saturno vivebant rege*, Plaut. *Mil.* 706, *Trinumm.* 65, Hor. *Ep.* 1.6.56, 1.11.29, 1.15.45, Mart. 12.17.9. Here, of course, the point is subtly different: the Epicurean notion is altered by the poet's insistence that only with the *puella* are woods and loneliness pleasing.

Via trita: the road not taken is a Callimachean trope (*Aet.* fr. 1.25–8; in Latin, Lucr. 1.926–7 *avia Pieridum peragro loca nullius ante/trita solo*); cf. Plin. *NH* pr.14 *praeterea iter est non trita auctoribus via*, Sen. *De Vit. Beat.* 1.2 and *Ep.*

122.9 of the philosophical life; other examples at Prop. 3.18.22 *ista terenda via est* (of death); Quint. *Inst.* 1.6.22, Sil. 2.356–7.

Humano...pede: elsewhere at Apul. *Met.* 11.11 of the gods, Plin. *NH* 8.155, and Suet. *Jul.* 61.1 of a horse. On **humano**, see *ad* 3.4.26 (where it is a contested reading).

    Tu mihi curarum requies, tu nocte vel atra
12   lumen, et in solis tu mihi turba locis.

Tu...tu...tu: the pathos of the repetition may emphasize the poet's, as opposed to the *puella*'s, feelings (she is not satisfied with him alone; see Wills 1996: 361–2 for the repetition). Cf. Prop. 1.11.23–4 *tu mihi sola domus, tu, Cynthia, sola parentes,/omnia tu nostrae tempora laetitiae*, and Ov. *RA* 579–91 on the dangers of solitary places for those in love (with Lee 1963: 9); the *topos* derives ultimately from Hom. *Il.* 6.429–30. **Curarum requies** is not a description of the normal elegiac relationship; again, the poem seems to withdraw wholly from elegy's urban setting, where part of the game is the knowledge that there are other options. Cf. Ov. *Tr.* 4.10.118 *tu curae requies*, *EP* 3.3.7 sleep as *requies curarum*, [Ov.] *Ep. Drus.* 306 *tu requies fesso grata laboris eras*.

    Nocte...atra: elsewhere in poetry at V. *A.* 4.570, Hor. *Epod.* 10.9, Ov. *Met.* 5.71, Manil. 2.46–7, 5.725, Sen. *HF* 282, *HO* 1294, [Sen.] *Oct.* 715, Stat. *Theb.* 8.691, Sil. 5.36, 5.127, 7.126. The delayed word-order of **vel** is perhaps intensifying. **Nocte...lumen**: similar sentiment at Prop. 4.1.143 *illius arbitrio noctem lucemque videbis*. On **atra**, see André 1949: 43–52 and Pichon 1991: 91. For **lumen** in an amatory sense, see Pichon 1991: 192; elsewhere at e.g. Apul. *Met.* 5.13.

    The idea of one person serving to fill the roles of many is not uncommon in poetry (see Prop. 1.11.23–4 (quoted above) and the *locus classicus* at Hom. *Il.* 6.429), but is not often phrased in terms of a **turba** (Lee 1963 objects strongly); Ov. *Met.* 1.335, *nos duo turba sumus*, is probably the closest parallel (spoken by one of the only two remaining humans to the other). The word in Ov. often signifies a group of people with common interests, such that two can be a sufficient 'crowd' (cf. *ad* 3.10.18); see too Mart. 12.21.10 *Romam tu mihi sola facis* and *AP* 12.60, which claims that Thero is all things to the author. Such passages as e.g. Prop. 1.13.36, *quotcumque voles, una sit ista tibi*, are actually rather different. **Solis...locis**: a common conjunction, e.g. Plaut. *Aul.* 673, *Rud.* 205, 1185, Ter. *And.* 406, Lucr. 4.573, 6.396, Ov. *Am.* 3.6.50, *Her.* 11.84 (same *sedes*), *RA* 579–80 (seen by Eisenhut 1977: 213 as a key intertext), *Met.* 7.819, 14.681, *Fas.* 1.502, 4.514 (same *sedes*), Sen. *Ag.* 436, Stat. *Theb.* 12.145.

    Nunc licet e caelo mittatur amica Tibullo,
14   mittetur frustra deficietque Venus.

Licet: introduces, as often, a subjunctive; here it is almost a conditional clause, 'even if'. **E caelo mittatur**: possibly proverbial; cf. Tib. 1.3.89–90 *tunc veniam* *subito, nec quisquam nuntiet ante./sed videar caelo missus adesse tibi*, Sil. 11.410–11 *lascivus et alto/mittit se caelo niveis exercitus alis*, and, more generally, Prop. 2.3.25–32. The phrase perhaps also picks up on the frequent *topos* in this book of the gods coming down to earth to examine particular mortals, or of goddesses who have affairs with human men, disastrously for the latter. More disturbingly, we may see a reference to the destructive Pandora, sent to mortals to wreak havoc (as Tränkle 1990 notes *ad loc.*, in the Greco-Roman imagination, gifts from the gods are far from positive). Note also Ov. *Ars* 1.43, where it is asserted that a *puella* will not simply drop out of the sky for the aspiring lover/elegist (*haec tibi non tenues veniet delapsa per auras*), with Lee 1963: 7.

Amica does not appear in the *CT*, but is regular in Cat. (not of Lesbia but of other women: 41.4, 43.5, 72.3, 110.1), Prop. (e.g. 1.6.10, 2.6.41–2, 2.29.31), and Ov. (e.g. *Am.* 1.6.45, 2.1.17, *Ars* 1.398, 1.417, 2.175, 2.288, *RA* 215, 441). Its absence from Ov. *Met.* suggests that it is not an elevated word; see Adams 1983: 348–50. **Tibullo**: it is perhaps strange that the poem mentions Tib., but not the *puella* (Tib. uses his own name in the nominative at 1.3.55 and 1.9.83, both epitaphs and both in the same *sedes*).

On **deficiet**, see *ad* 3.4.20, 3.9.6. **Deficietque Venus**: cf. Tib. 1.5.39–40 *saepe aliam tenui, sed tum cum gaudia adirem/admonuit dominae deseruitque Venus*.

> **Hoc tibi sancta tuae Iunonis numina iuro,**
> 16 **quae sola ante alios est mihi magna deos.**

Sancta... numina: poetic examples at e.g. Lucr. 2.434, 5.309, 6.70, V. A. 3.543, 8.382 (plural and singular seemingly interchangeable). **Tuae Iunonis**: see *ad* 3.6.48 for the Genius and Juno of individuals. Knoche 1956: 181 notes that *per* is expected here, and that the double accusative is a Graecism (with one Latin parallel, at V. A. 12.183). **Iuro**: famously problematic in elegy; see *ad* 3.1.26.

Sola: refers back to the phrasing of line 12; our poet likes extremes. **Ante alios**: see *ad* 3.4.93, 3.11.5. Postgate 1903 finds the conjunction of **sola** and **ante alios** redundant but, as Tränkle 1990 *ad loc.* notes, there are parallels (e.g. V. A. 3.321 and 11.821).

Mihi magna: for **magna** with the dative **mihi**, see e.g. Prop. 1.11.21. Here **magna** must have the force of a comparative. For **deos** of a single human see e.g. Ov. *EP* 4.8.23 *di tibi sunt Caesar iuvenis*.

> **Quid facio demens? Heu heu mea pignora cedo.**
> 18 **Iuravi stulte: proderat iste timor.**

Demens: see *ad* 3.6.27; cf. Ov. *Met.* 3.641 *quid facis, o demens?*, *Tr.* 5.10.51 *quid loquor, a! demens?*, *EP* 4.3.29 *quid facis, a! demens?*; the adjective is nearly always in this *sedes* in elegy. Because the elegiac relationship is not built upon mutual trust, the poet has lost ground by swearing fidelity (since she has done no such thing). For parallels, see e.g. Call. *Aet.* 74.2 with Harder 2012 *ad loc.*, and see Navarro Antolín 1994 for discussion of the *topos* in elegy.

Heu heu: Tibullan (1.4.81, 1.6.10, 2.3.2, 2.3.49, 2.5.108); repeated elsewhere in poetry at Plaut. *Pseud.* 1320, V. *E.* 2.58, 3.100, Hor. *Od.* 1.15.9, *Epod.* 15.23.

Pignora cedo: a legalistic phrase, occurring in Justinian. **Cedo** is only rarely transitive: Lucr. 5.986–7, Tib. 1.4.39–40, Manil. 2.584–5; **pignora** is usually concrete (e.g. Ov. *Ars* 3.486); see Lee 1963: 8–9. **Iuravi stulte**: not otherwise attested, but presumably colloquial. On **iuravi**: see above *ad* 3.19.15; **stulte**: see *ad* 3.18.3. **Proderat...timor**: not otherwise attested; meaning slightly obscure: '[your] fear was useful [for me]'.

    Nunc tu fortis eris, nunc tu me audacius ures:
20   hoc peperit misero garrula lingua malum.

Fortis: see *ad* 3.2.6, 3.6.62, and Tib. 1.4.13 *quia fortis adest audacia, cepit*. For the meaning, 'bold', perhaps even 'unpunished' (*TLL* 6.1.1152.66–82; it is usually more positive in nuance), see e.g. Ov. *Am.* 3.2.32. **Audacius ures**: this helps to complete the meaning of **fortis** (note too Tib. 1.2.16 and 1.4.13); cf. Ov. *Tr.* 2.267–8 *siquis tamen urere tecta/comparat, audaces instruit igne manus*; **ures**: see *ad* 3.8.11, 3.11.5, 3.12.17.

Garrula lingua: also at Ov. *Am.* 2.2.44 (of Tantalus; same *sedes*), Mart. 13.71.2, Val. Max. 7.2.ext.1c (of a mother-in-law). The adjective is regularly applied to a variety of noisy, and undignified, animals (V. *G.* 4.307 the *hirundo*; [V.] *Dir.* 74 the *rana*; Ov. *Met.* 8.237 the *perdix*). In elegy and Ov. *Met.*, loquacious characters are normally punished; in addition to the crow (*Met.* 2.547, *Am.* 3.5.22), cf. the tale of Echo (*Met.* 3.360), the partridge (*Met.* 8.237), Tantalus (Ov. *Am.* 2.2.44 and *Ars* 2.606), Corinna's parrot (*Am.* 2.6.26), and chatty servants (Prop. 4.7.42, Ov. *Am.* 2.2.60). Prop. 2.23.17 prefers a woman who is not *garrula*, but at 3.23.18, the *garrula* is more appealing, perhaps because she is also *volens*. For *garrula* of musical instruments, see *ad* 3.4.38; on **lingua**, see *ad* 3.4.88, 3.6.39, 3.6.46.

Peperit...malum: proverbial; cf. Plaut. *Cist.* 142 *ut aliae pariunt quae malum quaerunt sibi*, Zeno *Tract.* 1.1.8 *parit omne quod malum est et peperit omne quod peius*. **Peperit**: often in elegy without any procreative nuance: Tib. 1.6.27 wine brings sleep; 1.7.9 warfare brings glory; Prop. 1.18.23 girl brings misery; of birth at Prop. 2.3.28, 2.15.22, 4.1.102. **Malum**: see 3.2.8 and 3.4.82; **misero**: see *ad* 3.20.4; Pichon 1991: 202.

    Iam faciam quodcumque voles, tuos usque manebo,
22   nec fugiam notae servitium dominae,

Faciam: Müller's emendation *facias* would offer a nice counterpart to line 6 and is perhaps to be preferred. The sentiment as a whole is elegiac, but not often expressed with **tuos**. **Manebo**: used with erotic import at e.g. Cat. 32.7, of chastity at e.g. Tib. 1.3.83.

On **fugiam**, see Pichon 1991: 156–7. The couplet contains an explicit invocation of **servitium** *amoris*, which was before nascent; cf. e.g. Prop. 1.4.4, 2.13.36, Tib. 2.4.1, and *ad* 3.11.4 (with Introduction, Section I). **Notae...dominae**: elsewhere at Quint. *Decl. Min.* 363.2, where the adjective has implications about her reputation. **Notae** is amusing, as the *puella* is anything but, and her identity might help to fix authorship (note too Ov. *Am.* 3.9.31, which draws attention to the Tibullan peculiarity of double *puellae*). Cairns 2006a: 190 offers parallels to **servitium dominae**; see *ad* 3.4.74 on *domina*. **Dominae** is the only non-disyllabic pentameter end in this poem; see Maltby 2009: 337.

> sed Veneris sanctae considam vinctus ad aras:
> 24   haec notat iniustos supplicibusque favet.

Veneris sanctae: also at Cat. 36.3, 68.5; Sen. *Phaed.* 211. **Veneris**: see *ad* 3.19.1, on the repetition of this word as potentially closural. **Considam...ad aras**: elsewhere at Liv. 40.45.8, Ov. *Met.* 10.274 (not quite parallel). **Vinctus**: see *ad* 3.6.2 and 3.11.14; cf. Tib. 2.3.80 *non ego me vinclis verberibusque nego*.

notat iniustos: with the technical meaning 'brand' (*OLD* IIc); perhaps with a pun on *notae* of the previous couplet, suggesting the notoriety of the *puella*. See too Tib. 1.5.58 *saevit et iniusta lege relicta venus*.

Supplicibus...favet: cf. Tib. 1.4.71–2 *Venus ipsa: querelis/supplicibus, miseris fletibus illa favet*). Venus' help is asserted at Tib. 1.2.18 and sought at 3.3.34. **Favet**: see *ad* 3.3.33, 3.4.44, 3.10.19, 3.11.9, 3.12.7.

3.20:

This wholly anonymous poem (or fragment) is profoundly elegiac, expressing the lover's frustration at his *puella*'s unfaithfulness. His wish, also typical, is rather not to know than for the situation to be different (cf. e.g. Prop. 2.20, Ov. *Am.* 2.5, 3.14). See too Ov. *Am.* 3.12, which raises larger questions about the 'public' nature of both *puella* and poetry (with Introduction, Section VI). There may be a connection between this poem and 3.4, in which Apollo gives L. information about N.'s unfaithfulness which he would rather not have heard.

The poem is epigrammatic both in length and in the clever twist at the end. Potentially epigrammatic too is the repetition in the pentameter of the following couplet of a word found in the hexameter of the previous one (*rumor*)—but see *ad loc.* Some see *tace*, the final word of the poem (and of the collection), as offering a comment on the book as a whole: it enjoins against further poetry, but also, for some, points to the literary ventriloquism throughout the collection (Pearcy 2006). Among the arguments for seeing this as a 'closural' poem, most persuasive is the fact that this one summarizes the concerns of the book as a whole.

>   Rumor ait crebro nostram peccare puellam:
> 2   nunc ego me surdis auribus esse velim.

Rumor is surprisingly infrequent in amatory elegy, given the role of outsiders in the elegiac relationship: Prop. 1.5.26, 1.13.13, 2.18.38, 2.32.24, 4.4.47 *rumor ait*, 4.5.7, Ov. *Her.* 16.141—nearly all of gossip about lovers cheating on one another; the old men of Cat. 5.2, and Mart. 3.80.2 and 3.87.1 may suggest the lowbrow nature of the scenario. **Crebro**: can have an erotic tone, as at Ov. *Her.* 15.48, and is also used of lovers' anxiety and sufferings as at Tib. 1.5.72, Prop. 3.8.15, Ov. *Her.* 20.129. **Peccare puellam**: the phrase also occurs at Prop. 2.32.51, Ov. *Am.* 2.5.3–4; cf. *peccasse* at 3.13.9.

Surdis: sometimes used of those unresponsive to love. For **surdis auribus** of lovers unwilling to hear, see Prop. 2.16.35–6 *quod aiunt/turpis amor surdis auribus esse solet*, 2.16.47–8 *non semper…/Iuppiter et surda neglegit aure preces*, 2.20.13 *de te quodcumque, ad surdas mihi dicitur aures*; cf. Ov. *Am.* 3.7.61, where the charms of a *puella* have the same (non-)effect on Ov. as Phemius' singing on a deaf man and, in a non-erotic context, cf. Ov. *EP* 2.9.25 *Iuppiter oranti surdas si praebeat auris*, Germ. *Arat.* 99 *nec surdam praebes venerantibus aurem*.

>   Crimina non haec sunt nostro sine facta dolore:
> 4   quid miserum torques, rumor acerbe? Tace.

Crimina: prosaic, but also commonly used of the accusations of lovers; see *ad* 3.4.84. **Facta**: see Tränkle 1990 *ad loc.* for a defence of *iacta*. **Dolore**: see *ad* 3.2.3; **nostro…dolore**: not infrequent in poets or prose, but perhaps with a Propertian feel (five times: 1.16.21, 2.15.35, 2.16.13, 2.33.21, 4.5.73).

Miserum: see *ad* 3.19.20. **Torques**: see *ad* 3.9.12, and especially 3.10.11; note too Tib. 2.6.17 *tu miserum torques, tu me mihi dira precari*.

Rumor acerbe: not attested elsewhere; **rumor**: see Pichon 1991: 256. On the (non-closural) repetition of a word in the pentameter of a couplet after its use in the preceding couplet's hexameter, see Heyworth 2007: 281 (*ad* Prop. 3.1.6), with citations. **Acerbe**: used in the vocative of Venus at Tib. 1.2.100 (nominative at 1.6.84, and of a *puella* at 2.6.41); see Pichon 1991: 78 for its elegiac nuances.

Tace: frequent in comedy, less so in tragedy, and in other poetry only at Stat. *Silv.* 1.2.28, Juv. 2.61 and 8.97, and Mart. 2.27.4, 3.45.6, 5.52.6, and 10.101.4 (in Mart. at line-end, often at poem-end). For a 'silent' figure at what may be the end of another book of poetry, see Harpocrates in Cat. 102.4.

Works Cited

Abel, Walther. 'Die Anredeformen bei den römischen Elegikern: Untersuchungen zur elegischen Form'. Diss. Friedrich-Wilhelms Universitat, Berlin: 1930.
Adams, J.N. 'Latin Words for Woman and Wife'. *Glotta* 50 (1972): 234–55.
Adams, J.N. *The Latin Sexual Vocabulary*. Baltimore: 1982.
Adams, J.N. 'Words for "Prostitute" in Latin'. *RhM* 126 (1983): 321–58.
Adams, J.N. 'Female Speech in Latin Comedy'. *Antichthon* 18 (1984): 43–77.
Adams, J.N. 'Nominative Personal Pronouns and Some Patterns of Speech in Republican and Augustan Poetry'. *PBA* 93 (1999): 97–133.
Alfonsi, Luigi. *Albio Tibullo e gli Autori del* Corpus Tibullianum. Pubblicazioni dell'Università Cattolica del Sacro Cuore 13. Milan: 1946.
Allen, Archibald W. ' "Sincerity" and the Roman Elegists'. *CP* 45 (1950): 145–60.
Allen, Archibald W. '*Sunt Qui Propertium Malint*'. In Sullivan, J.P., ed. *Critical Essays on Roman Literature: Elegy and Lyric*. London: 1962: 107–48.
Allen, Samuel. 'Review of Némethy's *Tibullus and Lygdamus*'. *CR* 20 (1906): 449–56.
Amerasinghe, C.W. '*Saturnia Iuno*: Its Significance in the *Aeneid*'. *G&R* 22 (1953): 61–9.
Anderson, R.D., Parsons, Peter J. and Nisbet, R.G.M. 'Elegiacs by Gallus from Qaṣr Ibrîm'. *JRS* 69 (1979): 125–55.
Anderson, William S. 'The Suppliant's Voice and Gesture in Vergil and Ovid's *Metamorphoses*'. *ICS* 18 (1993): 165–77.
André, Jacques. *Etude sur les Termes de Couleur dans la Langue Latine*. Paris: 1949.
André, Jean-Marie. 'Mécène écrivain (avec, en appendice, les fragments de Mécène)'. *ANRW* II.30.3. Berlin: 1983: 1765–87.
Argetsinger, Kathryn. 'Birthday Rituals: Friends and Patrons in Roman Poetry and Cult'. *CA* 11 (1992): 175–93.
Arias Abellan, C. '*Albus-Candidus, Ater-Niger* and *Ruber-Rutilus* in Ovid's *Metamorphoses*: A Structural Research'. *Latomus* 43 (1984): 111–17.
Armstrong, Rebecca. 'Retiring Apollo: Ovid on the Politics and Poetics of Self-Sufficiency'. *CQ* 54 (2004): 528–50.
Ashby, Thomas. *The Aqueducts of Ancient Rome*. Washington, DC: 1973.
Austin, R.G. '*Ille Ego Qui Quondam*...' *CQ* 18 (1968): 107–15.
Austin, R.G. *P. Vergili Maronis:* Aeneidos *Liber Sextus*. Oxford: 1977.
Avrin, Leila. *Scribes, Script and Books: The Book Arts from Antiquity to the Renaissance*. Chicago: 1991.
Axelson, Bertil. *Unpoetische Wörter: Ein Beitrag zur Kenntnis der lateinischen Dichtersprache*. Lund: 1945.
Axelson, Bertil. 'Lygdamus und Ovid. Zur Methodik der literarische Prioritätsbestimmung'. *Eranos* 58 (1960a): 92–111.
Axelson, Bertil. 'Das Geburtsjahr des Lygdamus. Ein Rätsel der römischen Elegiendichtung'. *Eranos* 58 (1960b): 281–97.
Baehrens, Aemilius. *Elegiarum Libri Duo: Accedunt Pseudotibulliana*. Leipzig: 1878.
Baker, R.J. '*Miles Annosus*: The Military Motif in Propertius'. *Latomus* 27 (1968): 322–49.

Baligan, Giuseppe. *Il Terzo Libro del Corpus Tibullianum*. Studi Pubblicati dall'Istituto di Filologia Classica della Facoltà di Lettere e Filosofia dell'Università degli Studi di Bologna I. Bologna: 1948.
Baligan, Giuseppe. 'Ancora su Ligdamo'. *Aevum* 24 (1950): 270–90.
Baligan, Giuseppe. 'Il *Natalis* di Ligdamo'. *Vichiana* 4 (1967a): 84–6.
Baligan, Giuseppe. 'Le Bucoliche de Marco Valerio'. *Vichiana* 4 (1967b): 383–98.
Ball, Larry F. *The* Domus Aurea *and the Roman Architectural Revolution*. Cambridge: 2003.
Barchiesi, Alessandro. 'Endgames: Ovid's *Metamorphoses* 15 and *Fasti* 6'. In Roberts, Deborah H., Dunn, Francis M., and Fowler, Don, edd. *Classical Closure: Reading the End in Greek and Latin Literature*. Princeton, NJ: 1997: 187–208.
Barchiesi, Alessandro. *Speaking Volumes: Narrative and Intertext in Ovid and Other Latin Poets*. London: 2001.
Barnard, Sylvia. 'Hellenistic Women Poets'. *CJ* 73 (1978): 204–13.
Barthes, Roland. *A Lover's Discourse: Fragments*, trans. R. Howard. New York: 1978.
Batstone, William. 'Dry Pumice and the Programmatic Language of Catullus 1'. *CP* 93 (1998): 125–35.
Batstone, William. 'Sulpicia and the Speech of Men'. Forthcoming.
Bellandi, Franco. 'L'immagine di Mecenate protettore delle lettere nella poesia fra I e II sec. D.C.' . *Atene e Roma* 40 (1995): 78–101.
Bennett, Charles E. 'The Ablative of Association'. *TAPA* 36 (1905): 64–81.
Bernays, Ludwig. 'Zur Elegie Tib. 3.9 und zur Problematik der Sulpicia-Gedichte'. *Mnemosyne* 57 (2004): 209–14.
Berthet, Jean-François. 'L'*Etrusca disciplina* dans les élégies de Properce, Tibulle et Lygdamus'. In Guittard, Charles and Briquel, Dominique, edd. *Les écrivains du siècle d'Auguste et l'Etrusca disciplina*. Caesarodunum Suppl. 61 (1991): 89–99.
Besslich, Siegfried. 'Die "Hörner" des Buches: Zur Bedeutung von Cornua im Antiken Buchwesen'. *Gutenberg-Jahrbuch* 48 (1973): 44–50.
Besslich, Siegfried. 'Anrede an das Buch: Gedanken zu einem Topos in der römischen Dichtung'. In Świerk, Alfred, ed. *Beiträge zur Geschichte des Buches und seiner Funktion in der Gesellschaft; Festschrift für Hans Widmann zum 65 Geburtstag*. Stuttgart: 1974: 1–12.
Bessone, Federica. 'Latin Precursors'. In Thorsen, Thea S., ed. *Cambridge Companion to Latin Love Elegy*. Cambridge: 2013: 39–56.
Bickel, Ernst. 'Die Lygdamus-Elegien: Lygdamus appellativisch servus amoris, Messalla Messalinus als Verfasser der Elegien'. *RhM* 103 (1960): 97–109.
Birt, Theodor. *Das antike Buchwesen in seinem Verhältniss zur Litteratur*. Berlin: 1882.
Blümner, Hugo. 'Über die Farbenbezeichnungen bei den römischen Dichtern'. *Philologus* 2 (1889): 142–67.
Blümner, Hugo. 'Umbilicus und Cornua'. *Philologus* 73 (1916): 426–45.
Bodel, John. 'Death on Display: Looking at Roman Funerals'. In Bergmann, Bettina and Kondoleon, Christine, edd. *The Art of Ancient Spectacle*. New Haven, CT: 1999: 259–81.
Boisseuil, Didier. *Le Thermalisme en Toscane à la fin du moyen âge*. Collection de l'École française de Rome 296. Rome: 2002.
Bömer, Franz. *P. Ovidius Naso: Die Fasten: Herausgegeben, übersetzt und kommentiert*. Heidelberg: 1957 and 1958.
Bömer, Franz. *P. Ovidius Naso:* Metamorphosen. Bucher I–III. Heidelberg: 1969.

Bömer, Franz. *P. Ovidius Naso:* Metamorphosen. Bucher IV–V. Heidelberg: 1976.
Bömer, Franz. *P. Ovidius Naso:* Metamorphosen. Bucher VI–VII. Heidelberg: 1976.
Bömer, Franz. *P. Ovidius Naso:* Metamorphosen. Bucher VIII–IX. Heidelberg: 1977.
Bömer, Franz. *P. Ovidius Naso:* Metamorphosen. Bucher X–XI. Heidelberg: 1980.
Bömer, Franz. *P. Ovidius Naso:* Metamorphosen. Bucher XII–XIII. Heidelberg: 1982.
Bömer, Franz. *P. Ovidius Naso:* Metamorphosen. Bucher XIV–XV. Heidelberg: 1986.
Booth, Joan and Maltby, Robert. 'Light and Dark: Play on *Candidus* and Related Concepts in the Elegies of Tibullus'. *Mnemosyne* 58 (2005): 124–31.
Borriello, Mariarosaria and d'Ambrosio, Antonio. *Baiae-Misenum: Forma Italiae Regio I volumen XIV*. Florence: 1979.
Boucher, J.P. 'A propos de Cérinthus et de quelques autres pseudonyms dans la poésie augustéene'. *Latomus* 35 (1976): 504–19.
Bouquet, Jean. *Le songe dans l'épopée latine d'Ennius à Claudien*. Coll. Latomus 260. Brussels: 2001.
Bowerman, Helen C. 'The Birthday as a Commonplace of Roman Elegy'. *CJ* 12 (1917): 310–18.
Bowersock, Glen W. *Roman Arabia*. Cambridge, MA: 1983.
Boyd, Barbara Weiden. *Ovid's Literary Loves: Influence and Innovation in the* Amores. Ann Arbor, MI: 1997.
Bradley, James R. 'The Elegies of Sulpicia'. *New England Classical Newsletter and Journal* 22 (1995): 159–64.
Bréguet, Esther. *Le Roman de Sulpicia: Elégies IV, 2-12 du Corpus Tibullianum*. Geneva: 1946.
Bréguet, Esther. 'Le Thème *Alius... ego* chez les Poètes Latins'. *REL* 40 (1962): 128–36.
Brenk, Frederick E. '*Purpureos Spargam Flores*: A Greek Motif in the *Aeneid*?' *CQ* 60 (1990): 218–23.
Broukhusius, J. *Tibullus*. Amsterdam: 1708.
Brouwer, H.H.J. *Bona Dea: The Sources and a Description of the Cult*. Leiden: 1989.
Brouwers, J.H. '"*Ferreus ille fuit*": Sens et Structure de Tibulle 1.2.67–80'. *Mnemosyne* 31 (1978): 389–406.
Bücheler, F. 'Altes Latein'. *RhM* 46 (1891): 233–43.
Büchner, Karl. 'Die Elegien des Lygdamus'. *Hermes* 93 (1965): 65–112, 503–8.
Bürger, R. 'Eine Elegie des Gallus'. *Hermes* 38 (1903): 19–27.
Bürger, R. 'Studien zu Lygdamus und den Sulpiciagedichten'. *Hermes* 40 (1905): 321–35.
Burkowski, Jane M.C. 'The Symbolism and Rhetoric of Hair in Latin Elegy'. Diss. Oxford: 2012.
Butler, H.E. and Barber, E.A. *The Elegies of Propertius*. Oxford: 1933.
Butler, Judith. *Gender Trouble: Feminism and the Subversion of Identity*. New York: 1990.
Butler, Samuel. *The Authoress of the Odyssey: Where and When She Wrote, Who She Was, the Use She Made of the* Iliad, *and How the Poem Grew Under Her Hands*. London: 1897 (2nd ed. 1922).
Butrica, James L. 1993. 'Lygdamus, Nephew of Messalla?' *LCM* 18 (1993): 51–3.
Butrica, James L. 'The Fabella of Sulpicia (*Epigrammata Bobiensia* 37)'. *Phoenix* 60 (2006): 70–121.
Butterfield, D.J. 'The Poetic Treatment of *atque* from Catullus to Juvenal'. *Mnemosyne* 61 (2008): 386–413.

Cahoon, Leslie. 'The Bed as Battlefield: Erotic Conquest and Military Metaphor in Ovid's *Amores*'. *TAPA* 118 (1988): 293–307.
Cairns, Francis. 'Propertius 3.10 and Roman Birthdays'. *Hermes* 99 (1971): 150–5.
Cairns, Francis. *Generic Composition in Greek and Roman Poetry*. Edinburgh: 1972.
Cairns, Francis. *Tibullus: A Hellenistic Poet at Rome*. Cambridge: 1979.
Cairns, Francis. 'Lavinia's Blush (Vergil *Aeneid* 12.64–70)'. In Cairns, Douglas, ed. *Body Language in the Greek and Roman Worlds*. Swansea: 2005: 195–213.
Cairns, Francis. *Sextus Propertius: The Augustan Elegist*. Cambridge: 2006a.
Cairns, Francis. 'Propertius and the Origins of Latin Love-Elegy'. In Günther, Hans-Christian, ed. *Brill's Companion to Propertius*. Leiden: 2006b: 69–95.
Calame, Claude. *Choruses of Young Women in Ancient Greece: Their Morphology, Religious Role, and Social Function*, trans. Derek Collins and Janice Orion. Lanham, MD: 1997.
Calonghi, F. '*De Lygdamo Ovidii Imitatore*'. *RFIC* 29 (1901): 273–8.
Cameron, Alan. 'How Thin was Philetas?' *CQ* 41 (1991): 534–8.
Cameron, Alan. *Callimachus and his Critics*. Princeton, NJ: 1995.
Campbell, Malcolm. *Moschus*: Europa. Hildesheim: 1991.
Camps, W.A. *Propertius* Elegies *Book III*. Cambridge: 1966.
Cancik, Hubert. '*Idolum* and *Imago*: Roman Dreams and Dream Theories'. In Shulman, David and Stroumsa, Guy G., edd. *Dream Cultures: Explorations in the Comparative History of Dreaming*. New York: 1999: 169–88.
Carcopino, Jérome. 'Épitaphe en vers de la lectrice Pétalè, découverte à Rome'. *Bulletin de la société Nationale des Antiquaires de France*: 1929: 84–6.
Carey, Christopher. 'Archilochus and Lycambes'. *CQ* 36 (1986): 60–7.
Carroll, Maureen. *Spirits of the Dead*. Oxford: 2006.
Cartault, Augustin. *A Propos du Corpus Tibullianum: Un Siècle de Philologie Latine Classique*. Paris: 1906.
Cartault, Augustin. *Tibulle et les Auteurs du Corpus Tibullianum*. Paris: 1909.
Cartault, Augustin. *Le Distique élégiaque chez Tibulle, Sulpicia, Lygdamus*. Univ. de Paris Bibl. de la faculté des lettres 27. Paris: 1911.
Casali, Sergio. *P. Ovidii Nasonis*: Heriodum Epistula IX *Deianira Herculi*. Florence: 1995.
Casson, Lionel. *The Periplus Maris Erythraei: Text with Introduction, Translation and Commentary*. Princeton, NJ: 1989.
Castelli, Giovanni. 'Note a *Corp. Tibull.* III.6.2'. *RSC* 21 (1973): 114–16.
Caston, Ruth Rothaus. *The Elegiac Passion: Jealousy in Roman Love Elegy*. Oxford: 2012.
Cesareo, Emanuele. *Il Carme natalizio nella poesia Latino*. Palermo: 1929.
Ciaffi, Vincenzo. *Lettura di Tibullo*. Turin: 1944.
Clay, Diskin. *Archilochus Heros: The Cult of Poets in the Greek Polis*. Cambridge, MA: 2004.
Coleman, Robert. *Vergil:* Eclogues. Cambridge: 1977.
Connolly, Joy. 'Asymptotes of Pleasure: Thoughts on the Nature of Roman Erotic Elegy'. *Arethusa* 33 (2000): 71–98.
Conte, Gian Biagio. *The Rhetoric of Imitation: Genre and Poetic Memory in Virgil and Other Latin Poets*, ed. C. Segal. Ithaca, NY: 1986.
Courtney, Edward. 'Problems in Tibullus and Lygdamus'. *Maia* 39 (1987): 29–32.
Courtney, Edward. *The Fragmentary Latin Poets*. Oxford: 2003.

Cozzolino Andrea. 'Il Carme III 13 del Corpus Tibullianum e il Fragmentum Grenfellianum'. *Athenaeum* 80 (1992): 475–8.
Currie, H. MacL. 'The Poems of Sulpicia'. *ANRW* II.30.3. Berlin: 1983: 1751–64.
Currie, H. MacL. 'Closure/transition and the *nox erat* topos: Some notes'. *LCM* 18.6 (1993): 92–5.
D'Angour, Armand. *The Greeks and the New: Novelty in Ancient Greek Imagination and Experience*. Cambridge: 2011.
D'Arms, John H. *Romans on the Bay of Naples: A Social and Cultural Study of the Villas and Their Owners from 150 B.C. to A.D. 400*. Cambridge, MA: 1970.
Davies, Ceri. 'Poetry in the Circle of Messalla'. *G&R* 20 (1973): 25–35.
Davis, Gregson. *The Death of Procris:* Amor *and the Hunt in Ovid's* Metamorphoses. Rome: 1983.
Day, Archibald A. *The Origins of Latin Love-Elegy*. Oxford: 1938.
DeBrohun, Jeri Blair. *Roman Propertius and the Reinvention of Elegy*. Ann Arbor, MI: 2003.
Deferrari, Roy J., Barry, M. Inviolata, McGuire, Martin R.P., edd. *A Concordance of Ovid*. Washington, DC: 1939.
de Kleijn, Gerda. *The Water Supply of Ancient Rome: City Area, Water, and Population*. Amsterdam: 2001.
Della Corte, Francesco. 'Il poeta Lucio Giulio Calido'. *RCCM* 7 (1965): 416–31.
Della Corte, Francesco. 'Aspetti Sociali del III Libro del *Corpus Tibullianum*'. *Opuscula* III. Genoa: 1972: 690–5.
Della Corte, Francesco. 'L'Elegia del Sogni'. *Opuscula* III. Genoa: 1973: 17–28.
Della Corte, Francesco. 'Alle origini del Corpus Tibullianum'. In *Studi su Varrone sulla retorica storiografia e poesia latina. Scritti in onore di Benedetto Riposati* (Rieti), 143–52 = *Opuscula* VII. Genoa: 1983: 91–100.
Dell'Era, Antonio. '*Corpus Tibullianum* 3.14–15 (4.8–9)'. *RPL* 18 (1995): 57–9.
Dell'Era, Antonio. 'Note al III libro del *Corpus Tibullianum*'. *RPL* 19 (1996a): 97–100.
Dell'Era, Antonio. 'Per il testo del *Corpus Tibullianum*'. *BollClass* 17 (1996b): 119–25.
Delz, Josef. 'Apoll als verhinderter Sänger (zu [Tib.] 3, 4, 71)'. *MH* 48 (1991): 61–2.
Dettmer, Helena. 'The "Corpus Tibullianum"'. *ANRW* II.30.3. Berlin: 1983: 1962–75.
Diggle, James. *Euripides*: Phaethon. Cambridge: 1970.
Dinter, Martin. 'Inscriptional Intermediality in Latin Elegy'. In Keith, Alison, ed. *Latin Elegy and Hellenistic Epigram: A Tale of Two Genres at Rome*. Newcastle upon Tyne: 2011: 7–18.
Dissen, Ludolph. *Albii Tibulli Carmina*. Göttingen: 1835.
Dixon, Helen M. 'The Discovery and Disappearance of the Fragmentum Cuiacianum of Tibullus'. *Revue d'histoire des textes* 1 (2006): 37–72.
Dixon, Suzanne. *The Roman Mother*. London: 1988.
Doncieux, George. 'Sur la Personnalité de "Lygdamus"'. *Revue de Philologie, d'histoire, et de littérature anciennes* 12 (1888): 129–34.
Doncieux, George. 'De qui sont les elégies 2-6 du livre IV de Tibulle'? *Revue de Philologie, d'histoire, et de littérature anciennes* 15 (1891): 76–81.
Dougherty, Carol. 'Sowing the Seeds of Violence: Rape, Women, and the Land'. In Wyke, Maria, ed. *Parchments of Gender: Deciphering the Bodies of Antiquity*. Oxford: 1998: 267–84.

Drinkwater, Megan O. ' "His Turn to Cry": Tibullus' Marathus Cycle (1.4, 1.8 and 1.9) and Roman Elegy'. *CJ* 107 (2012): 423–48.

Dronke, Peter. 'Alcune osservazioni sulle poésie di Sulpicia'. *Giornate filologiche Francesco Della Corte* 3 (2003): 81–99.

Dufallo, Basil. *The Ghosts of the Past: Latin Literature, the Dead, and Rome's Transition to a Principate*. Columbus, OH: 2007.

Dumézil, Georges. *Archaic Roman Religion*, trans. Philip Krapp. Chicago: 1966.

Duret, Luc. 'Dans l'ombre des plus grands: Poets et prosateurs mal connus de l'époque augustéenne'. *ANRW* II.30.3. Berlin: 1983: 1448–560.

Dutsch, Dorota M. *Feminine Discourse in Roman Comedy: On Echoes and Voices*. Oxford: 2008.

Dyson, Julia T. 'Lilies and Violence: Lavinia's Blush in the Song of Orpheus'. *CP* 94 (1999): 281–8.

Edgeworth, Robert. 'Does *purpureus* mean "bright"?' *Glotta* 57 (1979): 281–91.

Ehwald, Rudolf. *Ad historiam carminum Ovidianorum recensionemque symbolae*. Gotha: 1889.

Ehwald, Rudolf. 'Zu Lydgamus, c. 1'. *Philologus* 60 (1901): 572–8.

Eisenhut, Werner. 'Die Autorschaft der Elegie 3.19 im Corpus Tibullianum'. *Hermes* 105 (1977): 209–23.

Ellerman, Karen. 'Sulpicia og hendes digte'. *Museum Tusculanum* 48 (1982): 61–91.

Enk, P.J. *Commentarius Criticus*. Leiden: 1946 (2nd ed. 1962).

Enk, P.J. 'À propos du poète Lygdamus'. *Mnemosyne* 4 (1950): 70–5.

Erasmo, Mario. *Reading Death in Ancient Rome*. Columbus, OH: 2008.

Erath, Wolfgang. *Die Dichtung des Lygdamus*. Inaugural-Dissertation der Philosophischen Fakultät der Friedrich-Alexander-Universität Erlangen-Nürnberg. Erlangen: 1971.

Ernout, Alfred and Meillet, Antoine. *Dictionnaire étymologique de la langue latine: Histoire des mots*, 4th ed. Paris: 2001.

Esposito, Elena. *Il* Fragmentum Grenfellianum: (*P. Dryton 50*). Eikasmos Studi 12. Bologna: 2005.

Evans, Harry B. *Water Distribution in Ancient Rome: The Evidence of Frontinus*. Ann Arbor, MI: 1994.

Évrard, Étienne. 'Vieux et Ancien chez Tibulle'. *Latomus* 37 (1978): 121–47.

Fabre-Serris, Jacqueline. 'Sulpicia: An/other Female Voice in Ovid's *Heroides*: A New Reading of *Heroides* 4 and 15'. *Helios* 36 (2009): 149–73.

Fairweather, Janet. 'Ovid's Autobiographical Poem, *Tristia* 4.10'. *CQ* 37 (1987): 181–96.

Fantham, Elaine. 'Roman Elegy: Problems of Self-Definition, and Redirection'. In *L'Histoire Littéraire immanente dans la Poésie Latine*. Fondation Hardt Entretiens 47. Vandoeuvres: 2001: 183–220.

Farrell, Joseph. 'Reading and Writing the *Heroides*'. *HSCP* 98 (1998): 307–38.

Farrell, Joseph. *Latin Language and Latin Culture: From Ancient to Modern Times*. Cambridge: 2001.

Farrell, Joseph. 'Calling out the Greeks: Dynamics of the Elegiac Canon'. In Gold, Barbara, ed. *A Companion to Roman Love Elegy*. Chichester: 2012: 11–24.

Fatucchi, Alberto. 'Le ferie aretine di Sulpicia (Nota topografia)'. *Orpheus* 23 (1976): 145–60.

Fedeli, Paolo. *Properzio: Elegie libro IV testo critico e commento*. Bari: 1965.
Fedeli, Paolo. *Sesto Properzio: Il primo libro delle Elegie: Introduzione, testo critico e commento*. Florence: 1980.
Fedeli, Paolo. *Properzio: Il libro terzo delle Elegie: Studi e commenti*. Bari: 1985.
Fedeli, Paolo. *Properzio: Elegie libro II introduzione, testo e commento*. Cambridge: 2005.
Feeney, Denis. *The Gods in Epic: Poets and Critics of the Classical Tradition*. Oxford: 1991.
Feeney, Denis. *Caesar's Calendar: Ancient Time and the Beginnings of History*. Berkeley, CA: 2007.
Findley, Samuel J. 'Studies in Loss: Theognis, Tibullus, and Textual Tradition'. Diss. Duke University: 2002.
Fisher, J.M. 'The Life and Work of Tibullus'. *ANRW* II.30.3. Berlin: 1983: 1924–61.
Fitzgerald, William. *Catullan Provocations: Lyric Poetry and the Drama of Position*. Berkeley, CA: 1995.
Flaschenreim, Barbara. 'Sulpicia and the Rhetoric of Disclosure'. *CP* 94 (1999): 36–54.
Flemming, Rebecca. 'Women, Writing and Medicine in the Classical World'. *CQ* 57 (2007): 257–79.
Fletcher, G.B.A. 'Latin Marginalia'. *CQ* 25 (1931): 49–51.
Fletcher, G.B.A. 'On Tibullus and Other Poets of the Corpus Tibullianum'. *Latomus* 24 (1965): 45–52.
Fontenrose, Joseph. *The Delphic Oracle: Its Responses and Operations*. Berkeley, CA: 1978.
Frazer, James G. *Publii Ovidii Nasonis*, Fastorum *libri sex*. Vol. III (*Fasti* 3-4). London: 1929.
Fredrick, David. 'Reading Broken Skin: Violence in Roman Elegy'. In Hallett, Judith P. and Skinner, Marilyn B., edd. *Roman Sexualities*. Princeton, NJ: 1997: 172–93.
Fredricks, S.C. 'A Poetic Experiment in the Garland of Sulpicia (*Corpus Tibullianum* 3.10)'. *Latomus* 35 (1976): 761–82.
Fulkerson, Laurel. *The Ovidian Heroine as Author: Reading, Writing, and Community in the* Heroides. Cambridge: 2005.
Fulkerson, Laurel. 'Apollo, *Paenitentia*, and Ovid's *Metamorphoses*'. *Mnemosyne* 59 (2006): 388–402.
Fulkerson, Laurel. '*Servitium Amoris*'. In Thorsen, Thea S., ed. *The Cambridge Companion to Latin Love Elegy*. Cambridge: 2013: 180–93.
Fulkerson, Laurel. 'Close Encounters: Divine Epiphanies on the Fringes of Latin Love Elegy'. In Trimble, Gail and Matzner, Sebastian, edd. *Breaking and Entering: Metalepsis and Classical Literature*. Oxford: forthcoming.
Fulkerson, Laurel and Stover, Tim, edd. *Repeat Performances: Ovidian Repetition and the* Metamorphoses. Madison, WI: 2016.
Fuss, Diana. *Essentially Speaking: Feminism, Nature and Difference*. New York: 1989.
Gaertner, Jan Felix. 'The Literary Background of an Amateurish Poetess: On [Tib.] 3.13'. *PP* 54 (1999): 198–200.
Gaertner, Jan Felix. '[Tib.] III.8 und Ovids *Fasti*'. *Mnemosyne* 53 (2000a): 88–9.
Gaertner, Jan Felix. 'Zu den Vorlagen von [Tib.] III.10'. *Latomus* 59 (2000b): 672–3.
Gaertner, Jan Felix. 'Zur Deutung von [Tib.] 3.19'. *Mnemosyne* 55 (2002): 346–9.
Gaertner, Jan Felix. *Ovid,* Epistulae Ex Ponto, *Book I: Edited with Introduction, Translation and Commentary*. Oxford: 2005.

Gagé, Jean. *Matronalia: Essai sur les devotions et les organisations cultuelles des femmes dans l'ancienne Rome*. Brussels: 1963.
Gale, Monica R. 'Propertius 2.7: *Militia Amoris* and the Ironies of Elegy'. *JRS* 87 (1997): 77–91.
Galinsky, G. Karl. *Augustan Culture: An Interpretive Introduction*. Princeton, NJ: 1996.
Ganzenmüller, Carl. 'Aus Ovids Werkstatt'. *Philologus* 70 (1911): 274–311.
Gardner, Hunter H. *Gendering Time in Augustan Love Elegy*. Oxford: 2013.
Giangrande, Giuseppe. 'Symptotic Literature and Epigram'. In *L'Épigramme Grecque*. Entretiens Hardt 14. Vandoeuvres: 1967: 97–134.
Gibson, Roy K. 'How to Win Girlfriends and Influence Them'. *PCPS* 41 (1995): 62–82.
Gibson, Roy K. *Ovid Ars Amatoria Book 3*. Cambridge: 2003.
Gibson, Roy K. 'Loves and Elegy'. In Thorsen, Thea S., ed. *Cambridge Companion to Latin Love Elegy*. Cambridge: 2013: 209–23.
Gigante, Marcello. 'Il Papiro di Grenfell e i Cantica Plautini'. *PP* 2 (1947): 300–8.
Gilbert, Sandra M. and Gubar, Susan. *The Madwoman in the Attic: The Woman Writer and the Nineteenth-Century Literary Imagination*. New Haven, CT: 1979.
Gipper, Helmut. '*Purpur*: Weg und Leistung eines umstrittenen Farbworts'. *Glotta* 42 (1964): 39–69.
Glatt, Martin. *Die 'andere Welt' der römischen Elegiker. Das personliche in der Liebesdichtung*. Studien zur klassischen Philologie 54. Frankfurt: 1991.
Gold, Barbara K. *Literary Patronage in Greece and Rome*. Chapel Hill, NC: 1987.
Gold, Barbara K. '"The Master Mistress of My Passion": The Lady as Patron in Ancient and Renaissance Literature'. In DeForest, Mary, ed. *Woman's Power, Man's Game: Essays on Classical Antiquity in honor of Joy K King*. Wauconda, IL: 1993: 279–304.
Gowers, Emily. *Horace Satires I*. Cambridge: 2012.
Grafton, Anthony. *Forgers and Critics: Creativity and Duplicity in Western Scholarship*. Princeton, NJ: 1990.
Green, R.P.H. 'Ausonius' Use of Classical Latin Poets: Some New Examples and Observations'. *CQ* 27 (1977): 441–52.
Greene, Ellen. *The Erotics of Domination: Male Desire and the Mistress in Latin Love Poetry*. Baltimore: 1998.
Grenfell, Bernard A. *An Alexandrian Erotic Fragment and other Greek Papyri Chiefly Ptolemaic*. Oxford: 1896.
Griffin, Jasper. 'Augustus and the Poets: *Caesar qui cogere posset*'. In Millar, F. and Segal, E., edd. *Caesar Augustus: Seven Aspects*. Oxford: 1984: 189–218.
Griffin, Jasper. *Latin Poets and Roman Life*. London: 1985.
Grillone, Antonino. *Il sogno nell'epica latina: Tecnica e poesia*. Palermo: 1967.
Grmek, Mirko D. *Diseases in the Ancient Greek World*, trans. M. Muellner and L. Muellner. Baltimore: 1989.
Gruen Erich S. *Studies in Greek Culture and Roman Policy*. Leiden: 1990.
Gruppe, Otto F. *Die romische Elegie*. Vol. 1. Leipzig: 1838.
Gubar, Susan. '"The Blank Page" and the Issues of Female Creativity'. In Abel, Elizabeth, ed. *Writing and Sexual Difference*. Chicago: 1982: 73–93.
Gurd, Sean Alexander. *Work in Progress: Literary Revision as Social Performance in Ancient Rome*. Oxford: 2012.
Habinek, Thomas N. *The Politics of Latin Literature: Writing, Identity, and Empire in Ancient Rome*. Princeton, NJ: 1998.

Hagen, Bolko. 'Stil und Abfassungszeit der Lygdamus-Gedichte'. Diss. Hamburg: 1954.
Hägg, Tomas. 'Hermes and the Invention of the Lyre: An Unorthodox Version'. *SO* 64 (1989): 36–73.
Haines-Eitzen, Kim. *The Gendered Palimpsest: Women, Writing, and Representation in Early Christianity*. Oxford: 2012.
Hälikkä, Riikka. '*Sparsis comis, solutis capillis*: "Loose" Hair in Ovid's Elegiac Poetry'. *Arctos* 35 (2001): 23–34.
Hallett, Judith P. *Fathers and Daughters in Roman Society: Women and the Elite Family*. Princeton, NJ: 1984.
Hallett, Judith P. 'The Eleven Elegies of the Augustan Poet Sulpicia'. In Churchill, Laurie J., Brown, Phyllis R., and Jeffrey, Jane E., edd. *Women Writing Latin: From Roman Antiquity to Early Modern Europe*. Vol. 1. New York: 2002a: 45–65.
Hallett, Judith P. 'Sulpicia and the Valerii: Family Ties and Poetic Unity'. In Amden, Bettina, et al., edd. *Noctes Atticae: 34 Articles on Greco-Roman Antiquity and its Nachleben: Studies Presented to Jorgen Mejer on his Sixtieth Birthday, March 18, 2002*. Copenhagen: 2002b: 141–9.
Hallett, Judith P. 'Sulpicia and her *Fama*: An Intertextual Approach to Recovering her Latin Literary Image'. *CW* 100 (2006): 37–42.
Hallett, Judith P. 'Ovid's Sappho and Roman Women Love Poets'. *Dictynna* 6 (2009a): 2–10.
Hallett, Judith P. 'Sulpicia and her Resistant Intertextuality'. In van Mal-Maeder, D., Burnier, A., and Núñez, L., edd. *Jeux de voix. Enonciation, intertextualité et intentionnalité dans la littérature antique*. Bern: 2009b: 141–53.
Hallett, Judith P. 'Absent Roman Fathers in the Writings of their Daughters'. In Hübner, S. and Ratzan, D., edd. *Growing up Fatherless in Antiquity*. Cambridge: 2009c: 175–91.
Hallett, Judith P. 'Scenarios of Sulpiciae: Moral Discourses and Immoral Verses'. *EuGeStA* 1 (2011): 79–97.
Hammer, Jacob. *Prolegomena to an Edition of the Panegyricus Messallae: The Military and Political Career of M. Valerius Messalla Corvinus*. New York: 1925.
Hanslik, Rudolf. 'Der Dichterkreis des Messalla'. *Anzeiger d. Öst. Akad. d. Wiss. Phil. Hist. Kl.* 89 (1952): 22–38.
Hanslik, Rudolf. 'M. Valerius Messalla Corvinus'. *RE* 8a (1955): 131–57.
Hanson, John S. 'Dreams and Visions in the Graeco-Roman World and Early Christianity'. *ANRW* II.23.2. Berlin: 1980: 1395–427.
Harder, Annette. *Callimachus*. Aetia. 2 vols. Oxford: 2012.
Hardie, Philip. *Virgil:* Aeneid *Book IX*. Cambridge: 1994.
Harris, William V. *Ancient Literacy*. Cambridge, MA: 1989.
Harris, William V. 'Roman Opinions about the Truthfulness of Dreams'. *JRS* 93 (2003): 18–34.
Harris, William V. *Dreams and Experience in Classical Antiquity*. Cambridge, MA: 2009.
Harrisson, Juliette. *Dreams and Dreaming in the Roman Empire: Cultural Memory and Imagination*. London: 2013.
Harvey, Elizabeth D. *Ventriloquised Voices: Feminist Theory and English Renaissance Texts*. London: 1992.
Haupt, Moritz. 'Varia'. *Hermes* 5 (1871): 21–47, reprinted in *Opuscula* III (1905).
Häußler, Reinhard. *Nachträge zu A. Otto*. Sprichwörter und sprichwörtlich Redensarten der Römer. Darmstadt: 1968.

Hawkins, Tom. 'Out-Foxing the Wolf-Walker: Lycambes as Performative Rival to Archilochus'. *CA* 27 (2008): 93–114.
Hellegouarc'h, J. '"*Parce, precor…*" ou Tibulle et la prière: Etude stylistique'. *ICS* 14 (1989): 49–68.
Hemelrijk, Emily A. *Matrona Docta: Educated Women in the Roman Élite from Cornelia to Julia Domna*. London: 1999.
Henderson, A.A.R. 'Tibullus, Elysium and Tartarus'. *Latomus* 28 (1969): 649–53.
Hermann, Léon. *L'âge d'argent doré*. Paris: 1951.
Hermann, Léon. '*Corpus Tibullianum* III.19 et 20'. *Latomus* 16 (1957): 462–4.
Heubeck, Alfred, West, Stephanie, and Hainsworth, J.B. *A Commentary on Homer's Odyssey: Volume I: Books I–VIII*. Oxford: 1988.
Heyne, C.G. *Albii Tibulli quae extant carmina nouis curis castigata*. 3rd ed. Leipzig: 1798.
Heyworth, Stephen J. 'Some Allusions to Callimachus in Latin Poetry'. *MD* 33 (1994): 51–79.
Heyworth, Stephen J. *Cynthia: A Companion to the Text of Propertius*. Oxford: 2007.
Heyworth, Stephen J. 'The Elegiac Book: Patterns and Problems'. In Gold, Barbara, ed. *A Companion to Roman Love Elegy*. Chichester: 2012: 219–33.
Heyworth, Stephen J. 'Keeping on Keeping on: Repetition in the Propertian Narrative'. ORA 2013: http://ora.ox.ac.uk/objects/uuid:0e07d210-8b2d-46f1-8b39-c19aae8b8b20/datastreams/bined81ca2e-5f6d-461a-8057-6c4de862dfee.
Hill, Timothy. Ambitiosa Mors: *Suicide and Self in Roman Thought and Literature*. New York: 2004.
Hinds, Stephen E. 'The Poetess and the Reader: Further Steps Towards Sulpicia'. *Hermathena* 143 (1987a): 29–46.
Hinds, Stephen E. *The Metamorphosis of Persephone: Ovid and the Self-Conscious Muse*. Cambridge: 1987b.
Hinds, Stephen E. 'Generalising About Ovid'. *Ramus* 16 (1987c): 4–31.
Hinds, Stephen E. *Allusion and Intertext: Dynamics of Appropriation in Roman Poetry*. Cambridge: 1998.
Hinds, Stephen E. 'First among Women: Ovid, *Tristia* 1.6 and the Traditions of "Exemplary" Catalogue'. In Braund, Susanna Morton and Mayer, Roland, edd. amor: roma: *Love and Latin Literature*. Cambridge: 1999: 123–42.
Hinds, Stephen E. 'Essential Epic: Genre and Gender from Macer to Statius'. In Depew, Mary and Obbink, Dirk, edd. *Matrices of Genre: Authors, Canons, and Society*. Cambridge, MA: 2000: 221–44.
Hinds, Stephen E. 'Dislocations of Ovidian Time'. In Schwindt, J.P., ed. *Zur Poetik der Zeit in Augusteischer Dichtung*. Heidelberg: 2005: 203–30.
Hinds, Stephen E. 'Venus, Varro and the *Vates*: Toward the Limits of Etymologizing Interpretation'. *Dictynna* 3 (2006): 175–210.
Hollis, Adrian S. *Ovid: Ars Amatoria I*. Oxford: 1977.
Hollis, Adrian S. *Fragments of Roman Poetry, c. 60 BC–AD 20*. Oxford: 2007.
Holmes, Nigel. '*Gaudia Nostra*: A Hexameter-Ending in Elegy'. *CQ* 45 (1995): 500–3.
Holst-Warhaft, Gail. *Women's Laments and Greek Literature*. London: 1992.
Holzberg, Niklas. 'Four Poets and a Poetess or Portrait of the Poet as a Young Man? Thoughts on Book 3 of the *Corpus Tibullianium*'. *CJ* 94 (1998): 169–91.
Holzenthal, Erhard. 'Das Krankheitsmotiv in der römischen Elegie'. Diss. Cologne: 1967.

Hooper, Richard W. 'A Stylistic Investigation into the Third and Fourth books of the *Corpus Tibullianum*'. Diss. Yale: 1975.
Hope, Valerie M. *Roman Death: The Dying and the Dead in Ancient Rome*. London: 2009.
Horsfall, Nicholas. 'The *Collegium Poetarum*'. *BICS* 23 (1976): 79–95.
Houghton, Luke B.T. 'Death Ritual and Burial Practice in the Latin Love Elegists'. In Hope, Valerie M. and Huskinson, Janet, edd. *Memory and Mourning: Studies on Roman Death*. Oxford: 2011: 61–77.
Housman, A.E. 'Horatiana III'. *JPh* 18 (1890): 1–35.
Housman, A.E. 'Prosody and Method II. The Metrical Properties of GN'. *CQ* 22 (1928): 1–10.
Housman, A.E. *The Classical Papers of A.E. Housman*. Vol. 1, ed. Diggle, J. and Goodyear, F.R.D. Cambridge: 1972.
Hubbard, Thomas K. 'Pindar, Theoxenus, and the Homoerotic Eye'. *Arethusa* 35 (2002): 255–96.
Hubbard, Thomas K. 'The Invention of Sulpicia'. *CJ* 100 (2004): 177–94.
Hunter, Richard. 'Callimachus and Roman Elegy'. In Gold, Barbara, ed. *A Companion to Roman Love Elegy*. Chichester: 2012: 155–71.
Hunter, Richard. 'Greek Elegy'. In Thorsen, Thea S., ed. *Cambridge Companion to Latin Love Elegy*. Cambridge: 2013: 23–38.
Hutchinson, Gregory O. *Talking Books: Readings in Hellenistic and Roman Books of Poetry*. Oxford: 2008.
Ingleheart, Jennifer. 'Ovid's *Scripta Puella*: Perilla as Poetic and Political Fiction in *Tristia* 3.7'. *CQ* 62 (2012): 227–41.
Irwin, Elizabeth. 'Biography, Fiction, and the Archilochean *ainos*'. *JHS* 118 (1998): 177–83.
Ishøy, Hanne. 'Bimsstein und Stirn, Horn und Nabel: Zu den Beschreibungen der Ausstattung der Papyrusrolle in römischer Poesie'. *Hermes* 134 (2006): 69–88.
Jacobson, Howard. *Ovid's* Heroides. Princeton, NJ: 1974.
James, Sharon L. 'Introduction: Constructions of Gender and Genre in Roman Comedy and Elegy'. *Helios* 25 (1998): 3–15.
James, Sharon L. *Learned Girls and Male Persuasion: Gender and Reading in Roman Love Elegy*. Berkeley, CA: 2003.
James, Sharon L. 'Elegy and New Comedy'. In Gold, Barbara, ed. *A Companion to Roman Love Elegy*. Chichester: 2012: 253–68.
Janan, Micaela. *The Politics of Desire: Propertius IV*. Berkeley, CA: 2001.
Janan, Micaela. 'Narcissus on the text: Psychoanalysis, exegesis, ethics'. *Phoenix* 61 (2007): 286–95.
Janan, Micaela. 'Lacanian Psychoanalytic Theory and Roman Love Elegy'. In Gold, Barbara, ed. *A Companion to Roman Love Elegy*. Chichester: 2012: 375–89.
Johnson, William A. *Bookrolls and Scribes in Oxyrhynchus*. Toronto: 2004.
Kaibel, George. *Epigrammata Graeca Ex Lapidibus Conlecta*. Berlin: 1878.
Kaster, Robert A. *Emotion, Restraint, and Community in Ancient Rome*. New York: 2005.
Keith, Alison M. *The Play of Fictions: Studies in Ovid's* Metamorphoses *Book 2*. Ann Arbor, MI: 1992.
Keith, Alison M. '*Corpus Eroticum*: Elegiac Poetics and Elegiac *Puellae* in Ovid's *Amores*'. *CW* 88 (1994): 27–40.

Keith, Alison M. '*Tandem venit amor*: A Roman Woman Speaks of Love'. In Hallett, Judith P. and Skinner, Marilyn B., edd. *Roman Sexualities*. Princeton, NJ: 1997: 295–310.
Keith, Alison M. 'Critical Trends in Interpreting Sulpicia'. *CW* 100 (2006): 3–10.
Keith, Alison M. 'Sartorial Elegance and Poetic Finesse in the Sulpician Corpus'. In Edmonson, Jonathan and Keith, Alison, edd. *Roman Dress and the Fabrics of Roman Culture*. Toronto: 2008: 192–201.
Keith, Alison M., ed. *Latin Elegy and Hellenistic Epigram: A Tale of Two Genres at Rome*. Newcastle upon Tyne: 2011.
Keith, Alison M. 'Naming the Elegiac Mistress: Elegiac Onomastics in Roman Inscriptions'. In Keith, Alison M. and Edmondson, Jonathan, edd. *Roman Literary Cultures: Domestic Politics, Revolutionary Poetics, Civic Spectacle*. Toronto: 2016: 73–111.
Kennedy, Duncan F. 'Gallus and the *Culex*'. *CQ* 32 (1982): 371–89.
Kennedy, Duncan F. *The Arts of Love: Five Studies in the Discourse of Roman Love Elegy*. Cambridge: 1993.
Kenney, Edward J. 'The Poetry of Ovid's Exile'. *PCPS* 191 (1965): 37–49.
Kenney, Edward J. 'Books and Readers in the Roman World'. *Cambridge History of Classical Literature: Latin*. Cambridge: 1982: 3–32.
Kenney, Edward J. *Ovidio* Metamorfosi. *Vol IV: lib. VII–IX*. Milan: 2011.
Kenyon, Frederic G. *Books and Readers in Ancient Greece and Rome*. Oxford: 1932.
Kershaw, Allen. 'Emendation and Usage: Two Readings of Propertius'. *CP* 75 (1980): 71–2.
Kershaw, Allen. 'A! and the Elegists: More Observations'. *CP* 78 (1983): 232–3.
Kessels, A.H.M. *Studies on the Dream in Greek Literature*. Utrecht: 1978.
Kleingünther, Adolf. ΠΡΩΤΟΣ ΕΥΡΕΤΗΣ: *Untersuchungen zur Geschichte einer Fragestellung*. Philol. Suppl. 26. Leipzig: 1933
Knoche, Ulrich. 'Tibulls früheste Liebeselegie? (Tibull 3, 19)'. In *Navicula Chiloniensis. Studia philologica Felici Jacoby professori Chiloniensi emerito octogenario oblata*. Leiden: 1956: 173–90.
Knox, Peter E. 'Wine, Water, and Callimachean Polemics'. *HSCP* 89 (1985): 107–19.
Knox, Peter E. 'Adjectives in *-osus* and Latin Poetic Diction'. *Glotta* 64 (1986): 90–101.
Knox, Peter E. 'The *Corpus Tibullianum*'. In Guenther, H.-C., ed. *Brill's Companion to Tibullus*. Leiden: forthcoming.
Koenen, Ludwig. 'Die Unschuldsbeteuerungen des Priestereides und die Römischen Elegie'. *ZPE* 2 (1968): 31–8.
Konishi, Haruo. 'Muse, Goddess of Literacy'. *LCM* 18 (1993): 116–21.
Kraus, Walther. 'Lygdamus und Ovid'. *WS* 70 (1957): 197–204.
Lachmann, Karl. *Kleinere Schriften*. Vol 2. Berlin: 1876.
Lamberton, Robert. *Hesiod*. New Haven, CT: 1988.
Landels, John G. *Music in Ancient Greece and Rome*. London: 1999.
Langlands, Rebecca. *Sexual Morality in Ancient Rome*. Cambridge: 2006.
La Penna, Antonio. 'Note sul linguaggio erotico dell'elegia latina'. *Maia* 4 (1951): 187–209.
La Penna, Antonio. 'Ancora su Ligdamo e Ovidio'. *Atene e Roma* 3 (1953): 105–10.
Lattimore, Richmond. *Themes in Greek and Latin Epitaphs*. Illinois Studies in Classical Literature, Vol. 28. Urbana, IL: 1942.
Lee, A. Guy. 'The Date of Lygdamus and his Relationship to Ovid'. *PCPS* 5 (1958–9): 15–22.
Lee, A. Guy. 'On [Tibullus] III.19 (IV.13)'. *PCPhS* 9 (1963): 4–10.
Lee. A. Guy. 'Tibulliana'. *PCPS* 20 (1974): 53–7.
Lee-Stecum, Parshia. *Powerplay in Tibullus: Reading Elegies Book One*. Cambridge: 1998.

Lenz, Friedrich Walther. 'Ein Liebesgedicht Tibulls (4.13)'. *SIFC* 10 (1932): 125–45.
Lenz, Friedrich Walther and Galinsky, G.K. *Albii Tibulli Aliorumque Carminum Libri Tres*. 3rd ed. Leiden: 1971.
Leonotti, Emilio. 'Semantica di *Durus* in Tibullo'. *Prometheus* 16 (1990): 27–42.
Levin, Susan. *Dorothy Wordsworth and Romanticism*. New Brunswick, NJ: 1987.
Lieberg, Godo. Puella Divina: *Die Gestalt der göttlichen Geliebten bei Catull im Zusammenhang der antiken Dichtung*. Amsterdam: 1962.
Lieberg, Godo. 'Catull 60 und Ps. Theokrit 23'. *Hermes* 94 (1966): 115–19.
Lieberg, Godo. 'Le Muse in Tibullo e nel Corpus Tibullianum'. *Prometheus* 6 (1980): 29–55, 138–52.
Lilja, Saara. *The Roman Elegists' Attitude to Women*. Annales Acad. Scient. Fennicae B 135.1. Helsinki: 1965.
Lilja, Saara. *The Treatment of Odours in the Poetry of Antiquity*. Commentationes Humanarum Litterarum 49. Helsinki: 1972.
Lipking, Lawrence. *Abandoned Women and Poetic Tradition*. Chicago: 1998.
Lissberger, Ewald. 'Das Fortleben der Römischen Elegiker in den Carmina Epigraphica'. Diss. Eberhard-Karls-Universität. Tübingen: 1934.
Littlewood, R.J. 'Two Elegiac Hymns: Propertius, 3.17 and Ovid, *Fasti*, 5.663-692'. *Latomus* 34 (1975): 662–74.
Lively, Genevieve. 'Narratology in Roman Elegy'. In Gold, Barbara, ed. *A Companion to Roman Love Elegy*. Chichester: 2012: 410–25.
Lowe, N.B. 'Sulpicia's Syntax'. *CQ* 38 (1988): 193–205.
Luck, Georg. *Albii Tibulli aliorumque* Carmina. Stuttgart: 1969.
Lyne, R.O.A.M. *Ciris: A Poem Attributed to Vergil*. Cambridge: 1978.
Lyne, R.O.A.M. '[Tibullus] Book 3 and Sulpicia'. *Collected Papers on Latin Poetry*. Oxford: 2007: 341–67.
Maas, Martha and McIntosh Snyder, Jane. *Stringed Instruments of Ancient Greece*. New Haven, CT: 1989.
McClure, Laura K. *Courtesans at Table: Gender and Greek Literary Culture in Athenaeus*. New York: 2003.
McCrea, Nelson Glenn. 'Ovid's Use of Colour and of Colour-Terms'. In *Classical Studies in Honour of Henry Drisler*. New York: 1894: 180–94.
MacFarlane, Katherine N. *Isidore of Seville on the Pagan Gods* (Origines VII.11). Transactions of the American Philosophical Society 70.3. Philadelphia: 1980.
McKay, Alexander G. *Houses, Villas, and Palaces in the Roman World*. Baltimore: 1998 (first ed. Ithaca, NY: 1975).
McKay, K.J. 'Lygdamus (Tibullus III) I.7f'. *Latomus* 46 (1987): 213–14.
McKay, L.A. 'Satvrnia Ivno'. *G&R* 3 (1956): 59–60.
McKeown, J.C. *Ovid: Amores: Text, Prolegomena and Commentary. Volume II: A Commentary on Book One*. Leeds: 1989.
McKeown, J.C. *Ovid: Amores: Text, Prolegomena and Commentary. Volume III: A Commentary on Book Two*. Leeds: 1998.
Malcovati, Henrica. *Oratorum Romanorum Fragmenta*. Turin: 1953.
Maleuvre, Jean-Yves. 'Un certain Lygdamus'. *LEC* 69 (2001): 171–88, 237–49.
Maltby, Robert. *A Lexicon of Ancient Latin Etymologies*. Leeds: 1991
Maltby, Robert. 'Technical Language in Tibullus'. *Emerita* 67 (1999): 231–49.
Maltby, Robert. *Tibullus: Elegies. Text, Introduction and Commentary*. Cambridge: 2002.

Maltby, Robert. 'The Unity of *Corpus Tibullianum* Book 3: Some Stylistic and Metrical Considerations'. *Papers of the Langford Latin Seminar* 14 (2009): 319–40.
Maltby, Robert. 'The Influence of Hellenistic Epigram on Tibullus'. In Keith, Alison, ed. *Latin Elegy and Hellenistic Epigram: A Tale of Two Genres at Rome.* Newcastle upon Tyne: 2011: 87–98.
Martelli, Francesca. *Ovid's Revisions: The Editor as Author.* Cambridge: 2013.
Martinon, Philippe. *Les Élégies de Tibulle, Lygdamus et Sulpicia.* Paris: 1895.
Mayer, Roland. *Horace*: Epistles *Book I.* Cambridge: 1994.
Mayer, Roland. 'Persona(l) Problems: The Literary Persona in Antiquity Revisited'. *MD* 50 (2003): 55–80.
Merkelbach, Reinhold. 'Ein Billet der Sulpicia'. *RhM* 127 (1984): 95.
Merriam, Carol U. 'Some Notes on the Sulpicia Elegies'. *Latomus* 49 (1990): 95–8.
Merriam, Carol U. 'The Other Sulpicia'. *CW* 84 (1991): 303–5.
Merriam, Carol U. 'Sulpicia and the Art of Literary Allusion: [Tibullus] 3.13'. In Greene, Ellen, ed. *Women Poets in Ancient Greece and Rome.* Norman, OK: 2005: 158–68.
Merriam, Carol U. 'Sulpicia: Just another Roman Poet'. *CW* 100 (2006): 11–16.
Michalopoulos, Andreas N. *Ovid,* Heroides *16 and 17: Introduction, Text and Commentary.* ARCA 47. Cambridge: 2006.
Miller, J. Innes. *The Spice Trade of the Roman Empire 29 B.C. to A.D. 641.* Oxford: 1969.
Miller, John F. 'Propertius' Hymn to Bacchus and Contemporary Poetry'. *AJP* 112 (1991): 77–86.
Miller, John F. 'The Lamentations of Apollo in Ovid's *Metamorphoses*'. In Schubert, Werner, ed. *Ovid: Werk und Wirkung: Festgabe für Michael von Albrecht zum 65. Geburtstag.* Frankfurt: 1998: 413–21.
Miller, John F. *Apollo, Augustus, and the Poets.* Cambridge: 2009.
Miller, Patricia Cox. *Dreams in Late Antiquity: Studies in the Imagination of a Culture.* Princeton, NJ: 1994.
Miller, Paul A. *Subjecting Verses: Latin Love Elegy and the Emergence of the Real.* Princeton, NJ: 2004.
Milnor, Kristina. 'Sulpicia's (Corpo)reality: Elegy, Authorship, and the Body in [Tibullus] 3.13'. *CA* 21 (2002): 259–82.
Milnor, Kristina. *Gender, Domesticity, and the Age of Augustus: Inventing Private Life.* New York: 2005.
Miralles Maldonado, José C. 'La Lengua de Sulpicia: *Corpus Tibullianum* 4.7–12'. *Habis* 21 (1990): 101–20.
Momigliano, Arnaldo. '*Panegyricus Messallae* and *Panegyricus Vespasiani*: Two References to Britain'. *JRS* 40 (1950): 39–42.
Monteil, Pierre. *Beau et Laid en Latin: Étude de Vocabulaire.* Paris: 1964.
Morgan, Llewelyn. Musa Pedestris: *Metre and Meaning in Roman Verse.* Oxford: 2010.
Morgante, Filippo. 'Lucio Giulio Calido e altri poeti'. *RCCM* 72 (1970): 127–61.
Morrison, A.D. *The Narrator in Archaic Greek and Hellenistic Poetry.* Cambridge: 2007.
Müller, Richard. *Motivkatalog der römischen Elegie: Eine Untersuchung zur Poetik der Römer.* Zurich: 1952.
Murgatroyd, Paul. *Tibullus* Elegies I. Pietermaritzburg: 1980.
Murgatroyd, Paul. 'Amatory Hunting, Fishing and Fowling'. *Latomus* 43 (1984): 362–8.
Murgatroyd, Paul. *Tibullus* Elegies II. Oxford: 1994.

Musurillo, Herbert. 'The Theme of Time as a Poetic Device in the Elegies of Tibullus'. *TAPA* 98 (1967): 253–68.
Myers, K. Sara. 'The Poet and the Procuress: The *Lena* in Latin Love Elegy'. *JRS* 86 (1996): 1–21.
Myers, K. Sara. *Ovid*: Metamorphoses *Book XIV*. Cambridge: 2009.
Näf, Beat. *Traum und Traumdeutung im Altertum*. Darmstadt: 2004.
Nagy, Gregory. 'Iambos: Typologies of Invective and Praise'. *Arethusa* 9 (1976): 191–205.
Nagy, Gregory. *Greek Mythology and Poetics*. Ithaca: 1990.
Navarro Antolín, Fernando. '*Iuraui stulte*: Tib. III.19 (= IV.13)'. In *Actas del VIII Congreso español de estudios clásicos (Madrid, 23–28 de septiembre de 1991)*. Madrid: 1994: 799–804.
Navarro Antolín, Fernando. *Corpus Tibullianum III.1–6: Lygdami Elegiarum Liber. Edition and Commentary*, trans. J.J. Zoltowski. Leiden: 1996.
Navarro Antolín, Fernando. 'Propercio en el libro tercero del *Corpus Tibullianum*'. In Santini, Carlo and Santucci, Francesco, edd. *Properzio nel genere elegiac: Modelli, motivi, riflessi storici*. Atti del Convegno Internazionale, Assisi, 27–29 maggio 2004. Assisi: 2005: 301–24.
Némethy, Geza. *Albii Tibulli Carmina*. Budapest: 1905.
Némethy, Geza. *Lygdami carmina. Accedit Panegyricus in Messallam. Edidit, adnotationibus exegeticis et criticis instruxit*. Budapest: 1906.
Némethy, Geza. 'Zur Ciris-Frage'. *RhM* 62 (1907): 484–5.
Newlands, Carole. 'The Role of the Book in *Tristia* 3.1'. *Ramus* 26 (1997): 57–79.
Newman, K.J. *The Concept of Vates in Latin Poetry*. Leuven: 1967.
Newton, Francis L. 'Tibullus in Two Grammatical Florilegia of the Middle Ages'. *TAPA* 93 (1962): 253–86.
Nisbet, R.G.M. and Hubbard, Margaret. *A Commentary on Horace*: Odes *Book I*. Oxford: 1970.
Nisbet, R.G.M. and Hubbard, Margaret. *A Commentary on Horace*: Odes *Book II*. Oxford: 1978.
Nisbet, R.G.M. and Rudd, Niall. *A Commentary on Horace*: Odes *Book III*. Oxford: 2004.
Nitzsche, Jane C. *The Genius-Figure in Antiquity and the Middle Ages*. New York: 1975.
Nochlin, Linda. *Women, Art and Power and Other Essays*. Boulder, CO: 1988: 147–58.
Norden, Eduard. *Römische Literatur*. 4th ed. Leipzig: 1952 (first ed. 1910).
Norden, Eduard. *Vergil. Aeneis Buch VI*. Leipzig: 1957.
Nugent, S. Georgia. '*Tristia* 2: Ovid and Augustus'. In Raaflaub, Kurt A. and Toher, Mark, edd. *Between Republic and Empire: Interpretations of Augustus and His Principate*. Berkeley, CA: 1990: 239–57.
Oebecke, Franz. *De vero elegiarum auctore quae tertio Tibulli libro vulgo continentur*. Jahresbericht des Gymnasium in Aachen. Aachen: 1832.
O'Gorman, Ellen. 'Love and the Family: Augustus and Ovidian Elegy'. *Arethusa* 30 (1997): 103–23.
O'Hara, James J. *Death and the Optimistic Prophecy in Vergil's Aeneid*. Princeton, NJ: 1990.
Öhrman, Magdalena. *Varying Virtue: Mythological Paragons of Wifely Virtues in Roman Elegy*. Lund: 2008.
Oliver, Revilo P. 'The Text of Ovid's *Amores*'. *Illinois Studies in Language and Literature* 58 (1969): 138–64.

O'Neil, Edward N. *A Critical Concordance of the Tibullan Corpus*. Ithaca, NY: 1963.
Otto, A. *Die Sprichwörter und sprichwörtlich Redensarten der Römer gesammelt und erklärt*. Leipzig: 1890.
Parca, Maryline. 'The Place of Lygdamus in Latin Poetry'. *SLLRH* 4 (1986): 461–74.
Parker, Holt N. 'Love's Body Anatomized: The Ancient Erotic Handbooks and the Rhetoric of Sexuality'. In Richlin, Amy, ed. *Pornography and Representation in Greece and Rome*. Oxford: 1992: 90–111.
Parker, Holt N. 'Sulpicia, the *Auctor de Sulpicia*, and the Authorship of 3.9 and 3.11'. *Helios* 21 (1994): 39–62.
Parker, Holt N. 'Catullus and the "Amicus Catulli": The Text of a Learned Talk'. *CW* 100 (2006): 17–29.
Paschalis, Michael. '*Aut Ego Fallor Aut Ego Laedor* (Ovid, *Metamorphoses* 1.607–8): A Witty Tautology'. *Eranos* 84 (1986): 62–3.
Pearcy, Lee T. 'Erasing Cerinthus: Sulpicia and her Audience'. *CW* 100 (2006): 31–6.
Pease, Arthur Stanley. *Publi Vergili Maronis:* Aeneidos Liber Quartus. Cambridge, MA: 1935.
Peirano, Irene. *The Rhetoric of the Roman Fake: Latin* Pseudepigrapha *in Context*. Cambridge: 2012.
Pepe, L. *Tibullo Minore*. Naples: 1948.
Perkins, Caroline A. 'The Figure of Elegy in *Amores* 3.1: Elegy as *Puella*, Elegy as *Poeta*, *Puella* as *Poeta*'. *CW* 104 (2011): 313–31.
Perotti, Pier Angelo. 'L'infinito perfetto in Tibullo e nel *Corpus Tibullianum*'. *Orpheus* 10 (1989): 141–9.
Petersen, A. *De Quarti Libri Tibulliani Eligidiis Eorumque Auctore*. Gluckstadt: 1849.
Petersen, Amy. 'Ovid's Wife in the *Tristia* and *Epistulae ex Ponto*: Transforming Erotic Elegy into Conjugal Elegy'. Master's Thesis: University of Georgia: 2005.
Phillimore, J.S. *Index Verborum Propertianus*. Darmstadt: 1961.
Piastri, Roberta. 'I carmi di Sulpicia e il repertorio topico dell'elegia'. In *Quaderni del Dipartimento di Filologia, Linguistica e Tradizione classica, Univiversità degli Studi di Torino*. Pubblicazioni del Dipartimento di Filologia, Linguistica e Tradizione Classica 11 (1998): 137–70.
Piastri, Roberta. 'Un appunto filologico in merito a Tib. 3.16.1 (= 4.10.1)'. *Sileno* 25 (1999): 323–8.
Pichon, René. *Index Verborum Amatoriorum*. Hildesheim: 1991.
Platnauer, Maurice. *Latin Elegiac Verse: A Study of the Metrical Usages of Tibullus, Propertius and Ovid*. Cambridge: 1951.
Poliakoff, Michael. 'Nectar, Springs, and the Sea: Critical Terminology in Pindar and Callimachus'. *ZPE* 39 (1980): 41–7.
Pollock, Griselda and Cherry, Deborah. 'Woman as sign in Pre-Raphaelite literature: The representation of Elizabeth Siddall'. In Pollock, Griselda, ed. *Vision and Difference: Femininity, Feminism, and the Histories of Art*. London: 1988: 91–114.
Ponchont, Max. *Tibulle et les auteurs du Corpus Tibullianum*, 7th ed. Paris: 1968.
Porte, D. 'Messalla'. *Orphea Voce* 4. Bordeaux: 1992.
Possanza, D. Mark. '*Cornua* and *Frontes* in [Tibullus] 3.1.13'. *CQ* 44 (1994): 281–2.
Postgate, J.P. 'On the Genuineness of Tibullus IV.13'. *Journal of Philology* 9 (1880): 280–5.
Postgate, J.P. 'Paralipomena: Tibullus'. *CQ* 6 (1912): 40–3.

Postgate, J.P. 'Neaera as a Common Name'. *CQ* 8 (1914): 121–2.
Postgate, J.P. *Tibullus*. 2nd ed. Oxford: 1915.
Postgate, J.P. *Selections from Tibullus and Others.* London: 1929.
Putnam, Michael C.J. 'Some Virgilian Unities'. In Hardie, Philip and Moore, Helen, edd. *Classical Literary Careers and their Reception.* Cambridge: 2010: 17–38.
Quinn, Kenneth. *Catullus: An Interpretation.* New York: 1973.
Racette-Campbell, Melanie. 'Marriage Contracts, *Fides* and Gender Roles in Propertius 3.20'. *CJ* 108 (2013): 297–317.
Radford, Robert S. 'The Juvenile Works of Ovid and the Spondaic Period of his Metrical Art'. *TAPA* 51 (1920): 146–71.
Radford, Robert S. 'Tibullus and Ovid: The Authorship of the Sulpicia and Cornutus Elegies in the Tibullan Corpus'. *AJP* 44 (1923): 1–26; 230–59; 293–318.
Radford, Robert S. 'The Ovidian Authorship of the Lygdamus Elegies'. *TAPA* 57 (1926): 149–80.
Radford, Robert S. 'The Ovidian Authorship of the Lygdamus Elegies'. *CP* 22 (1927): 356–71.
Ramorino, F. 'Ligdamo e Ovidio: Quistioncina cronologica'. *Rivista di Storia Antica e Scienze Affini* 4.3 (1899).
Ramsby, Teresa R. *Textual Permanence: Roman Elegists and the Epigraphic Tradition.* London: 2007.
Raucci, Stacie. *Elegiac Eyes: Vision in Roman Love Elegy.* New York: 2011.
Raymond, Emmanuelle. 'Caius Cornelius Gallus: "The Inventor of Latin Love Elegy"'. In Thorsen, Thea S., ed. *Cambridge Companion to Latin Love Elegy.* Cambridge: 2013: 59–67.
Rebelo Gonçalves, Maria Isabel. 'Helenismos onomásticos do *Corpus Tibullianum*. Aspectos métricos'. *Euphrosyne* 16 (1988): 309–21.
Reinhold, Meyer. *History of Purple as a Status Symbol in Antiquity.* Coll. Latomus 116. Brussels: 1970.
Reynolds, L.D., ed. *Texts and Transmission. A Survey of the Latin Classics.* Oxford: 1983.
Rhorer, Catherine C. 'Red and White in Ovid's Metamorphoses: The Mulberry Tree in the Tale of Pyramus and Thisbe'. *Ramus* 9 (1980): 79–88.
Richardson, Janette. 'The Function of Formal Imagery in Ovid's *Metamorphoses*'. *CJ* 59 (1964): 161–9.
Richlin, Amy. 'Julia's Jokes'. In Garlick, B., Dixon, S., and Allen, P., edd. *Stereotypes of Women in Power.* New York: 1992: 65–91.
Richlin, Amy. 'Emotional Work: Lamenting the Roman Dead'. In Tylawsky, Elizabeth and Weiss, Charles, edd. *Essays in Honor of Gordon Williams: Twenty-five Years at Yale.* New Haven, CT: 2001: 229–48.
Rimell, Victoria. *Ovid's Lovers: Desire, Difference and the Poetic Imagination.* Cambridge: 2006.
Riposati, Benedetto. *Introduzione allo studio di Tibullo.* 2nd ed. Milan: 1967.
Robinson, David M. 'The Wheel of Fortune'. *CP* 41 (1946): 207–16.
Roessel, David. 'The Significance of the Name Cerinthus in the Poems of Sulpicia'. *TAPA* 120 (1990): 243–50.
Rosati, Gianpiero. 'L'elegia al femminile: Le *Heroides* di Ovidio (a altre heroides)'. *MD* 29 (1993): 71–94.
Rose, H.J. 'On the Original Significance of the *Genius*'. *CQ* 17 (1923): 57–60.

Rosenmeyer, Patricia A. *The Poetics of Imitation: Anacreon and the Anacreontic Tradition.* Cambridge: 1992.
Ross, David O. *Style and Tradition in Catullus.* Cambridge, MA: 1969.
Ross, David O. *Backgrounds to Augustan Poetry: Gallus, Elegy, and Rome.* Cambridge: 1975.
Rossbach, A. *Albii Tibulli libri quattuor.* Leipzig: 1855.
Rostagni, Augusto. 'La *Vita* Suetoniana di Tibullo e la Costituzione del *Corpus Tibullianum*'. *RFIC* 13 (1935) 20–51 (= *Scritti Minori* Vol. 2.2; Turin: 1956: 304–41).
Ruiz Sánchez, Marcos. 'Poética y símbolo en el ciclo de Sulpicia (*Corpus Tibullianum*, 3.8–3.12 y 3.13–3.18)'. *Helmantica* 47 (1996): 379–413.
Russ, Joanna. *How to Suppress Women's Writing.* Austin, TX: 1983.
Russo, Joseph, Fernandez-Galiano, Manuel, and Heubeck, Alfred. *A Commentary on Homer's* Odyssey*: Volume II: Books 17–24.* Oxford: 1990.
Salanitro, Nino. *Tibullo.* Naples: 1938.
Sallares, Robert. *Malaria and Rome: A History of Malaria in Ancient Italy.* Oxford: 2002.
Salvatore A. 'Tecnica e motivi tibulliani nel Panegirico di Messalla'. *PP* 7 (1948): 48–63.
Santirocco, Matthew S. 'Sulpicia Reconsidered'. *CJ* 74 (1979): 229–39.
Scaliger, J.J. *Castigationes in Catullum, Tibullum, Propertium.* Paris: 1577.
Scheid, John. *Les Frères arvales.* Bibliothèque de l'École des Hautes Études: Section des Sciences Religieuses 77. Paris: 1975.
Schmatz, Joseph. *Baiae, das erste Luxusbad der Römer.* Part 1. Regensburg: 1905.
Schmidt, V. '*Hic ego qui iaceo*: Die lateinischen Elegiker und ihre Grabschrift'. *Mnemosyne* 38 (1985): 307–33.
Schneider, Fedor. 'Über Kalendae Ianuariae und Martiae im Mittelalter'. *Arch. f. Religionswissenschaft* 20 (1920): 82–134.
Schoonhoven, Henk. 'The 'Panegyricus Messallae': Date and Relation with Catalepton 9'. *ANRW* II.30.3. Berlin: 1983: 1682–707.
Schrijvers, Piet Herman. 'In Praise of Messalla: Hellenistic Geography in Three Panegyric Poems'. In Harder, M.A., Regtuit, R.F., and Walker, G.C., edd. *Nature and Science in Hellenistic Poetry.* Leuven: 2006: 149–76.
Schuster, Mauriz. *Tibull-Studien: Beiträge zur Erklärung und Kritik Tibulls und des Corpus Tibullianum.* Hildesheim: 1930 (reprint 1968).
Scodel, Ruth. 'Self-Correction, Spontaneity, and Orality in Archaic Poetry'. In Worthington, Ian, ed. *Voice into Text: Orality and Literacy in Ancient Greece.* Leiden: 1996: 59–79.
Sebesta, Judith Lynn. 'Tunica Ralla, Tunica Spissa'. In Sebesta, Judith Lynn and Bonfante, Larissa, edd. *The World of Roman Costume.* Madison, WI: 1994: 65–76.
Seelentag, Sabine. *Der pseudovergilische Culex: Text-Übersetzung-Kommentar.* Hermes Einzelschriften 105. Stuttgart: 2010.
Severy, Beth. *Augustus and the Family at the Birth of the Roman Empire.* New York: 2003.
Shackleton Bailey, D.R. 'On an Idiomatic Use of Possessive Pronouns in Latin'. *CR* 68 (1954): 8–9.
Sharrock, Alison. 'Womanufacture'. *JRS* 81 (1991): 36–49.
Sharrock, Alison. *Seduction and Repetition in Ovid's* Ars Amatoria II. Oxford: 1994.
Sihler, E.G. 'The *Collegium Poetarum* at Rome'. *AJP* 26 (1905): 1–21.
Sisman, Adam. *The Friendship: Wordsworth and Coleridge.* New York: 2006.
Skiadas, Aristoxenos. '*Periuria Amantum*: Zur Geschichte und Interpretation eines Motivs der augusteischen Liebesdichtung'. In Lefèvre, Eckard, ed. *Monumentum*

Chiloniense: Studien zur augusteischen Zeit: Kieler Festschrift für Erich Burck zum 70. Geburtstag. Amsterdam: 1975: 400–18.

Sklenár, Robert J. 'Ausonius' Elegiac Wife: Epigram 20 and the Traditions of Latin Love Poetry'. *CJ* 101 (2005): 51–62.

Skoie, Mathilde. '*Sulpicia Americana*: A reading of Sulpicia in the Commentary by K.F. Smith (1913)'. *Arethusa* 33 (2000): 285–311.

Skoie, Mathilde. *Reading Sulpicia: Commentaries 1475–1990*. Oxford: 2002.

Skoie, Mathilde. 'Reading Sulpicia: (Em)Plotting Love'. In Nilsson, Ingela, ed. *Plotting with Eros: Essays on the Poetics of Love and the Erotics of Reading*. Copenhagen: 2009: 59–82.

Skoie, Mathilde. '"The Woman"'. In Thorsen, Thea S., ed. *Cambridge Companion to Latin Love Elegy*. Cambridge: 2013: 83–96.

Skutsch, Otto. 'Zu Vergils Eklogen'. *RhM* 99 (1956): 193–201.

Skutsch, Otto. '*Cum cecidit fato consul uterque pari*'. *Philologus* 103 (1959): 152–4.

Skutsch, Otto. 'Zur Datierung des Lygdamus'. *Philologus* 110 (1966): 142–6.

Skutsch, Otto. 'Lygdamus 1.19'. *Philologus* 113 (1969): 156–7.

Skutsch, Otto. *The Annals of Q. Ennius. Edited with Introduction and Commentary*. Oxford: 1985.

Smith, Kirby Flower. *The Elegies of Albius Tibullus: The Corpus Tibullianum*. New York: 1913.

Snyder, Jane McIntosh. *The Woman and the Lyre: Women Writers in Classical Greece and Rome*. Carbondale, IL: 1989.

Solimano, Giannina. 'Il mito di Apollo e Admeto negli elegiaci latini'. In *Mythos: Scripta in honorem Marii Untersteiner*. Genoa: 1970: 255–68.

Solodow, Joseph. '*Raucae, tua cura, palumbes*: A Study of a Poetic Word Order'. *HSCP* 90 (1986): 129–53.

Spender, Dale. *The Writing or the Sex? Or, Why You Don't Have to Read Women's Writing to Know it's No Good*. New York: 1989.

Speyer, Wolfgang. *Die Literarische Fälschung im heidnischen und christlichen Altertum: Ein Versuch ihrer Deutung*. Munich: 1971.

Staples, Ariadne. *From Good Goddess to Vestal Virgins: Sex and Category in Roman Religion*. London: 1998.

Stearns, John Barker. 'Studies of the Dream as a Technical Device in Latin Epic and Drama'. Diss. Princeton: 1927.

Šterbenc Erker, Darja. 'Gender and Roman Funeral Ritual'. In Hope, Valerie M. and Huskinson, Janet, edd. *Memory and Mourning: Studies on Roman Death*. Oxford: 2011: 40–60.

Stevenson, Jane. *Women Latin Poets: Language, Gender, and Authority, from Antiquity to the Eighteenth Century*. Oxford: 2005.

Stroh, Wilfried. *Die römische Elegie als werbende Dichtung*. Amsterdam: 1971.

Swoboda, Michał. 'Autorzy Trzeciej Księgi tzw. *Corpus Tibullianum*'. *Eos* 58 (1969–70): 99–114.

Syme, Ronald. *Some Arval Brethren*. Oxford: 1980.

Syme, Ronald. 'A Great Orator Mislaid'. *CQ* 31 (1981): 421–7.

Syme, Ronald. *The Augustan Aristocracy*. Oxford: 1986.

Tarrant, R.J. 'Toward a Typology of Interpolation in Latin Poetry'. *TAPA* 117 (1987): 281–98.

Tarrant, R.J. 'The Reader as Author: Collaborative Interpolation in Latin Poetry'. In Grant, John N., ed. *Editing Greek and Latin Texts: Papers given at the Twenty-Third Annual Conference on Editorial Problems, University of Toronto, 6–7 November 1987.* New York: 1989: 121–62.

Tarrant, R.J. *Texts, Editors and Readers: Methods and Problems in Latin Textual Criticism.* Cambridge: 2016.

Thomas, Phillip L. 'Red and White: A Roman Color Symbol'. *RhM* 122 (1979): 310–16.

Thomas, Richard F. *Virgil*: Georgics *I-II*. Vol.1 and *Virgil*: Georgics *III-IV*. Vol. 2. Cambridge: 1988.

Thompson, Clara Louise. '*Taedium Vitae* in Roman Sepulchral Inscriptions'. Diss. University of Pennsylvania: 1911.

Thorsen, Thea S. 'Ovid the Love Elegist'. In Thorsen, Thea S., ed. *Cambridge Companion to Latin Love Elegy*. Cambridge: 2013: 114–29.

Thorsen, Thea S. *Ovid's Early Poetry: From His Single* Heroides *to his* Remedia Amoris. Cambridge: 2014.

Toynbee, J.M.C. *Death and Burial in the Roman World*. London: 1971.

Traina, Alfonso. '*Primus dies natalis*'. *Maia* 18 (1966): 279–80.

Tränkle, Hermann. *Die Sprachkunst des Properz und die Tradition der lateinischen Dichtersprache*. Hermes Einzelschriften 15. Wiesbaden: 1960.

Tränkle, Hermann. 'Zum ersten Lygdamusgedicht'. *ZPE* 35 (1979): 23–8.

Tränkle, Hermann. *Appendix Tibulliana*. Berlin: 1990.

Treggiari, Susan. *Roman Marriage:* Iusti Coniuges *from the Time of Cicero to the Time of Ulpian*. Oxford: 1991.

Tsantsanoglou, K. 'The Memoirs of a Lady from Samos'. *ZPE* 12 (1973): 183–95.

Tschiedel, Hans Jürgen. 'Die Gedichte der Sulpicia (Tib. 3.13–18) – Frauenlyrik?' *GB* 18 (1992): 87–102.

Ullman, B.L. 'Tibullus in the Mediaeval Florilegia'. *CP* 23 (1928): 128–74.

Ullman, B.L. 'A List of Classical MSS (in an Eighth Century Codex) perhaps from Corbie'. *Scriptorum* 8 (1954): 24–37.

Vahlen, Iohannes. *Opuscula Academica*. Vol. 1. Hildesheim: 1907.

Vahlen, Iohannes. *Opuscula Academica*. Vol. 2. Hildesheim: 1908.

Valvo, Alfredo. 'M. Valerio Messalla Corvino negli studi più recenti'. *ANRW* II.30.3. Berlin: 1983: 1663–80.

Van Berchem, Denis. 'Messalla, ou Messalinus? Note sur le Panégyrique de Messalla'. *MH* 2 (1945): 33.

van der Horst, P.C. '*Fatum, Tria Fata: Parca, Tres Parcae*'. *Mnemosyne* 11 (1943): 217–27.

van Lieshout, R.G.A. *Greeks on Dreams*. Utrecht: 1980.

Van Sickle, John. 'The Book-Roll and Some Conventions of the Poetic Book'. *Arethusa* 13 (1980): 5–42.

Verdière, Raoul. 'L'auteur du *Panegyricus Messalae* tibullien'. *Latomus* 13 (1954): 56–64.

Veremans, Jozef. 'Lygdamus III.1 et III.4: Essai d'interprétation'. *Euphrosyne* 26 (1998): 9–24.

Versnel, Henk S. 'What did Ancient Man see when He saw a God? Some Reflections on Greco-Roman Epiphany'. In Van der Plas, D., ed. Effigies Dei. Leiden: 1987: 42–55.

Veyne, Paul. *Roman Erotic Elegy: Love, Poetry, and the West*, trans. David Pellauer. Chicago: 1988.

Voss, J.H. *Tibull und Lygdamus nach den Handschriften berichtiget, mit Anmerk. P. Burmanns und den Konjekturen Schraders*. Heidelberg: 1811.
Vretska, Karl. 'Tibull IV.8.6'. *Gymnasium* 64 (1957): 83–9.
Wagenvoort, H. 'De Lygdamo poëta deque eius Sodalicio'. *Mnemosyne* 45 (1917): 103–22.
Walde, Christine. *Die Traumdarstellungen in der griechisch-römischen Dichtung*. Munich: 2001.
Ward-Perkins, J. 'Nero's Golden House'. *Antiquity* 30 (1956): 209–19.
Watson, Patricia. '*Puella* and *Virgo*'. *Glotta* 61 (1983): 119–43.
Watt, W.S. 'Five Notes on the *Corpus Tibullianum*'. *Maia* 43 (1991): 15–16.
Webster, T.B.L. 'The Myth of Ariadne from Homer to Catullus'. *G&R* 13 (1966): 22–31.
Weinrich, Otto. 'Catull c. 60'. *Hermes* 87 (1959): 75–90.
Welch, Tara S. 'Elegy and the Monuments'. In Gold, Barbara, ed. *A Companion to Roman Love Elegy*. Chichester: 2012: 103–18.
West, Martin L. *Theogony*. Oxford: 1966.
West, Martin L. *Studies in Greek Elegy and Iambus*. Berlin: 1974.
West, Martin L. 'Erinna'. *ZPE* 25 (1977): 95–119.
West, Martin L. *Ancient Greek Music*. Oxford: 1992.
West, Martin L. *Die griechische Dichterin: Bild und Rolle*. Stuttgart: 1996.
Wheeler, Stephen. *A Discourse of Wonders: Audience and Performance in Ovid's Metamorphoses*. Philadelphia: 1999.
Wheeler, Stephen. 'Before the *Aetas Ovidiana:* Mapping the Early Reception of Ovidian Elegy'. *Hermathena* 177/8 (2004–5): 9–26.
White, Peter. 'The Presentation and Dedication of the *Silvae* and the *Epigrams*'. *JRS* 64 (1974): 40–61.
White, Peter. *Promised Verse: Poets in the Society of Augustan Rome*. Cambridge, MA: 1993.
Williams, Craig A. *Roman Homosexuality: Ideologies of Masculinity in Classical Antiquity*. New York: 1999.
Williams, Frederick. *Callimachus:* Hymn to Apollo. Oxford: 1978.
Williams, Gareth D. 'Representation of the Book-Roll in Latin Poetry: Ovid, *Tr.* 1.1.3–14 and Related Texts'. *Mnemosyne* 42 (1992): 178–89.
Wills, Jeffrey. *Repetition in Latin Poetry: Figures of Allusion*. Oxford: 1996.
Wiseman, T.P. *Cinna the Poet and Other Roman Essays*. Leicester: 1974.
Wiseman, T.P. 'Sirmio, Sir Ronald, and the *Gens Valeria*'. *CJ* 88 (1993): 223–9.
Witczak, Krzysztof Tomasz. 'The Roman Elegist Servius Sulpicius: Known or Unknown?' *Eos* 81 (1993): 77–82.
Wordsworth, Dorothy. *Illustrated Lakeland Journals*. Introduction by Rachel Trickett. London: 1987.
Wyke, Maria. 'Written Women: Propertius' *Scripta Puella*'. *JRS* 77 (1987): 47–61 (= 2002: 46–77).
Wyke, Maria. 'Mistress and Metaphor in Augustan Elegy'. *Helios* 16 (1989a): 25–47 (= 2002: 11–45).
Wyke, Maria. 'Reading Female Flesh: *Amores* 3.1'. In Cameron, Averil, ed. *History as Text: The Writing of Ancient History*. Chapel Hill, NC: 1989b: 111–43 (= 2002: 115–54).
Wyke, Maria. 'Taking the Woman's Part: Engendering Roman Love Elegy'. *Ramus* 23 (1994): 110–28 (revised as 2002: 155–78).

Wyke, Maria. *The Roman Mistress: Ancient and Modern Representations*. Oxford: 2002.
Yardley, John C. 'Sick-Visiting in Roman Elegy'. *Phoenix* 27 (1973): 283–8.
Yardley, John C. 'The Roman Elegists, Sick Girls, and the Soteria'. *CQ* 27 (1977): 394–401.
Yardley, John C. 'Cerinthus' *Pia Cura* ([Tibullus] 3.17.1–2)'. *CQ* 40 (1990): 568–70.
Yardley, John C. *Minor Authors of the Corpus Tibullianum*. Bryn Mawr Commentaries. Bryn Mawr, PA: 1992.
Zagagi, Netta. 'Amatory Gifts and Payments: A Note on *Munus, Donum, Data* in Plautus'. *Glotta* 65 (1987): 129–32.
Zagagi, Netta. '*Exilium Amoris* in New Comedy'. *Hermes* 116 (1988): 193–209.
Zanker, Paul. *The Power of Images in the Age of Augustus*, trans. Alan Shapiro. Ann Arbor, MI: 1988.
Zetzel, James E.G. 'Poetic Baldness and Its Cure'. *MD* 36 (1996): 73–100.
Zgoll, Christian. 'Badefreuden und Liebesleiden. Zur Interpretation und Stellung der 5. Elegie im Lygdamus-Zyklus ([Tib.] 3.1–6)'. *RhM* 145 (2002): 108–19.
Zimmermann, Rudolf. 'Die Autorschaft Tibulls an den Elegien 2–6 des IV Buches'. *Philologus* 83 (1928): 400–18.
Zingerle, Anton. *Kleine Philologische Abhandlungen*, Vol. 2. Innsbruck: 1877.

Index Locorum

Aelian
   VH 12.19: 50 n. 113
Aeschylus
   Ch. 660–1: 140
   Eum. 19 fr 86R: 158
Accius
   Fr. 159: 145
   Fr. 22.2: 119
   Fr. 688R: 199
Afranius
   141R: 255
Alcaeus
   366: 200
Alcman
   1: 236
   3: 236
   362: 221
Anacreon
   352: 221
   363: 221
   396: 221
   397: 221
   410: 221
Anacreonta
   4: 227
Anaxilas
   Fr. 22K: 177
AP (see also particular authors)
   4.1: 76
   5.6.3–4: 216
   5.68: 259
   5.88: 259
   5.93: 198
   5.260: 229, 230
   5.286: 259
   6.154: 107
   6.283–5: 288
   9.15: 228
   9.258: 218
   9.279.1: 118
   9.331: 218
   11.49.3: 218
   12.49–50: 198
   12.60: 298
   12.205: 192
   207.1: 271
Apollodorus
   2.3.1: 179
Apollonius Rhodius
   1.1273: 143
   4.685: 138
   4.1235: 181
Apuleius
   *Apol.*10: 8, 27
   Met 5.13: 298
   Met 8.21: 283
   Met 8.27: 107
   Met 11.11: 298
Archilochus
   177.2–3W: 261
Aristophanes
   Av. 1731–4: 256
   Thes. 315: 153
Arrian
   Ind. 37.3: 121
Athenaeus
   13: 50
   13.567e: 28 n. 54
   13.590a: 28 n. 54
   13.591d: 28 n. 54
   13.596a: 9 n. 19
   13.596c: 50 n. 113
   13.598a–b: 9 n. 19
   13.599c: 50 n. 113
   13.599d: 50 n. 113
Augustus
   Fr. 5.2 Malcovati: 125
Ausonius
   Parent. 19.13: 290
   Bucolica Einsidlensia
   1.35: 157
   2.37: 205
   2.38: 138

Caesar
   BG 5.31.5: 287
   BG 6.17: 247
Caesar Strabo
   Fr. 2: 144
Caesius Bassus
   Fr. 2.1: 247
Callimachus
   Aet. Fr. 1 Pf.: 248
   Aet. 1.21–2: 273
   Aet. Fr. 1–2: 131
   Aet. Fr. 1.17: 123
   Aet. Fr. 1.25–8: 297
   Aet. Fr. 7: 76
   Aet. Fr. 67–75: 151
   Aet. Fr. 72: 297

Callimachus (cont.)
- Aet. Fr. 73: 297
- Aet. Fr. 74.2: 300
- Epig. 5: 128
- Epig. 29.3–4: 296
- Hymn 2.32–3: 153
- Hymn 2.32–42: 143, 145
- Hymn 2.38: 146
- Hymn 2.47–54: 168
- Hymn 2.48: 169
- Hymn 2.68: 159
- Hymn 2.253–4: 153
- Hymn 4.234: 161
- Hymn 4.249: 202
- Iamb 1.7–8: 156
- Fr. 814: 127

Calpurnius Siculus
- 1.93: 170
- 2.34: 159
- 3.42: 275
- 7.53–4: 242

Calvus
- Fr. 9: 210
- Fr. 27: 101

Cato the Elder
- Agr. 133.3: 288
- Agr. 144.1: 204
- Agr. 160: 249

Catullus
- 1: 83, 87
- 1.1: 76, 79, 80
- 1.2: 85
- 1.9: 76
- 2.10: 123
- 3.6–7: 160
- 3.14: 130
- 5: 116, 250
- 5.1: 81
- 5.2: 206, 277, 279, 302
- 5.2–3: 270, 276
- 5.6: 217
- 6.5: 288
- 6.8: 108
- 6.17: 83
- 7: 250
- 7.3: 250
- 8.1: 251, 287
- 8.6: 210
- 8.16: 296
- 10.3: 288
- 10.33: 287
- 11: 202
- 11.5: 109
- 11.6: 174
- 12.5: 208
- 13.2: 292
- 14.1–2: 93
- 14.2: 124
- 14.5: 285
- 16: 33
- 16.3: 83
- 16.5: 156
- 16.6: 83
- 22.1–8: 83
- 22.3: 83
- 22.7: 84
- 22.8: 85
- 22.16: 292
- 27.1: 219
- 27.1–2: 201
- 27.5–6: 206
- 29.19: 127
- 30.2: 202
- 30.10: 184, 208
- 32: 217
- 32.7: 301
- 34.13: 138
- 35.16–17: 157
- 35.17: 157
- 36.3: 301
- 37.11: 159, 220, 275
- 37.51–60: 160
- 41.4: 299
- 41.5: 283
- 42.3: 169
- 43.5: 299
- 44: 282
- 44.7: 247
- 45: 257, 267
- 45.14: 259
- 45.16: 93
- 45.20: 259
- 50: 19, 87
- 50.1: 134, 293
- 50.4: 83
- 50.11–16: 246
- 50.16: 124
- 51.3: 253
- 51.13: 281
- 55.2: 111
- 60: 177
- 60.1: 181
- 60.1–3: 177
- 60.3: 97
- 61: 286
- 61.10: 84
- 61.56: 149
- 61.78b: 164
- 61.169–71: 260
- 61.188: 84
- 61.196: 260
- 61.211: 240

Index Locorum

61.226: 297
62.26: 124
62.37: 267
62.47: 124
62.60–5: 266
63: 204
63–8: 104
63.48: 178
63.69: 106
63.92: 207
64: 2, 11, 210, 212, 256
64.31: 118
64.56: 136
64.60: 213
64.67: 152
64.95: 249
64.98: 258
64.103: 213
64.111: 195
64.130: 172, 210
64.135: 212
64.136–7: 165, 166
64.139: 173
64.142: 208
64.143–6: 93
64.144: 135
64.148: 212
64.154: 178, 181
64.154–7: 177
64.155: 180
64.156: 181
64.157: 181
64.162: 229
64.164: 216
64.166: 170
64.180: 212
64.183: 220
64.189: 250
64.195: 172, 210
64.200: 212, 293
64.223: 172, 210
64.227: 107
64.266: 161
64.292: 150
64.299: 212
64.303–22: 256
64.306: 129, 154
64.325: 159
64.325–6: 129
64.330: 105
64.341: 243
64.346: 212
64.374: 221
64.382: 105, 154
64.384: 164
64.392: 254

64.399: 105
65–8: 2
65–116: 2
65.2: 157
65.4: 176
65.5: 118, 194
65.5–6: 94
65.6: 186
65.9: 260
65.10: 183
65.11: 260
65.17: 79
65.19: 151
65.19–24: 273, 275
65.24: 150
66.10: 166
66.12: 109
66.13: 229
66.15: 290
66.19: 172
66.24: 91, 211
66.30: 211
66.33: 126
66.39: 40
66.81: 272
66.82: 124
66.87: 164
67.1: 124
67.4: 144
67.25: 163
68.5: 217, 301
68.8: 217
68.16: 124
68.56: 211
68.57: 170
68.68: 11 n. 22
68.70: 231, 263
68.71: 231
68.72: 120
68.83: 217
68.84: 97
68.98: 110
68.106–7: 98
68.110: 119
68.131: 233, 265
68.131–2: 279
68.132: 243, 275
68.136: 7, 241
68.142: 213
68.143: 149
68.144: 108, 109, 234
68.145: 241
68.147–8: 125
68.155: 208
68.159: 182
68.160: 243, 292

Catullus (*cont.*)
  69.8: 160
  70: 10, 216, 222
  70.3–4: 184
  70.4: 249
  72: 10, 216, 222
  72.3: 299
  72.3–4: 160
  73.1: 175
  73.3: 213
  76.1–6: 139
  76.2: 105
  76.6: 213
  76.9: 213
  76.13–14: 209
  76.25: 246, 291
  77.3: 245
  78.4: 160
  82.3: 96
  83.4: 267
  85: 211
  87.3: 216
  88.2: 217
  96.1: 293
  96.3: 268
  99.1: 245
  99.16: 245, 260
  102.1: 293
  102.4: 302
  107.1: 293
  107.6: 125
  109.1: 124
  109.4: 285
  110.1: 299
  116: 267
  116.1: 266, 282
Celsus
  3.15.6: 184
  3.22.8: 291
  7.26.5: 290
Cicero
  Arch. 19: 178, 181
  Att. 8.11.3: 176
  Att. 8.16.1: 250
  Att. 12.27.2: 287
  Att. 12.35.1: 91
  Att. 14.20.2: 286
  Att. 15.7.1: 286
  Att. 16.4.4: 284
  Cael. 9: 164
  Cael. 10: 293
  Cael. 25–30: 293
  Cael. 27: 187
  Cael. 35: 187
  Div. 1.3: 135
  Div. 1.13.11: 170
  Div. 1.39–70: 131
  Div. 2.120–50: 131
  Div. 2.121: 134
  Fam. 10.10.2: 91
  Fam. 13.16.4: 286
  Fam. 30: 280
  Fin. 2.101.7: 281
  Flacc. 21.14: 294
  Flacc. 92: 203
  De Leg. 3.19.2: 281
  Mil. 34.9: 109
  Mur. 54: 29 n. 55
  DND 2.66.1: 266
  DND 2.68: 138
  DND 2.69: 271
  De Or. 3.18: 243
  De Or. 3.45: 48
  Par. Sto. 49: 121
  Phaen. 3.4: 170
  Phaen. 34.288: 118
  Phaen. 34.385: 146
  Phil. 2.44: 288
  Phil. 3.10: 288
  Phil. 9.12: 29 n. 55
  Phil. 14.28.7: 94
  De Sen. 71: 192
  TD 1.118: 259
  TD 3.8.12: 141
  TD 3.51: 297
  TD 5.25: 123
  Verr. 1.21: 294
  Verr. 2.1.49: 122
  Verr. 2.2.51: 254
  Verr. 2.5.30: 107
  Verr. 2.5.31: 265
  Verr. 2.5.80: 107
  Verr. 2.5.86: 265
  Verr. 2.5.137: 265
  Verr. 2.5.150: 181
Claudian
  Carm. 15.213–14: 142
Columella
  DRR 6.1.3: 146
  DRR 6.5.2: 291
  DRR 7.6.3: 244
  DRR 10.256: 187
  DRR 10.430: 211
  DRR 12.15.1: 187
Crinagoras
  AP 6.227: 254
  AP 6.261: 254
  AP 6.345: 254
  CRF 57–8: 77
Curtius Rufus
  6.5.32: 244
  8.9.14: 121

8.9.21: 107
8.9.24: 107
10.2.13.5: 229

Decimus Iunius Silanius
　Fr. 41.6–7: 146
[Demosthenes]
　59: 28 n. 54
Diodorus Siculus
　3.59.5–6: 153
　5.75.3: 153
　6.1.4: 108
Dioscorides
　1.7.1: 146

Ennius
　Andr. 117: 140
　Ann. 1.3 Sk.: 131
　Ann. 1.32: 159
　Ann. 1.107: 178
　Ann. 5: 144
　Ann. 6.188: 123
　Ann. 6.190: 140
　Ann. 6.203: 117
　Ann. 12.63: 253
　Ann. 64: 128
　Ann. 124: 238
　Ann. 225: 178
　Ann. 361k: 147, 148, 150
　Ann. 487: 275
　Ath. 120: 211
　Med. 216: 167
　Tr. 121: 107
　Tr. 136: 152
　Tr. 216: 141
　Var. 103: 140
Euhemerus
　FGrHist 63 F2: 108
Euripides
　Alc. 1: 168
　Alc. 1–14: 168
　Bacc. 987–91: 178
　Hipp. 208–11: 242
　Ion 1150: 140, 161
　Med. 1341–3: 178
　Med. 1342–3: 181
　Med. 1358–60: 177
　Phaeth. 224–5: 143
　FPL 78.1: 141

Festus
　446.32–448.1–4: 19 n. 38
　De Verb. 147M: 78
　De Verb. 305M: 78
Frontinus
　Aq. 99: 219

Fronto
　De Ant. de Eloq. 2.14.2: 266
Fulgentius
　Myth. 2.1.40: 128

Galen
　De Prae. 2–3: 195
Gallus
　Fr. 2: 282
　Fr. 2.6: 271
　Fr. 2.6–7: 11 n. 22, 265
Gellius
　2.26.15: 84
　3.16.10: 256
　13.23.16: 28 n. 54
Germanicus
　Arat. 2: 88
　Arat. 99: 302
　Arat. 149: 204
　Arat. 213: 146
　Arat. 340: 142
　Arat. 510: 146
　Arat. 612: 159
Grattus
　Cyn. 19: 204
　Cyn. 25–33: 242
　Cyn. 373–4: 187
　Cyn 473: 250

Herodotus
　5.101: 127
Hesiod
　Scut. 203: 153
　Scut. 206: 79
　Th. 22–34: 131, 136
　Th. 26–8: 83
　Th. 27–8: 169
　Th. 66–8: 157
　Th. 198: 274
　Th. 211: 142
　Th. 311: 179
　Th. 319: 179
　Th. 319–25: 179
　Th. 570–93: 229
　Th. 758: 142
　Th. 905–6: 129
　Th. 933–7: 226
　WD 59–82: 229
　WD 267: 261
　WD 614: 200
Himerius
　48.10–11: 202
Hippocrates
　Prog. 20: 195
Homer
　Il. 2.8: 133

Il. 2.71: 142
Il. 3: 274
Il. 3.373–82: 273
Il. 3.410–12: 273
Il. 4.141–7: 147
Il. 5.311–14: 273
Il. 6.179–82: 179
Il. 6.429–30: 298
Il. 8.368: 179
Il. 11.416: 239
Il. 14.159–223: 225
Il. 14.233–91: 142
Il. 15.187–93: 193
Il. 16.33–5: 177, 178
Il. 20.39: 145
Il. 22.26–31: 186
Il. 23.69: 161
Il. 23.595–6: 91
Od. 1.1: 100
Od. 4.561–9: 193
Od. 5.306–7: 125
Od. 6.149–85: 147
Od. 6.154–9: 125
Od. 6.163: 147
Od. 7: 124
Od. 8: 124, 225, 226, 237
Od. 8.228: 274
Od. 8.256–366: 259
Od. 10.524–9: 197
Od. 11.14–19: 194
Od. 11.321: 211
Od. 11.405–56: 164
Od. 12.85–110: 180
Od. 12.90–2: 180
Od. 12.132–3: 28
Od. 19.457–8: 249
Od. 19.535–63: 132
Od. 19.562–7: 133
Od. 22.411: 297
Od. 23.177–204: 295
H.H.Ap. 185: 154
H.H.H. 33: 153
H.H.H. 41–54: 153
H.H.H. 471–2: 158
Horace
  AP 75: 1 n. 2
  AP 105: 211
  AP 105–6: 155
  AP 106: 217
  AP 128: 209
  AP 291: 85
  AP 320: 244
  AP 389: 84
  AP 393: 204
  AP 446: 103
  CS 6: 245

CS 14–15: 138
CS 25: 129, 174
CS 63–4: 250
Ep. 1.1.92–3: 292
Ep. 1.2.47: 123
Ep. 1.3.25: 199
Ep. 1.4.4: 297
Ep. 1.5.18: 285
Ep. 1.6.56: 297
Ep. 1.7.12: 202
Ep. 1.10.22: 121
Ep. 1.10.27–8: 248
Ep. 1.10.28: 93
Ep. 1.11.29: 297
Ep. 1.13: 91
Ep. 1.13.1–5: 91
Ep. 1.15.45: 297
Ep. 1.18.75: 92
Ep. 1.19.4: 157
Ep. 1.19.9: 205
Ep. 1.20: 76, 83, 272
Ep. 1.20.2: 85
Ep. 2.1.21–2: 118
Ep. 2.1.132: 245
Ep. 2.2.123: 89
Ep. 2.2.132: 183
Ep. 2.4.25–6: 217
Epod. 2.29–38: 238
Epod. 3: 202
Epod. 4.17–18: 119
Epod. 5.37: 93
Epod. 9.37–8: 107
Epod. 9.38: 107
Epod. 10.9: 298
Epod. 10.18: 126
Epod. 13.15–16: 129
Epod. 14.1–4: 94
Epod. 15.3: 140
Epod. 15.9: 146
Epod. 15.11: 28
Epod. 15.23: 300
Epod. 16.19: 182
Epod. 16.35: 126
Od. 1.1.25–6: 237
Od. 1.1.29: 107, 199, 213
Od. 1.1.29–30: 157
Od. 1.3: 178
Od. 1.3.14: 183
Od. 1.4.1–10: 187
Od. 1.4.9: 152
Od. 1.4.13: 94
Od. 1.4.18: 202
Od. 1.5.2: 105
Od. 1.7.6: 111, 162
Od. 1.7.28–9: 174
Od. 1.8.3–4: 241

Index Locorum

Od. 1.12.48: 147
Od. 1.13.2–3: 241
Od. 1.13.17–18: 260
Od. 1.13.18–20: 264
Od. 1.15.9: 300
Od. 1.16.1: 160
Od. 1.17.13–14: 156
Od. 1.18.3: 206
Od. 1.18.5: 203
Od. 1.18.11: 199
Od. 1.20.9: 201
Od. 1.21: 154
Od. 1.21.2: 145
Od. 1.22.5: 181
Od. 1.23.9–10: 204
Od. 1.25.7: 217
Od. 1.26.6: 128
Od. 1.27.17: 278
Od. 1.27.21–4: 179
Od. 1.28.3–4: 92
Od. 1.28.17: 205
Od. 1.30.5: 292
Od. 1.31: 145
Od. 1.31.3–8: 113
Od. 1.32.4–5: 154
Od. 1.32.13–14: 153
Od. 1.33: 44, 57, 294, 295
Od. 1.33.2: 172
Od. 1.33.10–12: 259
Od. 1.34.10: 120
Od. 1.35: 123
Od. 1.35.22: 202
Od. 1.36.15–16: 221
Od. 1.36.18–19: 264
Od. 1.38: 219
Od. 1.38.1: 200
Od. 2.5.10: 192
Od. 2.5.18–20: 147
Od. 2.6.3: 181
Od. 2.6.6: 117
Od. 2.7.7–8: 108, 221
Od. 2.7.21–5: 221
Od. 2.7.25–6: 202
Od. 2.8.18: 256
Od. 2.9.11: 91
Od. 2.9.13: 183
Od. 2.9.17–18: 173
Od. 2.11.10: 147
Od. 2.11.14–17: 221
Od. 2.11.16: 108
Od. 2.11.16–17: 146
Od. 2.11.18: 219
Od. 2.11.18–20: 201
Od. 2.12.20: 254
Od. 2.12.21–8: 124
Od. 2.15.1: 115

Od. 2.16.9–12: 123
Od. 2.16.11–12: 121
Od. 2.16.35–7: 122
Od. 2.17.14–5: 264
Od. 2.18.1–2: 121
Od. 2.18.1–5: 120
Od. 2.18.1–11: 113
Od. 2.19: 197
Od. 2.19.1–2: 157
Od. 2.19.29–33: 179
Od. 2.20.1: 280
Od. 3.1.41: 120
Od. 3.2.26–7: 189
Od. 3.3.13–14: 204
Od. 3.3.31: 124
Od. 3.4.15–16: 119
Od. 3.4.32: 108
Od. 3.4.61: 88
Od. 3.4.74–5: 130
Od. 3.6.40: 284
Od. 3.6.41–2: 102
Od. 3.8: 76
Od. 3.8.1–3: 77
Od. 3.9: 7, 92
Od. 3.9.3–4: 221
Od. 3.9.10: 155
Od. 3.9.24: 116
Od. 3.10.5–6: 121
Od. 3.10.11–12: 178
Od. 3.11.3: 153
Od. 3.11.3–5: 153
Od. 3.11.17–18: 180
Od. 3.11.37: 149
Od. 3.11.51: 110
Od. 3.12.3: 282
Od. 3.14.17: 200
Od. 3.14.21: 28
Od. 3.16.18–19: 115
Od. 3.16.33–8: 113
Od. 3.17.14–16: 257
Od. 3.19.10: 200
Od. 3.19.20: 153
Od. 3.20.10: 239
Od. 3.21.14–20: 203
Od. 3.21.15–16: 205
Od. 3.21.18: 203
Od. 3.23.20: 137
Od. 3.24.22: 162
Od. 3.25: 157, 197
Od. 3.25.14: 218
Od. 3.25.19: 211
Od. 3.27.4: 110
Od. 3.27.12: 142
Od. 3.27.13: 208
Od. 3.27.13–14: 196
Od. 3.27.53–4: 248

Horace (cont.)
  Od. 3.29.2: 201
  Od. 3.29.60: 128
  Od. 3.30.1–9: 270
  Od. 3.30.6–7: 105
  Od. 3.30.6–10: 280
  Od. 3.30.16: 221
  Od. 4.1.37: 162
  Od. 4.3.17–18: 153
  Od. 4.4.14: 204
  Od. 4.5.21: 164
  Od. 4.5.39: 205
  Od. 4.6.37: 171
  Od. 4.7.27–8: 118
  Od. 4.8.11–12: 82
  Od. 4.9.8: 275
  Od. 4.9.27: 217
  Od. 4.11: 254
  Od. 4.11.15–17: 255
  Od. 4.11.34–5: 170
  Od. 4.15.25: 121
  Od. 4.15.26: 206
  Ser. 1.1.18: 210
  Ser. 1.1.79: 291
  Ser. 1.2.47: 8
  Ser. 1.2.63: 278, 288
  Ser. 1.2.80–2: 30, 288
  Ser. 1.3.45: 287
  Ser. 1.3.139–40: 202
  Ser. 1.4.66: 287
  Ser. 1.5.51–4: 80
  Ser. 1.10.18–19: 213
  Ser. 1.10.31–5: 131
  Ser. 1.10.33: 140
  Ser. 1.10.85–6: 29 n. 55
  Ser. 2.1.5: 283
  Ser. 2.2.10: 115
  Ser. 2.2.125: 217
  Ser. 2.3.47: 292
  Ser. 2.3.99: 253
  Ser. 2.3.218: 283
  Ser. 2.5.99: 123
  Ser. 2.5.109–10: 187
  Ser. 7.13–14: 232
Hyginus
  Fab. 57.3: 179
  Fab. 151.1: 179
  Fab. 191: 127
  Fab. 203: 144

Ilias Latina
  3: 130
  126: 159
  158: 152
  396: 181
  654: 238
  736: 118
  867: 142
  891: 179
Isidore
  Nat. 4.2: 78
  Or. 6.11.4: 84
  Or. 8.11.57: 77
  Or. 16.2.3: 137

Juvenal
  2.61: 302
  2.67: 122
  2.98: 215
  3.318: 110
  4.34: 80
  4.66–7: 281
  6.62: 127
  7.23: 84
  7.198: 197
  8.16: 85
  8.97: 302
  9.50: 77
  9.95: 85
  10.343–4: 292
  11.13: 170
  12.64–6: 129
  12.98: 290
  13.46: 254
  13.50: 205
  13.160: 292
  14.307: 120
  15.101: 248
  15.131: 205

Laberius
  Salin. 99: 106
Licinius
  3.1–2 Ribb.: 28 n. 54
Livius Andronicus
  Od. 1.1: 275
  Od. 21.1: 171
Livy
  1.9–11: 77
  2.42.10: 141
  4.12.7: 282
  5.22.4: 262
  5.45.4: 94
  6.12.8: 158
  8.38.15: 207
  9.1.11: 190
  9.9.7: 259
  10.36.3: 229
  21.44.7: 229
  23.26.8: 91
  27.37.7: 19 n. 38
  28.41.9: 91
  28.42.15: 263
  39: 269

Index Locorum

39.9.5: 288
39.15.4: 272
40.45.8: 301
40.51.7: 248
41.16.3: 185
Lucan
  1.222: 196
  1.367: 181
  2.39: 97
  2.136: 117
  2.153: 241
  2.544: 197
  3.239: 107
  4.161: 238
  4.623: 250
  5.125: 88
  5.140: 190
  5.221: 94
  5.491: 208
  5.497: 125
  6.42: 240
  6.487: 204
  6.648: 120
  6.768: 94
  6.806: 190
  7.22: 137
  7.442: 109
  7.676: 129
  8.79: 254
  8.232: 205
  8.854: 109
  9.36: 120
  9.87: 188
  9.115: 176
  9.140: 135
  9.201: 164
  9.234: 117
  9.762–3: 111
  10.72: 173
  10.113: 121
  10.434: 142
  10.525: 207
Lucilius
  11.419: 162
  730 M: 11 n. 22
Lucretius
  1.8: 178
  1.10–27: 78
  1.23: 183
  1.33–8: 227
  1.83: 213
  1.590: 177
  1.926: 79
  1.926–7: 297
  2.23–33: 121
  2.192: 267
  2.361: 84
  2.365: 123
  2.417: 108
  2.434: 299
  2.600: 157
  2.772: 178
  3.52–3: 197
  3.486: 158
  3.634: 177
  3.681: 117
  3.939: 128
  3.973: 278
  3.990: 97
  3.999: 167
  4.1: 79
  4.255: 207
  4.573: 298
  4.577: 170
  4.848: 250
  4.884: 278
  4.908: 285
  4.1201: 90
  4.1205: 90
  4.1216: 90
  5.6.5: 99
  5.264: 107
  5.301: 267
  5.309: 299
  5.346–7: 111
  5.699: 217
  5.854: 90
  5.890–924: 178
  5.892: 180
  5.901: 204
  5.905–6: 179
  5.963: 90
  5.986–7: 300
  5.1215: 91
  6.51: 137
  6.70: 299
  6.224: 267
  6.396: 298
  6.440: 178
  6.506–7: 107
  6.623–4: 107
  6.627–8: 107
  6.766: 241
  6.767: 207
  6.795: 240
  6.1134: 161

Macrobius
  Sat. 1.12.7: 77
  Sat. 1.12.3–6: 78
  Sat. 2.5: 50
  Sat. 6.4.13: 77, 286
Maecenas
  Fr. 3.1–2: 93

Manilius

- 1.56: 123
- 1.77: 208
- 1.166: 178
- 1.286: 119
- 1.323: 212
- 1.358: 268
- 2.46–7: 298
- 2.49: 157
- 2.87: 135
- 2.584–5: 300
- 3.214: 279
- 3.548: 209
- 4.12: 123
- 4.203: 118
- 4.263: 152
- 4.527: 155
- 4.577: 216
- 5.204: 240
- 5.263a: 212
- 5.264: 108
- 5.451: 279
- 5.568: 125
- 5.725: 298
- 5.1064: 239

Martial

- 1.11.3: 219
- 1.15.1: 125
- 1.15.4: 292
- 1.25.2: 89
- 1.53.9: 121
- 1.55.5: 120
- 1.64.4: 160
- 1.66: 83
- 1.66.10: 85
- 1.66.11: 84, 89
- 1.70.15: 157
- 1.76.1: 125
- 1.88.1: 193
- 1.88.7: 200
- 1.117.16: 85, 89
- 2.27.4: 302
- 2.87.1: 160
- 3.2: 83
- 3.2.11: 85
- 3.20: 80
- 3.20.8: 19 n. 38
- 3.45.6: 302
- 3.47.3: 128
- 3.57.2: 197
- 3.65.5–6: 109
- 3.80.2: 302
- 3.87.1: 302
- 4.10.1–2: 85
- 4.18.5: 197
- 4.25.7: 117
- 4.33.4: 106
- 4.57.1–3: 185
- 4.57.7: 187
- 4.57.8: 187
- 4.61.2: 19 n. 38
- 4.78.3: 79
- 4.82.6: 219
- 4.88.1: 92
- 4.141–2: 253
- 5.2.7: 150
- 5.20.2: 160
- 5.37.4: 122
- 5.52.6: 302
- 5.65.9: 119
- 5.84: 77
- 6.27.5: 106
- 6.42.7: 187
- 6.42.11: 120
- 6.43: 185
- 6.43.1–2: 196
- 6.43.2: 218
- 6.47.1: 218
- 6.53.3: 111
- 6.58.7–8: 129
- 6.63: 82
- 7.17.9: 92
- 7.30.4: 234
- 7.54.2: 190
- 7.54.5: 262
- 7.68.1: 275
- 7.80.5: 92
- 7.99.7: 213
- 8.3: 80
- 8.3.17: 206
- 8.7.2: 260
- 8.28.14: 122
- 8.33.15: 79
- 8.39.1: 220
- 8.39.4: 197
- 8.46.2: 245
- 8.64: 255
- 8.72.1–2: 89
- 8.72.2: 85
- 8.73.8: 213
- 8.77.3: 109
- 9.2.9: 122
- 9.12.5: 122
- 9.18.6: 219
- 9.29.2: 94
- 9.42.3: 157
- 9.52: 255
- 9.53.1–2: 92
- 9.54.11: 92
- 9.75.6–9: 120
- 9.75.7: 120
- 9.75.8: 120

9.93.1: 201, 219, 221
10.13.9: 90
10.17.5: 122
10.20: 76, 80
10.24: 255
10.35: 26, 34
10.38: 26, 34
10.58.13: 19 n. 39
10.98.1: 219, 221
10.101.4: 302
10.103.2: 249
11.1: 83
11.1.1–2: 89
11.11.3: 219
11.26.1: 125
11.36.5: 219
11.39.16: 89
11.107.1: 87
12.11: 76, 80
12.11.1: 91
12.17.9: 297
12.18.23: 297
12.21.10: 298
12.32.6: 94
12.60: 255
12.60.8: 221
13.71.2: 300
14.100.1: 213
14.152.1: 213
14.170.2: 201, 221
Spect. 12.6: 284
Martianus Capella
  2.149: 138
Meleager
  AP 4.1.1: 79
Menander Rhetor
  334.25–336.4: 197
Moschus
  Eur. 1.27: 183
  Eur. 2–3: 140

Naevius
  Fr. 18.1: 194
Nonnus
  7.275: 271
  16.82–5: 242
  16.91–3: 241
  48.107: 271

ORF
  Fr. 176: 32 n. 63
Ovid
  Am. 1.*Epig*.: 41
  Am. 1.*Epig*.2: 87
  Am. 1.1: 75
  Am. 1.1.1: 77, 144, 227

Am. 1.1.1–2: 227
Am. 1.1.4: 245
Am. 1.1.5: 167
Am. 1.1.6: 159, 252
Am. 1.1.12: 225
Am. 1.1.13: 256
Am. 1.1.20: 87
Am. 1.1.24: 87, 159
Am. 1.2: 271
Am. 1.2.1–4: 142
Am. 1.2.3: 217
Am. 1.2.6: 203
Am. 1.2.46: 292
Am. 1.2.47–8: 204
Am. 1.3.2: 251
Am. 1.3.6: 135
Am. 1.3.9: 115
Am. 1.3.11: 156
Am. 1.3.13: 135
Am. 1.3.14: 148
Am. 1.3.16: 135
Am. 1.3.17–18: 116, 217
Am. 1.3.21: 174
Am. 1.4.11–12: 184
Am. 1.4.12: 183
Am. 1.4.22: 148
Am. 1.4.23: 267
Am. 1.4.25: 243
Am. 1.4.43: 241
Am. 1.4.52: 221
Am. 1.4.64: 241
Am. 1.5: 14, 140, 148, 217, 270
Am. 1.5.10: 230
Am. 1.6.7–8: 203
Am. 1.6.9: 134, 138
Am. 1.6.34: 167
Am. 1.6.45: 299
Am. 1.6.52: 209
Am. 1.6.54: 247
Am. 1.6.58: 256
Am. 1.7: 87
Am. 1.7.3–4: 105
Am. 1.7.6: 167
Am. 1.7.7–12: 254
Am. 1.7.15: 212
Am. 1.7.16: 212
Am. 1.7.18: 156
Am. 1.7.19: 266
Am. 1.7.40: 191
Am. 1.7.50: 242
Am. 1.7.56: 183
Am. 1.7.63: 173
Am. 1.8: 8
Am. 1.8.19: 189
Am. 1.8.23: 243
Am. 1.8.26: 89

Ovid (*cont.*)
Am. 1.8.29–30: 77
Am. 1.8.41–2: 77
Am. 1.8.43: 92, 156, 286
Am. 1.8.50: 249
Am. 1.8.53: 116
Am. 1.8.57: 159, 274
Am. 1.8.59: 159
Am. 1.8.59–60: 145, 152
Am. 1.8.60: 154
Am. 1.8.69: 82
Am. 1.8.85–6: 216
Am. 1.8.91: 104
Am. 1.8.94: 266
Am. 1.8.95: 127, 287
Am. 1.8.97: 229
Am. 1.8.107–8: 118
Am. 1.8.112: 194
Am. 1.8.113: 116
Am. 1.9: 12
Am. 1.9.4: 116
Am. 1.9.6: 160
Am. 1.9.7: 217
Am. 1.9.27: 180
Am. 1.9.27–8: 265
Am. 1.9.33: 239
Am. 1.9.38: 103
Am. 1.9.39: 265
Am. 1.9.43: 130
Am. 1.10.15: 118, 271
Am. 1.10.17–18: 82
Am. 1.10.32: 82, 163
Am. 1.10.33: 205
Am. 1.10.47: 82
Am. 1.10.48: 215
Am. 1.10.55–6: 192
Am. 1.10.59: 162
Am. 1.10.59–64: 82
Am. 1.10.62: 273
Am. 1.10.63: 82
Am. 1.10.64: 175
Am. 1.11: 88
Am. 1.11.7: 278
Am. 1.11.9: 96, 173
Am. 1.11–12: 90
Am. 1.11.15: 278
Am. 1.11.21: 83
Am. 1.11.23–4: 277
Am. 1.12: 277
Am. 1.12.1: 278
Am. 1.12.4: 253
Am. 1.12.7: 278
Am. 1.12.21: 190
Am. 1.13: 116, 274
Am. 1.13.6: 252
Am. 1.13.18: 241
Am. 1.13.25: 100
Am. 1.13.40: 141
Am. 1.14.6: 107
Am. 1.14.36: 287
Am. 1.14.50: 273
Am. 1.15: 270
Am. 1.15.2: 87
Am. 1.15.4: 105
Am. 1.15.7: 273
Am. 1.15.10: 249
Am. 1.15.17: 182
Am. 1.15.34: 127
Am. 1.15.35: 122
Am. 1.15.36: 88
Am. 1.15.38: 142, 220
Am. 1.15.42: 196, 280
Am. 2.1.1: 229
Am. 2.1.2: 171
Am. 2.1.3: 206
Am. 2.1.5: 278
Am. 2.1.5–8: 277
Am. 2.1.17: 299
Am. 2.1.21: 114, 173
Am. 2.1.21–35: 82
Am. 2.1.23: 147
Am. 2.1.34: 82, 159
Am. 2.1.38: 148
Am. 2.2: 265
Am. 2.2.9: 226
Am. 2.2.10: 134
Am. 2.2.14: 145, 156
Am. 2.2.18: 294
Am. 2.2.21: 143, 195
Am. 2.2.35: 190
Am. 2.2.41–60: 154
Am. 2.2.44: 300
Am. 2.2.45: 262
Am. 2.2.63–5: 188
Am. 2.2.66: 173
Am. 2.3.2: 90, 163, 244
Am. 2.315: 281
Am. 2.4.8: 249
Am. 2.4.10: 251
Am. 2.4.15: 209
Am. 2.4.17: 153
Am. 2.4.18: 157
Am. 2.4.21: 159
Am. 2.4.41: 146
Am. 2.5: 272, 301
Am. 2.5.3–4: 302
Am. 2.5.4: 125
Am. 2.5.7: 175
Am. 2.5.26: 160
Am. 2.5.29: 163
Am. 2.5.34: 148
Am. 2.5.34–42: 149

Index Locorum 337

Am. 2.5.35-6: 148
Am. 2.5.35-41: 150, 151
Am. 2.5.37-8: 148
Am. 2.5.43: 230
Am. 2.5.44: 232
Am. 2.5.46: 149
Am. 2.6.4: 149, 242
Am. 2.6.12: 182
Am. 2.6.25: 123
Am. 2.6.44: 183, 208
Am. 2.6.55: 262
Am. 2.6.56: 160
Am. 2.7.8: 294
Am. 2.7.19-20: 278
Am. 2.7.27-8: 114
Am. 2.8.3: 124
Am. 2.8.5: 116
Am. 2.8.18: 206
Am. 2.8.19-20: 184
Am. 2.8.20: 183
Am. 2.8.27: 280
Am. 2.9.1-6: 167
Am. 2.9.2: 175
Am. 2.9.16: 253
Am. 2.9.19: 250
Am. 2.9.24: 118
Am. 2.9.34: 148
Am. 2.9.44: 163
Am. 2.9.45: 190
Am. 2.9.50: 135, 163
Am. 2.9.53: 256
Am. 2.10.19: 167
Am. 2.10.29: 90
Am. 2.10.35: 143
Am. 2.10.35-8: 117
Am. 2.10.37: 110
Am. 2.11.7: 220
Am. 2.11.18: 180
Am. 2.11.20: 181
Am. 2.11.37: 110
Am. 2.11.46: 126
Am. 2.11.49: 107
Am. 2.11.52: 183
Am. 2.11.55: 152
Am. 2.12: 270
Am. 2.12.1: 144
Am. 2.12.2: 246
Am. 2.12.3: 98
Am. 2.12.13: 202
Am. 2.12.16: 247
Am. 2.12.25-6: 169
Am. 2.13-14: 95, 246
Am. 2.13.15: 173, 253
Am. 2.13.21: 253
Am. 2.13.24: 250
Am. 2.14.7: 194

Am. 2.14.13: 192
Am. 2.14.23-4: 192
Am. 2.14.24: 193
Am. 2.14.31: 111
Am. 2.14.35: 204
Am. 2.15.11: 117
Am. 2.15.14: 117
Am. 2.15.27: 92
Am. 2.16.22: 183
Am. 2.16.42-6: 215
Am. 2.16.43: 93
Am. 2.16.47: 290, 292
Am. 2.17.10: 229
Am. 2.17.11: 256
Am. 2.17.18: 243
Am. 2.17.23: 243
Am. 2.17.27: 154
Am. 2.18.18: 159
Am. 2.18.22: 212
Am. 2.18.29: 252
Am. 2.18.35: 159
Am. 2.19.1-2: 175
Am. 2.19.4: 96
Am. 2.19.9-18: 98
Am. 2.19.12: 191
Am. 2.19.15: 290
Am. 2.19.19: 96
Am. 2.19.22: 217
Am. 2.19.25: 100
Am. 2.19.29: 262
Am. 2.19.55: 220
Am. 2.19.58: 163
Am. 3.1: 198
Am. 3.1.12: 205, 266
Am. 3.1.16: 175
Am. 3.1.19: 159
Am. 3.1.23: 157
Am. 3.1.32: 125
Am. 3.1.34: 146
Am. 3.1.46: 114
Am. 3.1.49: 265
Am. 3.1.62: 126
Am. 3.1.67: 159
Am. 3.2.3: 217
Am. 3.2.27: 241
Am. 3.2.29: 241
Am. 3.2.31: 241
Am. 3.2.32: 300
Am. 3.2.46: 247
Am. 3.2.49: 77
Am. 3.2.61: 93
Am. 3.2.71: 210
Am. 3.2.76: 246
Am. 3.3.1: 93, 221
Am. 3.3.5-6: 148
Am. 3.3.9-14: 215

338 Index Locorum

Ovid (*cont.*)
  Am. 3.3.11: 93, 216
  Am. 3.3.13: 93
  Am. 3.3.44: 159, 210
  Am. 3.3.45: 93
  Am. 3.4: 265, 301
  Am. 3.4.3: 156
  Am. 3.4.11: 134
  Am. 3.4.32: 296
  Am. 3.4.36: 156
  Am. 3.4.41: 156
  Am. 3.4.43: 206, 226
  Am. 3.4.43–8: 175
  Am. 3.5: 132
  Am. 3.5.11: 117
  Am. 3.5.22: 154, 300
  Am. 3.5.31: 162
  Am. 3.5.33: 162
  Am. 3.5.45: 175
  Am. 3.6: 274
  Am. 3.6.17: 138, 159
  Am. 3.6.48: 242
  Am. 3.6.50: 298
  Am. 3.6.51: 249
  Am. 3.6.58: 190
  Am. 3.6.80: 249
  Am. 3.6.83: 258
  Am. 3.6.88: 163
  Am. 3.7: 14
  Am. 3.7.1: 89
  Am. 3.7.27: 250
  Am. 3.7.46: 293
  Am. 3.7.61: 126, 302
  Am. 3.7.63: 163, 267
  Am. 3.8: 7
  Am. 3.8.1–8: 274
  Am. 3.8.30: 82
  Am. 3.8.31: 182, 206
  Am. 3.8.50: 193
  Am. 3.9: 22, 35, 123, 191
  Am. 3.9.5: 159, 273
  Am. 3.9.6: 104
  Am. 3.9.11: 110
  Am. 3.9.17: 155, 159
  Am. 3.9.26: 159
  Am. 3.9.28: 104
  Am. 3.9.29: 159
  Am. 3.9.31: 239, 301
  Am. 3.9.32: 294
  Am. 3.9.41: 159
  Am. 3.9.46: 110
  Am. 3.9.59: 143
  Am. 3.9.49–54: 95
  Am. 3.9.49–56: 101
  Am. 3.9.51: 104
  Am. 3.9.55: 239
  Am. 3.9.60: 194
  Am. 3.9.62: 213
  Am. 3.10: 76
  Am. 3.10.3: 143
  Am. 3.10.40: 234
  Am. 3.10.46: 262
  Am. 3.11.1: 98
  Am. 3.11.7: 193
  Am. 3.11.17: 98
  Am. 3.11.21: 220
  Am. 3.11.24: 294
  Am. 3.11.29: 143
  Am. 3.11.31: 134
  Am. 3.11.39: 97
  Am. 3.11.43: 273
  Am. 3.11.48: 257
  Am. 3.12: 301
  Am. 3.12.7: 297
  Am. 3.12.7–10: 162
  Am. 3.12.21: 180
  Am. 3.12.41: 159
  Am. 3.13: 9 n. 19, 76, 262
  Am. 3.13.3: 156, 266
  Am. 3.13.13: 169
  Am. 3.13.23: 156
  Am. 3.13.26: 152
  Am. 3.13.29: 117
  Am. 3.13.30: 229
  Am. 3.13.60: 156
  Am. 3.14: 269, 292, 301
  Am. 3.14.1: 278
  Am. 3.14.1–2: 175
  Am. 3.14.6: 273
  Am. 3.14.7: 240, 240
  Am. 3.14.17–18: 272
  Am. 3.14.24: 265
  Am. 3.14.36: 273
  Am. 3.14.50: 215
  Am. 3.15.1: 159, 185
  Am. 3.15.3: 229
  Am. 3.15.7–8: 163
  Am. 3.15.12: 115
  Am. 3.15.17: 157
  Ars 1.1–2: 19
  Ars 1.7–30: 144
  Ars 1.12: 204
  Ars 1.14: 106, 139
  Ars 1.18: 167
  Ars 1.23–30: 168
  Ars 1.29: 87
  Ars 1.30: 174
  Ars 1.31–4: 78
  Ars 1.33: 296
  Ars 1.42: 295
  Ars 1.43: 299
  Ars 1.46: 238

Index Locorum 339

Ars 1.47: 242
Ars 1.53: 235
Ars 1.55–50: 296
Ars 1.61: 193
Ars 1.63: 268
Ars 1.99: 225
Ars 1.101–32: 77
Ars 1.110: 175
Ars 1.127: 202
Ars 1.137: 155
Ars 1.146: 253
Ars 1.156: 241
Ars 1.174: 296
Ars 1.229: 220
Ars 1.231–2: 200
Ars 1.232: 148
Ars 1.237: 203, 291
Ars 1.237–44: 203
Ars 1.240: 194
Ars 1.251: 122
Ars 1.255–6: 187
Ars 1.266: 153
Ars 1.270: 243
Ars 1.276: 260, 294
Ars 1.306: 287
Ars 1.310: 165
Ars 1.322: 278
Ars 1.333: 180
Ars 1.359: 117
Ars 1.360: 119
Ars 1.363: 117
Ars 1.372: 190
Ars 1.387: 214
Ars 1.392: 244
Ars 1.398: 299
Ars 1.405: 255
Ars 1.405–9: 78
Ars 1.417: 299
Ars 1.429: 266
Ars 1.437–86: 90
Ars 1.438: 114
Ars 1.445: 94
Ars 1.457–8: 151
Ars 1.459: 214
Ars 1.504: 204, 284
Ars 1.506: 85
Ars 1.509: 213
Ars 1.511: 89
Ars 1.525: 157
Ars 1.526: 258
Ars 1.532: 149
Ars 1.550: 204
Ars 1.556: 212
Ars 1.559: 204
Ars 1.565: 200
Ars 1.581–2: 202

Ars 1.591: 190
Ars 1.602: 267
Ars 1.612: 135
Ars 1.631–4: 184, 216
Ars 1.633: 216
Ars 1.633–4: 216
Ars 1.635: 93
Ars 1.710: 114
Ars 1.718: 100
Ars 1.720: 241
Ars 1.732: 291
Ars 1.733: 248
Ars 1.735–6: 142
Ars 1.739: 216
Ars 1.741–2: 297
Ars 1.752: 296
Ars 2.13–14: 184
Ars 2.14: 153
Ars 2.58: 296
Ars 2.66: 167
Ars 2.107: 183, 207
Ars 2.117: 191
Ars 2.118: 194
Ars 2.175: 89, 299
Ars 2.183: 204
Ars 2.239: 159, 169
Ars 2.239–41: 168
Ars 2.256: 92
Ars 2.261–2: 92
Ars 2.272: 165
Ars 2.288: 299
Ars 2.297: 161
Ars 2.297–8: 230, 231
Ars 2.303: 229
Ars 2.315–36: 246
Ars 2.319–36: 184
Ars 2.321: 290
Ars 2.322: 234
Ars 3.323: 291
Ars 2.325: 100
Ars 3.325–6: 251
Ars 3.327: 250
Ars 2.328: 136
Ars 2.336: 250
Ars 2.340: 98
Ars 2.346: 100
Ars 2.358: 241
Ars 2.385: 264
Ars 2.403: 239
Ars 2.418: 106
Ars 2.443: 287
Ars 2.447–8: 125
Ars 2.452: 149
Ars 2.453: 205
Ars 2.459: 244
Ars 2.492: 253

Ovid (*cont.*)
  Ars 2.493–510: 132
  Ars 2.494: 153, 154
  Ars 2.515: 251
  Ars 2.530: 100
  Ars 2.536: 91
  Ars 2.539: 98
  Ars 2.557: 265
  Ars 2.592: 293
  Ars 2.601: 189
  Ars 2.606: 154, 300
  Ars 2.632: 243
  Ars 2.640: 199
  Ars 2.652: 98
  Ars 2.660: 248
  Ars 2.670: 116, 191
  Ars 2.679: 295
  Ars 2.686: 258
  Ars 2.692: 143
  Ars 2.723: 183
  Ars 2.734: 146, 221
  Ars 3: 229
  Ars 3.35–6: 212
  Ars 3.40: 111
  Ars 3.43–4: 274
  Ars 3.51: 89
  Ars 3.56: 91
  Ars 3.59–100: 116
  Ars 3.73: 194
  Ars 3.74: 152
  Ars 3.75–6: 85
  Ars 3.79–80: 227
  Ars 3.88: 160
  Ars 3.101: 89
  Ars 3.124: 122
  Ars 3.127: 89
  Ars 3.129–30: 234
  Ars 3.133: 230
  Ars 3.133–68: 230
  Ars 3.135: 230
  Ars 3.135–58: 230
  Ars 3.147: 153
  Ars 3.158: 212
  Ars 3.169–92: 231
  Ars 3.170: 122
  Ars 3.172: 240
  Ars 3.173: 117
  Ars 3.179: 161
  Ars 3.203: 100
  Ars 3.218: 139
  Ars 3.236: 230
  Ars 3.267: 248
  Ars 3.302: 256
  Ars 3.322: 180
  Ars 3.344: 249
  Ars 3.345: 19
  Ars 3.347: 175
  Ars 3.347–8: 156
  Ars 3.374: 175
  Ars 3.377: 216
  Ars 3.386: 196, 249
  Ars 3.405: 155, 193
  Ars 3.433: 89
  Ars 3.455: 214
  Ars 3.456–8: 215
  Ars 3.457: 212
  Ars 3.460: 212
  Ars 3.472: 142, 220
  Ars 3.477–8: 94
  Ars 3.484: 165
  Ars 3.486: 300
  Ars 3.494: 165
  Ars 3.509: 256
  Ars 3.516: 239
  Ars 3.522: 243
  Ars 3.523–4: 292
  Ars 3.524: 243
  Ars 3.526: 139
  Ars 3.533–4: 81
  Ars 3.534: 182
  Ars 3.539–50: 156
  Ars 3.548: 79, 157
  Ars 3.568: 149
  Ars 3.571: 258
  Ars 3.600: 142, 220
  Ars 3.609: 287
  Ars 3.611–66: 265
  Ars 3.613: 164
  Ars 3.645: 107
  Ars 3.664: 280
  Ars 3.675: 258
  Ars 3.681: 89
  Ars 3.723: 102
  Ars 3.753: 215
  Ars 3.765: 221
  Ars 3.775: 241
  Ars 3.784: 103
  Ars 3.785: 138, 194
  Ars 3.790: 174
  Ars 3.797–8: 244
  Ars 3.805: 244
  EP 1.1.1–4: 130
  EP 1.1.51–8: 188
  EP 1.1.57: 259
  EP 1.2.15: 111
  EP 1.2.54: 141
  EP 1.2.71: 261
  EP 1.2.75–8: 32 n. 66
  EP 1.3.32: 205
  EP 1.3.36: 161
  EP 1.3.38: 181
  EP 1.4.2: 194

Index Locorum 341

EP 1.4.28: 250
EP 1.4.29: 142
EP 1.4.35: 178
EP 1.4.44: 140, 207
EP 1.5: 32
EP 1.5.58: 236
EP 1.5.85: 117
EP 1.6.19: 293
EP 1.6.24: 134
EP 1.7: 32, 32 n. 66
EP 1.7.94: 257
EP 1.8.12: 250
EP 1.8.15: 225
EP 1.8.31: 202
EP 1.8.32: 128
EP 1.8.35: 115
EP 1.8.63: 91
EP 1.9: 32
EP 1.9.31: 100
EP 1.9.51–4: 108
EP 1.10.28: 249
EP 1.13: 88
EP 1.17.57: 216
EP 2.1.32: 254, 262
EP 2.2: 32, 32 n. 66
EP 2.2.9–16: 188
EP 2.2.13: 189
EP 2.2.30: 196
EP 2.3: 32
EP 2.3.51: 123
EP 2.3.68: 140
EP 2.4.23–4: 94
EP 2.4.30: 208
EP 2.5.63: 283
EP 2.6.8: 250
EP 2.6.11: 114
EP 2.7.14: 134
EP 2.7.15: 123
EP 2.7.20: 123
EP 2.7.23: 159
EP 2.7.41: 123
EP 2.7.56: 250
EP 2.7.69: 182
EP 2.8.51: 128
EP 2.8.76: 207
EP 2.9.25: 126, 302
EP 2.9.29: 161
EP 2.9.67–72: 188
EP 2.10.17: 19 n. 39
EP 3.1.20: 176
EP 3.1.26: 122, 189
EP 3.1.39: 91
EP 3.1.56: 115
EP 3.1.127: 142
EP 3.1.131: 174
EP 3.1.156: 139

EP 3.1.161–2: 262
EP 3.2: 32
EP 3.2.18: 126, 190
EP 3.2.32: 104
EP 3.2.49: 119
EP 3.3: 130, 141, 144, 149
EP 3.3.5: 140
EP 3.3.7: 298
EP 3.3.7–8: 141
EP 3.3.9: 142
EP 3.3.12: 175
EP 3.3.14: 153
EP 3.3.16: 146
EP 3.3.17–18: 147
EP 3.3.21: 259
EP 3.3.53: 165
EP 3.3.70: 176
EP 3.3.93: 175
EP 3.3.106: 122
EP 3.4.45–6: 170
EP 3.4.67–76: 19 n. 39
EP 3.5: 32
EP 3.6.21: 160
EP 3.6.36: 253
EP 3.6.43: 134, 138
EP 3.6.44: 196
EP 3.6.45: 192
EP 3.9.48: 284
EP 4.1.17: 94
EP 4.3.29: 208, 299
EP 4.3.113: 158
EP 4.6.3: 197
EP 4.6.11: 111
EP 4.6.22: 125
EP 4.7.12: 111
EP 4.8.22: 273
EP 4.8.23: 299
EP 4.8.35: 92
EP 4.8.75: 154
EP 4.8.81: 19 n. 39
EP 4.9.34: 125
EP 4.9.86: 115
EP 4.9.127–8: 261
EP 4.10.1–2: 194
EP 4.10.14: 243
EP 4.10.43: 183
EP 4.10.69–74: 21 n. 44
EP 4.11.22: 174
EP 4.12.24: 241
EP 4.12.31: 173
EP 4.13.1: 125
EP 4.13.33: 275
EP 4.13.38: 253
EP 4.13.48: 253
EP 4.16.3: 273
EP 4.16.48: 134

Ovid (*cont.*)
 EP 5.16: 103
 Fas. 1.115: 159
 Fas. 1.128: 137
 Fas. 1.137: 115
 Fas. 1.138: 137
 Fas. 1.159: 115
 Fas. 1.197: 195
 Fas. 1.247: 117
 Fas. 1.268: 153
 Fas. 1.292: 249
 Fas. 1.329: 145
 Fas. 1.367: 259
 Fas. 1.417: 258
 Fas. 1.444: 155
 Fas. 1.468: 202, 253
 Fas. 1.482: 191
 Fas. 1.502: 298
 Fas. 1.556: 250
 Fas. 1.571–2: 154
 Fas. 1.576: 125
 Fas. 1.622: 213
 Fas. 1.629: 253
 Fas. 1.657: 125
 Fas. 1.711: 143
 Fas. 2.15: 282
 Fas. 2.34: 117
 Fas. 2.38: 213
 Fas. 2.63: 249
 Fas. 2.86: 253
 Fas. 2.107: 233
 Fas. 2.127: 249
 Fas. 2.232: 243
 Fas. 2.242: 253
 Fas. 2.269: 80
 Fas. 2.300: 183
 Fas. 2.339: 204
 Fas. 2.340: 139
 Fas. 2.404: 275
 Fas. 2.431: 114
 Fas. 2.449–50: 138
 Fas. 2.462: 117
 Fas. 2.507: 254
 Fas. 2.519: 234
 Fas. 2.523: 103
 Fas. 2.534: 92
 Fas. 2.565: 102
 Fas. 2.571: 106
 Fas. 2.592: 243
 Fas. 2.618–19: 283
 Fas. 2.658: 249
 Fas. 2.667–8: 254
 Fas. 2.706: 234
 Fas. 2.716: 252
 Fas. 2.752: 278
 Fas. 2.760: 215
 Fas. 2.794: 164
 Fas. 2.798: 91
 Fas. 2.813: 140
 Fas. 2.850: 190
 Fas. 3: 222, 225
 Fas. 3.11–42: 225
 Fas. 3.16: 253
 Fas. 3.23: 175
 Fas. 3.68: 253
 Fas. 3.135–48: 78
 Fas. 3.167–258: 77
 Fas. 3.169: 77
 Fas. 3.171: 225
 Fas. 3.171–6: 254
 Fas. 3.173: 141
 Fas. 3.247: 78
 Fas. 3.253–5: 77
 Fas. 3.255: 138
 Fas. 3.269: 143
 Fas. 3.284: 137
 Fas. 3.301: 201
 Fas. 3.346: 159, 202
 Fas. 3.353: 159, 202
 Fas. 3.361: 142
 Fas. 3.363: 161
 Fas. 3.391–2: 276
 Fas. 3.675–96: 225
 Fas. 3.404: 118
 Fas. 3.461: 212
 Fas. 3.462: 213
 Fas. 3.465–516: 211
 Fas. 3.473: 212
 Fas. 3.484: 264
 Fas. 3.487: 215
 Fas. 3.507: 221
 Fas. 3.549: 111
 Fas. 3.561: 108
 Fas. 3.593–4: 208
 Fas. 3.634: 267
 Fas. 3.652: 249
 Fas. 3.670: 266
 Fas. 3.714: 157, 253
 Fas. 3.721: 207
 Fas. 3.734: 254
 Fas. 3.738: 169
 Fas. 3.769–72: 199
 Fas. 3.772: 199
 Fas. 3.789–90: 157
 Fas. 3.804: 250
 Fas. 3.820: 153
 Fas. 3.827: 247
 Fas. 3.856: 155
 Fas. 4.1: 253
 Fas. 4.7: 267
 Fas. 4.32: 243
 Fas. 4.116: 207

Index Locorum 343

Fas. 4.120: 241
Fas. 4.126: 187
Fas. 4.151: 107
Fas. 4.153: 149
Fas. 4.172: 243
Fas. 4.207: 221
Fas. 4.222: 80
Fas. 4.240–1: 165
Fas. 4.260: 245
Fas. 4.282: 120
Fas. 4.296: 254
Fas. 4.309: 263
Fas. 4.312: 252
Fas. 4.324: 245
Fas. 4.409: 137
Fas. 4.419: 178
Fas. 4.439: 150
Fas. 4.442: 150
Fas. 4.493: 228
Fas. 4.499: 181
Fas. 4.500: 180
Fas. 4.514: 298
Fas. 4.551: 203
Fas. 4.569: 109
Fas. 4.584: 193
Fas. 4.601: 166
Fas. 4.612: 120
Fas. 4.661: 143
Fas. 4.751–3: 121
Fas. 4.774: 241
Fas. 4.853: 108
Fas. 4.865: 196
Fas. 4.898: 254
Fas. 4.939: 186
Fas. 4.954: 250
Fas. 5.30: 279
Fas. 5.58: 194
Fas. 5.59: 225
Fas. 5.79: 143
Fas. 5.86: 243
Fas. 5.144: 106
Fas. 5.178: 207
Fas. 5.220: 221
Fas. 5.273: 117
Fas. 5.341: 217
Fas. 5.345: 219
Fas. 5.363: 187
Fas. 5.426: 110
Fas. 5.434: 102
Fas. 5.449: 159
Fas. 5.532: 99
Fas. 5.537: 239
Fas. 5.548: 125
Fas. 5.549–51: 226
Fas. 5.561: 226
Fas. 5.563: 226

Fas. 5.565: 226
Fas. 5.567: 226
Fas. 5.589: 117
Fas. 5.596: 254
Fas. 5.625: 117
Fas. 5.683: 123
Fas. 5.704: 192
Fas. 6.39: 138
Fas. 6.228: 249
Fas. 6.244: 139
Fas. 6.249: 253
Fas. 6.251: 160
Fas. 6.253: 138
Fas. 6.228: 253
Fas. 6.290: 245
Fas. 6.304: 105
Fas. 6.320: 169
Fas. 6.322: 250
Fas. 6.389: 175
Fas. 6.408: 210
Fas. 6.426: 159
Fas. 6.464: 91
Fas. 6.501: 80
Fas. 6.509: 91
Fas. 6.538: 91
Fas. 6.574: 243
Fas. 6.584: 203
Fas. 6.635: 117
Fas. 6.662: 153
Fas. 6.709: 88
Fas. 6.732: 117
Fas. 6.751: 117
Fas. 6.755: 121, 203
Fas. 6.799: 80
Fas. 6.811: 157
Her. 1.2: 226
Her. 1.5: 117
Her. 1.8: 212
Her. 1.12: 142, 220
Her. 1.14: 94
Her. 1.41: 206
Her. 1.54: 119
Her. 2.12: 183
Her. 2.26: 126
Her. 2.39–41: 215
Her. 2.42: 199
Her. 2.58: 183
Her. 2.76: 212
Her. 2.93: 215
Her. 2.101: 202
Her. 2.103: 207, 210
Her. 2.146: 111
Her. 3.23: 117
Her. 3.26: 160
Her. 3.45: 225
Her. 3.66: 212

Ovid (*cont.*)
  Her. 3.90: 111
  Her. 3.109: 116
  Her. 3.137: 220
  Her. 3.139: 100
  Her. 4: 236, 269
  Her. 4.8: 253
  Her. 4.9: 272
  Her. 4.18: 272
  Her. 4.19: 271
  Her. 4.19–20: 257
  Her. 4.28: 259
  Her. 4.35–6: 246
  Her. 4.38: 245
  Her. 4.40: 239
  Her. 4.41: 242
  Her. 4.41–2: 242
  Her. 4.41–4: 236
  Her. 4.42: 243
  Her. 4.59: 212
  Her. 4.70: 228
  Her. 4.72: 148
  Her. 4.87–8: 241, 244
  Her. 4.131: 158
  Her. 4.156: 99
  Her. 4.162: 238
  Her. 4.167: 238
  Her. 5.2: 86
  Her. 5.3: 253
  Her. 5.4: 278
  Her. 5.19–20: 242
  Her. 5.29: 212
  Her. 5.60: 114
  Her. 5.92: 256
  Her. 5.109: 117
  Her. 5.129: 160
  Her. 5.149–50: 169
  Her. 5.151: 169
  Her. 5.151–2: 168
  Her. 6.21: 252
  Her. 6.44: 199
  Her. 6.84: 234
  Her. 6.115: 143
  Her. 6.122: 138
  Her. 6.124: 157
  Her. 7.1: 129
  Her. 7.4: 126, 190
  Her. 7.37–9: 177
  Her. 7.38: 245
  Her. 7.51: 166
  Her. 7.67: 212
  Her. 7.70: 103
  Her. 7.84: 212
  Her. 7.143: 250
  Her. 7.182: 165
  Her. 7.195: 111

  Her. 7.195–6: 112
  Her. 8.15: 290
  Her. 8.24: 226
  Her. 8.32: 284
  Her. 8.39: 287
  Her. 8.41: 193
  Her. 8.86: 239
  Her. 8.96: 241
  Her. 9.20: 139
  Her. 9.39–40: 137
  Her. 9.74: 139
  Her. 9.90: 119
  Her. 9.93–4: 179
  Her. 9.101: 122
  Her. 9.142: 189
  Her. 10.1: 177
  Her. 10.32: 183
  Her. 10.43: 212
  Her. 10.53: 229
  Her. 10.75–6: 212
  Her. 10.80: 212
  Her. 10.85: 204
  Her. 10.99–100: 213
  Her. 10.111: 183
  Her. 10.119: 110
  Her. 10.129: 212
  Her. 10.131–2: 177
  Her. 11.51: 210
  Her. 11.55: 138
  Her. 11.60: 253
  Her. 11.76: 183
  Her. 11.84: 298
  Her. 11.125: 110
  Her. 11.127: 110
  Her. 12.29: 181
  Her. 12.35: 145
  Her. 12.84: 126
  Her. 12.97: 94
  Her. 12.124: 213
  Her. 12.141: 139
  Her. 12.142: 91
  Her. 12.148: 209
  Her. 12.156: 229
  Her. 12.196: 283
  Her. 13.4: 220
  Her. 13.46: 296
  Her. 13.58: 120
  Her. 13.107: 138
  Her. 13.108: 209
  Her. 13.137: 110
  Her. 13.159: 126
  Her. 14.16: 190
  Her. 14.55: 182
  Her. 14.93: 210
  Her. 14.118: 110
  Her. 14.125–6: 118

Her. 14.127: 105, 110
Her. 15: 51, 236, 244, 269
Her. 15.1: 266
Her. 15.9–10: 257
Her. 15.25: 212, 219
Her. 15.39–40: 279
Her. 15.48: 210, 302
Her. 15.62: 110
Her. 15.76: 109
Her. 15.79: 205
Her. 15.80: 251
Her. 15.92: 225
Her. 15.95: 247
Her. 15.109: 163
Her. 15.109–10: 276
Her. 15.124: 125
Her. 15.133–4: 279
Her. 15.169–70: 291
Her. 15.202: 134
Her. 15.216: 241
Her. 16.20: 274
Her. 16.42: 159
Her. 16.141: 302
Her. 16.143: 142
Her. 16.158: 275
Her. 16.167: 215
Her. 16.170: 98
Her. 16.178: 250
Her. 16.204: 243
Her. 16.231–2: 198
Her. 16.243–6: 277
Her. 16.246: 171
Her. 16.249–54: 227
Her. 16.253: 227
Her. 16.257: 268
Her. 16.317: 217
Her. 16.320: 125
Her. 16.343: 239
Her. 16.344: 138
Her. 16.349: 213
Her. 16.352: 139
Her. 16.372: 225
Her. 17.54: 115
Her. 17.109: 291
Her. 17.111: 134
Her. 17.175: 266
Her. 17.181: 217
Her. 17.193: 213
Her. 17.218: 176
Her. 17.254: 251
Her. 18.8: 250
Her. 18.90: 258
Her. 18.107: 250
Her. 18.162: 250
Her. 18.177: 258
Her. 18.196: 142, 220

Her. 18.200: 111
Her. 19.5: 257
Her. 19.37: 129
Her. 19.44: 119
Her. 19.48: 196
Her. 19.55–6: 142
Her. 19.56: 250
Her. 19.62: 246
Her. 19.82: 196
Her. 19.95: 208
Her. 19.105: 165
Her. 19.109: 127, 287
Her. 19.165: 126
Her. 19.193: 134, 162
Her. 19.193–202: 132
Her. 19.195: 143
Her. 19.195–6: 133, 140, 142
Her. 19.200: 144
Her. 20: 151
Her. 20–21: 263
Her. 20.1: 251
Her. 20.10: 245
Her. 20.57: 146
Her. 20.57–8: 228
Her. 20.72: 128
Her. 20.79: 243
Her. 20.83: 100
Her. 20.86: 98
Her. 20.97: 239
Her. 20.122: 148
Her. 20.129: 302
Her. 20.134: 253
Her. 20.137: 253
Her. 20.181: 160
Her. 20.224: 243
Her. 20.233: 253
Her. 20.236: 122
Her. 21: 151
Her. 21.1: 139
Her. 21.14: 250
Her. 21.15: 249
Her. 21.33: 256
Her. 21.46: 187
Her. 21.48: 191
Her. 21.72: 208
Her. 21.133: 114
Her. 21.139: 174
Her. 21.161: 146
Her. 21.170: 119
Her. 21.191: 253
Her. 21.215–7: 151
Her. 21.217: 148
Her. 21.229: 173
Ib. 8: 161
Ib. 12: 161
Ib. 34: 183

346   Index Locorum

Ovid (*cont.*)
  Ib. 78: 249
  Ib. 100: 106
  Ib. 129: 126
  Ib. 123: 111
  Ib. 173: 194
  Ib. 215: 225
  Ib. 217: 281
  Ib. 318: 111
  Ib. 329: 211
  Ib. 431: 220
  Ib. 477: 147
  Ib. 514: 249
  Ib. 584: 100
  Ib. 589: 196
  Ib. 615: 115
  MFF 7: 89
  MFF 100: 149
  Met. 1: 228
  Met. 1.64: 181
  Met. 1.110: 115
  Met. 1.147: 130
  Met. 1.172: 195
  Met. 1.179: 125
  Met. 1.181: 190
  Met. 1.216: 181
  Met. 1.264–5: 183
  Met. 1.304–5: 204
  Met. 1.306: 243
  Met. 1.335: 298
  Met. 1.387: 140
  Met. 1.414: 201
  Met. 1.452–76: 130
  Met. 1.452–567: 144, 228
  Met. 1.454: 235
  Met. 1.470: 239
  Met. 1.473: 93
  Met. 1.475: 241
  Met. 1.491: 169
  Met. 1.495: 91
  Met. 1.497–8: 230
  Met. 1.498–9: 228
  Met. 1.508: 241
  Met. 1.508–9: 241
  Met. 1.509: 242
  Met. 1.523–4: 169
  Met. 1.549: 86
  Met. 1.593: 241
  Met. 1.606–7: 80
  Met. 1.611: 161
  Met. 1.612: 128
  Met. 1.637: 155
  Met. 1.685: 291
  Met. 1.708: 170
  Met. 1.747: 254
  Met. 1.762: 215

  Met. 2: 132
  Met. 2.3: 85
  Met. 2.49: 125
  Met. 2.112: 142
  Met. 2.125: 220
  Met. 2.145–6: 166
  Met. 2.224: 181
  Met. 2.241: 193
  Met. 2.252: 162
  Met. 2.322: 215
  Met. 2.327: 112
  Met. 2.442: 235
  Met. 2.447: 209
  Met. 2.547: 154, 300
  Met. 2.612–15: 162
  Met. 2.618: 169
  Met. 2.631–2: 162
  Met. 2.679–83: 168
  Met. 2.737: 153
  Met. 2.784: 189
  Met. 2.856: 266
  Met. 2.872: 178
  Met. 2.874: 87
  Met. 3–4: 206
  Met. 3.6: 265
  Met. 3.141: 123
  Met. 3.146: 238, 242
  Met. 3.161: 266
  Met. 3.164: 105
  Met. 3.167: 266
  Met. 3.176: 121
  Met. 3.177: 241
  Met. 3.238: 215
  Met. 3.275–8: 191
  Met. 3.276: 194
  Met. 3.284: 207
  Met. 3.316: 157
  Met. 3.336–7: 158
  Met. 3.360: 154, 300
  Met. 3.370: 242
  Met. 3.375–6: 173
  Met. 3.389: 215
  Met. 3.397: 248
  Met. 3.420–3: 143
  Met. 3.421–3: 148
  Met. 3.423: 151
  Met. 3.428–9: 215
  Met. 3.442: 165
  Met. 3.473: 253
  Met. 3.482–4: 151
  Met. 3.482–5: 143
  Met. 3.520: 157
  Met. 3.607: 180
  Met. 3.641: 299
  Met. 3.650: 152
  Met. 3.668: 204

Met. 3.733: 262
Met. 4: 206, 237, 247
Met. 4.8: 207
Met. 4.9–30: 199
Met. 4.14: 211
Met. 4.18: 200
Met. 4.34: 129
Met. 4.41: 126
Met. 4.77: 126
Met. 4.102: 181
Met. 4.135: 94, 249
Met. 4.157: 110
Met. 4.221: 129
Met. 4.226: 171
Met. 4.261: 103
Met. 4.267: 130
Met. 4.313: 170
Met. 4.331: 151
Met. 4.342: 152
Met. 4.348: 152
Met. 4.353–5: 196
Met. 4.355: 150
Met. 4.404: 245
Met. 4.411: 170
Met. 4.429–30: 207
Met. 4.438: 94
Met. 4.464: 205
Met. 4.483: 266
Met. 4.515: 172
Met. 4.574: 155
Met. 4.655: 153
Met. 4.678–9: 260
Met. 4.734: 125
Met. 4.765: 201
Met. 4.782: 153
Met. 5.10: 98
Met. 5.43: 115
Met. 5.71: 298
Met. 5.105–6: 155
Met. 5.112: 155
Met. 5.131: 262
Met. 5.140: 123
Met. 5.146: 158
Met. 5.235: 91
Met. 5.255: 157
Met. 5.336: 102
Met. 5.368: 193
Met. 5.373: 98
Met. 5.381: 239
Met. 5.392: 150
Met. 5.395: 94
Met. 5.476: 182
Met. 5.488: 146
Met. 5.549: 135
Met. 5.667: 98
Met. 5.678: 154

Met. 5.576: 268
Met. 6.49: 142
Met. 6.57: 129
Met. 6.62: 102
Met. 6.133: 125
Met. 6.149: 117
Met. 6.195: 123
Met. 6.222–3: 233
Met. 6.272: 118
Met. 6.321: 143
Met. 6.325: 103
Met. 6.415: 205
Met. 6.479: 215
Met. 7.18: 267
Met. 7.32–3: 177
Met. 7.37: 133
Met. 7.53: 181
Met. 7.62–5: 180
Met. 7.75: 297
Met. 7.84: 145
Met. 7.96–7: 158
Met. 7.118: 119
Met. 7.183: 230
Met. 7.190–1: 190
Met. 7.241: 153
Met. 7.244–50: 197
Met. 7.250: 192
Met. 7.290: 248
Met. 7.357: 153
Met. 7.373: 204
Met. 7.387: 245
Met. 7.428: 114
Met. 7.601: 291
Met. 7.637: 144
Met. 7.643: 175
Met. 7.662–3: 209
Met. 7.672–865: 240
Met. 7.692: 128
Met. 7.766: 240
Met. 7.814: 241
Met. 7.819: 298
Met. 7.826: 252
Met. 7.855: 111
Met. 8.1–151: 180
Met. 8.15: 154
Met. 8.19: 117
Met. 8.23: 182
Met. 8.35: 267
Met. 8.108: 212
Met. 8.120: 181
Met. 8.120–5: 177
Met. 8.121: 204
Met. 8.174: 213
Met. 8.208: 202
Met. 8.220–1: 153
Met. 8.237: 300

Ovid (*cont.*)
   Met. 8.270–424: 238
   Met. 8.320: 153
   Met. 8.331–3: 242
   Met. 8.451–525: 258
   Met. 8.451–6: 256
   Met. 8.452–3: 129
   Met. 8.488: 105
   Met. 8.493: 296
   Met. 8.533–4: 154
   Met. 8.586: 110
   Met. 8.628–9: 232
   Met. 8.702: 121
   Met. 8.703: 155
   Met. 8.724: 155
   Met. 8.741–2: 121
   Met. 8.882: 87
   Met. 9.44: 91
   Met. 9.66: 152
   Met. 9.82: 153
   Met. 9.90: 230
   Met. 9.147: 216
   Met. 9.217: 125
   Met. 9.225: 145
   Met. 9.244: 91
   Met. 9.294: 138
   Met. 9.322: 210
   Met. 9.333: 174
   Met. 9.382: 128
   Met. 9.427–8: 190
   Met. 9.446: 179
   Met. 9.459: 215
   Met. 9.472: 175
   Met. 9.476: 296
   Met. 9.527: 296
   Met. 9.536: 248
   Met. 9.542: 267
   Met. 9.546: 128
   Met. 9.558: 257
   Met. 9.600: 267
   Met. 9.605: 215
   Met. 9.613–15: 178, 181
   Met. 9.675: 126
   Met. 10: 243
   Met. 10.1: 161
   Met. 10.13: 120
   Met. 10.24: 193
   Met. 10.38: 128
   Met. 10.120: 182
   Met. 10.171: 172
   Met. 10.191: 150
   Met. 10.203: 157
   Met. 10.209: 159
   Met. 10.212: 150
   Met. 10.260–1: 92
   Met. 10.267: 122
   Met. 10.274: 301
   Met. 10.309: 108
   Met. 10.336: 210
   Met. 10.380: 111
   Met. 10.399: 207
   Met. 10.443: 91
   Met. 10.478: 108, 109
   Met. 10.482: 100
   Met. 10.510: 182
   Met. 10.519–739: 238
   Met. 10.535: 242
   Met. 10.545: 237
   Met. 10.551: 204
   Met. 10.558: 117
   Met. 10.594–6: 148
   Met. 10.625: 100
   Met. 10.634: 128, 197
   Met. 10.635: 116
   Met. 10.642: 114
   Met. 10.645: 128
   Met. 10.650–77: 151
   Met. 10.698–9: 204
   Met. 10.704: 204
   Met. 10.710: 241
   Met. 11.48: 107
   Met. 11.132: 211
   Met. 11.134–45: 127
   Met. 11.154: 154
   Met. 11.165–6: 144
   Met. 11.165–8: 143
   Met. 11.166: 152
   Met. 11.167–8: 153
   Met. 11.386: 215
   Met. 11.388: 253
   Met. 11.423: 212
   Met. 11.496: 186
   Met. 11.592–3: 194
   Met. 11.592–673: 142
   Met. 11.593: 175
   Met. 11.614: 134
   Met. 11.624: 142
   Met. 11.624–5: 250
   Met. 11.672–3: 144
   Met. 11.727: 128
   Met. 11.734–5: 170
   Met. 11.793: 248
   Met. 11.794: 146
   Met. 12.56: 126
   Met. 12.133: 125
   Met. 12.152: 136
   Met. 12.198: 244
   Met. 12.288: 125
   Met. 12.357: 106
   Met. 12.403: 241
   Met. 12.405: 183
   Met. 12.577: 155

Met. 12.586: 125
Met. 13–14: 180
Met. 13.132–3: 129
Met. 13.290: 153
Met. 13.347: 153
Met. 13.380: 110
Met. 13.592: 117
Met. 13.604: 103
Met. 13.639: 221
Met. 13.732: 180
Met. 13.732–4: 169
Met. 13.733: 180
Met. 13.767: 279
Met. 13.838: 152
Met. 13.900–14.74: 180
Met. 14.18–19: 173
Met. 14.33: 152
Met. 14.40: 251
Met. 14.44: 189
Met. 14.96: 194
Met. 14.99: 212
Met. 14.102: 153
Met. 14.112: 202–3
Met. 14.116: 130
Met. 14.178: 283
Met. 14.206: 125
Met. 14.254: 115
Met. 14.262: 266
Met. 14.263: 161
Met. 14.318: 159
Met. 14.341: 154
Met. 14.349: 227
Met. 14.424: 275
Met. 14.428–9: 154
Met. 14.441–2: 108
Met. 14.538: 204
Met. 14.578: 248
Met. 14.623: 772, 231
Met. 14.634: 244
Met. 14.642: 232
Met. 14.654: 143
Met. 14.656: 241
Met. 14.675: 226
Met. 14.681: 298
Met. 14.693: 173
Met. 14.711: 178
Met. 14.716: 97, 98
Met. 14.717: 91
Met. 14.725: 118
Met. 14.726: 135
Met. 14.730: 110
Met. 14.758: 173
Met. 14.810–11: 276
Met. 14.843–4: 158
Met. 15.21: 143
Met. 15.30: 152

Met. 15.32: 144
Met. 15.86: 204
Met. 15.106: 192
Met. 15.125: 115
Met. 15.163: 153
Met. 15.186: 140
Met. 15.465: 126
Met. 15.516: 126
Met. 15.550–9: 143
Met. 15.619: 142
Met. 15.620–1: 87
Met. 15.653: 144
Met. 15.664: 175
Met. 15.672: 121
Met. 15.793: 121
Met. 15.846: 105
Met. 15.871–9: 270
Met. 15.875–6: 106
Met. 15.879: 196, 280
RA 11: 294
RA 16: 153
RA 26: 189
RA 35: 190
RA 71: 117
RA 81: 291
RA 108: 268
RA 109: 141
RA 115: 247, 291
RA 125: 117
RA 138: 124
RA 143: 219
RA 151: 202
RA 153: 225
RA 181: 154
RA 199–200: 244, 245
RA 213: 98
RA 213: 259
RA 213–48: 202
RA 215: 299
RA 245: 98
RA 260: 200
RA 294: 259
RA 313–4: 141
RA 317: 241
RA 322: 289
RA 343: 89
RA 359: 99
RA 376: 255
RA 379: 114
RA 380: 284
RA 387: 205
RA 407: 295
RA 441: 299
RA 472: 287
RA 493: 267
RA 497: 209

Ovid (cont.)
  RA 503: 241
  RA 504: 267
  RA 511: 250
  RA 526: 232
  RA 530: 167
  RA 531: 134
  RA 539: 100
  RA 546: 267
  RA 549–58: 130
  RA 552: 228
  RA 555–75: 132
  RA 557: 142, 220
  RA 564: 255
  RA 579–91: 298
  RA 583: 212
  RA 591: 297
  RA 602: 94
  RA 621: 267
  RA 630: 255
  RA 679: 229
  RA 686: 253
  RA 688: 250
  RA 697: 98
  RA 739: 181
  RA 768: 289
  RA 772: 162
  RA 774: 164
  RA 777: 239
  RA 785: 212
  RA 794: 267
  RA 809–10: 198
  Tr. 1.1: 76, 273
  Tr. 1.1.1–12: 83
  Tr. 1.1.5–14: 86
  Tr. 1.1.7: 85
  Tr. 1.1.9: 86, 263
  Tr. 1.1.11: 85
  Tr. 1.1.12: 85
  Tr. 1.1.48: 176
  Tr. 1.1.50: 296
  Tr. 1.2.15: 183
  Tr. 1.2.17: 208
  Tr. 1.2.27: 142
  Tr. 1.2.30: 183
  Tr. 1.2.37: 163
  Tr. 1.2.45: 267
  Tr. 1.2.53: 192
  Tr. 1.3: 112
  Tr. 1.3.56: 191
  Tr. 1.3.61: 181
  Tr. 1.3.66: 125
  Tr. 1.3.75: 117
  Tr. 1.3.80: 155, 211
  Tr. 1.4.19: 153
  Tr. 1.5.1: 125
  Tr. 1.5.9: 93
  Tr. 1.5.27: 123
  Tr. 1.5.38: 191
  Tr. 1.5.47: 100
  Tr. 1.5.84: 140, 207
  Tr. 1.6.1–2: 9 n. 19
  Tr. 1.7.2: 107, 199
  Tr. 1.7.8: 263
  Tr. 1.8.26: 170
  Tr. 1.8.37–44: 178
  Tr. 1.8.39–40: 181
  Tr. 1.10.42: 191, 207
  Tr. 2.5.19–20: 19
  Tr. 2.13: 157
  Tr. 2.72: 254
  Tr. 2.133: 155, 211
  Tr. 2.140: 296
  Tr. 2.142: 125, 209
  Tr. 2.160: 254
  Tr. 2.259–60: 19
  Tr. 2.267–8: 300
  Tr. 2.295: 225
  Tr. 2.318: 290
  Tr. 2.361–2: 229
  Tr. 2.377: 225
  Tr. 2.441: 29 n. 55
  Tr. 2.447–50: 265
  Tr. 2.453: 155
  Tr. 2.461–2: 165
  Tr. 2.490: 221
  Tr. 2.536: 295
  Tr. 3.1: 76, 83
  Tr. 3.1.13: 85
  Tr. 3.1.13–16: 83
  Tr. 3.3: 184
  Tr. 3.3.9: 141
  Tr. 3.3.22: 250, 253
  Tr. 3.3.43–4: 116
  Tr. 3.3.45–76: 95
  Tr. 3.3.56: 100
  Tr. 3.3.57: 99
  Tr. 3.3.69: 108
  Tr. 3.3.83–4: 102
  Tr. 3.4.1: 125
  Tr. 3.4.3: 293
  Tr. 3.4.16: 196
  Tr. 3.4.34: 208
  Tr. 3.4.42: 250
  Tr. 3.4.53: 128
  Tr. 3.4.64: 215
  Tr. 3.5.15: 214
  Tr. 3.5.23–4: 289
  Tr. 3.5.55: 152
  Tr. 3.6.23: 207
  Tr. 3.7: 53
  Tr. 3.7.12: 53

Index Locorum 351

Tr. 3.7.18: 53
Tr. 3.7.34: 194
Tr. 3.7.35: 192
Tr. 3.7.35–6: 117
Tr. 3.7.47: 104
Tr. 3.8.25: 141
Tr. 3.8.33: 141
Tr. 3.9.27: 264
Tr. 3.9.32: 284
Tr. 3.10.65: 239
Tr. 3.10.73: 151
Tr. 3.11.3–4: 178
Tr. 3.11.7: 181
Tr. 3.11.20: 190
Tr. 3.11.27: 117
Tr. 3.11.59: 100
Tr. 3.13.1–10: 281
Tr. 3.13.2: 261
Tr. 3.13.17: 266
Tr. 3.13.19–20: 281
Tr. 3.13.24: 176
Tr. 3.14.1: 249
Tr. 3.14.7: 283
Tr. 4.1: 32 n. 66
Tr. 4.1.19: 259
Tr. 4.1.47: 94
Tr. 4.1.49: 259
Tr. 4.1.54: 254
Tr. 4.1.88: 176
Tr. 4.2: 145
Tr. 4.2.27: 122
Tr. 4.3.9: 152
Tr. 4.3.10: 110
Tr. 4.3.22: 175
Tr. 4.3.24: 161
Tr. 4.3.70: 148
Tr. 4.4.22: 284
Tr. 4.4.27–30: 32 n. 66
Tr. 4.4.38: 176
Tr. 4.5.1: 125
Tr. 4.6.5: 204
Tr. 4.6.13: 115
Tr. 4.7.1: 180
Tr. 4.7.11–20: 178
Tr. 4.7.12: 179
Tr. 4.7.13: 180
Tr. 4.8.2: 191
Tr. 4.8.6: 190
Tr. 4.8.11–12: 117
Tr. 4.10: 40, 285
Tr. 4.10.1: 171
Tr. 4.10.6: 39, 192
Tr. 4.10.11–14: 39
Tr. 4.10.12: 266
Tr. 4.10.27: 191
Tr. 4.10.63: 117

Tr. 4.10.65–6: 205
Tr. 4.10.73–4: 116
Tr. 4.10.81: 283
Tr. 4.10.86: 102, 104
Tr. 4.10.93–4: 191
Tr. 4.10.118: 298
Tr. 5.1.1: 283
Tr. 5.1.8: 229
Tr. 5.1.33: 100
Tr. 5.1.57: 147
Tr. 5.2.11: 106
Tr. 5.2.31: 181
Tr. 5.3: 19 n. 39, 157, 197
Tr. 5.3.10: 236
Tr. 5.3.14: 256
Tr. 5.3.15: 199
Tr. 5.3.17: 129
Tr. 5.3.24: 234
Tr. 5.3.25: 129
Tr. 5.3.25–6: 256
Tr. 5.3.43: 199, 247
Tr. 5.3.45–6: 107
Tr. 5.3.47: 254
Tr. 5.3.50: 197
Tr. 5.4.7: 111
Tr. 5.4.24: 91
Tr. 5.5.2: 105
Tr. 5.5.13: 261
Tr. 5.5.36: 103
Tr. 5.7.4: 208
Tr. 5.7.25: 19
Tr. 5.8.7: 123
Tr. 5.8.15: 123
Tr. 5.8.25: 142
Tr. 5.8.28: 173, 205
Tr. 5.9.27: 243
Tr. 5.10.51: 208, 299
Tr. 5.11.27: 260
Tr. 5.12.14: 207
Tr. 5.12.23: 115
Tr. 5.12.31–2: 98
Tr. 5.12.46: 289
Tr. 5.13: 184
Tr. 5.13.19–29: 166
Tr. 5.14.2: 125
Tr. 5.14.6: 104
Tr. 5.14.11–12: 118
[Ovid]
Cons. ad Liv. 73–4: 108
Cons. ad Liv. 336: 115
Ep. Dr. 38: 134
Ep. Dr. 51: 123
Ep. Dr. 65: 105
Ep. Dr. 164: 129
Ep. Dr. 296: 254
Ep. Dr. 301: 264

[Ovid] (cont.)
   Ep. Dr. 306: 298
   Ep. Dr. 321: 117
   Ep. Dr. 334: 199
   Ep. Dr. 458: 111
   Ep. Dr. 459: 144
   Hal. 50: 138
   Hal. 60: 188
   Hal. 117: 186
   Nux 7: 117
   Nux 159: 100

Parthenius
   Erot. 14: 144
Pausanias
   8.54.7: 153
   10.7.8: 144
Persius
   1.9: 117
   2.1: 125
   2.3: 257
   4.37: 117
   5.23: 202
Petronius
   18.5: 196
   25.4: 215
   26.5: 196
   37.3: 257
   53.4: 257
   57.11: 257
   62.14: 257
   71.7: 108
   74.14: 257
   75.2: 257
   79.8: 258
   89.1.17: 137
   92.5: 205
   127.9: 150
   128.6: 136
   132.3: 288
   133.3: 188, 190
   138.2: 196
   Fr. 30.1–2: 136
Philemon
   Fr. 49: 28 n. 54
Philumenus Medicus
   1.109.9: 146
   2.139.2: 146
Philostratus
   VA 2.37: 140
Pindar
   Ol. 14.24: 221
   P. 1.1–2: 153
   P. 1.39: 88
   P. 4.64: 187
   P. 4.272: 248

   P. 9.5: 242
   Fr. 123 S–M: 33 n. 71
   Fr. 123.13–15 S–M: 228
Plato
   Phlb. 65c: 216
Plautus
   Amph. 422: 140
   Asin. 606: 130
   Aul. 673: 298
   Aul. 692: 138
   Aul. 732: 175
   Bacch. 676: 209
   Capt. 313: 261
   Capt. 454: 286
   Capt. 977: 257
   Cas. 23: 285
   Cas. 408: 215
   Cist. 142: 300
   Cist. 222: 99
   Epid. 396: 137
   Men. 902: 175
   Men. 1060: 215
   Merc. 225–6: 136
   Merc. 858–63: 167
   Mil. 456: 165
   Mil. 691: 77
   Mil. 706: 297
   Mil. 1241: 97
   Pers. 515: 197
   Pers. 656: 287
   Poen. 1258: 209
   Poen. 1400: 133
   Pseud. 94: 97
   Pseud. 1320: 300
   Rud. 1–2: 170
   Rud. 170: 196
   Rud. 205: 298
   Rud. 702–4: 128
   Rud. 1185: 298
   Stich. 736: 183
   Trin. 65: 297
   Truc. 454: 285
   Truc. 476: 138
   Vid. 17e: 146
Pliny Maior
   NH pr 14: 297
   NH 2.16: 215
   NH 2.236: 179
   NH 4.16: 120
   NH 4.64: 120
   NH 5.100: 179
   NH 6.28: 121
   NH 7.186: 100
   NH 8.155: 298
   NH 9.53: 122
   NH 9.60.125–65.141: 122

NH 9.106–124: 121
NH 9.135–41: 233
NH 10.37: 240
NH 12.41: 109
NH 12.70: 121
NH 13.23.74–26.83: 84
NH 14.36: 282
NH 14.62: 201
NH 14.88: 107
NH 16.235: 138
NH 17.98: 288
NH 18.87: 282
NH 19.10: 107
NH 21.46: 84
NH 21.47: 150
NH 23.40: 106
NH 26.87: 282
NH 28.119: 244
NH 31.41: 219
NH 34.34: 231
NH 35.1–3: 119
NH 35.3: 120
NH 35.115: 279
NH 35.150: 107
NH 36.4–8: 119
NH 36.44–63: 119
NH 36.48:120: 121
NH 36.49: 120
NH 36.102: 120
NH 36.121: 219
NH 36.135: 120
NH 36.156: 203
NH 36.158: 120
NH 36.184–189: 121
Pliny Minor
　Ep. 1.16.6: 48
　Ep. 2.20.3: 279
　Ep. 3.5.3: 29 n. 55
　Ep. 3.16.5: 279
　Ep. 4.19.4: 53
　Ep. 5.3.5: 32 n. 63
　Ep. 6.11.3: 125
　Ep. 7.1.6: 279
　Ep. 7.17: 19 n. 37
　Ep. 9.39.4: 121
　Pan. 26.4.1: 94
　Pan. 36.1: 207
　Pan. 68.2: 160
　Pan. 95.3: 202
Plutarch
　Cons. Apoll. 106b–c: 9 n. 19
　De Mus. 1135f: 153
　Num. 4.8: 168
　QR 19: 78
Polybius
　6.53–4: 95

Pomponius Mela
　3.81: 108
Porphyry
　3.22.2–3: 138
Porcius Licinius
　Fr 7: 228
Posidippus
　SH 705.8: 88
Pratinas
　708.4: 218
Propertius
　1.1: 167, 200, 236, 242, 271
　1.1.1: 82, 215
　1.1.1–4: 274
　1.1.1–6: 112
　1.1.5: 92, 156, 167
　1.1.7: 240, 268
　1.1.8: 126, 190
　1.1.9: 167
　1.1.9–12: 297
　1.1.10: 204
　1.1.11: 184
　1.1.23: 176
　1.1.25–6: 202
　1.1.26: 267
　1.1.27: 167
　1.1.31: 126
　1.1.32: 296
　1.1.33: 142
　1.1.35–6: 214
　1.1.37: 126
　1.1.59–68: 112
　1.2: 14, 86, 222
　1.2.1: 114, 263
　1.2.2: 86
　1.2.3: 105
　1.2.5: 89, 229
　1.2.8: 118, 271
　1.2.26: 89
　1.2.27–8: 53
　1.2.28: 258
　1.2.29: 124
　1.2.32: 100
　1.2.71–80: 112
　1.3: 22, 51, 197, 286
　1.3.1: 212
　1.3.1–2: 211
　1.3.2: 143
　1.3.9: 197
　1.3.13–14: 197
　1.3.17: 244
　1.3.18: 190
　1.3.23: 163
　1.3.24: 151
　1.3.27: 220
　1.3.28: 134, 252

354 Index Locorum

Propertius (cont.)
1.3.37: 217
1.3.38: 143
1.3.42: 250
1.4: 202
1.4.3: 157
1.4.4: 301
1.4.7: 145
1.4.11: 106, 240
1.4.16: 135
1.4.17: 190
1.5: 202
1.5.1: 190, 281
1.5.7: 242
1.5.9: 176
1.5.15: 104
1.5.16: 248
1.5.24: 112, 161
1.5.26: 302
1.5.125: 229
1.6: 202
1.6.8: 212
1.6.10: 213, 299
1.6.12: 291
1.6.16: 190, 242
1.6.23–4: 275
1.6.25: 123, 197
1.6.30: 197
1.6.31–6: 196
1.6.32: 127
1.7.4: 202
1.7.5: 163
1.7.7–8: 99
1.7.11: 157, 296
1.7.12: 259
1.7.13–14: 277
1.7.19: 229
1.8: 112, 280
1.8.12: 218
1.8.16: 165
1.8.28: 274
1.8.29: 209
1.8.32: 127
1.8.33: 217
1.8.37–8: 275
1.8.39: 166
1.8.41–2: 274
1.8.42: 296
1.8.45: 295
1.9.6: 238
1.9.7: 218
1.9.11: 83
1.9.11–12: 81
1.9.13: 229
1.9.16: 190
1.9.19: 204

1.9.21: 93
1.9.26: 228
1.10: 276
1.10.7: 143
1.10.8: 147
1.11: 96, 187
1.11.5: 110
1.11.11–12: 196
1.11.15: 265
1.11.21: 299
1.11.23: 298
1.11.23–4: 298
1.11.29: 156, 218
1.12: 96
1.12.9: 123
1.12.11: 102
1.12.13: 217
1.12.16: 163
1.12.17: 291
1.13: 270
1.13.2: 96
1.13.13: 302
1.13.15: 143
1.13.25–6: 208
1.13.35: 208
1.13.36: 298
1.14: 112, 186
1.14.11: 127
1.14.12: 121
1.14.14: 197
1.14.15: 126
1.14.15–24: 124
1.14.16: 244
1.14.17–21: 203
1.14.18: 97
1.14.23–4: 127
1.14.24: 124
1.15.4: 291
1.15.5: 229
1.15.9–22: 212
1.15.10: 212
1.15.11: 103, 104
1.15.25: 134
1.15.33: 215
1.16.15: 217
1.16.21: 302
1.16.35: 289
1.16.40: 217, 220
1.16.41: 81, 83
1.16.48: 123
1.17.1: 218, 220
1.17.12: 246
1.17.19–24: 95
1.17.27: 252
1.18: 297
1.18.9: 102

Index Locorum

1.18.10: 111
1.18.18: 135
1.18.23: 300
1.18.25: 235, 256
1.18.25–6: 172
1.18.29: 276
1.19.17: 116
1.19.18: 110
1.19.19: 103
1.19.23: 110
1.19.24: 166
1.20.1: 214
1.20.13–14: 238
1.20.15–16: 100
1.20.36: 151
1.20.37–8: 150
1.20.41–2: 162
1.20.47: 196
1.21.6: 110
1.22.7: 283
2.1: 223
2.1.1: 216
2.1.3–4: 168
2.1.4: 99
2.1.5–8: 230
2.1.5–16: 230
2.1.8: 163, 235, 247, 256
2.1.13: 118
2.1.15–16: 228
2.1.45: 239
2.1.55–6: 101
2.1.58: 246, 291
2.1.71–8: 95
2.1.72: 115
2.1.77: 110
2.2.15: 116
2.2.16: 159
2.3.6: 205
2.3.10: 150
2.3.11–12: 148
2.3.13: 146
2.3.14: 228
2.3.20: 157
2.3.21–2: 53
2.3.23–32: 228
2.3.25–32: 299
2.3.28: 300
2.3.43: 230
2.3.46: 228
2.3.51: 159
2.4.3: 139
2.4.5: 105
2.4.9–16: 246
2.4.11: 141
2.4.15: 159
2.4.16: 136

2.4.19: 296
2.4.21: 102
2.5.5–6: 82
2.5.14: 259
2.5.18: 188
2.5.19: 99
2.6.3: 252
2.6.7: 283
2.6.28: 156, 164
2.6.32: 190
2.6.36: 248
2.6.37–9: 265
2.6.38: 218
2.6.41–2: 299
2.6.42: 93
2.7: 20
2.7.19: 296
2.8: 95, 99, 101
2.8b: 271
2.8.1: 96
2.8.13: 136
2.8.16: 235
2.8.17–28: 95, 101
2.8.18: 163
2.8.29: 93, 96, 98
2.8.33: 248
2.8.36: 97
2.9: 140
2.9.3: 251
2.9.3–4: 97
2.9.19–20: 163
2.9.20: 140
2.9.25: 250
2.9.25–8: 246
2.9.33: 181
2.9.35–6: 166
2.9.38: 239
2.9.42: 241
2.9.44: 218
2.10.12: 87
2.10.19: 159
2.10.24: 124
2.11.6: 157
2.12.9: 242
2.12.12: 267
2.12.17: 93
2.12.20: 102
2.13.11: 157
2.13.14: 296
2.13.15: 126
2.13.15–6: 101
2.13.16: 218
2.13.17: 101
2.13.17–36: 95, 101
2.13.20: 108
2.13.25: 85

356 Index Locorum

Propertius (*cont.*)
2.13.29: 108
2.13.36: 301
2.13.45: 188
2.13.52: 251
2.13.53–4: 238
2.13.56: 103
2.14: 270, 271
2.14.7: 213
2.14.14: 291
2.14.18: 190
2.14.22: 291
2.14.27: 263
2.14.29: 243
2.15.5: 118, 272
2.15.8: 291
2.15.13–16: 118
2.15.16: 243
2.15.20: 104
2.15.22: 300
2.15.24: 217
2.15.25–6: 260
2.15.26: 260
2.15.35: 97, 98, 302
2.16.5: 220
2.16.7: 226
2.16.35–6: 126, 302
2.16.47–8: 216, 302
2.16.47–56: 216
2.16.48: 126
2.16.55: 122
2.17.3: 159
2.17.3–4: 142
2.17.10: 226
2.17.11: 123
2.17.13: 140
2.17.14: 189
2.17.15: 217
2.18.6: 194
2.18.7: 116
2.18.17: 116
2.18.18: 85
2.18.20: 192
2.18.28: 287
2.18.29: 134
2.18.36: 263
2.18.37: 276
2.18.38: 302
2.19: 236, 280
2.19.2: 238
2.19.3: 156
2.19.17: 242
2.19.17–18: 241, 244
2.19.32: 278
2.20: 301
2.20.1: 239, 284
2.20.3: 190

2.20.4: 135
2.20.13: 126, 302
2.20.14: 166
2.20.15: 104
2.20.18: 135
2.20.34: 135
2.21.6: 252
2.21.7: 235
2.21.9: 293
2.21.19: 217
2.22.16: 190
2.22.18: 251
2.22.20: 123
2.22.22: 89
2.22.47–8: 142
2.23.9: 265
2.23.17: 300
2.23.26: 153
2.24.5: 258
2.24.16: 169
2.24.17: 163
2.24b.21–2: 81
2.24.26: 151
2.24.27: 258
2.24.34: 188
2.24.35–6: 110
2.24.35–8: 95, 101
2.24.39: 99, 102
2.24.43: 213
2.24.46: 212, 293
2.24.50: 106
2.25.3: 85
2.25.9: 116
2.25.9–10: 268
2.25.18: 139
2.25.22: 164, 252
2.25.29–30: 297
2.26a: 132
2.26.9: 117
2.26.15: 123
2.26.23: 127
2.26.27: 135
2.26.35: 100
2.26.45: 183
2.28: 246
2.28.1: 247
2.28.1–2: 248
2.28.3: 226
2.28.9–12: 190
2.28.10: 123
2.28.15: 290
2.28.41–2: 253
2.28.42: 117
2.28.44: 251
2.28.47–8: 187, 188
2.28.59: 243
2.28.59–62: 250

Index Locorum

2.28.60: 254
2.29.1: 134, 242, 243
2.29.6: 259
2.29.8: 203
2.29.13: 218
2.29.15: 122
2.29.17: 234
2.29.17–18: 228
2.29.18: 109
2.29.25: 145
2.29.27: 156
2.29.31: 299
2.29.35: 229
2.29.45: 229
2.30.1: 208
2.30.7–9: 239
2.30.13: 116
2.30.27–30: 156
2.30.28: 257
2.30.33–6: 79, 156
2.30.40: 99
2.31: 133, 145, 154
2.31.5–6: 133
2.31.6: 115, 154
2.31.9: 115
2.31.15–16: 133
2.31.16: 152
2.32.17: 80, 241
2.32.24: 302
2.32.48: 144
2.32.51: 302
2.32.55–6: 97
2.32.60: 156
2.33: 76
2.33.9: 262
2.33.17: 113
2.33.21: 302
2.33.39: 201
2.34: 81
2.34.42–2: 134
2.34.48: 167
2.34.61: 239
2.34.65: 19
2.34.69: 151
2.34.79: 157
2.34.80: 159
2.34.91–2: 93, 129
3.1.6: 302
3.1.7: 248
3.1.8: 85, 86
3.1.21: 123
3.1.23–4: 273
3.2: 274
3.2.1–2: 82
3.2.2: 164
3.2.9: 156
3.2.11–12: 115, 120

3.2.11–14: 120, 121
3.2.11–26: 112
3.2.14: 219
3.2.15–16: 156
3.2.17: 85, 162
3.3: 79, 132, 274
3.3.1: 144
3.3.10: 105
3.3.13: 88
3.3.13–26: 156
3.3.14: 153
3.3.18: 109
3.3.19: 85
3.3.19–20: 277
3.3.28: 153
3.3.34: 240
3.5.2: 239
3.5.5: 119
3.5.14: 118
3.5.21: 107
3.5.24: 191
3.5.23–6: 116
3.6: 27, 88
3.6.8: 126
3.6.9: 103
3.6.18: 190
3.6.23: 163
3.6.31: 134, 174
3.6.39: 242
3.7.1: 220
3.7.6: 125
3.7.9: 105
3.7.48: 240, 241
3.7.63: 249
3.8.2: 190
3.8.6: 242
3.8.9: 291
3.8.15: 302
3.8.19: 190
3.8.20: 291
3.8.24: 251
3.8.28: 94
3.8.35: 163
3.8.36: 235, 256
3.9.3: 178
3.9.15: 118
3.9.29: 102
3.10: 14, 76, 79, 132, 217
3.10.1: 275
3.10.2: 148
3.10.4: 125
3.10.13: 262
3.10.18: 256
3.11.3: 130
3.11.4: 259
3.11.15: 272
3.11.31: 82

Propertius (*cont.*)
  3.12.8: 250
  3.12.15: 156
  3.12.22: 215
  3.12.35: 115
  3.12.37: 156
  3.13.1: 82
  3.13.6: 121, 122
  3.13.8: 234
  3.13.14: 82
  3.13.15: 125
  3.13.17: 189
  3.13.18: 105, 230, 254
  3.13.23: 164, 165
  3.13.29: 85
  3.13.52: 145
  3.14.13: 272
  3.14.29: 252
  3.15.10: 259
  3.15.20: 100
  3.16.4: 218
  3.16.11: 251
  3.16.15: 111
  3.16.23: 108
  3.16.23–30: 95
  3.17: 197, 211
  3.17.3: 190
  3.17.3–4: 198
  3.17.5: 198
  3.17.11: 242
  3.17.12: 94
  3.17.13: 292
  3.17.31: 146
  3.17.32: 152
  3.17.42: 220
  3.18.22: 298
  3.18.31: 105
  3.19.11: 99
  3.19.15: 116
  3.19.22: 85
  3.19.27: 130
  3.20: 96, 295
  3.20.1: 203
  3.20.7: 156
  3.20.10: 246
  3.20.21: 295
  3.20.23: 259
  3.21: 96, 202
  3.21.32: 297
  3.22.4: 94, 219
  3.22.35–6: 262
  3.23: 277
  3.23.4: 278
  3.23.11: 277
  3.23.12: 291
  3.23.13: 145
  3.23.18: 154, 203, 300
  3.23.23: 221
  3.24.2: 235, 256
  3.24.3: 253
  3.24.4: 115
  3.24.7–8: 147
  3.24.17: 250
  3.24.18: 267
  3.24–25: 92
  3.25.1: 220
  3.25.8: 160
  3.25.11–14: 194
  3.25.15: 235
  4: 3, 13, 76, 269
  4.1: 198
  4.1.34: 190
  4.1.51: 159
  4.1.62: 157, 199
  4.1.67: 87, 253
  4.1.75: 159
  4.1.79: 283
  4.1.88: 256
  4.1.99: 138
  4.1.99–102: 262
  4.1.102: 300
  4.1.117: 159
  4.1.135: 87
  4.1.135–46: 131, 132
  4.1.143: 284, 298
  4.2: 3, 11
  4.2.2: 159
  4.2.3: 293
  4.2.4: 231
  4.2.13: 231
  4.2.20: 166
  4.2.21–4: 231
  4.2.25–6: 232
  4.3: 22, 34, 35, 49, 51, 280
  4.3.10: 235
  4.3.27: 248
  4.3.29: 142
  4.3.41: 104
  4.3.47: 181
  4.3.61: 188
  4.3.64: 107
  4.3.69–70: 245
  4.3.72: 251
  4.4.21: 227
  4.4.23: 137
  4.4.28: 242
  4.4.32: 296
  4.4.39: 180
  4.4.47: 302
  4.5: 8
  4.5.7: 302
  4.5.29: 82
  4.5.43: 82
  4.5.47: 265

4.5.49: 296
4.5.53–4: 82
4.5.57: 83
4.5.57–8: 82
4.5.59: 194
4.5.67: 194
4.5.73: 302
4.6: 145, 197
4.6.1: 159
4.6.5: 114
4.6.6: 125
4.6.9: 134
4.6.10: 159
4.6.27–54: 132
4.6.30: 125
4.6.31–2: 145
4.6.32: 235
4.6.72: 146
4.6.75–6: 156
4.7: 22, 27, 51, 94, 132
4.7.2: 130
4.7.3: 144
4.7.10: 194
4.7.13: 161
4.7.15: 241
4.7.16: 203
4.7.21–2: 208
4.7.21–34: 95
4.7.28: 110
4.7.32: 108
4.7.34: 107
4.7.41: 288
4.7.42: 154
4.7.52: 180
4.7.69: 110
4.7.77: 83
4.7.83–4: 111
4.7.91: 194
4.8: 22
4.8.13: 156
4.8.16: 262, 264
4.8.47: 272
4.8.48: 252
4.8.63: 163
4.8.69: 257
4.8.72: 250
4.8.75: 89
4.8.82: 235, 256
4.8.86: 125
4.9: 197, 236
4.9.24: 121
4.9.24–7: 238
4.9.25–6: 188
4.9.33: 121
4.9.38: 171
4.9.43: 262
4.9.47: 122

4.9.52: 85
4.9.57: 159
4.9.71–2: 262
4.10.30: 234
4.11: 22: 51
4.11.1: 110, 134
4.11.8: 130
4.11.36: 279
4.11.46: 115
4.11.54: 107
4.11.57: 110
4.11.60: 110
4.11.64: 116, 117
4.11.98: 180

Publilius Syr
 A5: 284
 A21: 82
 A29: 176
 A34: 289
 L5: 123

Quintilian
 Decl. Mai. 1.11: 248
 Decl. Min. 363.2: 301
 Inst. 1.6.22: 298
 Inst. 1.11.19: 229
 Inst. 8.3.42: 87
 Inst. 9.1.21: 279
 Inst. 10.1.113: 32 n. 63
 Inst. 10.5.2: 32 n. 63
 Inst. 11.3.22: 201

Rhianus
 Fr. 10 Pow., *Schol*: 168
Rutilius Namatianus
 1.248: 196

Sallust
 Cat. 24.3: 293
 Cat. 25.2–5: 47
 Cat. 36.1: 282
Sappho
 1: 202, 269
 2.44: 257
 2.46: 271
 16: 278
 86: 274
 96.7–9: 147
 105: 151
 112: 149
 140a: 274
 208: 202
Seneca Maior
 Cont. 1.1.5: 123
 Cont. 1.3: 287
 Cont. 2.4.3.5: 275
 Cont. 2.4.8: 32 n. 63

Sappho (*cont.*)
  Cont. 3.pr.10.4: 196
  Cont. 7.1.11.1: 182
  Cont. 10.praef.4–5: 17 n. 33
  Suas. 6.17: 100
Seneca Minor
  Ag. 436: 298
  Ag. 493: 143
  Ag. 584: 155
  Ben. 7.27.3: 194
  De Vita Beat. 1.2: 297
  Dial. 1.6.3: 136
  Dial. 2.9.4: 202
  Dial. 3.20.5: 137
  Dial. 12.17.1: 279
  Ep. 12.2: 257
  Ep. 24.22: 100
  Ep. 51.3: 287
  Ep. 60.4: 108
  Ep. 66.5: 279
  Ep. 88.37: 50 n. 116
  Ep. 90.41: 113
  Ep. 105.3: 297
  Ep. 107.8: 209
  Ep. 110.1: 215
  Ep. 122.9: 298
  HF 18: 212
  HF 133: 142
  HF 138: 163
  HF 175: 128
  HF 282: 298
  HF 587: 120
  HF 609: 193
  HF 621: 290
  HF 663: 120
  HF 664: 190
  HF 697: 290
  HF 722: 105
  HF 813: 120
  HF 833: 193
  HF 909–10: 234
  HF 1001: 170
  HF 1136: 284
  HO 143: 181
  HO 241–2: 204
  HO 377: 258
  HO 652: 128
  HO 724: 190
  HO 793: 234
  HO 1061: 120
  HO 1294: 298
  HO 1771: 120
  HO 1933: 204
  Ira 1.1.6: 238
  Ira 1.6: 239
  Ira 3.23.4–8: 17 n. 33
  Ira 8.6.2: 91
  Laus Pis. 159: 125
  Med. 1–2: 139
  Med. 47: 163
  Med. 142: 110
  Med. 717–8: 189
  Med. 846: 114
  Med. 850: 167
  Med. 930: 208
  Oed. 39: 186
  Oed. 226: 105
  Oed. 419: 209
  Oed. 430: 143
  Oed. 436: 207
  Oed. 563: 102
  Oed. 657: 284
  Oed. 712–13: 88
  Oed. 780: 192
  Oed. 787: 192
  Oed. 837: 135
  Oed. 920: 204
  Oed. 1006: 207
  Phaed. 62: 243
  Phaed. 110–11: 236, 242
  Phaed. 135: 172
  Phaed. 166: 181
  Phaed. 211: 301
  Phaed. 261: 245
  Phaed. 262: 117
  Phaed. 296–8: 168
  Phaed. 344–8: 204
  Phaed. 346–7: 239
  Phaed. 376: 152
  Phaed. 393: 108
  Phaed. 394–7: 242
  Phaed. 415: 257
  Phaed. 438: 190
  Phaed. 496–7: 121
  Phaed. 506: 240
  Phaed. 521: 128
  Phaed. 694: 125
  Phaed. 826: 135
  Phaed. 978: 123
  Phaed. 1082: 137
  Phaed. 1201: 120
  Phoen. 113: 173
  Phoen. 141: 173
  Phoen. 222: 245
  Phoen. 465: 100
  Thy. 347: 121
  Thy. 413: 240
  Thy. 457: 121
  Thy. 665–6: 129
  Thy. 839: 138, 139
  Thy. 843: 254
  Troad. 174: 121

Troad. 185: 227
Troad. 402: 120
Troad. 470: 125
Troad. 491: 119
Troad. 511: 129
Troad. 521: 275
Troad. 745: 99
Troad. 836: 120
Troad. 979: 290
Q. Nat. 1 pr 1: 287
[Seneca]
  Oct. 86: 204
  Oct. 101: 111
  Oct. 225: 163
  Oct. 351: 111
  Oct. 522: 102
  Oct. 715: 298
  Oct. 820: 196
  Oct. 980: 181
Servius
  ad *Aen.* 3.262: 137
  ad *Aen.* 5.118: 179
  ad *Aen.* 6.395: 179
  ad *Geor.* 1.198: 183
  ad *Geor.* 2.59: 183
  ad *Geor.* 2.194: 136
Sidonius Apollinaris
  Carm. 9.261–2: 26
Silius Italicus
  1.107: 129
  2.193–4: 204
  2.356–7: 298
  2.527: 128
  2.572: 178
  3.233–4: 203
  3.555: 141
  3.666: 121
  3.675–6: 121
  3.688: 121
  4.55: 195
  4.80: 178
  4.475: 200
  4.596: 249
  4.635: 129
  4.680: 121
  5.36: 161, 298
  5.127: 298
  5.267–9: 118
  6.67: 155
  6.116: 129
  6.481: 117
  6.537: 200
  7.77: 266
  7.126: 298
  7.288: 204
  7.447: 161
  7.687: 161
  8.116: 193
  8.118: 123
  9.18: 129
  9.159: 125
  9.250: 193
  10.80: 240
  10.272: 250
  10.321: 178
  10.518–19: 99
  10.592: 254
  11.40–1: 233
  11.189: 126
  11.402: 108
  11.410–11: 299
  11.481–2: 173
  11.484: 144
  12.613: 161
  13.141: 240
  13.399: 163
  13.415: 94
  13.437: 193
  13.560: 130
  13.573: 129
  13.587: 94
  14.69: 103
  14.368: 240
  14.495: 240
  14.648: 121
  14.661: 197
  15.223: 142
  15.276: 162
  15.284: 161
  15.455: 190
  16.237: 204
  16.363: 152
  16.502: 122
  17.188: 253
  17.339–40: 190
  17.341: 208
Simonides
  511a.5: 153
Sophocles
  El. 114: 295
  El. 410: 138
  Phil. 393: 127
  Trach. 1046–1102: 105
Statius
  Ach. 1.161–2: 148
  Ach. 1.218: 208
  Ach. 1.252: 200
  Ach. 1.255: 129
  Ach. 1.273: 200
  Ach. 1.459–60: 240
  Ach. 1.524–5: 190
  Ach. 1.549: 129

Statius (cont.)
  Ach. 1.582: 111
  Ach. 1.620: 175
  Ach. 1.743–4: 180
  Ach. 2.5: 266
  Ach. 2.23: 104
  Silv. 1.2.28: 302
  Silv. 1.2.90: 268
  Silv. 1.2.118: 128
  Silv. 1.2.122–9: 232
  Silv. 1.2.133: 212
  Silv. 1.2.148–50: 120
  Silv. 1.2.152: 120
  Silv. 1.2.163: 125
  Silv. 1.3.35: 121
  Silv. 1.3.65: 219
  Silv. 1.3.71: 161
  Silv. 1.4.78–9: 181
  Silv. 1.5.2: 156
  Silv. 1.5.4: 169
  Silv. 1.5.26–7: 219
  Silv. 1.5.34: 120
  Silv. 1.5.34–50: 119
  Silv. 1.5.37: 120
  Silv. 1.5.51: 141
  Silv. 2.1.8: 204
  Silv. 2.1.19: 106
  Silv. 2.1.21: 262
  Silv. 2.1.45: 173
  Silv. 2.1.54: 188
  Silv. 2.1.132: 161
  Silv. 2.1.147: 187
  Silv. 2.1.157–62: 108
  Silv. 2.1.184: 179
  Silv. 2.2.83: 120
  Silv. 2.2.85–97: 119
  Silv. 2.3.16: 161
  Silv. 2.3.22: 243
  Silv. 2.4.34: 108
  Silv. 2.5.8: 240
  Silv. 2.6.86–93: 108
  Silv. 2.6.88: 108
  Silv. 2.7: 254
  Silv. 3.1.108–9: 254
  Silv. 3.2.84: 196
  Silv. 3.2.86: 180
  Silv. 3.2.139–40: 233
  Silv. 3.3.3: 161
  Silv. 3.3.21: 129
  Silv. 3.3.27: 180
  Silv. 3.3.33–5: 108, 109
  Silv. 3.3.58: 168
  Silv. 3.3.179–80: 212
  Silv. 3.3.212: 108
  Silv. 3.4.5: 128
  Silv. 3.4.55: 161
  Silv. 3.4.60: 200
  Silv. 3.5.39: 117
  Silv. 4.2.38: 119
  Silv. 4.376–7: 171
  Silv. 4.4.10–11: 91
  Silv. 4.5.58–9: 110
  Silv. 4.6.18: 122
  Silv. 4.6.54: 205
  Silv. 4.6.80: 211
  Silv. 4.7.21: 275
  Silv. 4.9.7–9: 83
  Silv. 5.1.19: 106
  Silv. 5.1.25–6: 156
  Silv. 5.1.43–4: 260
  Silv. 5.1.196: 143
  Silv. 5.1.210–16: 108
  Silv. 5.1.232: 212
  Silv. 5.2.67: 161
  Silv. 5.2.84–5: 129
  Silv. 5.3.43: 234
  Silv. 5.3.92: 168
  Silv. 5.3.119: 161
  Silv. 5.4: 142
  Silv. 5.5.3–7: 188
  Silv. 5.5.79: 200
  Theb. 1.96: 120
  Theb. 1.110: 266
  Theb. 1.128: 167
  Theb. 1.212–3: 119
  Theb. 1.397: 204
  Theb. 1.398–9: 158
  Theb. 1.502–3: 135
  Theb. 1.574: 116
  Theb. 1.602: 105
  Theb. 1.613: 173
  Theb. 1.706: 129
  Theb. 2.31: 180
  Theb. 2.32: 120
  Theb. 2.44: 120
  Theb. 2.59: 142
  Theb. 2.286: 229
  Theb. 2.527: 266
  Theb. 2.533: 240
  Theb. 3.125: 161
  Theb. 3.241–2: 129
  Theb. 3.282: 116
  Theb. 3.295: 125
  Theb. 3.393: 143
  Theb. 3.416: 161
  Theb. 4.291: 94
  Theb. 4.419: 191
  Theb. 4.536: 117
  Theb. 5.248: 238
  Theb. 5.257: 201
  Theb. 5.274: 129
  Theb. 5.366–7: 208

Theb. 5.608: 125
Theb. 6.59–60: 109
Theb. 6.209: 108
Theb. 6.210–12: 107
Theb. 6.372: 165
Theb. 6.787–8: 204
Theb. 7.363: 125
Theb. 7.370: 120
Theb. 7.464: 100
Theb. 7.658: 107
Theb. 7.697: 94
Theb. 7.782: 94
Theb. 7.783: 180
Theb. 8.10: 187
Theb. 8.12: 129
Theb. 8.691: 298
Theb. 9.16: 204
Theb. 9.317: 157
Theb. 9.432: 105
Theb. 9.881: 125
Theb. 10.58: 266
Theb. 10.162: 128
Theb. 10.238: 290
Theb. 10.603: 111
Theb. 11.222: 262
Theb. 11.394: 125
Theb. 11.495: 266
Theb. 12.145: 298
Theb. 12.220: 111
Theb. 12.451: 240
Theb. 12.676: 212
Theb. 12.811: 125
Strabo
  5.2.3: 186
  5.2.9: 186, 187
  8.5.7: 120
  10.1.6: 120
  12.8.14: 120
  13.4.5: 127
  16.3.5: 121
Solon
  13.62: 248
Suetonius
  Cal. 16.1: 17 n. 33
  Cal. 50.1: 279
  Aug. 23.2: 183
  Aug. 79.2: 27
  Aug. 94.3: 27
  Jul. 61.1: 298
  Jul. 73: 17
  Nero 31: 120
  Tib. 7.2–3: 112
  Vesp. 19.1: 77

Tacitus
  Ann. 1.7.3: 279
  Ann. 1.24: 209
  Ann. 1.72.3: 17 n. 33
  Ann. 4.21.2: 17 n. 33
  Ann. 6.11: 32 n. 65
Terence
  And. 180: 209
  And. 260: 163
  And. 289: 257
  And. 406: 298
  And. 493: 203
  And. 556: 209
  And. 956: 125
  Heaut. 48–50: 82
  Hec. 49–51: 82
  Hec. 505: 91
  Hec. 842: 209
Tertullian
  De Idol. 14.6: 77, 79
Theocritus
  2: 51 n. 118
  3.15: 172
  7.117: 147, 151
  12.15: 259
  23: 177
  29.1: 200
[Theocritus]
  23: 95
  23.19–26: 94
Theognis
  1.891.4: 30
Theophrastus
  CP 1.13.5–6: 186
Tibullus
  1.1: 75, 81, 84, 113, 281
  1.1.1: 119
  1.1.1–6: 234
  1.1.5: 124
  1.1.2: 89, 115
  1.1.7–8: 192
  1.1.9: 262
  1.1.10: 119, 127
  1.1.19: 124
  1.1.25: 97
  1.1.27: 186
  1.1.37: 124
  1.1.40: 110
  1.1.43: 295
  1.1.46: 275
  1.1.48: 128
  1.1.51: 165
  1.1.52: 272
  1.1.55: 82, 145
  1.1.56: 253
  1.1.57: 81
  1.1.57–60: 217
  1.1.59: 187

Tibullus (cont.)
  1.1.59–62: 104
  1.1.59–68: 95
  1.1.62: 110
  1.1.63–4: 96
  1.1.64: 178
  1.1.67: 140
  1.1.67–8: 230
  1.1.68: 149
  1.1.69: 295
  1.1.71: 245
  1.1.71–2: 116
  1.1.72: 191
  1.1.76: 134, 160
  1.1.77: 110, 128, 262, 266
  1.2: 139, 189, 197
  1.2.1: 198, 221
  1.2.2: 248, 250
  1.2.5: 265
  1.2.9: 172, 173
  1.2.10: 229, 241
  1.2.12: 226
  1.2.15: 265, 265
  1.2.16: 300
  1.2.17: 238
  1.2.17–22: 203
  1.2.18: 301
  1.2.19: 229
  1.2.20: 144
  1.2.22: 110
  1.2.25: 242
  1.2.33: 167
  1.2.42: 249
  1.2.46: 249
  1.2.49: 180
  1.2.53: 110
  1.2.54: 125
  1.2.55: 229
  1.2.62: 197
  1.2.63: 90
  1.2.65: 96
  1.2.65–78: 124
  1.2.68: 293
  1.2.69: 180
  1.2.70: 263
  1.2.72: 97
  1.2.75: 126
  1.2.75–80: 142
  1.2.77–8: 265
  1.2.78: 113, 217
  1.2.79: 139
  1.2.80: 190, 196
  1.2.81–2: 190
  1.2.81–4: 188
  1.2.82: 139
  1.2.84: 245, 254, 258
  1.2.85: 139
  1.2.87–96: 116
  1.2.89: 227
  1.2.92: 85
  1.2.93: 229
  1.2.94: 191
  1.2.99–100: 259
  1.2.100: 302
  1.3: 95, 96, 175, 184, 189, 195, 297
  1.3.1: 184
  1.3.2: 109
  1.3.3: 141, 185
  1.3.4: 187
  1.3.5–6: 104
  1.3.5–8: 95
  1.3.5–10: 101
  1.3.6: 104, 106
  1.3.7: 108, 109
  1.3.7–8: 108
  1.3.11: 125
  1.3.13: 126
  1.3.15: 277
  1.3.23: 113
  1.3.32: 115
  1.3.35: 297
  1.3.50: 119
  1.3.51: 212
  1.3.51–2: 188, 190
  1.3.52: 139, 190, 250
  1.3.53–6: 101
  1.3.54: 111
  1.3.55: 299
  1.3.55–6: 95, 101
  1.3.58: 193
  1.3.60: 126
  1.3.61: 89
  1.3.62: 116
  1.3.64: 239
  1.3.66: 146, 221
  1.3.70: 139
  1.3.71: 179
  1.3.71–2: 180
  1.3.73–4: 262
  1.3.80: 118, 194
  1.3.83: 156, 301
  1.3.85–7: 288
  1.3.88: 250
  1.3.89–90: 298
  1.3.92: 272
  1.4: 5, 50, 96, 132
  1.4.3: 82
  1.4.4: 89, 182
  1.4.6: 186
  1.4.9: 252
  1.4.12: 148, 196
  1.4.13: 300

Index Locorum

1.4.14: 149
1.4.16: 100
1.4.21: 212
1.4.21–4: 93
1.4.21–6: 216
1.4.24: 287
1.4.25–6: 79
1.4.29: 187
1.4.29–38: 116
1.4.33: 238
1.4.34: 293
1.4.35: 183
1.4.38: 145, 230
1.4.39–40: 300
1.4.42: 186
1.4.47: 167, 293
1.4.48: 241
1.4.49: 240
1.4.49–50: 242
1.4.59: 96
1.4.61: 157, 213
1.4.61–6: 79
1.4.62: 82
1.4.66: 249
1.4.71: 172
1.4.71–2: 173, 301
1.4.73: 155
1.4.79–80: 116
1.4.80: 252
1.4.81: 242, 300
1.5.2: 297
1.5.5: 172, 242
1.5.7: 241, 257, 295
1.5.7–8: 295
1.5.9: 171, 290, 291
1.5.9–20: 246
1.5.10: 250
1.5.12–14: 136
1.5.15–16: 250
1.5.17: 128
1.5.18: 166
1.5.19: 251
1.5.26: 154
1.5.35: 183
1.5.35–6: 208
1.5.36: 234
1.5.37–8: 198
1.5.39–40: 299
1.5.42: 276
1.5.49–50: 189
1.5.58: 259, 301
1.5.60: 173
1.5.61: 124
1.5.63: 124
1.5.65: 124, 229, 241
1.5.66: 148

1.5.72: 302
1.5.75: 241
1.6: 116
1.6.2: 252
1.6.3: 167
1.6.5: 229, 244
1.6.5–6: 241, 245
1.6.9: 136
1.6.10: 265, 300
1.6.15: 136, 216
1.6.16: 278
1.6.22: 186, 188, 189
1.6.27: 300
1.6.29: 226
1.6.31: 171
1.6.34: 177
1.6.35: 185, 258
1.6.37–8: 167, 168, 172
1.6.39: 297
1.6.41: 176
1.6.43–56: 132
1.6.51: 239
1.6.54: 208, 245
1.6.57–64: 104
1.6.67: 156
1.6.71: 278
1.6.72: 139, 188
1.6.74: 291
1.6.75: 156
1.6.76: 90, 239
1.6.77: 191
1.6.77–86: 116
1.6.78: 129
1.6.81: 164, 180
1.6.82: 218
1.6.84: 302
1.6.86: 85
1.7: 32, 76, 84, 96, 197, 198, 254
1.7.1–2: 129, 256
1.7.9: 300
1.7.14: 196
1.7.19: 178
1.7.21: 186
1.7.30: 160
1.7.35: 249
1.7.45: 143
1.7.46: 152
1.7.49: 199, 247, 257
1.7.51: 146
1.7.52: 221
1.7.55–6: 116, 194
1.7.63: 261
1.8: 5, 50, 96, 238, 246
1.8.3–4: 135
1.8.7: 134, 183
1.8.9: 113, 182

Tibullus (*cont.*)
  1.8.9–12: 114
  1.8.11: 263
  1.8.15–16: 230
  1.8.16: 152
  1.8.26: 279
  1.8.31–2: 172
  1.8.34: 127
  1.8.35: 229, 243
  1.8.42: 116, 191
  1.8.48: 191
  1.8.49: 242, 250
  1.8.49–50: 116
  1.8.52: 248
  1.8.53: 104, 172, 173
  1.8.55: 265
  1.8.56: 265
  1.8.61: 114
  1.8.62: 220
  1.8.64: 142
  1.8.69: 214
  1.8.70: 113, 114, 254, 258, 262
  1.8.75: 296
  1.8.77: 235, 256
  1.9: 5, 50, 96
  1.9.1–2: 295
  1.9.1–6: 216
  1.9.3: 212
  1.9.4: 191
  1.9.6: 82
  1.9.24: 203
  1.9.26: 155
  1.9.28: 272
  1.9.31: 93
  1.9.31–2: 119
  1.9.32: 135
  1.9.33: 82
  1.9.37: 165
  1.9.45: 293
  1.9.47: 253
  1.9.50: 249
  1.9.51: 297
  1.9.52: 82
  1.9.55: 238
  1.9.56: 143, 250
  1.9.57: 229
  1.9.65: 165, 293
  1.9.71: 160, 264, 296
  1.9.74: 89, 116, 182, 220
  1.9.76: 295
  1.9.79: 117
  1.9.80: 235, 256, 279
  1.9.83: 136, 299
  1.9.83–4: 267
  1.9.84: 268
  1.10: 95

1.10.1: 96
1.10.2: 96
1.10.6: 245
1.10.7: 119
1.10.13: 226
1.10.19: 117, 124, 127
1.10.28: 146
1.10.33: 240
1.10.34: 191
1.10.35: 89
1.10.38: 94
1.10.39: 117
1.10.39–48: 116
1.10.40: 191, 248
1.10.43–4: 194
1.10.44: 195
1.10.50: 248
1.10.53: 258
1.10.54: 216
1.10.55: 149
1.10.57–8: 265
1.10.60: 245
1.10.63: 125
2.1: 111
2.1.3–4: 199
2.1.5: 243
2.1.11: 297
2.1.12: 133
2.1.13: 156
2.1.16: 252
2.1.25: 135
2.1.25–6: 135
2.1.29: 255
2.1.29–30: 201
2.1.33: 111, 162, 253
2.1.35: 199, 247
2.1.37: 279
2.1.39: 110
2.1.46: 197
2.1.53: 154, 170
2.1.62: 233
2.1.74: 116, 206
2.1.75–6: 265
2.1.81: 249, 255, 258
2.1.83: 111, 253
2.1.84–85: 260
2.1.85: 205
2.1.87: 140
2.1.89: 161
2.1.89–90: 142
2.2: 14, 31, 32, 76, 221, 254, 261, 294
2.2.1: 261
2.2.1–10: 31 n. 60
2.2.3: 108
2.2.3–4: 234
2.2.4: 234

Index Locorum
367

2.2.5: 257
2.2.6: 221
2.2.7: 146, 221
2.2.8: 201, 266
2.2.9: 261
2.2.10: 261
2.2.15–16: 234, 235
2.2.18–19: 259
2.2.19: 116
2.2.19–20: 117, 192, 194
2.2.21: 261, 265
2.3: 31, 32, 246, 282
2.3.1: 282
2.3.2: 96, 300
2.3.5: 175
2.3.6: 119
2.3.9: 250
2.3.10: 168, 240
2.3.11: 169
2.3.11–28: 168
2.3.12: 169, 247
2.3.13–14: 248
2.3.14: 173
2.3.14a: 247
2.3.27: 171
2.3.29–30: 259
2.3.30: 250
2.3.31–2: 169
2.3.32: 272
2.3.33: 252
2.3.42: 115
2.3.44: 119
2.3.49: 164, 300
2.3.52: 263
2.3.61: 239, 284
2.3.64: 258
2.3.64–7: 281
2.3.65: 82
2.3.66: 282
2.3.79: 167, 204
2.3.80: 167, 301
2.4.1: 301
2.4.3: 260
2.4.4: 259
2.4.6: 257
2.4.7: 97, 175
2.4.11: 142
2.4.13: 88
2.4.14: 82
2.4.15: 79, 134
2.4.19–20: 81
2.4.20: 79, 134
2.4.21–6: 188
2.4.24: 182
2.4.27: 165
2.4.27–8: 122, 148

2.4.27–31, 122
2.4.30: 121, 122
2.4.32–3: 265
2.4.33: 82
2.4.35–6: 82
2.4.38: 268
2.4.39: 82
2.4.43–6: 82
2.4.44: 104
2.4.45–50: 116
2.4.46: 104
2.4.47: 268
2.4.51: 114, 135, 214
2.4.52: 182
2.4.53: 144
2.4.60: 119
2.5: 84, 133, 145, 154, 254
2.5.1: 253
2.5.4: 253
2.5.5: 144
2.5.6: 226
2.5.11: 158
2.5.18: 159
2.5.29–30: 153
2.5.36: 255
2.5.38: 231
2.5.46: 271
2.5.58: 142
2.5.60: 141
2.5.63: 174
2.5.65: 159
2.5.83: 164
2.5.87: 201, 255
2.5.89: 262
2.5.91–4: 116
2.5.93–4: 194
2.5.94: 260
2.5.96: 102
2.5.99: 255
2.5.108: 300
2.5.109–10: 246
2.5.110: 291
2.5.111: 83
2.5.113: 156
2.5.114: 159
2.5.117: 279
2.5.121: 261
2.5.122: 110, 156
2.6.15: 228
2.6.17: 242, 302
2.6.17–18: 190
2.6.18: 190
2.6.19: 100
2.6.19–28: 94
2.6.25: 260
2.6.29–34: 95

Tibullus (*cont.*)
  2.6.29–40: 104
  2.6.32: 110, 221
  2.6.36: 291
  2.6.37: 134
  2.6.38: 104, 141
  2.6.41: 115, 302
  2.6.43: 233, 265
  2.6.45: 28
  2.6.49: 250
  2.13.27–30: 104
[Tib.]
  3.1: 6, 9, 13, 37, 37 n. 78, 38, 112, 132, 156, 218, 223, 225, 235, 255, 262
  3.1.1: 9, 138, 224, 225, 235, 255, 286
  3.1–6: 25, 38, 39, 55
  3.1.1–14: 76
  3.1.2: 261
  3.1.4: 28
  3.1.5: 88, 89, 91, 157, 235
  3.1.6: 96, 160, 165, 203, 214, 218, 265, 278
  3.1.7: 79, 145, 162, 214, 296
  3.1.7–8: 76, 162
  3.1.8: 75, 86, 89, 116, 164, 233, 244, 265, 297
  3.1.9: 102, 107, 125, 169, 215, 231
  3.1.10: 59, 103, 146, 221, 278, 293
  3.1.11: 102
  3.1.12: 75, 81, 111
  3.1.13: 59
  3.1.14: 89, 103, 156, 262
  3.1.15–28: 76
  3.1.16: 156
  3.1.17: 127, 215, 224
  3.1.18: 175, 248
  3.1.19: 7, 78, 89, 163, 208, 275, 290
  3.1.19–20: 208, 259
  3.1.20: 156, 173, 252
  3.1.21: 218
  3.1.23: 7, 9, 78, 156, 164, 245, 266
  3.1.25–6: 128, 218
  3.1.26: 78, 92, 98, 105, 172, 299
  3.1.26–7: 9, 164
  3.1.28: 130, 193, 197
  3.2: 6, 7, 13, 112, 113, 117
  3.2.1: 218, 250, 282
  3.2.1–2: 172, 264
  3.2.1–6: 270
  3.2.2: 204, 239, 243, 284, 293
  3.2.3: 98, 99, 193, 200, 201, 214, 239, 289, 302
  3.2.4: 112
  3.2.5: 78, 189, 270
  3.2.6: 97, 104, 112, 190, 214, 289, 300
  3.2.7–10: 270
  3.2.8: 175, 249, 279, 291, 300
  3.2.9: 166

  3.2.10: 106, 130, 141, 187, 234, 241, 252
  3.2.11: 146
  3.2.11–15: 293
  3.2.13: 97, 160, 214, 218, 289
  3.2.15: 59
  3.2.15–16: 106
  3.2.16: 115, 290
  3.2.17: 250
  3.2.18: 59, 106, 187, 241
  3.2.19: 59, 219
  3.2.20: 197
  3.2.20–1: 106
  3.2.22: 115
  3.2.23: 221
  3.2.23–4: 146, 234
  3.2.24: 234
  3.2.25: 196, 252
  3.2.26: 210, 229, 264, 279
  3.2.27: 129, 155, 249, 252, 281
  3.2.29: 97, 214, 289, 290
  3.2.29–30: 102
  3.2.30: 93, 98, 128, 284
  3.2.61: 166
  3.3: 13, 188
  3.3.1: 119, 128, 160, 176, 208, 250, 258, 268
  3.3.2: 166, 214
  3.3.3: 108, 113, 250
  3.3.4: 28, 182
  3.3.6–10: 113
  3.3.7: 209
  3.3.8: 28, 191, 246, 297
  3.3.9: 243
  3.3.10: 194
  3.3.11: 113, 234
  3.3.12: 232
  3.3.13: 113, 115, 121
  3.3.16: 108
  3.3.17: 128, 234
  3.3.17–18: 90
  3.3.18: 231, 233, 241
  3.3.20: 297
  3.3.21: 166, 240, 290
  3.3.22: 119
  3.3.23: 126, 127
  3.3.23–4: 233
  3.3.25: 118, 208, 243
  3.3.26: 154, 174, 196, 208, 232, 254
  3.3.27: 130, 155, 202, 257, 281
  3.3.29: 124, 129
  3.3.32: 160, 209, 218, 287
  3.3.33: 114, 253, 301
  3.3.33–4: 264
  3.3.34: 122, 253, 301
  3.3.35: 126, 155, 209, 249, 252, 281
  3.3.36: 59, 157
  3.3.37: 102

Index Locorum 369

3.3.38: 175, 234
3.4: 5, 11, 13, 35, 77, 195, 198, 202, 222, 246
3.4.1: 136
3.4.2: 143, 293
3.4.3: 201, 207, 220, 239
3.4.4: 175, 250, 262
3.4.5: 158, 263
3.4.6: 185, 195
3.4.7: 208, 214, 216
3.4.8: 240
3.4.9: 159, 290
3.4.10: 139, 162
3.4.11: 135
3.4.12: 176
3.4.13: 78, 134, 138, 220
3.4.14: 188, 218
3.4.15: 210, 227, 240
3.4.16: 163, 190, 191, 207, 213, 251
3.4.17: 133, 142
3.4.17–42: 133
3.4.17–80: 133
3.4.19: 141, 143, 183, 240
3.4.20: 160, 190, 220, 289, 290, 299
3.4.21–2: 140
3.4.22: 131, 134, 195, 250
3.4.23: 92, 156, 245, 266
3.4.24: 78, 144, 152
3.4.25: 133
3.4.26: 298
3.4.27–8: 235
3.4.28: 108, 150, 221
3.4.29–36: 146
3.4.30: 103, 150, 187, 250, 265
3.4.31: 208
3.4.32: 151, 241, 247, 248
3.4.33: 148, 149
3.4.33–4: 150
3.4.34: 199, 208, 231, 241
3.4.35: 231, 265
3.4.36: 119, 250
3.4.37: 247
3.4.37–8: 235
3.4.38: 162, 300
3.4.39: 143
3.4.40: 208, 232
3.4.41: 154
3.4.42: 202, 209, 249, 252, 257, 282
3.4.43: 92, 119, 245, 290
3.4.43–80: 133
3.4.44: 199, 253, 301
3.4.45: 213, 262
3.4.47: 123
3.4.49: 214, 216
3.4.50: 174, 239
3.4.51: 218
3.4.52: 163, 265, 296

3.4.53: 114, 250
3.4.54: 127, 209, 287
3.4.56: 80, 134, 214, 220
3.4.57: 82, 83, 111, 145, 195
3.4.58: 7, 160
3.4.59: 139, 176, 213, 240, 290
3.4.60: 92, 170, 245, 266, 297
3.4.61: 183, 295
3.4.62: 80, 214, 240
3.4.63: 7, 93, 240
3.4.64: 59, 114, 172, 202, 214
3.4.65: 171, 172, 201, 204, 260
3.4.66: 99
3.4.68: 134, 206, 220
3.4.69: 297
3.4.71: 169, 190, 266
3.4.72: 170
3.4.73: 40, 188, 203
3.4.74: 179, 182, 204, 250, 301
3.4.75: 114, 214
3.4.76: 97, 182, 201, 239
3.4.78: 78
3.4.79: 164, 202, 239
3.4.80: 134, 208, 232
3.4.81: 90, 130, 250
3.4.82: 165, 249, 291, 300
3.4.83: 250
3.4.84: 173, 302
3.4.86: 172
3.4.87: 143
3.4.88: 300
3.4.91: 178
3.4.92: 97, 201, 224, 239
3.4.92–4: 9 n.18
3.4.93: 104, 203, 257, 299
3.4.94: 203
3.4.96: 213
3.5: 1, 132, 191, 198, 246, 293
3.5.2: 184
3.5.3: 13, 185
3.5.5: 102
3.5.6: 139, 172, 218
3.5.7: 290
3.5.7–14: 139
3.5.9: 233
3.5.11: 141, 188
3.5.12: 160
3.5.13: 240
3.5.14: 126, 139, 213
3.5.15: 140, 207
3.5.17: 78, 117
3.5.18: 39
3.5.19: 241
3.5.21: 94, 188
3.5.22: 97, 201, 239
3.5.23: 194

[Tib.] (cont.)
3.5.24: 118
3.5.27: 134, 220, 296
3.5.28: 143, 249, 250
3.5.29: 111, 160, 186, 187, 253
3.5.30: 219
3.5.31: 110, 208, 232
3.5.33: 94, 102
3.5.33–4: 107
3.5.34: 189, 221, 266
3.5.39: 136
3.5.57–8: 186
3.5.72: 171
3.6: 4, 11, 37 59, 132, 191, 197, 198, 282, 292
3.6.1: 10, 205, 231, 241
3.6.2: 301
3.6.3: 97, 214, 289
3.6.4: 205
3.6.5: 189, 198, 218, 233
3.6.7: 97, 134, 207, 239, 290
3.6.8: 174
3.6.9: 185, 253, 257, 281
3.6.12: 80 214, 218
3.6.14: 284
3.6.15: 181
3.6.16: 99, 173
3.6.17–18: 200
3.6.18: 189
3.6.22: 160, 191
3.6.25: 239
3.6.26: 140
3.6.27: 136, 165, 250, 299
3.6.28: 245
3.6.29: 140, 290
3.6.30: 232
3.6.31: 127
3.6.32: 209
3.6.33–6: 198, 200
3.6.34: 206, 240, 249, 252, 281
3.6.35: 110, 138, 159, 279
3.6.36: 142, 160, 220, 289
3.6.37: 139, 172, 214, 216, 227, 290
3.6.38: 155, 209, 249, 252, 281
3.6.39: 214, 218, 300
3.6.39–40: 213
3.6.40: 293
3.6.41: 130, 157, 214
3.6.42: 139, 163
3.6.43: 97, 208, 232, 289
3.6.46: 80, 166, 300
3.6.47: 85, 93, 136, 214, 217, 257
3.6.48: 257, 262, 299
3.6.49: 135, 184, 212
3.6.51: 136, 214
3.6.52: 207

3.6.57: 211, 220
3.6.58: 106, 187, 221, 266
3.6.59: 78
3.6.59–61: 142
3.6.60: 134, 289
3.6.61: 160, 258, 289
3.6.62: 200, 266, 300
3.6.63: 108, 146, 233
3.7: 25, 35, 37, 38, 45, 282
3.7.7: 92
3.7.12–13: 229
3.7.17: 110
3.7.35: 110
3.7.64: 194
3.7.68: 102
3.7.100: 110
3.7.182: 123
3.7.191: 275
3.7.198–9: 127
3.8: 3, 8, 10–11, 11, 14, 37, 42, 42 n. 91, 75, 76, 78, 243, 255, 261, 267, 271, 276
3.8–12: 6, 25, 27, 37, 38, 39, 42, 44 n. 96, 45, 49, 54, 56, 237, 247, 268, 276
3.8–18: 42, 268
3.8.1: 77, 182, 222, 227, 232, 258, 263, 286
3.8.2: 297
3.8.4: 139
3.8.5: 263
3.8.5–6: 282
3.8.5–12: 223, 231
3.8.6: 234, 258, 293
3.8.8: 110, 210, 230, 241, 257, 264
3.8.9: 232
3.8.9–10: 221, 231
3.8.10: 87, 226, 262
3.8.11: 300
3.8.11–12: 148, 256
3.8.12: 226, 230, 241
3.8.13: 152, 208, 223
3.8.13–18: 231
3.8.15: 83, 218, 265
3.8.16: 122, 221
3.8.19: 121, 234
3.8.22: 153, 154, 247, 256
3.8.24: 83, 265
3.9: 6, 12, 22, 26, 27, 31, 37, 42, 42 n. 91, 52 n. 120, 231, 254, 256, 258, 268, 275, 280
3.9.1: 188
3.9.3: 97, 201
3.9.4: 264
3.9.5: 159, 283, 284, 290
3.9.6: 258, 299
3.9.7–8: 238
3.9.8: 191, 262
3.9.9: 242, 245, 247, 257
3.9.11: 243, 281, 290

Index Locorum

3.9.12: 250
3.9.13: 229
3.9.14: 259
3.9.15: 118, 292
3.9.17: 241
3.9.18: 160, 209, 276
3.9.19: 281
3.9.20: 92, 156, 201, 242, 266
3.9.21: 229, 241, 257
3.9.22: 258
3.9.23: 226, 244
3.9.24: 78, 275, 297
3.10: 8, 11, 42, 42 n. 91, 95, 184, 222, 223, 237, 247, 276, 289
3.10.1: 241, 291
3.10.2: 235, 256
3.10.4: 82
3.10.5: 117
3.10.6: 226
3.10.7: 209, 241, 278, 281, 291
3.10.8: 282
3.10.9: 254, 255, 258, 262, 264
3.10.10: 290
3.10.11: 242
3.10.12: 247
3.10.13: 195
3.10.15: 140, 191, 207, 246
3.10.16: 166
3.10.17: 262
3.10.18: 6, 286, 298
3.10.19: 301
3.10.20: 250
3.10.21: 110, 282
3.10.22: 209, 249
3.10.23: 111, 263
3.10.24: 249, 262, 263, 263
3.10.25: 208, 232, 252, 290
3.11: 11, 22, 26, 27, 31, 37, 42, 42 n. 91, 52 n. 120, 76, 231, 237, 261, 262, 266, 280
3.11.1: 249, 258, 262, 268, 275
3.11.3: 129
3.11.4: 235, 301
3.11.5: 167, 267, 299, 300
3.11.5–6: 258, 293
3.11.6: 90
3.11.7: 202, 229, 241, 281
3.11.8: 119, 215
3.11.8–9: 262
3.11.9: 250, 253, 264, 301
3.11.12: 249, 254, 262, 263
3.11.13: 292
3.11.13–15: 264
3.11.13–16: 273
3.11.14: 301
3.11.17: 267, 272
3.11.19: 226

3.11.20: 267
3.12: 9, 11, 42, 42 n. 91, 222, 223, 237, 261, 266, 276
3.12.1: 215, 249, 258
3.12.2: 157, 213, 240, 241, 247
3.12.4: 252, 254, 258
3.12.7: 226, 249, 253, 258, 262, 301
3.12.8: 90, 257
3.12.9: 110, 210
3.12.10: 83, 259
3.12.11: 160, 217, 239
3.12.12: 214
3.12.13: 170, 261
3.12.14: 92, 156, 221, 245
3.12.15: 104, 282
3.12.16: 240
3.12.17: 300
3.12.19: 218
3.12.20: 250
3.13: 2, 11, 26, 37, 39, 42 n. 90, 222, 223, 243, 260, 286, 292, 293, 294
3.13–18: 6, 25, 31 n. 60, 38, 39, 42, 44 n. 96, 48, 49, 56, 260, 268
3.13.1: 99, 274, 279, 293
3.13.1–2: 152, 243
3.13.2: 93, 291
3.13.3: 57, 276
3.13.3–5: 226
3.13.4: 78, 117, 246, 276, 289, 293, 297
3.13.5: 209, 244, 270
3.13.5–6: 244, 273
3.13.6: 224
3.13.7: 288
3.13.8: 272
3.13.9: 110, 210, 302
3.13.10: 83, 243, 265
3.13.13: 87
3.13.14–18: 278
3.14: 76, 243
3.14–15: 297
3.14.1: 271, 284
3.14.2: 202, 209, 249, 252, 285
3.14.3: 257, 296
3.14.5: 45, 182, 266
3.14.6: 239
3.14.7: 239
3.15: 76, 280
3.15.1: 209, 252, 280
3.15.1–3: 281
3.15.2: 284
3.15.3: 234
3.15.13: 170
3.16: 31, 6, 96, 285
3.16.1: 127, 209
3.16: 31, 6, 96, 285.2: 293
3.16.3: 290

Index Locorum

[Tib.] (cont.)
  3.16.3–4: 272, 291
  3.16.4: 29, 256, 264, 265
  3.16.5: 160, 214, 220, 272, 285
  3.16.6: 220
  3.17: 6, 7, 184, 246, 247, 267, 292
  3.17.1: 289, 292
  3.17.2: 250, 281
  3.17.3: 165, 175, 209, 249, 252, 281
  3.17.4: 272
  3.17.5: 113, 287
  3.17.6: 78, 219, 249
  3.17.17: 257
  3.18: 31, 59, 260, 273, 279
  3.18.1: 118, 259, 290
  3.18.3: 300
  3.18.5: 134, 252, 272
  3.18.6: 220
  3.19: 3, 6, 25, 26, 38, 43, 44, 57, 59, 94
  3.19.1: 301
  3.19.2: 78
  3.19.3: 296
  3.19.5: 160, 195, 215
  3.19.7: 123, 207, 239
  3.19.8: 226, 246
  3.19.9: 97
  3.19.11: 290
  3.19.12: 252
  3.19.13: 294
  3.19.15: 249, 262, 300
  3.19.15–18: 93
  3.19.16: 182
  3.19.17: 208
  3.19.18: 293
  3.19.19: 257
  3.19.20: 154, 249, 291
  3.19.22: 220, 295
  3.19.23: 249, 258, 262
  3.19.24: 253, 259
  3.20: 6, 12, 25, 38, 43, 44, 57, 162, 175
  3.20.1: 78, 278
  3.20.3: 78, 176, 214, 289
  3.20.4: 242, 300
Timocles
  Fr. 25–6: 28 n. 54

Valerius Aedituus
  2.5–6: 244
Valerius Flaccus
  1.43: 181
  1.46: 110
  1.104–5: 253
  1.112: 128
  1.132: 266
  1.260: 201
  1.278: 143
  1.315–6: 99
  1.385: 152
  1.648: 111
  1.659: 161
  1.718: 117
  1.750: 254
  1.766: 97
  2.106: 266
  2.167: 114
  2.180–1: 256
  2.249: 105
  3.227: 141
  3.682: 293
  4.53: 200
  4.334: 144
  4.386: 170
  4.475: 117
  4.603–4: 207
  5.52: 208
  5.83: 253
  5.334: 143
  5.423: 107
  6.112: 94
  6.148: 181
  6.225: 107
  6.492: 150
  6.626–7: 254
  6.726: 114
  6.745: 161
  7.65: 117
  7.213: 136
  7.279: 213
  7.307: 167
  7.437: 207
  7.607–8: 119
  8.10: 125
  8.24–5: 121
Valerius Maximus
  1.1.7: 107
  1.7.ext.9: 136
  2.5.6: 190
  3.7.11: 19 n. 38
  7.2.ext.1c: 300
  7.2.2.5: 227
Varro
  DLL 5.46: 231
  DLL 5.69: 77, 138
  DLL 5.100: 204
  DLL 6.42: 163
  DLL 6.75: 275
  DLL 6.80: 280
  DLL 7.26–7: 275
  DLL 9.24.7: 78
  DRR 3.5.13: 170
  Fr. 388.1: 122
  Men. Fr. 27.1: 245

Index Locorum

Men. Fr. 204: 228
Varro of Atax
  Fr. 15.5: 170
  Fr. 15.4–5: 171
Vegetius
  Mulom. 4.3.6: 291
Velleius Paterculus
  2.103.1.1: 94
Vergil
  Aen. 1.1a–b: 171
  Aen. 1.20: 193
  Aen. 1.23: 128
  Aen. 1.53: 169
  Aen. 1.239: 176
  Aen. 1.263: 204
  Aen. 1.342: 85
  Aen. 1.398: 154
  Aen. 1.409: 170
  Aen. 1.412: 161
  Aen. 1.544–5: 183
  Aen. 1.684: 203
  Aen. 1.717: 91
  Aen. 1.726: 121
  Aen. 2.268–9: 142
  Aen. 2.270–1: 144
  Aen. 2.302: 85
  Aen. 2.448: 121
  Aen. 2.458: 85
  Aen. 2.519: 240
  Aen. 2.536: 290
  Aen. 2.538: 254
  Aen. 2.623: 206
  Aen. 2.722: 204
  Aen. 2.738: 98
  Aen. 2.758: 85
  Aen. 2.780: 178
  Aen. 3.12: 140
  Aen. 3.42: 105
  Aen. 3.81: 143, 144
  Aen. 3.113: 204
  Aen. 3.141: 186
  Aen. 3.150–1: 144
  Aen. 3.191: 178
  Aen. 3.251–2: 158
  Aen. 3.297: 289
  Aen. 3.321: 182, 299
  Aen. 3.330–1: 98
  Aen. 3.354: 201
  Aen. 3.405: 161
  Aen. 3.420–1: 180
  Aen. 3.476: 155
  Aen. 3.489: 125
  Aen. 3.493: 196
  Aen. 3.543: 299
  Aen. 3.545: 161
  Aen. 3.641: 207

  Aen. 4: 128, 237
  Aen. 4.1–5: 290
  Aen. 4.22: 283
  Aen. 4.35–8: 289
  Aen. 4.41: 181
  Aen. 4.66: 93
  Aen. 4.83–5: 274
  Aen. 4.91: 128
  Aen. 4.121: 240
  Aen. 4.159: 204
  Aen. 4.172: 257
  Aen. 4.191–2: 279
  Aen. 4.207: 211
  Aen. 4.262: 122
  Aen. 4.305–30: 286
  Aen. 4.365–7: 177
  Aen. 4.365–87: 286
  Aen. 4.467: 144
  Aen. 4.511: 138
  Aen. 4.517: 105
  Aen. 4.522–3: 250
  Aen. 4.569–70: 164, 166
  Aen. 4.570: 298
  Aen. 4.589: 125
  Aen. 4.596: 213
  Aen. 4.644: 94
  Aen. 4.698–9: 187
  Aen. 5.97: 197
  Aen. 5.246: 144
  Aen. 5.253: 243
  Aen. 5.499: 168
  Aen. 5.539: 144
  Aen. 5.721: 140
  Aen. 5.772: 144
  Aen. 5.729–30: 99
  Aen. 5.736: 197
  Aen. 5.745: 137
  Aen. 5.751: 253
  Aen. 5.761: 121
  Aen. 5.803–4: 90
  Aen. 6.12: 158
  Aen. 6.127: 94
  Aen. 6.136: 159
  Aen. 6.153: 197
  Aen. 6.164: 183
  Aen. 6.227: 107
  Aen. 6.228: 106, 108
  Aen. 6.249: 197
  Aen. 6.306: 118
  Aen. 6.343–4: 159
  Aen. 6.359: 165
  Aen. 6.419: 180
  Aen. 6.429: 188
  Aen. 6.437: 167
  Aen. 6.441–9: 194
  Aen. 6.460: 40

Vergil (*cont.*)
  Aen. 6.464: 97
  Aen. 6.513–4: 209
  Aen. 6.535: 140, 141
  Aen. 6.566: 193
  Aen. 6.647: 155
  Aen. 6.657: 236
  Aen. 6.689: 170
  Aen. 6.714–15: 94
  Aen. 6.853: 204
  Aen. 6.893–901: 133
  Aen. 7.82: 121
  Aen. 7.228: 178
  Aen. 7.243–4: 92
  Aen. 7.341: 189
  Aen. 7.356: 91
  Aen. 7.389: 232
  Aen. 7.415: 205
  Aen. 7.568: 94
  Aen. 7.649–50: 183
  Aen. 7.704–5: 208
  Aen. 7.717: 165
  Aen. 7.778: 121
  Aen. 8.30: 143
  Aen. 8.33: 144, 161
  Aen. 8.34: 107
  Aen. 8.64: 141
  Aen. 8.291: 167
  Aen. 8.303: 162
  Aen. 8.377: 128
  Aen. 8.382: 299
  Aen. 8.389: 93
  Aen. 8.550: 135
  Aen. 8.552–3: 204
  Aen. 8.560: 125
  Aen. 8.581: 200
  Aen. 8.597–9: 121
  Aen. 8.617: 80
  Aen. 8.627: 158
  Aen. 8.667: 94
  Aen. 8.686: 234
  Aen. 8.702: 266
  Aen. 8.709: 94
  Aen. 9.24: 114
  Aen. 9.138: 98
  Aen. 9.187: 163
  Aen. 9.276: 91
  Aen. 9.326: 91
  Aen. 9.382: 247
  Aen. 9.425–6: 97
  Aen. 9.480: 114
  Aen. 9.603: 201
  Aen. 9.618: 154
  Aen. 9.772: 183
  Aen. 10.90: 112
  Aen. 10.92: 202
  Aen. 10.273: 186
  Aen. 11.165–6: 117
  Aen. 11.180: 116
  Aen. 11.379: 117
  Aen. 11.497: 152
  Aen. 11.776: 107
  Aen. 11.821: 182, 299
  Aen. 11.839: 111
  Aen. 12.17: 289
  Aen. 12.64–71: 147
  Aen. 12.67–9: 147, 150
  Aen. 12.68–9: 150
  Aen. 12.120: 199
  Aen. 12.139: 169
  Aen. 12.147: 129
  Aen. 12.155: 125
  Aen. 12.183: 299
  Aen. 12.199: 94
  Aen. 12.391: 182
  Aen. 12.402: 248
  Aen. 12.405: 123
  Aen. 12.411–22: 249
  Aen. 12.487: 163
  Aen. 12.639: 183
  Aen. 12.712: 169
  Aen. 12.753: 265
  Aen. 12.802: 155
  Aen. 12.819: 157
  Aen. 12.885: 161
  Aen. 12.908–9: 143
  Ecl. 1.2: 170
  Ecl. 1.5: 219
  Ecl. 1.6–10: 203
  Ecl. 1.57: 201
  Ecl. 1.58: 289
  Ecl. 1.70–1: 182
  Ecl. 1.74: 134
  Ecl. 1.79: 217
  Ecl. 2.6: 165
  Ecl. 2.20: 107
  Ecl. 2.29: 182
  Ecl. 2.45: 247
  Ecl. 2.58: 300
  Ecl. 2.60: 208
  Ecl. 2.69: 208
  Ecl. 3.3: 28
  Ecl. 3.11: 193
  Ecl. 3.59: 275
  Ecl. 3.78: 182
  Ecl. 3.100: 300
  Ecl. 4: 254
  Ecl. 4.10: 138, 266
  Ecl. 4.13: 202
  Ecl. 4.25: 108, 109
  Ecl. 4.46–7: 256
  Ecl. 4.47: 129

Ecl. 4.53: 125
Ecl. 4.57: 145
Ecl. 5.14: 154
Ecl. 5.27–9: 204
Ecl. 5.29: 204
Ecl. 5.33: 119
Ecl. 5.35: 258
Ecl. 6.1–5: 131
Ecl. 6.3: 159
Ecl. 6.8: 102, 170
Ecl. 6.46: 169
Ecl. 6.47: 210
Ecl. 6.69: 159
Ecl. 6.73: 121
Ecl. 6.74: 180
Ecl. 6.75: 180
Ecl. 6.82: 170
Ecl. 7.9: 247
Ecl. 7.24: 153
Ecl. 7.44: 134
Ecl. 7.62: 146
Ecl. 8.10: 232
Ecl. 8.20: 188
Ecl. 8.43: 172
Ecl. 8.43–5: 178
Ecl. 8.47–8: 167
Ecl. 8.63: 80
Ecl. 8.86: 121
Ecl. 9.39: 247
Ecl. 9.40: 187
Ecl. 9.43: 247
Ecl. 10: 162, 236
Ecl. 10.1: 167, 201
Ecl. 10.6: 142
Ecl. 10.21–3: 162
Ecl. 10.22: 190, 201, 208
Ecl. 10.28: 201
Ecl. 10.46: 239
Ecl. 10.48: 241
Ecl. 10.49: 241
Ecl. 10.50–1: 170
Ecl. 10.50–4: 297
Ecl. 10.51: 154
Ecl. 10.56: 238
Ecl. 10.60: 240
Ecl. 10.69: 173, 200, 271
Ecl. 10.77: 89, 134
Geor. 1.1–5: 78
Geor. 1.8: 119
Geor. 1.15: 169
Geor. 1.28: 146
Geor. 1.38: 193
Geor. 1.43–4: 187
Geor. 1.63: 201
Geor. 1.166: 199
Geor. 1.181: 152

Geor. 1.261–2: 239
Geor. 1.277: 130
Geor. 1.349: 143
Geor. 1.405: 180
Geor. 1.467: 152
Geor. 1.469: 178
Geor. 2.4: 211
Geor. 2.7: 211
Geor. 2.113: 219
Geor. 2.115: 109
Geor. 2.128: 189
Geor. 2.139: 108
Geor. 2.151–2: 204
Geor. 2.257: 209
Geor. 2.259: 211
Geor. 2.296: 166
Geor. 2.353: 186
Geor. 2.378–9: 239
Geor. 2.386: 103
Geor 2.4.61–6: 114
Geor. 2.490: 214
Geor. 2.524: 164
Geor. 3.2: 169
Geor. 3.85: 179
Geor. 3.245–6: 181
Geor. 3.271: 93
Geor. 3.292: 88
Geor. 3.349: 181
Geor. 3.359: 141
Geor. 3.455: 248
Geor. 3.510: 211
Geor. 3.513: 133
Geor. 3.526–7: 200
Geor. 4.62: 249
Geor. 4.63: 30 n. 57
Geor. 4.127–8: 115
Geor. 4.130–1, 150
Geor. 4.131: 147
Geor. 4.252: 291
Geor. 4.307: 300
Geor. 4.346: 257
Geor. 4.348: 82
Geor. 4.379: 108
Geor. 4.384: 266
Geor. 4.408: 204
Geor. 4.425: 186
Geor. 4.430: 178
Geor. 4.467: 120
Geor. 4.475: 118
Geor. 4.516: 244
Geor. 4.546: 197
Aet. 4: 88
Aet. 4–8: 87
Aet. 62: 254
Aet. 339: 160
Aet. 411: 98

Vergil (*cont.*)
  Aet. 637: 125
  Aet. 643: 94
  Catal. 9: 33 n. 68, 38 n. 81
  Catal. 9.1: 148
  Catal 9.13–20: 32 n. 63
  Catal 9.23-4: 32 n. 63
  Catal. 9.59–60: 156
  Cir. 23: 266
  Cir. 28: 125
  Cir. 37–8: 147
  Cir. 59: 180
  Cir. 71: 180
  Cir. 100: 86
  Cir. 121: 144
  Cir. 135: 204
  Cir. 135–6: 167
  Cir. 144: 152
  Cir. 185: 208
  Cir. 199: 157
  Cir. 229: 201
  Cir. 250: 161
  Cir. 255: 170
  Cir. 269: 80
  Cir. 286: 125
  Cir. 287: 117
  Cir. 291: 167
  Cir. 333: 94
  Cir. 512: 108
  Cul. 12: 88
  Cul. 12–19: 87
  Cul. 14: 105
  Cul. 17: 88
  Cul. 18–19: 88
  Cul. 42: 140
  Cul. 63–4: 121
  Cul. 87: 108
  Cul. 102: 140
  Cul. 107: 140
  Cul. 148: 186
  Cul. 172: 161
  Cul. 202: 140
  Cul. 209: 111
  Cul. 232: 194
  Cul. 331: 180
  Cul. 372: 94
  Cul. 374: 129
  Cul. 411–12: 111
  De Rosc. Nasc. 47: 292
  Dir. 66: 94
  Dir. 67: 218
  Dir. 74: 300
  Eleg. in Maec. 1.6: 129
  Eleg. in Maec. 2.14: 196
  Lyd. 3: 258
  Lyd. 6: 170
  Lyd. 59: 244
  Lyd. 176: 161
  Mor. 1: 140
  Priap. 3.9: 92
  Priap. 16.6: 160
Vitruvius
  2.8.10: 108
  5.9.6: 108
  8.2.4: 108

Xenophanes
  Fr. 1.4: 201
Xenophon
  Kyn. 2.4–9: 242
  Kyn. 10: 238
  Kyn. 10.6: 241
  Mem. 2.1.21: 198

Zenobius
  Tract. 1.1.8: 300

Index

Achelous 143
Achilles 100, 129, 161, 177–8, 199, 204
Acontius 151, 263, 297
Actaeon 238, 245
Actium 132
Admetus 130, 159, 168–9, 171, 173
Adonis 237–8, 241, 243, 256, 274
Aegean 212
Aeneas 97, 102, 112, 120, 143, 150, 164–6, 273, 279
Aeneid 75, 128, 227
Aeolus 183
Agamemnon 133, 164
Agave 207
Alcimede 97
Alcinous 124, 127
Alcyone 142
Alexandrian see Callimachus
Alexis 247
Allecto 205
Alma 253
'amateur' poets 20–1, 26, 38, 40, 57
amator 2, 5–8, 12, 15, 24, 80, 92, 96, 99, 101, 112, 115, 119, 123, 142, 163, 172, 229, 233–4, 251, 255, 269, 278, 293–4, 296–7
'*amicus*' (of S.; see also *ad* [Tib.] 3.8–12) 6–11, 13, 25–7, 42 and n. 90, 43, 50, 56, 222, 231, 235, 237, 255, 270
Ammon 174
A/amor (see also Cupid) 10–11, 126, 130, 146–9, 167, 172–3, 178, 182, 197–200, 202–5, 218, 222–3, 225, 228–9, 238–9, 254, 259, 265, 269–71, 274, 277, 292
Anacreonta 33 and n. 69
Anchises 155, 274
Andromache 275
Andromeda 98, 268
anger 6–7, 92, 125, 130, 205–7, 218, 239, 286
Antimachus 1, 9 n. 19
Antony 20 n. 42
Aphrodite (see also Venus) 51, 178, 206, 237, 276
Apollo 5, 7, 11, 13, 27, 30, 79, 83, 87–8, 93, 120, 130–3, 136, 141–75, 177, 183, 185, 202, 224, 228, 230, 235–6, 239, 241, 246–51, 253–4, 256, 261, 265, 274, 301
Appendix Vergiliana 18, 45, 58
apple 150–1, 192–3
Ara Maxima 236

Arabia and Arabian Sea 109, 121, 233–4
Archilochus 33, 34 n. 72
Ares (see also Mars) 237, 243
Arethusa 51–2, 104, 188, 245
Argo 181
Argus 291
Ariadne 136, 177, 181, 183, 198, 211–16, 218
Aristophanes 48 n. 105
Armenia 177, 181, 204, 234
Arno 282
Arretium 281–2
Artemis (see also Diana) 138, 146–7, 151
Asclepius 121
Assyria (see also Syria) 108–9, 146, 233–4
Atalanta 114, 148, 151
Atellan farce 286
Athenaeus 50
Athens 96
Attis 165
Augustan age 2, 15–21, 23 n. 46, 24, 29, 33 n. 68, 35–6, 41, 44 n. 96, 47, 53, 55–6, 89, 97, 101, 120, 127, 131, 134, 152
Augustan marriage laws 8–9, 15–16, 23, 176
Augustus 8, 15, 17, 21, 27, 32, 40 n. 86, 42, 50, 97, 130, 145, 249
Aurora 140–2, 149
Ausonius 44, 58, 176
Aventine 231
Avienus 44, 58

Bacchus (see also other cult titles) 10, 106–7, 111, 148, 155–7, 197–9, 200–2, 205–7, 211, 218–19, 230, 232, 249, 253, 258
Bacchylides 113
Baiae 184–6, 196
Bassareus (see also Bacchus) 198
Baucis 121, 155
Bellerophon 179
Bellona 132
biography/(auto-)biographical statements 8–10, 20, 21 and n. 44, 22–3, 29, 38, 40, 51 n. 117, 164, 168, 191, 246, 270, 276
Bion 238
birthdays 14–15, 31, 39–40, 51, 76, 92, 192, 194, 221, 249, 254–7, 261, 266–7, 275, 280–1, 283–5
Bittis 9 n. 19
black (also *ater*, *niger*, etc.) 102–3, 106, 125, 129–30, 141, 161, 187–8, 191, 197, 234, 298

378   *Index*

blush 146–51
boar 205, 236, 238–9, 241–4
Bona Dea 188–9
Boreas 247
Briseis 93, 100, 239
Brutus (D.) 32
Byblis 181

Cadmus 206–7
Caecilius Metellus 97
Caesar 17, 35, 254, 285, 299
Calenus 26
Callimachus/Callimachean poetics 1–2, 4 and n. 10, 46 n. 98, 49 n. 112, 86, 148, 151, 156, 168, 171, 180, 214, 219, 236, 248, 249, 263, 273, 297
Callinus 1
Callisto 244
Calvus 152
Calydon 238
Calypso 103, 212
Camenae (see also Muses) 273–6
Campania 119, 201
cara of beloved 92–3, 95–6, 104, 127–8, 159–60, 202–3, 218
carmen, canere, cantus 6, 81–2, 90, 111, 126, 154, 174, 212–13, 229, 249, 256, 270
Carystos 119
Cassandra 103
Cassius Parma 41–2
Cassius Severus 17 n. 33
casta (see also infidelity, *pudor*) 7 and n. 16, 92, 143–4, 155–6, 163–4, 244–5, 265–6, 286,
Cato 181
Catullus 2, 4 n. 10, 6–8, 10–11, 17, 20, 24, 37, 40 n. 86, 43, 50, 84, 110, 163, 176–7, 211–16, 231–2, 244, 246, 268–9, 274, 290, 292
Caucasus 177
Centaurs 178
Cephalus 240
Cepheus 279
Cerberus 118, 177–80
Ceres (see also Demeter) 228
Cerinthus 6–7, 9, 11–12, 25, 30 and nn. 57–9, 31, 42, 45, 110, 220–3, 229, 236–8, 241–7, 250–7, 260–4, 268, 272, 274, 277, 280–1, 284–7, 289–90
Cestus 244
Ceyx 128
Charis 228
Charybdis 177, 179–80
Chimaera 177–9
Chiron 204
Chloris 147
Cicero 48, 57, 131, 187, 263
Cimmerians 193–4

Circe 180, 189, 227, 266
Claudia Quinta 253, 263
Cleopatra 49 n. 110, 94
Clodia 8
Cnossos 211–12
Cos 230–1
Coleridge, Samuel 19 n. 39, 52
componere 19, 109–10, 210, 228–30, 232, 262, 264–5, 278–9, 295,
coniugium, coniunx 9, 75, 78, 92–4, 97–8, 104, 111–12, 126–8, 163–4, 171–2, 174–5, 226, 228
Corinna (Ov.) 14, 21, 27, 30 n. 59, 81, 95, 115, 123, 151, 162, 184, 246, 270, 300
Corinna (poet) 27
Cornelia 51
Cornutus 30–32, 42, 162, 168–9, 221–2, 234, 236, 259, 261, 265–6, 282
country see rural
courtesan 8, 24 and n. 48, 28 and n. 54, 30, 50 nn. 113 and 116, 223, 252, 288
Crete 212
Creusa 98
Croesus 127
cultus 88–9, 115, 127, 181–2, 222, 224, 230, 232, 263,
Cumae 187
Cupid (see also Amor) 93, 132, 134, 144, 153, 227, 239, 241–2, 245, 253, 256, 258, 271, 292
cura 54, 90, 111, 123, 125, 127, 137, 142, 155–6, 162–3, 165, 169, 201, 208, 210, 214, 239–40, 245, 248, 286–8, 290, 292, 294, 298
custos 9, 13, 23, 156, 238–9, 265
Cybele 204
Cydippe 151, 263, 297
Cynthia 8, 14, 27, 29, 30 n. 59, 42, 51, 76, 79–80, 101, 103–4, 108, 110, 112, 116, 124, 126–7, 132, 134, 140, 156, 159, 161, 163, 174, 176, 190, 226, 238, 244, 248, 253, 274–5, 288, 290, 296, 298
Cynthius 174
Cyparissus 169
Cypassis 124
Cytherea (see also Venus) 273–5
Cyzicus 98

Danae 182
Daphne 86, 144, 147, 167–9, 171, 228, 241
death 14, 40, 93–7, 100–4, 106, 109–12, 115, 117–18, 120, 126, 129–30, 142–4, 164–5, 184, 187–8, 192, 194, 194, 196, 198, 217, 239–40, 268, 283
Decor 110, 228–30, 232
Deianeira 216
Delia 5, 8, 27, 29, 44, 81, 84, 96, 103–4, 113, 124, 126, 132, 148, 159, 171–2, 183–4, 198, 245, 263, 294–5, 297

Delia (Diana) 239
Delius 174, 201
Delos 147, 159
Delphi 88, 158, 174, 254
Demeter 166
Diana 146, 205, 216, 235, 237–41, 244, 254, 266
Dickinson, Emily 49, 268
didactic (also *docere*) 13, 96, 103, 132, 165, 167–8, 171, 188–9, 198, 206, 213–14, 249, 265, 277, 297
Dido 11, 51, 94, 97, 112, 122, 164, 166, 177, 210, 247, 269, 273, 274, 279, 286, 289
dies 124–5, 129, 134, 160, 188, 195, 208–9, 217, 255–6, 260, 281, 285, 291–2, 294
digna/us 81–2, 148, 208, 232–3, 235–6, 260, 264–5, 269, 278–9, 293
Diomedes 189
Dionysus 145, 179–80, 198, 203–4, 206
Dipsas 159
Dis (see also Hades, underworld) 93–4, 197 and earlier
Discordia 266
dog-star/Sirius 185–6
dolor 97–9, 104, 111–12, 118, 154, 172, 175, 184, 199–200, 203, 213–14, 289, 302,
domina 3, 11 n. 22, 12, 171–2, 203–4, 250, 296, 300–1
Domitius Marsus 25 and n. 50, 35, 194
dragon/snake 179
dream 130–3, 135–6, 138, 142–4, 149
drink/drunkenness (see also wine) 191, 198–9, 206, 208–10, 214, 221, 233
Drusus 115
Dryope 128

Echidna 177
Echo 154, 300
economics of elegy, status of elegist 8, 12, 24, 84, 109, 112–15, 118–24, 126–7, 165, 230
Egypt 113
Elegia 198, 284
elegy
  family in 8, 9 and n. 18, 29, 39, 41, 43, 81, 104, 107, 110, 141, 159–60, 168, 178, 182–3, 192, 194–5, 207, 223, 246, 264, 266–7, 281–3, 288–9
  and lament (see also *dolor, tristitia*) 1–2, 7, 10, 12, 45, 96–7, 100, 154–5, 169, 172, 210, 216, 264, 267, 286
  post-Ovidian 2 and n. 6, 4, 45, 58, time in (see also old age and youth) 14 and n. 27, 76, 119, 227, 268
  topoi of (see also under particular *topoi*) 3, 5–7, 10–15, 22, 36, 50, 51 n. 117, 52, 94, 97, 119, 169, 176–9, 201, 203, 298–9, 300
elision 55–6, 106, 158, 171

Eloise and Abelard 268
Elysium 193–4
Eos (see also Aurora) 116, 231, 234–5
epic 4, 17, 75, 77, 79, 99, 140, 167–8, 171, 175, 181–2, 193, 213, 225, 227, 238, 240, 249
Epicurus 297
epigram 2, 4 and n. 10, 76, 198, 301
epitaph 1, 81, 95, 100–1, 108–12, 128, 279
Erinna 49 n. 112
Etruscan 185–6, 231
etymology 1 n. 2, 28, 31 n. 61, 97, 107, 119, 121, 137–8, 141, 156, 179, 186, 210, 226, 230–2, 239, 256, 259, 271, 275, 287
Euboea 120
Euhemerus 108
Euripides 48 n. 105, 205–6, 236
Europa 174, 177
Eurus 183–4

Fabius 253
Falernum 201, 219
fallere see trickery
fama 110, 269–70, 272–4, 276–80
fata/Fates 39, 123, 128–9, 157, 176, 188, 196–7, 208, 250, 256
fear 7, 90, 94, 134, 137–9, 179, 198, 249, 300
feet (see also metre) 4, 14, 148, 178, 229, 245
felix 109, 124–5, 154–5, 174, 183, 196, 207–8, 210, 213–14, 231–2, 234, 254, 259–60
female voice 3, 5 and n. 13, 22, 26, 34, 43, 46–53, 236–7, 269–70
feminization of elegiac poet 11, 30, 94, 211, 213, 241, 256, 268, 275, 281
fire (also metaphorical, and see illness for fevers) 93, 108, 179, 183, 189–90, 227–8, 256–8, 267, 282, 290, 292–3, 300
flowers 150–1 and earlier
freed slaves and freed people (see also slaves) 8, 10, 16, 27 and n. 51, 28, 30, 257
funeral (see also death) 1, 81, 94–5, 101, 104–5, 107–10, 117, 128, 221, 234, 286
Furor 240

Gabes 181
Galatea 196, 247
Gallus 2–3, 4 n. 10, 17 n. 33, 28, 35, 46 n. 98, 56, 93, 112, 129–30, 142, 159, 161, 167, 170–1, 176, 190, 201, 207–8, 208, 236, 238–42, 248, 265, 270–1, 274, 276, 279, 289, 291, 297
genethliacon 254–5, 280
Genius 198, 215, 249, 257–8, 261–2, 299
genre (elegy), see also epic 14–15, 75, 127, 131, 169
Geryon 178, 180
giants 178

380 Index

gifts 77–9, 80, 82–4, 91–2, 112, 121, 124, 165, 173, 199, 205, 225, 233, 235, 254–5, 274–5, 299
Glaucus 180
Glycera 44, 172, 294–5
gods (see also specific gods) 1, 105, 113, 115, 126–8, 130–1, 133, 135–7, 140–1, 144–5, 148, 151, 154–6, 158, 160, 163–6, 168, 171, 174, 179, 183, 188, 190–1, 193, 197–9, 203, 205–7, 210, 215–16, 218–19, 222, 225–32, 235–7, 240, 246–8, 250–1, 253–4, 258–9, 261, 263–6, 272–3, 299
Graces 75
Greek poetry (all genres except epic) 1–2, 4, 18, 33–4, 48–9 and n. 112, 76, 111, 198, 211, 219, 286
guardianship of women (see also *custos*) 13, 29 n. 56, 32, 96, 216, 239, 252, 266, 280, 282–4
Gyes 178

Hades (see also underworld) 130, 166, 193, 275
Hagisilas 228
hair 14 and n. 26, 85, 87, 95m 101, 103, 114, 125, 145–6, 169, 182, 187, 191, 194, 229–30, 247, 262
harpy 177–8
Hecate 139
Hector 275
Helen 120, 164, 227, 269, 273–4, 277
Helios 143
Hellenistic see Callimachus
hendiadys 80, 129, 137, 288
Hephaestus 128, 259
Hera (see also Juno) 225
Herculaneum 121
Hercules 139, 171, 198, 262
Hermaphroditus 151
Hermes (see also Mercury) 152
Hermione 98, 284
Hermus 127
Heroides (Ov.) 19–20, 22, 35, 43, 49, 51–2, 237, 280
Hesiod 33 and n. 71, 83, 130–1, 131, 136, 157, 165
Hesperides 151
Hesperios 231
hiatus 106, 175
Hippocratic texts 34 n. 72, 251
Hippolytus 205–6, 237, 240, 244–5, 246
Hippomenes 114, 151
Hispala Faecinia 288
Historia Augusta 35
Homer 18, 49 n. 112, 79, 81, 130, 131, 133, 147, 149, 157, 159, 169, 171, 175
homoioteleuton 157, 160, 192
Horace 7, 18, 30, 32, 88, 131, 197, 219
hunting (also amatory) 6, 12, 31, 82, 229, 236, 238–40, 242–6, 250

Hyacinthus 150, 169, 172
Hydra 177
Hymn, hymnic structure 197–8, 203, 222, 235, 238

Ilia 77
Iliad 19, 269, 286
illness (also amatory) 1, 8, 12–13, 40–1, 94–5, 101, 113, 141, 143, 169, 173, 184–6, 189–91, 193, 195–6, 199, 214, 240, 246–51, 253, 267, 282, 289–92
impotence 14
India, Indian Ocean 234–5
infelix 207, 210, 214 and earlier
infidelity and fickleness (see also trickery) 7 and n. 16, 8–10, 13, 16, 44, 80, 99, 101, 132, 135–6, 140, 149, 156, 162, 164, 166, 169, 171, 175, 178, 183–4, 187, 198, 211, 214, 226, 264–7, 272, 278, 284–5, 289, 296, 299–301
invidia see jealousy
Io 174, 241, 262
Isis 2, 76, 254
Ismene 262
Iulus 274
iuvenis 96, 145, 149, 172, 191, 237–8, 242, 250, 260, 264, 267–8
Iuventa 292–3
Ixion 262

Jason 145, 177, 283
jealousy 6–7 and n. 17, 23 n. 47, 123, 128, 180, 197, 222, 226, 237, 240, 258, 267, 277, 296–7
Julia 50
Julius Calidus 42
Julius Marathus 27
Juno 11, 77–8, 80, 110, 128, 138, 187, 198, 205, 215, 226, 246, 249, 261–4, 266–7, 299
Jupiter 10, 78, 88, 126, 135, 155, 157, 158, 170–1, 182, 184, 215–16, 226, 241, 246–7, 254, 266, 302,
Justinian 300
Juvenal 18

Kalends 14, 77–8, 80, 223–5, 235, 255

'late' words in *AT* 36, 40–2, 56, 108, 120–2, 150, 179, 194, 207, 234, 237
Labienus 17 n. 33
Laconia 120
Laodamia 97, 138
Lavinia 98, 148, 150, 232, 267
Leda 174
legal language 93, 171, 174, 202, 281, 284, 286–7, 300
lena 8, 82, 104, 223, 233
Lenaeus 210–11

Index

Leonidas 107
Lesbia 6, 8, 10, 27, 37, 81, 84, 120, 231, 246, 299
Lethe 117–18, 193–4
Leto 146–7, 149, 170–1
Leucothoe 171
Liber 156, 197–8, 205, 247, 254
lies, see truth
lions 177–81, 204–5, 239
Livius Andronicus 19 n. 38
Lucifer 139, 142, 152
Lucina 77–8, 138–9, 262, 266
Lucretia 164
Lucretius 137, 214
Luna 139, 146–7, 149
lux 42 n. 91, 118, 125, 138, 243, 292, 293
Lyde 9 n. 19
Lyaeus 198, 205
Lycoris 29, 51, 162, 245, 274
Lydia 92, 126–7
Lydgamus 1–2, 4–7, 9, 11–13, 20–1, 25–8, 36, 37 and n. 78, 39–42 and nn., 44 and n. 96, 45, 54–6, 75, 78, 80–96, 98–103, 106, 109–14, 116–20, 124–5, 127–45, 149, 154–6, 159–66, 168–9, 171–9, 181–97, 200, 203–21, 253, 262, 287, 289, 301
lyre 152, 154–5, 157, 169, 171, 235
lyric poetry (Roman) 30, 198, 202, 206, 218–19, 222

Macer 32 n. 67, 159
Maecenas 17–18, 32, 42, 102, 181
magic 103, 125, 189, 229–30, 249, 252
makarismos 125
Mantua 163
Marathus (see also *puer*) 27, 50, 135–6, 166, 250
March 235, 255
Marcian aqueduct 218–19
Marcus Plautius 279
marriage 8, 9 n. 19, 10, 20, 30–1, 54, 77, 80, 84, 90, 92, 97, 104–5, 112, 117, 128, 138–9, 149–50, 163–4, 174, 176, 178, 182, 228, 234, 236, 260, 263–7, 286, 289
Mars 75, 77–8, 141, 205, 222–8, 235, 237, 243, 254, 258–9, 274,
Martial 18, 34, 41, 76
matrona/matron (see also puella, legal status) 77–8, 83, 223, 231, 252, 288
Matronalia 9, 76–8, 84, 138–9, 223, 235–6, 262
Mausolus 108
Medea 51, 94, 141, 167, 177, 181, 189, 264
Medusa 178–9
Meleager 258
Meliboeus 170, 247
Menander 182
Menelaus 147, 164, 227

Mercury 122, 145, 164, 166, 168, 171
Messalla, and sons 3, 17–18, 25, 27–8, 29 and n. 55, 31, 32 and nn. 63–5 and 67, 33 and n. 68, 35–7, 38 and nn. 80–1, 41, 45, 59, 76, 81, 84, 102, 110–11, 116, 127, 133, 162, 198, 219, 247, 253, 266, 281–4
Messina 180
metapoetic gestures 13–14, 24, 75, 83–5, 86–8, 95, 103, 110, 123, 152, 169, 183, 186, 199, 209, 219, 221–2, 224–5, 230, 242–3, 248–9, 262–3, 269, 271–5, 278, 282, 290
metre 2, 4, 25, 41, 49, 53–7, 77, 144, 154, 156–7, 171, 182, 225, 227, 245, 294, 302
Midas 127
Milanion 242
militia amoris (also warfare) 12, 16, 77, 82, 95–6, 125, 167, 172–3, 184, 199, 202, 225–7, 229, 239, 242, 263, 274, 300
Mimnermus 1, 83
Minerva 88, 216, 225, 254, 266
Minos 177, 212–13
Minotaur 178
misogyny 13, 46, 132, 229
Mt. Cynthus 158–9
Muses 13, 20 n. 40, 75–6, 79–83, 86–9, 91, 112, 120, 131–2, 136, 153, 155–7, 164, 169, 213, 224, 230, 235–6, 240, 246, 271, 274–7
Myrrha 108

Narcissus 148, 150
Natalis 261, 265
Nausicaa 147
Naxos 212
Neaera 1, 4–7, 9, 13, 20, 25, 28 and n. 54, 29, 45, 75–8, 81–3, 88–95, 98, 101, 103–4, 106–7, 109, 111–14, 116–17, 119, 124, 126–9, 132–4, 149, 156, 159–64, 166, 171, 173–7, 180–2, 184–5, 195–8, 203, 207–8, 211, 214, 218–20, 301
Nemesis 5, 27, 29, 44, 83–4, 95, 104, 124, 141, 168, 263, 294–5
Neptune 183
Nero 17, 120–1, 163
Nestor 155
Nisus 180
North Africa 181
Notos 183
Nox/night 110, 118, 125, 133–4, 136–8, 140–3, 161–2, 203, 217, 220, 241, 245, 250, 265–6, 291, 293, 298
Numidia 204

Ocean 141
Octavia 163
Odysseus 147, 175–6, 212, 295
Odyssey 49 n. 112

Oenone 169, 171, 253
old age (see also elegy, time in) 14, 116–17, 119, 136, 154, 191–2, 194, 268
Olympus 231–2, 259, 264, 266
Orpheus, Orphic texts 34 n. 72, 178
Osiris 143, 198, 247
Ovid 2–4, 10–14, 17–19, 21, 26, 32, 35–7, 39, 40 and n. 85, 41 and n. 88, 42, 51, 53–6, 59, 81, 83, 85, 88, 100, 112, 124, 128, 130, 132, 141, 144, 148, 151, 154, 160, 163, 172–3, 175–6, 178, 185, 191–4, 198, 204, 213–14, 227, 236–7, 241, 245, 257, 289, 296, 298, exile of 21, 32, 40–1, 85, 95, 130, 176, 181, 236, wife of 4, 9 and n. 19, 21, 112, 128, 148

Pactolus 127
Paelignia 163, 219
Paetus 240
Palatine 133, 143, 145, 152, 154–5
palla 144–5, 151–2, 222, 231, 233, 265–6
Pallas 199
Panchaia 108
Pandora 165, 229, 299
panegyric 17, 25, 38
Parcae 128–9, 256
Paris 120, 171, 227, 251, 269, 273–4, 277
Pasiphae 165, 210
pastoral 169–71, 201, 219, 238, 247
Patroclus 161, 177–8
patron/patronage 15–20, 32, 75, 83–4, 152, 185, 282
Peitho 228
Penelope 51, 94, 97, 132–3, 252, 295,
Pentheus 207
perfume 95, 105, 107–9, 146, 221, 228, 233–4
Perilla 53 and n. 124
Perithoos 212
Persephone 139, 150, 187–8, 193
Perseus 268
Persia, Persian Gulf 109, 121, 234
persona, poetic 21–2, 25–7, 33, 34 n. 72, 78, 100, 127, 160, 210, 240
Petale 43 n. 93
Phaeacia 120
Phaedra 237, 242, 245, 257
Phaon 51, 163, 247, 256
Phemius 302
Philaenis 50 and n. 114
Philemon 121, 155
Philitas 1
philosophy 113–14, 118, 122–3, 128, 135, 297–8
Philitas 9 n. 19
Phoebe/Phoebus (see also Apollo) 147, 152, 155–6
Phrygia 119–20

Phryne 28 and n. 54
Phyllis 94
Picus 227
Pierides (see also Muses) 154, 297
Pindar 33 and n. 71
Plautus 278–81
Pliny 53
Pluto 205
poeta 5–6, 15 n. 28, 18–20 and nn., 26, 44, 53, 155–6, 181, 236, 269, 277, 284
poetic claims to immortality 104–6, 112, 196, 270, 280
Polyphemus 279
Pontus 181
Poseidon (see also Neptune) 193
Postumus 125
praeceptor amoris see didactic
prayer (*preces, precor*) 59, 105, 109, 113–14, 116, 119, 125–6, 139, 161, 166, 172–3, 183, 190, 198–9, 203, 207–8, 210, 214, 216–17, 239, 246–7, 258, 262, 273
presentation copy 76, 79, 86, 111
priamel 95, 113
Priapea and Priapus 25 and n. 50, 92
Procris 128, 240
Prometheus 181
propempticon 196
Propertius 2–3, 10–11, 13–14, 17–18, 20 n. 42, 21, 26, 32, 35–6, 51, 54, 80, 84, 101–2, 110–11, 117, 126–7, 129, 160, 167, 172, 182, 185, 190, 276, 295–6
prostitute, see courtesan
Protesilaus 97, 220
proverbs 82, 94, 96–7, 99, 123–4, 126, 133, 209, 212–13, 251, 283, 297–8, 300
Psyche 226
public/*publica* (see also Callimachus, *fama*) 18–19, 47, 50, and n. 116, 75, 162, 222–3, 231, 243, 249, 263, 269, 272–3, 277, 294, 301
pudor 12, 99–100, 149, 260, 270–3, 293
puella 2, 5–8, 11, 13–14, 15 and n. 28, 20, 24 and n. 48, 25, 28–9, 31, 50 and n. 115, 53, 75–6, 78, 80–3, 86, 89, 92–3, 95–6, 98, 100, 101, 104, 109, 112–13, 115, 119, 128, 135–6, 140, 148–50, 153, 156–7, 159–66, 169, 171, 176, 178, 182, 184–5, 188, 190–1, 196, 202–3, 213, 215–27, 229–35, 239, 244, 246–7, 250–3, 255–6, 261–3, 265, 269, 273–4, 276–8, 280–4, 289–91, 293, 295–9, 301–2
  adornment of, luxury of (see also wealth) 6, 81–2, 86, 100, 120–2, 222–3, 229, 232–4, 263, 287
  docta 20, 50 and n. 115, 89, 157, 224, 261–2, 266–7, 273

legal status of 8–9, 11, 16, 24, 78, 80, 171, 176, 222–3, 227, 232, 252, 269, 286–7, 289
puer (*delicatus*), male beloved 2, 5, 30, 82, 96, 146, 168, 172, 185, 196, 200–1, 238, 250
Punic 204
Punic war 188
purpureus (purple, see also wealth) 84, 120, 122, 147–8, 150–1, 161, 186–7, 231, 233–4, 265–6
Pygmalion 92
Pyramus 110, 237

querellae, queror 114, 170–3, 190, 210, 214, 216, 264, 301
Quirinus 131

rape (see also violence) 77, 79, 96, 114, 150, 218, 222, 225, 241, 280
recusatio 127, 227
red sea 234
religion (Roman) 5, 76, 78, 105, 113, 135, 137, 152, 156, 160, 188–90, 198, 224, 235–6, 257, 262
Remus 275
Rhea Silvia 224–5
rival 2, 5–7, 11, 31, 82, 98, 109, 112, 163, 184, 202, 239–40, 244–5, 252, 256, 263, 267, 274, 280, 285, 287, 289, 295
Roma 253
Roman comedy 4, 7–8, 47 and n. 104, 283, 302
Roman education 34, 46–7 and n. 99–100
Roman elite 43, 53, 101, 122, 127, 288
Rome (see also *urbs*) 13, 15, 42–3, 184, 188, 284–5, 297–8
Romulus 275
Rosetti, Christina 52
Rosetti, Dante Gabriel 52
rumor (see also *fama*) 277, 301–2
rural life 13, 96, 115–16, 168, 186, 198, 238, 245, 280–1, 283, 297

Sabines 77, 79, 225, 296
Sappho 11, 27, 50 nn. 113 and 116, 51, 147, 253, 269, 273–4, 276
Sardis 127
Sarmatia 178
Saturnalia 77
Saturnia (see also Juno) 264
Saturnus 297
Scylla 177–8, 180–1
Scythia 178, 181
Sea of Azov 194
[Sallust] 35
Salmacis 151

Semele 157
Sempronia 47, 293
Seneca 41, 149, 154, 176, 236
servitium amoris (see also slaves) 11–12, 20, 28–9, 167, 171–2, 204, 256, 259–60, 264–5, 294, 300–1
Servius Sulpicius and the Sulpicii (see also Sulpicia, Valerian *gens*) 28–9 and nn. 55–6, 31–2, 41–2, 46, 230, 256, 264, 282–3, 286, 288
sex 14, 21, 49–50, 76, 79, 82, 99 100, 116–17, 128, 133, 163–4, 180, 206, 209, 218, 224–5, 229, 236–7, 241, 244, 250, 275–6, 279–80, 286, 293
showing/hiding 14, 30, 49, 99, 152, 243, 263, 268, 270–2, 279, 292–3
Sibyl 159, 174
Sicily 170, 180
Sidonian 233
Sidonius 122
Sidra 181
slave (see also *servitium amoris*) 11–12, 23–4, 27–8, 31, 42, 77, 79–80, 88–9, 91–3, 111, 113, 134, 154, 199, 219, 260, 288, 300
Solon 1
Somnus (personified) 141–2, 143, 161, 183
song, poetry as (see *cantus*)
Sophocles 232
Sphinx 177
Statius 15, 41, 76
suicide (see also violence) 13–14, 94–5, 100, 129
Sulpicia 6–15, 18, 22, 23 n. 47, 25–7, 29 and nn. 55–6, 31–4, 37 and n. 78, 42, 43 and nn. 45–7, 50, 52–7, 99, 110, 182, 220–9, 231–7, 240–6, 248, 250, 253–64, 266–8, 280–2, 266–75, 284, 292–4
Sulpicia (the later) 34, 44
sun (see also Phoebus) 5, 102, 141–3, 147–9, 171, 187, 194, 202
symposium 11, 28, 197–9, 202–3, 209, 211, 217, 219, 221
Synnas 120
Syria (and adjective *Syrius*) 146, 221
Syrtis 177, 181

Taenarum 120
Tagus 127
Tantalus 154, 300
Tarpeia 227, 242
Tatius 227, 242
Terminus 249
Thebes 207
Theocritus 51 n. 117
Theognis 1, 33
Thero 298

384

Index

Theseus 107, 139, 165, 183, 211–13, 215, 220, 249, 293
Thessaly 207
Thetis 266
Thisbe 94, 110, 237, 247
Tibullus 2, 3, 10–11, 13, 17–18, 20, 22, 25–8, 35–6, 38, 41–2, 44 and n. 94, 50, 54–8, 59 and n. 126, 81, 84, 101–2, 104, 115, 123, 136, 159, 165, 167–8, 171–2, 182–5, 188, 191, 194–5, 198, 213, 239–40, 268, 294, 297–9, 301
Tiber 136, 143
Tiberius 112
Tibur 185–6
tigers 177–8, 181, 204–5
Timagenes 17 n. 33
Tisiphone 266
Tithonus (see also old age) 116, 148, 151
Tityrus 170
Tmolus 127
toga 122, 152, 286, 288
Tragoidia 198, 205, 266
transvestism and transvestite ventriloquism (see also female voice, Vertumnus) 22, 45, 51 n. 117, 52, 188, 223, 231, 301
trickery, elegiac 5, 113–14, 21–7, 169, 183, 186, 203, 214–17, 245, 261, 265, 279, 294
tristitia (see also elegy, lament and) 111, 123, 128–9, 150, 154–5, 189, 208–9, 211, 252, 281, 284, 291
Trojan war, Troy 120, 193, 279
truth (see also trickery) 8–9, 114, 136–8, 159, 173–5
Tullus 186
Turnus 150
Tuscan, Tuscany 135–6, 186, 195
Tyre/*Tyrius* 122, 126, 146, 148, 152, 161, 222, 231–3,
Tyrtaeus 1

underworld (see also death, Dis, Hades) 93–5, 97, 118, 120, 129–30, 139, 164, 179, 187–8, 193–4, 197
urban life, *urbs* 96, 115, 280–2, 296–8

Valerian gens 29 nn. 55–6, 31, 32, 247, 267, 290
Valgius Rufus 42
ventriloquism, see transvestite ventriloquism
Venus 11, 77, 78, 103–4, 114, 128, 136, 146–7, 149, 173, 194, 196, 202, 215–16, 219, 222, 224–7, 230, 232, 237–8, 240–1, 243–4, 246–7, 249, 256, 259, 263–4, 266, 270–1, 273–7, 295, 298–9, 301
Vergil 11, 18–19, 25, 32, 35, 38 n. 79, 118, 122, 133, 148, 163, 167, 171, 187, 194, 222, 269, 286, 290
Verona 163
Vertumnus 3, 11, 223, 226, 231–2
Vesta 105, 253
Vicus Tuscus 231
violence (see also rape, suicide) 12–13, 77, 101, 151, 165, 216, 223, 226
Violentilla 232
vir 5, 8–9, 13, 16, 92, 96, 104–5, 156, 160, 162–5, 174–5, 221, 251, 267, 294
virginity/*virgo* 76, 79, 105, 147, 149–50, 180, 210, 241, 287
Volumnia Cytheris 29, 274
Vulpius 118

weaving 129, 150, 170, 256
white (*candidus, niveus*, etc.) 28, 85, 90, 102, 106–7, 124–5, 147–8, 150–2, 161, 168–9, 191, 197–8, 202, 208, 231, 241, 248, 252
wine 10, 106–7, 197, 205, 213, 217–21, 281, 292, 300
Wordsworth, Dorothy 52 and nn. 121–2
Wordsworth, William 19 n. 39, 52 and nn. 121–2

Xenophon 34

youth, see also elegy, time in 40, 191–2, 194, 280

zeugma 288
Zeus (see also Jupiter) 193